THE LAW OF
SUCCESSION

THE LAW OF SUCCESSION

by

Anthony R. Mellows

T.D., B.D., LL.M., Ph.D., A.K.C.

Solicitor, Reader in Law in the University of London
Director of Conveyancing Studies at King's College, London

SECOND EDITION

LONDON
BUTTERWORTHS
1973

ENGLAND:	BUTTERWORTH & CO. (PUBLISHERS) LTD.
	LONDON: 88 KINGSWAY, WC2B 6AB
AUSTRALIA:	BUTTERWORTH PTY. LTD.
	SYDNEY: 586 PACIFIC HIGHWAY, CHATSWOOD, NSW 2067
	MELBOURNE: 343 LITTLE COLLINS STREET, 3000
	BRISBANE: 240 QUEEN STREET, 400
CANADA:	BUTTERWORTH & CO. (CANADA) LTD.
	TORONTO: 14 CURITY AVENUE, 374
NEW ZEALAND:	BUTTERWORTHS OF NEW ZEALAND LTD.
	WELLINGTON: 26/28 WARING TAYLOR STREET, 1
SOUTH AFRICA:	BUTTERWORTH & CO. (SOUTH AFRICA) (PTY.) LTD.
	DURBAN: 152/154 GALE STREET

First edition February, 1970
Second edition June, 1973

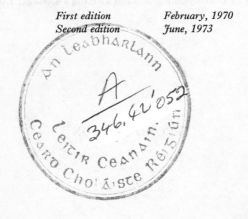

ISBN—Casebound: 0 406 62372 4
Limp: 0 406 62373 2

PRINTED IN GREAT BRITAIN BY
EYRE & SPOTTISWOODE LTD, THANET PRESS, MARGATE

PREFACE

I have followed the general approach of the first edition of this book in attempting to present as a chronological sequence and logical unity the various elements which are commonly thought to constitute the law of succession. The law of wills and of intestacy has generally been considered as part of the Law of Property. Probate law has usually been regarded as an independent topic of little academic import. And Administration of Estates is frequently presented as part of Equity. Yet these elements combine to form a unity, which is a striking amalgam of the various sources of English law. The law and practice of the church courts, common law, and equity, as well as statute law and the more recent discipline of taxation are here joined together, but with their separate origins and influences still apparent.

With few exceptions, the existing books in this field cover only individual aspects of the topic, and even so are either short or very substantial. In this book I have attempted to adopt a midway course by dealing with the whole field in a length which admits of discussion without being too bulky.

I have tried not only to explain the law, but to show how sometimes the likely result can be avoided when the interests of the client so require, for a good lawyer is not one who can merely understand and interpret the law, but one who is able to use the law in the best interests of his client. For this reason I have tried to present the law not just as a series of rather dead propositions, but for its significance in overall wealth planning. This has necessarily involved considering the taxation implications where these have been appropriate.

This branch of the law has seen a number of developments since the first edition was prepared. New legislation has included the Administration of Justice Acts 1969 and 1970; the Guardianship of Minors Act 1971; the Law Reform (Miscellaneous Provisions) Acts 1970 and 1971; and the Proceedings Against Estates Act 1970. There have been a number of statutory instruments, including an important one varying the amount of the "statutory legacies" payable on intestacy. The taxation provisions have been affected by the Taxes Act 1970, and the subsequent Finance Acts, and I have attempted to include reference to all the significant judicial decisions since the first edition was prepared. I have also taken the opportunity to re-arrange or re-write some of the material where, in the light of experience, this seemed desirable.

Although I have wished to keep the book to manageable size, I have taken space in several places to explain the nature of the problems with which the law is faced, as well as the solutions. In doing so, I have had in mind particularly those students who are trying to study this subject without any other tuition. I have only discussed problems which are of practical, as well as academic, importance, and I have been able to deal with certain questions which were not included in the first edition, as well as expanding the treatment of some others. The writer of any textbook has difficulty in the selection of material to be included and I have been faced with two problems in particular. In the first place there is a substantial overlap between the position of personal representatives and that of trustees. I have assumed that the reader of this book will not be unfamiliar with the law of trusts, and I have therefore felt justified in merely referring on some occasions to the equivalent position of trustees, rather than giving an exhaustive exposition. In the same way I have had to omit discussion of such topics as the perpetuities and accumulations rules, and the equitable rules as to apportionment. In the second place I would have liked to have included a section on Estate Duty, but I have always thought that a brief outline account is virtually useless. An account in comparable detail to the rest of the book would have required at least 150 pages, and this would have caused too great an increase in the length of the book.

The manner in which I have dealt with the material which is included is bound to reflect my own experience as a university teacher and a partner in a London firm of solicitors. The result will, I hope, be interesting and useful to students reading for degrees, and subsequently while undergoing professional training. I also hope that they will find it worth keeping by them after qualification. By the same token, I should like to think that the book will also be of assistance to practitioners, both in the law itself, and in other fields, such as accountancy, where legal problems are never far away. But above all I hope that whoever is the reader will find this subject alive and interesting.

The law is stated at 1 January, 1973.

King's College, London WC2.   A.R.M.

TABLE OF CONTENTS

PART III: INTESTACY

PART IV: THE EXTENT OF TESTAMENTARY FREEDOM

PART VI: THE POSITION OF THE PERSONAL REPRESENTATIVES

APPENDIX

TABLE OF STATUTES

References in this Table to "*Statutes*" are to Halsbury's Statutes of England (Third Edition) showing the volume and page at which the annotated text of the Act will be found. Page references printed in bold type indicate where the Act is set out in part or in full.

TABLE OF CASES

In the following Table references are given where applicable to the English and Empire Digest where a digest of the case will be found.

A

F

G

N

O

PAGE

PAGE

Part I

THE LAW OF WILLS

CHAPTER 1

THE WILL AS AN INSTRUMENT OF WEALTH PLANNING

Probably the most outstanding feature of the development of property law in the twentieth century is the process of dividing the old concept of ownership into the twin concepts of "ownership", in an emaciated sense, and "control". The old concept of ownership involved[1] (a) the power of enjoyment, or control (that is, the power to determine the use to which the property is to be put; the power to deal with its produce, and the power to destroy it); (b) possession, which includes the right to exclude others; (c) the power to alienate *inter vivos*; and, (d) the power to leave the property by will.

This century has seen the whittling away of the owner's first power, to control, and in some cases the powers of control have been transferred to others. Thus, a person may "own" the freehold in land, although many of the powers of control over that land are vested not in him but in the local authority under the Town and Country Planning Acts.[2] Likewise, the right of possession has been modified. In extreme cases an owner can even be excluded from his own property, without ceasing to be the owner.[3] Permanent legislation has given numerous authorities powers of entry[4] onto land, and to some authorities power to acquire, compulsorily, rights over land without acquiring the land itself.[5]

So far the powers to alienate *inter vivos*, and to dispose by will have been relatively untouched. There have been times when gifts

---

[1] Paton, Jurisprudence, 2nd ed., p. 420.
[2] See Mellows (1963), 2 Solr. Qtrly. 109.
[3] As in the case of a control order made under the Housing Act 1961.
[4] E.g. under the Public Health Act 1936 and the Housing Act 1957.
[5] E.g. compulsory rights orders in favour of the National Coal Board under the Opencast Coal Act 1958.

1

inter vivos or by will to donees of a particular class have been restricted[1] but in general there has been no direct attempt to restrict alienation.

Both types of alienation, *inter vivos* and by will, have been subject to contrary tendencies. On the one hand a prime object of much property legislation, particularly that of 1925, has been to simplify, and so encourage, dispositions. On the other hand, taxation often has the result of discouraging dispositions. Capital gains tax[2] and stamp duty[3] are payable on many *inter vivos* dispositions, and so discourage them. There are certain restrictions on testamentary freedom, particularly under the Family Provision legislation whereby the court can override the terms of the will to make provision for dependants.[4] Nevertheless, despite these restrictions, there is a wide power of disposition which most people seek to use to advantage.

To what extent, then, is this wide testamentary power used? Here again there are conflicting trends. A person who owns a few hundred pounds or less may well still not bother to make a will, although in future such persons are likely to make wills in increasing numbers.[5] But it is probable that most people who own their own homes, albeit with the aid of a mortgage, make a will, for, in owning their home, their assets are often transformed from being reckoned in hundreds of pounds to being reckoned in thousands of pounds. With the dramatic growth in home ownership,[6] the proportion of the population which dies testate increases.[7] On the other hand, for many people of medium wealth or more, the will is by no means the only means of transferring property to other members of the family. Estate duty rates, which, depending on one's viewpoint, are either vicious or tough, constitute a substantial tax liability on assets at death: but while capital gains tax imposes a limited tax in respect of some dispositions *inter vivos*, it leaves untouched others, particularly those in cash of any amount. The present taxation rules, as well as the fear of a

---

[1] E.g. The Mortmain and Charitable Uses Acts.

[2] Introduced by the Finance Act 1965.

[3] The Stamp Act 1891, as amended.

[4] Under the Family Provision legislation, considered in Ch. 13.

[5] As a result of the operation of the Legal Advice and Assistance Act 1972, poor people are now able to obtain legal aid to make a will.

[6] In 1972, over half the houses in England and Wales were owner-occupied.

[7] In 1971, 65% of all grants were in respect of testate estates.

future wealth tax, induce a person to dispose of his assets in his lifetime. Therefore, a person of means can be expected to give *inter vivos* a substantial part of his wealth to his children or grand-children. But he will not give away all his wealth, so that there is always a place for a will. A will, then, is becoming more and more not an isolated transaction, but one instrument of several in overall wealth planning.

In planning any will the intending testator, with his professional advisers, will have regard to:

1. the persons to be benefited;
2. the circumstances in which they are to be benefited;
3. the amount of that benefit;
4. the type of that benefit; and
5. the means by which that benefit can be conferred with the greatest taxation advantage.

In most cases, the intending testator will only have a very general idea of what is to happen. His professional adviser must seek first to clarify his own thoughts; envisage circumstances which might arise, and ascertain whether account is to be taken of them; and then plan the way in which that result is best to be achieved. Perhaps the most common example is that of a married man with two children, who decides to make a will. He may have decided only that he wants all his property to go to his wife, and then to his children. Does he in fact want his wife only to have a life interest, and so no right to the capital? What is to happen if his wife remarries: is she (and her future husband) to continue to benefit, or are his children to benefit at that stage? If on the death of his wife one of his children is dead, but that child has children of his own, are those children to take the share of the deceased child? The professional adviser has rapidly considered eventualities which probably have not even entered the head of his client.

When the testator's intentions are ascertained in this way, the taxation implications are then considered. In general, estate duty is payable on all the property which a person owns or in which he has a life interest[1] and it is payable on each death. Thus, if the intending testator leaves all his property to his wife, and she

---

[1] Finance Act 1894, s. 1.

makes a will leaving all her property to the children, then in the event of the husband dying first, duty will be payable on the death of the husband,[1] and again on the death of the wife. There is, however, an exemption, known as the "surviving spouse exemption"[2] under which if a surviving spouse has a life interest only, although duty is payable in the normal way on the death of the testator, no duty is payable on the death of the surviving spouse in respect of property received under the will of the testator.

This, then, may point to the desirability of giving the wife a life interest only. On the other hand, she may at some stage have need of capital. This need may be met by giving the executors power to take part or the whole of the capital out of the trust and to pay it to the wife.[3] The estate duty advantage will be lost in respect of the property taken out of the trust, but the remaining property will still attract the benefit.

At the outset, then, the intending testator may have thought only of a will leaving everything to his wife, and then to his children. He may end up with a will which in essence provides:

  (i) a life interest to his wife if she survives him;

 (ii) a provision for capital to be advanced to her at the discretion of the executors;

(iii) subject to the wife's rights, a gift of his property to his children in equal shares; and

(iv) a proviso that if either of his children should not survive his wife and himself, but leave issue so surviving, then that issue take the share which the deceased child would have taken.

If the property is not to be left to the wife and children in succession, but is to be split up in some other way, questions may arise as to the incidence of estate duty. A beneficiary who receives realty is liable to pay the estate duty on it, unless there is any contrary provision in the will, whereas a beneficiary of personalty takes free of duty.[4] If the testator wishes to give his house to his wife and the residue to his children, does he want to alter the normal incidence of duty, so that his wife takes the house free of

---

[1] Except in respect of the first £30,000 left to the wife: Finance Act 1972, s. 121.

[2] Finance Act 1894, s. 5 (2); Finance Act 1898, s. 13; Finance (1909–10) Act 1910, s. 55; Finance Act 1914, s. 14.

[3] Though this power must not be exercisable by the surviving spouse alone: *Re Penrose*, [1933] Ch. 793.

[4] Finance Act 1894, s. 9.

estate duty, or does he want her, perhaps, to have to arrange a mortgage on it so that she can pay the duty.

From these simple examples it will be seen that a professional adviser must himself be able to envisage what might happen: know what can be done; and know how best it can be done.

The skill in envisaging what might happen is a combination of the logical consideration of possibilities, coupled with the ability to balance a desire on the one hand to make provision for such contingencies and on the other hand not to make the will too complicated. Logically, there is no end to the circumstances which might happen, and provision can only be made for some.

In the second phase, considering what can be done, a will can consist of simple gifts, or it can create a trust. A person can by will tie up wealth for the benefit of his family, either in fixed proportions or in proportions to be fixed later by the exercise of powers of appointment or of selection. Provision can be made for persons outside the family to whom a moral obligation is owed, or even, to a limited extent, for animals and causes.[1] In fact, any type of express trust can be created by will. Nevertheless, the repeated forays of the taxation legislation now make it desirable to leave as much flexibility in the trust as possible.

Even a provision which looks like a simple gift may lead to a trust if the beneficiary is not *sui iuris* when the will comes into effect. Thus, if a man makes a will leaving £1,000 to each of his three sons, and the residue to his wife, and at the date of his death any of the sons is under 18,[2] the legacies for the minors will have to be held in trust until they reach that age. A wide investment clause may be desirable, including, in times of currency uncertainty, the power to invest abroad, and clauses designed to facilitate the administration of the estate, such as by excluding the various equitable rules as to apportionment.

The third general point, how best the testator's wishes can be brought into effect, will appear from the remainder of this book.

---

[1] *Pettingall* v. *Pettingall* (1842), 11 L.J. Ch. 176; *Re Dean* (1889), 41 Ch. D. 552.
[2] Family Law Reform Act 1969, s. 1.

CHAPTER 2

THE NATURE OF A WILL

A. DEFINITION OF A WILL

1. DUALITY OF MEANING

The word "will" has two distinct meanings. The first, and strict, meaning is metaphysical, and denotes the sum of what the testator wishes, or "wills", to happen on his death. The second, and more common, meaning is physical, and denotes the document or documents, in which that intention is expressed. Where there is more than one document which complies with the provisions of the Wills Act 1837, it is customary to refer to the main instrument as the will, and to subsidiary instruments as codicils. However, as the Privy Council observed in *Douglas-Menzies* v. *Umphelby*,[1] all unrevoked testamentary instruments which a man may leave together constitute one will in the strict sense.[2]

2. CHARACTERISTICS OF WILL

A will in the physical sense may, then, be defined as a declaration in prescribed form of the intention of the person making it of the matters which he wishes to take effect on or after his death, until which time it is revocable.[3] This definition indicates the following characteristics of a will:

1. the scope of a will is not confined to dispositions of property;
2. a will operates only as a declaration of intention;
3. it must, usually, be in prescribed form;
4. it is always revocable;

---

[1] [1908] A.C. 224, at p. 233.

[2] See e.g., *Lemage* v. *Goodban* (1865), L.R. 1 P. & D. 57, at p. 62; *Green* v. *Tribe* (1878), 9 Ch. D. 231, at p. 234; *Re Elcom, Layborn* v. *Grover Wright*, [1894] 1 Ch. 303, at p. 314, CA.

[3] This definition is based on that of Hanbury, namely, "a declaration in prescribed manner of intention of the person making it with regard to matters which he wishes to take effect on his death".

5. it takes effect on death; and
6. it is ambulatory.

These characteristics must now be considered further.

3. SCOPE NOT LIMITED TO PROPERTY

Although the primary aim of a will is almost always to dispose of property, a will can also:

a. appoint executors;

b. appoint trustees where a trust will arise under the will. The trustees are usually the same persons as the executors, although their function is different,[1] but other persons may be appointed if the testator wishes;

c. appoint special personal representatives of settled land;[2]

d. appoint guardians of infant children, under the Guardianship of Minors Act 1971;[3]

e. revoke previous wills;

f. confer special powers on executors and trustees, such as the power to invest outside the provisions of the Trustee Investments Act 1961, or the power to distribute the estate *in specie*, without requiring any consent.[4]

g. exclude various equitable rules, such as the rules of apportionment known as the rules in *Howe* v. *Earl of Dartmouth*[5] or the rule in *Re Earl of Chesterfield's Trusts*;[6]

h. give directions as to burial or cremation; sanction the use of the body or eyes for purposes of transplant or other therapeutic or educational use. In many cases directions of this nature are merely declarations of desire, without legal effect, and it is for the executor to decide as to the disposal

---

[1] See *post*, p. 317; in essence, the function of an executor is to administer the estate and distribute the assets, whereas the function of a trustee is to retain assets, often for a long period of time.

[2] See *post*, p. 358; special personal representatives are the persons who are responsible for vesting settled land in the next tenant for life entitled under the settlement following the death of the previous tenant for life.

[3] Under s. 4(1), (2), either parent may appoint a testamentary guardian: see *post*, p. 291.

[4] See *post*, p. 551. Administration of Estates Act 1925, s. 41, confers a power of appropriation which can in general be exercised only with the consent of the beneficiary.

[5] (1802), 7 Ves. 137.

[6] (1883), 24 Ch. D. 643.

of the body. Where, however, the testator has by will or otherwise declared that his body must not be cremated, that declaration is binding;[1]

i. exercise a testamentary power of appointment, that is, a power which the testator has been given under a previous will or settlement and which is exercisable either by deed or will, or by will alone.

A document which effects one or more of the foregoing objects, without disposing of any property, is a will.[2]

4. DECLARATION OF INTENTION ONLY

The courts have said repeatedly that a will operates only as a declaration of intention.[3] There are two aspects of this. In the first place, by making a will the testator does not in any way interfere with his power of disposition *inter vivos*. Accordingly, if the testator makes a will leaving his house to Arthur, he may nevertheless sell the house in his lifetime: in this case Arthur will generally receive nothing under the will even though this provision is not formally revoked.[4]

In the second place, the executor has a supervening authority to sell property in the course of the administration of the estate, even if it is the subject of a specific gift in the will.[5] Further, the amount of the deceased's liabilities may be sufficiently large to absorb all of his assets, in which case the dispositive parts of his will will have no effect.[6]

5. PRESCRIBED FORM

With one exception, a will must be in writing, signed at its foot or end by the testator or by someone at his direction and in his presence, and it must be witnessed by two persons. These formalities are considered in detail in Chapter 5. The exception

---

[1] Regn. 4, Cremation Regulations 1930.

[2] The fact that it is a will does not necessarily mean that it will be admitted to probate. See *post*, p. 266.

[3] *A.-G.* v. *Jones and Bartlett* (1817), 3 Price 368, at p. 391; *Re Baroness Llanover*, [1903] 2 Ch. 330, at p. 335; *Re Thompson*, [1906] 2 Ch. 199, at p. 202; *Re Westminster's Deed of Appointment*, [1959] Ch. 265, at p. 271.

[4] This is as a result of the doctrine of ademption.

[5] See *post*, p. 351.

[6] See *post*, p. 383.

enables military personnel when on actual military service and sailors at sea to make wills without formality. This type of will, known as a privileged will, is considered in Chapter 6.

6. REVOCABLE

A will can always be revoked, unless after making it the testator ceases to be of sound mind, and so loses his testamentary capacity. In *Vynior's Case*[1] the will contained a declaration that it was not revocable, but this declaration was held to be invalid. Even if there is a contract not to revoke the will, the will itself may be revoked although an action for damages for breach of contract may lie.[2]

7. TAKES EFFECT ON DEATH

A will takes effect only on death. Therefore, until death, the beneficiaries and executors have no interest whatever in the testator's property, and they do not acquire any interest until death. Accordingly, if a beneficiary dies between the time when the will is made and the testator's death, his estate will, generally, derive no benefit under the will.[3] On the other hand, as is explained below, it does not necessarily follow that a document which only takes effect on death is necessarily a will.

8. AMBULATORY

A will is said to be "ambulatory", that is, that it is capable of dealing with property acquired after the date when it was made, provided, of course, that it is owned by the testator at his death. Thus, a gift by will made in 1966 of "all my omnibuses" will include buses acquired in 1969.[4]

B. WILLS DISTINGUISHED FROM OTHER TRANSACTIONS

1. GIFT *inter vivos*

A will is distinguishable from a gift *inter vivos* both as regards the time when it takes effect, and the formalities required. Generally, a gift *inter vivos* takes effect forthwith, whereas a gift by will

---

[1] (1609), 8 Co. Rep. 81b.

[2] See e.g., *Synge* v. *Synge*, [1894] 1 Q.B. 466.

[3] Subject to any provision against lapse: see *post*, p. 453. See also *Re Currie's Settlement*, [1910] 1 Ch. 329, at p. 334.

[4] Unless there is evidence of a contrary intention.

takes effect only on death, although a future interest can be conferred by *inter vivos* gift. The formalities are also different. The
only formal requirements of a will are those relating to writing,
signature, and attestation.[1] Various formalities are necessary for
gifts *inter vivos*. Thus a gift of land must be by deed;[2] a gift of
land where the title is registered at the Land Registry must be
effected by an instrument of transfer which is registered;[3] a gift
of shares in a company must be by transfer and registration;[4]
and so on according to the type of property.

Usually, of course, there is no problem in deciding whether a
document is intended to effect a gift *inter vivos* or to operate as a
will. In some cases, however, this has caused difficulty. In *Milnes
v. Foden*[5] Sir James Hannen, P., laid down this test: "The true
principle appears to be that if there is proof, either in the paper
itself or from clear evidence *dehors*, first that it was the intention
of the writer of the paper to convey the benefits by the instrument
which would be conveyed by it if considered as a will; secondly,
that death was the event which was to give effect to it, then whatever may be its form it may be admitted to probate as testamentary.
It is not necessary that the testator should intend to perform or be
aware that he has performed a testamentary act."

Thus, in *In the Goods of Morgan*[6] a settlor executed three deeds
of gift under which property was given to trustees for the benefit
of children, and the deeds provided that they were not to take
effect before the settlor's death. These deeds were held to amount
to wills, and probate was granted accordingly. In *In the Goods of
Slinn*[7] a woman granted her savings to her niece by a deed which
also complied with the formal requirements of the Wills Act 1837.
The Court admitted extrinsic evidence that she wished to settle
her affairs, and held that this document could be admitted to
probate.[8]

---

[1] *Supra*, and see Ch. 5.
[2] Law of Property Act 1925, s. 51.
[3] Land Registration Act 1925, ss. 19 to 23.
[4] Stock Transfer Act 1963.
[5] (1890), 15 P.D. 105.
[6] (1866), L.R. 1 P. & D. 214.
[7] (1890), 15 P.D. 156.
[8] See also *In the Goods of Montgomery* (1846), 5 Notes of Cases, 99; *Robertson
v. Smith* (1870), L.R. 2 P. & D. 43; *Re Anziani*, [1930] 1 Ch. 407; *Re Walshaw*
(1879), 48 L.J.P. 27; *Green* v. *Andrews* (1877), 41 J.P. 105.

If, however, an attempt has been made to create a gift *inter vivos*, but the attempt has been ineffective, then the document by which that attempt has been made will not be regarded as a will, even though it refers to the person's death.[1] This is because a person must intend a document to take effect on death if it is to be admitted as a will.

The courts, therefore, attempt to ascertain the intention of the donor, and then to examine whether the formal requirements of the method of disposition which he attempted to make have been satisfied.

2. REVOCABLE SETTLEMENT *inter vivos*

If Andrew wishes to leave his house to Benjamin, he may do so by will in the usual way. He may also achieve a result which is similar in many respects by conveying the house *inter vivos* to trustees to hold upon trust for Andrew for life with remainder to Benjamin. Andrew may also include a power of revocation in the deed. If Benjamin survives Andrew, the result would for many purposes be the same as if the gift had been made by will.[2] But Benjamin has, on the making of the settlement, received an interest in remainder. If, therefore, Benjamin predeceases Andrew, without Andrew revoking the settlement, Benjamin's estate will take the interest which Benjamin would have taken if he had survived.[3] Thus, a revocable settlement creates a present interest in property, whereas a will only confers an interest upon death.

3. DONATIO MORTIS CAUSA

A *donatio mortis causa* is a revocable gift by a person made in contemplation of his impending death, and conditional upon that death. It is considered fully in Chapter 33.

---

[1] *Dillon* v. *Coppin* (1839), 4 My. & Cr. 647; *In the Goods of Halpin* (1873), 8 R.I. Eq. 567.

[2] There are differences. The property subject to a settlement, unless the settlement could be avoided as having been made in defraud of creditors (under Bankruptcy Act 1914, s. 42 or Law of Property Act 1925, s. 172) cannot be taken as assets for the payment of creditors (see *post*, p. 378), nor would it abate on an insufficiency to pay legacies (see *post*, p. 468).

[3] As to the doctrine of lapse which applies where a similar position arises by will, see *post*, p. 453.

4. NOMINATIONS

A nomination is a direction to a person who holds funds on behalf of another to pay those funds in the event of death to a nominated person. In many cases, nominations operate by statute, and their effect is considered at p. 368. However, there can also be non-statutory nominations, particularly in connexion with pension schemes.[1] The rules of many pension schemes provide, in essence, that if the employee dies during the course of his employment the amount of his contributions will be paid to a person nominated by the employee in writing, and in the absence of any nomination, to the employee's personal representatives. Where a nomination is made, it does not operate as a will. While the document does affect the devolution of property on death, the property passes directly from the fund to the nominee, and at no time forms part of the estate. The nomination operates by virtue of the rules of the scheme, and not as a will, and it does not, therefore, have to satisfy the requirements of the Wills Act.[2]

C. DISPOSITIVE EFFECT OF WILL

Wills Act 1837, s. 3, provides that every person may dispose of his real and personal property, whether legal or equitable, by will. When a will became operative following the passing of that Act, therefore, the will itself operated to pass the legal estate in property where the testator himself had the legal estate vested in him. This was modified by Sched. 9, Law of Property (Amendment) Act 1924, which provides that "the Wills Act 1837 takes effect to enable equitable interests to be disposed of subject and without prejudice to the estate and powers of a personal representative". Although it could have been expressed more clearly, the result of this provision is that a will operates only to confer an equitable interest on the beneficiary.[3] The legal interest devolves on the executor,[4] and if he does not require the property for the purposes of the administration of the estate, he transfers it to the beneficiary.

---

[1] See Administration of Estates Act 1925, s. 1.

[2] Chappenden, [1972] J.B.L. 20.

[3] *Bennett* v. *Slater*, [1899] 1 Q.B. 45; *Eccles Provident Industrial Co-operative Society, Ltd.* v. *Griffiths*, [1912] A.C. 483, at p. 490; *Re Danish Bacon Co., Ltd.'s Staff Pension Fund, Christensen* v. *Arnett*, [1971] 1 All E.R. 486.

[4] Although even this "equitable interest" is only of a limited type: see *post*, p. 439.

In view of this, it is sometimes said that a will now takes effect only in equity.[1] Although this is true in so far as property is concerned, a will does have significance for the legal estate, because the legal estate will devolve upon the executors named in the will merely by virtue of their appointment as such.[2]

D. TERMINOLOGY

It may be convenient at this stage to indicate the meaning of terms frequently used.

1. CODICIL

Any document which complies with the formal requirements of the Wills Act, and is intended to operate on death, may be described as a will.[3] As has been said,[4] however, it is more usual to refer to the document which is the primary testamentary instrument as the will, and to any testamentary document which modifies or varies it as a codicil.

2. EXECUTORS, ADMINISTRATORS AND PERSONAL REPRESENTATIVES

In general terms, an executor is the person appointed by the will to administer the estate.[5] Where the deceased dies intestate, that is, without leaving a will which disposes of property,[6] or where he leaves a will without appointing executors, the person who administers the estate is known as the administrator. Their functions are the same, and their positions similar.[7] Executors and administrators are known collectively as personal representatives.

3. BEQUESTS AND DEVISES

A bequest is a gift by will of personalty, and a devise is gift by will of realty. Although both terms are still met frequently, the word "gift" itself is appropriate to cover both.

---

[1] E.g. Williams on Wills, 3rd ed., p. 8.
[2] See *post*, p. 333.
[3] *Douglas-Menzies* v. *Umphelby*, [1908] A.C. 224, at p. 233.
[4] *Ante*, p. 6.
[5] See *post*, p. 239, for a more detailed definition.
[6] Administration of Estates Act 1925, s. 55 (1) (vi).
[7] See *post*, p. 317.

CHAPTER 3

CONDITIONAL, JOINT AND MUTUAL WILLS

The usual will is one made by one person alone, and is intended to take effect unconditionally upon his death. There are, however, other types of will which can be made, and these are considered in this chapter.

A. CONDITIONAL WILLS

1. THE PRINCIPLE

A will may be made with the intention that it shall become operative only upon the happening of a specified event. For example, the will may provide that it is to come into force only if the testator survives his wife, or if he returns from a dangerous mission. If the condition is not fulfilled, the will is of no effect[1] so that if a conditional will is expressed to revoke a previous will, it is inoperative to revoke that previous will if the contingency does not happen.[2]

The principle governing conditional wills is easy to state, but often difficult to apply in practice. Wills which may be conditional are often made in the face of unusual danger, but there is often difficulty in knowing whether in fact the testator intended the will only to come into force upon the happening of that event, or whether the prospect of death from that cause was merely the motive for making an unconditional will. The question arises for consideration where the deceased does not die as a result of the contemplated danger, but from some other cause.

---

[1] *Parsons* v. *Lanoe* (1748), 1 Ves. Sen. 189; *In the Goods of Winn* (1861), 2 Sw. & Tr. 147; *Roberts* v. *Roberts* (1862), 2 Sw. & Tr. 337; *In the Goods of Robinson* (1870), L.R. 2 P. & D. 171.
[2] *In the Goods of Hugo* (1877), 2 P.D. 73.

A useful discussion of the cases[1] is contained in *In the Goods of Spratt*.[2] In *In the Goods of Spratt* itself the testator was an Army officer serving in New Zealand at the time of the Maori war. During the course of the war, he wrote to his son saying that more English officers would be killed if they stayed in New Zealand much longer. He also said[3] that if anything happened to him, his son was to have everything. The testator was not killed in the war, but survived for thirty-two years, without having revoked his previous will and without having made a new one. The result depended on whether the testator intended his son to take his property only if he was killed in the war, or whether he was to take in any case. The Court held the will to be unconditional, so that the son took.[4]

In *Re Govier*[5] on the other hand, a husband and wife made a joint will which commenced "in the event of our two deaths". The will was made in 1941, and it was held to be conditional upon them dying at the same time, as, for example, by being blown up by the same bomb.[6]

2. THE JUDICIAL APPROACH

At this point it is as well to consider the judicial approach to many questions involving the construction and validity of wills. There are a number of principles which are usually expressed as a series of logical propositions applied by the judge to give a result which flows readily from them. Undoubtedly some judges follow this approach, and perhaps more have done so in the past than do now. Others, perhaps, allow the circumstances of a particular case to influence their decision. This is a personal impression—and it is stressed that it is a personal impression only, and not a statement which can be proved—but it seems that frequently a judge

---

[1] *Strauss v. Schmidt* (1820), 3 Phillim. 209; *Burton v. Collingwood* (1832), 4 Hag. Ecc. 176; *In the Goods of Hobson* (1861), 7 Jur. N.S. 1208; *In the Goods of Thorne* (1864), 5 Sw. & Tr. 36; *In the Goods of Dobson* (1866), L.R. 1 P. & D. 88; *In the Goods of Martin* (1867), L.R. 1 P. & D. 380; *In the Goods of Mayd* (1880), 6 P.D. 17.

[2] [1897] P. 28.

[3] As he was a soldier on actual military service, he could make a will informally: see *post*, Ch. 6. His letter could, therefore, operate as a will.

[4] See also *In the Estate of Vines, Vines v. Vines*, [1910] P. 147.

[5] [1950] P. 237.

[6] See also *Re Rowland, Smith v. Russell*, [1963] 1 Ch. 1; and note at 79 L.Q.R. 1.

will seek to reach a result in which the testator's spouse or children will benefit. It is always prudent to remember the form which a probate action takes. By the time that the judge is called upon to make any decision, the whole argument from all sides represented has been put to him, and almost always he knows what will be the result of the possible decisions open to him. Suppose, then, that a married man with two children proposes to undertake a dangerous trans-arctic journey, and before doing so makes a will providing that "in the event of my death all my property shall go to my fourth cousin Rosemary". If he dies after his return from natural causes, it may well be that a judge would be more willing to hold that will to be conditional than if he had provided that his property should go to his wife. In each case it is for the judge to decide whether a particular will is conditional. The mere fact that the matter is being litigated probably shows that the position is by no means clear: this in fact gives the judge a wide discretion as to the decision which he will reach. What better circumstances are there for a judge to make a decision which he considers to be, broadly, just?

This is not to argue that all judges take this broad approach— they do not. But it does perhaps help to explain some cases in which the decision appears on its facts to have been easily capable of a contrary result.

It is suggested, therefore, that in the case of conditional wills, it is as important to bear in mind who will take the testator's property as to examine the terms of the will itself. The same considerations apply to several of the decisions on the formal requirements of a will.[1]

B. JOINT WILLS

When two or more persons incorporate their testamentary wishes in one document, and if the formalities prescribed by the Wills Act are observed, they are said to have made joint wills. These must be clearly distinguished from mutual wills which are discussed in the next section of this chapter.

A joint will does not take effect as one will, but as the separate wills of the parties who made it. Thus, if a husband and wife make a joint will, and the husband dies first, the document can

---

[1] See, e.g. *post*, p. 60.

be admitted to probate first as the will of the husband on his death, and secondly as the will of the wife on her death.[1] A joint will which is not a mutual will can be revoked by either or both parties at any time, and without the consent of the other. A joint will which is also a mutual will can still be revoked without the consent of the other party, although adverse results ensue.[2] Apart from the mere fact that a joint will is written on the same piece of paper, it is for all purposes regarded as the separate wills of the parties who made it. Thus, one party can make a separate codicil to a joint will[3] and can republish[4] a joint will by a separate will.[5]

A joint will is generally clumsy, and inconvenient, because on the death of the first person to die, the will itself is retained at the Probate Registry.[6] Its use can be recommended in only two circumstances. First, where a mutual will is made, it may be convenient for this to be made as a joint and mutual will. Secondly, a joint will may be convenient to exercise a joint power of appointment, in which case the power is deemed to have been exercised when the second person dies.[7] A joint will may, of course, also exercise a power of appointment given to one party alone.[8]

There is no merit in having a joint will where the parties own property jointly. In the case of a joint tenancy, the property passes automatically on the death of one party to the survivor, even if there is only *scintilla temporis* between the deaths of the parties.

C. MUTUAL WILLS

1. TYPES OF MUTUAL WILL

Mutual wills are wills made by two or more persons, usually in substantially the same terms and conferring reciprocal benefits, following an agreement between them to make such wills and not

---

[1] *Re Duddell*, [1932] 1 Ch. 585; see also *In the Goods of Stracey* (1855), Dea. & Sw. 6; *In the Goods of Lovegrove* (1862), 2 Sw. & Tr. 453; *In the Goods of Miskelly* (1869), 4 I.R. Eq. 62; *In the Goods of Piazzi-Smyth*, [1898] P. 7; *In the Estate of Heys*, [1914] P. 192.

[2] Unilateral revocation can lead to actions for breach of contract or breach of trust. See *post*, pp. 21 and 22.

[3] *In the Goods of Crofton* (1897), 13 T.L.R. 374.

[4] As to republication, see *post*, p. 112.

[5] *In the Goods of Fletcher* (1883), 11 L.R. Ir. 359.

[6] This, however, does not prevent its revocation by the survivor.

[7] *Re Duddell*, [1932] 1 Ch. 585; in this case it was confirmed by a testator's separate will, but this is not necessary.

[8] *In the Goods of Stracey* (1855), Dea. & Sw. 6.

to revoke them without the consent of the other.[1] Mutual wills may be made either in the form of a joint will, or as separate wills.

There are two basic types of mutual will:

a. reciprocal life interests, with remainder over. Thus, husband and wife may make mutual wills giving a life interest to the survivor, with remainder to their son.

b. absolute gifts, with alternative provisions in the event of the predecease of the other person. Husband and wife may each make wills leaving the whole of their property to the survivor, but providing that if the spouse does not survive, then the whole of the property shall go to their son.

Although mutual wills are often made by husband and wife, they can be made by any two or more persons and are sometimes found made by other relatives, such as two sisters, who might, for example, wish to confer life interests on each other, with remainders to charity.

2. REVOCATION

Mutual wills involve a conflict of principle. Wills are mutual wills only if made in pursuance of a prior agreement not to revoke without the consent of the other. This is a contract and is enforceable.[2] On the other hand, it is a cardinal principle of the law of wills that a will may always be revoked.[3] The solution to the conflict which has been evolved is that the will itself may always be revoked, but such revocation may give rise to an action for breach of contract. Furthermore, it is established that on the death of the first person to die, a trust arises in favour of the beneficiaries, and if there is any attempt by the survivor to revoke, proceedings may also be taken for breach of trust.

Actions in respect of breach of contract or breach of trust relate only to the dispositive part of the will. The new will is fully effective to deal with non-dispositive matters, such as the appointment of executors or guardians. Suppose, therefore, that Winnie and Wendy make mutual wills under which they leave a life interest to each other, with remainder to Wilfred, and appoint Edward to be the executor. Suppose also that after the death of Winnie, Wendy revokes her will and makes a new one leaving all

---

[1] Burgess (1970), 34 Conv. (N.S.) 230.
[2] See *post*, p. 19.
[3] *Ante*, p. 9; see also *Forse and Hembling's Case* (1588), 4 Co. Rep. 60 b.

her property to Roger, and appointing Theodore to be her executor. The revocation of the first will is effective, and Theodore will obtain probate of the second will. However, as a trust arose on the death of Winnie, Theodore will hold Wendy's property upon the trusts declared by the mutual will.

3. AGREEMENT NOT TO REVOKE

In order for wills to be mutual wills, there must be a prior agreement not to revoke without the consent of the other, and such agreement must be strictly proved.

a. *The agreement*

The agreement itself may relate to the whole will, or merely to part. Thus, in *Re Green*[1] a husband and wife made wills leaving their property to each other, with the proviso that the survivor was to leave half of that property to certain specified charities. The wife died first, and the husband remarried, making a second will practically wholly in favour of his second wife. Vaisey, J., held that the second will was effective to deal only with half of the husband's property, the other half being subject to the trusts of the mutual will.

The essential nature of the agreement is not that identical wills should be made, but that there should not be any unilateral revocation. In *Re Oldham*,[2] for example, where a husband and wife made almost identical wills leaving their property to each other, with provision for various relatives if the other died first, it was held that an agreement to make the wills could be proved from the letters written to the solicitor who prepared the wills, but that there was no proof of an agreement not to revoke. Thus, when the husband died first, and the wife remarried, her new will in favour of her second husband was held to be effective.

b. *Proof of agreement*

If there is an agreement not to revoke, that agreement may be oral or in writing,[3] and it may or may not be recited in the will itself. The most satisfactory way of recording the agreement is to

---

[1] [1951] Ch. 148.
[2] [1925] Ch. 75.
[3] *Stone* v. *Hoskins*, [1905] P. 194; *In the Estate of Heys*, [1914] P. 192; *Re Oldham*, [1925] Ch. 75; *Gray* v. *Perpetual Trustee Co.*, *Ltd.*, [1928] A.C. 391.

recite it in the will itself,[1] for where the agreement is not recorded in the will, it is easy for it to be overlooked on the death of the survivor. Consider again the example of Winnie and Wendy given at p. 18. If there is no mention of the agreement in the wills, then the remainderman would know that he was mentioned in Winnie's will, but this would not give any indication that it was made in pursuance of a prior agreement. If Wendy made a new will, probate would be granted of that new will, without any reference to the previous will. There is no way which ensures that the remainderman in these circumstances will ever learn that he is a beneficiary under the mutual will. It may well be that the comparative dearth of reported cases on mutual wills is due to the fact that in many cases an unrecited agreement has gone unnoticed.

Where there is some doubt whether there was a prior agreement not to revoke, it seems that the court leans against finding that there was a definite agreement in two circumstances. The first is where under the wills each party has an absolute interest in the event of him surviving. This was the position in *Re Oldham*[2] where Astbury, J., drew a distinction between the situation where the survivor only has a life interest, and where he has an absolute interest. The judge observed: "If the spouses intended to do what the plaintiff suggests (i.e., create mutual wills) it is difficult to see why the mutual[3] wills give the survivor an absolute interest in the whole of the property of the one who dies first." The reason behind this statement appears to be the difficulty of determining the extent of the property subject to the trust. This is considered later.[4]

The other situation in which the court may lean against finding that there was an agreement is where the whole of the property of

---

[1] As in *Re Green* where the husband, in his will, provided that his wife "will provide in her will for the carrying out of my wishes as expressed in this my will for the event that I shall survive her and in consideration of such promise by me she has agreed to leave me all her property on my undertaking to provide for the carrying out of the terms of the will as expressed in her will of even date herewith for the event that she shall survive me and for that purpose I have provided . . . ". See also *Re Hagger* where the will contained a recital of an agreement not to revoke unilaterally.

[2] [1925] Ch. 75.

[3] The judge was using the expression "mutual wills" in the wide sense of identical wills.

[4] See *post*, p. 23.

the parties is covered by the mutual provisions. This may, but does not necessarily, overlap with the position where absolute interests are conferred. In *Lord Walpole* v. *Lord Orford*[1] the court rejected the contention that there were mutual wills because of lack of evidence of any agreement, but it also said that such an arrangement would have been inequitable because it covered all the property of the parties. There is indeed difficulty as to the extent of the property covered[2] but it probably overstates the position to describe the arrangement as inequitable. If there is clear evidence of agreement to make mutual wills covering all the property of the parties, this will be binding.[3]

It has been said repeatedly that the requisite agreement not to revoke will not be implied from the fact that the wills are made in identical or largely identical terms.[4]

4. UNILATERAL REVOCATION DURING JOINT LIFETIMES

If there is an agreement not to revoke, this can clearly be varied or cancelled by mutual agreement. The agreement will also be revoked if one party unilaterally alters his will in the joint lifetimes. Where this occurs, the other party is released from his obligation not to revoke his own will. Thus, in *Stone* v. *Hoskins*[5] a husband and wife made mutual wills leaving most of their property to the survivor. The wife changed her mind, and secretly made a new will revoking the previous will. She died first. Her husband claimed that the first will was not revoked because he had no notice of revocation, but this contention was rejected. The revocation was effective. The court went on to say that where the revoker is the first to die, the survivor can alter his will.

As well as being entitled to make a new will, the other party also has a right to sue the revoker, or his estate, for damages for breach of contract. But what does this amount to? The object of damages for breach of contract is to compensate for loss, but in this case it is very difficult to calculate the loss. Where one party revokes unilaterally, the other has lost the possibility[6] of receiving

---

[1] (1797), 3 Ves. 402.
[2] See *post*, p. 23.
[3] *Re Hagger*, [1930] 2 Ch. 190.
[4] *Re Oldham*, [1925] Ch. 75, at p. 87; *Gray* v. *Perpetual Trustee Co., Ltd.*, [1928] A.C. 391, at p. 400.
[5] [1905] P. 194.
[6] "Possibility" because he might survive.

an unascertained amount[1] at an unspecified time.[2] In addition, the innocent party has been released from his obligations. The problem of calculating damages may be so difficult, and the likely amount of those damages so small, as to make the threat of an action for breach of contract no serious deterrent.

5. THE TRUST

a. *Commencement*

Until the death of the first person to die, the relationship between the parties is solely contractual. Where the wills are unrevoked at the death of the first to die, a trust arises at that time. Accordingly, where the wills confer life interests, with remainders over, the remainderman acquires a vested interest on the death of the first to die. Thus, in *Re Hagger, Freeman v. Arscott*[3] a husband and wife made a joint mutual will under which the whole of the property was to be held upon trust for the survivor for life, and thereafter upon trust for nine persons of whom one was Eleanor Palmer. The wife died in 1904, and the husband died in 1928. Eleanor Palmer died in 1923. Clauson, J., held that although she did not survive the husband, her share became vested upon the death of the wife, and so her estate became entitled on the death of the husband to the share which she would have taken herself had she been alive at that time.

b. *Basis of trust*

Why should Equity impose a trust upon the death of the first to die? In the old case of *Dufour* v. *Pereira*[4] Lord Camden said: "he, that dies first, does by his death carry the agreement on his part into execution. If the other then refuses, he is guilty of a fraud, can never unbind himself, and becomes a trustee of course. For no man shall deceive another to his prejudice. By engaging to do something that is in his power, he is made a trustee for the performance, and transmits that trust to those that claim under him."

But *Dufour* v. *Pereira* was also considered to be based on the ground that Equity intervened solely because the survivor had

---

[1] Unless a fixed amount is specified in the will.
[2] "Unspecified" because the date of revoker's death is not known.
[3] [1930] 2 Ch. 190.
[4] (1769), 1 Dick. 419.

taken the benefit of the agreement, and it would then be inequitable to allow him to revoke his own will. It now seems clear,
however, that whether or not a benefit is actually taken is irrelevant
to the question whether or not the trust exists. On the one hand,
the fact that a benefit is taken does not *per se* lead the court to
declare the existence of a trust. In *Re Oldham, Hadwen* v. *Miles*,[1]
for example, the survivor took a benefit, but her property was not
subject to a trust because the court was not satisfied that there
was an agreement not to revoke. On the other hand, it seems that
the survivor cannot be released from his obligation by refusing to
take any benefit. In *Re Hagger, Freeman* v. *Arscott*[2] where the
wife died first, Clauson, J., was rather hesitant. He said: "Therefore I am bound to hold that from the death of the wife the
husband held the property, according to the tenor of the will,
subject to the trusts imposed upon it, at all events if he took
advantage of the provisions of the will."

In *Gray* v. *Perpetual Trustee Co., Ltd.*[3] it was said that in the
absence of a definite agreement, it is irrelevant that the benefits
under the will of the first to die have been accepted. This seems
clearly in accord with principle. The survivor is only one of the
beneficiaries under the trust; it would be surprising if renunciation
of benefit by him could prejudice the position of the remainderman.

The basis for the trust is, therefore, the more general consideration that it would be inequitable for the survivor to allow the
other to die in the belief that the arrangement was firm, if he
could subsequently resile.

It must be admitted, however, that a contrary view has been
reached in some other jurisdictions, where a subsequent benefit
is essential.[4]

c. *Scope of trust property*

The trust which arises under a mutual will on the death of the
first to die is an implied trust. The scope of the implied trust
depends on the type of interest conferred by the mutual will.

---

[1] [1925] Ch. 75.
[2] [1930] 2 Ch. 190.
[3] [1928] A.C. 391.
[4] See e.g. *Denyssen* v. *Mostert* (1872), L.R. 4 P.C. 236; *Minakshi Ammal* v.
V swanatha Aiyar (1909), I.L.R. 33 Mad. 406.

Suppose, first, that husband and wife make mutual wills leaving
a life interest to the survivor, with remainder to their son, and that
the wife dies first. The wife's property will be subject not to an
implied trust, but to the express trusts of her will. In this case, it
is her husband's property only which becomes subject to the
implied trust. If, however, the husband and wife made mutual
wills leaving an absolute interest to the survivor, but with a
proviso that if the other spouse dies first, the property goes to the
son, and the wife dies first, the whole of the property, both what
was his own, and what was derived from his wife, will be subject
to the implied trust.

In the light of this, it is now appropriate to consider in greater
detail the facts of *Re Hagger*.[1] It will be recalled that in this case
husband and wife made a joint mutual will, leaving a life interest
to each other, and thereafter upon trusts for various persons
including Eleanor Palmer. The property concerned was situate
at Wandsworth.[2] It was agreed that so far as the property could
be shown to be the property of the wife, Eleanor Palmer obtained
a vested interest at her death, but it was also argued that so far as
the property could be shown to have belonged to her husband,
Eleanor Palmer took no interest because as regards his part, the
document only became effective on his death. Clauson, J., said:
"So far as the husband's interest in the property is concerned, the
will operated as a trust from the date of the wife's death." In
reaching this decision he was influenced by what he considered to
be the intention of the parties.

In view of this, it is not difficult to see why the courts have
leant against upholding wills as mutual where all the property is
included. Consider further the example of the husband and wife
making mutual wills leaving a life interest to the survivor, with
remainder over. If the wife dies first, all the property of the
husband from the date of her death is, in principle, subject to
the trust under which he is life tenant. In strict principle it appears
that the surviving husband would be obliged to treat this as any
other trust fund. He would, for example, be obliged to convert
all the property into authorised investments, and thereafter
merely to enjoy the income. He would be obliged to sell his house,

---

[1] [1930] 2 Ch. 190.
[2] It was held on a joint tenancy.

for a house for occupation is not an authorised investment.[1] He would even be forced to sell his pyjamas, and invest the proceeds of those in trustee investments. Clearly the court would strive to find some way to avoid the absurdity. As so much depends on what the court considers was the intention of the parties, it may be that the husband would be deemed to have had implied authority to spend the money during his lifetime. This overcomes one difficulty, but only raises another in its place: is the husband to be entitled to defeat the whole arrangement by spending the whole trust fund, or at least the whole of his property? And if he can spend it, presumably he can give it away, and so achieve by *inter vivos* disposition—perhaps by revocable settlement[2]—what he could not achieve by will.

There is, however, a further difficulty. If the mutual wills cover the whole of the property, although the trust arises at the date of death of the first to die, it appears that after acquired property will become subject to it. It could, perhaps, even be argued that income from the capital is after acquired property in the hands of the survivor, and so ought also to be regarded as capital.

Some assistance can be derived from a recent case on secret trusts. In *Ottaway* v. *Norman*[3] the testator, Harry Ottaway, owned a bungalow where he and his housekeeper, Eva Hodges, lived as man and wife. He wanted the property to go to William, his son by his predeceased wife, and discussions took place between all three. Harry made a will leaving the bungalow to Eva, on the basis that Eva would hold it on trust for herself, and thereafter it would pass to William. The essence of the decision was that Eva took the property on the secret trust. However, it was also suggested that the secret trust governed Eva's money at the time of her death. There were two possibilities. It might include all money which Eva had at her death, including money which she had acquired before Harry's death, and money which she had acquired afterwards from all sources. There was not sufficient evidence, however, to show that that was intended. The second possibility was that Eva should be bound by a trust affecting only

---

[1] *Re Power*, [1947] Ch. 572.
[2] See *ante*, p. 11.
[3] [1971] 3 All E.R. 1325.

money derived from Harry's will. Brightman, J., said,[1] "I am content to assume for present purposes but without so deciding that if property is given to the primary donee on the understanding that the primary donee will dispose by his will of such assets, if any, as he may have at his command at his death in favour of the secondary donee, a valid trust is created in favour of the secondary donee which is in suspense during the lifetime of the primary donee, but attaches to the estate of the primary donee at the moment of the latter's death". But this arrangement is meaningless and unworkable unless it includes the requirement that the primary donee should keep the money separate and distinct from his own money. On this point also there was no evidence, and the judge therefore decided that the trust did not attach to the money.

If a mutual will is to be made, it is therefore most important that clauses to deal with these difficulties should be included. The law can only imply a trust where there is no express provision.

6. OTHER EFFECT

It appears that where a joint tenant makes a mutual will, he thereby severs the joint tenancy in property subject to the will.[2]

7. MARRIAGE AND MUTUAL WILLS

The effect of subsequent marriage on a mutual will is open to some doubt. Wills Act 1837, s. 18, provides that a will is revoked by subsequent marriage unless that will is made in contemplation of that marriage. If, therefore, a person who had made a mutual will, not in contemplation of marriage, subsequently marries, does that revoke the will, and if so does the person who marries render himself liable to an action for damages?

In *Re Green*[3] it will be remembered that all the property of the first to die went to the survivor, who was obliged to leave half of it to certain charities. The husband survived and remarried, making a second will in favour of his new wife. It was held that the second will was effective only to deal with the other half of the husband's property. The trust had arisen previously on the death of the first wife, and the husband's subsequent marriage

---

[1] *Ibid.*, at p. 1334.
[2] *In the Estate of Heys*, [1914] P. 192.
[3] [1951] Ch. 148.

did not affect it. This seems correct in principle, although the possible effect of s. 18 does not appear to be have been mentioned in argument.

The nearest case which illustrates the effect of the subsequent marriage on the contractual liability is *Re Marsland*.[1] In that case a husband in a deed of separation made with his wife covenanted not to revoke his will. After his first marriage came to an end, he remarried. The will was revoked, and the Court of Appeal held that the contractual remedy did not lie. A distinction was drawn between intentional revocation, which did give rise to an action for damages, and revocation by operation of law, which did not. These principles will probably apply to mutual wills.

---

[1] [1939] Ch. 820, C.A.

CHAPTER 4

MAKING A WILL — THE MENTAL ELEMENT

To make a valid will a person must:

    a. be over 18;[1]

    b. have an *animus testandi*; and *Intention of making will*

    c. observe the requirements as to form laid down in the Wills Act 1837.[2]

The only exception to the rule that a person must be over 18 applies in the case of privileged wills, and the exception is considered in Chapter 6. The requirements as to form are considered in the next chapter, and this chapter deals with the *animus testandi.* An *animus testandi* means in effect that:

    a. the testator must understand the nature of the act in which he is engaged, that is, making a will;

    b. the testator must be free of vitiating mental disorder; and

    c. the testator must exercise his genuine free choice in the making of the will.

A. INTENTION TO MAKE A WILL

1. REQUISITE INTENTION

The testator must intend to make a will. There have been a number of loose statements as to the nature of the requisite intention, and in his celebrated exposition of the test of a testator's mental capacity, which is considered further at p. 32, Cockburn, C.J., in *Banks* v. *Goodfellow*[3] said that a testator "ought to be capable of making his will with an understanding of the nature of the business in which he is engaged". It is clear, however, that the testator need not know that he is making a will. All that is

---

[1] Wills Act 1837, s. 7; Family Law Reform Act 1969, s. 1.

[2] Unless the will is a "privileged will": see *post*, Ch. 6.

[3] (1870), L.R. 5 Q.B. 549, at p. 567.

necessary is that he should intend by his act to make a disposition
of his property, or to do any of the other things capable of being
done by will, which will be effective on his death.[1]

2. DOCUMENTS NOT APPARENTLY WILLS

In some cases it is clear that the testator intended to dispose of
his property, but there is doubt whether the disposition is intended
to take effect only on death. Where the transaction is effected by a
document which has been executed in a manner satisfying the
formal requirements of the Wills Act, but there is doubt whether
it was intended to be a will, the court will admit extrinsic evidence
of the testator's intention. Thus, in *In the Goods of Slinn*,[2] where
the document was executed as a deed, but also in a manner which
complied with the Wills Act, the Court admitted evidence that the
testatrix wished to settle her affairs, and on that evidence it admitted the document to probate.

In this type of case, there is usually no doubt that the testator
intended to dispose of his property: the doubt is whether the
disposition is to take effect on death, for, to be a valid will, that
must be the intention.[3] The person's intention must be firm and
beyond the stage of mere contemplation.[4] Thus where the testator
is still considering alternative drafts, he does not at that time have
an intention to make a valid will.[5]

Where the testator's wishes are fixed, however, and the formal
requirements are satisfied, a document will be regarded as a will
even if it was intended to be replaced by a more formal document.
The position is analagous to the cases in the law of contract where
a distinction is drawn between negotiations conducted "subject
to contract" and cases where it is intended to replace an informal,
but binding, agreement with a more formal document.[6] If, there-

---

[1] See *Re Stable, Dalrymple* v. *Campbell*, [1919] P. 7; *post*, p. 80.

[2] (1890), 15 P.D. 156; see *ante*, p. 10.

[3] *Nichols* v. *Nichols* (1814), 2 Phillim. 180; *King's Proctor* v. *Daines* (1830),
3 Hag. Ecc. 218; *In the Goods of Webb* (1864), 3 Sw. & Tr. 482; *Milnes* v. *Foden*
(1890), 15 P.D. 105.

[4] *Theakston* v. *Marson* (1832), 4 Hag. Ecc. 290; *Whyte* v. *Pollok* (1882), 7
App. Cas. 400; *Godman* v. *Godman*, [1920] P. 261; *In the Estate of Beech*,
[1923] P. 46.

[5] *Broughton-Knight* v. *Wilson* (1915), 32 T.L.R. 146.

[6] *Winn* v. *Bull* (1877), 7 Ch. D. 29; *Chillingworth* v. *Esche*, [1924] 1 Ch. 97;
Eccles v. *Bryant and Pollock*, [1948] 1 Ch. 93. cf. *Branca* v. *Cobarro*, [1947]
K.B. 854.

fore, instructions for a will are intended to operate as a will, pending completion of a more formal will, then those instructions will amount to a valid will.[1]

3. DOCUMENTS APPARENTLY WILLS

If a document appears on its face to be a will, and satisfies the formal requirements, there is a presumption that the testator intended to make a will. This presumption can be rebutted by evidence of a contrary intention.[2] Thus, it was said in *Lister* v. *Smith*:[3] "If the fact is plainly and conclusively made out that the paper which appears to be the record of a testamentary act was in reality the offspring of a jest, or the result of a contrivance to effect some collateral object, and never seriously intended as a disposition of property, it is not reasonable that the court should turn it into an effective instrument. . . There must be *animus testandi*[4]".

B. UNSOUNDNESS OF MIND

1. THE PROBLEM

There is no direct correlation between the mental capacity required to make a will, and mental disorder for the purposes of the Mental Health Act 1959.[5] As will be seen, a person who is competently detained under that Act can, in some circumstances, make a valid will, and a person who has never been near a mental hospital can have such unsoundness of mind as to vitiate any will he purports to make. Accordingly, each case is considered on its own facts. This flexibility is desirable, but it throws upon the Court the need to hold a balance. On the one hand, if the Court sets too high a standard, those who are dissatisfied with a will are

---

[1] *Godman* v. *Godman*, [1920] P. 261, at p. 271.

[2] *Trevelyan* v. *Trevelyan* (1810), 1 Phillim. 149; *In the Goods of English* (1864), 3 Sw. & Tr. 586; *Lister* v. *Smith* (1868), 3 Sw. & Tri. 282; *In the Goods of Nosworthy* (1865), 4 Sw. & Tr. 44; *Cock* v. *Cooke* (1866), L.R. 1 P. & D. 241; *In the Goods of Coles* (1871), L.R. 2 P. & D. 362.

[3] (1868), 3 Sw. & Tr. 282, at p. 288.

[4] *Nichols* v. *Nichols* (1814), 2 Philim. 180 is authority for the simple proposition that a will must not be made as a joke.

[5] See Fridman (1963), 79 L.Q.R. 502.

encouraged to allege mental unsoundness on the part of the testator. On the other hand, if the Court sets too low a standard, effect will be given to the most absurd wills. The balance between these two extremes has not, however, been constant. It is probably true that the degree of mental capacity now required is lower than was previously the case.

As will be seen, sometimes the result of a case may depend largely on whether the will is rational on its face.[1] This, however, needs great care. It follows from the fundamental notion of testamentary freedom that a testator can make a will in such terms as he wishes. "By the laws of this country, every testator, in disposing of his property, is at liberty to adopt his own nonsense".[2] And whether or not the will contains nonsense, in principle the motive behind a provision is also irrelevant. "Testators are not bound to have good or any reasons for what they do".[3] This salutary principle is established because the testator may have made his will from a motive which is completely unknown to the court. The position was summarised by Wigram, V.C., in *Bird* v. *Luckie*[4] in the following terms:[5] "No man is bound to make a will in such a manner as to deserve approbation from the prudent, the wise, or the good. A testator is permitted to be capricious and improvident, and is moreover at liberty to conceal the circumstances and the motives by which he has been actuated in his dispositions. Many a testamentary provision may seem to the world arbitrary, capricious, and eccentric, for which the testator, if he could be heard, might be able to answer most satisfactorily."

Yet the fact remains that if the will is irrational on its face, it will be easier to set it aside. Sir Joseph Jekyll, a former Master of the Rolls, left his fortune to pay the National Debt. His will was set aside on an application by relatives, the judge observing that the bequest was "a very foolish one. He might as well have attempted to stop the middle arch of Blackfriars bridge with his

---

[1] See particularly the rules as to the burden of proof: *post*, p. 34.
[2] *Vaughan* v. *Marquis of Headfort* (1840), 10 Sim. 639, *per* Shadwell, V.C., at p. 641; cf. *Jeffries* v. *Alexander* (1860), 8 H.L. Cas. 594, *per* Lord Campbell, at p. 648.
[3] *Hart* v. *Tulk* (1852), 2 De G.M. & G. 300, *per* Knight-Bruce, L.J., at p. 313.
[4] (1850) 8 Hare 301.
[5] *Ibid.*, at pp. 306, 307.

full bottomed wig".[1] The cases are often difficult to distinguish, although the principle is clear. A testator may make an apparently irrational will, and such irrationality will affect the will if, and only if, it indicates unsoundness of mind. Yet, in practice, what apparent irrationality, which cannot be explained, would not indicate unsoundness of mind?

2. THE TEST OF MENTAL CAPACITY

In the *Marquess of Winchester's Case*[2] it was said "It is not sufficient that the testator be of memory when he makes a will to answer familiar and usual questions, but he ought to have a disposing memory, so that he is able to make a disposition of his lands with understanding and reason." This test was expanded by Cockburn, C.J., in *Banks* v. *Goodfellow*[3] where he said: "As to the testator's capacity, he must, in the language of the law, have a sound and disposing mind and memory. In other words, he ought to be capable of making his will with an understanding of the nature of the business in which he is engaged, a recollection of the property he means to dispose of, of the persons who are the objects of his bounty, and the manner in which it is to be distributed between them. It is not necessary that he should view his will with the eye of a lawyer, and comprehend its provisions in their legal form. It is sufficient if he has such a mind and memory as will enable him to understand the elements of which it is composed, and the disposition of his property in its simple forms."

But Cockburn, C.J.'s formulation itself raises problems. What is meant by "a recollection of the property he means to dispose of"? Probably, this indicates that the testator ought to have in mind his property with a particularity appropriate to his level of wealth. A poor university teacher would easily be able to have in contemplation, for example, every item of real property which he owns: usually just his house. On the other hand, the Charlie Clores of this world might own so much property that one of them could not be expected to remember where it all is. In this case, he may merely recall that he owns office blocks in various parts of the country and it may be sufficient if he intends to leave all

---

[1] Quoted in Croake James, "Curiosities of Law and Lawyers", p. 491.

[2] (1598), 6 Co. Rep. 23a.

[3] (1870), L.R. 5 Q.B. 549. at p. 567, quoting from *Harrison* v. *Rowan*, 3 Washington at p. 595.

his office blocks in, say, London, to make a will in those terms, without having in mind each of the buildings that will pass under that description.

Another problem is raised by the expression "the persons who are the objects of his bounty". This does not mean merely the beneficiaries named in the will, but the persons who have a moral claim upon the testator.[1] The testator should, then, consider all who have moral claims, and select his beneficiaries from that class, as well as from outside it. In order to make this workable at all, and to prevent unhelpful enquiry into who have moral claims, the courts in practice restrict the class of those who have moral claims for this purpose to wives, children, and those to whom the testator stood *in loco parentis*. If, therefore, he does not have in contemplation any of such persons, except, probably, those who have lived apart from him for a considerable time, and have forfeited their claim, the will is vitiated.[2]

Provided the four tests in *Banks* v. *Goodfellow*, namely, that he is aware that he is making a will, and that he has in mind his property, the beneficiaries, and the manner of distribution between them, are satisfied, a person who is insane may nevertheless make a valid will in a lucid interval.

An interesting illustration of the degree of mental capacity required is provided by *In the Estate of Park*.[3] In that case, the testator was a rich old man who had been married for over fifty years. His wife died in January 1948, leaving him with no close relatives, his nearest relative being a nephew of the half-blood.[4] In March 1948 he executed a complicated will, leaving large benefits to his solicitors. The will also conferred substantial benefits on the step-nephew. In May 1948 he had a stroke and had another in May 1949, by which time he was incapable of looking after himself. He then became engaged to the cashier of his club. He settled shares worth £6,000 on her, and on 30 May 1949 he married her. The marriage operated to revoke the 1948 will.[5] The ceremony of marriage took place on the morning of

---

[1] *Harwood* v. *Baker* (1840), 3 Moo. P.C.C. 282; *Banks* v. *Goodfellow* (1870), L.R. 5 Q.B. 549, at p. 569. See also *Boreham* v. *Prince Henry Hospital* (1955), 29 A.L.J. 179.

[2] An example is *In the Estate of Walker, Watson* v. *Treasury Solicitor* (1912), 28 T.L.R. 466; see *post*, p. 36.

[3] [1954] P. 89.

[4] The expression "half-blood" denotes step-relationship, not acute anaemia.

[5] By virtue of s. 18, Wills Act 1837; see *post*, p. 101.

30 May: he celebrated in the afternoon by making a new and complicated will in favour of his new wife, under which she was left £1,000. He died shortly afterwards. There was then a contest between the second wife and the step-nephew. The second wife alleged that the second will was invalid, because the deceased was not capable of appreciating the complicated will that he had made. If this was so, she would take the whole estate under the intestacy rules.[1] The step-nephew retaliated by asserting that if there was insufficient mental capacity to make a will in the afternoon, there was also insufficient mental capacity to contract a valid marriage in the morning. Therefore there was no valid marriage, and the 1948 will remained effective. At first instance, Karminski, J., held that the testator understood the nature of the ceremony of marriage, which he held to be valid, and he therefore found in favour of the wife. The judge also said that a lesser degree of capacity was required for marriage than to make a will. While the Court of Appeal upheld the decision, it disapproved of this statement by the judge, and drew a distinction between the capacity required to make a simple will and that required to make a complicated will, as in this case.[2]

3. THE BURDEN OF PROOF

Where a question of possible mental incapacity arises, it is important to know where the burden of proof lies. The following rules may be deduced:

   a. In every case the person propounding a will must satisfy the court that the will is valid, that is, that it complies with the formal requirements of the Act and that the requisite mental element is present. This was expressed by Parke, B., in *Barry* v. *Butlin*[3] as: "the *onus probandi* lies in every case upon the party propounding a will; and he must satisfy the conscience of the court that the instrument so propounded is the last will of a free and capable testator."

   b. If the will is rational on its face, it is presumed that the

---

[1] *Post*, p. 175.

[2] In cases such as this, even if the will in favour of the spouse is not upheld, an application can be made to the court under the Inheritance (Family Provision) legislation: see *post*, Ch. 13.

[3] (1838), 2 Moo. P.C.C. 480; see also *Cleare* v. *Cleare* (1869), L.R. 1 P. & D. 655; *Harmes* v. *Hinkson* (1946), 62 T.L.R. 445.

testator was sane at the time when it was made.[1] Accordingly, where a will, rational on its face, is being attacked on this ground, the person attacking may either prove that the testator did not have adequate mental capacity generally, or that he lacked that capacity at the particular time that the will was made.

c. If the person attacking the will proves generally that the testator did not have mental capacity, the burden of proof shifts once again to the propounder to establish that notwithstanding the general incapacity, there was adequate capacity at the time when the will was made.

d. If the will is irrational on its face, there is a presumption that the testator did not have adequate mental capacity, so that those propounding it must satisfy the court of the testator's capacity at the time when the will was made.[2] This proposition itself causes difficulty because there is considerable authority that eccentricity or mere foolishness is not sufficient to show mental incapacity.[3] What is the distinction between an irrational will on the one hand, and eccentricity or foolishness on the other? In *Mudway* v. *Croft*[4] it was said that what is eccentricity in one person may amount to mental incapacity in another, and that eccentricity must be tested against the whole life and habits of the testator.

e. There is also a presumption of the continuance of a mental state. Therefore, where a court is satisfied that a testator had full mental capacity some time before making a will, it will presume, until evidence is shown to the contrary, that he continued to have that capacity until the will was made.[5] Likewise, where there was incapacity before the making of the will, that state, in the absence of contrary evidence, will be presumed to have continued to the time when the will was made.[6]

---

[1] *Wellesley* v. *Vere* (1841), 2 Curt. 917; *Symes* v. *Green* (1859), 1 Sw. & Tr. 401.

[2] *Harwood* v. *Baker* (1840), 3 Moo. P.C.C. 282, at p. 291.

[3] *Wellesley* v. *Vere* (1841), 2 Curt. 917; *Mudway* v. *Croft* (1843), 3 Curt. 671; *Frere* v. *Peacocke* (1846), 1 Rob. Eccl. 442; *Pilkington* v. *Gray*, [1899] A.C. 401.

[4] (1843), 3 Curt. 671.

[5] *Chambers and Yatman* v. *Queen's Proctor* (1840), 2 Curt. 415.

[6] *Smee* v. *Smee* (1879), 5 P.D. 84; *Groom* v. *Thomas* (1829), 2 Hag. Ecc. 433; *Banks* v. *Goodfellow* (1879), L.R. 5 Q.B. 549, at p. 570.

4. WILL MADE DURING LUCID INTERVAL

It follows from paragraphs c. and e. above that where the testator was of unsound mind prior to the making of the will, it is for those propounding the will to show either that by the time the will was made the testator had recovered from that unsoundness, or that the will was made during a lucid interval. A lucid interval does indeed mean "interval", so that it is not necessary to show final recovery.[1] In *Chambers and Yatman* v. *Queen's Proctor*,[2] for example, the court admitted to probate a will made during a lucid interval on one day, even though the insanity had returned to the extent that the deceased killed himself on the following day.

The cases before the Mental Health Act 1959 are full of references to the old terms idiot and lunatic.[3] In future, cases of this nature are most likely to arise where an order for the control and management of the testator's property has been made under the provisions of s. 103 of the 1959 Act. An illustration of the general position derived from the old law is *In the Estate of Walker*.[4] In that case, a large amount of property had been settled on a young woman who had always had to be kept under supervision and who, when she was 21, was found lunatic by inquisition.[5] She had periods of delusion during which she was violent and dangerous, but apart from these delusions she took a general interest in affairs. While not affected by delusions, she made a will which three doctors certified she was capable of making, and the will was admitted to probate.

There is some old authority[6] that the burden of proving a lucid interval is less where the person suffered from intermittent un-

---

[1] *Ex parte Holyland* (1805), 11 Ves. 10, at p. 11; *Creagh* v. *Blood* (1845), 8 I. Eq. 434, at p. 439; *Prinsep and East India Co.* v. *Dyce Sombre* (1856), 10 Moo. P.C.C. 232.

[2] (1840), 2 Curt. 415.

[3] At common law an idiot was a person of unsound mind from the time of his birth, and a lunatic was a person who became of unsound mind at some time during his life. However, as a result of the Mental Deficiency Act 1913, the common law definition of idiot was extended to any person who became unsound at any age up to eighteen.

[4] (1912), 28 T.L.R. 466.

[5] One of the old procedures.

[6] *Cartwright* v. *Cartwright* (1793), 1 Phillim. 90; *Steed* v. *Calley* (1836), 1 Keen 620; *Tatham* v. *Wright* (1831), 2 Russ. & M. 1; *Borlase* v. *Borlase* (1845), 4 Notes of Cases 106; *Kinleside* v. *Harrison* (1818), 2 Phillim. 449.

soundness of mind than where it is sought to prove that the lucid interval was an isolated period in otherwise unbroken mental ill health.

5. DELUSIONS

In *Dew* v. *Clark and Clark*[1] it was said that a delusion is a belief in the existence of something which no rational person could believe, and which could not be eradicated from the testator's mind by reasoned argument. It will be clear that delusion may or may not affect the person's mental capacity.

Where the delusion does not affect either the testator's property or the objects of his bounty, it will not prevent him making a valid will.[2] Where the delusion does affect either of these matters, it is a question of degree whether the delusion is so strong that his powers of critical judgment are so overborne that he has lost his power of considering rationally the circumstances which he ought to consider in making the will.[3] On the one hand, therefore, a person may take a view of the objects of his bounty which is harsh, but can be said to be rational. On the other hand, the view may be so harsh and irrational that the will cannot be allowed to stand. In *Dew* v. *Clark and Clark*[4] a daughter alleged that her father was not capable of making a valid will because of his attitude towards her. The will was rational on its face, and the burden of proof was therefore on the daughter.[5] She was able to discharge this by showing that the father refused even to see her for the first three years of her life; that he forced her to sleep with an insane woman; and that he himself was found lunatic by inquisition some time after he had made the will.

Probably the best statement of the position is again from the judgment of Cockburn, C.J., in *Banks* v. *Goodfellow*.[6] He said:

---

[1] (1826), 3 Add. 79.
[2] *Jenkins* v. *Morris* (1880), 4 Ch. D. 674; *Frere* v. *Peacocke* (1846), 1 Rob. Eccl. 442; *Smith* v. *Tebbitt* (1867), L.R. 1 P. & D. 398; *Boughton* v. *Knight* (1873), L.R. 3 P. & D. 64; *Smee* v. *Smee* (1879), 5 P.D. 84; *Murfett* v. *Smith* (1887), 12 P.D. 116.
[3] *Banks* v. *Goodfellow* (1870), L.R. 5 Q.B. 549; *Hope* v. *Campbell*, [1899] A.C. 1; *In the Estate of Walker* (1912), 28 T.L.R. 466; *Re Belliss* (1929), 141 L.T. 245.
[4] (1826), 3 Add. 79.
[5] *Ante*, p. 34.
[6] (1870), L.R. 5 Q.B. 549, at p. 565.

"Here, then, we have the measure of the degree of mental power which should be insisted on. If the human instincts and affections, or the moral sense, become perverted by mental disease; if insane suspicion, or aversion, take the place of natural affection; if reason and judgment are lost, and the mind becomes a prey to insane delusions calculated to interfere with and disturb its functions, and to lead to a testamentary disposition, due only to their baneful influence—in such a case it is obvious that the condition of the testamentary power fails, and that a will made under such circumstances ought not to stand."

A delusion which impairs testamentary capacity may affect only part of a will or codicil, in which case probate may be granted of the remainder. *In the Estate of Bohrmann*,[1] for example, a man had made a will and three codicils in which he made substantial gifts to charity. Towards the end of his life, he began to suffer from a delusion that he was being persecuted by the L.C.C.[2] Shortly before his death he made a fourth codicil, in one clause of which he said that all references to English charities were to be read as references to the corresponding American charities. Langton, J., omitted this clause from probate, but granted probate of the remainder.

The existence of a delusion may, and usually will, be proved by extrinsic evidence, for there is often no indication on the face of the will that the testator is suffering from a delusion. For example, if a testator refuses to accept that his daughter exists, and leaves all his property to charity, there will be nothing in the will itself to cast doubt upon the testator's capacity. For this reason, the court has refused to grant probate of some wills which on their face appear rational.[3]

In many ways it is unfortunate that the law developed for the most part in the nineteenth century, when the courts were convinced that there was a sharp distinction between those who were rational and those who were not, and when the courts were only too happy to pass judgment on what was rational and what was not. As a result, many pronouncements are unsatisfactory to modern ears, which recognise the many gradations between the

---

[1] [1938] 1 All E.R. 271.

[2] The forerunner of the Greater London Council.

[3] *Symes* v. *Green* (1859), 1 Sw. & Tr. 401; *Smith* v. *Tebitt* (1867), L.R. 1 P. & D. 398.

extremes of rationality and irrationality. Accordingly, perhaps more importance should now be placed on the actual facts of a case than some statements of principle might suggest.

6. INSANITY FOLLOWING WILL

To make a valid will it is only necessary for a person to have full mental capacity at the time when the will is made, so that if he becomes mentally ill after the will is made, the will will remain effective. Where the mental illness is such as to deprive him of *animus testandi*, he will also not have *animus revocandi*. Thus, mental illness following the will can make the will irrevocable.[1]

7. WILL MADE BY COURT

Section 17 of the Administration of Justice Act 1969 gives to the Court of Protection power to make a will on behalf of an adult[2] mental patient where it believes that the patient is incapable of making a valid will for himself. A will made under this provision can serve all or any of the purposes for which the will of a sane person can serve. Thus, it may dispose of property; exercise a power of appointment; or appoint executors.[3]

The formalities required for the execution of a will made by the court are considered later.[4]

C. THE RULE IN *PARKER* v. *FELGATE*[5]

As it is only necessary for a person to have full mental capacity at the time when the will is executed, it might be thought that this is the only time which is relevant. In a lenient mood, however, the courts have evolved a rule, known as the rule in *Parker* v. *Felgate*. Under this rule, if a testator, when competent, has given instructions to another person, usually his solicitor, to prepare a will, and the will is in fact prepared in accordance with those instructions, then the will is valid even though, when he actually executes it, the testator is no longer competent to make a will.

---

[1] See *post*, p. 97.

[2] Mental Health Act 1959, s. 103(3)(a) added by Administration of Justice Act 1969, s. 17(2).

[3] Mental Health Act 1959, s. 103(1) added by Administration of Justice Act 1969, s. 17(1).

[4] See *post*, p. 65.

[5] (1883), 8 P.D. 171.

This rule is objectionable in principle, for in principle the requisite testamentary capacity should accompany the execution of the will, but it is a means of upholding wills in circumstances in which the courts favour them being saved.

In *Parker* v. *Felgate*[1] a testatrix, when ill, gave her solicitor instructions to prepare a will leaving legacies to her father and brother. The testatrix went into a coma, but she was brought out of it when the new will was ready. She was told that the document shown to her was her will, and she was asked whether she wanted someone to sign on her behalf. This was done. It was established that at the time when the will was signed, the testatrix did not remember the instructions which she had given to the solicitor, and it was also established that if each particular disposition had been put to her separately, she would not have been able to understand it. It was also established, however, and this is the basis of the decision, that when the will was executed she did know that at some time previously she had given instructions for a will to her solicitor, and that she believed she was executing a will made in accordance with those instructions. On this finding, the will was held to be valid.

While, as in *Parker* v. *Felgate* itself this doctrine saves wills in *bona fide* circumstances, the scope for abuse is manifest. Accordingly, it seems that the court will only apply the rule where there is no ground for suspicion. In particular, the court will inquire into the circumstances very closely where instructions are given through third persons, or where the person drawing the will takes some significant benefit under it. *Battan Singh* v. *Amirchand*[2] was an appeal to the Privy Council from Fiji. The testator had made several previous wills benefiting his four nephews. Then, shortly before he died, and when he was very ill with the last stage of consumption, he made a will saying that he had no relatives, and leaving all his property to two creditors. Instructions had been sent through an intermediary. The Privy Council refused to uphold the will, both on the ground of the attendant suspicion, and also because there was a suspicion that he did not understand what he was doing.

---

[1] (1883), 8 P.D. 171.
[2] [1948] A.C. 161.

D. KNOWLEDGE OF CONTENTS OF WILL

Although *Banks* v. *Goodfellow*[1] was a decision on mental incapacity, it is a general principle of the law of wills that a testator must understand not only that he is making a will, but also that he understands the property of which he is disposing and the manner of its disposition. It is sufficient if he understands the general effect of his will, even if he does not understand the full legal significance of each part.[2] It seems that where no question of mental incapacity arises, it will be presumed that the testator did know the contents of the will.

In certain circumstances, however, it is necessary to prove that the testator knew of the contents of the will. This is so where, in the opinion of the court the circumstances give rise to suspicion, or the need for inquiry. It is not possible to give an exhaustive categorisation of these circumstances, but they include those now considered.

1. DRINK AND DRUGS

There is no presumption that even a habitual drunkard, or, presumably, drug addict, has no testamentary capacity at the time when the will is made.[3] A person opposing the will may, however, prove that at the time when the will was made the testator was under the influence of drink or drugs,[4] and where this is done the court will require evidence that notwithstanding the inebriation, the testator had the necessary capacity.

2. BLINDNESS AND ILLITERACY

The usual professional practice when making a will for a blind or illiterate person is to read over and explain the will to him prior to execution. The court may refuse probate where this has not been done, or at least a summary given to the testator. Where it is shown that the testator was blind or illiterate, the burden of proof is on the propounder to show that the testator did understand its

---

[1] (1870), L.R. 5 Q.B. 549, *ante*, p. 32.
[2] (1870), L.R. 5 Q.B. 549, at p. 567.
[3] *Ayrey* v. *Hill* (1824), 2 Add. 206; *Handley* v. *Stacey* (1858), 1 F. & F. 574.
[4] *Ayrey* v. *Hill*, *ante*; *Handley* v. *Stacey*, *ante*; *Wheeler and Batsford* v. *Alderson* (1831), 3 Hag. Ecc. 574; *Brunt* v. *Brunt* (1873), L.R. 3 P. & D. 37.

contents. *Christian* v. *Intsiful*[1] was an appeal from the Gold Coast[2] to the Privy Council. A testator, aged 86, had handed a document to someone who had been a solicitor's clerk, asking him to have the contents typed out as a will. The clerk had read it over to the testator, whose eyesight was so defective that he could not read the will. There were no suspicious circumstances, and the will was upheld. The case is significant for two reasons. First, it shows that the attitude of the court will depend very much on the contents of the will. Where, as here, there are no suspicious circumstances, and the will is of a type which the court would expect the testator to make, it will strive to uphold a will as valid, even where there is no positive proof that the testator knew the contents. Secondly, the case was concerned with Ordnance 49 of the Courts Ordinance of the Gold Coast which read: "Where the testator was blind or illiterate, the court shall not grant probate of the will, or administration with the will annexed, unless the Court is first satisfied, by proof or by what appears on the face of the will, that the will was read over to the deceased before its execution, or that he had at that time knowledge of its contents." In the course of his judgment, Lord Porter declared[3] that to be a principle of English law, and it is now represented by rule 11 of the Non-Contentious Probate Rules 1954.

3. OLD AGE AND INFIRMITY

Old age and infirmity do not generally give grounds for suspicion or enquiry of themselves, and are more usually used to strengthen suggestions that the testator had no knowledge of the contents, brought on some other ground such as undue influence,[4] or that the will was prepared by a principal beneficiary.[5] Where, however, it is alleged that the testator did not have knowledge of the contents because of old age or infirmity, the courts inquire into the state of the testator's memory.[6]

---

[1] [1954] 1 W.L.R. 253.
[2] The previous name for Ghana.
[3] [1954] 1 W.L.R. at p. 255.
[4] *Ashwell* v. *Lomi* (1850), L.R. 2 P. & D. 477.
[5] *Re Holtam* (1913), 108 L.T. 732.
[6] This at least is the position in certain Commonwealth jurisdictions. See *Murphy* v. *Lamphier* (1914), 32 O.L.R. 19; *Lamb* v. *Brown* (1923), 54 O.L.R. 443.

E. WILL PREPARED BY BENEFICIARY

Whenever a person who prepares a will benefits under it, the court will require evidence that the testator knew and approved its contents.[1] This is a separate question from whether the testator was subject to undue influence[2] and while the two points may be taken together, it is by no means necessary to allege undue influence as well as requiring the propounder to show that the testator knew and approved of the contents of the will.

It had previously been thought that evidence that a will had been read over to the testator prior to signature would be sufficient. Indeed, Sir J. P. Wilde in *Atter* v. *Atkinson*[3] had said: "Once get the facts admitted or proved that a testator is capable, that there is no fraud, that the will was read over to him, and that he put his hand to it, and the question whether he knew and approved of its contents is answered." While this may remain correct where the will is simple, when the will is more complicated, the propounder must now also show that the effect of the will was appreciated by the testator.[4]

Perhaps the best example of the operation of this principle is *Wintle* v. *Nye*.[5] In this case there was at no time any suggestion of fraud or undue influence, the case depending solely on whether the testatrix knew and approved the contents of her will. The testatrix made her will in 1937, shortly after the death of her brother. During her brother's lifetime, she had apparently had no experience of dealing with her own financial affairs, and naturally turned to Mr. Nye, the family solicitor. At first she instructed him to prepare a will under which he and a bank were to be joint executors, and the residue of the estate was to go to certain named charities. She was not content with the draft will prepared by the solicitor, and had a long series of interviews with him, at the end of which a will was prepared under which the solicitor was appointed to be the sole executor. Certain annuities and charitable legacies were given, and the residue was given to the solicitor.

---

[1] *Wintle* v. *Nye*, [1959] 1 All E.R. 552, *infra.*

[2] *Post*, p. 46.

[3] (1869), L.R. 1 P. & D. 665.

[4] This follows Lord Cairns, L.C., in *Fulton* v. *Andrew* (1875), L.R. 7 H.L. 448 who referred to the duty "to bring home to the mind of the testator the effect of his testamentary act".

[5] [1959] 1 All E.R. 552

When questioned about this, the solicitor said that the testatrix's first concern was for her sister Mildred, to whom she had left an annuity, that she did not wish Mildred to get control of more than that, but that if the testatrix left the residue to him, he could supply further sums for her maintenance. This explanation was, perhaps, less than convincing. Sometime later, the testatrix executed a codicil revoking the charitable legacies contained in her will. Her motive in so doing was to ensure that adequate funds were available for the payment of the annuities, which might otherwise have abated.[1] In fact there were ample funds for the payment of the annuities, and the only effect of the codicil was to increase the size of the residuary estate, which went to the solicitor. When the testatrix died, her estate was valued for estate duty purposes at £115,000. There then enters upon the scene Colonel Alfred Daniel Wintle, a retired cavalry officer, who in no uncertain terms thought that the solicitor Nye had behaved shabbily. His first attack was a frontal charge—literally so, for it ended in him debagging Nye, and proceedings being taken against him. The second attack was against the will itself. Colonel Wintle purchased the interest of a beneficiary who had a small share in the estate, and three days later issued process against Nye. He admitted in court that he purchased this share with the sole object of getting Nye into court. He lost at first instance, and in the Court of Appeal, but was successful in the House of Lords. It is worth quoting part of the judgment of Viscount Simmonds *in extenso*.[2] He said:[3] "It is not the law that in no circumstances can a solicitor or other person who has prepared a will for a testator take a benefit under it. But that fact creates a suspicion that must be removed by the person propounding the will. In all cases the court must be vigilant and jealous. The degree of suspicion will vary with the circumstances of the case. It may be slight and easily dispelled. It may, on the other hand, be so grave that it can hardly be removed. In the present case, the circumstances were such as to impose on the respondent as heavy a

---

[1] See *post*, p. 468, for the doctrine of abatement.

[2] Because it brings home the caution which solicitors must exercise in the preparation of wills under which they benefit. Advocates will also see this as an example of the technique of releasing in rapid sequence a succession of charges, so that the opponent withers under the attack.

[3] [1959] 1 All E.R. 552, at p. 557.

burden as can well be imagined. Here was an elderly lady who might well be called old, unversed in business, having no one on whom to rely except the solicitor who had acted for her and her family; a will made by him under which he takes the bulk of her large estate; a will made, it is true, after a number of interviews extending over a considerable time . . . but [having] a complexity which demanded for its comprehension no common understanding; on her part a wish disclosed in January 1937 to leave her residuary estate to charity which was by August superseded by a devise of it to him; and on his part an explanation of the change which was calculated as much to aggravate as to allay suspicion; the will retained by him and no copy of it given to her; no independent advice received by her and, even according to his own account, little pressure exercised by him to persuade her to get it; a codicil cutting out legacies to charities allegedly for the benefit of annuitants, but, in fact, as was reasonably foreseeable, for the benefit of the residuary beneficiary. All these facts and others that I do not presume to enumerate demanded a vigilant and jealous scrutiny by the judge . . . ''

The same principle will apply if the benefit is for a close member of the family of the person who prepares the will. In *Thomas* v. *Jones*[1] the testatrix executed a will appointing her solicitor to be the executor and leaving most of her property to the solicitor's daughter. The court held that the circumstances were so suspicious that the will was not to be upheld.

F. LACK OF FREE WILL

1. COERCION

Where a will is accompanied by force, fraud, fear or undue influence, that will, or the affected part which is produced in this way, is not regarded as the act of the testator, and so probate will be refused. There is little authority on force and fear—but little is needed to show that a will signed only because the testator is being banged on the head with a truncheon until he does sign will not be regarded as valid.[2]

---

[1] [1928] P. 162.
[2] See, however, *Mountain* v. *Bennet* (1787), 1 Cox, Eq. Cas. 353; *Nelson* v. *Oldfield* (1688), 2 Vern. 76.

2. UNDUE INFLUENCE

a. *Absence of presumption*

By contrast with some other branches of the law[1] there is never a presumption that a will is made under undue influence because there is a relationship between the testator and beneficiary: it must always be proved. Thus, in *Parfitt* v. *Lawless*[2] a testatrix left all her property to a Roman Catholic priest who had lived with the testatrix and her husband as their chaplain, and who was her confessor. An attempt was made to raise a presumption of undue influence[3] although there was no positive evidence that he had exercised any influence at all over the testatrix. It was held that there was not even a case to go to the jury.[4]

The reason for this difference from the law of contract is that many of the usual relationships which in contract give rise to the presumption, such as parent and child, husband and wife, solicitor and client, are just those relationships which would naturally give rise to the testator's bounty. Furthermore, in the case of an *inter vivos* transaction, the parties can protect themselves by taking independent advice, whereas in the case of a gift by will, the beneficiary may well not know of the gift until after the testator has died. Although undue influence will not be presumed from the existence of a relationship between testator and beneficiary, the circumstances surrounding the making of the will can give rise to such a presumption.

Re Craig, Meneces v. *Middleton*[5] is an example of such a case. The case in fact related to gifts made by the deceased *inter vivos* and not by will, but had they been made by will, the same principles would have applied. Mrs. Craig died in 1958, and left her estate to her husband, the deceased, who was then worth about £40,000. In January 1959 the deceased employed Mrs. Middleton as his secretary/companion, and she continued in that employment until the deceased died in 1964. In 1959 the deceased was aged

---

[1] E.g., contract.

[2] (1872), L.R. 2 P. & D. 462.

[3] Cf. *Archer* v. *Hudson* (1844), 7 Beav. 551.

[4] See also *Wheeler and Batsford* v. *Alderson* (1831), 3 Hag. Ecc. 574; *Wyatt* v. *Ingram* (1832), 3 Hag. Ecc. 466; *Walker* v. *Smith* (1861), 20 Beav. 394; *Croft* v. *Day* (1838), 1 Curt. 782; *Tuckwell* v. *Cornick* (1844), 2 L.T.O.S. 336; *Greville* v. *Tylee* (1851), 7 Moo. P.C.C. 320; *Ashwell* v. *Lomi* (1850), L.R. 2 P. & D. 477.

[5] [1970] 2 All E.R. 390.

84. Within one month of her employment commencing, the deceased gave her £1,000; by the end of 1959 he had given her £13,600; in 1960 he gave her shares worth over £5,000; and so on. By the time of his death he had given her a total of £27,851, and his estate was reduced to about £9,500. Major General and Mrs. Meneces were the residuary beneficiaries under the will, and they asked the court to set aside the gifts made to Mrs. Middleton because of undue influence. There was no evidence that pressure had been applied to produce any particular gift, although Mrs. Middleton had applied pressure to get her way in other matters, such as to prevent the deceased making a gift to General Meneces of a tea set. There was considerable difference in temperament between the deceased and his companion. The deceased was "a very gentle, dependent and vulnerable old man, deteriorating as he aged." Mrs. Middleton, by contrast, emerges as "a middle aged woman at the height of her powers. She is markedly able and competent, of a managing disposition and strong personality . . . She is physically and mentally tough and powerful, and combines these formidable qualities with a charming manner."

Ungoed-Thomas, J., found that a presumption of undue influence was raised because of the existence of two factors. First, there was a relationship between the deceased and his companion which involved such confidence by the deceased in her that she was in a position to exercise undue influence; and secondly the gifts could not "be reasonably accounted for on the ground of the ordinary motives on which ordinary men act".[1] Because no presumption of undue influence arises from relationships in relation to testamentary gifts, the first aspect of the case need not be considered further. But the Judge went on to consider whether General Meneces could have succeeded, as he did, without relying on the presumption. The Judge said:[2] "The onus of establishing such behaviour as the exercise of undue influence is heavy, because the more objectionable the behaviour the more unlikely normally is it to occur, and, therefore, the heavier the onus of establishing it. But at the end of the day the finder of fact, whether jury or judge, has to review the evidence as a whole and conclude

---

[1] [1970] 2 All E.R. 390 at p. 408.
[2] *Ibid.*, at p. 409.

whether undue influence, unlikely though it normally be, is established. The absence of direct evidence of a gift being obtained by undue influence in circumstances such as those in this case is far from indicating that it did not occur. For my part the amount of the gifts, the circumstances in which they were made, the vulnerability of Mr. Craig to pressure by Mrs Middleton, the evidence of the direct exercise of that pressure on other occasions and for other purposes, the knowledge of Mr. Craig and Mrs. Middleton of his utter dependence on her, and the whole history of the relationship of Mr. Craig and Mrs. Middleton persuade me that were it not for undue influence by Mrs. Middleton the gifts would never have been made."[1]

b. *Difference from persuasion*

In *Hall* v. *Hall*[2] Sir J. P. Wilde said:[3] "Persuasion is not unlawful, but pressure of whatever character if so exerted as to overpower the volition without convincing the judgment of the testator, will constitute undue influence, though no force is either used or threatened." Regard is paid particularly to the effect of persuasion on the testator. While he retains his freedom of choice, there will be no undue influence. Where, however, he gives in to the continued exhortation because he cannot tolerate it any longer, then that will amount to undue influence. Similarly, the court will more readily find that undue influence has been exercised where the testator is of weak mental capacity or in a weak state of health.[4]

c. *Burden of proof*

Although it is always for the person propounding a will to satisfy the court that it is valid[5] this does not extend to disproving undue influence. It is always for the person alleging undue influence to prove it.[6] In *Re Cutcliffe's Estate*[7] the Court of Appeal made it clear that an allegation of undue influence should only be made where there is strong evidence, and that if an allegation is made on insufficient evidence, the person making the allegation will probably be condemned in the costs.

---

[1] See also Baker (1970), 86 L.Q.R. 447.
[2] (1868), L.R. 1 P. & D. 481.
[3] At p. 482.
[4] *Hampson* v. *Guy* (1891), 64 L.T. 778.
[5] *Ante*, p. 34.
[6] *Boyse* v. *Rossborough* (1857), 6 H.L. Cas. 2; *Low* v. *Guthrie*, [1909] A.C. 278; *Tyrrell* v. *Painton*, [1894] P. 151; *Craig* v. *Lamoureux*, [1920] A.C. 349.
[7] [1959] P. 6.

d. Did the testator know and approve the contents of the will?

It is important to contrast the position where there is undue influence, and where the testator did not know and approve the contents of his will. As has been shown,[1] if undue influence is alleged, it must be proved by the person making the allegation. If, however, a person opposing the will can satisfy the court that the circumstances surrounding its making are suspicious, the burden of proof shifts. It is for those opposing the will to show that the circumstances are suspicious. If they do so, in effect the burden is then shifted to those propounding the will to show that the testator knew and approved the contents. But the degree of proof is different in the two cases. A finding of undue influence involves at least a moral condemnation of the person using that influence. Strictly, a finding that the testator did not know and approve the contents of his will is morally neutral, although in the circumstances of a particular case moral guilt might be present. But because moral guilt is necessarily present in undue influence, the judge will require clear evidence of it, and where there is any doubt about the strength of the evidence it is, where appropriate, better to issue process only requiring the executor to prove that the testator knew and approved the contents of the will.[2]

G. MISTAKE

There are three situations in which mistake may arise:
1. the wrong document may be executed;
2. there may be mistake going to the motive for a provision in a will;
3. there may be mistake as to the effect of a will, or of one or more of its provisions.

1. EXECUTION OF WRONG DOCUMENT

Where a document is executed by mistake, probate of it will be refused. Thus, in *In the Estate of Meyer*[3] two sisters executed similar codicils. Then by mistake they each executed the document intended for the other. The Court refused to grant probate.

[1] *Ante*, p. 46.
[2] As in *Wintle* v. *Nye*, *ante*, p. 43.
[3] [1908] P. 353.

This is as far as the English courts will go, although in Canada on similar facts probate was granted of the correct document.[1]

2. MISTAKE AS TO MOTIVE

If the testator intended certain words to be included in the will, and they are so included, then probate of the will is granted including those words, although the testator is mistaken as to their legal effect. In *Collins* v. *Elstone*[2] the testatrix was given incorrect information as to the effect of a revocation clause, but as she intended those words to appear in the document, they were admitted to probate.[3]

3. MISTAKE AS TO CONTENTS

Where a word or clause has been included in the will by mistake, and without the knowledge of the testator, probate will be granted of the will with these words omitted.[4] In *Re Swords*[5] the testatrix gave instructions for a draft will to be prepared. On her instructions, the original excluded one of the clauses, with the remaining clauses being correspondingly renumbered. The testatrix kept a copy of the draft, but not a copy of the will as executed. She then made a codicil revoking a clause in the will. Because of the numbering, she did not in fact wish to revoke that clause, and probate of the codicil was granted with that revocation clause omitted.

The court will not, however, omit part of the will from probate if the effect of the remainder of the will is altered. In *Re Horrocks*[6] a solicitor drew up for a testatrix a will which contained a gift of residue for such charitable or benevolent objects as her trustees might select. After her death, the solicitor, who was also the executor, said that this was a typing error, and he sought to omit the word "or". This would have the effect of making the words "charitable" and "benevolent" cumulative. The court refused to make the deletion, for it altered the effect of what remained.

---

[1] *Re Brander*, [1952] 4 D.L.R. 688.

[2] [1893] P. 1.

[3] See also *Fulton* v. *Andrew* (1875), L.R. 7 H.L. 448; *Harter* v. *Harter* (1873), L.R. 3 P. & D. 11; *Rhodes* v. *Rhodes* (1882), 7 App. Cas. 192; *Gregson* v. *Taylor*, [1917] P. 256.

[4] *Re Oswald* (1874), L.R. 3 P. & D. 162; *Morrell* v. *Morrell* (1882), 7 P.D. 68; *In the Goods of Moore*, [1892] P. 378; *In the Goods of Boehm*, [1891] P. 247; *In the Goods of Reade*, [1902] P. 75; *Vaughan* v. *Clerk* (1902), 87 L.T. 144; *Marklew* v. *Turner* (1900), 17 T.L.R. 10.

[5] [1952] P. 368.

[6] [1939] P. 198.

CHAPTER 5

MAKING A WILL—THE FORMAL REQUIREMENTS

Section 9 of the Wills Act 1837, provides that in order to be valid:

1. a will must be in writing;
2. it must be
   a. signed
   b. at the foot or end thereof
   c. by (i) the testator; or
        (ii) some other person in his presence and by his direction
3. the will must be so signed, or the signature acknowledged, by the testator in the presence of two or more witnesses.

This requirement applies to all wills, with the sole exception of privileged wills, which are considered in the next chapter. Although in some jurisdictions[1] a holograph will, that is, a will in the testator's own handwriting, is treated as valid without further formality, this is not so under English law, and, in fact, it makes no difference to the validity of a will if it is written in the testator's own hand.

It should be stressed that the formal requirements explained in this chapter are the corollary to the mental requirements discussed in the last: whatever formalities are observed, a document can only operate as a valid will if it is intended to take effect as a will.

A. THE NEED FOR FORMALITIES

There have been a large number of cases on almost all aspects of the formal requirements for a will. These show how easy it is for the ordinary testator to fall into error, and there has resulted

---

[1] E.g., Scotland.

51

the undignified spectacle of the courts indulging in schizophrenia, sometimes bending backwards to save a will despite apparent formal defect, and sometimes standing firm on trivial and highly technical defects.

There is, of course, no objection to prescribing formalities to be observed where a document is to be professionally prepared.[1] There is a strong, but perhaps, unpopular argument for requiring all wills to be prepared by a solicitor. In view of the many pitfalls— by no means confined to formalities—an overall benefit to the public would probably ensue if all wills were professionally drawn. But if this is politically unacceptable, it may be questioned whether the type of formality prescribed by the Wills Act is needed in current conditions.

The main arguments for these formalities are first that forgery is made more difficult; secondly that there can be no dispute as to the identity of the testator; and thirdly that the likelihood of a will being signed under coercion is reduced. Prevention of forgery is no longer a sound reason. If a person is determined to prove a forged will, he can also forge signatures of some bogus witnesses. Although it is often useful when proving a will to have affidavits from at least one of the attesting witnesses, if they have disappeared the will may still be proved under the maxim *omnia praesumuntur rite esse acta.* This is considered later.[2] There may be little difference in practical effect between a will with two genuine witnesses who have disappeared and a "will" with the "signatures" of two "invented" witnesses who never existed.

The second argument in favour of formalities, to confirm the identity of the testator, no longer has efficacy, in a society where there is rigid documentation and recording. The third reason, to prevent coercion again lacks conviction—if a will is made under coercion there is nothing to prevent the testator revoking it as soon as the coercion ceases, unless he has died in the meantime. In certain circumstances the formal requirements may be useful to prevent coercion, but it is hardly a sufficient reason by itself to justify the retention of these formalities.

There are left two other reasons for formalities. The first is to achieve certainty of the testator's intention, and this is indeed

---

[1] As in the case of deeds, which, by virtue of the Solicitors Acts, may only be prepared for reward by solicitors.

[2] *Post*, p. 277.

a reason for a will being in writing, and signed at some place.[1] The second is that by requiring the formality of witnesses, a person will think carefully about what he is doing, as there will be little doubt as to what was in fact intended to operate as a will. It may be thought by the end of this chapter that the cases do not bear this out. It may also be thought that the only formalities which really are necessary are that the will should be in writing, and signed in some place by the testator. At least, it is important not to become so bemused by the statute and case law on formalities that the possibility of some other situation is overlooked.

Against this background, we can now consider the various requirements of the Wills Act.

B. WRITING

The requirement that a will must be in writing does not mean that it must be in the testator's handwriting. Nor does it mean that it must necessarily be in anyone's handwriting. Probably any permanent form of visual representation will be sufficient. A will may, therefore, be handwritten, typed, printed, or be in any combination of these.[2] If it is handwritten, it may be in ink, or pencil, or partly one and partly the other.[3]

There is no requirement as to the material on which the will must be written. Thus, a will may be written on the shell of an egg.[4] There is also no requirement as to the language in which the will is written. It may be written in a foreign language, or even in Welsh, or indeed, partly in code, provided this can be deciphered from extrinsic evidence.[5]

Suppose therefore that a person seeking to produce a modern rival to the Elgin marbles chips out his will in the form of a strip cartoon over 176 blocks of marble and then signs it at the end. It may cause havoc with the Probate Registry's filing system— but will it nevertheless not be valid?

---

[1] Not necessarily at the end.

[2] Interpretation Act 1889, s. 20; see also *In the Goods of Moore*, [1892] P. 378; *Re Smithers*, [1939] Ch. 1015, at p. 120; [1939] 3 All E.R. 689, at p. 692.

[3] *In the Goods of Lawson* (1842), 6 Jur. 349; *In the Goods of Hall* (1871), L.R. 2 P. & D. 256; *In the Goods of Adams* (1872), L.R. 2 P. & D. 367; *In the Goods of Tonge* (1891), 66 L.T. 60.

[4] *In the Goods of Barnes* (1926), 43 T.L.R. 71.

[5] *Kell v. Charmer* (1856), 23 Beav. 195.

C. SIGNATURE OF TESTATOR

1. MEANING OF SIGNATURE

Although the Wills Act says that the will must be "signed" by
the testator, the courts have decided that this does not mean what
it says.[1] This provision has been construed as meaning that the
testator must put some mark on the document which he *intends*
to be his signature. A "signature" made by a rubber stamp is
satisfactory.[2] A mark is acceptable as a signature,[3] even, it appears
from a Canadian case, if the hand of the testator is guided when
the mark is made.[4] In *Re Finn*[5] the testator, who was admittedly
illiterate, went even further: he dipped his thumb in the ink pot,
and made a blot on the will with his inky thumb. That was
accepted as a valid signature.

A testator may sign just his initials,[6] or part of his signature,
provided in every case that the actual mark he did make was
intended to be his signature. Thus, in *In the Goods of Chalcraft*[7]
the testatrix was on the verge of death. Her normal signature was
"E Chalcraft". She began to sign her name, and had got as far as
"E Chal" when she could not go on. On a liberal construction,
the court held that this was all that she intended to put as her
signature, and the will was admitted to probate.

If the testator intends to use a full name, apparently it need
not be his own.[8] Thus, in *In the Goods of Glover*[9] a will was
admitted to probate where it was signed by a woman in the name
of her first husband after her second marriage, and in *In the Goods
of Redding*[10] the will was held to be effectively signed where the
testatrix had used an assumed name. Further, it seems that to
be a "signature" it is not necessary to use a name at all. In *In the*

---

[1] See, generally, Sherrin (1970), 114 S.J. 198.

[2] *Re Jenkins* (1863), 3 Sw. & Tr. 93.

[3] *Lemaine* v. *Staneley* (1681), 1 Freem. K.B. 538; *Baker* v. *Dening* (1838),
8 Ad. & El. 94; *Hindmarsh* v. *Charlton* (1861), 8 H.L. Cas. 160; *Re Kieran*,
[1933] I.R. 222.

[4] *Re White*, [1948] 1 D.L.R. 572.

[5] (1935), 105 L.J.P. 36.

[6] *In the Goods of Savory* (1851), 18 L.T.O.S. 280; *In the Goods of Emerson*
(1882), 9 L.R. Ir. 443.

[7] [1948] P. 222.

[8] *In the Goods of Clarke* (1858), 1 Sw. & Tr. 22.

[9] (1847), 5 Notes of Cases 553.

[10] (1850), 2 Rob. Eccl. 339.

Estate of Cook[1] the court accepted as a valid signature the words
"your loving mother" and in *Rhodes* v. *Peterson*[2] the word "Mum".
The testator must, however, make some mark. Accordingly,
it is not effective to pass a dry pen over a signature already on the
paper, in the form of a mock signing,[3] though this might perhaps
be valid as an acknowledgement.[4]

The result of these decisions is that it is necessary for the
testator to make a mark on the paper, but the courts will accept
as a signature whatever mark was intended by him as a signature.

2. POSITION OF SIGNATURE

a. *Single sheet of paper*

The Wills Act 1837 required the signature to be "at the foot
or end thereof". If the words "the foot or" are tautologous, the
meaning would seem clear. It is, however, almost as if there was
an underground organisation of troublesome testators who plotted
together to see where else they could place their signatures.
Signatures were placed lengthwise and sideways in the margin,
in the middle of the text, at the top, on the back, and in almost
every conceivable place. As a result the Wills Act Amendment Act
was passed in 1852. This Act provides that a signature is valid if
it "is so placed at or after or following or under or beside or
opposite to the end of the will" and it is apparent on the face of
the will that the testator intended to give effect to the document
as his will. This, however, did not put an end to the litigation.
In *In the Goods of Ainsworth*[5] a will was held valid where the last
part of it was written in short lines confined to the left hand side
of the sheet, with the signature opposite those lines on the right
hand side. One line on the left was below the signature. In this
case it was proved that the last line was written before the signature, and the whole will was valid.

Re Hornby[6] went further. In that case the testator wrote out a
will and as he did so he left in the text towards the end a "box",

---

[1] [1960] 1 All E.R. 689.
[2] 1972 S.L.T. 98.
[3] *Playne* v. *Scriven* (1849), 1 Rob. Eccl. 772; *Kevil* v. *Lynch* (1874), 9 I.R. Eq.
249; *Re Maddock* (1874), L.R. 3 P. & D. 169.
[4] See *post*, p. 59.
[5] (1870), L.R. 2 P. & D. 151.
[6] [1946] P. 171.

in which, when he had finished the whole text, he wrote his signature. This will too was upheld, on the basis that the signature was intended to validate the whole will.

In *In the Estate of Roberts*,[1] when the testator was writing out his own will, he came to the end of the page, and found that there was no room for his signature. He therefore turned the paper sideways, and wrote both the attestation clause and the signature along the margin. His signature appeared at the top of the paper. This was held to be valid. By contrast, in *Re Stalman*[2] where the testatrix just signed at the top because there was no room at the bottom, the will was held to be defective.

b. *"End"—in space, or time, or intention?*

There is little doubt that the Wills Act 1837 envisaged that a will would be signed physically at the end, or, as it may be called, at the end in space. In *Re Ainsworth*, *Re Hornby* and *In the Estate of Roberts* discussed above the signature was in each case elsewhere than at the end. The wills were nevertheless admitted as valid because the court was satisfied that the signature was placed later in time than the remainder of the will.

An alternative explanation, and the express ground of the decision in *Re Hornby* is that the court is satisfied that the signature was at the end of the will "in the intention of the testator". It is necessary to prove this intention to the court. A case which is in some ways similar to *Re Hornby* is *Re Dilkes*[3] where the signature was in the middle of the document, but was held to be ineffective. In *Re Dilkes* the intention of the testator was not proved to the court.

The cases are inconsistent. One certainly cannot say that if a signature is proved to be at the end in time or intention, but not in space, then it will necessarily be held to be valid. All that can be said is that some wills may be saved if the judge wishes to save them.

c. *More than one page*

A will is frequently written either on folded paper, or on separate sheets. The 1852 Act says that a will shall not be made

---

[1] [1934] P. 102.
[2] (1931), 145 L.T. 339.
[3] (1874), L.R. 3 P. & D. 164.

ineffective because "a blank space shall intervene between the concluding word of the will and the signature". Can whole pages intervene? And if so, in what order were the pages written? In *In the Goods of Wotton*[1] the testatrix used a will form. This had been printed on a sheet of paper folded in two, so that one side formed pages 2 and 3 of the document, and the other side formed pages 1 and 4. Page 1 was printed with the standard heading of a will, and had other printed material, including a space for signature. The other three pages were left blank. The testatrix wrote on pages 2 and 3 and signed in the space provided on page 1. This was held to be valid. The court accepted evidence that the testatrix regarded pages 2 and 3 as the first two pages, so that the signature on page 1 was in fact the last, notwithstanding that it was headed with the commencing words of the will. There was clear evidence that the document was in fact signed after the remainder had been written.

This was followed in *Re Long*[2] where a will was written on two pages. One page contained a list of bequests. On the other page was the heading, the appointment of executors, and the signature. Probate of the will was granted, Sir Boyd Merriman, P., saying:[3] "Provided that the court is satisfied that the whole document was written before the signatures were made, and that the dispositive part of the document may be fairly read as preceding and leading up to the part containing the signatures and in no sense as a mere annexe or schedule thereto, I think that it would be transgressing what Sir James Hannen, in *In the Goods of Wotton*[4] called 'the spirit of the Act' to insist, as a criterion of valid execution, upon proof that the several parts of the document were actually written in any particular order."

On similar facts, however, only the page which was signed was admitted to probate in *Royle* v. *Harris*.[5] This was followed in *In the Goods of Gee*[6] where the will was written on two pages. The first page was signed, and the signature witnessed, and the dispositive part was continued on the second page. Even though

---

[1] (1874), L.R. 3 P. & D. 159; see also *Re Smith*, [1931] P. 225.
[2] [1936] P. 166; see also *In the Goods of Mann*, [1942] P. 146; *Re Denning*, [1958] 2 All E.R. 1; *Re Little*, [1960] 1 All E.R. 387.
[3] [1936] P. 166, at p. 173.
[4] (1874), L.R. 3 P. & D. 159, at p. 161.
[5] [1895] P. 163.
[6] (1898), 78 L.T. 843.

the sentence at the end of the first page was not finished, and was completed on the second page, probate was granted only of the first page.

There thus grew up a liberal school, illustrated by *In the Goods of Wotton* and *Re Long*, and a narrow school illustrated by *Royle* v. *Harris* and *Re Gee*. The former sought to give effect to what the testator clearly intended at the expense of the strict meaning of the Wills Act, while the latter sought to follow the Act. In 1953, however, the Senior Registrar issued a Practice Direction[1] to the effect that probate will not be granted of pages after the signature unless there is some specific reference above the signature which incorporates the later pages by reference.[2] Accordingly, it has long been established that if there is a sign of interpolation, and the interpolated matter follows the signature, that can be admitted.[3] Thus in *Palin* v. *Ponting*[4] where the testator wrote "see other side for completion" the words on the other side were included in the probate.

While the Practice Direction may have brought some degree of certainty, it does not have the force of law so far as questions of substance are concerned, and it is still open to litigants to rely upon the earlier cases if appropriate.

There is no requirement in the Wills Act 1837 that a will must be written on one sheet of paper only. The courts, however, developed a requirement that if the will was written on more than one sheet then all sheets on which it was written should be attached at the time of execution.[5] This rule was relaxed so that it is now sufficient if the sheets are held together at the time of execution, for example, by holding them with finger and thumb, even though there is no permanent means of attachment.[6]

In some cases the courts have been concerned with the situation where a will is placed in an envelope and the envelope itself, but not its enclosure, is signed and the signature witnessed. If it can be shown that the envelope and its enclosure were held together at

---

[1] 103 L.J. 314.

[2] See *post*, p. 67, for the doctrine of incorporation by reference.

[3] *In the Goods of Kimpton* (1864), 3 Sw. & Tr. 427.

[4] [1930] P. 185.

[5] *Cook* v. *Lambert* (1863), 3 Sw. & Tr. 46; *In the Goods of West* (1863), 32 L.J.P.M. & A. 182; *In the Goods of Horsford* (1874), L.R. 3 P. & D. 211; *Lewis* v. *Lewis*, [1908] P. 1.

[6] *Lewis* v. *Lewis, ante*; *Re Little, Foster* v. *Cooper*, [1960] 1 All E.R. 387.

the time of execution then the signature on the envelope will be
effective if it was intended by the deceased as the signature to the
will. It is in each case a question of fact whether the signature on
the envelope is intended to be the signature of the will or whether
it is merely a means of identification of the contents of the envelope.
In *In the Goods of Mann*[1] the testatrix wrote on the envelope
"Last Will and Testament of J. C. Mann". She signed this and
her signature was witnessed. This envelope was then placed into
a larger envelope and sealed. Probate was granted. In other cases[2]
probate has been refused where it could not be shown that the
signature was intended as the signature to the will.

The testator must either sign his will in the presence of two or
more witnesses or if he has previously signed it he may acknowledge his signature in the presence of such witnesses. The acknowledgment is of the signature and not of the will itself. It is therefore not necessary that the witnesses should know that the document is a will.[3] It is sufficient if the testator merely asks the
witnesses to sign the document which he produces and they see his
signature upon it.[4] Alternatively the acknowledgment may be
merely by gesture.[5] It was stated earlier[6] that to draw a dry pen
over a signature on a will did not constitute a signing of the will
for the purposes of the Act. It may be, however, that such a
gesture would amount to an acknowledgment of the signature.[7]

A signature can only be acknowledged if the witnesses either see
or have the opportunity of seeing the signature.[8] In *Re Groffman*[9]
the deceased said to two friends at a coffee party "I should like
you now to witness my will"; at the same time gesturing to his
coat pocket where the folded will was, but not taking it out. The
only table in the room was covered with coffee cups and cakes, so
the deceased and one of the friends went into an adjoining room,
where the deceased took the will out of his pocket, revealing the
signature on it. As the friend was the only person present in that

---

[1] [1942] P. 146.
[2] E.g., *In the Estate of Bean*, [1944] P. 83.
[3] *Keigwin* v. *Keigwin* (1843), 3 Curt. 607.
[4] *Gaze* v. *Gaze* (1843), 3 Curt. 451.
[5] *In the Goods of Davies* (1850), 2 Rob. Eccl. 337; *In the Goods of Owston*
1862), 2 Sw. & Tr. 461.
[6] *Ante*, p. 55.
[7] *Lewis* v. *Lewis*, [1908] P. 1.
[8] *In the Goods of Gunstan* (1882), 7 P.D. 102.
[9] [1969] 2 All E.R. 108.

other room, the production of the will by the deceased was not a valid acknowledgment, but although there was no doubt that the deceased intended to make his will, it was rejected.[1]

D. ATTESTATION

1. PRESENCE OF WITNESSES

The testator must sign his will or acknowledge his signature in the presence of two witnesses who are both present when the signature is made or acknowledged. The witnesses must both sign the will. They must sign in the presence of the testator but they need not sign in the presence of each other. It is therefore sufficient if the testator signs his will in the presence of two witnesses; one goes out of the room while the other signs; and then the other comes back and signs while the first one goes out of the room.

2. MEANING OF "PRESENCE"

Although the Wills Act requires the testator to sign, or acknowledge his signature, in the presence of witnesses, and the witnesses to sign in the presence of the testator, this provision has been construed narrowly so that it is now clear that the witnesses need not actually see the testator sign, nor need he see them sign.[2] The test is whether the person in whose presence the signature is made could have seen the other signing had he wished to do so. Thus, if the testator is in one room and the witnesses are in another room, but there is a hole in the wall, then if the witnesses from where they were standing in the room could have looked through the hole in the wall and seen the testator signing that is sufficient.[3] If, however, the witnesses would have needed to have moved in order to see through the hole in the wall, and there is no evidence that they did alter their position, the attestation is bad.[4] In *Casson* v. *Dade*[5] in 1781 a testatrix drove to her solicitor's office to sign a will. She signed it but found the office hot and went outside to sit in her carriage. When she was in the carriage she

---

[1] See Baker (1969), 85 L.Q.R. 462.

[2] *Tod* v. *Earl Winchelsea* (1826), 2 C. & P. 488; *Jenner* v. *Ffinch* (1879), 5 P.D. 106; *Carter* v. *Seaton* (1901), 85 L.T. 76.

[3] *Shires* v. *Glascock* (1688), 2 Salk. 688.

[4] *Norton* v. *Bazett* (1856), Dea. & Sw. 259.

[5] (1781), 1 Bro. C.C. 99.

could not in fact see the witnesses through the window of the office but at the very moment when the witnesses were signing the horses backed just so that there was a line of sight through the window of the carriage and the window of the office in such a way that had she so wished the testatrix could have seen the witnesses signing. The attestation was good.

This and similar cases are clear examples of the extent to which the Courts will go in order to save a will if possible. Indeed, in *Winchilsea* v. *Wauchope*[1] it was stated that where a line of sight exists there is a presumption of good attestation if there is no evidence to the contrary.

The extent of this doctrine is open to some speculation. For example, if a person, thinking he is alone, signs his will but is in fact being observed by two people watching through closed circuit television, can it be said that he is signing in their presence? Again, if a person signs a will by himself at the bottom of a valley and is observed by two others at the top of the adjoining hill, who are watching carefully through binoculars, is that valid execution? When considering the position of a blind man as a witness, Pearce, J., said:[2] "In the light of common sense, and without authority, I should be inclined to hold that for the purposes of the Act a 'witness' means . . . in regard to things visible one who has the faculty of seeing. The signing of a will is a visible matter." It was decided in that case that a blind person is not a competent witness for the purposes of the Act, but by Pearce, J.'s test the corollary may seem to admit the bizarre circumstances just discussed.

3. COMPETENCE OF WITNESSES

Under the legislation in force until 1752, a will was not valid unless it was witnessed by three persons who were "credible". Whether or not a person was credible appears to have been largely determined by whether he received any benefit under the will. The Wills Act 1752 altered the previous position by providing that if an attesting witness received any benefit under the will then the attestation was good but he could not take that benefit. This provision of the 1752 Act was repealed and re-enacted in the 1837 Act. It extends to any benefit. Because of the rule

---

[1] (1827), 3 Russ. 441.
[2] *Re Gibson*, [1949] P. 434.

which prevents a trustee deriving any benefit from his office in
the absence of express provision[1] where there is no express
provision in the will enabling him to do so, a solicitor or other
professional person who is appointed to be the executor of the
will cannot make a charge for his services. It is therefore customary
for a solicitor who is also appointed the executor of the will to
include in the will a charging clause, which is a clause enabling
him to make a proper professional charge in connection with the
work done by him as executor. Such a charging clause is however
regarded as conferring a benefit on him under the terms of the
will so that notwithstanding the presence of such a clause he
cannot in fact make a charge if he also witnesses the will.[2]

Section 15 of the Act also provides that a beneficial gift to the
wife or husband of an attesting witness shall be void. The courts
have sought to construe this as narrowly as possible. Accordingly
in *Thorpe* v. *Bestwick*[3] the testator left property to a woman beneficiary. One of the attesting witnesses married her after the
execution of the will but before the testator's death. It was held that
the gift remained effective.

A further illustration of the way in which the courts have
construed this provision of s. 15 narrowly, is provided by
the fact that the courts will uphold a gift if it can be said to have
arisen under any testamentary instrument which the witness did
not attest. In several cases it has been decided that if a beneficiary
attests the will and the will is confirmed by a codicil which he does
not attest then he is entitled to take the gift as it can be said that
he takes under that codicil.[4] In *Re Trotter*[5] it was even held that
in these circumstances the beneficiary could take notwithstanding
the fact that he witnessed a subsequent codicil as well as the will
itself. Likewise, if a beneficiary takes a gift under a will and
witnesses not the will but a codicil to it the gift remains effective.[6]

There is some inconsistency as to the position where a gift is
altered. In *Gaskin* v. *Rogers*[7] the will provided for a beneficiary

---

[1] See e.g., *Robinson* v. *Pett* (1734), 3 P. Wms. 249, at p. 251.
[2] *Re Barber* (1886), 31 Ch.D. 665; *Re Pooley* (1888), 40 Cn.D. 1.
[3] (1881), 6 Q.B.D. 311.
[4] *Anderson* v. *Anderson* (1872), L.R. 13 Eq. 381; *Re Trotter, Trotter* v. *Trotter*,
[1899] 1 Ch. 764; *Re Elcom, Layborn* v. *Grover Wright*, [1894] 1 Ch. 303.
[5] [1899] 1 Ch. 764.
[6] *Gaskin* v. *Rogers* (1866), L.R. 2 Eq. 284.
[7] (1866), L.R. 2 Eq. 284.

to receive a contingent gift. He did not witness the will but witnessed a codicil where the nature of the gift was altered from a contingent to an absolute gift. On these facts he was held not entitled to take. By contrast in *Gurney* v. *Gurney*[1] the will provided for the payment of a legacy and for the residue to be divided equally between two named persons. The residuary beneficiaries did not witness the will but they did witness a codicil which revoked the legacy. This obviously had the result of increasing the residuary estate, and accordingly their benefit, but they were nevertheless held entitled to take the whole of the residuary estate as provided by the codicil.

For a gift to be avoided on the ground that a beneficiary attests the will it must be shown that the beneficiary is to take the gift beneficially and not as a trustee.[2] Thus, in *Re Ray's Will Trusts, Public Trustee* v. *Barry*[3] the testatrix, who was a nun, left her property to the person who should be the abbess of her convent at the date of her death upon trust for the convent. The will was witnessed by two other nuns one of whom at the date of death of the testatrix was the abbess. In holding that the gift was effective the court gave two reasons, first that the gift was not a beneficial legacy and secondly that the gift was to a person identified by a formula under which the testatrix could not know at the time the will was made who in fact would take the gift. It is uncertain whether in these circumstances the gift would have been effective had this formula been used but the gift had been intended to be beneficial.

The cases are not consistent where one of the witnesses is to take a benefit under the will under a secret trust. In *Re Fleetwood, Sidgreaves* v. *Brewer*[4] it was held that the beneficiary under the secret trust could not take a gift under the will but this was not followed in the more recent case of *Re Young, Young* v. *Young*.[5] The decision in *Re Young* is more in keeping with the general liberal construction of this section.

Where there are at least two witnesses to a will who do not take a benefit under it, and the gift is made to another witness, or to

---

[1] (1855), 3 Drew. 208.
[2] *Cresswell* v. *Cresswell* (1868), L.R. 6 Eq. 69; *Re Ryder* (1843), 2 Notes of Cases 462; *Re Ray's Will Trusts, Public Trustee* v. *Barry*, [1936] Ch. 520.
[3] [1936] Ch. 520.
[4] (1880), 15 Ch.D. 594.
[5] [1951] Ch. 344.

his wife, the attestation by that "surplus" witness is disregarded, so that he can take his benefit.[1]

4. INTENTION TO ATTEST

Section 14 of the Wills Act 1837 provides that if a person who witnesses a will is not at the time of such attestation, or at any time subsequently, competent to be called as a witness to prove the execution of the will then the will is not on that ground invalid. It is not clear whether this provision relates to the general credibility of the witness or, as may seem more likely on its face, to the mental capacity of that witness. If, however, this section does relate to mental capacity there is the surprising result that the execution of the will would not be invalid if one of the witnesses could not understand the nature of the act in which he was engaged. It can be said in favour of this construction however that the need for an intending testator to satisfy himself of the mental capacity of the witness is obviated.

If this section does relate to mental capacity it will have the effect of restricting the meaning of the word "presence" in s. 9. One would, at least at first sight, expect "presence" in this section to relate both to physical and to mental presence. Whether or not it does relate to mental presence depends on the true construction of s. 14. There is remarkably little authority on this point but it is likely that the witness must attest *animo testandi*.[2]

5. THE ATTESTATION CLAUSE

It is desirable although not essential that a will should conclude with an attestation clause. This clause, which may be adapted to the circumstances, is designed to provide *prima facie* evidence that in the particular circumstances of the case the requirements of the Act have been fulfilled. The usual clause reads: "signed by the above named Alfred Brown as his last will in the presence of us both present at the same time who at his request in his presence and in the presence of each other have hereunto subscribed our names as witnesses." A more streamlined clause[3] is: "Signed by

---

[1] Wills Act 1968, s. 1, reversing *In the Estate of Bravda, Bravda v. Bravda*, [1968] 2 All E.R. 217.

[2] *In the Goods of Eynon* (1873), L.R. 3 P. & D. 92; *In the Goods of Smith* (1889), 15 P.D. 2.

[3] As approved in *Re Selby-Bigge*, [1950] 1 All E.R. 1009.

the above named Alfred Brown in our presence and attested by us in the presence of him and each other." If there is no such clause showing that the statutory requirements have been fulfilled, although the will will not be necessarily invalid, it will be necessary to prove in some other way that the requirements of the Act have been fulfilled.[1] This will usually involve tracing one of the attesting witnesses, or someone else who was present at the time of execution, and to obtain from that person an affidavit confirming exactly what happened at the time of execution.[2] If such evidence cannot be obtained because it is impossible to trace the witnesses the will may nevertheless be admitted to probate under the presumption considered later.[3]

E. EXECUTION OF WILL OF MENTAL PATIENT

Section 17 of the Administration of Justice Act 1969 conferred upon the Court of Protection power to make a will on behalf of a mental patient. Where the power is exercised the Court directs or authorises a person, known as "the authorised person", to make the will on the patient's behalf. The will is signed by the authorised person who signs the name of the patient, and also signs his own name. The will must be attested by two witnesses in the usual way, who must sign in the presence of the authorised person. Thereafter the will is sealed with the official seal of the Court of Protection.[4] A will executed in this way takes effect as if it were executed by the patient, and he had the capacity to make a valid will,[5] except that it cannot govern immovable property outside England and Wales[6] and except also that it is of limited effect where the patient is domiciled outside England and Wales.[7]

The authorised person may also sign a statement on behalf of

---

[1] Non-Contentious Probate Rules 1954, r. 10. An affidavit of handwriting may be necessary: *Baxendale* v. *De Valmer* (1887), 57 L.T. 556.

[2] If the attesting witness refuses to swear an affidavit, the court can order his attendance, or it may dispense with the affidavit, *Re Ovens* (1929), Ir.R. 451.

[3] See *post*, p. 277.

[4] Mental Health Act 1959, s. 103A(1), added by Administration of Justice Act 1969, s. 18.

[5] Mental Health Act 1959, s. 103A(3).

[6] Mental Health Act 1959, s. 103A(4)(a).

[7] Mental Health Act 1959, s. 103A(4)(b): See Hunt and Reed (1970) 34 Conv. (N.S.) 150.

the deceased for the purposes of s. 1(7) of the Inheritance (Family Provision) Act 1938.[1,2]

F. REQUIREMENTS WHERE WILL EXECUTED ABROAD

Where a testator who made a will abroad dies on or after 1 January, 1964, the position is governed by the Wills Act 1963. In respect of pre-1964 deaths, the provisions of the Wills Act 1861, still apply, but those provisions are not considered in this book. The 1963 Act applies to all deaths after 1963, even if the will was made before that date.

The 1963 Act seeks to save as many wills as possible. It adopts the well established distinction of Private International Law between requirements of form, such as whether the will must be holograph, or whether it must be witnessed, and requirements as to essential validity, such as whether the testator had full mental capacity. Where there is doubt as to the nature of the requirement, there is a tendency for it to be regarded as a requirement of form only. Thus, where a will can only be witnessed by persons holding certain qualifications, or where particular categories of testators are required to satisfy special formalities, those requirements are regarded as matters of form only.[3]

The Act then lays down the general principle[4] that as regards formal validity, a will is to be regarded as properly executed, if it was made in accordance with the internal law of the country or territory:

a. (i) where the testator was domiciled; or

   (ii) where the testator had his habitual residence; or

   (iii) of which the testator was a national.

b. (i) at the time when the will was made; or

   (ii) at the date of his death.

There can be any combination of situations within categories a. and b. In respect of immovable property, a will is also valid if it is formally valid by the law of the territory in which the property

---

[1] Considered at p. 211.
[2] Mental Health Act 1959, s. 103A(5).
[3] Wills Act 1963, s. 3.
[4] Wills Act 1963, s. 1.

is situated, even if none of the general conditions just mentioned is satisfied.[1]

Where a will is executed on board a ship or aircraft, it is regarded as valid if the execution conformed to the law in force in the territory "with which, having regard to its registration (if any) and other relevant circumstances, the vessel or aircraft may be taken to have been most closely connected".[2] This provision appears to leave ample scope for argument and dispute.

G. INCORPORATION BY REFERENCE

1. REQUIREMENTS

It is convenient to deal here with the doctrine of incorporation by reference. Under this doctrine, documents which satisfy certain conditions are regarded as forming part of the will, even though they themselves are unattested. The conditions are:

    a. the document must be in existence at the date of the will;[3]

    b. the document must be referred to in the will as being in existence at that date; and

    c. the document must be clearly identified in the will.

The courts have, with few exceptions, demanded strict compliance with these conditions. Otherwise it would be possible for the testator to make a will in outline reserving to himself the power to alter the incorporated document at some future date. This would clearly defeat the object of the Wills Act.

It is necessary to consider the conditions further.

a. *Existence of document*

A document cannot be incorporated into the will if it is not in existence at that date.[4] Where a document comes into existence after the date of the will, but before a codicil confirming it, it will be incorporated if the will in its republished form refers to it as being in existence at that time.[5] The doctrine of republication is considered in Chapter 8.

---

[1] Wills Act 1963, s. 2 (1) (*b*).

[2] Wills Act 1963, s. 2 (1) (*a*).

[3] *Re Keen, Evershed* v. *Griffiths*, [1937] Ch. 236; *Singleton* v. *Tomlinson* (1878), 3 App. Cas. 404; *Re Sunderland* (1866), L.R. 1 P. & D. 198.

[4] *Singleton* v. *Tomlinson* (1878), 3 App. Cas. 404.

[5] *In the Goods of Lady Truro* (1866), L.R. 1 P. & D. 201; *Re Reid* (1868), 38 L.J. P. & M. 1; *In the Goods of Rendle* (1899), 68 L.J.P. 125; *In the Estate of Phillips, Boyle* v. *Thompson* (1918), 34 T.L.R. 256.

b. *Reference to existence of document*

The document must not only actually be in existence when the will is made, but it must be referred to as being in existence at that time. Thus in *In the Goods of Smart*[1] the testatrix made a will in which she gave a life interest in property to a beneficiary, and subject thereto said: "I direct my trustees to give to such of my friends as I may designate in a book or memorandum that will be found with this will." The will was made in 1895. On the death of the testatrix a book was found written in 1898 and 1899 which was headed "hints for executors" and which complied with the description in the will. The will was republished in 1900. The book was not incorporated, because although it was actually in existence in 1900, it was referred to in the will as being a future document. Again, in *University College of North Wales* v. *Taylor*[2] the testator left a substantial legacy to the University College, with a direction to use the income for scholarships and prizes, the gift being conditional on compliance with "any memorandum found with my papers". Because this expression could refer to a document not in existence at that date, it was held to be not validly incorporated. A similar result was reached in *Re Bateman's Will Trusts, Brierley* v. *Perry*[3] where the executors were directed to pay the income from a fund to such persons "as shall be stated by me in a sealed letter in my own handwriting and addressed to my Trustees".

A very liberal, and exceptional, decision is *In the Estate of Saxton.*[4] The testator left all his property "to the following persons". There was no following list of persons, but on death lists of legacies were found, headed by the testator's note that he wished those persons to benefit. This list was held to be incorporated, but the decision is wrong in principle.

Where the document is referred to as being in existence at the time when the will is made, but cannot be found at the date of death, it is regarded as never having been incorporated, and the provision purporting to incorporate the document is without effect.[5]

---

[1] [1902] P. 238.
[2] [1908] P. 140.
[3] [1970] 3 All E.R. 817
[4] [1939] 2 All E.R. 418.
[5] *Re Barton, Barton* v. *Bourne* (1932), 48 T.L.R. 205; cf. *Willoughby* v. *Storer* (1870), 22 L.T. 896.

c. *Identification of document*

It was said in *Croker* v. *Marquis of Hertford*[1] that identification is of the very essence of incorporation, but perhaps a slightly lower standard of identification is accepted than might be expected. In *In the Estate of Mardon*[2] the testatrix made a codicil in which she referred to the "schedule hereto". That reference was held to be sufficient. In *In the Estate of Saxton*[3] the will contained the words "to the following persons" and the document began "I wish to leave the following amounts". That was held to be a sufficient cross-reference.

2. EFFECT OF INCORPORATION

When a document is incorporated it will normally be included in the probate. Exceptionally, however, the document will not be included in the probate if it would be unduly inconvenient to do so. Thus, in *In the Goods of Balme*,[4] where the document incorporated was a substantial library catalogue, this was omitted from probate.[5] Whether or not the incorporated document is included in the probate, it becomes testamentary, and must be construed with the will itself.[6]

Difficult problems arise where the document incorporated itself leaves the disposition of the property open to doubt. In *Re Jones*[7] the testator left a legacy on the terms of a deed of trust "executed by me bearing even date with this my will and testament or any substitution therefor". As this left room for a future document to be substituted, the whole incorporation was held by Simonds, J., to be ineffective. The position was more complicated in *Re Edwards Will Trusts*.[8] The testator directed his residuary estate to be held upon the trusts declared by an identified trust instrument which was in existence at the date of the will. The trust instrument gave the testator, who was the settlor, power to direct

---

[1] (1844), 4 Moo. P.C.C. 339, at p. 366.
[2] [1944] P. 109.
[3] [1939] 2 All E.R. 418.
[4] [1897] P. 261.
[5] See also *Re Marquis of Lansdowne* (1863), 3 Sw. & Tr. 194; *In the Goods of Jones* (1920), 123 L.T. 202.
[6] *A.-G.* v. *Jones and Bartlett* (1817), 3 Price 368; *Watson* v. *Arundel* (1877), 11 I.R. Eq. 53.
[7] [1942] Ch. 328.
[8] [1948] Ch. 440.

by memorandum to whom the capital and income were to be paid, and provided that subject thereto, the fund was to be held for his wife and children. The Court of Appeal held that because the document itself satisfied the conditions it was incorporated. However, when incorporated it could only have effect to the extent that a document could form a valid part of a testamentary disposition, and while it was admitted to probate with the will, the clause enabling the settlor to appoint by memorandum was held to be ineffective. Accordingly, the fund passed to the testator's wife and children.[1]

3. USE OF DOCTRINE

Because the document will usually be admitted to probate and will always form part of the testamentary instrument, it is not an effective way of making testamentary gifts without them becoming public knowledge. This must be done by a secret trust. The practical importance of the doctrine is in fact confined to the case where complicated questions of detail arise, and which are too bulky to be included conveniently in the will.

There is an overlap between the operation of this doctrine and revival of revoked wills.[2] In the first place a revoked will may be incorporated by reference in a later will rather than itself being revived. Thus, in *Re White, Knight* v. *Briggs*[3] the testator by will directed his trustees to hold property on certain trusts. This will was subsequently revoked, and he made a later will leaving property on the trusts declared by the previous will. The previous will was held to be incorporated into the later. In other cases the possibility of showing that a will has not been revived or republished, but has been incorporated, must be kept in mind. This is particularly important where the previous will is in itself defective, and so has not taken effect. If it is the subject of a basic deficiency, it will not be effectively republished, but there is no reason why, as a document, it should not be incorporated if the testator's intention to that effect can be shown.

4. STATUTORY WILL FORMS

Law of Property Act 1925, s. 179, authorises the Lord Chancel-

---

[1] *Re Schintz's Will Trusts*, [1951] Ch. 870.
[2] Considered, *post*, p. 116.
[3] [1925] Ch. 179.

lor to publish forms to which the testator may refer in his will, and if they are incorporated in this way, they form part of the will in accordance with normal rules. The object of the rules is to enable the length of a will to be reduced by obviating the need to set out provisions at length. These are, however, inconvenient because it is preferable to have all the provisions of the will in one document, and the Statutory Will Forms are therefore little used in practice.

CHAPTER 6

PRIVILEGED WILLS

1. CONCEPT

Although in most cases formalities may be thought necessary for making a will, and when the Wills Act was passed the need for those formalities was far greater than at present,[1] it is realised that in certain exceptional cases a person should be able to make a will without formality. This is where the testator is usually in grave danger, which accentuates the desire to make a will, and where he is deprived of the normal means of consultation before making his will.

There is no general principle that a person in unusual danger or deprived of consultation may make an informal will, but s. 11 Wills Act 1837, provides that "any soldier being in actual military service, or any mariner or seaman being at sea, may dispose of his personal estate as he might have done before the making of this Act". That is, he may make a will without any formal requirements whatever. A privileged will may, therefore, be nuncupative, that is, completely oral, or it may be written, and if written it need not be signed or witnessed. Although there are no formal requirements, however, it is still necessary to show an intention to make a will.[2]

To many, the decisions on privileged wills may seem to be unduly liberal. It is then well to remember that a judge is a member of society, and must be, to a greater or lesser degree, influenced by the feelings of society. Most of the decisions on privileged wills have been made during a time of war, or shortly after the end of hostilities. At such times, if at no other, soldiers are popular and respected. In common with the society in which they lived the judges have adopted the most liberal approach to soldiers, and their wills.

---

[1] *Ante*, p. 52.
[2] *Post*, p. 80.

72

A second general feature of the decisions is that in this field as in others,[1] the court seeks to uphold as valid those wills where the dispositive effect accords with what the courts seek to encourage. Where an unmarried soldier wishes to benefit his parents or fiancée, or a married soldier his wife or children, the courts will be inclined even more to find for the validity of the will.

Whatever may have been the historical origin of the doctrine, the institution of privileged wills may be justified on pragmatic grounds. It can be a source of comfort to a soldier facing battle to know that should he not return, arrangements have been made for his affairs. Cynics have suggested that the privilege is more for the beneficiaries than the testator, for it is the persons named in the will who appear to derive all the benefit. This is to ignore the psychological benefit to the soldier in the field.

2. HISTORY

Immediately prior to the passing of the Statute of Frauds in 1677 there were no formal requirements for any will disposing of personalty. The Statute of Frauds altered this position by prescribing various formalities for a will disposing of personalty worth more than £30. Thereafter, the will had to be either in writing, or if nuncupative, had to be made in the presence of three witnesses and put into writing within six days of its making. The only exception to this was in respect of the wills of soldiers on actual military service and sailors at sea.

The 1837 Act preserved the position under the Statute of Frauds so far as privileged wills were concerned, so that there were no formal requirements, but these wills were only adequate to dispose of personalty.

Section 3 of the Wills (Soldiers and Sailors) Act 1918, however, extended the scope of the exception to wills of realty for persons dying after 5 February, 1918. At the same time the Act extended the scope of the privilege to members of what is now the Royal Air Force.[2] Accordingly, at present a privileged will may dispose of any type of property. It may also be used to appoint testamentary guardians.[3]

---

[1] *Ante*, p. 15.
[2] Wills (Soldiers and Sailors) Act 1918, s. 5 (2).
[3] Wills (Soldiers and Sailors) Act 1918, s. 4.

3. "ACTUAL MILITARY SERVICE"

Whether a person is on "actual military service" is a question of fact, and it does not necessarily depend on the legal position of the forces concerned. Thus, almost certainly a soldier cannot make a privileged will merely because he is stationed in a country with whom we are at war. Still, in 1973, no Peace Treaty has been signed with Germany, although it is most unlikely that a soldier attached to B.A.O.R. could make a privileged will.[1] Likewise, the expressions "actual military service" and "active service" are not co-terminous, for again "active service" is a term determining the legal status of the forces, including such matters as whether they are eligible to win certain decorations, such as the V.C.

It was at one time thought that a soldier on actual military service was in the same position as a Roman soldier *in expeditione*.[2] A Roman soldier *in expeditione* was entitled to make a privileged will, on the basis that he was *inops concilii*, and so unable to obtain proper assistance to discuss and make a formal will. However, the respectability of the Roman analogy was discredited by Denning, L.J., in *Re Wingham, Andrews* v. *Wingham*.[3] He said: "The words of our statute are in plain English: 'in actual military service.' I find them easier to understand and to apply than the Latin: 'in expeditione.' If I were to inquire into the Roman law, I could perhaps after some research say how Roman law would have dealt with its soldiers on Hadrian's Wall or in the camp at Chester, but I cannot say how it would have dealt with an airman in Saskatchewan, who is only a day's flying from the enemy."

The meaning given to the expression "actual military service" has altered with the changing nature of warfare. Prior to 1939, a soldier had to be either serving overseas in a campaign, or to be about to serve overseas following mobilisation.[4] Thus, in *White* v. *Repton*[5] a soldier being in barracks in peacetime was held not to be entitled to the privilege, because he might have had the same

---

[1] See, however, *Re Colman*, [1958] 2 All E.R. 35.
[2] See *Drummond* v. *Parish* (1843), 3 Curt. 522; *White* v. *Repton* (1844), 3 Curt. 818; *In the Goods of Hill* (1845), 1 Rob. Eccl. 276.
[3] [1949] P. 187.
[4] *In the Goods of Hiscock*, [1901] P. 78; *Gattward* v. *Knee*, [1902] P. 99; *Re Booth, Booth* v. *Booth*, [1926] P. 118; *In the Estate of Rippon*, [1943] P. 61.
[5] (1844), 3 Curt. 818.

assistance as a civilian, and in *Re Stable, Dalrymple* v. *Campbell*[1] it was said that in order to qualify, the soldier must be under orders to go to the front.

The cases arising out of the 1939-45 War extend this test markedly. Some suggest that merely by being in uniform a person is entitled to make a privileged will. Thus, in *In the Estate of Spark*[2] Hodson, J., decided that a soldier who was killed during an air-raid on his camp in the United Kingdom was entitled to make a privileged will. In principle, however, the circumstances in which the deceased died should be irrelevant: the relevant circumstances are those in which the will was made, but these do not appear from the report. By contrast, Henn Collins, J., in *In the Goods of Gibson*[3] decided that an officer of the Royal Army Dental Corps, who lived at home but attended daily at his camp, and who was killed by a bomb on his house, was not entitled to make a privileged will.[4]

In *In the Estate of Rowson*[5] a squadron officer, W.A.A.F., who was in charge of a W.A.A.F. depot in England was held to be entitled to make a will. In that case, while in England, she had sent instructions to her solicitors to make for her a formal will. They had prepared a draft but it was not executed. Her instructions were treated as a valid will. Wallington, J., observed: "I want to make it quite clear . . . that the few observations I wish to make are not to be understood as indicating a view, even remotely, that everybody in the W.A.A.F. is in actual military service." He did not, however, indicate why Squadron Officer Rowson was regarded as being in actual military service. The facts that she *had* seen active service, and *had* been mentioned in despatches were regarded as important, even though in principle they should have been just as irrelevant as the circumstances in which she died.

The most important of the cases to emerge from the 1939-45 War is *Re Wingham, Andrews* v. *Wingham*.[6] In that case, a member of the R.A.F. was sent to Canada for flying training and while

[1] [1919] P. 7.
[2] [1941] P. 115.
[3] [1941] P. 118, n.
[4] See article by R. E. Megarry (1941), 57 L.Q.R. 481.
[5] [1944] 2 All E.R. 36.
[6] [1949] P. 187.

there he made an informal will. He later died in a flying accident. At first instance it was held that because the will was made outside a theatre of war it was not privileged. This was unanimously reversed by the Court of Appeal, but on various grounds. Cohen, L.J., adopted as his test that "the deceased was liable at any time to proceed to some area in order to take part in active warfare and that under these circumstances he was in actual military service".

Denning, L.J., went further. He said: "The plain meaning[1] of the statutes is that any soldier, sailor or airman is entitled to the privilege, if he is actually serving with the Armed Forces in connexion with military operations which are or have been taking place or are believed to be imminent. It does not, of course, include officers on half-pay or men on the reserve, or the territorials, when not called up for service. They are not actually serving. Nor does it include members of the Forces serving in this country, or on routine garrison duty overseas, in time of peace, when military operations are not imminent. They are actually serving, but are not in actual 'military' service,[2] because no military operations are afoot. It does, however, include all our men serving—or called up for service—in the wars; and women too, for that matter. It includes not only those actively engaged with the enemy but all who are training to fight him. It also includes those members of the Forces who, under stress of war, both work at their jobs and man the defences, such as the Home Guard. It includes not only the fighting men but also those who serve in the Forces, doctors, nurses, chaplains, W.R.N.S., A.T.S., and so forth. It includes them all, whether they are in the field or in barracks, in billets or sleeping at home. It includes them although they may be captured by the enemy or interned by neutrals. It includes them not only in time of war but also when war is imminent. After hostilities are ended, it may still include them, as, for instance, when they garrison the countries which we occupy, or when they are engaged in military operations overseas. In all these cases they are plainly 'in actual military service'. Doubtful cases may arise in peacetime when a soldier is in, or is about to be sent to, a disturbed area or an isolated post, where he may be involved in military operations. As to these cases, all

---

[1] When a judge refers to the "plain meaning" of anything, it is a sure sign that it is anything but plain.

[2] If the service is not military, it is difficult to know what it is.

I say is that, in case of doubt, the serving soldier should be given the benefit of the privilege."

In some respects the narrower test of Cohen, L.J., may be preferred, as it permits a clear distinction to be drawn between cases where on the one hand the privilege should certainly be granted because fighting is in progress or imminent, and the Home Guard type of case on the other.[1] Despite some criticisms,[2] however, it seems likely that Denning, L.J.'s test will be followed.

It appears both from *Re Wingham* and from earlier cases that the position with regard to the privilege is the same where war is imminent though not declared as where it is in progress. Thus, in *In the Estate of Rippon*[3] a Territorial Army officer received orders in August 1939 to rejoin his battalion, whereupon he made an informal will. The Territorial Army was not embodied until 1 September, and war was not declared until 3 September, but the will was held to be privileged.

There is little authority as to the position in post-1945 conditions. The present organisation of the Army depends on allocating part of the Regular Army to a strategic reserve, which is kept in readiness to be flown to trouble areas anywhere. It seems likely that members of the strategic reserve, put on, say, 72 hours standby, would be entitled to make a privileged will while stationed in England. The nearest authority appears to be the Australian decision *In the Will of Anderson*[4] where a soldier was held to be entitled to make a privileged will when under orders to proceed to Malaya following the declaration of a state of emergency. It is more difficult to know whether British troops used in Internal Security operations, such as Cyprus between 1955 and 1959, in Aden between 1963 and 1967 and Northern Ireland from 1970 would be entitled to make privileged wills. In theory, such operations may be regarded as policing only, but often verge more into war and the areas concerned were declared to be active service areas.

4. "AT SEA"

The second limb of privileged wills under s. 11 of the 1837 Act relates to mariners or seamen "at sea". Section 2 of the Wills

---

[1] *In the Estate of Anderson*, [1944] P. 1.
[2] E.g., D. C. Potter at 12 M.L.R. 183.
[3] [1943] P. 61.
[4] (1958), 75 W.N. (N.S.W.) 334.

(Soldiers and Sailors) Act 1918 extended this to enable a member of the Royal Navy or Royal Marines to make a privileged will not only when he is at sea, but also when he is "so circumstanced that if he were a soldier he would be deemed to be in actual military service". On this basis, it seems that if the wider test in *Re Wingham, Andrews* v. *Wingham* is applied, any member of the Royal Navy or Royal Marines during wartime would be entitled. In *In the Estate of Yates*[1] an officer of the Royal Navy who was ordered to join his ship told his son when bidding him goodbye at the railway station that if anything happened to him, he wanted everything to go to his wife. Something did happen to him, and this oral wish was held to be a valid will under the 1918 Act.

Section 2 of the 1918 Act applies only to members of the Royal Navy and Royal Marines: it does not apply to merchant seamen, although the 1837 Act does.[2]

5. PERSONS ENTITLED TO MAKE PRIVILEGED WILLS

It remains to decide who is entitled to make a privileged will, assuming that the requirements of being in actual military service, or being at sea, are fulfilled. Here again the construction has been wide. It has already been seen that the term "soldier" includes officers[3] and it also includes members of the Royal Air Force of any rank.[4] A barman on a liner is a "sailor at sea"[5] as is a sailor serving on board a vessel stationed permanently in habour,[6] and even it was suggested in *In the Goods of Barnes, Hodson* v. *Barnes*[7] serving as a pilot on duty on the Manchester Ship Canal.[8]

Women may qualify either as soldiers on actual military service, or as sailors at sea. In *In the Estate of Stanley*[9] an army nurse was held entitled to the privilege when, on leave, she wrote a letter

---

[1] [1919] P. 93.

[2] *In the Goods of Milligan* (1849), 2 Rob. Eccl. 108; *In the Goods of Parker* (1859), 2 Sw. & Tr. 375; *In the Goods of Hale,* [1915] 2 I.R. 362.

[3] *In the Estate of Rippon,* [1943] P. 61.

[4] Wills (Soldiers and Sailors) Act 1918, s. 5 (2).

[5] *In the Estate of Knibbs,* [1962] 2 All E.R. 829 (although in that case there was no valid will).

[6] *In the Goods of M'Murdo* (1868), L.R. 1 P. & D. 540.

[7] (1926), 96 L.J.P. 26.

[8] See also *In the Goods of Austen* (1853), 2 Rob. Eccl. 611; *In the Goods of Patterson* (1898), 79 L.T. 123.

[9] [1916] P. 192.

asking the addressee to deal with her affairs. *In the Estate of Rowson*[1] has already been mentioned[2] as a further example. In *In the Goods of Hale*[3] a woman who was employed as a typist on a Cunard liner was held entitled to make a privileged will.

There are two special provisions which apply to seamen. Formerly, members of the Royal Navy and Royal Marines could only dispose of money payable by the Admiralty, such as arrears of wages, prize money and bounties, if the will complied with all the formalities of a written will,[4] but this restriction has now been repealed as regards persons dying after 14 August, 1953.[5]

Secondly, in order for a merchant seaman to make a will at sea disposing of assets under the control of the Department of Trade and Industry, he must make a will which complies with s. 177, Merchant Shipping Act 1894. By that section, if the will is made on board ship, it is necessary for it to be in writing and attested by the master or mate.

6. CONFLICT WITH OTHER PROVISIONS

There are apparent inconsistencies between s. 11, and several other sections of the 1837 Act. There is no general principle as to how these inconsistencies are to be resolved, it depending in each case on what the courts have thought to accord with public policy.

a. *Infants*

Section 7 of the 1837 Act declares simply: "No will made by any person under the age of 18 years shall be valid."[6] *Re Wernher, Wernher v. Beit*[7] was concerned with an informal will made by an infant, who, had he been an adult, would clearly have been entitled to make a privileged will. It is very doubtful whether the legislature in 1837 intended s. 11 to override s. 7, thereby enabling a military infant to make a valid privileged will, and so thought Younger, J., at first instance. However, before the case reached

---

[1] [1944] 2 All E.R. 36.

[2] *Ante*, p. 75.

[3] [1915] 2 I.R. 362.

[4] Navy and Marines (Wills) Act 1865, s. 5, as amended by Navy and Marines (Wills) Act 1930.

[5] Navy and Marines (Wills) Act 1953.

[6] See *ante*, p. 28. The age of 18 was substituted for the age of 21 by the Family Law Reform Act 1969, s. 3 (1).

[7] [1918] 1 Ch. 339.

the Court of Appeal, Parliament rushed through the 1918 Act s. 1 of which declares that the privilege has always extended to infant soldiers and infant mariners and seamen.

If an infant soldier ceases to be on military service before he reaches the age of 18, he cannot make a new formal will until he reaches that age. He can, however, revoke his will before reaching that age.[1]

b. *Revocation*

One of the methods prescribed for revoking a will is by another instrument in writing "executed in the manner in which a will is hereinbefore required to be executed".[2] It was held in *In the Estate of Gossage, Wood* v. *Gossage*,[3] however, that an informal privileged will can revoke an earlier formal will.

Although s. 11 thus overrides s. 20, s. 18 overrides s. 11. S. 18 provides that with certain exceptions[4] a will is revoked by a subsequent marriage. In *Re Wardrop*[5] the privileged will was held to be revoked by subsequent marriage, though the reasoning seems inconsistent with *In the Estate of Gossage, Wood* v. *Gossage*.

7. ANIMUS TESTANDI

Difficulty has arisen in several cases as to the mental element required for a privileged will. In principle, the deceased should intend that as a result of his words his property should devolve in the manner which he states.[6] Thus, in *Re Stable, Dalrymple* v. *Campbell*[7] a young lieutenant was engaged during the First World War to a certain Blanche Dalrymple. To her, in a romantic moment, he said: "If I stop a bullet everything of mine will be yours". Another person was present,[8] and Blanche, being nicely brought up, replied: "I wish you would not speak of such things to outside people". Horridge, J., admitted the officer's words to probate, and observed in so doing that it is not necessary that a testator should think that he is making a will

---

[1] S. 3 (3) Family Law Reform Act 1969.
[2] S. 20, Wills Act 1837.
[3] [1921] P. 194.
[4] *Post*, p. 101.
[5] [1917] P. 54.
[6] *Drummond* v. *Parish* (1843), 3 Curt. 522; *In the Estate of Vernon* (1916), 33 T.L.R. 11.
[7] [1919] P. 7.
[8] The witness was able to give evidence confirming the words spoken.

Where, however, the deceased makes an informal statement showing that he only intends at some time in the future to make a will that statement will not amount to a will. On the other hand, such a statement will be effective if the statement shows that the deceased merely intends in the future to make a formal will repeating the terms of the present informal one.[1] Likewise, a statement that a result will occur by some other means, such as by operation of the intestacy rules, will not amount to a will, and this is so whether or not the belief or statement as to the intestacy rules is correct. In *Re The Estate of Donner*[2] the deceased was discussing with a friend making a will and was told that if he died, his mother would take everything. He replied: "That is just what I want. I want my mother to have everything", but it was held that these words did not constitute an intention to make a will, but a statement of approbation of what he understood to be the position without a will.

Similarly, in *In the Estate of Knibbs, Flay* v. *Trueman*[3] where a sailor said "if anything happens to me Iris will get anything I have got", Iris got nothing because this statement proceeded on the basis that Iris would take because of arrangements already made, and not as a result of these very words.

Although the position in principle is as has just been stated, the courts are prepared in some cases to relax their requirements, and to admit to probate almost any expression of testamentary wish. It is, however, quite impossible to know in advance of the trial whether the court will relax the principle. One case where it did was *Re Spicer, Spicer* v. *Richardson*.[4] Army pay books issued to officers and soldiers contain a page upon which a soldier may write out his will if he so wishes. In this case a soldier produced his pay book, and said that if anything happened to him, his property would go to a named person. The pay book could not be found on the soldier's death, but those present when the statement was made thought that the deceased's wishes were recorded in it. If this had been so then his oral statement could not have amounted to a will, but in the absence of production of the book, the court accepted the words spoken as a will.

---

[1] *Gattward* v. *Knee*, [1902] P. 99.
[2] (1917), 34 T.L.R. 138.
[3] [1962] 2 All E.R. 829.
[4] [1949] P. 441.

The facts of *In the Estate of Rowson*[1] have already been given.[2] In that case, instructions for a will were accepted as a valid will, though it is highly likely that the officer concerned intended her instructions only to amount to instructions, and not as a will itself.

8. THE PRIVILEGE RECONSIDERED

It may be thought that the scope of privileged wills should in in one respect be restricted, and in another respect extended. The restriction would involve a limitation on the period of time for which a privileged will should remain effective.

There would be much to be said for an enactment that a privileged will should remain effective only for, say, twelve months after the person making it ceased to be on actual military service or at sea. He would in that time have ample opportunity to make a formal will, and so avoid the difficulties attaching to an informal one. There is, however, no such provision in English law. A privileged will remains fully effective until it is revoked or until the deceased dies.

On the other hand, it might also be thought that informal wills, similarly limited in life, could be made by any person in an emergency. A spy in an enemy prison; a round-the-world yachtsman contemplating Cape Horn; explorers in the Amazon; and spacemen cavorting around the planets should all be able to make emergency wills without any formality. Perhaps the old Roman idea could be resurrected, and anyone could make an informal will who was not able to obtain proper assistance to discuss and make a formal will.

---

[1] [1944] 2 All E.R. 36.
[2] *Ante*, p. 75.

CHAPTER 7

REVOCATION AND ALTERATIONS

Provided that the testator has full mental capacity, his will can always be revoked. As in the case of mutual wills[1] the making of a will may be accompanied by an agreement or covenant not to revoke, but while breach of this agreement or covenant may give rise to an action for damages, the will itself remains revocable.

A will can only be revoked in one of four ways:

Voluntary revocation:

    a. by a document executed with the same formalities as are needed for a will;

    b. by an informal declaration where the testator is entitled to make a privileged will;

    c. by actual destruction.

Involuntary revocation:

    d. by marriage, except where the will was made in contemplation of marriage.[2]

Just as with a will it is necessary to show the presence of the two elements—intention and formality—so in the case of voluntary revocation these two elements must also be present. Accordingly, for example, if a will is ripped to pieces in a state of mental derangement or drunkenness,[3] the will will not be revoked. The same degree of mental capacity is needed to revoke a will as to make one,[4] but this probably equates the capacity to revoke

---

[1] *Ante*, p. 19.
[2] And in certain cases except where the will exercises a power of appointment: see *post*, p. 104.
[3] *In the Goods of Brassington*, [1902] P. 1.
[4] *Re Sabatini* (1969), 114 Sol. Jo. 35.

with that to make a *simple* will. Because voluntary revocation must always be accompanied by an *animus revocandi* it is only where a person, having made a will, subsequently becomes of incurable unsoundness of mind that a will can become irrevocable.

Marriage is the only circumstance in which a will is automatically revoked. It is important to note that no revocation occurs on divorce, or on the birth of issue.

In general the revocation must be by the testator himself. In no circumstances can the intention to revoke be delegated.[1] However, the act of revocation may be delegated in two circumstances:

a. where the revocation is by destruction, the act of destruction may be carried out by another person in the presence of the testator and by his direction;[2] and

b. where the testator sends to the person having custody of the will a document executed in testamentary form requesting him to revoke that person may destroy it.[3]

A. WHEN WILL IS NOT REVOKED

This chapter is concerned primarily with the circumstances in which a will can be revoked. It is, however, essential to keep in mind the fact that a will will not be revoked in any other circumstances. Two situations in particular cause difficulty in practice.

The first is when a marriage breaks down. Although, generally, marriage automatically revokes a will,[4] divorce does not. If therefore, the testator does not take steps to revoke his will by one of the prescribed means, his wife or former wife will still be entitled under a will made in her favour when the marriage was happy. A solicitor advising a client about a divorce or separation should consider also the revocation of any existing will.

The second situation is where there is a substantial alteration in the financial position of the deceased between the time when the will was made, and the time of death. For example, a testator

---

[1] *Stockwell* v. *Ritherdon* (1848), 1 Rob. Eccl. 661.

[2] See *post*, p. 94.

[3] *In the Goods of Durance* (1872), L.R. 2 P. & D. 406; *Re Spracklan's Estate*, [1938] 2 All E.R. 345.

[4] See *post*, p. 101.

owning assets worth, say, £550, might leave a legacy of £500 to his son, and his residue to his brother. If he then wins the first prize in the Premium Savings Bond draw, and dies from the shock, his son will still receive the £500, but his brother will take £50,050. Another example is a little less obvious. The testator might have built up a family company, and made a will leaving the shares to his employees, when they were of little value, and the remainder of his estate to his wife. The company may prosper, and the shares increase in value quite disproportionately to the value of the remainder of the estate. But estate duty on personalty is, in general, payable from the residue of the estate. The employees will, then, take their shares free of duty, and the amount left for the wife might be negligible. Wills should, therefore, be reviewed at, say, five-yearly intervals, rather than as being made for life.

B. REVOCATION BY DOCUMENT

1. EXPRESS REVOCATION

a. *Revocation clause*

Section 20 of the Wills Act 1837 provides that no will or codicil, and no part of any will or codicil, shall be revoked otherwise than in one of two ways. The first is by actual destruction, and this is considered later. The other way is "by another will or codicil executed in manner hereinbefore required, or by some writing declaring an intention to revoke the same, and executed in the manner in which a will is hereinbefore required to be executed". It will be seen that s. 20 contemplates the revocation either of the whole will, or of some part of it.

It is common for a will to commence with an express revocation clause.[1] Such a clause may be confined to the revocation of some part of a previous will, or to the revocation of only one of several previous testamentary instruments, so that, for example, if the testator has property in England and France, and he makes separate wills dealing with his properties in those countries, he may wish to confine his revocation clause in a subsequent will to the previous English will.

The usual form of this clause is to revoke all previous wills. In the most common form it reads: "I hereby revoke all former

---

[1] See Sherrin (1972), 122 N.L.Jo. 6.

wills and testamentary instruments made by me and declare this
to be my last will." Even where there has been no previous will,
this clause is often included in a will for it confirms to those who
are administering the estate that they need not search for an earlier
will.

b. *Nature of revoking document*

The instrument in which the revocation clause is contained
need not be a will, and therefore it need not be a document which
is admissible to probate. The only requirement is that it should
be executed in the same way as a will. Thus, in *Re Howard,
Howard* v. *Treasury Solicitor*[1] a testator had made a will in 1923
leaving his property to his son. In 1940 he executed two separate
wills, both of which contained an express revocation clause. In
one will he left all his property to his wife, and in the other he
left all his property to his son. There was no indication which
will was made first. The object of this curious procedure was so
that whether his wife or son survived him, the survivor would
be able to produce a will completely in his or her favour. The
court held that the two wills were irreconcilable, and so neither
could be admitted to probate, but they were both sufficient to
revoke the 1923 will.[2]

An attested document asking for a will to be destroyed may be
an effective express revocation. As will be seen,[3] where a document is to be revoked by actual destruction, the destruction must
take place by the testator, or by someone in his presence. This can
cause difficulties if the testator is, for example, abroad, and the
will is in England. In such circumstances, the testator may execute
a document revoking the will.[4] By extension it has been held that
an attested letter may be construed as showing a present intention
to revoke. Thus, in *Re Durance*[5] the testator was in Canada, and
his will was in England. He sent a letter, attested by two witnesses,

---

[1] [1944] P. 39.

[2] See also *Biddles* v. *Biddles* (1843), 3 Curt. 458; *Townsend* v. *Moore*, [1905]
P. 66; *Loftus* v. *Stoney* (1867), 17 I. Ch.R. 178.

[3] *Post*, p. 96.

[4] Whether or not that document is also a will.

[5] (1872), L.R. 2 P. & D. 406.

to his brother in England asking him to collect the will and to burn it. This was held to be an effective revocation.[1] It is necessary, however, to show that the testator intended the will to be revoked by the letter, and not by the following act of destruction.

c. *Intention to revoke*

In principle, an intention to revoke must be shown as well as the act of revocation, but where there is an express revocation clause, there is also a strong presumption that the testator had an intention to revoke. It is, therefore, only in the clearest case that a previous testamentary instrument will remain effective notwithstanding a subsequent express revocation clause. Thus, in *Sotheran v. Denning*[2] a wife had a general power of appointment over realty. In 1877 she made a will exercising the power. In 1878 she made a new will which contained an express revocation clause, but disposed only of her personalty. It was probably her intention not to revoke the previous will in so far as it exercised the power of appointment, but this limitation of her intention could not be proved, with the result that the revocation clause was effective and the realty devolved in default of appointment.[3]

There are three situations in which the previous testamentary instrument will not be revoked by the revocation clause. These are:

a. where a contrary intention can be proved;

b. in some cases where the revocation clause was inserted by mistake; and

c. where the doctrine of dependent relative revocation applies.

In the Estate of Wayland[4] is an example of a case where the contrary intention could be proved. In that case a British subject domiciled in England made a will in Brussels in accordance with Belgian law and expressed to deal only with his Belgian property. Two years later he made a will which expressly said that it was disposing only of his property in England, but also containing a general revocation clause. It was held that the testator

---

[1] See also *Re Spracklan's Estate*, [1938] 2 All E.R. 345.

[2] (1881), 20 Ch. D. 99.

[3] See also *Cottrell* v. *Cottrell* (1872), L.R. 2 P. & D. 397; *Re Kingdon, Wilkins* v. *Pryer* (1886), 32 Ch. D. 604.

[4] [1951] 2 All E.R. 1041.

had no intention by this clause of revoking his previous Belgian will, so that the revocation clause was effective only to revoke the previous English will. However, had he used words which were sufficiently clear, he could have revoked even the Belgian will by a revocation clause in the English will.[1]

The position was summarised by Langton, J., in *Lowthorpe-Lutwidge* v. *Lowthorpe-Lutwidge*,[2] who said: "It is a heavy burden upon a plaintiff who comes into court to say: 'I agree that the testator was in every way fit to make a will, I agree that the will he has made is perfectly clear and unambiguous in its terms, I agree that it contains a revocatory clause in simple words: nevertheless I say that he did not really intend to revoke the earlier bequest in earlier wills.' Quite obviously the burden must be heavy upon anybody who comes to assert a proposition of that kind." In considering the intention of the testator, it is permissible to consider declarations which he made.[3]

Considerable difficulty is caused where the revocation clause is included in the will by mistake. The strict rule is that if a revocation clause was included without the knowledge or approval of the testator, then it is ineffective, but that if it was included with his knowledge and approval, then it is effective, even though the testator may have misunderstood its legal effect. In *Collins* v. *Elstone*[4] for example, a testatrix had made a will. Later she took out a policy of assurance and wanted to make a new will leaving this policy. Although she intended to revoke her previous will only to the extent necessary to make a new will dealing with the policy, the new will contained a general revocation clause. It was held that because she intended that clause to be included in the new will, then it must take its effect notwithstanding that the testatrix thought that it only had a limited effect. This decision has been criticised in *Lowthorpe-Lutwidge* v. *Lowthorpe-Lutwidge*[5] and while it is in accord with the general principle that mistake of legal effect is not itself a reason for failing to give effect to the terms of a will[6] it is inconsistent with the other principle that a clause

---

[1] Cf. *Re Feis, Guillaume* v. *Ritz-Remorf*, [1964] Ch. 106.
[2] [1935] P. 151.
[3] *Clarke* v. *Scripps* (1852), 2 Rob. Eccl. 563.
[4] [1893] P. 1.
[5] [1935] P. 151.
[6] See *ante*, p. 50.

should operate only so far as is necessary to effectuate the intention of the testator.[1]

The whole or part of a revocation clause in a will will be omitted from probate if there is no *animus revocandi*. A good illustration of this is *Re Morris, Lloyds Bank, Ltd.* v. *Peake*[2] the facts of which are given later.[3]

A further recent example is provided by *Re Phelan*.[4] The deceased was an Irishman. He made a will leaving all his property to the people with whom he lodged. He then appears to have been given some advice that separate holdings of shares had to be dealt with by separate wills. So he acquired three will forms, and left each of his three blocks of shares to his landlord and land-lady. The wills were all executed on the same day. However, the forms contained revocation clauses, and the deceased had not deleted them. Stirling, J., held that the surrounding facts showed that the deceased did not know and approve of the contents of the wills so far as they related to revocation, and he admitted the three wills to probate with the revocation clauses omitted.

The doctrine of dependent relative revocation is considered later.[5]

2. IMPLIED REVOCATION

a. *The principle*

There is a general rule of construction that where there are inconsistent testamentary instruments, the later instrument revokes the earlier to the extent of the inconsistency.[6] It follows that where there is no express revocation clause, but two or more testamentary instruments, there are three basic situations:

    (i) the instruments are not mutually inconsistent, and all wills must be read together as the last "will" of the deceased.[7] There is no rule that a testator revokes a previous will merely by making a later one.[8]

---

[1] *In the Goods of Lewis* (1850), 7 Notes of Cases 436; *Doe d. Evers* v. *Ward* (1852), 18 Q.B. 197.

[2] [1971] P. 62.

[3] See *post*, p. 268.

[4] [1972] Fam. 33.

[5] See *post*, p. 9 [1972] Fam. 33.

[6] *Birks* v. *Birks* (1865), 4 Sw. & Tr. 23.

[7] *Simpson* v. *Foxon*, [1907] P. 54; *Pepper* v. *Pepper* (1870), 5 I.R. Eq. 85.

[8] *Simpson* v. *Foxon*, *Supra*; *Re Wyatt*, [1952] 1 All E.R. 1030.

(ii) the instruments are partially inconsistent, in which case the later instrument is completely effective, and the earlier only effective to the extent that the later is not inconsistent.[1]

(iii) the two instruments are totally inconsistent, in which case the whole of the earlier will will be impliedly revoked.[2]

It is, in each case, a question of construction whether the previous disposition is to be revoked entirely, or whether it is only to be revoked in part. Where the later will covers practically the same ground as the earlier, then the earlier will almost always be revoked. However, there is a difference in the position of documents which are wills in the colloquial sense, that is, testamentary documents which are intended to be complete in themselves on the one hand, and of codicils on the other hand. In the case of codicils, under the rule in *Hearle* v. *Hicks*[3] the court will seek to construe codicils so as to interfere as little as possible with the will. In *Hearle* v. *Hicks* itself the testator left by will his copyhold house to his wife for life. In a later codicil he left all his freehold and copyhold land to his daughter for life. It was held that as the gift in the will was clear and specific, and the terms of the codicil were general, the will would take effect to leave the house to the wife, the daughter taking the remainder of the property.[4]

With this may be contrasted *Re Stoodley, Hooson* v. *Locock*.[5] A clergyman made numerous specific bequests and subject thereto left his estate as to one third to the Society for the Propagation of Christian Knowledge and as to two thirds to the vicar for church purposes. Three years later he made a codicil leaving the residue not bequeathed by will to Miss Mabel Locock. The words of this codicil were clear enough to revoke the whole gift of residue in the will, for otherwise the codicil would have had no effect. It is common for a codicil to be worded on the basis that the

---

[1] *Lemage* v. *Goodban* (1865), L.R. 1 P. & D. 57; *Re Petchell* (1874), L.R. 3 P. & D. 153; *In the Goods of Summers* (1901), 84 L.T. 271; *Re Bund*, [1929] 2 Ch. 455.

[2] *In the Goods of Palmer, Palmer* v. *Peat* (1889), 58 L.J.P. 44; *Cadell* v. *Wilcocks*, [1898] P. 21; *In the Estate of Bryan*, [1907] P. 125.

[3] (1832), 1 Cl. & Fin. 20.

[4] See also *Re Stoodley, Hooson* v. *Locock*, [1916] 1 Ch. 242, C.A.; *Re Picton, Porter* v. *Jones*, [1944] Ch. 303, at p. 306; *Re Crawshay, Hore-Ruthven* v. *Public Trustee*, [1946] Ch. 327, at pp. 330, 331; *Re Wray, Wray* v. *Wray*, [1951] Ch. 425.

[5] [1915] 2 Ch. 295.

will is to be read as if a particular person's name was omitted. In general, this type of provision will be restricted to direct beneficial interests taken under the will. In *Re Wray, Wray* v. *Wray*[1] the testator made a will appointing A to be his executor, and left him a legacy. He left his residue to B, but included a proviso that if B predeceased him, then the residue should devolve as part of B's estate. The testator subsequently made a codicil in which he directed that his will should be read as if A's name was omitted from it and as if A were dead. A in fact became the tenant for life under the will of B. It was held that the codicil revoked the appointment of A as executor, and also revoked the legacy to him, but he was not excluded from the life interest in the residue.[2]

It follows from general principles that if a gift is made by codicil, and the gift is ineffective, the will continues to take effect, unless there is a revocation clause.[3] The approach is illustrated by *Re Robinson, Lamb* v. *Robinson*[4] although that case was concerned with two wills, and not a will and a codicil. The testatrix made a will containing certain provisions, and subsequently made a further will leaving all her property to C. The second will was witnessed by C's wife, and the effect was not to invalidate the second will but to prevent C from benefiting under it.[5] Accordingly, the provisions of the first will continued to take effect, though they would not have done so had the second will contained a revocation clause.

A rather different problem arises where the testator declares a document to be "my last will". These words, by themselves, do not show an intention to revoke previous wills.[6] So in *Re Hawksley's Settlement, Black* v. *Tidy*[7] where the testatrix made a will in 1922, a codicil to it in 1925, and a further will in 1927 described as her last will, the previous instruments remained effective.

b. *Function of Court of Probate*

Normally, questions of construction are dealt with in the

---

[1] [1951] Ch. 425.
[2] See also *Re Spensley's Will Trusts*, [1952] Ch. 886.
[3] *Ward* v. *Van der Loeff*, [1924] A.C. 653; *Re Ransome's Will Trusts, Moberley* v. *Ransome*, [1957] Ch. 348, at pp. 366, 367.
[4] [1930] 2 Ch. 332.
[5] See *ante*, p. 62.
[6] *Kitcat* v. *King*, [1930] P. 266.
[7] [1934] 1 Ch. 384.

7

Chancery Division after probate has been obtained.[1] It will be
seen, however, that in order to decide whether a previous testamentary instrument is still effective the Family Division[2] must
construe the documents before it in order to ascertain whether,
and if so, to what extent an earlier instrument has been impliedly
revoked by a later one.[3] There is, therefore, sometimes a double
process of construction. In the first place, the Family Division
makes its construction when probate is sought. Secondly, where
several testamentary instruments are admitted to probate, there
may still be some inconsistencies between them, and these will be
dealt with by the Chancery Division. The process is cumulative,
so that once the Family Division has decided that part of an
earlier instrument has been expressly or impliedly revoked, the
Chancery Division is precluded from looking at it.

3. LOST WILL

intention of revoking will.

Where a will was last known to be in the possession of the
testator, but it cannot be found when he dies, there is a presumption that the testator destroyed it *animo revocandi*, unless the
contrary can be shown.[4] Where the will itself cannot be found
but codicils to that will are found, there is no presumed intention
that the testator intended to revoke the codicils as well as the will.[5]

Where this presumption as to a lost will does apply, it can be
rebutted by evidence to the contrary. Thus, in *Re Webb, Smith* v.
Johnston[6] the presumption was rebutted when it was shown that
the will was destroyed not by the testator, but by enemy air attack.

The presumption is both with regard to the fact of destruction
by the testator, and to the intention to revoke. Thus, the presumption can also be rebutted if it can be proved that through mental
incapacity or otherwise the testator did not have the *animus
revocandi*.[7]

---

[1] *Post*, p. 125.

[2] Administration of Justice Act 1970, s. 1(1).

[3] *Re Murray, Murray* v. *Murray*, [1956] 2 All E.R. 353.

[4] E.g., *Re Booth, Booth* v. *Booth*, [1926] P. 118.

[5] See the Australian decision *West Australian Trustee Executor and Agency
Co., Ltd.* v. *O'Connor* (1955), 57 W.A.L.R. 25.

[6] [1964] 2 All E.R. 91.

[7] *Brunt* v. *Brunt* (1873), L.R. 3 P. & D. 37; *In the Goods of Hine*, [1893]
P. 282; *In the Goods of Downer* (1853), 1 Ecc. & Ad. 106; *In the Goods of Brassington*, [1902] P. 1.

There is also a rule that where an instrument revokes a will, and that later instrument is itself revoked, the earlier will is not thereby revived.[1] Difficulty can therefore arise where an instrument has been lost. If it contained a revocation clause, the previous will will be permanently revoked:[2] if it did not, the previous will will remain effective. Extrinsic evidence may be admitted to prove the contents of the lost instrument, such as the instructions to the solicitor who drew up the document, his draft, and declarations by the testator.[3] The cases, however, are not entirely consistent.

In *Re Wyatt*[4] the testatrix made a will leaving everything to her husband for life, with remainder over. The will was deposited in her bank. In 1927 she gave instructions for a new will to be prepared, and, when executed, this was also deposited in the bank. Later the testatrix withdrew the will from the bank, and it was never seen again. No exact copy of the will could be produced, but the solicitor who prepared the will swore an affidavit to the effect that he usually included a revocation clause in any will which he prepared. Collingwood, J., held that there was not sufficient evidence to show that the 1927 will did in fact contain an express revocation clause, so that the 1925 will remained valid. On very similar facts, however, in *In the Estate of Hampshire*[5] Karminski, J., thought it so unlikely that a will prepared by a solicitor would not contain a revocation clause that he held that the missing will had effectively revoked the earlier one.

C. REVOCATION BY INFORMAL DECLARATION

Warrington, J., held in *In the Estate of Gossage, Wood* v. *Gossage*[6] that a person who is entitled to make a privileged will may informally revoke a will. This informal revocation can be either of an informal or of a formal will. In *In the Estate of Gossage, Wood* v. *Gossage* itself the soldier had made a formal will, and while on actual military service sent a letter to his son asking him

---

[1] *Bell* v. *Fothergill* (1870), L.R. 2 P. & D. 148; *Barkwell* v. *Barkwell*, [1928] P. 91.
[2] See *post*, p. 98.
[3] *Barkwell* v. *Barkwell*, [1928] P. 91.
[4] [1952] 1 All E.R. 1030.
[5] [1951] W.N. 174.
[6] [1921] P. 194.

to burn the will, the letter using words which were construed to show an intention thereby to revoke. The revocation was held to be effective.

An interesting point arises with regard to the ability of a person under the age of 18 to revoke a will which was validly made while he was on actual military service. It is clear that a privileged will normally remains effective however long the testator lives after having ceased to be in a privileged position.[1] It is also clear that a privileged will of an infant is revoked on his marriage.[2] There was formerly a doubt as to the position of the infant who wishes to revoke by some further instrument, or by destruction.

This doubt has now been resolved by Family Law Reform Act 1969, s. 3 (3). This sub-section provides that an infant may revoke a privileged will even if he could not at the time of revocation make a new privileged will. The sub-section does not, however, say whether such revocation in the case of a person no longer in a privileged position must be in one of the normal ways of revocation, or whether it can be by informal declaration. Presumably informal declaration is only sufficient where the infant is still entitled to the privilege.

D. REVOCATION BY ACTUAL DESTRUCTION

1. REQUIREMENTS

Section 20 of the Wills Act 1837, also authorises revocation by "burning, tearing, or otherwise destroying the same by the testator, or by some person in his presence and by his direction, with the intention of revoking the same". It is, therefore, necessary to show:

a. an act of physical destruction within the terms of the Act;

b. that the act of destruction was carried out

    (i) by the testator; or

    (ii) by some other person in his presence and by his direction; and

c. *animus revocandi.*

---

[1] See *ante*, p. 82.
[2] *In the Estate of Wardrop*, [1917] P. 54.

a. *Act of destruction*

(i) Types of act

The words "or otherwise destroying" must be read *eiusdem generis* with "burning, tearing", so that it has been held that an act such as writing across the will the word "cancelled" is not effective to revoke, even if this is done with an intention to revoke.[1] The clearest illustration of this is *Cheese* v. *Lovejoy*.[2] In that case the testator had made his will and various codicils to it. Many years afterwards, he took them out, drew a pen through part of the will, and wrote on the back "revoked". In the presence of his housekeeper and maid he said that he had cancelled his will, and he then threw it into a pile of waste paper. He reckoned without the natural curiosity of most maids. After the testator left the room, the maid retrieved the will, and kept it. The testator died thinking that the will had been revoked, but the maid produced the document after his death. It was admitted to probate. The testator had at most attempted to revoke his will by a symbolic destruction, and this was not sufficient.

Although the mere crossing through of a signature or other part of the will is not an effective revocation, the complete scratching out of a signature will be regarded, liberally, as a lateral cutting off, and so will be effective.[3] The word "tearing" includes cutting.[4]

(ii) Extent of Act

While symbolic destruction is not sufficient, it is not necessary so to mutilate the document that it is rendered entirely illegible. There is a double test of the extent of the act of destruction: (a) there must be *some* actual burning, tearing or other destruction; and (b) the destruction which has actually occurred must be all that the testator intended to do by way of destruction.

Thus, it has been held that the mere tearing off of the signatures and the attestation clause may be a sufficient act.[5] If, however, some other part is torn off, that will only be sufficient to revoke the will if the part torn off is so important that the will could not

---

[1] *Stephens* v. *Taprell* (1840), 2 Curt. 458.

[2] (1877), 2 P.D. 251.

[3] *In the Goods of Morton* (1887), 12 P.D. 141.

[4] *Hobbs* v. *Knight* (1838), 1 Curt. 768; *In the Goods of Simpson* (1859), 5 Jur. N.S. 1366; *In the Goods of Lady Slade* (1869), 20 L.T. 330.

[5] *In the Goods of Lewis* (1858), 1 Sw. & Tr. 31.

fairly be allowed to stand without it. In *In the Goods of Woodward*,[1] for example, the testator made a will consisting of seven sheets of paper. He tore off eight lines of one page, and probate was granted of the remainder.[2]

The importance of the testator's intention as to the extent of the act of destruction is shown by *Doe d. Perkes v. Perkes*.[3] During a quarrel with one of the beneficiaries, the testator tore his will into four pieces. The beneficiary, choosing discretion rather than valour, apologised. The testator stopped tearing and fitted the pieces together again. It was held that when he stopped tearing the testator had not done all that he intended to do in order to revoke, and accordingly the will had never been revoked.[4]

(iii) Partial revocation

It follows from *Re Woodward*[5] mentioned above that a document may be partially revoked by actual destruction, leaving the remainder effective. In *In the Estate of Nunn*[6] a testatrix made a will, and at some time had cut a piece out of the middle of a sheet of paper, and had sewn the two remaining pieces together. She was held to have revoked the part cut out, and probate was granted of the remainder.[7]

b. *Presence of testator*

The destruction must be by the testator, or by someone in his presence and by his direction. This requirement is construed strictly. In *In the Goods of Dadds*[8] the testatrix was on her deathbed, and said that she wished to revoke a codicil. She confirmed this to her executor and a neighbour who was called in, and they decided that the codicil should be burned. They therefore took it into the kitchen and burned it there. This was held not to be an effective revocation, as it had not been destroyed in her presence.[9]

---

[1] (1871), L.R. 2 P. & D. 206.

[2] Cf. *Treloar v. Lean* (1889), 14 P.D. 49; *Leonard v. Leonard*, [1902] P. 243; *In the Estate of Green, Ward v. Bond* (1962), 106 Sol. Jo. 1034.

[3] (1820), 3 B. & Ald. 489.

[4] See also *Elms v. Elms* (1858), 1 Sw. & Tr. 155.

[5] *Supra.*

[6] [1936] 1 All E.R. 555.

[7] The presumption that she had revoked that part *animo revocandi* was applied.

[8] (1857), Dea. & Sw. 290.

[9] See also *In the Goods of Bacon* (1859), 23 J.P. 712.

c. *Intention*

It will be appreciated that in connexion with revocation by destruction, two questions of intention arise. First, the act of destruction must be all that the testator intended to do in order to destroy. This has already been considered. Secondly, the testator must actually intend to revoke.

(i) Intention to revoke

There will be no revocation where the testator had no *animus revocandi* at the time of destruction. In the first place, the intention and the act of destruction must be concurrent. Thus, in *Gill* v. *Gill*[1] a husband made a will leaving everything to his wife. During an argument, the wife lost her temper and tore up the will. The husband laughed about it, and said that he would not make another one. Although he acquiesced in her act afterwards, because the will was not destroyed at his direction, and because he had no intention to revoke at the time, the will remained effective. It has been held, however, that the testator can consciously adopt his own act of destruction even if at the time of destruction he did not intend to destroy.[2]

Mental illness or similar incapacity can be effective both to prevent revocation[3] and to provide therapy for the judges. *Re Aynsley*[4] was reported under the headline: "Judge solves a jigsaw puzzle with torn will." When she was suffering from such mental confusion that she did not know what she was doing, the testatrix, who was an elderly widow, tore her will into more than forty pieces. Counsel for the executors, who were propounding the will, handed the pieces to Megarry, J., who spent an hour putting them together again. Pleased with his success, he declared that the will was valid.

(ii) Mistake

It has been mentioned above that a distinction must be drawn between an act of revocation or destruction which was not intended on the one hand, and an act which was intended although there

---

[1] [1909] P. 157; see also *Re Booth, Booth* v. *Booth,* [1926] P. 118.

[2] *James* v. *Shrimpton* (1876), 1 P.D. 431.

[3] *Brunt* v. *Brunt* (1873), L.R. 3 P. & D. 37; See also *In the Goods of Hine,* [1893] P. 282; *In the Goods of Downer* (1853), 1 Ecc. & Ad. 106; *In the Goods of Brassington,* [1902] P. 1.

[4] The Times, February 6, 1973.

was a misunderstanding of legal effect on the other hand. Thus, in *Collins* v. *Elstone*[1] where the latter applied, the revocation was held to be effective.

Where there has been destruction while the testator was under a misapprehension as to legal effect, however, the courts have shown a marked willingness to hold that such destruction was conditional on the legal result being as the testator understood it, with the result that as that was not the case, the revocation was not effective. Thus, in *In the Estate of Southerden, Adams* v. *Southerden*[2] the testator believed, mistakenly, that on his death intestate, his widow would be entitled to the whole of his property, and he therefore destroyed the will by burning. As he misunderstood the effect of the intestacy rule the revocation was not effective. Again, in *Re Davies, Thomas* v. *Thomas-Davies*[3] the testatrix thought she had made a valid second will, and in this belief, she destroyed her first will. In fact the second will was not valid and the first will was held to be effective. Further cases of this nature are considered in connexion with the doctrine of dependent relative revocation.

(iii) Presumption of revocation *animo revocandi*

The presumption that where a will cannot be found it is presumed to have been revoked *animo revocandi* has already been mentioned.[4] A further presumption applies where the will is found in a mutilated condition. This is that the testator intended to revoke, provided that the act of mutilation is sufficient to amount to an act of destruction.[5]

E. DEPENDENT RELATIVE REVOCATION

The intention to revoke a will may be absolute or conditional.[6] Where the revocation is by an act of destruction, the testator's intention is a question of fact,[7] and in any other case it is a question of construction.[8] There is, in theory, no limit to the type of

---

[1] [1893] P. 1.

[2] [1925] P. 177.

[3] [1928] Ch. 24.

[4] *Ante*, p. 92.

[5] *In the Goods of Lewis* (1858), 1 Sw. & Tr. 31; *Magnesi* v. *Hazelton* (1881), 44 L.T. 586; *North* v. *North* (1909), 25 T.L.R. 322.

[6] See, generally, Henderson (1969), 32 M.L.R. 447.

[7] *Dixon* v. *Treasury Solicitor*, [1905] P. 42.

[8] *In the Estate of Zimmer* (1924), 30 T.L.R. 502.

condition which may be imposed, but it is customary to divide cases of conditional revocation into:

1. cases where the revocation is conditional upon some other disposition; in which case it is known as dependent relative revocation; and

2. other types of condition.

The rules as to both types of conditional revocation are the same.

1. WHERE DOCTRINE APPLIES

The principle of dependent relative revocation may be stated as follows: where the testator purports to revoke a will on the basis that a new will is valid, or that the intestacy rules make the desired provision, but the new will is not valid, or the intestacy rules do not have that effect, then the old will remains effective. The principle is extended to cover the revocation of parts of the will.

At first, the doctrine applied only where the beneficiaries under the old and the new wills were the same, but, perhaps, there was some change in the amount of the benefit to be received. Thus, if the testator made a will leaving £5,000 to his wife, and later, wishing to increase her benefit, he made another will revoking the first will and leaving £10,000 to his wife, then if the second will is ineffective, the courts strive to preserve the first gift. In both cases the testator intended that beneficiary to have a benefit. In *Onions* v. *Tyrer*,[1] for example, the testator made a will containing certain devises. He later made a subsequent will altering some of the administrative provisions of the will, but not altering its dispositive effect, and destroyed the first will. The second will was not valid because it was not attested in his presence, and he was held to have revoked his first will only conditionally. The cases have not been confined to wills where the beneficiaries are the same. So, in *Re Middleton*[2] the testator made a will leaving a legacy to his niece. He then attempted to make a second will excluding his niece, but the second will was invalid for want of proper attestation. The first will was then destroyed. It was held that the revocation of the first will was to be conditional on the

---

[1] (1716), 2 Vern. 741.
[2] (1864), 3 Sw. & Tr. 583.

second will coming into force, so that the first will remained operative. The doctrine now applies whenever the second will ceases to have effect, and for whatever reason.[1]

In *In the Estate of Bromham*,[2] for example, the testator destroyed his will intending to make another. He became too ill to make the new will, however, and Lord Merriman, P., held that the first will remained effective. A similar result was reached in *Dixon* v. *Treasury Solicitor*[3] where a testator destroyed his old will because he thought he could not make a new will until the old one was destroyed. In fact, the new one was never completed and the old one was therefore held to remain effective.

The rule also applies where the testator relies upon the intestacy rules. *In the Estate of Southerden, Adams* v. *Southerden*[4] has already been mentioned briefly.[5] The testator made a will leaving everything to his wife. Later, he took the will, and thinking that the wife would take all his assets under the intestacy rules, he burnt it. It was held that the testator revoked conditionally on the intestacy rules having the effect which he thought they had, and, as they did not, the will was not revoked.

2. INTENTION

It is difficult to know exactly how far the actual intention of the testator is important. The doctrine is stated to depend entirely on the testator's intention. In many cases this is clearly true. Thus, in *Re Feis, Guillaume* v. *Ritz-Remorf*[6] the testator had property in England and abroad, and had made a will dealing with both types of property. He then expressly revoked the will in so far as it dealt with foreign property believing that other arrangements applied to the disposal of that property. In fact, they did not. The court refused to accept that the revocation clause was conditional upon such other arrangements applying, and therefore held the clause to be unconditionally effective.

Nevertheless, in many cases the courts have intervened to save

---

[1] *Scott* v. *Scott* (1859), 1 Sw. & Tr. 258; *Beardsley* v. *Lacey* (1897), 67 L.J.P. 35; *Giles* v. *Warren* (1872), L.R. 2 P. & D. 401; *In the Goods of Thornton* (1889), 14 P.D. 82; *Clarkson* v. *Clarkson* (1862), 2 Sw. & Tr. 497.

[2] [1952] 1 All E.R. 110, n.

[3] [1905] P. 42.

[4] [1925] P. 177.

[5] *Ante,* p. 98.

[6] [1964] Ch. 106.

provisions of earlier wills where there is not the slightest evidence of the testator's actual intention. Indeed, in the typical case of a man who revokes a will because he thinks a subsequent will is valid, it never occurs to him that the subsequent will might not be valid, so that there is no actual conditional element in his intention to revoke the former will. The operation of the doctrine is, in most cases, in accordance with common sense, but it is only achieved by flagrant invention on the part of judges of an element of intention which in most cases was not present.

F. REVOCATION BY MARRIAGE

1. THE RULE

The combined effect of Wills Act 1837, s. 18, and Law of Property Act 1925, s. 177, is as follows:

a. a will is revoked upon subsequent marriage; unless

b. it is made in contemplation of the particular marriage which does occur, in which case it is not revoked; or

c. unless and to the extent that it exercises a power of appointment under which the wife[1] and issue would not be entitled in default of appointment.

Marriage is the only act which causes the revocation of the will without the testator's intention, and, indeed, even contrary to his intention.[2] This is a rule of law, and not a question of intention or construction. Section 18 operates to revoke privileged wills.[3]

In each case it is necessary to prove a valid marriage, which means not merely a ceremony of marriage but a marriage which is fully effective for the purposes of English law. In *Mette* v. *Mette*[4] the testator made a will, and then married his deceased wife's half sister. At the time that relationship made the marriage void, and the will was not revoked.[5] There is no English authority on the effect of a voidable marriage.

---

[1] Subject to the correctness of *Re Gilligan*, [1950] P. 32; see *post*, p. 105.

[2] *Marston* v. *Roe d. Fox* (1838), 8 Ad. & El. 14; *Israell* v. *Rodon* (1839), 2 Moo. P.C.C. 51.

[3] *In the Estate of Wardrop*, [1917] P. 54.

[4] (1859), 1 Sw. & Tr. 416.

[5] See also *Warter* v. *Warter* (1890), 15 P.D. 152.

2. WILLS IN CONTEMPLATION OF MARRIAGE

Section 177 of the Law of Property Act 1925, which applies to wills made on or after 1 January, 1926, provides that "a will expressed to be made in contemplation of a marriage . . . shall not be revoked by the solemnization of the marriage contemplated". It is, therefore, not sufficient to show that the testator contemplated marriage in general: he must have contemplated the actual marriage which took place. Thus, in *Sallis* v. *Jones*,[1] where the last line of the will read "this will is made in contemplation of marriage", and where the testator married a few months later, the will was revoked. In his harsh judgment, Bennett, J., said: "In my judgment section 177 of the Law of Property Act 1925, upon its true construction excludes the operation of section 18 of the Wills Act if the will made before a marriage is expressed to be made in contemplation of a particular marriage and is followed by the solemnization of that marriage". This decision can be justified only on the basis that s. 177 refers to a will expressed to be made in contemplation of "a", that is, of a specified marriage.

The marriage contemplated must be a future marriage. So in *In the Estate of Gray*[2] the testator was married, but went through a bigamous ceremony of marriage with a woman Edith Annie Gray in 1927. In 1958 she executed a will, being at that time unaware of the fact that her marriage was invalid. The testator's wife died in 1960, and Edith Annie then learned of the true position. She married the testator later that year, and it was held that her will was revoked, because at the time when she made her will she thought that she was married. This case illustrates that where it applies, s. 177 is absolute, and does not only revoke those wills under which the future wife would not benefit.

In *In the Estate of Gray* the testator himself made a will in favour of "my wife Edith Annie Gray" in 1935. This too was revoked on the marriage in 1960, because Simon, P., was not satisfied that at the time when the will was made the testator had an intention to marry her. In other cases, however, the courts have accepted that to call a woman "my wife" when she is not shows an intention to marry her. So in *Pilot* v. *Gainfort*[3] where the testator

---

[1] [1936] P. 43.
[2] (1963), 107 Sol. Jo. 156.
[3] [1931] P. 103.

left all his property to "Diana Featherstone Pilot my wife", and married her three years later, the will was not revoked. In *Pilot* v. *Gainfort* the testator was married at the time when the will was made to another woman who had disappeared, but he did not marry until she had disappeared for a total of seven years, whereafter he could have applied for a decree of presumption of death.

Pilot v. *Gainfort* should be carefully compared with *Re Gray*. In both cases at the time when the wills were made the testators were not legally in a position to marry, yet *Pilot* v. *Gainfort* shows that a person may "contemplate" marriage when he is not in a position to marry. The distinction between the two cases is that in *In the Estate of Gray* the judge did not accept that merely by using the expression "my wife" showed such a contemplation.

A reference to a named person as "my future wife"[1] or as "my fiancée"[2] will be sufficient to save the will from revocation.

3. WILLS CONDITIONAL ON MARRIAGE

A will made in contemplation of marriage is not thereby made conditional on marriage. In *Ormiston* v. *Laws*[3] the testator made a will leaving a legacy to his named fiancée, but the marriage did not take place. The will was held to be unconditional, so that the woman took the legacy. It is, of course, open to the testator to make a will which is both conditional on and in contemplation of marriage.

4. COVENANT NOT TO REVOKE

A covenant not to revoke a will may be a valid covenant,[4] but an action for damages will only lie where the breach is the result of an intentional act, and not by operation of law. In *Re Marsland, Lloyds Bank, Ltd.* v. *Marsland*[5] the testator made a will for the benefit of his young children, and covenanted not to revoke it. Several years later his wife died and he remarried, making a new will partly in favour of his new wife. The children by the first marriage sued on the covenant. It was held that the

---

[1] *Re Knight*, not reported but mentioned in *Re Langston*, [1953] P. 100.
[2] *Re Langston*, [1953] P. 100.
[3] 1966, S.C. 47.
[4] *Re Marsland, Lloyds Bank, Ltd.* v. *Marsland*, [1939] Ch. 820.
[5] [1939] Ch. 820.

covenant not to revoke did not amount to a covenant not to re-
marry, for that would be a covenant void for public policy, and
as the revocation was by operation of law, and not intentional act,
no action for damages would lie.

5. POWERS OF APPOINTMENT

The position with regard to the revocation on marriage of
testamentary instruments exercising powers of appointment is
complicated. The reason for the existence of s. 18 so far as the
wife is concerned is that at common law a married woman was
incapable of making a will, and therefore incapable of revoking
one. Accordingly, unless her will was revoked on marriage, it
would become irrevocable. This need not concern us here. So far
as the man is concerned, the effect of automatic revocation, together with the intestacy rules, is to confer a benefit on, in the
first instance, his wife and children. The intention of the legislature so far as powers of appointment are concerned is in broad
terms again to try to benefit the class of spouse and children.
Powers of appointment may be divided into two types: those
where this class does benefit in default of appointment, and those
where it does not. Where the class does benefit in default, then
the object of the legislature was for the will to be revoked, so that
the power would not be exercised (in the absence of a further will)
with the result that the class would benefit. Where the class
would not benefit in default of appointment, there was no point
in making marriage revoke a will to the extent that it exercised
the power.

If this is the general approach to the problem, s. 18 itself
provides that a will shall be revoked on marriage "except a will
made in exercise of a power of appointment, when the real or
personal estate thereby appointed would not in default of such
appointment pass to his or her heir, customary heir, executor, or
administrator, or the person entitled as his or her next of kin,
under the Statute of Distributions, 1670". It is, therefore, important to know who is entitled as heir or next of kin.

Before 1925 a widow had a statutory entitlement on intestacy,
but she did not take it as next of kin. Does, therefore, a widow
come within the class of those entitled for the purposes of the

exception to s. 18? The point arose for decision in *Re Gilligan*.[1] In that case the testator made a settlement in contemplation of his first marriage under which he had a general power of appointment exercisable by will among certain persons, and in default of appointment the fund was to be held in trust for "such persons as would have been entitled under the statutes for the distribution of the personal estates of intestates on the death of the said Harry Gilligan had he died possessed thereof intestate and without having been married". His first wife died, and thereafter he made a will exercising the power in favour of certain nephews and nieces, who were within the scope of the appointment. He then remarried. Pilcher, J., held that a widow came within the class of those entitled under the Statutes of Distribution. Accordingly, as the widow was within the class, and she would not benefit by any revocation of the will exercising the power, that appointment was not revoked.[2]

G. ALTERATIONS AND OBLITERATIONS

1. EFFECT

Alterations, interlineations and obliterations are of two types: those made before the execution of the will, and those made after. Where the alteration, etc., is made before execution, then the will takes effect as altered, although in this type of case there is often difficulty in proving that it was made before execution. Where the alteration is made after execution the position is governed by Wills Act 1837, s. 21. By this section, no alteration interlineation or obliteration made after the execution of the will takes effect unless:

a. "the words or effect of the will before such alteration shall not be apparent"; or

b. the alteration is executed in the same manner as the will itself.

a. *Words or effect not apparent*

Words are apparent for the purposes of s. 21 where they can be read from the face of the instrument, if necessary with the aid

---

[1] [1950] P. 32.

[2] See articles at (1951), 67 L.Q.R. 351 and (1952), 68 L.Q.R. 455, where the decision is criticized.

of a magnifying glass.[1] Any way of looking at the document is accepted, provided there is no physical interference with it. So, in *Ffinch* v. *Combe*[2] the court allowed the will to be read by surrounding an obliteration with brown paper and holding the document against a window pane. It follows, that if necessary, the will can be held up to the light, and read through the back.

Except where the doctrine of dependent relative revocation applies, extrinsic evidence is not admissible to ascertain the state of the document before the alteration.[3] Accordingly, if the testator has pasted a strip of paper over part of the will, and written over that strip, the strip cannot be removed[4] and the effect of the instrument before alteration will not be apparent unless it is possible to read through that strip. The difference between apparent, which means "apparent on the face of the instrument in the condition in which it was left by the testator"[5] and discoverable was illustrated by *Re Itter, Dedman* v. *Godfrey*.[6] In that case the testatrix pasted strips of paper over parts of her will, with alterations on them. An infra-red photograph of the document was taken, and by examining this photograph it was possible to see what had been written in the first place. It was nevertheless held that the effect of the document before alteration was not "apparent".

The exact scope of *Re Itter* is uncertain. In that case, a new document, the photograph, had been created, and the effect of the original will was apparent not from the face of the will but from the photograph. If, however, the instrument itself is examined under ultra violet or infra-red light, and by this process it is possible to see the state of the original will, it is difficult to see why that should not be allowed in the same way that the use of a magnifying glass is.

This general position is altered where the doctrine of dependent relative revocation applies, for in this case the court does not regard itself as bound by s. 21, and it will resort to more drastic

---

[1] *In the Goods of Ibbetson* (1839), 2 Curt. 337; *In the Goods of Brasier*, [1899] P. 36.

[2] [1894] P. 191.

[3] *In the Goods of Ibbetson* (1839), 2 Curt. 337; *In the Goods of Horsford* (1874), L.R. 3 P. & D. 211; *Re Itter, Dedman* v. *Godfrey*, [1950] P. 130.

[4] *In the Goods of Horsford* (1874), L.R. 3 P. & D. 211.

[5] Per Sir James Hannen in *In the Goods of Horsford, supra.*

[6] [1950] P. 130.

methods of ascertaining the original state of the document. *Re Itter, Dedman* v. *Godfrey* itself was a case of dependent relative revocation, the court accepting that the testatrix only wished the provisions in the original will not to take effect if the provisions on the pasted-over strips took effect. Accordingly, the meaning of the original will was ascertained from the infra-red photograph. A further example of the application of the doctrine of dependent relative revocation is *Sturton* v. *Whetlock*.[1] In that case the testator wished to make certain gifts to his grandchildren, to vest when they attained the age of twenty-five. Such gifts would have contravened the perpetuity rule as it then stood[2] and accordingly the solicitor prepared the will on the basis that the gifts would vest when the grandchildren attained twenty-one. After execution, the testator obliterated the word "one" in "twenty-one", and substituted the word "five". Probate was granted of the will as it had originally been prepared.

b. *Execution of alteration*

The second exception to the general rule laid down by s. 21 that alterations after execution are ineffective is where the alterations are themselves attested. The section is rather wider than this, for it provides that an alteration is deemed to be duly executed if the signature of the testator, and of the witnesses, is made in the margin or near to the alterations, or at the foot or end of a memorandum referring to the alteration. The memorandum itself must be written on the will.

Strict observance of the formalities of execution is necessary. A hard case was *In the Goods of Shearn*.[3] In that case the testatrix properly executed her will, which was duly attested. Immediately afterwards, it was found that a small part had been omitted, and this was corrected by an interlineation. The testatrix acknowledged the document as her last will, and the two witnesses placed their initials in the margin by the interlineation. The testatrix did not herself initial the insertion, and it was held that this was not validly executed. So far as it is possible to make sense of the decision, it seems to depend on the fact that the testatrix neither signed (or initialled) the alteration herself, nor acknowledged her

---

[1] (1883), 52 L.J.P. 29.
[2] But see now Perpetuities and Accumulations Act 1964, s. 4.
[3] (1880), 50 L.J.P. 15.

previous signature in respect of that alteration. While the decision does not stand alone[1] the earlier decision of *In the Goods of Dewell*[2] seems preferable. In that case, on similar facts, the testator was held to have acknowledged his previous signature, so that it was sufficient for the witnesses alone to place their initials in the margin.

2. PRESUMPTIONS AS TO EXECUTION

a. *Alterations and additions*

There is a general presumption that unattested alterations interlineations and erasures are made after execution of the will and so are ineffective.[3] This presumption may be rebutted either by evidence from the document itself or by extrinsic evidence. The following are examples of the circumstances in which the presumption has been rebutted:

(i) Internal evidence

    a. where without an alteration or interlineation the will does not make sense. Thus, where the will was originally written out with blanks, and those blanks have been completed, they have been accepted as having been completed before execution;[4]

    b. where the alteration or interlineation is proved to have been written in the same hand and with the same ink as the remainder of the document.[5] Although there is no decision, the same would be the case where a document examiner could prove that the alteration was made either before or at the same time as the will itself.

(ii) External evidence

    a. in exceptional cases, such as the will of a lawyer, evidence that the testator knew the statutory requirements has been accepted as evidence that the alteration was made before execution;[6]

---

[1] *Re Martin* (1849), 1 Rob. Eccl. 712.

[2] (1853), 1 Ecc. & Ad. 103.

[3] *Cooper* v. *Bockett* (1846), 4 Moo. P.C.C. 419.

[4] *Greville* v. *Tylee* (1851), 7 Moo. P.C.C. 370; *Kell* v. *Charmer* (1856), 23 Beav. 195.

[5] *Re Tonge* (1891), 66 L.T. 60.

[6] *In the Goods of Jacob* (1842), 1 Notes of Cases 401; *Re Thomson* (1844), 3 Notes of Cases 441; *O'Meagher* v. *O'Meagher* (1883), 11 L.R. Ir. 117.

b. direct proof from an attesting witness that the alterations had been made prior to execution of the will, is, of course, accepted, as is the evidence of the person who prepared the will that it contained alterations when it left his hands prior to execution;[1]

c. declarations by the testator before or at the time of execution are admissible,[2] but not subsequent declarations.

A subsequent codicil operates to republish the will[3] so that if the will was altered prior to the execution of the codicil, the codicil will republish the will as altered. It is necessary, however, to distinguish between a codicil which takes notice of the alteration, and one which does not.

In the Goods of Heath[4] is an example of the first type of case. The testator gave a legacy of £10,000 to one of his executors. He subsequently made an unattested alteration giving him a further legacy of £1,000. Later, he made a codicil reciting the fact that he had given the executor a legacy of £11,000. On this basis it was held that probate of the will should be granted with the alteration included, for the codicil republished it in its altered form.[5]

Conversely, where the codicil does not refer to the alterations, they will be presumed to have been made after the date both of the will and of the codicil.[6]

b. *Pencilled alterations*

There is a presumption that where a will is written both in ink and in pencil, the part written in pencil is intended to be deliberative only, and not intended to have final effect. Thus, in *In the Goods of Bellamy*[7] where the will was first written out in pencil, and then parts only written over in ink, probate was only

---

[1] *Keigwin* v. *Keigwin* (1843), 3 Curt. 607.

[2] *Doe d. Shallcross* v. *Palmer* (1851), 16 Q.B. 747; *In the Goods of Foley* (1855), 2 Ecc. & Ad. 206; *In the Goods of Hardy* (1861), 30 L.J.P.M. & A. 142; *In the Goods of Sykes* (1873), L.R. 3 P. & D. 26; *Re Jessop*, [1924] P. 221.

[3] See *post*, p. 112.

[4] [1892] P. 253.

[5] See also *Tyler* v. *Merchant Taylors' Co.* (1890), 15 P.D. 216.

[6] *Lushington* v. *Onslow* (1848), 6 Notes of Cases 183; *In the Goods of Sykes* (1873), L.R. 3 P. & D. 26; *Christmas and Christmas* v. *Whinyates* (1863), 3 Sw. & Tr. 81, at p. 89; *Rowley* v. *Merlin* (1860), 24 J.P. 824.

[7] (1866), 14 W.R. 501.

granted of the words which had been so inked over. Where, therefore, pencil alterations have been made to a will written in ink, they will be presumed to have been deliberative, and probate will not be granted of them.[1] This does not in any way modify the rule that a will can be written in whatever medium the testator wishes, so that probate will be granted of a whole will written in pencil.[2]

c. *Alterations to privileged wills*

In accordance with the general practice of stretching the rules as far as possible in favour of privileged wills, alterations in a privileged will are presumed to have been made while the testator was still in a position to make a privileged will, and so are valid without further formality.[3]

All these presumptions may be rebutted by contrary evidence.

3. INEFFECTUAL ALTERATIONS

The scope of the Act has in fact been modified slightly by the Non-Contentious Probate Rules 1954. Rule 12 (1) enables the registrar to grant probate of a will with alterations which are un-attested, and where there is no evidence that they were made prior to execution, where the alteration "appears to the registrar to be of no practical importance".

4. EFFECT OF UNATTESTED ALTERATIONS

Where an alteration is unattested, and it cannot be shown that it was made before the execution of the will, probate will be granted of the will in its original form. Where the original has been obliterated, probate will be granted with a blank space. A good illustration of this is *In the Estate of Hamer*.[4] In that case the testator made a will which contained a legacy of "the sum of two hundred and fifty pounds". The testator subsequently obliterated the words "two hundred and" so that probate was granted showing a legacy of "the sum of   fifty pounds". Where

---

[1] *Rymes* v. *Clarkson* (1809), 1 Phillim. 22.
[2] *In the Goods of Usborne* (1909), 25 T.L.R. 519.
[3] *In the Goods of Tweedale* (1874), L.R. 3 P. & D. 204; *In the Goods of Newland*, [1952] P. 71.
[4] (1943), 113 L.J.P. 31.

the original words can be read, probate will be granted in the original form.

To prevent the difficulties which arise with regard to alterations, it is always prudent for the testator and witnesses to initial the alterations which are made, whether they are in fact made before the execution of the will or subsequently.

CHAPTER 8

REPUBLICATION AND REVIVAL

A. REPUBLICATION

1. REQUIREMENTS

Republication is a means of making a will take effect as if it had been written not at the date when it was written, but at the subsequent date of republication. Republication can only be effected by an act attended by the same formalities as are necessary to make a will, and, therefore, there are only two ways in which republication can take place:

a. re-execution of the original will; or

b. making a codicil to that will.

In both cases it must be shown that the testator intended to republish his will. The fact of re-execution of the original will leads to the presumption that the testator intended to republish although that intention may be rebutted.[1] More positive proof of intention to republish is required where a codicil is made to the will, although the standard of proof required is slight. Thus merely by referring in a codicil to the will, such as by describing it as "the codicil to my will dated . . . " will be sufficient to republish.[2] There is no need for the codicil to contain words of express republication of the will.[3]

---

[1] *Dunn* v. *Dunn* (1866), L.R. 1 P. & D. 277.

[2] *Re Champion, Dudley* v. *Champion,* [1893] 1 Ch. 101; *Re Taylor, Whitby* v. *Highton* (1888), 57 L.J. Ch. 430.

[3] *Potter* v *Potter* (1750), 1 Ves. Sen. 437, at p. 442.

2. EFFECT

Republication was introduced into the law of wills before the 1837 Act. Under the pre-1837 law, a will was not ambulatory in respect of realty, so that it could not dispose of realty which the testator acquired between the date when the will was made, and the date of his death. It became fairly common to republish the will, so that it took effect at the date of republication, and included realty acquired in the meantime. The main reason for republication disappeared with the passing of the 1837 Act, but republication is still common.

a. *General position*

The general effect of republication was stated by the Privy Council in *Goonewardene* v. *Goonewardene*,[1] an appeal from Ceylon on a Ceylon Ordinance which contained a similar provision to s. 34 of the 1837 Act. This section provides that every will which is re-executed or republished, as well as one which is revived[2] shall "be deemed to have been made at the time at which the same shall be so re-executed republished or revived". In *Goonewardene* the Privy Council said:[3] "the effect of confirming a will by codicil is to bring the will down to the date of the codicil, and to effect the same disposition of the testator's property as would have been effected if the testator had at the date of the codicil made a new will containing the same dispositions as in the original will but with the alterations introduced by the codicil."

With this must be contrasted the dictum of Romer, J., in *Re Hardyman, Teesdale* v. *McClintock*.[4] He said: "The authorities . . . lead . . . to the conclusion that the courts have always treated the principle that republication makes the will speak as if it had been re-executed at the date of the codicil not as a rigid formula or technical rule, but as a useful and flexible instrument for effectuating a testator's intentions . . "

The difficulty in understanding many of the cases is due to the fact that the courts require such a low standard of proof that the testator did intend to republish. In many situations a testator

---

[1] [1931] A.C. 647.
[2] See *post*, p. 116.
[3] [1931] A.C. 647, at p. 650.
[4] [1925] Ch. 287.

makes a codicil dealing with a particular matter, and referring in that codicil to his will. This will usually be sufficient to republish the whole will, even though it is likely that the testator only directed his attention to the part of the will which was being altered. It would be more satisfactory to require positive proof of an intention to republish.

Subject to this qualification it is possible to illustrate the operation of the rule.

b. *Persons*

Where the rule applies, descriptions in the will of persons will relate to those persons who fit the description at the date of republication. In *Re Hardyman, Teesdale* v. *McClintock*[1] the testatrix made a will leaving property to the wife of her cousin. After the will was made, the cousin's wife died, and the testatrix thereafter made a codicil republishing the will in general, but without referring to this gift in particular. The cousin subsequently re-married, and it was held that his second wife could benefit.

There is one statutory exception to the general principle. There is a presumption that in wills and other dispositions references to children and other relatives include references to illegitimate children, and to persons related through them.[2] This presumption applies, however, only where the will was made after 1969. The Family Law Reform Act 1969, s. 15 (8) provides that a will is not to be treated as having been "made" for this purpose merely because it is confirmed by a codicil made after 1969.

c. *Property*

The same principle applies to property. Thus, in *Re Reeves, Reeves* v. *Pawson*[3] the testator bequeathed his interest in "my present lease". At the time of making the will the lease had an unexpired term of three and a half years. The testator subsequently took a new lease for twelve years and then made a codicil republishing the will. This was effective to give the beneficiary the residue of the term of the new lease. A similar result was

---

[1] *Ante*, p. 113.
[2] Family Law Reform Act 1969, s. 15.
[3] [1928] Ch. 351.

reached in *Re Champion, Dudley* v. *Champion*[1] where the testator devised certain freehold property "now in my own occupation". He later acquired some further land which he occupied with the remainder, and republished the will. The beneficiary was held to be entitled to the additional land as well as that occupied by the testator at the date of the original will.

d. *Exceptions to rule*

(i) Property adeemed

The effect of gifts of property which are adeemed is considered later,[2] but, while the authorities are by no means clear, it is probably true that where the gift has been adeemed, and another asset of the same description is subsequently acquired, then republication of the will is not sufficient to save the gift. In *Re Bower, Bower* v. *Mercer*[3] the testatrix had a power to appoint a life interest in property to her husband, and she made a will exercising the power in his favour. After she made the will she was given a further power by a new *inter vivos* settlement made by her father, and she then republished the will. This was held to be effective to exercise both the original and the new power.[4] In *Re Viscount Galway's Will Trusts*[5] the testator made a will in 1927 leaving all his unsettled estates in certain counties to his eldest son. By virtue of the Coal Act 1938, the coal was appropriated to the State, and the owner given a right to compensation. The codicil was executed republishing the will after the date when the right to compensation arose, but it was held that the son was not entitled to this compensation. It is difficult to see the principle behind these cases.

(ii) Illegitimate relations

There is a presumption that in wills made before 1970, references to persons are to be construed as references to legitimate persons only. The presumption is reversed in the case of post-1969 wills.[6] However, a will made before 1970 but republished after

---

[1] [1893] 1 Ch. 101.
[2] *Post*, p. 461.
[3] [1930] 2 Ch. 82.
[4] See also *Re Wells, Trusts, Hardisty* v. *Wells* (1889), 42 Ch.D. 646; *Doyle* v. *Coyle*, [1895] 1 I.R. 205.
[5] [1950] Ch. 1.
[6] *Post*, p. 154.

that date is not automatically regarded as being made after 1969 for the purpose of this presumption.[1]

(iii) Contrary to testator's intention

A will is not republished where to do so would be contrary to the testator's intention. *Re Heath's Will Trusts, Hamilton* v. *Lloyds Bank*[2] was a sympathetic decision of Harman, J. In that case the testator executed a will before 1936 containing a gift to his daughter with restraint upon anticipation. By s. 2, Law Reform (Married Women and Tortfeasors) Act 1935, it became impossible to create new restraints upon anticipation after 1935. After 1935 the testator executed a codicil to his will, but the judge held that if the original will was regarded as republished it would defeat the testator's intention, and accordingly he held that it had not been republished.

e. *Intermediate codicils*

Generally a codicil republishing a will republishes it as altered by any subsequent codicils,[3] and, in some cases, as altered by even unattested alterations.[4] The decisions on unattested alterations are explicable on the basis that because the codicil refers to the will as altered the court can accept that as evidence that the alteration had been validly made before the codicil was executed. With this qualification, however, the will can only be republished in the form in which it was immediately before republication. So, in *Burton* v. *Newbery*[5] where a gift to an attesting witness in an intermediate codicil was void, the republishing codicil did not save that irregularity.

B.   REVIVAL

1. REQUIREMENTS

Republication is the bringing forward in time of a will which has throughout remained valid. Revival is the restoration to effect of a will or codicil which has been revoked. The result of s. 22 of

---

[1] Family Law Reform Act 1969, s. 15 (8).

[2] [1949] Ch. 170.

[3] *Re Fraser, Lowther* v. *Fraser*, [1904] 1 Ch. 726; see also *Green* v. *Tribe* (1878), 9 Ch.D. 231; *Follett* v. *Pettman* (1883), 23 Ch.D. 337.

[4] *In the Goods of Wollaston* (1845), 3 Notes of Cases 599; *Re Barke* (1845), 4 Notes of Cases 44; *Re Tegg* (1846), 4 Notes of Cases 531.

[5] (1875), 1 Ch.D. 234.

the 1837 Act is that an instrument can be revived only in the same ways as republication, namely

a. re-execution; or

b. subsequent codicil.

Accordingly, to show revival, it is necessary for three elements to be shown:

a. formal act of revival;

b. intention to revive; and

c. existence of document to be revived.

2. INTENTION

Stronger evidence of intention to revive is required than to republish. Accordingly, although the mere reference in a codicil to a former will is sufficient to show an intention to republish, it is not sufficient to show an intention to revive.[1] It is necessary to show more than a mere reference, such as an express confirmation of the original will,[2] or some other statement which makes this intention clear.[3] The court is very much more willing in the case of revival than in the case of republication to enquire into the actual intention of the testator.

It is not the case, however, that the words of the reviving instrument must contain express words of revival. Thus, in *In the Estate of Davis*[4] the testator made a will in favour of a woman to whom he was not married. He subsequently married her, and his will was revoked.[5] After his marriage he endorsed on the envelope containing the will a statement that the woman "is now my lawful wedded wife". This statement was signed and attested. The court accepted this as showing an intention to revive the will, Willmer, J., commenting not unfairly "I am baffled when I try to think what other intention the deceased could possibly have had except to revive the will".

---

[1] *Re Smith, Bilke* v. *Roper* (1890), 45 Ch.D. 632.

[2] *Marsh* v. *Marsh* (1860), 1 Sw. & Tr. 528; *In the Goods of Steele* (1868), L.R. 1 P. & D. 575; cf., however, *Goldie* v. *Adam*, [1938] P. 85, where the word "confirm" was described as very inappropriate to revive a will.

[3] *In the Goods of Steele* (1868), L.R. 1 P. & D. 575; *Re Courtenay* (1891), 27 L.R. Ir. 507.

[4] [1952] P. 279.

[5] Wills Act 1837, s. 18; see *ante*, p. 101.

3. EXISTENCE OF DOCUMENT

In order to be revived, the revoked will must be physically in existence at the date of the reviving instrument.[1]

4. REVOCATION OF REVOKING INSTRUMENT

Section 22 of the 1837 Act provides that a revoked will can be revived by re-execution, or by codicil, and in no other way. Accordingly, where it was revoked by an instrument, the revocation of that revoking instrument is not sufficient to revive it.[2] For this purpose it is essential to remember that a will is revoked by a subsequent inconsistent will. In *In the Goods of Hodgkinson*[3] by a will made in June 1881 the testator gave all his property to "my dear friend Jane", and he appointed her to be his sole executrix. Three months later, with male fickleness, he made another will leaving, in effect, his realty to his sister, Emma, and appointed her to be his sole executrix. Will No. 2 made no provision as to personalty, and it did not contain a revocation clause. The testator then revoked the second will by cutting off his signature. The effect of will No. 2 was, therefore, to revoke will No. 1 in so far as it related to realty. But the revocation of will No. 2 did not revive will No. 1. Probate was, therefore, granted of will No. 1, limited to personalty.

The mere fact that a codicil which revives an earlier will is stated to be a codicil to that will, does not necessarily revoke an intervening will. Whether the intervening will is revoked will depend on the terms of the first will as revived. Take a basic example:

The testator makes will No. 1 in 1950; will No. 2, revoking No. 1, in 1960; and codicil reviving No. 1 in 1970. It is clear that probate will be granted of the 1950 will and the 1970 codicil, but the fate of the 1960 will depends on the terms of the 1950 will or of the 1970 codicil. If the 1970 codicil *expressly* revokes the 1960 will, that revocation is clearly effective. If the 1950 will itself contains an express revocation clause, upon revival in 1970 it will be deemed to have been made in 1970, and so

---

[1] *Rogers and Andrews* v. *Goodenough and Rogers* (1862), 2 Sw. & Tr. 342; *Re Reade*, [1902] P. 75.

[2] *Major and Munday* v. *Williams and Iles* (1843), 3 Curt. 432; *In the Goods of Brown* (1858), 1 Sw. & Tr. 32; *Powell* v. *Powell* (1866), L.R. 1 P. & D. 209.

[3] [1893] P. 339.

will revoke the (prior) will of 1960.[1] If neither the 1950 will, nor the 1970 codicil contain express revocation clauses, the 1960 will will remain valid to the extent that it is not inconsistent with the combined 1950 will and 1970 codicil. If the court is satisfied that it is totally inconsistent, it will refuse probate of the 1960 will, but if it is not satisfied it will grant probate of all three documents, leaving the exact effect to be determined by the Chancery Division.[2]

5. EFFECT OF REVIVAL

The effect of revival is the same as republication, namely the will takes effect as if it had been written at the date of revival,[3] except in those circumstances in which a republished will would not take effect as if written at the date of republication.[4] This, however, is subject to two qualifications. Revival may involve the revocation of an intermediate instrument, as has just been considered. Secondly, it is possible for only part of a document to be revived. If it is clear that the mind of the testator was directed not to the whole will but only to some part of it, then only that part will be revived.[5]

---

[1] *Re Pearson, Rowling v. Crowther,* [1963] 3 All E.R. 763.
[2] *In the Goods of Dyke* (1881), 6 P.D. 205; *In the Goods of Reynolds* (1873), L.R. 3 P. & D. 35; *Re Baker, Baker v. Baker,* [1929] 1 Ch. 668.
[3] *Ante,* p. 113.
[4] *Ante,* pp. 115 *et seq.*
[5] *In the Estate of Mardon,* [1944] P. 109.

Part II

THE CONSTRUCTION OF WILLS

CHAPTER 9

THE GENERAL PRINCIPLES

A. GENERAL CONSIDERATIONS

1. THE PROBLEM

The meaning of a will may not be clear. The testator may have used words which are imprecise: if there is a gift "to John's relations", are these John's brothers and children, or are his cousins included? The testator may have used expressions which appear to be inconsistent: if there is a gift of "my car to Albert" in one clause, and a gift of "all my personalty to Victoria" in another clause, does the car go to Albert or to Victoria? There may be doubt as to the person who is intended to take a benefit. If the testator leaves a legacy to "my employees", are the people to qualify those who are employees both at the date when the will was made and at the date of death, or at either of those dates? If there is a gift of "my cactus", and between the date of making the will and the date of death the cactus dies and the testator acquires a new one, does the new one pass under that provision? Gaps may have been left in the will, which the testator intended to fill in later, but did not. Words with a precise technical meaning may have been used but in the incorrect sense. A testator with a perverted sense of humour may have written parts of the will in the form of a quasi-algebraic equation. As early as 1613, Coke, C.J., lamented: "Wills and the construction of them do more perplex a man than any other learning, and to make a certain construction of them, this *excedit juris prudentum artem*."[1] The Law Reports are full of examples of every conceivable way of making the meaning of the will uncertain and obscure.

Faced with such a situation, the obvious and natural reaction is to attempt to ascertain the testator's real meaning. But how

---

[1] *Roberts* v. *Roberts* (1613), 2 Bulstr. 123, at p. 130.

may this be done? If one looks outside the will, the requirement that a will must be in writing is seriously threatened. It is clear, for example, that provided a word used in a will is given a clear definition in the will, then that word will be given the meaning attached to it by that definition, and not its normal meaning. Thus, if the testator gives "£1,000 to my banana", and adds a definition clause showing that wherever he uses the word "banana" he means his son, then the son takes. If, however, there is a gift in the same terms, but no definition clause, can one admit extrinsic evidence to show that the testator always called his son "banana"? If so, in principle it would be possible to draw a will full of such apparently meaningless phrases, leaving the meaning of all of them to be determined by extrinsic evidence. The requirement for a will to be in writing could then be made an empty formality. For this reason, the general principle is that one must deduce the testator's intention only from the will itself.

Sometimes the doubt does not appear on the face of the will itself, but only when its effect is considered in conjunction with surrounding circumstances. For example, the testator may have left "£500 to my niece Jane". On its face, the will is clear: but when the surrounding circumstances are considered there may be two nieces called Jane. Can the surrounding circumstances of the testator's intention be adduced to show which one he intended?

2. PRINCIPLES AND RULES OF CONSTRUCTION

If the Court is able to deduce the testator's intention from the will, that will prevail. If the court cannot deduce his intention— and only if it cannot—it adopts the so-called "rules of construction". These are not in any sense rules of law which are binding on the testator: they are more rules of convenience applied by the court, more often than not in order to give some, rather than no, meaning to the will.

These rules and principles are often set forth in a neat tabulated form, and the impression is given that in any particular case a question of construction is solved by a logical application of these rules. Life is not like that. In this subject it is more important than in any other to remember how a case is tried, and in particular that all contentions are before the judge before he has to make any decision. Before he makes his decision he knows what its effect will be. The rules of construction are so numerous that he ought to be able to find some which enable him to reach the conclusion that he wishes to reach. This is not to suggest that in all such cases judges come to a decision which they wish to reach, and then construct the reasoning for it, so that when the judgment is read, it appears to be a logical sequence starting with the principles, which appear to point, inevitably, to the conclusion. While it is not suggested that all judges approach the matter in this way, and there is positive evidence that some do not, nevertheless the suspicion remains that in many cases this is what happens.

3. THE COURT OF CONSTRUCTION

As will be seen, the Chancery Division of the High Court is the usual "court of construction". In some respects this is unfortunate. All lawyers become increasingly conscious of the exact meaning of words. It is part of the result of construing documents, distinguishing and drafting. A lawyer can see what he imagines to be a real difference between two similar words, whereas to the layman who can see no difference this is but splitting hairs. The consciousness of the meaning of words is particularly true of Chancery lawyers and Chancery judges. It is also worth recalling that the Chancery Division is used to the construction of complex trust deeds, settlements, conveyances, and commercial documents almost all of which will have been professionally prepared. Although the Chancery Division attempts, or sometimes attempts, to shake off this background when construing a "home made" will, it is unrealistic to expect that a lifetime's background can be put aside. This may help to explain why some decisions appear to be unduly narrow, and to lead to a result far removed from what might be thought to be the testator's intention. A judge may complain testily that "the numerous class of persons who, in wills and otherwise, speak as if the office of language were to conceal their thoughts, have no right to complain of being taken to mean what their language expresses".[1] Instead of indulging in such arrogance, it is better to recall that few testators set out to conceal their thoughts: lack of ability with a pen, rather than intention to obscure, is the usual cause of the difficulty, and it is lack of ability

---

[1] Knight-Bruce, L.J., in *Lowe* v. *Thomas* (1854), 5 De G.M. & G. 315, at p. 317.

which should meet with sympathy, not irritation, on the part of the court. Fortunately, a more liberal attitude has prevailed since the often harsh and unattractive Victorian era, and effect is perhaps now more frequently given to the testator's intention. But Lord Atkin may have been a little too optimistic when, in *Perrin* v. *Morgan*[1] he anticipated[2] "with satisfaction that henceforth the group of hosts of dissatisfied testators who, according to a late Chancery judge, wait on the other bank of the Styx to receive the judicial personnages who have misconstrued their wills may be considerably diminished".

B. THE COURT OF CONSTRUCTION

1. DIVISION OF FUNCTIONS

There is an apparently curious division of function between the "court of probate", which is concerned with the validity of the will, and the "court of construction" which is concerned with the meaning and effect of a valid will. The former function is now usually exercised by the Family Division of the High Court,[3] whereas the latter function is exercised by the Chancery Division. This division of function is the result of historical development.

By the end of the twelfth century the ecclesiastical courts were recognised as having jurisdiction over the interpretation of a will, as well as over the validity of a will of personalty.[4] The common law courts were content not to interfere, and accepted the grant of probate by the Bishop as conclusive evidence that the will was valid.

The Court of Chancery made one or two rather weak attempts to interfere with the probate jurisdiction of the ecclesiastical courts, their main interest being with regard to interpretation. In due course the Court of Chancery became the accepted court of construction of wills of personalty, while the ecclesiastical courts continued to exercise their probate function.

The common law courts had never accepted the need for probate of wills of realty. Where a will disposed both of realty and personalty, and probate was granted by the church courts, this had no effect on the realty. The common law courts and the

---

[1] [1943] A.C. 399, H.L.
[2] *Ibid.*, at p. 415.
[3] Administration of Justice Act 1970, s. 1(4)(a).
[4] At that time there was no possibility of making a will of realty.

Court of Chancery had concurrent jurisdiction over the interpretation of wills of realty. The Judicature Acts assigned the construction of all wills, whether of realty or personalty, to the Chancery Division and the Judicature Act 1873 assigned probate jurisdiction to the then Probate Divorce and Admiralty Division. The Probate, Divorce and Admiralty Division was renamed the Family Division by the Administration of Justice Act 1970.

2. EFFECT OF HISTORICAL BACKGROUND

The ecclesiastical courts borrowed heavily from Roman Law, and many of the rules of Roman Law were applied in the construction of wills of personalty. When the Court of Chancery became concerned with the interpretation of wills of personalty, and the common law courts became concerned with the interpretation of wills of realty, they adopted many of the Roman based rules of the ecclesiastical courts. Roman Law has, therefore, influenced considerably the construction of wills of personalty, although it has played little part in the construction of wills of realty. The general tendency since the Judicature Acts has been for the principles of construction of realty and personalty to be equated, but some differences still remain.

3. INTER-RELATION WITH PROBATE COURT

In practice it is not always possible to separate the probate and construction functions. In the first place the Family Division has to construe a document to ensure that it is intended to operate as a will;[1] and in the second place, where two wills are inconsistent, the Family Division must construe both documents to decide the extent to which the earlier will has been impliedly revoked.[2] Any construction of the Family Division is not binding on the Chancery Division, except to the extent that the Chancery Division is obliged to accept the will in the form in which Probate has been granted. If there is any error in it, the Probate can only be altered by the Family Division.

In exceptional cases, such as where the estate is small, the

---

[1] See *ante*, p. 29, and *Re Hawksley's Settlement*, [1934] Ch. 384.
[2] See *ante*, p. 89, and *In the Estate of Fawcett*, [1941] P. 85.

Family Division may determine a question of construction if all parties agree.[1]

C. FUNDAMENTAL PRINCIPLES

1. COURTS WILL NOT MAKE WILLS

The function of the court is to interpret the words which the testator has used, and not to make the will itself. An illustration of this was considered earlier[2] where the court is prepared to delete part of a will where it has been inserted without the knowledge of the testator, although it is not prepared to insert what it thinks he intended.

There are two reasons for the Courts' attitude. In the first place, it was shown earlier[3] that a testator may make a will in such terms as he wishes, even if the court does not think that he has been wise in so doing. The second reason for the attitude of the courts is that if the court departs from the words of the testator, it upsets the basic rule that the testator is himself entitled to determine the destiny of his property.

The result of this approach is that if the words which the testator has used are clear, effect will be given to them, even though the court might suspect that the result is not what the testator intended. Some examples of this have already been given. Thus, where the testator intended certain words to be included in his will, effect will be given to them even if he did not intend that effect.[4] In *Scalé* v. *Rawlins*[5] the testator left three houses to his niece for life, and provided that if she should die leaving no children, the houses were then to go to his nephews. It seems clear that the testator intended that if the niece died leaving children of her own, then on her death the property should go to her children. It was held by the House of Lords, however, that because the testator had not expressly made any provision for the niece's children, they could not take in any event.

---

[1] *In the Estate of Last,* [1958] P. 137.
[2] *Ante,* p. 49.
[3] *Ante,* p. 31.
[4] See, e.g., *ante,* p. 87.
[5] [1892] A.C. 342.

2. WILL AS A WHOLE TO BE CONSTRUED

Having established that the courts seek to interpret the intention of the testator, it is next necessary to note that in general they are prepared only to interpret that intention as expressed in the will itself.[1] This means that the will as a whole must be considered, and not merely the particular part upon which doubt arises.[2] By looking at the will as a whole, other provisions in it may make it more easy to determine what the testator intended by the part in dispute. Furthermore, the testator may himself have given a definition of a word in another part of the will.[3]

D. MEANING OF WORDS AND PHRASES

1. USUAL MEANING

A word or phrase is in the first place given its ordinary grammatical meaning.[4] This rule was stated by Kindersley, V.C., in *Re Crawford's Trusts*[5] as "a rule of universal application, which admits of no exception, and which ought never under any circumstances to be departed from". This considerably overstates the position, which has been better described as "The most general of rules; a rule of great utility".[6] Consideration of the ordinary grammatical meaning is part of the enquiry to ascertain the meaning which the testator himself placed on the words,[7] but in the absence of some indication that the deceased used the words in a special sense, they are given their normal meaning. Thus, in *Gilmour* v. *MacPhillamy*[8] a testator left his residuary estate to be divided between his nine children equally. Each child was given a life interest in his share, and the testator then provided that the

---

[1] *Lowen* v. *Cocks* (1627), Het. 63; *Bowen* v. *Lewis* (1884), 9 App. Cas. 890; *Beaudry* v. *Barbeau*, [1900] A.C. 569.

[2] *Baddeley* v. *Leppingwell* (1764), 3 Burr. 1533; *Thellusson* v. *Woodford* (1799), 4 Ves. 227, at p. 329; *Martin* v. *Lee* (1861), 14 Moo. P.C.C. 142, at p. 153; *Crumpe* v. *Crumpe*, [1900] A.C. 127.

[3] The so-called "dictionary principle" discussed below.

[4] *Villar* v. *Gilbey*, [1907] A.C. 139, at p. 147; *Hamilton* v. *Ritchie*, [1894] A.C. 310, at p. 313; *Higgins* v. *Dawson*, [1902] A.C. 1, at p. 12; *Gorringe* v. *Mahlstedt*, [1907] A.C. 225, at p. 227.

[5] (1854), 2 Drew 230.

[6] *Gether* v. *Capper* (1855), 24 L.J.C.P. 69, at p. 71.

[7] *Shore* v. *Wilson* (1842), 9 Cl. & Fin. 355, at p. 563.

[8] [1930] A.C. 712.

share of such child should pass to his children, but that if any of his, the testator's, children should die without issue, the share of that child should be divided among the survivors. The testator probably intended to regard the issue of his children as standing in the stead of the children themselves, with the result that the issue of the deceased children would participate with the surviving children in taking the share of those who had died without issue. In fact, the testator had only used the word "survivors" of his children. Accordingly, when two of his children died without issue, the two children who were still then living took the share of the deceased children, without the issue of other predeceased children participating.

Although this insistence on giving effect to the strict meaning of the words used often causes a result which the testator did not intend, it seems necessary to have some such approach if the whole requirement that a will must be in writing should be preserved. Otherwise, the testator could express himself in the most vague and general terms, leaving scope for the admission of outside evidence to determine what he really intended.

The meaning which the court seeks to establish is the ordinary meaning at the time when the will was made,[1] it being remembered that with the passage of time words can alter their meaning. It follows from this that care must be exercised in the use of precedents: they can only show what meanings have in the past been given to a particular word.[2] Furthermore, of course, each case depends on its own facts, and the intention which the particular testator had.

2. SECONDARY MEANINGS

The courts will adopt a secondary meaning:
a. where there is, in effect, a definition clause in the will itself; and
b. where, when the apparent effect of the will is applied to the surrounding circumstances, it appears that the testator must have used the word in some other sense.

---

[1] *Cave* v. *Horsell*, [1912] 3 K.B. 533; *Pigg* v. *Clarke* (1876), 3 Ch.D. 672.
[2] *Perrin* v. *Morgan*, [1943] A.C. 399 and the authorities referred to in that case.

a. *Definition clause*

The testator may, when preparing his will, as in the case of the preparation of any other document incorporate an express definition clause attributing to certain words a specified meaning. The same result occurs where he does not do this expressly, but clearly uses words in a particular sense. A good example is provided by *Re Helliwell, Pickles* v. *Helliwell*[1]. The testator left property to his "nephews". It will be seen later[2] that normally where a person is described by reference to a relationship to the deceased, that expression means only legitimate relationships. In this case, however, in another part of the will the testator provided that the illegitimate son of his illegitimate sister was to participate "equally with my other nephews". The testator had, therefore, shown that he used the word "nephew" in a sense wider than normal.[3]

b. *Application to surrounding circumstances*

It will be seen shortly that the court is always entitled to take into account the circumstances in which the will was made, and to take note of the circumstances known to the testator at that time. Where this is done, it may show that the testator used a word in an unusual sense, and in this case, the word will bear the meaning which the testator gave to it. In *Re Smalley, Smalley* v. *Scotton*,[4] for example, the testator left his property to "my wife E.A.S.". When the will was considered in the light of the surrounding circumstances, it appeared that E.A.S. was bigamously married to the testator, so the Court of Appeal was able to hold that the testator used the word "wife" to mean "reputed wife". In *Thorn* v. *Dickens*,[5] the court was concerned with what has been described as the shortest known will, which merely read "All for mother". Evidence was admitted to show that the testator referred to his wife as "mother", and the wife took.[6]

---

[1] [1916] 2 Ch. 580.
[2] *Post*, p. 154. This applies only in pre-1970 instruments.
[3] See also *Re Davidson, National Provincial Bank, Ltd.* v. *Davidson*, [1949] Ch. 670.
[4] [1929] 2 Ch. 112.
[5] [1906] W.N. 54.
[6] See also *Charter* v. *Charter* (1874), L.R. 7 H.L. 364; *Re Bailey, Barclay's Bank, Ltd.* v. *James*, [1945] Ch. 191.

N.B. The same result could have been reached by disregarding the words "my wife" under the *falsa demonstratio* rule considered *post*, p. 139.

3. WORDS WITH MORE THAN ONE MEANING

A word may have more than one usual or ordinary meaning. In this case the court will adopt the meaning which it regards as most probable,[1] which in effect leaves a wide discretion to the judge.

An example of this is the expression "stocks and shares". In *Re Everett, Prince* v. *Hunt*[2] the testatrix had made provision in her will for the disposal of her "stocks and shares". Her investments consisted partly of stocks and shares in limited companies, but they also included redeemable debentures[3] and Government securities. Cohen, J., held that the gift passed only stocks and shares in the limited companies. He could have founded his decision on the basis that in that case the other investments were required for the payment of legacies, but he expressly said that he was not basing his decision on that. By contrast, in *Re Purnchard's Will Trusts, Public Trustee* v. *Pelly*[4] Jenkins, J., held that the testator must be presumed to have wished to dispose of the whole of his estate, and therefore the expression "stocks and shares" included all his investments.

Further examples are provided by the use of the word "money". This was originally restricted to coin of the realm, but the word has now ceased to have any *prima facie* meaning.[5] As Goulding, J., has observed[6] "the use of a word like 'money' varies between persons of different classes, possibly between different parts of the country, certainly in the mouth of one and the same individual under differing circumstances, and a judge would need to be more of a philologist than I am to feel confident in relying in all cases on his own knowledge of the contemporary use of the English language. Nonetheless, it seems to me that the House of Lords[7] has directed that a judge should apply his own knowledge of the

---

[1] *Perrin* v. *Morgan*, [1943] A.C. 399 especially the judgment of Lord Atkin at p. 414.

[2] [1944] Ch. 176.

[3] Debentures are technically a loan to the company, rather than an equity participation in the company.

[4] [1948] Ch. 312.

[5] *Re Trundle*, [1961] 1 All E.R. 103, *per* Cross, J., *Re Barnes's Will Trusts, Prior* v. *Barnes*, [1972] 2 All E.R. 639.

[6] In *Re Barnes's Will Trusts, Prior* v. *Barnes*, [1972] 2 All E.R. 639, at p. 644.

[7] The reference is to the decision of the House of Lords in *Perrin* v. *Morgan*, [1943] A.C. 399.

language in the light of such context and circumstances as may assist him". So, where the testator made a gift of his money, but no gift of residue, the expression was held to pass all the personalty;[1] and where the testator directed his debts to be paid, and then left "the remainder of my money", this was effective to leave also his realty.[2] In the most recent decision, *Re Barnes's Will Trusts, Prior* v. *Barnes*[3] there was a gift of "my money" and a residuary gift of "any other personal property". The judge had no difficulty in deciding that balances with Barclays Bank, and with the Abbey National Building Society were included. But what of premium bonds? The judge tried to put himself in the position of the testatrix, who was a "small trader". "If I am . . . to apply my experience of the contemporary and vulgar use of the English language, I think on the whole that a testatrix in the position of Mrs. Barnes would have included (the bonds) as part of her money. It is certainly not unfamiliar[4] to hear persons speak of a purchase of premium savings bonds as 'placing my money with Ernie' ".[5]

4. TECHNICAL WORDS AND SYMBOLS

Where the testator uses words which have a technical legal meaning, such as "heir" there is a strong presumption that the words will carry that technical meaning[6] particularly if they appear in a professionally drawn will.[7] Thus, in *Re Smith, Bull* v. *Smith*[8] the testatrix left her property "to my own right heirs" other than R. J. Smith and his issue. When she died the son of R. J. Smith was her heir at common law, but if R. J. Smith or his issue had never existed then her nephew would have been her heir. It was held, however, that one could not have a "right heir" excluding the "right heir", so that the whole gift was void.[9]

---

[1] *Perrin* v. *Morgan*, [1943] A.C. 399.

[2] *Re Mellor, Porter* v. *Hindsley*, [1929] 1 Ch. 446; *Re Shaw, Mountain* v. *Mountain*, [1929] W.N. 246.

[3] [1972] 2 All E.R. 639.

[4] Although the writer admits that he has never heard anyone so speaking.

[5] [1972] 2 All E.R. 639, at p. 645.

[6] *Re Athill, Athill* v. *Athill* (1880), 16 Ch.D. 211; *Re Fetherston-Haugh-Whitney's Estate*, [1924] 1 I.R. 153.

[7] *Read* v. *Backhouse* (1831), 2 Russ. & M. 546; *Hall* v. *Warren* (1861), 9 H.L. Cas. 420.

[8] [1933] Ch. 847.

[9] See also Family Law Reform Act 1969, s. 15 (2).

The meaning of scientific technical terms is a question of fact, and will *prima facie* be given the technical meaning which they bear according to the evidence of experts in that field.[1]

Where the testator uses special words or symbols which have a recognised significance in the locality trade or business to which the testator belonged, evidence will be given of their significance.[2] Where, however, the testator uses symbols which are known only to himself, evidence will not be admitted to prove their meaning.[3] Thus, in *Clayton* v. *Lord Nugent*[4] the donees in the will were described by letters which referred to a card index system maintained by the testator which was not incorporated by reference. It was not possible to admit evidence of the significance of those letters.

5. CUSTOM

Where the testator belonged to a special group of persons, and a word has a special meaning among persons of that group, the meaning of the word for that group will be taken to be the ordinary meaning of the word for the purposes of the will, and not the meaning attributed to it in common parlance. In the same way, where the testator has used the symbols of a trade to which he belonged, these symbols will be given their meaning current among persons who carry on that trade.[5] But the principle is not confined to a trade: for example, it also applies to members of a particular religious community. So in *Shore* v. *Wilson*[6] where the testator was a member of a dissenting sect, his expression "godly persons" was given the meaning current among members of that sect.[7]

6. SUMMARY

The position is, therefore:

a. Where the testator has expressly or impliedly defined his

---

[1] *Gobley* v. *Beechey* (1829), 3 Sim. 24; *Clayton* v. *Gregson* (1836), 5 Ad. & El. 302.
[2] *Kell* v. *Charmer* (1856), 23 Beav. 195; *Shore* v. *Wilson* (1842), 9 Cl. & Fin. 355, at p. 525; *Re Rayner, Rayner* v. *Rayner*, [1904] 1 Ch. 176.
[3] *Goblet* v. *Beechey* (1829), 3 Sim. 24.
[4] (1844), 13 M. & W. 200.
[5] *Kell* v. *Charmer* (1856), 23 Beav. 195.
[6] (1842), 9 Cl. & Fin. 355.
[7] Cf. *Re How, How* v. *How*, [1930] 1 Ch. 66.

word, the meaning given will be in accordance with that definition. Likewise, where there is no definition, but by reference to the surrounding circumstances it can be seen that he uses the word in a special sense, the court will adopt that special sense.

Subject to that:

b. If the testator came from a special group, and used a word having a special significance among members of that group, the word will have that special meaning.

c. If the testator has used a technical word, it will be presumed to bear that technical meaning.

d. Subject to all the foregoing, the word will carry its ordinary general meaning, or, if it has more than one ordinary general meaning, such meaning as the court considers most appropriate in the circumstances.

E. SUBSIDIARY GENERAL PRINCIPLES OF CONSTRUCTION

1. INCONSISTENT CLAUSES

There is a general rule that if two parts of a will are mutually inconsistent then the later clause is to prevail.[1] The reason for this arbitrary rule is that the last clause is said to be the last expression of the testator's wish but this reasoning appears to be specious and it is perhaps better to regard the rule either as a mere rule of thumb[2] or a "rule of despair".[3]

Although the acceptance of the rule has been recognised for a long time[4] because of its arbitrary nature the Courts are in fact reluctant to apply it. Accordingly, the rule will not apply in any of the following circumstances:—

a. Where upon construction of the will as a whole it appears that the testator intended the first clause to apply. This in fact gives the judge more or less complete freedom to reach whichever

---

[1] *Paramour v. Yardley* (1579), 2 Plowd 539; *Sherratt v. Bentley* (1834), 2 My. & K. 149; *Brocklebank v. Johnson* (1855), 20 Beav. 205; *Re Hammond, Hammond v. Treharne*, [1938] 3 All E.R. 308.

[2] *Per* Jessel, M.R., in *Re Bywater, Bywater v. Clarke* (1881), 18 Ch.D. 17.

[3] *Per* Lord Greene, M.R., in *Re Potter's Will Trusts*, [1944] Ch. 70, at p. 77.

[4] See authorities cited in footnote 1, *supra*.

conclusion he wishes. If there are clauses in a will which are inconsistent, if the judge wishes to follow the former clause he has only to say that this is in accordance with the testator's intention. In many cases however there is no clear indication of what the testator intended. An illustration of this is *Re Bywater, Bywater v. Clark.*[1] In that case the testator bequeathed an annuity to his second wife but provided that the annuity should not be payable until the daughters of his first wife had reached the age of 21. The final clause of the will indicated that the annuity should be paid at once and there was therefore this inconsistency. Jessel, M.R., at first instance, basing his decision not upon the arbitrary rule but upon what he held to be the testator's intention derived from the will as a whole, held that the final clause prevailed. The Court of Appeal however held that the first clause prevailed, they themselves basing their decision on what they took to be the testator's intention. Where there is this type of inconsistency it is usually anyone's guess to determine from the will itself what the testator actually intended.

b. There is Commonwealth authority that if by following the arbitrary rule an intestacy occurs then the former clause is to be preferred.[2] This is in accordance with the presumption against intestacy referred to at p. 137.

c. Where the inconsistency lies in a gift of the same thing to two persons both donees will take some interest in that thing. They may both take at once as joint tenants or tenants in common[3] or, if the nature of the thing so demands, they will take in succession.[4] In *Re Alexander's Will Trusts, Courtauld-Thomson v. Tilney,*[5] for example, where the same bracelet was given to one person in one clause and to another person in another clause both clauses were construed together as giving both persons a moiety each. It seems however that separate considerations affect gifts of residue. In *Re Gare, Filmer v. Carter*[6] where there were inconsistent gifts of residue the first of the gifts was held to prevail.

---

[1] (1881), 18 Ch.D. 17.

[2] *Piper* v. *Piper* (1886), 5 N.Z.L.R. 135.

[3] *Ridout* v. *Pain* (1747), 3 Atk. 486; cf. *Sherratt* v. *Bentley* (1834), 2 My. & K. 149.

[4] *Gravenor* v. *Watkins* (1871), L.R. 6 C.P. 500; *Re Bagshaw's Trusts* (1877), 46 L.J. Ch. 567.

[5] [1948] 2 All E.R. 111.

[6] [1952] Ch. 80.

There was substantial previous authority to support this decision[1] and this rule may be justified on the basis that if there are lapsed shares of the first gift of residue these would pass under the second gift. Alternatively it may be possible to show that all lapsed legacies fall into residue.[2]

d. If one gift is in the will and the other in a codicil the court will usually conclude that to that extent the codicil has revoked the will.[3]

In most cases the difficulty which arises from inconsistent provisions could be resolved if the courts were prepared to admit extrinsic evidence as to the testator's intentions. It is shown later[4] that the courts will only admit extrinsic evidence of a testator's intention where there is an ambiguity. This does not apply where there is an inconsistency. It may be thought however that it would be far better for the courts to admit extrinsic evidence of the testator's intentions in the case of an inconsistency rather than to indulge in speculation of this unattractive kind. In *Re Bywater*,[5] for example, there was evidence that the final clause had been inserted in the will by mistake and indeed directly contrary to the testator's express instructions to his solicitor. That evidence was not admissible.

2. THE GOLDEN RULE

The so-called Golden Rule is that the court will endeavour to adopt a construction which gives a sensible meaning to the provisions of the will and which will not lead to an intestacy. It is, of course, accepted that a testator has a right to be capricious if he so wishes[6] and if he uses words which are clear and unambiguous then the court has no alternative but to give effect to the testator's words unless an application is made under the Family Provision legislation. The Golden Rule operates where there are at least

---

[1] *Davis* v. *Bennett* (1861), 30 Beav. 226; *Re Spencer, Hart* v. *Manston* (1886), 54 L.T. 597; *Re Isaac, Harrison* v. *Isaac*, [1905] 1 Ch. 427.

[2] *Re Jessop* (1859), 11 I. Ch.R. 424; *Re Gare*, [1952] Ch. 80.

[3] *Earl Hardwicke* v. *Douglas* (1840), 7 Cl. & Fin. 795; *Re Stoodley, Hooson* v. *Locock*, [1916] 1 Ch. 242.

[4] *Post*, p. 141.

[5] *Ante*, p. 136.

[6] *Bird* v. *Luckie* (1850), 8 Hare 301; *Varley* v. *Winn* (1856), 2 K. & J. 700, at p. 707; *Jenkins* v. *Hughes* (1860), 8 H.L. Cas. 571, at p. 589; *Re Hamlet* (1888), 39 Ch.D. 426, at p. 434.

two possible constructions. The rule was expressed by Esher, M.R., in *Re Harrison, Turner* v. *Hellard* in the following words:[1] "Where a testator has executed a will in solemn form you must assume that he did not intend to make it a solemn farce—that he did not intend to die intestate when he had gone through the form of making a will. You ought, if possible, to read the will so as to lead to a testacy, not an intestacy." This is the golden rule. Thus, in *Re Arnould, Arnould* v. *Lloyd*[2] the court could only make sense of the testator's will by construing his full stops as commas. This was done.

3. *EJUSDEM GENERIS*

The so-called *ejusdem generis* rule provides that where a wide word is used in conjunction with and following several narrow words then the scope of the wide word will be controlled by the narrow words. In *Re Miller, Daniel* v. *Daniel*[3] the testator made specific bequests of his books and wine, and his plate, and then made a residuary gift of "all the rest of the furniture and effects at my residence". By itself the word "effects" will include all personal property but in this case the court decided that the word must be construed *ejusdem generis* with the preceding words books, wine, plate and furniture, so that the beneficiary did not take the share certificates and bank notes which were at the testator's residence.

The *ejusdem generis* rule can only operate where there is no other expression of the testator's intention. If by considering the phrase or the will as a whole it appears that the general word is not to be restricted by the preceding narrow words then the *ejusdem generis* rule will not apply. Again it is for the courts to decide whether there is that contrary intention. Thus in *Re Fitzpatrick*[4] where there was a gift of "my house and all my furniture and effects" the word "effects" was not construed *ejusdem generis* and was held to include all the personalty of the testatrix.

---

[1] (1885), 30 Ch.D. 390, at p. 393.
[2] [1955] 2 All E.R. 316.
[3] (1889), 61 L.T. 365.
[4] (1934), 78 Sol. Jo. 735.

It has been suggested[1] that the rule is no more than an illustration of the general principle of construction that a word must be construed in a secondary sense if the will shows that this was the testator's meaning.

4. AMBIGUOUS WORDS DO NOT CONTROL A CLEAR GIFT

A clear gift in a will will not be reduced in scope by any subsequent words which are ambiguous or not equally clear. In *Re Freeman*[2] the testator appointed A to be one of his executors and gave him a legacy of £1,000 and a share in the residue. The appointment of A to be the executor and the specified legacy to him were revoked by a subsequent codicil. The codicil provided that B should be the executor and should have a legacy of £200 and that the will should take effect as if the name of B were inserted throughout instead of the name of A. No specific mention was made in the codicil of the share of residue given to A. There was accordingly a gift of residue to A in the will and the general statement in the codicil that the will should take effect as if the name of B were substituted for the name of A. The court held that the general statement in the codicil did not revoke the specific gift of residue in the will and accordingly A took.[3]

5. *FALSA DEMONSTRATIO*

The full maxim is *falsa demonstratio non nocet cum de corpore constat*. The doctrine applies to all written instruments but with regard to wills there are two limbs of it. The first limb provides that where the description of a person or property is made up of more than one part, and one part is true and the other false, then if the part which is true describes the person or property with sufficient certainty the untrue part will be rejected and will not vitiate the gift.[4]

In order to ascertain whether part of the description is true the court has regard to the will as a whole and to the surrounding circumstances. Accordingly, where there was a gift to "my wife Caroline" and the testator had a wife Mary but lived with a woman named Caroline with whom he had gone through an invalid ceremony of marriage the word "wife" was held not to

---

[1] S. J. Bailey, The Law of Wills, 6th edn., at p. 217.
[2] [1910] 1 Ch. 681, at p. 691.
[3] See also *Re Gouk, Allen v. Allen*, [1957] 1 All E.R. 469.
[4] *Re Brocket, Dawes v. Miller*, [1908] 1 Ch. 185.

affect the validity of the gift and Caroline took.[1] The rule also applies to property. Thus where a gift of stock was stated to be in the joint names of a testator and/or another, and in fact the stock was standing in the name of the testator alone but all other description of it was correct, the gift was effective.[2] Further, where the testator devised all his freehold houses in a named place and it appeared that the testator had no freehold houses there but leasehold houses the gift was sufficient to pass the leaseholds.[3]

A more extreme example is *Re Price, Trumper v. Price*.[4] In that case the testatrix bequeathed "My £400 5% War Loan 1929-1947". She had in fact never held any War Loan but had held £400 National War Bonds which had been converted into other Government securities before she made her will. It was found as a fact that she regarded as "War Loan" any securities which represented the investments she had made to assist the country during the first world war. Accordingly her words were sufficient to cover the proceeds of her National War Bond, and the words "Five per cent . . . 1929/1947" were rejected as *falsa demonstratio* and the word "Loan" was read in a secondary sense to enable effect to be given to the testatrix's wishes.

The second limb of the *falsa demonstratio* rule is that additional words are not rejected as importing a false description if they can be read as words of restriction. So, in *Wrightson v. Calvert*,[5] where the testator made a gift to his grandchildren living near B, the testator had three grandchildren but only two lived near B and the third was held not to be entitled.

The usual situation in which the main part of the *falsa demonstratio* rule applies, that is the first rule, is where words of the will themselves contain an accurate description as well as a further false description.

The principle, has however, been extended so that if the description in the will is wholly false but the context of the will and the surrounding circumstances show unambiguously what the testator meant then the description in the will is rejected and

---

[1] *Pratt* v. *Mathew* (1856), 22 Beav. 328; *Re Petts* (1859), 27 Beav. 576; *In the Goods of Howe* (1884), 48 J.P. 743.

[2] *Coltman* v. *Gregory* (1870), 40 L.J. Ch. 352.

[3] *Day* v. *Trig* (1715), 1 P. Wms. 286.

[4] [1932] 2 Ch. 54.

[5] (1860), 1 John. & H. 250.

the intention of the testator is given effect.[1] In one case there was
a gift to the "resident apothecary" but there was only a resident
dispenser and he was held entitled to take.[2] In several cases a gift
to the children of A has been held to take effect as a gift to the
children of B provided that the context and circumstances show
that that was what was intended.[3] The rule is likewise with regard
to property. Thus the description "War Loan" was held to pass
holdings of Conversion Stock and Treasury Bonds[4] and a devise
was held to pass the interest in the proceeds of sale of the
land.[5]

Re Price, Trumper v. *Price* and many of the other decisions
show the lengths to which the court will go in order to give effect
to the testator's intention. The reasoning for such decisions
represents intellectual acrobatics of an unconvincing kind and
while one does not quarrel with the decision itself this type of
intellectual acrobatics shows the great scope which the courts in
fact have if they wish to use it in order to give a decision which
they consider to be fair and in many cases it is extremely difficult
for professional advisers to give firm advice as to the likely outcome of a case. Again one comes to the point[6] when in many
cases the courts are able to reach their decision first and then to
construct the reasoning which appears to support it.

The principles so far discussed have been evolved by the courts
themselves. Two sections of the Wills Act 1837, ss. 24 and
27, are very important in the construction of wills but these are
considered in the next chapter on gifts of property and gifts to
persons.

F. USE OF EXTRINSIC EVIDENCE

1. GENERAL RULE

The general rule is that the court is entitled to ascertain the
testator's intention only from the words of the will itself, and that

---

[1] *Morrell* v. *Fisher* (1849), 4 Exch. 591; *Cowen* v. *Truefitt*, [1899] 2 Ch. 309.
[2] *Ellis* v. *Bartrum* (1857), 25 Beav. 109.
[3] *Bradwin* v. *Harpur* (1759), Amb. 374; *Bristow* v. *Bristow* (1842), 5 Beav.
289; *Lord Camoys* v. *Blundell* (1848), 1 H.L. Cas. 778.
[4] *Re Price, Trumper* v. *Price*, [1932] 2 Ch. 54; *Re Gifford, Gifford* v. *Seaman*,
[1944] Ch. 186.
[5] *Re Glassington, Glassington* v. *Follett*, [1906] 2 Ch. 305.
[6] *Ante*, p. 125.

it may not admit extrinsic evidence of what the testator intended. There are, however, three exceptions to this principle, when extrinsic evidence will be admitted:

 a. where the surrounding circumstances are taken into account under the armchair principle;

 b. where there is a latent ambiguity as to the testator's meaning; and

 c. to rebut certain presumptions which equity raises.

2. THE ARMCHAIR RULE

In construing a will, the court has the right to ascertain all the facts which were known to the testator at the time when he made the will, and thus to place itself in the testator's position at that time. In *Boyes* v. *Cook*,[1] James, L.J., said: 'You may place yourself, so to speak, in (the testator's) armchair, and consider the circumstances by which he was surrounded when he made his will to assist you in arriving at his intention."

The method in which the rule is applied is that the will is first construed without any reference to the surrounding circumstances. The apparent effect of the will is then applied to the surrounding circumstances so that the court can confirm to itself that the conclusion drawn from the terms of the will itself is in accordance with the circumstances existing at the date when it was made.[2] The rule is also adopted to identify more particularly the person or property named in the will.

Suppose, therefore, in a will a testator makes a gift "to the wife of my cousin John". On its face, the effect of the will seems clear. The court is then entitled to check its conclusion by sitting in the testator's armchair. If, therefore, the testator knew that at that time John's wife had died, the will is construed as meaning any subsequent wife of John.[3]

It is by the application of this rule that it can sometimes be seen that the testator uses words in a particular way.[4] A further example is provided by *Re Fish, Ingham* v. *Rayner*[5] where a testator bequeathed property "to my niece Eliza Waterhouse".

---

[1] (1880), 14 Ch.D. 53, at p. 56.

[2] *Blackwell* v. *Pennant* (1852), 9 Hare. 551.

[3] See *post*, p. 149.

[4] *Ante*, p. 131.

[5] [1894] 2 Ch. 83.

When the apparent effect of the will was checked in the light of surrounding circumstances, it appeared that he had no niece of this name, but that his wife had a grand-niece of that name. It was held that the testator used the word "niece" in this wide sense, so that Eliza took.

The armchair rule is also applied when the description of the person or property in the will is not in precise terms.[1] Thus, where the testator gives property "to my friend Bonzo", evidence will be admitted of the testator's practice of calling a particular person by the nickname Bonzo.[2] Again, where the description of the property is vague, such as "my estate called Ashford Hall", evidence will be admitted to show the exact extent of what the testator regarded as his Ashford Hall estate.[3]

While it is true that evidence of the surrounding circumstances in which the will was made will always be admitted[4] this evidence can only be used to confirm the apparent effect of the will, or to clarify imprecise terms in the will. It cannot be used to alter the effect of the words used in the will if they are clear and unambiguous.[5] So, in *Evans* v. *Angell*[6] the testator devised his freehold land "situate in the parish of C with their appurtenances". It was found that at the date when the will was made, the testator held with that property certain pieces of land in two other parishes, all of which had been occupied as one unit. Nevertheless, because the words of the will were clear, the land in these other parishes could not pass under the devise.

3. LATENT AMBIGUITY

Where the subject matter of a gift, or the beneficiary, is described in terms which are applicable to two or more persons or

---

[1] *Thomson and Baxter* v. *Hempenstall* (1849), 1 Rob. Eccl. 783; *Grant* v. *Grant* (1870), L.R. 5 C.P. 727; *Kingsbury* v. *Walter*, [1901] A.C. 187.

[2] *Mostyn* v. *Mostyn* (1854), 5 H.L. Cas. 155, at p. 168; *Re Ofner, Samuel* v. *Ofner*, [1909] 1 Ch. 60.

[3] *Ricketts* v. *Turquand* (1848), 1 H.L. Cas. 472. See also *Doe d. Beach* v. *Earl of Jersey* (1825), 3 B. & C. 870; *Webb* v. *Byng* (1855), 1 K. & J. 580; *Re Vear, Vear* v. *Vear* (1917), 62 Sol. Jo. 159.

[4] *In the Estate of Davis*, [1952] P. 279.

[5] *Higgins* v. *Dawson*, [1902] A.C. 1.

[6] (1858), 26 Beav. 202.

things, extrinsic evidence may be admitted to prove which person or thing was intended.[1] In this case there is an ambiguity.

The rule applies usually only where there is a latent ambiguity that is, where the description on the face of the will appears to be precise, but that when it is applied to the surrounding circumstances, it appears that it can apply to more than one person or thing. In this type of ambiguity it is possible to admit extrinsic evidence of the person or thing intended by the testator. On the other hand, if the description contained in the will is sufficient to point to one person or thing only, then it will be taken to refer to that person or thing, even if this is contrary to the likely intention of the testator.[2]

If, however, the words are not sufficient to point to one, and only one, person or thing, then evidence of the testator's intention may be adduced to identify the correct person. If that does not identify the person intended, the gift will be void.

The best example of the operation of the rule is *Re Jackson, Beattie* v. *Murphy*.[3] In her will the testatrix gave property to "my nephew Arthur Murphy". By adopting the armchair rule, it became apparent that there were two legitimate nephews Arthur Murphy, as well as one illegitimate one. There was therefore a latent ambiguity, and at this stage it was possible to admit extrinsic evidence of the testatrix's intention. This was that the illegitimate nephew should take, the testatrix having used the word "nephew" in a wide sense. If there had been only one legitimate nephew of this name, then at the first stage of this process, the application of the armchair principle, that nephew would have taken. It was only because there were two legitimate nephews of the same name that the latent ambiguity arose. If there had been only the two legitimate nephews, and the extrinsic evidence did not indicate that either of them was entitled to take, the whole gift would have been void.

It is a little difficult to know the extent of the rule when the ambiguity appears on the face of the will. It is clear that in most cases of patent ambiguity, extrinsic evidence will not be admitted. Thus, if there is a gift to "Mr. . . . ." evidence cannot be adduced

---

[1] *Per* Lord Russell, C.J., in *Re Stephenson, Donaldson* v. *Bamber*, [1897] 1 Ch. 75, at p. 80.

[2] *Re Jackson, Beattie* v. *Murphy*, [1933] Ch. 237.

[3] [1933] Ch. 237.

to show who was intended.[1] Nor can evidence of intention be adduced where there is a gift "to one of my nephews", although in such a case the courts will strive to give some effect to the provision.[2]

The case which gives rise to difficulty is *Doe d. Gord* v. *Needs*.[3] In that case the testator gave one of his two houses to "George Gord the son of George Gord"; a pecuniary legacy to "George Gord the son of John Gord", and his other house to "George Gord the son of Gord". Evidence was admitted to show that the testator intended the second house to go to the son of George Gord, and he accordingly took. This appears to be a case of patent ambiguity, yet extrinsic evidence of intention was admitted. On the other hand, in most cases extrinsic evidence of intention is not admitted in the case of patent ambiguity. It seems better to regard this case as deciding that the gift in dispute may for this purpose be considered in isolation, as if the only provision in the will had been to "George Gord the son of Gord". There would then be an inadequate description, which, when applied to the circumstances surrounding the making of the will would bring forth the two George Gords, both of whom would appear to be equally entitled. At that stage extrinsic evidence of intention could be admitted in the usual way. In other words, it was coincidental that the fact of the ambiguity in this case appeared on the face of the will.

It will therefore be seen that if evidence of intention is to be admitted, there are three separate and progressive stages:—

a. construction of the will itself;

b. examination of the surrounding circumstances in which the will was made; and

c. in some cases, admission of evidence of the testator's intention.

4. EVIDENCE TO REBUT EQUITABLE PRESUMPTIONS

Equity raises certain presumptions against double portions,[4] and as the satisfaction of portion debts by legacies,[5] and legacies by

[1] *Baylis* v. *A.-G.* (1741), 2 Atk. 239.
[2] See *post*, p. 152.
[3] (1836), 2 M. & W. 129.
[4] *Post*, p. 484.
[5] *Post*, p. 480.

portions.[1] These are, however, only presumptions of the testator's intention, and evidence may be admitted either to support or rebut the presumptions.[2]

5. NATURE OF ADMISSIBLE EVIDENCE

Where it is admissible to adduce evidence of the testator's intention, the evidence may be contemporaneous with the making of the will, or prior to or subsequent to it. Any type of evidence is admissible, so that it may consist of declarations by the testator[3] or, for example, correspondence between the testator and his solicitor as to the provisions which he wanted to be included in his will.

6. SUMMARY

The position may be summarised as follows:—

1. Is the meaning of the will apparently clear on its face? If so, in all cases reference should be made to the surrounding circumstances to see whether that description fits exactly, or subject only to insignificant misdescription,[4] one, and only one, person or item of property.

    a. If it does, that meaning will prevail, even if there is available extrinsic evidence that this is contrary to the testator's intention.

    b. If it does not, there is either:

        (i) a statement which is too vague to be given effect, in which case the gift is void; or

        (ii) a latent ambiguity, in which case evidence of the testator's actual intention may then be admitted. If the extrinsic evidence indicates the person or property, the gift will take effect accordingly. If it does not, then the gift also fails.

---

[1] *Post,* p. 482.

[2] *Hurst* v. *Beach* (1821), 5 Madd. 351; *Hall* v. *Hill* (1841), 4 I. Eq.R. 27; *Kirk* v. *Eddowes* (1844), 3 Hare. 509, at p. 51; *Re Tussaud's Estate* (1878), 9 Ch.D. 363.

[3] *Dwyer* v. *Lysaght* (1812), 2 Ball. & B. 156, at p. 162; *Charter* v. *Charter* (1874), L.R. 7 H.L. 364; *Re Taylor, Cloak* v. *Hamond* (1886), 34 Ch.D. 255; *Re Nesbitt's Will Trusts,* [1953] 1 All E.R. 936.

[4] Which can be ignored under the *falsa demonstratio* rule.

2. If the meaning of the will is not apparently clear on its face:

    a. reference may be made to the surrounding circumstances. If more than one person is indicated at that stage, a latent ambiguity arises, and one may proceed as in 1. b. (above).

    b. if the will is too vague to be explained by the surrounding circumstances, the gift will be void.

CHAPTER 10

GIFTS TO PERSONS AND OF PROPERTY

The last chapter was concerned with general principles of the construction of wills. This chapter is concerned with the application of those principles to gifts to persons, and to gifts of property, and also with the particular considerations which apply to these gifts.

I. GIFTS TO INDIVIDUAL PERSONS

A. GIFTS TO PERSONS IDENTIFIED BY NAME OR DESCRIPTION

In many cases, a gift will be to a person or persons in a defined relationship to the testator, such as "my wife", or "my children"; or to a person holding office by reference to that office, such as "my servants" or "the vicar". If nothing else is said, is the person entitled to take that person who fulfils the description at the date of the will, or at the date of death? The general rule is that where there is a person who fulfils the description at the date of the will, that person takes. Wills Act 1837, s. 24 provides that with regard to the property disposed of, the will speaks from death unless there is a contrary intention,[1] but this section does not apply to the persons entitled.[2]

The rules may be stated more specifically as follows:

1. PERSON FULFILLING DESCRIPTION AT DATE OF WILL

Where a person fulfils the description at the date of the will, there is a presumption that that person is to take. So, in *Re*

---

[1] *Post*, p. 162.
[2] *Bullock* v. *Bennett* (1855), 7 De G.M. & G. 283; *Gibson* v. *Gibson* (1852), 1 Drew. 42.

Whorwood, Ogle v. *Lord Sherborne*[1] a testator bequeathed a cup to "Lord Sherborne". Lord Sherborne was alive at the time when the will was made, but predeceased the testator, leaving a son who took the title. The Court of Appeal held that the gift was to the Lord Sherborne who was alive when the will was made, and that as he himself had predeceased the testator, the gift lapsed.[2]

This principle is, however, subject to there being no contrary intention. It may be that the Court will be less willing to find a contrary intention if the relation of the beneficiary to the testator is close. Accordingly, there will be a strong presumption that a gift to " my wife" or "to the wife of A" is a gift to the person who is the wife at the date of making the will, and a weaker presumption if the gift is to "the vicar".[3]

2. NO PERSON FULFILLING DESCRIPTION AT THE DATE OF THE WILL

Where no person fulfils the description at the date of the will, there are four possibilities:

a. the description is wrong. In this case the gift may be saved under the *falsa demonstratio* principle,[4] in which case the relevant time will be either the date of the will, or the date ascertained in accordance with c. below;

b. the context indicates that the designated beneficiary could only take if he fulfilled the description at the date of the will. In this case, the gift will fail;

c. the context indicates that the designated beneficiary is to be ascertained at a specified time. This will usually be the death of the testator, or the death of some life tenant, but some other future date may be chosen.[5] In *Re Daniels,*

---

[1] (1887), 34 Ch.D. 446.

[2] See also *Lomax* v. *Holmden* (1749), 1 Ves. Sen. 290; *Thompson* v. *Thompson* (1844), 1 Coll. 381; *Amyot* v. *Dwarris*, [1904] A.C. 268. In the last of these cases, a gift to the eldest son lapsed, in view of the fact that the son who was the eldest at the time when the will was made died before the testator, even though the testator left other sons him surviving.

[3] But even "wife" may be subject to a contrary intention—*Peppin* v. *Bickford* (1797), 3 Ves. 570; *Meredith* v. *Treffry* (1879), 12 Ch.D. 170; *Bathurst* v. *Errington* (1887), 2 App. Cas. 698.

[4] *Ante*, p. 139.

[5] *Re Earl Cathcart* (1912), 56 Sol. Jo. 271.

London City and Midland Executor and Trustee Co., Ltd. v. *Daniels*[1] there was a gift to "the Lord Mayor of London for the time being", and it was held that the words "for the time being" indicated the person who was Lord Mayor at the date of the testator's death;

d. the context indicates that the designated beneficiary is to be ascertained at some unspecified time in the future. In this case, the first person to fulfil the description will take.[2] So, in *Radford* v. *Willis*[3] where there was a gift "to the husband of A", and at the date of the will A had no husband but later acquired one, that person took. As this case shows, where no person fulfils the description at the date of the will, and none of the preceding paragraphs applies, the courts will strain to save the gift by bringing it within this head.

3. REPUBLICATION

Where a will is republished[4] and, it seems, the testator knew of the facts, the republication can make the will speak as to persons from the date of republication. In *Re Hardyman, Teesdale* v. *McClintock*[5] there was a gift by will to the wife of A. The will was republished by codicil after the testator knew of the death of A's wife. A's subsequent wife was held entitled to take.

4. DESCRIPTION SUBSEQUENTLY BECOMING INAPPROPRIATE

Where a person appears to be entitled under the rules so far considered, then, unless there is a contrary intention in the will, that person continues to be entitled even if the description is no longer applicable. So in *Re Hickman, Hickman* v. *Hickman*[6] there was a gift "to the wife of my grandson". At the date of the will the grandson was not married, but he subsequently married twice, the first marriage being brought to an end by divorce. The

---

[1] (1918), 87 L.J. Ch. 661.
[2] *Ashburner* v. *Wilson* (1850), 17 Sim. 204.
[3] (1871), 7 Ch. App. 7.
[4] *Ante*, p. 112.
[5] [1925] Ch. 287.
[6] [1948] Ch. 624.

first wife became entitled under paragraph d. above, and in this case she continued to be entitled, although she had ceased to be the grandson's wife by the testator's death.

5. GIFTS TO PERSONS BY NAME

There may sometimes be a dispute between two persons of the same name. Suppose the will contains a gift to William Silver. Suppose also that there was a William Silver alive at the date of the will, but between the date of the will William Silver died, leaving a son also called William Silver. As has already been shown[1] in the absence of a contrary intention the will would indicate William Silver the elder, and the gift would therefore lapse. Where the name of the beneficiary is accurate, the same rules apply as previously considered.

B. INACCURATE NAMES OR DESCRIPTIONS

From what was said in the previous chapter, the following procedure with regard to persons should be followed:

1. ascertain from the face of the will the person entitled to benefit. (At this stage there has been no reference whatever to the surrounding circumstances.)

2. attempt to identify in the surrounding circumstances which existed at the relevant date, ascertained as above, the person who fulfils the description.

    a. if there is one such person, who was known to the testator, he will take;

    b. if there were two or more such persons, both known to the testator, and an equivocation arises, extrinsic evidence of the testator's intention will be admitted;[2]

    c. if there was no such person attempt to establish from the surrounding circumstances whether part, or even the whole, of the name or description was inaccurate:

        (i) if that can be done, and the correct name ascertained, apply rules a. and b. above as if the correct name had been stated in the will;

        (ii) if that cannot be done, the gift fails.

---

[1] *Ante*, p. 148.
[2] *Ante*, p. 141.

To illustrate the operation of these rules, we may consider the facts of two cases. In *Doe d. Hiscocks* v. *Hiscocks*[1] there was a gift to "John Hiscocks eldest son of John Hiscocks". On the face of the will it appeared who was entitled to benefit. However, when there was an attempt to identify this individual in the surrounding circumstances, it appeared that John Hiscocks had two sons, the elder named Simon and the younger named John. There was no equivocation, because the description as given in the will did not apply to either son. Extrinsic evidence of the testator's intention could not be admitted. Could, then, part of the description be rejected under the *falsa demonstratio* rule? As it could not be shown which part of the description was false, the rule did not apply, and as a result the gift failed.

In *Re Halston, Ewen* v. *Halston*[2] there was a gift to "John William Halston the son of Isaac Halston". When the terms of the will were applied to the surrounding circumstances at the date when the will was made it appeared that John William Halston was by then already dead, and that the fact of death was known to the testator. It was then necessary, under rule 2. c. to ascertain whether part of the description was false. Under the *falsa demonstratio* rule it was held that the words "John William" could be rejected. Isaac Halston, however, had several sons, so that the expressions "the son of Isaac Halston" gave rise to an equivocation, and by applying rule 2. b. it was possible to admit extrinsic evidence to show which son was actually intended.

C. RELATIONSHIPS

Where a person is described by a relationship to the testator, it is presumed in the absence of intention to the contrary that the testator intended:

1. both lawful and unlawful relations;
2. blood relations; and
3. only relations of the actual degree specified.

---

[1] (1839), 5 M. & W. 363.
[2] [1912] 1 Ch. 435.

1. LEGITIMATE RELATIONS

a. *Illegitimate relations*

The Family Law Reform Act 1969, has completely reversed the position with regard to illegitimate relations. In respect of wills made before 1970, there is a presumption that illegitimate relations do not take. In respect of post-1969 wills, there is a presumption that they do take.

(i) *Pre-1970 wills*. It was laid down in *Hill* v. *Crook*[1] that if illegitimate relations are to be treated as legitimate, and so to take, there must be either:

(a) no legitimate relatives to satisfy the description; or

(b) an intention appearing from the will itself to include illegitimates.

If there are no legitimate relations at the relevant date[2] illegitimate ones can take unless the testator contemplated future legitimate relations.[3] Any knowledge of the testator that a woman was past childbearing or a man was incapable of procreating children will be taken into account.[4]

In order to take, however, an illegitimate person must show that no legitimate person could take, and it is not sufficient to establish in the mind of the court the probability that the illegitimate person was intended. So, in *Re Fish, Ingham* v. *Rayner*,[5] which was mentioned earlier,[6] the testator left property "to my niece Eliza Waterhouse". He had no nieces, but two grandnieces, both called Eliza Waterhouse. As one was legitimate and the other illegitimate, the legitimate one took, even though the Court of Appeal appeared to think that the illegitimate one was intended.

An intention on the part of the testator to include illegitimate relations may appear on the face of the will. So, in *O.* v. *D.*[7] an

---

[1] (1873), L.R. 6 H.L. 265.
[2] I.e., usually at the date of the will: see *ante*, p. 148.
[3] *Dorin* v. *Dorin* (1875), L.R. 7 H.L. 568; *Re Brown, Penrose* v. *Manning* (1890), 63 L.T. 159; *Re Dieppe, Millard* v. *Dieppe* (1915), 138 L.T. Jo. 564.
[4] *Paul* v. *Children* (1871), L.R. 12 Eq. 16; *Re Eve, Edwards* v. *Burns*, [1909] 1 Ch. 796; *Re Brown, Penrose* v. *Manning* (1890), 63 L.T. 159; *Re Wohlgemuth, Public Trustee* v. *Wohlgemuth*, [1949] Ch. 12.
[5] [1894] 2 Ch. 83.
[6] *Ante*, p. 142.
[7] [1916] 1 I.R. 364.

illegitimate girl was described in one clause as "my daughter". In another clause there was a gift to "my children", and she was held entitled to join with legitimate children in taking.[1] It must, however, be shown that the testator treated the claimant himself as legitimate, not that he treated other illegitimate relations as legitimate.[2]

(ii) *Post-1969 wills.* Family Law Reform Act 1969, s. 15, provides that in a will which is made on or after 1 January, 1970[3] a reference to a child or relative includes an illegitimate child or relative. For the purposes of this legislation, a will is made at the time when it is signed, not when the testator dies. A will executed before 1970 is treated as having been made before that date even if it is confirmed by a post-1969 codicil.[3] This applies where the illegitimate person is the beneficiary, and also where the beneficiary claims through an illegitimate person.[4] Exceptionally where the word "heir" is used, or an entail is created, there is still a presumption against illegitimate persons taking.

b. *Legitimated children*

A person born illegitimate but legitimated under the provisions of the Legitimacy Acts 1926 and 1959 is legitimated either from 1 January 1927, or from the date of his parents marriage, whichever is the later. Legitimated persons will take as "children" if they were legitimated before the testator's death,[5] provided there is no contrary intention in the will. Special rules apply where an illegitimate person dies before the marriage of his parents, but leaving a spouse, children or remoter issue living at the date of that marriage. If the deceased had been living at the date of marriage of his parents, and would thereupon have become legitimated, his spouse, children and remoter issue are entitled to take interest in property as if he was legitimated as from the date of the marriage.[6] However, if the illegitimate person was born at a

---

[1] See, however, *Re Jodrell, Jodrell* v. *Seale* (1890), 44 Ch.D. 590.
[2] *Mortimer* v. *West* (1827), 3 Russ. 370; *Re Wells' Estate* (1868), L. R. 6 Eq. 599. See also *Re Jackson, Beattie* v. *Murphy, ante,* p. 144.
[3] Family Law Reform Act 1969, s. 15 (8).
[4] Family Law Reform Act 1969, s. 15 (2).
[5] Legitimacy Act 1926; *Re Hepworth, Rastall* v. *Hepworth,* [1936] Ch. 750.
[6] Legitimacy Act 1926, s. 5.

time when either of his parents was married to a third person, this
rule only applies if he died after 28 October, 1959.[1]

The children of bigamous and certain other void marriages
are legitimated if either party or both parties to the marriage
reasonably believed at the date of the operative act of intercourse,
or at the date of marriage if later, that the marriage was valid.[2]

There was an absurd rule affecting seniority. Where seniority is
relevant, legitimated persons ranked as if they were born not on the
date when they were in fact born, but on the date of legitimation.[3]
However, with certain exceptions, this rule is abolished for wills
made after 1969.[4]

c. *Adopted children*

The position of adopted children depends on whether or not
the adoption order was made after the date of the will or codicil.
For the purposes of this provision, a will is treated as having
been made on the death of the testator.[5] If it was made before the
will, then in the absence of contrary intention, an express or
implied reference in the will to child or children will include a
reference to the adopted child.[6] This applies for all purposes
except a disposition of property limited to pass with a title of
honour.[7] The Adoption Act 1958, does not entitle a child adopted
after the making of the will to benefit: such a child will benefit
only if there was an intention in the will to benefit him.[8] Where a
power of appointment is exercised, to be an object of the power,
in the absence of any contrary intention, the child must be adopted
before the instrument creating the power becomes operative, and
not merely before the instrument exercising the power is operative.[9]

2. RELATIONSHIP BY BLOOD AND AFFINITY

Relationship arising by marriage is known as relationship by
affinity. The presumption is that where a relationship is specified
in a will, the only persons to take are the relations by blood, and

---

[1] See Legitimacy Act 1959, s. 1 (2).
[2] Legitimacy Act 1959, s. 2.
[3] Legitimacy Act 1926, s. 3 (2).
[4] Family Law Reform Act 1969, s. 15 (4) (b).
[5] Adoption Act 1958, s. 17 (2).
[6] Adoption Act 1958, s. 16 (2).
[7] Adoption Act 1958, s. 16 (3).
[8] *Best* v. *Best*, [1956] P. 76.
[9] *Re Brinckley's Will Trusts, Westminster Bank* v. *Brinkley*, [1967] Ch. 407.

not by affinity.[1] This is subject to the same exceptions as in the case of legitimate relations, namely relations by affinity may be included if there are no relations by blood,[2] or if there is an intention that they should. There may be a considerable difficulty in knowing whether a contrary intention is shown. In several cases a niece by affinity has been called for the purposes of a specific bequest or legacy "my niece A", but such person has been held not entitled to share in a subsequent gift to "my nephews and nieces".[3] These decisions have not been followed in others,[4] so that little may be said by way of general rule, each decision depending on its context.

It is also difficult to state the position affecting relations of the half-blood. In *Re Reed*[5] it was said that there is a presumption that relations of the half-blood are included and that "the context must be overriding to exclude the half-blood". On the other hand, in some cases the context has very easily displaced the presumption. So where the testator said "my own brothers and sisters" this was held sufficient to exclude step-brothers and step-sisters.

3. DEGREE OF RELATIONSHIP

There is a presumption that the testator only intended relations of the exact degree to benefit. Thus, if he refers to nieces, it is presumed he meant nieces and not, for example, great nieces.[6] Again the presumption may be displaced by the context or contrary intention.

4. INCORRECT STATEMENT OF RELATIONSHIP

The *falsa demonstratio* rule applies, whereby it may be possible to ignore incorrect descriptions.

---

[1] *Hibbert* v. *Hibbert* (1873), L.R. 15 Eq. 372; *Hussey* v. *Berkeley* (1763), 2 Eden. 194; *Smith* v. *Lidiard* (1857), 3 K. & J. 252; *Merrill* v. *Morton* (1881), 17 Ch.D. 382.

[2] *Frogley* v. *Phillips* (1861), 3 De G.F. & J. 466; *Hogg* v. *Cook* (1863), 32 Beav. 641; *Adney* v. *Greatrex* (1869), 38 L.J. Ch. 414; *Sherratt* v. *Mountford* (1873), 8 Ch. App. 928; *Re Gue, Smith* v. *Gue* (1892), 61 L.J. Ch. 510.

[3] *Smith* v. *Lidiard* (1857), 3 K. & J. 252; *Wells* v. *Wells* (1874), L.R. 18 Eq. 504.

[4] *Re Gue, Smith* v. *Gue* (1892), 61 L.J. Ch. 510; *Re Cozens*, [1928] S.C. 371.

[5] (1888), 57 L.J. Ch. 790.

[6] *Seale-Hayne* v. *Jodrell*, [1891] A.C. 304; *Re Cozens*, [1928] S.C. 371.

D. PARTICULAR WORDS

There has been a considerable amount of litigation as to the meaning of particular words used to designate beneficiaries. It is not intended even to begin to give an exhaustive statement of the position, but as illustrations four examples may be taken.

1. "CHILDREN"

The word "children" *prima facie* means immediate descendants, and not grandchildren or remoter issue.[1] If, however, it can be shown that the testator has confused the strict meaning of the word children with remoter issue, grandchildren will be entitled to take.[2] A child *en ventre sa mere* is included in the description of children born or living at a particular date if it is to the child's own benefit that he should be included.[3]

The position of legitimated and adopted children has already been considered.

2. "SURVIVORS"

Where property is to be divided among the survivors of a particular group, the *prima facie* meaning of that expression is that they should be living at and after[4] the moment of distribution.[5] In the case of an immediate gift, the moment of distribution is, for this purpose, the death of the testator, but in other circumstances it may be the death of a life tenant. Thus, a gift to "the surviving children of Winnie" means a gift to such of her children as are living at the date of death of the testator, but a gift to "Winnie for life, with remainder to her surviving children" enables the children living at the death of Winnie to take. Until that time, their interest does not vest, so that if they predecease Winnie, they will take no benefit, even if they survive the testator.[6]

The context of the will may, of course, show that the word is used in a special or secondary sense.

---

[1] *Loring* v. *Thomas* (1861), 1 Dr. & Sm. 497.

[2] *Wyth* v. *Blackman* (1749), 1 Ves. Sen. 196; *Re Marshall*, [1957] Ch. 507.

[3] *Villar* v. *Gilbey*, [1907] A.C. 139; *Elliot* v. *Joicey*, [1935] A.C. 209; *Re Stern's Will Trusts*, [1962] Ch. 732.

[4] *Elliott* v. *Joicey*, [1935] A.C. 209, at p. 218; see also *Re Castle, Public Trustee* v. *Floud*, [1949] Ch. 46.

[5] *Cripps* v. *Wolcott* (1819), 4 Madd. 11.

[6] *Re McKee, Public Trustee* v. *McKee*, [1931] 2 Ch. 145.

3. "ISSUE"

The technical meaning of the word "issue" is descendants in every degree.[1] This meaning may, however, be restricted to "children", where the context so indicates. Thus, a gift to "the issue of our marriage" has been confined to the children of the marriage[2] and wherever the testator uses an expression which shows that he used the word other than in its technical meaning, the word will bear that meaning. An example of this occurred where the testator used the expression "issue of such issue".[3]

4. "NEXT OF KIN"

The expression "next of kin" *simpliciter* does not have a technical meaning, but merely denotes the most nearly related relative of kin. On the other hand, the expression "statutory next of kin" indicates the persons who would be entitled to succeed to the property on intestacy, and in the proportions and subject to the same conditions as they would have taken under the intestacy rules.[4] Although the expression has this meaning by statute,[5] the statutory definition is nevertheless subject to a contrary intention being shown.

II. GIFTS TO GROUPS OF PERSONS

A. GIFTS BY NUMBER

A testator may attempt to identify the beneficiaries by describing them as members of a class or group, and adding their number, such as a gift to "the four children of A". Clearly in this case no problem arises if A in fact has four children, but what is the position if he has three or five? The position is as follows:

a. The relevant date is the same as for individuals, so that

---

[1] *Edyvean* v. *Archer*, [1903] A.C. 379; *Re Burnham, Carrick* v. *Carrick*, [1918] 2 Ch. 196; *Re Swain, Brett* v. *Ward*, [1918] 1 Ch. 399; *Re Hipwell, Hipwell* v. *Hewitt*, [1945] 2 All E.R. 476.

[2] *Re Noad, Noad* v. *Noad*, [1951] Ch. 553.

[3] *Pope* v. *Pope* (1851), 14 Beav. 591; *Fairfield* v. *Bushell* (1863), 32 Beav. 158.

[4] *Re Hart's Will Trusts, Public Trustee* v. *Barclays Bank, Ltd.*, [1950] Ch. 84; *Re Kilvert, Midland Bank Executor and Trustee Co., Ltd.* v. *Kilvert*, [1957] Ch. 388; and see *Re Krawitz's Will Trusts, Krawitz* v. *Crawford*, [1959] 3 All E.R. 793.

[5] Administration of Estates Act 1925, s. 50.

usually regard is paid to the position when the will is made;

b. the Court considers the surrounding circumstances to see with which of the members of the class the testator was acquainted. If that number corresponds to the number specified in the will, those persons will take.[1] This is part of a more general rule that where persons are misdescribed in number, an attempt should be made from the surrounding circumstances to see whether it is possible to say which of the class were meant. In *Re Mayo, Chester* v. *Keirl*[2] for example, there was a bequest to the three children of A. A had four children, but the testator had admitted paternity only of the younger three. The eldest child did not take;

c. where it is not possible to say which of the class is meant, all persons who answer the description take. Thus, in *Sleech* v. *Thorington*[3] the testatrix left a gift to "the two servants living with me at my death". She in fact had three servants, all of whom took.

B. CLASS GIFTS

1. NATURE OF RULE

Special rules apply to gifts which are, strictly so-called, "class gifts". The general object of these rules is to facilitate the distribution of the estate or fund at the earliest opportunity. The general situation may be described by an example. Suppose a testator leaves a fund to "my sisters". Suppose also that he has three sisters alive at the date of his death, and two born afterwards. There are two possibilities: the gift may be divided between the three who are alive at the date of his death; or the fund may be retained until it is impossible for any more sisters to be born, and then distributed. It is a fundamental principle of English property law that property and assets of every description should circulate as much as possible, and not be tied up. In accordance with this thinking, the class is deemed to close at the earliest opportunity, that is, at the date of death of the testator. On the example given, the two sisters born afterwards take nothing.

---

[1] *Newman* v. *Piercey* (1876), 4 Ch.D. 41.
[2] [1901] 1 Ch. 404.
[3] (1754), 2 Ves. Sen. 560.

Although the purpose behind the class closing rules can be clearly understood, they are nevertheless curious. They may be excluded by an expression of contrary intention[1] but apart from that they do not even purport to be an interpretation of the testator's intention. They are, frankly and blatantly, rules of convenience.[2]

2. STATEMENT OF THE RULE

The classic statement of the nature of a class is that of Lord Davey in *Kingsbury* v. *Walter*,[3] where he said *"prima facie* a class gift is a gift to a class, consisting of persons who are included and comprehended under some general description and . . . it may be none the less a class because some of the individuals of the class are named". Examples of "classes" are gifts "to all my sisters";[4] "to the grandchildren of A";[5] "to the children of A including his son B";[6] and "to my late husband's nephews and nieces other than A and B".[7]

The rule may be stated as follows:

1. a. Where the shares of members of the class are to vest at birth, the class will remain open indefinitely; unless

   b. (i) a member of the class was born before the testator's death; *or*

   b. (ii) a member of the class was born before the end of some intermediate period of limitation.

2. Where the shares of members of the class are to vest upon the happening of any event other than birth and where the exceptions within rule 1. b. apply, the class closes when the first member becomes entitled to an interest in possession.

3. No person may take a benefit after the class has closed.[8]

---

[1] *Scott* v. *Earl of Scarborough* (1838), 1 Beav. 154; *Hodson* v. *Micklethwaite* (1854), 2 Drew. 294; *Re Kebty-Fletcher's Will Trusts*, [1967] 3 All E.R. 1076.

[2] *Re Emmet's Estate, Emmet* v. *Emmet* (1880), 13 Ch.D. 484, at p. 490; S.J. See also Bailey (1958), Camb. L.J. 39, at p. 42.

[3] [1901] A.C. 187.

[4] *Weld* v. *Bradbury* (1715), 2 Vern. 705.

[5] *Re Knapp's Settlement, Knapp* v. *Vassall*, [1895] 1 Ch. 91.

[6] *Re Jackson, Shiers* v. *Ashworth* (1883), 25 Ch.D. 162.

[7] *Dimond* v. *Bostock* (1875), 10 Ch. App. 358.

[8] The rule governing the position where the gift to the class is postponed or is subject to the members of the class attaining a qualifying age, is known as the rule in *Andrews* v. *Partington* (1791), 3 Bro. C.C. 401.

The particular situations likely to arise are:

a. Immediate gift to a class without qualification—e.g. "to all my grandchildren". If the testator has a grandchild alive at his death, the class closes at his death (rule 1. b. (i)) but if he has no grandchildren alive then, all grandchildren whenever born will take (rule 1. a.).

b. Immediate gift to class with qualification—e.g. "to all my grandchildren who attain the age of 21". The class will close at the date of death of the testator if any grandchild attained the age of 21 during the testator's lifetime (rule 1. b. (i)). If grandchildren are alive during the testator's lifetime, but have not reached the age of 21 by his death, the class closes when the first one reaches that age (rule 2). It will be seen that rule 1. can only apply where vesting is to be at birth, and not at some other time. This is quite illogical.

c. Mediate gift without qualification—e.g. "to A for life, with remainder to all my grandchildren". The class will close on the death of A (the time when a child may acquire an interest in possession) if there is any grandchild then alive (rule 1. b. (ii)), but if there is no grandchild upon the death of A, the class will remain open indefinitely (rule 1. a.).

d. Mediate gift with qualification—e.g. "to A for life, with remainder to all my grandchildren who attain 21". The class will close on the death of A if there is any grandchild aged 21 (rule 2.). The class cannot close earlier than the death of A, because until then no member of the class can obtain an interest in possession. If there is no grandchild who has attained 21 at the death of A the class will close when the first grandchild does so (rule 2.).

3. EFFECT OF CLOSING RULE

Where there is a gift, whether immediate or mediate, with qualification, all persons who may attain that qualification at the date when the class closes are *prima facie* included. Thus if there is a gift "to all my grandchildren who attain the age of 21" and at the testator's death there are four grandchildren aged 23, 19, 10 and 2, the class then closes because one has fulfilled the qualifying condition. Each of the others *then alive* will participate if they in due course attain the qualifying age. Thus, when the class closes, the minimum amount payable to each member of

the class is ascertained and one quarter of the fund can be paid
to the eldest forthwith. If one of the others dies before attaining
the age of 21, his share lapses, and is divided among the others.
Thus the eldest, who would already have received one quarter,
will receive a further one third of the lapsed quarter.

4. CONTRARY INTENTION

It has been mentioned[1] that the rules can be excluded by a
contrary intention: the result is often an inelegant game of coin
tossing to see whether the testator in fact had a contrary intention.[2]
A good example is *Re Edmondson's Will Trusts, Baron Sandford* v.
Edmondson.[3] There was, in effect, a gift to "such of my grandchildren, whenever born, as should attain the age of 21." At the
time of the gift there were two children, and one grandchild, a
few months old. By the time of the application to the court,
there were eight grandchildren, with the possibility of more to
follow. Was the class to close, the eldest grandchild having reached
the age of 21? Or was it to remain open, and so admit any grandchild who might be born in the future? At first instance[4] Goulding,
J., held that the class closed: the Court of Appeal held that it
did not.[5] The decision of the Court of Appeal centred on the
proposition that an expression such as "born or hereafter to be
born" was merely a general reference to the future, not sufficient
to exclude the rule, whereas the expression "whenever born"
was sufficiently specific and emphatic to exclude the rule. This
type of dispute shows a detachment from reality meriting approval
from the mediaeval Schoolmen, but from no one else. It is possible
to formulate the principle that *Andrews* v. *Partington*[6] should
only be excluded if it can be shown that the testator appreciated
the nature of the problem that would arise by its exclusion, that
is, that the shares of persons with vested interests might have
to be retained in case further members of the class come to reduce
the size of each share. But in this sphere no rule is likely to be

---

[1] *Ante*, p. 148.
[2] Sherrin (1972), 122 N.L.J. 144.
[3] [1972] 1 All E.R. 444, C.A.
[4] [1971] 3 All E.R. 1121.
[5] The court was concerned with two documents, but there was no dispute
that for the purposes of one of them the class did close.
[6] (1791), 3 Bro. C.C. 401.

satisfactory, for the mind of the testator is rarely directed to the problem—and the mind of the draftsman not much more frequently.

III. GIFTS OF PROPERTY

A. THE RELEVANT DATE

1. THE GENERAL RULE

The general rule is that a reference to a person in a gift by will is to the person who fulfils that description at the date of the will.[1] So far as references to property are concerned, the rule is the reverse. By virtue of Wills Act 1837, s. 24, unless there is a contrary intention, a will must be construed with reference to the property comprised in it, to speak and take effect as if it had been executed immediately before the death of the testator. Accordingly, a gift of "all my horses" will include all horses owned by the testator at the date of his death, even if he acquired some of them after the date of the will. The reason for s. 24 was probably the rule relating to leaseholds. Before 1837, a gift of a leasehold interest would pass only that interest in existence at the date of the will. If, therefore, after the date of the will the lease expired and the testator was granted a new lease before his death, the new lease would not pass, because it was a different, new, interest. By virtue of s. 24, therefore, a new lease will pass provided the words of the will are appropriate to describe it.[2]

2. CONTRARY INTENTION

Section 24 reads: "Every will shall be construed . . . to speak and take effect as if it had been executed immediately before the death of the testator, unless a contrary intention shall appear by will." In the light of this, suppose a testator makes a gift of "my present piano". Does one apply the section narrowly, and read this clause as if the will had been executed just prior to death, or does one interpret the words "my present" as imparting a contrary intention, and to indicate the piano owned at the date of the will?

---

[1] *Ante*, p. 148.

[2] If, for example, the testator refers not merely to his leasehold property, but to the property demised by a lease dated 1950, the property will not pass if between the date of making the will and the date of death the term expires, and a new lease is granted in 1965.

Although s. 24 does not distinguish between general and specific gifts, the courts will be far more ready to find a contrary intention in specific gifts than in general gifts. A gift of "my house and land at A", where the word "my" forms an essential part of the description will be regarded as a specific gift, whereas a gift of "all my houses and lands at A" will be regarded as general. This distinction is important. If the testator uses the word "my" or some other possessive adjective, that may convert an otherwise general gift into a specific one.

The confusion which abounds in this field is illustrated by some of the many cases which have been concerned with the use of the word "now". There have been three approaches:

a. *to ignore it.* In *Wagstaff* v. *Wagstaff*,[1] where there was gift of an article "which I now possess", the expression "which I now possess" was treated as meaning "which I possess". An alternative route to reach the same result is to construe such words not as an essential part of the description, but as mere additional description, which may be rejected. So, in *Re Willis, Spencer* v. *Willis*[2] there was a devise to the testator's wife of "all that my freehold house and premises situate at Oakleigh Park, Whetstone, in the County of Middlesex, and known as 'Ankerwyke', and in which I now reside". Between the date of the will and the date of death the testator acquired two other plots which he enjoyed with the house. Eve, J., asked whether the expression "in which I now reside" was "an essential part of the gift, or (was) simply added as an additional description, inaccurate at the date when the will came into operation". Deciding on the facts that the latter was the case, he held that the two additional plots passed with the house to the wife.

b. *to interpret "now" expressly as referring to the deemed time of execution, that is immediately before death.* In *Hepburn* v. *Skirving*,[3] for example, a gift of "all the shares which I now possess in the Union Bank of Calcutta" was read as referring to assets held immediately before death.

c. *to interpret "now" as imputing a contrary intention.* So, in *Re Fowler, Fowler* v. *Wittingham*[4] there was a gift of "my house

---

[1] (1869), L.R. 8 Eq. 229.
[2] [1911] 2 Ch. 563.
[3] (1858), 32 L.T.O.S. 26.
[4] (1915), 139 L.T. Jo. 183.

and land wherein I now reside". Between the date of the will and the date of death further fields were acquired, and added to the grounds, but they did not pass under the gift. Similarly, in *Re Edwards, Rowland* v. *Edwards*[1] there was a gift of "my house and premises where I now reside". After the date of the will, part of the property was let, but the beneficiary was entitled to the whole premises occupied as at the date of the will.

A good explanation of the contrary intention rule was given by Stuart, V.C., in *Lady Langdale* v. *Briggs*.[2] He said: "Where . . . a testator by a will . . . devises lands by the description of 'all the lands now vested in me' and in the same will speaks of other lands which shall be vested in him at the time of his death, the language affords sufficient evidence of an intention to distinguish after acquired lands from lands vested at the time of the date and making of his will . . . ".

Although there are the three approaches, it will be appreciated that the result of following either of the first two will be the same. It is in cases such as this where the great freedom of action given to the judge is seen. Again, take the example of a gift of "the house in which I now reside". The judge may follow courses a. or b., and take the house as it stands at the date of the will,[3] or he may take the words as relating to the date of the will.[4] The construction of the will as a whole may control the judge's discretion, but if it is unfettered, one may speculate on the reasons which may lead a judge to one decision or to the other. This is of course speculation, but it may be expected that the court will be influenced by any material alteration in the value of the asset, and by the destruction of the property. Suppose the testator makes a gift of "my piano". Suppose also that at the date of the will the piano was an old upright piano worth £7·50, but that this was subsequently sold and a grand piano worth £450 purchased. It may well be that if the beneficiary was a casual friend, the gift would be construed as one relating to the date of the will, whereas

---

[1] (1890), 63 L.T. 481.

[2] (1855), 3 Sm. & G. 246, at p. 254.

[3] E.g., *Hutchinson* v. *Barrow* (1861), 6 H. & N. 583; *Noone* v. *Lyons* (1862), 1 W. & W. 235.

[4] *Re Midland Rail. Co.* (1865), 34 Beav. 525; *Re Champion, Dudley* v. *Champion*, [1893] 1 Ch. 101.

if it is to the testator's son it may speak from death. If this contention is correct, it shows how considerations which are technically irrelevant may affect the result, but nevertheless enable a just result to be reached.

B. SCOPE OF A GENERAL GIFT

1. NATURE OF A GENERAL GIFT

A general gift may be a gift of all the testator's assets, such as "all my property";[1] or a gift of all the testator's assets of a particular nature, such as "all my realty"; or a gift of the testator's residuary estate, or of his residue of a particular nature, such as "all my property remaining after the payment of my legacies" or "all my personal property remaining after the payment of my legacies".

The characteristic of all general gifts is that no particular item of the specified property is identified.

2. INTERESTS INCLUDED

In the absence of a contrary intention, a general gift will include all interests of the testator in the property comprised in the gift, whether legal or equitable.[2] It will also include all interests whether vested or contingent, and whether in possession, in remainder or in expectancy. So in *Re Egan, Mills* v. *Penton*[3] where the word "money" was given a very wide meaning[4] a gift of "money in my possession at my death" passed a reversionary interest held at the date of death.

In some cases technical words are used which, strictly, are applicable only to realty alone or to personalty alone, but which appear to apply to both realty and personalty. For example, the word "devise" is strictly applicable only to realty, and "bequest" to personalty. What, then, is the effect if the testator says: "I bequeath all my property to X", and dies leaving both realty and personalty. Such technical words, or technical words of limitation,

---

[1] *Re Bridgen, Chaytor* v. *Edwin*, [1938] Ch. 205.
[2] *Atcherley* v. *Vernon* (1723), 10 Mod. Rep. 518; *Potter* v. *Potter* (1750), 1 Ves. Sen. 437; *Capel* v. *Girdler* (1804), 9 Ves. 509.
[3] [1899] 1 Ch. 688.
[4] See *ante*, p. 132.

will be a factor in showing whether a gift is of all property, or is to be restricted,[1] but usually more force is given to the general nature of the gift than to the technical words used.[2] In the example given, it could be expected that the words would be sufficient to pass both realty and personalty.[3]

C. PROPERTY SUBJECT TO A POWER OF APPOINTMENT

1. POWERS SUBJECT TO WILLS ACT, S. 27

It is not intended to discuss here the law relating to powers of appointment, but it may be useful to summarize the classification of powers. Powers may be classified:

a. *according to the width of class of possible appointees:*
   (i) general—e.g. "to such persons as X shall select";
   (ii) special—e.g. "to such of my children as X shall select";
   (iii) hybrid—e.g. "to such persons, other than Y, as X shall select".

b. *according to the method of exercise:*
   (i) by deed only;
   (ii) by will only;
   (iii) by deed or will.

c. *according to the number of persons who must join in or concur:*
   (i) exercisable by the donee of the power alone;
   (ii) exercisable by the donee of the power jointly with another, that is, where there are two donees; and
   (iii) exercisable by the donee of the power, either with the consent of, or subject to veto by, another.

In principle, there may be any combination of these possibilities. Section 27 of the Wills Act 1837, which deals with the exercise of powers of appointment, governs property "which he [the testator]

---

[1] *Fullerton* v. *Martin* (1853), 1 Eq. Rep. 224; *Prescott* v. *Barker* (1874), 9 Ch. App. 174; *Kirby-Smith* v. *Parnell*, [1903] 1 Ch. 483.

[2] *Ackers* v. *Phipps* (1835), 3 Cl. & Fin. 665.

[3] *Barclay* v. *Collett* (1838), 4 Bing. N.C. 658; *Hamilton* v. *Buckmaster* (1866), L.R. 3 Eq. 323; *Stein* v. *Ritherdon* (1868), 37 L.J. Ch. 369; *Lloyd* v. *Lloyd* (1869), L.R. 7 Eq. 458; *Longley* v. *Longley* (1871), L.R. 13 Eq. 133.

may have power to appoint in any manner he may think proper".
It is necessary to consider to which powers this applies.

a. *Width of class of possible appointees*

The general meaning of "in any manner he may think proper"
refers to the class of possible objects. Accordingly it is established
that a special power is not within the scope of the section.[1] It also
seems that a hybrid power is excluded.[2] It would seem, however,
that in certain circumstances a hybrid power can become a general
power. Thus, if only one person (not being the donee of the power)
is excepted, and that persons dies[3] or if the excepted person does
not exist[4] then the power will be, or will become, general. Presumably, by applying s. 24, the relevant date is the date of death of
the testator, so that if a power is hybrid when the will is made,
but has become general by the date of death, that power will fall
within s. 27.

b. *Method of execution*

Section 10 of the Wills Act 1837 provides that the formalities
required for making a will are sufficient formalities to exercise a
power of appointment by will, even if the instrument creating the
power requires additional formalities. Subject to that, any requirement as to execution contained in the instrument creating the
power takes precedence over the Wills Act provisions. Accordingly,
if a power is exercisable by deed only, it cannot be exercised at all
by will. A power exercisable by will only, or by deed or will, can
fall within s. 27.[5] Also, in accordance with the general principle
that the requirements contained in the instrument creating the
power take priority, if the instrument of creation requires express
reference to the power, that power does not come within s. 27,
for if the testator must refer to the power, he does not, within the

---

[1] *Cloves* v. *Awdry* (1850), 12 Beav. 604; *Re Penrose, Penrose* v. *Penrose*,
[1933] Ch. 793.
[2] *Re Byron's Settlement, Williams* v. *Mitchell*, [1891] 3 Ch. 474; *Re Harvey,
Banister* v. *Thirtle*, [1950] 1 All E.R. 491; *Re Jones, Public Trustee* v. *Jones*,
[1945] Ch. 105.
[3] *Re Byron's Settlement, Williams* v. *Mitchell*, [1891] 3 Ch. 474.
[4] *Re Harvey, Banister* v. *Thirtle*, [1950] 1 All E.R. 491.
[5] *Re Powell* (1869), 39 L.J. Ch. 188.

terms of s. 27, have a power to appoint "in any manner he may think proper".[1]

c. *More than one person to join in*

Where the power of appointment is to be exercised by two persons, it can be validly exercised by the joint will of those persons. In *Re Duddell, Roundway* v. *Roundway*[2] a power was executed by two persons. They made a joint will which was admitted to probate on the death of the first to die. It was held that provided the survivor did not revoke the will, and it was also admitted to probate on his death, that would be a good exercise of the joint power. Whether the power has to be exercised by a joint will, or whether it can be exercised by two separate wills, depends on the requirements of the instrument creating the power.

As the words "in any manner" in s. 27 refer to the objects of the power, it is thought that if the exercise of a power is subject to consent, then, provided that consent is given, there may be a valid exercise under s. 27.

2. OPERATION OF SECTION 27

Section 27 provides that in respect of those powers which are subject to it, a general devise or a general bequest shall, in the absence of a contrary intention, operate as an exercise of the power without any express reference to the power being made.

To exercise a power of appointment under s. 27, a general gift need not be of the whole of the testator's estate, nor, indeed, of the whole of his realty or personalty. So far as realty is concerned, the section applies to a general devise of the whole of the testator's real estate; to his real estate in any particular place or in the occupation of any particular person; and to the real estate of the testator "otherwise described in any general manner". In the case of personalty, it applies to a general bequest of the personal estate of the testator, or to any bequest of personal property described in any general manner.

In order for a power to be exercised by a general gift, the property subject to the power must come within the description

---

[1] *Phillips* v. *Cayley* (1889), 43 Ch.D. 222; *Re Davies, Davies* v. *Davies*, [1892] 3 Ch. 63; *Re Lane, Belli* v. *Lane*, [1908] 2 Ch. 581.
[2] [1932] 1 Ch. 585.

of the gift. So, where the testator has a general power of appointment over shares, this power would be exercised by a gift of all
his property; or of all his personalty; or of all his investments;
but it would not be exercised by a gift of all his furniture.

The principle has been developed that the power will be
exercised by the narrowest gift in the will sufficient to cover the
property subject to the power. So, in *Re Doherty-Waterhouse*[1]
the testator had a power of appointment over stock, and by his
will made a gift of "all my stock to X" and "all the residue of my
property to Y". Both gifts, by themselves, would have been
sufficient to exercise the power, but the stock passed under the
former.

Section 27 applies only in the absence of a contrary intention,
but the courts will be slow to find such a contrary intention. This is
shown by numerous cases concerned with wills which appear
to refer only to property which belongs to the testator. Thus,
a gift of property "which I possess or to which I am entitled"
will be sufficient to include property over which the testator has
a power of appointment.[2] Likewise a gift of "all my stock" will
exercise a general power of appointment over stock.[3]

3. POWERS OUTSIDE SECTION 27

In the case of a power within s. 27, there is a presumption that
the power is intended to be exercised. In the case of a power outside the section, the burden of proof is reversed: it is upon the
person claiming that the power has been exercised to prove that
it has been.

In the case of a non-s. 27 power, there must always be an expression of intention to exercise the power. But it was stated in *Re
Weston's Settlement, Neeves v. Weston,*[4] and the same applies to
any non-s. 27 power, that a special power may be exercised in
any one of four ways, that is, by express exercise; by reference to
the power itself even if there is no express exercise of it; by
reference to the property subject to the power; or by showing
an intention to exercise the power in any other way.

---

[1] [1918] 2 Ch. 269.
[2] *Re Jacob, Mortimer* v. *Mortimer,* [1907] 1 Ch. 445.
[3] *Re Doherty-Waterhouse, Musgrave* v. *De Chair,* [1918] 2 Ch. 269.
[4] [1906] 2 Ch. 620.

It seems that the testator need not intend actually to exercise the power: his intention must be to transfer the property to the beneficiary. Thus, if a person has a special power over property, and specifically disposes of that property, he is deemed to have intended to exercise the power.[1] If, however, the property is only mentioned generally, that will not be sufficient to exercise the power.[2] In this case it is necessary to show that the testator had no property of his own which could pass under the general words.[3]

D. SCOPE OF GIFT OF RESIDUE

A residuary gift is a gift of such of the testator's property which he has not purported to dispose of by specific gifts. If the will itself does not dispose of the whole of the testator's property, that part which is not disposed of devolves in accordance with the intestacy rules.

Provided that the words of the gift are sufficient, and no contrary intention is shown, a residuary gift will include all property and all interests in property which are not effectively otherwise disposed of. If, therefore, a person is given a life interest, and there is no gift in remainder, upon the death of the life tenant, the property will fall into residue. Likewise, if there is a gift to a person upon attaining the age of, say, 21, and no prior gift of that property, the income until the beneficiary attains the age of 21 will form part of residue.[4]

Where a specific gift fails for any reason, such as lapse, then in the absence of a contrary intention the property subject to that gift will fall into residue. The result is the same whatever the reason for the failure of the specific gift. The testator may, of course, expressly provide for certain eventualities. Thus, "£500 to A but if she predeceases me, then to B". Alternatively, the testator may show a contrary intention to prevent it falling into

---

[1] *Forbes* v. *Ball* (1817), 3 Mer. 437; *Davies* v. *Davies* (1858), 28 L.J. Ch. 102; *Elliott* v. *Elliott* (1846), 15 Sim. 321; *Re David's Trusts* (1859), John. 495; *Re Mackenzie, Thornton* v. *Huddleston*, [1917] 2 Ch. 58.

[2] *Re Huddleston, Bruno* v. *Eyston*, [1894] 3 Ch. 595.

[3] *Bennett* v. *Aburrow* (1803), 8 Ves. 609; *Re Mattingley's Trusts* (1862), 2 John. & H. 426.

[4] Subject to the rules with regard to intermediate income.

residue, in which case it would devolve as on intestacy, but such a contrary intention is often hard to establish. It is clear that the mere attempt to leave the property elsewhere is not a sufficient contrary intention.[1] Furthermore, where the testator uses conventional expressions such as, "I give all my property not otherwise disposed of" the words "otherwise disposed of" are treated in the absence of a contrary intention as meaning "otherwise effectively disposed of", and previous specific gifts which have lapsed will therefore come within the residuary gift.

Where the whole residuary gift fails, then the residuary property passes as on intestacy. Where, however, part of the residuary gift fails, the effect of the gift depends on the testator's intention. If there is no expression of his intention, then the undisposed of part devolves as on intestacy.[2] Alternatively, the testator may show an intention for that part to fall back into residue, and so, in effect, be added to the other parts. Accordingly, if the residue is to be divided among four people, and one predeceases the testator, the share of that person will, if there is a sufficient expression of intention, be added to the shares of the other three.[3]

---

[1] *Re Spooner's Trust* (1851), 2 Sim. N.S. 129.

[2] *Sykes* v. *Sykes* (1868), 3 Ch. App. 301; *Re Bentley, Podmore* v. *Smith* (1914), 110 L.T. 623; *Re Forrest, Carr* v. *Forrest*, [1931] 1 Ch. 162.

[3] *Re Woods*, [1931] 2 Ch. 138.

Part III

INTESTACY

CHAPTER 11

TOTAL INTESTACY

The rules relating to beneficial entitlement on intestacy are designed to reflect the wishes of the average testator, and are in fact based upon an analysis of a large number of wills. Thus, the three most common situations are where the deceased left a spouse, but no children, in which case the spouse takes all; where the deceased left a spouse and children, in which case, provided the total estate exceeds £15,000, the property is divided between the spouse and children; and where the deceased left neither spouse nor children, in which case near relatives benefit.

The intestacy rules are changed from time to time, and different rules have applied in the case of deaths:

a. up to 31 December 1925, when the old Rules of Inheritance applied to realty, and Rules of Succession applied to personalty;

b. between 1 January 1926, and 31 December 1952, when the position was governed by the Administration of Estates Act 1925;

c. between 1 January 1953 and 31 December 1966, when the governing legislation was the Administration of Estates Act 1925, as amended by the Intestates Estates Act 1952;

d. between 1 January 1967 and 30 June 1972, when the 1925 and 1952 Acts, as amended by the Family Provision Act 1966, applied.

e. after 30 June 1972 when the 1925, 1952 and 1966 Acts apply, as amended by The Family Provision (Intestate Succession) Order 1972.

The account of the intestacy rules in this chapter is confined to the post-June 1972 situation. The provisions of the 1925 Act, as amended by the 1952 and 1966 Acts and the 1972 Order are reproduced in the Appendix. Although it has been modified by the 1952 and 1966 Acts, the Administration of Estates Act 1925 remains the basis of the law.

In addition to making provision for a total intestacy, the rules also deal with the case of a partial intestacy, that is where the testator makes a will which for one reason or another fails effectively to dispose of the whole of his assets.

A. STATUTORY TRUST FOR SALE

Section 33 of the Administration of Estates Act 1925 provides that the personal representatives hold all the deceased's property upon trust for sale. The personal representatives have a power to postpone sale for as long as they think proper. There are two qualifications to the general requirement to sell. First, the personal representatives are directed not to sell reversionary interests before they fall into possession, unless they "see special reason" for sale; and secondly, "personal chattels" are also not to be sold unless the proceeds are required for administrative purposes because there are no other assets, or because the personal representatives again see special reason for the sale.[1] The expression "personal chattels" is considered later.[2]

From the fund produced by the sale, the personal representatives pay the funeral, testamentary and administration expenses, debts and other liabilities of the deceased, and in the case of a partial intestacy, they also pay the legacies bequeathed by the will.[3] The residue, which will be available either for immediate distribution or where a minority or life interest arises, and which will be invested, is called by the Act "the residuary estate of the intestate".[4] The entitlement of the beneficiaries is to the residuary estate, and not to the gross estate.

B. RIGHTS OF SPOUSE

1. ENTITLEMENT

Where the intestate leaves a spouse[5]—the rules are the same whether the spouse is a widow or widower—the entitlement of that spouse depends on which of three situations apply:

---

[1] Administration of Estates Act 1925, s. 33 (1).
[2] *Post*, p. 177.
[3] Administration of Estates Act 1925, s. 33 (2).
[4] Administration of Estates Act 1925, s. 33 (4).
[5] As to the position of a wife under a polygamous marriage, see Hartley (1969), 32 M.L.R. 135.

a. if the intestate leaves neither issue, nor parent, nor brother or sister of the whole blood or their issue;[1]

b. if the intestate does leave issue (whether or not there are also relatives);

c. if the intestate does not leave issue, but does leave a parent, or brother or sister of the whole blood.

a. *Intestate leaving neither issue, nor near relative*

If the intestate leaves neither issue, nor a relative of the near class specified above, the residuary estate is held upon trust for the surviving spouse absolutely. Special provisions apply, however, where the spouses were legally separated.[2]

b. *Intestate leaving issue*

Where the intestate leaves issue as well as a spouse, the spouse is entitled to:

(i) the "personal chattels" absolutely. The expression "personal chattels" is defined by s. 55 (1) (x) of the 1925 Act, and means, broadly, articles of household or personal use or ornament, such as clothes, furniture, jewellery, motor cars and domestic animals. The expression does not include any article used by the intestate at the date of his death for business purposes, nor does it include money or securities. It is, therefore, necessary to have regard both to the nature of the asset itself, and also the purpose for which it is used at the date of death. If an antique dealer keeps part of his stock at home, that stock will not be within the expression, but if he retires, and continues to keep at home those items which were formerly part of his stock, those items will be included. The expression is, however, widely construed. So, in *Re Reynolds' Will Trusts, Dove* v. *Reynolds*[3] it was held to include a stamp collection worth £1,800. This was followed in *Re Collins Settlement Trusts, Donne* v. *Hewetson*[4] where the expres-

---

[1] A relation of the "whole" blood is distinguished from a step-relation, who is of the "half blood".

[2] *Post*, p. 183.

[3] [1965] 3 All E.R. 686.

[4] [1971] 1 All E.R. 283.

sion "personal effects" as used in a will was held to include a stamp collection insured for £15,000, and which formed part of an estate with the net total value of £25,000;

(ii) a "statutory legacy" of £15,000 absolutely, this sum to be paid free of deduction for estate duty or costs;

(iii) interest on the statutory legacy at £4% p.a. from the date of death to the date of payment. This interest is primarily payable out of the income of the estate[1] but if there is insufficient income, the balance is payable out of capital. Although the rate of interest is very low, the right of the surviving spouse to be paid interest is to be contrasted with the position where he or she would be entitled to a legacy under a will: in that case no interest would be paid.[2] Where the interest has to be made good out of capital, this will lead to disadvantageous taxation results, which are explained later,[3] with the result that the spouse might well wish to disclaim her right to interest;[4]

(iv) a life interest in one half of the residue. Thus, after setting aside from the residuary estate the personal chattels, the statutory legacy, and interest on it, the residuary estate is divided into two parts. One moiety is held upon trust for the issue absolutely, and the other half is held upon trust for the spouse for life, with remainder to the issue.

c. *Intestate leaving no issue, but near relative*

Where the intestate leaves, in addition to the spouse, a parent, or brother or sister of the whole blood, or their issue, the spouse is entitled to:

(i) the personal chattels, as defined above;

(ii) a statutory legacy, in this case of £40,000;

(iii) interest on the statutory legacy, as above; and

(iv) one half of the residue. This right is to one half of the capital, and not merely, as in the case where there are issue, to a life interest in one half. The other half of the residue

---

[1] Intestates Estates Act 1952, s. 1 (4).
[2] See *post*, p. 498.
[3] See *post*, p. 405.
[4] See *post*, p. 452.

is divided between the parents, or if there are none, to the brothers and sisters of the whole blood.

2. RIGHT TO REQUIRE CAPITAL PAYMENT IN LIEU OF LIFE INTEREST

A surviving spouse who has a life interest, that is, where the deceased also left issue, has a right to require the personal representatives to pay a capital sum in lieu of the life interest.[1] This right must be exercised within twelve months from the date on which a grant of representation is obtained, unless the court extends the period for special reasons.[2] The notice exercising the right must be in writing, and is revocable only with the consent of the personal representatives.[3] To safeguard the situation where the surviving spouse is also the sole personal representative, in this case the spouse must give notice of election to the Principal Registrar of the Family Division, and this notice is entered in a public register.[4] The surviving spouse may make this election even if he or she is an infant, and although the election is valid, the capital can only be paid when the spouse reaches the age of 18.[5]

The amount of the lump sum to which the surviving spouse is entitled is intended to be, broadly, the capitalized value of that life interest. The calculation of this capital sum is made as follows:[6]

  (i) take the value of the part of the residuary estate in which the spouse has a life interest at the "date of redemption", that is, the date when the election becomes operative, or the earlier death of the spouse;[7]

 (ii) calculate the annual income which would be produced by investing that capital sum in $2\frac{1}{2}\%$ Consols;

(iii) calculate the amount which would be required to purchase an immediate savings bank annuity under the Government Annuities Act 1929 to produce the same sum as in (ii);

(iv) reduce the capital sum in (iii) by 5%. This capital sum as reduced will be the amount payable to the spouse;

---

[1] Added by the Intestates Estates Act 1952, s. 47A.
[2] Administration of Estates Act 1925, s. 47A (5).
[3] *Ibid.*, s. 47A (6).
[4] *Ibid.*, s. 47A (7).
[5] *Ibid.*, s. 47A (8).
[6] *Ibid.*, s. 47A (2).
[7] *Ibid.*, s. 47A (4).

(v) where the age of the spouse exceeds 80, the capital sum
in (iii) is reduced by a further 5% for each year in excess
of 80, subject to a limit that the capital value must not be
reduced below one and a half times the annual value.

Where the issue are all over 18, and *sui iuris*, and if they agree,
it is not necessary for these complicated provisions to be used.
The spouse and the issue may agree between themselves as to a
capital sum to be paid to the spouse, and effect will be given to
that under the rule in *Saunders* v. *Vautier*.[1] Whether the statutory
procedure is followed, or the life interest redeemed by agreement,
there will often be advantages in redeeming the life interest.[2] The
whole of the estate may be distributed forthwith,[3] and the spouse
will not pay income tax on the capital sum, although income tax
would be payable on the whole of the income of the life interest.
If *Saunders* v. *Vautier* is used in this situation, then because of
the rules as to capital gains tax, the compromise should if possible
be made within two years from death.[4]

3. RIGHT TO MATRIMONIAL HOME

The surviving spouse is given special rights where part of the
residuary estate includes an interest in a dwelling-house in which
the surviving spouse was resident at the time of the intestate's
death. The spouse has a right by notice in writing to require the
personal representatives to appropriate to him or her that dwelling-
house in or towards satisfaction of any absolute interest which he
or she has in the intestate's estate,[5] or in or towards the capital
value of a life interest which the spouse has elected to have
redeemed.[6] The spouse may, therefore, make an election on the
basis just discussed, and then require that capital entitlement to
be satisfied by a transfer of the house. This right may only be
exercised within twelve months from the grant of representation
being issued,[7] unless this period is extended by the court,[8]

---

[1] (1841), Cr. & Ph. 240.
[2] See George (1968), 32 Conv. (N.S.) 246.
[3] Or appropriated to beneficiaries if they are under disability.
[4] Finance Act 1965, s. 24 (11); see *post*, p. 412.
[5] Intestates Estates Act 1952, sched. 2, para. 1 (1).
[6] *Ibid.*, para. 1 (4).
[7] *Ibid.*, para. 3 (1) (a).
[8] *Ibid.*, para. 3 (3).

and for this reason the personal representatives may not sell the property within twelve months from the date of death without the written consent of the surviving spouse, unless, through lack of other assets, it is needed for the purposes of administration.[1]

Where the property is to be transferred, it is transferred at its open market value.[2] Before committing himself, the spouse may require the deceased's interest in the property to be valued, and to be notified of that value, before deciding whether to exercise the right.[3]

It is not necessary for the deceased to have owned the property outright. It is sufficient if he had only an interest in it, as, for example, a joint tenant. The right is not generally exercisable where the interest of the deceased was leasehold with less than two years to run from the date of death, or where the lease contains a provision enabling the landlord to determine the lease within that period. The surviving spouse does, however, have the right to take a short lease where an application can be made for a long lease or the freehold under the Leasehold Reform Act 1967. In other circumstances the surviving spouse may, nevertheless, wish to take over the deceased's interest in short leasehold property. For example, the spouse may hope to obtain a new tenancy, or a protected tenancy under the Rent Acts. Although the spouse has no right to demand the transfer of the deceased's interest in such cases, the personal representatives have a discretion to appropriate to the spouse under s. 41 of the 1925 Act[4] and this power could be used in this situation.[5]

In some cases the right of the surviving spouse is only exercisable if the court is satisfied that the exercise of the right will not diminish the value of the remainder of the assets in the residuary estate, or make them more difficult to dispose of.[6] The application to the court may be made either by the personal representative or by the spouse.[7] The consent of the court is necessary in the following circumstances:

---

[1] Intestates Estates Act 1952, sched. 2, para. 4 (1).
[2] Administration of Estates Act 1925, s. 41.
[3] Intestates Estates Act 1952, sched. 2, para. 3 (2).
[4] See *post*, p. 551.
[5] Intestates Estates Act 1952, sched. 2, para. 1 (3).
[6] *Ibid.*, para. 2.
[7] *Ibid.*, para. 4 (2).

a. where the dwelling-house forms part only of a building, and an interest in the whole of the building is comprised in the residuary estate;

b. where the dwelling-house is held with agricultural land and an interest in the agricultural land is comprised in the residuary estate;

c. where the whole or a part of the dwelling-house was at the time of the intestate's death used as a hotel or lodging house; and

d. where part of the dwelling-house was at the time of the intestate's death used for non-domestic purposes.[1]

The right itself is not expressly to require a transfer of the matrimonial home, but the "dwelling-house in which the surviving husband or wife was resident at the time of the intestate's death". This will usually be the matrimonial home, but need not be. It seems, however, that "resident" is not equivalent to merely "living". "Residence" normally implies some degree of permanence or regularity[2] and this will probably be the case here.

Where the spouse is also a personal representative the right to take the home would appear at first sight to conflict with the rule that a trustee may not purchase trust property. It is specifically provided that this rule does not prevent the exercise of the right where the spouse is one of two or more personal representatives[3] though presumably it does apply if the spouse is the sole personal representative. In this case, it would be necessary to apply to the court for consent, or obtain the consent of all other persons entitled, provided that they were all *sui iuris*.

As in the case of election to redeem a life interest, a spouse who is a minor has the same right as an adult spouse to insist that the matrimonial home is transferred to her, and also, where the personal representatives wish to sell within twelve months from the grant of representation, an infant spouse may also give a valid consent.[4]

---

[1] Intestates Estates Act 1952, sched. 2, para. 2.

[2] For cases by analogy, see *Re Young* (1875), 1 T.C. 57; *Rogers* v. *Inland Revenue* (1879), 1 T.C. 225; *Lloyd* v. *Sulley* (1884), 2 T.C. 37; *Levene* v. *Inland Revenue Comrs.*, [1928] A.C. 217.

[3] Intestates Estates Act 1952, sched. 2, para. 5 (1).

[4] *Ibid.*, para. 6 (2).

4. SEPARATED SPOUSES

A special rule applies where a wife dies intestate after an order for judicial separation has been made.[1] In either of these cases, but not where there is only a separation agreement, any property which the wife acquired after that separation devolves as if her husband were then dead. This legislation does not affect property acquired before the separation order, nor does it apply to the property of the husband acquired after a separation order. In these cases the normal rules apply.

If while the decree of judicial separation is in force and the separation continues, one of the spouses dies after 1970, for the purposes of devolution on intestacy the other spouse is treated as having predeceased the intestate. This rule does not apply if there is a separation order in the magistrates court.[2]

5. COMMORIENTES

The general rule that in the case where a husband and wife die in circumstances which make it uncertain which survived the other the younger is deemed to have survived the elder[3] does not apply to the estates of intestate spouses.[4] Irrespective of ages, it is presumed that each spouse predeceased the other. This rule applies only in the case of husband and wife, and the general rule under Law of Property Act 1925, s. 184, applies in the case of other intestacies. So, if father and son die virtually simultaneously, the son will be deemed to have survived the father, and will take under his estate.

C. RIGHTS OF ISSUE

Where the intestate left issue, the issue will take:

a. if there is also a surviving spouse, the whole of the residuary estate subject to the rights of the spouse;

b. in any other case, the whole of the residuary estate.

In either case, the whole or part of the residuary estate to which the issue are entitled is held upon "the statutory trusts". These are prescribed by Administration of Estates Act 1925, s. 47.

---

[1] Matrimonial Proceedings and Property Act 1970, s. 40(1).
[2] *Ibid.*, s. 40(2).
[3] Law of Property Act 1925, s. 184. See *post*, p. 459.
[4] Administration of Estates Act 1925, s. 46 (3).

1. THE STATUTORY TRUSTS

Property held upon the statutory trusts for issue is to be divided in equal shares among such of the children of the intestate who are alive at the date of the death of the intestate, and who either attain the age of 18 or marry under that age. Where a child predeceases the intestate, but leaves issue at the date of death of the intestate, then those children, if they attain the age of 18 or marry under that age, will take the share in the residuary estate which their parent would have taken had he attained a vested interest. The issue therefore take *"per stirpes"*.

It will be seen that in order to benefit under the statutory trusts, the beneficiary must:

    (i) be alive at the date of death of the intestate; and

    (ii) either attain the age of 18, or marry under that age.

Suppose, therefore, that Andrew has three children, Peter, James and John, of whom Peter and James survive him, and John predeceases him leaving his daughters Mary and Martha surviving him, and surviving Andrew. Andrew's wife predeceased him. The residuary estate, or £30,000 will be divided:

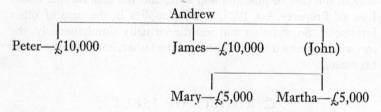

Andrew

Peter—£10,000   James—£10,000   (John)

Mary—£5,000   Martha—£5,000

This example assumes that Peter, James, Mary and Martha all attain the age of 18 or marry under that age. If, however, Martha, although alive at the death of Andrew died before attaining the age of 18, or marrying (and without herself leaving issue who take), her £5,000 would accrue on her death to Mary.

The effect of requiring that a beneficiary shall be alive at the date of death of the intestate is the same as the operation of the class closing rules[1] in that the minimum amount which may accrue to each beneficiary is ascertained at the date of death of the intestate. If a beneficiary who is alive at that date nevertheless

[1] *Ante*, p. 159.

fails to attain a vested interest by attaining the age of 18, or marrying under that age, as from the date when the contingent beneficiary dies, the estate is distributed as if that beneficiary had never been alive.

Suppose, then, that Edward left a wife Deirdre and an infant son, so that Deirdre takes a life interest in the residue. If before attaining a vested interest the son dies, from that date Deirdre will become entitled to the whole estate.

2. HOTCHPOT

It will be seen that in the case of legacies, children must, in the absence of contrary intention, bring into account sums received by way of advancement.[1] A similar provision applies in the case of intestacy. The same distinction must be drawn between gifts which represent an "advancement", and smaller or other casual payments which are outside that concept. It is only necessary to bring into account gifts by way of advancement, although the advancement may consist of the settlement of money or property on the child even if for only a life or less interest.

Where an advancement has to be brought into hotchpot, the gift is valued as at the date of death of the intestate, and not at the date of gift. If, therefore, your father is proposing to make to you an advancement, be guided as to the nature of the property. If it is of a wasting nature, such as a leasehold or copyright, take it in that form, for its value at his death will almost certainly be lower. In any other case take cash. A cross-cheque transaction may be used. So if your father proposes to give you a freehold house worth £5,000, take a gift of £5,000 by cheque, and then, with that money buy the house from him for £5,000. Even if the house is worth £15,000 by the time he dies, you will only have to bring into hotchpot the gift, that is, £5,000 cash. If the house itself is given, its value will be that at death.

Because of the terms of the Act, it is only necessary for an advancement to be brought into hotchpot if it was to the child of the deceased. If a substantial gift was made to a grandchild, then even if that grandchild claims because his father predeceases the intestate, he will not have to bring into account that gift. On the other hand, if his father received an advancement, that must be

---

[1] *Post*, p. 480.

brought into account, even though the grandchild himself derives no benefit from it.

The operation of these rules may be illustrated by an example. Stephen dies intestate, leaving a net estate of £43,000. He is survived by his widow, Emma, two sons Thomas and Titian, and two grandchildren, Edward and Edwina, the children of his deceased son Wilfred. During his lifetime he had made advancements of £10,000 to Thomas, £6,000 to Wilfred, and had made a gift of £2,000 to Edwina. Ignoring the personal chattels, and interest on the statutory legacy, the estate will be distributed as follows:

	£
Net estate	43,000
Less: statutory legacy to widow	15,000
	28,000
Appropriate to provide life interest in half of residue	14,000
Balance remaining for immediate distribution among children	14,000

To calculate entitlement of each child and grandchild:

	£	£
Balance brought down		14,000
Add: advances to children to be brought into account		
Thomas	10,000	
Wilfred	6,000	
		16,000
		30,000

Entitlement:

	Thomas	Titian	Estate of Wilfred
	£	£	£
⅓ × £30,000	10,000	10,000	10,000
Less: advances	10,000	—	6,000
	Nil	10,000	4,000

	£
Wilfred's share: Edwina	2,000
Edward	2,000

So: the actual £14,000 available for immediate distribution is payable to:

	£
Thomas	nil
Titian	10,000
Edwina	2,000
Edward	2,000
	14,000

3. ADMINISTRATIVE PROVISIONS

Where the statutory trusts operate, the trustees are given the usual powers of maintenance and advancement, and the duty to accumulate surplus income.[1] When an infant marries, and so acquires a vested interest, he can then give a receipt for income, but not for capital.[2]

The personal representatives are given an express power to permit any infant contingent beneficiary to use any personal chattels subject to the trusts[3] but there is no power enabling them to allow beneficiaries to reside in any house forming part of the estate.[4]

D. RIGHTS OF PARENTS

Parents will be entitled:

a. if the intestate leaves a spouse, but no issue, then the parents will be entitled to the half of the residue not taken by the wife.[5] If there is only one parent, that parent takes all.

b. if the intestate leaves neither spouse, nor issue, then the parents take all. If both parents are alive, they take in equal shares.[6]

In both cases the parents take outright, and not upon the statutory trusts.

E. RIGHTS OF OTHERS

1. BROTHERS AND SISTERS

The position of brothers and sisters is the same as that of parents, if there are no parents, save that brothers and sisters take upon the statutory trusts. Accordingly, if there is no issue, and no parents, the brothers and sisters, or their issue, take the half of the residue not taken by the wife. If there is no spouse, issue, or parent, the brothers and sisters and their issue take the whole upon the statutory trusts.

2. REMOTER RELATIVES

Where there is no spouse, issue, parent, or brother or sister of

---

[1] Administration of Estates Act 1925, s. 47 (1) (ii).   [2] *Ibid.*

[3] That is, if they are not taken by the surviving spouse.

[4] Administration of Estates Act 1925, s. 47 (1) (iv).

[5] *Ante,* p. 178.

[6] Administration of Estates Act 1925, s. 46 (1) (iii), (iv).

the whole blood, the following are entitled. If there is only one person in a category, he takes all, and no person in a lower class can take if there is any person in the previous class:

a. brothers and sisters of the half blood on the statutory trusts;

b. grandparents in equal shares;

c. uncles and aunts of the whole blood upon the statutory trusts

d. uncles and aunts of the half blood on the statutory trusts.

All relationships here described are blood relationships. Thus the wife of an uncle, bearing the courtesy title "aunt" cannot take.

The statutory trusts for brothers and sisters, and uncles and aunts, are the same as the trusts for issue. Thus deceased members of the class may be represented by their issue, and entitlement is dependent upon attaining the age of 18 or marrying under it.[1] As an exception, the provisions as to hotchpot do not apply.

3. THE CROWN

Where there is no one in the foregoing categories entitled to take, the estate goes to the Crown, or Duchy of Lancaster or Duchy of Cornwall as *bona vacantia*, and the Crown may at its discretion provide for persons who were actually dependent on the intestate whether related or not, or for such other persons for whom the intestate may have been expected to provide.[2]

F. SPECIAL PROVISIONS AS TO CHILDREN

1. ADOPTED CHILDREN

Where a child is adopted under an adoption order made in England, Scotland or Northern Ireland, and the death occurs after 1949, the adopted child is regarded as the lawful child of the adopter, and not of its natural parents.[3] This rule does not apply:

a. to adoption elsewhere than in England, Scotland or Northern Ireland;[4]

---

[1] Administration of Estates Act 1925, s. 47 (3).
[2] *Ibid.*, s. 46 (1) (vi).
[3] Adoption Act 1958, s. 16 (1).
[4] *Re Wilby*, [1956] P. 174.

b. to the estates of intestates dying before 1950 (when the rule was the reverse);

c. to property limited to devolve with a title of honour, which will continue to devolve with that title, and so preserve the link with the natural and not adoptive parents.[1]

Because of the change in position at 1950, a child whose natural parent died before 1950 would have been entitled to take under that intestacy, and he will also be entitled to take under the the intestacy of the adoptive parent if he dies after 1949.

2. ILLEGITIMATE CHILDREN

By virtue of Family Law Reform Act 1969, s. 14, an illegitimate child is now treated for most purposes in the same way as a legitimate child. Until that Act came into force, illegitimate children could benefit on intestacy only in exceptional circumstances.

The position of illegitimate children is governed by Family Law Reform Act 1969. On the death of either parent of an illegitimate child, that child takes in the same way as if he had been legitimate, and if he is dead, his issue stand in his stead.

The personal representatives may not know of the intestate's youthful escapades, and they are entitled to distribute the estate upon the basis that the only illegitimate children who can take are those known to them.[2] Any others may, however, trace the property into the hands of the other children.[3]

When an illegitimate child dies before his parents, each of them is entitled to share in his estate to the same extent as if he had been legitimate.[4] However, to cover the situation where the father was a stranger in the night, s. 14 (4) provides that unless the contrary is shown the child is presumed to have survived his father (but not his mother).

---

[1] Adoption Act 1958, s. 16 (3).

[2] Family Law Reform Act 1969, s. 17.

[3] *Ibid.*

[4] *Ibid.*, s. 14 (2).

G. INTESTACY AND FAMILY PROVISION

Section 1 (8) of the Inheritance (Family Provision) Act 1938 as amended by the Intestates Estates Act 1952 provides that where the applicant is entitled to benefits under the intestacy rules in the case of a total intestacy, or by virtue of a combination of the terms of the will and the intestacy rules in the case of a partial intestacy, the court is not bound to assume that the intestacy rules make reasonable provision for the dependent. Accordingly, a person who both benefits under the intestacy rules, and is a dependent within the terms of the Family Provision legislation may make an application under that legislation.

CHAPTER 12

PARTIAL INTESTACY

A. MEANING

A partial intestacy occurs when a person dies leaving a will which effectively disposes of some, but not all, of his property. The test is not whether there is a will, but whether there is a will effectively disposing of property.[1] Thus, if a person makes a will appointing executors, but not effectively disposing of any part of his property, the executors hold the property upon the trusts declared by the total intestacy rules.[2]

B. OPERATION OF WILL

1. GENERAL PRINCIPLE

In general, in the first instance full effect is given to the will, and the intestacy rules are then applied as a second stage to the extent that the will has not disposed of the property.[3] The operation of the intestacy rules does, however, cause difficulty. Partial intestacy is governed by s. 49 of the Administration of Estates Act 1925, which Danckwerts, J., has described[4] as being "as bad a piece of draftsmanship as one could conceive". Some of the difficulties which arise from that draftsmanship are now considered.

2. WILL DEALING WITH UNDISPOSED OF PROPERTY

This heading might be considered curious: how can a will deal with property which is undisposed of? The legislation envisages that sometimes this can happen, for the opening part of s. 49 (1) provides that the rules as to intestacy shall have effect

---

[1] Property is defined to include any interest in real or personal property. Administration of Estates Act 1925, s. 55 (1)(xvii).

[2] Re Ford, Ford v. Ford, [1902] 2 Ch. 605; Re Cuffe, Fooks v. Cuffe, [1908] 2 Ch. 500; Re Skeats, Thain v. Skeats, [1936] Ch. 683.

[3] Administration of Estates Act 1925, ss. 33 (7); 49 (1).

[4] In Re Morton, Morton v. Warham, [1956] Ch. 644, at p. 647.

as respects property undisposed of "subject to the provisions contained in the will". The expression was considered by the Court of Appeal in *Re Thornber*,[1] where it was shown that the expression "subject to the provisions contained in the will" means provisions which remain operative and effective. In this case the testator left certain annuities, and directed his trustees to accumulate the surplus income for the period of twenty-one years, or until the death of his wife, for the benefit of his children. He died without issue, and the question arose whether the surplus income should be treated as undisposed of, and not subject to the terms of the will, or whether it should be accumulated in accordance with the testator's direction. The Court of Appeal held that the trustees should not accumulate. Romer, L.J., said: "when you have ascertained what interest has been undisposed of by the testator you then look at the will to see whether as regards that interest he has given any directions, and, if he has, those directions must be attended to. For instance, it is conceivable that a testator bearing in mind the provisions of the Administration of Estates Act 1925 might insert a direction something to this effect in his will: 'In the event of any of my property being undisposed of by this my will and the provisions of s. 49 taking effect I direct that any such property shall be dealt with' in a particular way; but the provisions in this testator's will relating to accumulation are not provisions relating to any interest of which the testator had failed to dispose." It is, therefore, necessary to draw a distinction between an interest which has not been disposed of effectively, and other directions in the will. The line is often a fine one.

C. TRUST FOR SALE

1. DOES A STATUTORY TRUST FOR SALE ARISE?

The provisions as to total intestacy in the Administration of Estates Act 1925, are dealt with in two parts. Part III of the Act[2] deals with the *administration* of the intestate's estate, while Part IV[3] deals with the *distribution* of the estate. Although the general intention seems to have been to incorporate so far as appropriate all the rules as to intestacy to partially intestate estates s. 49 only

---

[1] [1937] Ch. 29.
[2] Administration of Estates Act 1925, ss. 32 to 44.
[3] *Ibid.*, ss. 45 to 52.

applies "this Part", that is, Part IV, to such estates and there is no corresponding provision applying Part III. There is, then, no statutory provision for the whole of the deceased's property to be held upon a trust for sale. While, however, there is no provision applying all the administrative provisions to a partial intestacy, s. 33 on its terms does apply to the extent that any property is undisposed of, subject to the provisions of the will.[1,2] There will, then, usually be a trust for sale of that part of the property which is undisposed of, although it seems that the will could validly direct that no trust for sale should arise.

2. WHICH TRUST FOR SALE?

It may be necessary to decide which of an express trust for sale and a statutory trust for sale shall apply, for there will not be more than one effective trust for sale in respect of the same property.[3] It is important to know which applies, for the terms of the trust may differ. The position seems to be that if the will contains an express trust for sale of the whole of the property, but a partial intestacy arises because a share in the proceeds of sale is undisposed of, the express trust for sale in the will operates. If, however, the property undisposed of in the will is not subject to a trust for sale, the statutory trust for sale applies to that property, subject to a contrary direction in the will. It is possible, then, for the will to create an express trust for sale in respect of part of the property, and for there to be a statutory trust for sale in respect of another part.

D. HOTCHPOT

1. BENEFITS TO BE BROUGHT INTO HOTCHPOT

In three situations, benefits have to be brought into hotchpot in applying the rules as to partial intestacy. These are:
   a. the surviving spouse must bring into account the beneficial interest received under the operative provisions of the will,

---

[1] Administration of Estates Act 1925, s. 33 (7).
[2] Cf. Williams and Mortimer, *Executors Administrators and Probate*, at p. 875.
[3] *Re Plowman, Westminster Bank, Ltd.* v. *Plowman*, [1943] Ch. 269; *Re Taylor's Estate and Will Trusts, Taylor* v. *Taylor*, [1969] 2 Ch. 245.

except that personal chattels specifically bequeathed are left out of account;[1]

b. children must bring into account substantial benefits which they received from the deceased during his lifetime. This is the general rule which applies in the same way as on total intestacy.[2] This rule does *not* require account to be taken of substantial benefits given by the deceased in his lifetime to remoter issue; and

c. children *and* remoter issue must bring into account beneficial interests acquired under the operative provisions of the will.[3]

The issues which arise must now be considered in greater detail.

2. BENEFITS OF SPOUSE

It will be recalled that in the case of total intestacy, a spouse may become entitled to benefit from the estate in four respects,[4] the statutory legacy; interest on the statutory legacy; personal chattels; and an absolute or a life interest in half the remainder. In the case of a partial intestacy, it is necessary to value the total beneficial interests received under the will, with the exception of personal chattels which are specifically bequeathed. That aggregate is then used to reduce the statutory legacy, of £15,000, or £40,000, so that if the benefit under the will exceeds the limit of the statutory legacy, none is payable. Where the statutory legacy is reduced, but not eliminated, the interest to which the spouse is entitled is calculated on the reduced amount of the legacy. The spouse is still entitled to the personal chattels which are undisposed of.

In so far as they relate to life interests, the rules are curious. The position is:

a. where the spouse takes a life interest under the will, that interest is actuarially valued, and is added to the other benefits, if any, which the spouse received under the will. The actuarial value of the life interest will, therefore, totally or partially eliminate the entitlement to the statutory legacy;

---

[1] Administration of Estates Act 1925, s. 49 (1) (aa), which applies only to post-1951 deaths.

[2] See *ante*, p. 185.

[3] Administration of Estates Act 1925, s. 49 (1) (a).

[4] See *ante*, pp. 177, 178.

b. if the benefits under the will exceed the amount of the statutory legacy, the remaining benefits are ignored and do *not* reduce the absolute or life interest in the remainder.

3. SUCCESSIVE INTERESTS TO CHILDREN AND REMOTER ISSUE

Suppose that the will creates a life interest for the son of the testator, with remainder to the issue of that son. What is to be brought into account? Section 49 (1) (a) requires that there shall be brought into account "any beneficial interests acquired by any issue of the deceased". This does not necessarily mean that the interests of the issue are to be separately valued, and brought into account at that valuation. In *Re Young, Young* v. *Young*,[1] where there was, in effect, a gift to the testator's son for his life, and thereafter for his issue, Harman, J., made a surprising decision. He held that it was necessary to treat the whole fund which was given by the deceased to the son and the descendants of the son as one gift, and that it was the capital value of that fund that was to be brought into account. In effect, then, the son had to bring into account the capital value of the fund, even though he only enjoyed a life interest in it. A different approach was adopted by Danckwerts, J., in *Re Morton, Morton* v. *Warham.*[2] In this case the fund was limited not merely to the son, and his issue, but other persons were also entitled to take a benefit. There was no question, then, on any view, of including the whole value of the fund. However, Danckwerts, J., approached the problem of valuation in more general terms. He said[3] that "the life interests or less interests which are brought in at a valuation, must be brought in at a valuation appropriate to the nature of the interest... and they cannot be brought in as if they were equivalent to an absolute interest in the capital. To value the interest as being equivalent to a gift of capital in a case where a person takes no more than a life interest seems to be contrary to fairness, common sense and everything else".

In a later decision,[4] Danckwerts, J., is stated to have taken it

---

[1] [1951] Ch. 185.
[2] [1956] Ch. 644.
[3] *Ibid.*, at pp. 648, 649.
[4] *Re Grover's Will Trust, National Provincial Bank, Ltd.* v. *Clarke*, [1971] Ch. 168 *per* Pennycuick, J., at p. 178.

for granted that the interests of the remoter issue should be brought into account as well as that of the child. If this is so the difference between his approach and that of Harman, J., is as to valuation, and not as to the nature of the interest to be brought into account. At the heart of the dispute is the fact that when separate interests exist in the same property, the aggregate value of those interests will only rarely be equivalent to the value of the property itself. The present position of the authorities is, then:

a. a child must give credit for benefits received both by himself and by his children or remoter issue under the will;
b. if the child and his issue are the only persons who could benefit, the child must give credit for the whole capital value of the fund; but
c. if persons other than the child and his issue can benefit, then, subject to what is said below, each interest is to be valued, and the child must give credit for the aggregate of the values of his interest and that of his issue.

While this approach produces a fair stirpital distribution, it seems to stretch the legislation well beyond its apparent meaning.

4. INTEREST LIABLE TO DIVESTING

The problem has been considered so far on the basis that the first interest is an absolute life interest. Suppose, however, that the interest is less than an absolute life interest, and that some person other than the child and his issue may become entitled? In general, it is suggested that the interest must be valued having full regard to its terms, and not as a life interest. In two cases, however, the life interest was not absolute, but was held on protective trusts, with the result that the spouse of the child could have benefited. Both in the first case, *Re Young*,[1] and in the later decision, *Re Grover's Will Trusts, National Provincial Bank, Ltd.* v. *Clarke*[2] Harman and Pennycuick, JJ., respectively, blithely disregarded the fact that the interests were held on protective trusts, and treated them for this purpose as absolute life interests.

5. EXAMPLE

The application of the rules may be illustrated by an example.

---

[1] [1951] Ch. 185; *ante*, p. 195.
[2] [1971] Ch. 168.

Andrew died in 1967 leaving an estate (after payment of debts and estate duty) of £50,000. By his will he left his wife his set of Chippendale chairs, worth £1,000 and an annuity of £300 p.a. He also left legacies of £5,000 to each of his two children Arnold and Abraham. In his lifetime, he had made an advancement of £2,000 to Arnold. The actuarial value of the widow's annuity is £5,350.

	£	£
Net estate		50,000
Legacies and bequests		
Specific bequest to wife	1,000	
Arnold	5,000	
Abraham	5,000	
		11,000
		39,000
Set aside fund to provide annuity		6,000
		33,000
Widow's statutory legacy	15,000	
Less: value of annuity under will	5,350	
		9,650
		23,350

(Note: chairs are not brought into account)

Half residue to provide fund for wife's life interest	11,675
Balance available for children	11,675
Entitlement of children is:	23,350
balance brought down	11,675
Add:	
Advance to Arnold	2,000
Legacies to children	10,000
	12,000
	23,675

	Arnold £	Abraham £
$\frac{1}{2} \times$ £23,675	11,837·50	11,837·50
Less: advancement	2,000	—
	9,837·50	11,837·50
Less: legacies	5,000	5,000
	4,837·50	6,837·50

On the death of the wife, there will be available for the children the fund set aside to provide for the annuity, and the other half of capital (£11,675).

6. DISCLAIMER AND INTESTACY

A disclaimer of an interest under a will does not prevent the person disclaiming taking a benefit under the intestacy rules. In many cases it will make no difference to his position. If a wife is entitled to a statutory legacy of £15,000, and is given a legacy of £5,000, in principle her position is the same whether she receives £5,000 under the will and £10,000 on intestacy, or disclaims her legacy under the will and receives £15,000 on intestacy. In some cases, however, it can be in her interest to disclaim and take on intestacy. These situations are discussed later.[1] It is appropriate to note here, however, *Re Sullivan*, *Dunkley* v. *Sullivan*.[2] In that case the widow was entitled to receive under the will certain royalties, but the effect of the will was to treat these as capital. She disclaimed the legacy under the will and became entitled on intestacy. However, the provision in the will affecting the royalties no longer took effect, so that the widow received them as income, as part of her life interest.

E. INTESTACY AFTER LIFE INTEREST

1. APPLICATION OF PARTIAL INTESTACY RULES

In some cases, a partial intestacy arises after the death of a life tenant. Suppose a person dies leaving a net estate of £10,000. Suppose also that he gives £3,000 to his only son absolutely, and directs that the other £7,000 shall be held upon trust for his wife for life, but that he does not make any disposition of that £7,000 after her death. There is no property undisposed of on the death of the deceased, but there is on the death of the wife. There are two possibilities. If effect is given to the will, the personal representatives are obliged to apply the intestacy rules at that time. On this basis, the wife's estate will be entitled to the statutory legacy, less the value of the life interest, together with interest at £4% p.a. from the date of death. So in *Re McKee*, *Public Trustee* v. *McKee*[3] a testator directed his executors to hold his residuary

---

[1] *Post*, p. 450.
[2] [1930] 1 Ch. 84.
[3] [1931] 2 Ch. 145.

estate upon trust for his wife for life, with remainder to such of his brothers and sisters as should be living at her death. All his brothers and sisters had died before the death of his wife, so that an intestacy arose at that time. The Court of Appeal held that the intestacy rules should be applied on her death, and that her estate should receive the statutory legacy and interest. (The intestacy rules in force at the time did not require the spouse to bring into account benefits received under the will, although she would have to bring this into account were the case to be decided on the same facts now.)

The other possibility is to give the wife her statutory legacy at once. On this basis her life interest under the will is actuarially valued, and is brought into hotchpot at that figure. This result was reached by Goff, J., in *Re Bowen-Buscarlet's Will Trusts, Nathan* v. *Bowen-Buscarlet*[1] where the wife was left a life interest in the whole residuary estate, but there was no provision as to what should happen after her death. The decision in *Re Bowen-Buscarlet* is to be preferred to that in *Re McKee*, and will probably now be followed.

The effect of following *Re Bowen-Buscartlet* is in practice to require different methods of calculation according to whether the life interest is in a fund greater or less than the amount of the statutory legacy. If the fund is less than the amount of the statutory legacy the widow can claim immediate payment of the whole fund. Suppose, for example, that Bernard dies leaving a net estate of £20,000, which he directs to be held on trust for his wife Celia, but that he makes no gift over on her death. There are no children. Celia is entitled to say that she has a charge on the fund for a statutory legacy of the full amount of the estate.

The charge is postponed to her life interest, but she can merge the two, and claim immediate payment.[2] Suppose, however, that the facts are the same, but that Bernard left two children, so that the wife's statutory legacy is £15,000. In this case, an actuarial valuation is made of the wife's life interest under the will, and the normal intestacy rules applied. Suppose that the life interest is worth £6,000. The wife cannot be compelled to disclaim her life interest under the will, and it seems that she is entitled to insist on the income from £15,000 being paid to her for life, but

[1] [1972] Ch. 463; [1971] 3 All E.R. 636.
[2] [1971] 3 All E.R. at p. 640.

also to an immediate capital payment of £9,000. The only way in which this could be produced would be for the personal representatives to sell the reversionary interest. But as the aggregate of the value of the life interest and the value of the reversion will not be equal to the value of the fund, the reversionary interest may not produce enough to pay the £9,000 in full. There is no problem if the widow disclaims her life interest under the will, and takes the capital sum of £15,000.

2. VALUATION OF LIFE INTEREST

The preceding remarks have been on the basis that whenever it is necessary to bring into account the value of a life interest, it is appropriate to take the actuarial value of the life interest at the date of the deceased's death. If the interest is not taken in possession at the date of death of the deceased, the value of the life interest is ascertained at the date when it does fall into possession.[1] An actuarial valuation is made, even though on the facts which happen it would be possible to calculate the exact amount received.[2]

---

[1] *Re Morton, Morton v. Warham*, [1956] Ch. 644.
[2] *Re Thomson Settlement Trusts, Robertson v. Makepeace*, [1953] Ch. 414 and (1956), 72 L.Q.R. 483.

Part IV

THE EXTENT OF TESTAMENTARY FREEDOM

CHAPTER 13

RESTRICTIONS ON TESTAMENTARY FREEDOM

A. THE FUNDAMENTAL PROBLEM

In much the same spirit as people refer, quite inaccurately, to an Englishman's home being his castle, people also seem convinced that a person has an inalienable right to leave his property to whomsoever he wishes. Both notions were derived from the nineteenth century, but are commonly thought to represent immutable principles of English law. In neither case is this so.[1] So far as testamentary freedom is concerned, long before the nineteenth century there was a period at which severe restrictions were imposed. And the provisions of other legal systems, by which a fixed proportion is given to a surviving wife and children, show that complete testamentary freedom is by no means the only principle, and perhaps by no means the norm, even among western legal systems.

There are two broad issues. First, legal systems which provide for the transmission of property on death may either allow complete testamentary freedom, or make some overriding provision for the nearest relatives, such as wives and children. Secondly, if a legal system is to make some overriding provision for relatives, this may be either on the basis of a fixed entitlement, such as giving the wife a right to one third of the estate, or it may be in the discretion of the court.

At first sight it may seem surprising that English law is moving away from complete testamentary freedon. One discernible trend in English law over the last century is a movement away from consideration of the family as an entity, to consideration of the

---

[1] See Mellows (1963), 2 Solr. Qtrly. 109.

individual. The evolution of methods of defeating entails,[1] the conferment of separate property rights on married women,[2] and the recognition of duties to support by wives as well as by husbands[3] all indicate this.[4] Yet by far a stronger trend is that to restrict the rights of private property. Just as these are widely restricted during life,[5] it is not surprising that they are also restricted on death.

It is far more difficult to decide whether, say, a wife or child should have a fixed right to part of the estate or only a right in the discretion of the court. If a fixed right is conferred, the rules must be blunt: they perhaps cannot cater adequately for each situation. A slightly absurd result ensues if a wife, although rich, is nevertheless entitled to receive in addition a percentage of her late husband's estate, even if he would have preferred his limited resources to be applied for his niece. But there are disadvantages also in the discretionary system.

It is of the essence of the discretionary system that the applicant must persuade the court that the deceased failed to make reasonable provision for him. This frequently involves consideration of the conduct of the deceased, and of the principal contestants, often to the great distress of all. Take a typical situation. The husband marries, and after some years separates from his wife and thereafter lives with a mistress. He makes substantial provision by will for his mistress, and the wife seeks to interfere with the will. A slanging match between wife and mistress can easily follow. The wife may allege that the mistress is a wanton who lured the husband away, and that she ought to receive nothing: in her turn the mistress may allege that the wife was a complete shrew who positively drove the husband away.

---

[1] As by the collusive actions of common recovery and fine, and the Fines and Recoveries Act 1833.

[2] See Married Women's Property Act 1882; Law Reform (Married Women and Tortfeasors) Act 1935; and Married Women (Restraint upon Anticipation) Act 1949.

[3] National Assistance Act 1948, s. 42.

[4] Further, while the incomes of husband and wife are usually assessed jointly (apart from the earned income of the wife), they may apply for separate assessments, although this does not affect the total tax payable: Income and Corporation Taxes Act 1970, ss. 37 to 42.

[5] Particularly under the Town and Country Planning legislation: see article noted on p. 203.

Despite this, and the other disadvantages of the often substantial costs of the application—substantial because full enquiry must be made—and of the time involved in dealing with an application, the advantages still probably lie with the discretionary system. Only the discretionary system can deal adequately with the particular conditions of each individual case. Nevertheless, the question remains open.

B. HISTORICAL BACKGROUND

The history of the English law of wills since the Norman Conquest falls into three phases: fixed rights of the family; complete testamentary freedom; discretionary rights of the family. So far as personalty is concerned, in the thirteenth century the general rule was that a man could leave only one third of his property if his wife and children survived him; one half if either his wife or children but not both survived him; and the whole of his estate if he was survived by neither. These restrictions ceased to apply over much of the country in the fourteenth century, but the position was governed by local custom. The restrictions were not abolished in the ecclesiastical province of York until 1704, and in the City of London until 1724. Complete testamentary freedom as to personalty existed throughout the country from that date until the passing of the Inheritance (Family Provision) Act 1938.

Wills of personalty had been under the control of the church courts, but a similar trend appears with regard to wills of realty. At first, it was thought essential that freehold land should remain in the family. In feudal times land represented both power and wealth, and in most places a freehold estate devolved automatically upon the heirs. Again, exceptions existed in particular localities, such as the City of London, usually as the result of a Royal charter. In 1540, however, the Statute of Wills allowed all freehold land to be devised, subject to restrictions in the case of land held by military tenures, and these restrictions themselves disappeared with the passing of the Act for the Abolition of Military Tenures 1660. Thereafter, there was complete testamentary freedom as to realty, again until the Inheritance (Family Provision) Act 1938.

C. THE FAMILY PROVISION LEGISLATION

1. BASIS OF LEGISLATION

There have been three Family Provision Acts. The Inheritance (Family Provision) Act 1938 followed earlier legislation in New Zealand and Australia, and it applies to persons dying between 13 July 1939 and 31 December 1952. The second Act, the Intestates Estates Act 1952, applies to persons dying between 1 January 1953 and 31 December 1966; and the Family Provision Act 1966 applies[1] to persons dying after 31 December 1966. The 1938 Act as amended by the subsequent Acts is reprinted as Schedule 3 to the 1966 Act.

The keynotes of the legislation have remained constant. They are:

    a. to give the courts a *discretion*;
    b. to award *maintenance*;
    c. for specified and insufficiently provided for *dependants*;
    d. out of *income*.

Each Act, however, has extended the scope of the previous one. Thus, the 1952 Act extended the legislation to cover complete intestacies, and the 1966 Act extended the power to make lump sum payments.

In addition to the Acts of 1938, 1952 and 1966, account must also be taken of the Matrimonial Causes Act 1965, under ss. 26 and 27 of which orders may be made in favour of a former spouse. This is considered later.

In the remainder of this chapter it is proposed to deal only with the provisions of the 1966 Act, and not the earlier Acts.

2. APPLICATIONS UNDER THE 1966 ACT

In order to succeed in an application under the legislation, the applicant must:

    a. prove that he has a *locus standi*; that is
       (i) that the deceased died domiciled in England; and
      (ii) that the applicant is a member of the class prescribed by
          s. 1 (1) of the Act;

---

[1] Except ss. 3 and 7.

b. convince the court that the will of the deceased, or the intestacy rules, or a combination of both, do not make reasonable provision for the maintenance of the applicant.

3. DOMICILE OF DECEASED

The Act only applies where the deceased died domiciled in England.[1] Curiously, there is no power for the court to interfere if the deceased was not domiciled in England, even if he had been resident here for a substantial time.[2] This may cause hardship where it is sought to make an application against the estate of a married woman who automatically takes the domicile of her husband. This is particularly so when it is remembered that it is for the applicant to prove the domicile of the deceased. Thus, in *Mastaka* v. *Midland Bank Executor and Trustee Co., Ltd.*[3] a daughter made an application in respect of the estate of her late mother. The mother had married a Russian, from whom she had been separated for a considerable period, and of whom she had heard nothing. There was no evidence before the court to show whether he was alive or dead. As the woman would be domiciled in the U.S.S.R. if her husband was alive, it was held that the daughter had not proved that the deceased's domicile was English, and accordingly she had no *locus standi* for making an application.

4. CLASS OF APPLICANTS

The Act enables, by s. 1 (1), an application to be made by:

a. a wife or husband;

b. a daughter who has not been married, or who is, by reason of some mental or physical disability, incapable of maintaining herself;

c. a son who has not attained the age of 21; or

d. a son of any age who is, by reason of some mental or physical disability, incapable of maintaining himself.

---

[1] Inheritance (Family Provision) Act 1938, s. 1 (1).

[2] Cf. the provisions in the matrimonial causes legislation which although basing divorce jurisdiction on domicile here also allow proceedings to be brought by married women resident in England for three years immediately prior to the presentation of the petition.

[3] [1941] Ch. 192.

a. *Wife or husband*

A wife or husband making an application against the estate of his or her deceased spouse must prove that the marriage was valid. A marriage certificate is accepted as *prima facie* evidence of marriage unless this is challenged, when further evidence is required. In *Re Peete, Peete* v. *Crompton*[1] a woman who thought she was a widow went through a ceremony of marriage with her second husband, and she was described on that marriage certificate as a widow. The wife had not seen her first husband for several years, and had been told by a member of her first husband's family that he had been killed in an explosion. However, no body had been identified. The court was not satisfied that the first husband was dead at the time of the second marriage, and therefore the application was not successful. On the other hand, in *Re Watkins, Watkins* v. *Watkins*[2] a husband deserted his wife in 1922 and was never heard of again. The wife remarried in 1948. In view of the length of time which had elapsed, and of the fact that the wife kept in touch with her first husband's family during that period, and they had heard nothing of him, the court presumed that the first husband was dead by 1948, so that the application could be made.

A party to a void marriage has a *locus standi*[3] unless the marriage was annulled during the lifetime of the deceased, or unless the applicant has remarried before the order is made[4]

While applications from husbands are sometimes discouraged, they have a clear *locus standi* to make an application.

b. *Daughter*

A daughter must prove:

   (i) that she is a legitimate or illegitimate[5] daughter; and
   (ii) *either* that she has not been married;

        or that by reason of some mental or physical disability she is incapable of maintaining herself.

In order to qualify as a "lawful" daughter, a girl may be legiti-

---

[1] [1952] 2 All E.R. 599.
[2] [1953] 2 All E.R. 1113.
[3] Law Reform (Miscellaneous Provisions) Act 1970, s. 6 (1).
[4] *Ibid.*, s. 6 (3).
[5] Illegitimate daughters only have a *locus standi* where the deceased died on or after 1 January 1970: Family Law Reform Act 1969, s. 18.

mate, or legitimated, or adopted in any part of the United Kingdom, Isle of Man, or Channel Islands. The child must either be born by the date of death of the deceased, or be *en ventre sa mere* at that date.

An illegitimate daughter may only make an application if her parent died on or after 1 January 1970.

If a daughter is making an application on the ground that she has not been married, she need show only that she has not been validly married. Thus, in *Re Rodwell, Midgley* v. *Rumbold*[1] Pennycuick, J., held that a daughter whose marriage was terminated by a decree of nullity could make an application.

The requirement that a daughter must be incapable of maintaining herself applies only to the second limb of the rule, relating to mental or physical incapacity, and not to unmarried daughters. An unmarried daughter earning a high salary has, therefore, a *locus standi*, although the court may not be disposed to exercise its discretion on her behalf. It should be noted that once a daughter has contracted a valid marriage, her right to apply under this head is lost, even if her marriage has come to an end before the death of the deceased. The reasoning appears to be that upon marriage a daughter ceases to have any moral claim on her parents for support, and must thereafter look to her husband. This is unsatisfactory. In certain circumstances, a daughter may, after the breakdown of her marriage, again become *de facto* dependent on her parents, but she is not entitled to make an application.

On the other hand, so long as the daughter does not marry, she can be the mistress of as many men as she likes, and still not lose her right to make an application. In *Re Andrews, Andrews* v. *Smorfitt*[2] a daughter lived with a married man for forty years, and had six children by him. She never married. At the age of 69 she made an application in respect of her late father's estate. It was held that she had a *locus standi* to make the application, although on the merits the court was not prepared to exercise its discretion in her favour.

Where a daughter is mentally or physically incapable of maintaining herself, she may make an application even if she has been

---

[1] [1970] Ch. 726.
[2] [1955] 3 All E.R. 248,

married. Whether or not a person is incapable of maintaining herself is a question of fact.

c. *Son*

A son must prove that he is lawful, in the same way as a daughter, except that, if the parent died on or after 1 January 1970, he also has a *locus standi* if he is illegitimate.[1]

A son may apply under one of two heads: that he is under 21; or that by reason of mental or physical disability he is incapable of maintaining himself. The latter ground is the same as for a daughter. It is difficult to understand why, under the first head, a son should be treated differently from a daughter. It will be noticed that the marriage of the son is irrelevant. Why should a married son under 21 be given a *locus standi* and not a married daughter under 21? Why should the attainment of the age of twenty-one disbar a son but not a daughter? This discrepancy is quite out of keeping with modern social conditions.

Where a son wishes to apply under the first head, it will be seen that he can do so when he is an infant, or between the ages of 18 and 21.[2]

d. *Mistresses and other dependants*

The Act seeks to provide maintenance for dependants; its class of persons who may make an application may seem far too narrowly drawn. Why, for example, should a woman who has lived with a man for forty years as his mistress, and borne him umpteen children, not make an application?

The law does not deny that the deceased may have had a moral obligation to other persons. Accordingly, if a will is made in their favour, the deceased's moral obligation to them will be taken into account when determining any application made by a member of the specified class.[3] But if they are not mentioned in the will, they may not make an application. It may be of some comfort that those who are able to make an application may nevertheless not be successful.[4]

But is there any workable alternative? The immediate reaction

---

[1] Family Law Reform Act 1969, s. 18.
[2] *Ibid.*, s. 5 (1).
[3] *Re Joslin, Joslin v. Murch*, [1941] Ch. 200.
[4] See e.g., *post*, p. 215.

may be to suggest that any person who can prove actual dependence should have the right to make an application. But what is "dependence", bearing in mind that in most cases dependence is only partial? And would there not be an intolerable increase in the number of applications made under the Act? Although the present rules are unsatisfactory, there may be no workable alternative if the discretionary system is to be retained.

5. REASONABLE PROVISION

a. *The deceased's reasons*

The wishes of the deceased are irrelevant, but the court is directed by s. 1 (7) to "have regard to" the deceased's reasons for making the will which he made, or for not making any, or any other, provision for the applicant. The court may accept such evidence of those reasons as it considers sufficient, particularly a statement in writing which is signed by the deceased and dated. Although the sub-section specifically refers to a written statement, the court may nevertheless accept evidence of the deceased's oral statements.[1] The statement may be in the will itself, or in a separate document, and it is not conclusively presumed that where a statement was made that it contained all the deceased's reasons. Accordingly, further evidence of other reasons may be admitted.[2]

The court is not obliged to accept the deceased's statement on its face, but may take into account the accuracy or otherwise of the statement. As a result, if the deceased leaves a statement which is inaccurate, the fact that it is inaccurate may in itself indicate that inadequate provision is made for the applicant.[3] An example of this occurred in *Re Clarke, Clarke* v. *Roberts*.[4] The testator married at the age of 49, when he was still a bachelor living with his mother. His wife was a school teacher aged 36. After the marriage the parties lived with the testator's mother for seven months, but she made his wife feel unwanted. In his will the testator left her £1,000, and said: "I hereby declare that the reason why I have not made further provision in this my will for (my wife) is that having before our marriage after due considera-

---

[1] *Re Pugh, Pugh* v. *Pugh*, [1943] Ch. 387; *Re Smallwood, Smallwood* v. *Martins Bank, Ltd.*, [1951] Ch. 369.
[2] *Re Searle, Searle* v. *Siems*, [1949] Ch. 73.
[3] *Re Borthwick, Borthwick* v. *Beauvais*, [1949] Ch. 395.
[4] [1968] 1 All E.R. 451.

tion agreed the matrimonial home should be in the home of my mother who is a partial invalid she has seen fit to leave me and set up a home by herself." However, Plowman, J., found that the wife went to live in the mother's house as a temporary measure intended to last only long enough to get the mother used to the idea that her forty-nine year old bachelor son had got married, and that it was not intended to be a permanent arrangement. Indeed the judge said that had the case been a matrimonial dispute, he would have found the husband to have been in constructive desertion of the wife. He therefore rejected the reason given in the will, and awarded one half of the income of the estate for the rest of her life, or until remarriage. The court will also not regard as a valid reason for not making provision feebleness of mind, even if that feebleness is such as to deprive the deceased of the mental capacity which would be required to make a will.[1]

Where a will is made on behalf of a mental patient by a person authorised by the Court of Protection, the authorised person may sign a statement of reasons for the purposes of s. 1 (7), but only on the directions of the court.[2]

b. *A subjective or objective test?*

The court may make an order in favour of the applicant if it is of opinion that the existing disposition of the deceased's estate "is not such as to make reasonable provision for the maintenance" of the applicant.[3] The section leaves open whether the test of reasonableness is subjective or objective. The fact that account is to be taken of the deceased's reasons suggests, but does not prove, that a subjective test was intended. The general approach has been to adopt a subjective test: the court has placed itself in the position of the deceased at the time of his death, and has examined the reasonableness of the disposition at that time. On this basis, both the facts known to the deceased, and the circumstances which were reasonably foreseeable by him were relevant. *Re Howell, Howell* v. *Lloyds Bank, Ltd.*[4] was concerned with the will

---

[1] *Re Blanch, Blanch* v. *Honhold*, [1967] 2 All E.R. 468.
[2] Mental Health Act 1959, s. 103A (5), added by Administration of Justice Act 1969, s. 18.
[3] Inheritance (Family Provision) Act 1938, s. 1 (1).
[4] [1953] 2 All E.R. 604.

of a testator who was a married man with children, and who left all his property to his second wife. After his death, his second wife became seriously ill, and could not look after the children, who then went to live with the former wife. As the deceased could not have reasonably foreseen the illness of his second wife, the provisions of his will remained unaltered.

Circumstances are considered at the moment of death. In *Re Franks, Franks* v. *Franks*[1] a woman who had been previously married left a small part of her estate to her second husband and the substantial balance to her son by her first marriage. She then had a child by her second husband, and died two days later. Even though it was not practicable for her to alter her will to make provision for her new baby, Wynn Parry, J., held that the child could successfully make an application. The wife was deemed to have been able to have made a new will.

A recent decision caused some confusion. In *Re Goodwin, Goodwin* v. *Goodwin*[2] the testator made a will leaving his residuary estate to his second wife. He anticipated that this would amount to between £8,000 and £9,000, but after the payment of estate duty, it in fact only amounted to about £1,500. Of that, £1,100 was represented by an unsecured interest free loan made by the testator to his wife's son by a previous marriage. After the testator's death the son became seriously ill, and ceased making repayments in respect of the loan. It was uncertain whether he would be able to recommence making payments. Megarry, J., held that even if there had been no uncertainty as to the £1,100, the provision would still have been unreasonable. He then took into account the supervening uncertainty of the debt, and made an order in favour of the widow. The decision accords with principle on the basis that if the provision was not reasonable as at the date of death of the testator, then in deciding what order should be made, the court may take into account subsequent events. However, the judge did not say that if the provision was reasonable as at the date of the death of the testator, then the court would not have had jurisdiction to make an order.[3]

The judge also had to consider the general question whether the

---

[1] [1948] Ch. 62.
[2] [1969] 1 Ch. 283; [1968] 3 All E.R.
[3] *Dun* v. *Dun*, [1959] A.C. 272.

test was subjective or objective. He said:[1] "The question is simply whether the will or the disposition has made reasonable provision, and not whether it was unreasonable on the part of the deceased to have made no provision or no larger provision for the dependant. A testator may have acted entirely reasonably; he may have taken skilled advice on the drafting of his will, intending to make a fully reasonable provision; and yet through some blunder of the draftsman (perhaps as to the incidence of estate duty) or by some change of circumstance unknown to the testator in his lifetime, the provision in fact made may have been wholly unreasonable. Conversely, the testator may have acted wholly unreasonably in deciding what provision to insert in the will, but by some happy accident, such as the lapse of a share of residue which then passed to the widow as on intestacy, the provision in fact made may be entirely reasonable. In my judgment the question is not subjective but objective. It is not whether the testator stands convicted of unreasonableness, but whether the provision in fact made is reasonable."

The approach of Megarry, J., was expressly approved by Winn, L.J., in *Re Gregory, Gregory* v. *Goodenough*[2] and more recently by Lord Denning, M.R., in *Millward* v. *Shenton*.[3] The latter case is instructive. A widow aged over 80 was survived by six children. In 1970 she made a will leaving her estate, which was just over £3,000, to the British Empire Campaign for Cancer Research. She did not leave anything to her children for two reasons. First, she appears to have been under the impression that they were all self supporting. Secondly, they had begun to quarrel among themselves over the money which would become available after her death, and she did not want her estate to be dissipated in the costs of proceedings which might ensue. Subjectively, then, it could not be said that the widow behaved unreasonably. An application was made to the court, however, by one son aged 52. Since 1966 he had suffered from dystrophia syotonica and could not do anything for himself. He lived on various social security benefits, and his wife was also severely handicapped with osteo-arthritis. The Court of Appeal unani-

---

[1] [1969] 1 Ch. 283 at p. 287; [1968] 3 All E.R. 12, at p. 15.
[2] [1971] 1 All E.R. 497; see *post*, p. 216.
[3] [1972] 2 All E.R. 1025, C.A.

mously held that he should receive 11/12ths of the estate, after the payment of the costs. But the attitude of the members of the Court of Appeal as to the test differed. As stated, Lord Denning approved the objective test. Megaw, L.J., made no reference to the nature of the test. Stamp, L.J., left the matter open, saying that it was not necessary for him to express an opinion whether the test was subjective or objective.[1] The point cannot yet be regarded as finally settled, although the indications are strongly in favour of the objective approach.[2]

6. RELEVANT CONSIDERATIONS

a. *Moral obligation*

The Act nowhere specifies all the circumstances to be taken into account in deciding whether an applicant should be successful. However, it is clearly established that in order to succeed, an applicant must show that the deceased had a moral obligation to support him. In *Re Andrews, Andrews* v. *Smorfitt*,[3] considered above, the daughter failed because by living with a man as his "wife", the daughter had thereby ceased to have any moral claim on her father.[4] A person may be under a moral obligation to support a dependant who is working. So in *Re Clarke*,[5] mentioned earlier,[6] the wife, who was a school teacher, earned over £1,000 p.a., but was nevertheless awarded the income from one half of the testator's net estate of £23,000.

In certain circumstances a dependant will be owed a moral obligation where he or she looks after the deceased. So, in *Re Blanch, Blanch* v. *Hornhold*,[7] where a wife, aged 71, looked after her husband, aged 68, for about a year while he was ill, and notwithstanding his irrational jealousy of a young man aged 20, Buckley, J., directed that she should receive benefit from the estate.

In exceptional circumstances, a person who is entirely responsible for the breakdown of the marriage may nevertheless

---

[1] [1972] 2 All E.R. 1025, C.A. p. 1028.
[2] See generally (1971) 35 Con. 72; and Hall (1972) 30 Camb. L.J. 248.
[3] [1955] 3 All E.R. 248.
[4] See also 72 L.Q.R. 18.
[5] [1968] 1 All E.R. 451.
[6] *Ante*, p. 211.
[7] [1967] 2 All E.R. 468.

not owe any moral duty to his spouse. In *Re Gregory, Gregory* v. *Goodenough*[1] the husband married in 1926. In 1927 they had a daughter and the husband left. He did not pay any maintenance to his wife or daughter, and cohabited with another woman. The other woman died in 1950, and the husband then asked his wife to come back. She refused because she was at the time looking after her mother. Shortly thereafter, the daughter went to live in South America and in 1955 the wife joined her there. From 1958 the husband wrote letters to his wife asking her to return. She did not do so and rarely answered his letters. He died in 1968, worth about £2,500, having left his wife nothing. The wife applied unsuccessfully to the county court, and her appeal to the Court of Appeal was unanimously dismissed. Although it was accepted that the husband was solely responsible for the breakdown of the marriage in 1927, he was held to have owed no moral obligation in respect of services or assistance in his later years. The other reasons for the decision were the length of the separation itself, and the fact that the wife had not relied in any way on the deceased for maintenance or support.

The court also considers the testator's moral obligation to those whom he has benefited by his will. Thus, where a testator has made provision for an illegitimate child[2] or a mistress of twenty years standing[3] (if that is the correct expression for a mistress) his moral obligation to those persons was recognized. This is so even though such persons may not themselves be entitled to make an application.

b. *Conduct of applicant*

Sub-section 1 (6) requires the court to have regard to the conduct of the applicant in relation to the deceased, and otherwise. This relates both to whether the applicant should receive any benefit from the deceased, and also to the size of that benefit.

c. *Financial position of estate and applicant*

Sub-section 1 (6) also requires the court to have regard to the past, present or future capital or income from any source of the

---

[1] [1971] 1 All E.R. 497.
[2] *Re Joslin, Joslin* v. *Murch*, [1941] Ch. 200 (under the pre-1970 law).
[3] *Re E, E.* v. *E.*, [1966] 2 All E.R. 44.

applicant.[1] The size of the estate is clearly relevant. The court may make provision only out of the "net estate" of the deceased, which means the property of which the deceased had power to dispose by will, after deducting his funeral and testamentary expenses, estate duty and other taxes such as capital gains tax, payable out of his estate on death; debts, and other liabilities. "Net estate" includes property over which the deceased had a general power of appointment exercisable by will, but not over which he had only a special power.[2]

The court appears reluctant to interfere with small estates. In *Re Howell, Howell* v. *Lloyds Bank, Ltd.*[3] and *Re Gregory, Gregory* v. *Goodenough*[4] where the estates were both less than £3,000, the Court of Appeal stated that they would be very slow to interfere with the testator's disposition of his estate, but in principle there is no reason why the size of the estate should affect the court's approach.

If there is a total or partial intestacy, the court is not bound to assume that the intestacy rules[5] make reasonable provision for the deceased's dependents.[6] The court may, therefore, in effect alter in a particular case the intestacy rules.

d. *Applications by husbands*

Applications by husbands used to be discouraged.[7] Each case is considered on its merits, but previously a husband would only be successful in exceptional cases. Such a case was *Re Sylvester, Sylvester* v. *Public Trustee*[8] where a husband gave up his employment in order to nurse his sick wife. Her net estate was £19,000, but she left her husband an annuity of only £1 a week. On his application, this was increased to £4 a week. A husband may also

---

[1] *Re Clayton, Clayton* v. *Howell*, [1966] 2 All E.R. 370; *Re Styler, Styler* v. *Griffith*, [1942] Ch. 387, at p. 390; *Re Charman, Charman* v. *Williams*, [1951] 2 T.L.R. 1095.

[2] 1938 Act, s. 5 (1).

[3] [1953] 2 All E.R. 604.

[4] [1971] 1 All E.R. 497.

[5] *Ante*, p. 190.

[6] 1938 Act, s. 1 (8), as amended.

[7] See Farwell, J., in *Re Sylvester, Sylvester* v. *Public Trustee*, [1941] Ch. 87, at p. 89; and see Morton, J., in *Re Styler, Styler* v. *Griffith*, [1942] Ch. 387, at p. 389. *Re Lawes* (1946), 62 T.L.R. 231.

[8] [1941] Ch. 87.

be successful in less extreme cases where he is poor.[1] However, in *Re Clayton, Clayton* v. *Howell*[2] Ungoed-Thomas, J., established the modern approach by stating that there was no greater onus of proof on a husband than on a wife.

e. *Source of deceased's funds*

Where the deceased had been married more than once, it is relevant for the court to take into account whether the deceased derived his funds mainly from one spouse.[3] So in *Sivyer* v. *Sivyer*[4] the deceased owed moral obligations to his widow, who was his third wife, and to his daughter by his second wife. The deceased had a net estate of about £4,000, and died intestate. The widow would, under the intestacy rules,[5] have taken the total estate, and an application was made on behalf of the daughter. Pennycuick, J., was at first minded to award the daughter £2,000, but increased this to £2,500 solely because most of the deceased's wealth was derived from his second wife, the girl's mother.

f. *State supported dependants*

It used to be thought that a testator was entitled to make no or little provision for dependants who were being cared for under the National Health Service. In *Re Watkins, Watkins* v. *Watkins*[6] a man left an estate of £23,000. His daughter was a mental in-patient and he had during his lifetime allowed her £250 p.a. In his will he left her £72 only. Roxburgh, J., refused an application to increase. However, in *Re Pringle, Baker* v. *Matheson*[7] it was held that even though the testator's mentally defective son was being cared for in a National Health Service home, it was nevertheless reasonable for the testator to make some provision for him and in *Millward* v. *Shenton*[8] it was held that a testatrix should make provision for a son aged 52 who was totally incapacitated, and was entirely dependent on social security payments.

---

[1] *Re Pointer, Pointer and Shonfield* v. *Edwards*, [1941] Ch. 60; *Re Clayton, Clayton* v. *Howell*, [1966] 2 All E.R. 370.

[2] [1966] 2 All E.R. 370; [1966] 1 W.L.R. 969.

[3] *Re Styler, Styler* v. *Griffith*, [1942] Ch. 387, at p. 390; *Re Sivyer, Sivyer* v. *Sivyer*, [1967] 3 All E.R. 429.

[4] [1967] 3 All E.R. 429.

[5] *Ante,* p. 178.

[6] [1953] 2 All E.R. 1113.

[7] [1946] Ch. 124.

[8] [1972] 2 All E.R. 1025, C.A.; discussed, *ante*, p. 214.

Further, in *Sivyer* v. *Sivyer*[1] Pennycuick, J., awarded half the estate to a girl who was in the care of the local authority.

On the other hand, it has been held that where the applicant is in receipt of a Social Security pension or allowance, and the only result of an allowance from the estate would be to reduce that allowance, then it is not unreasonable for the deceased to make no provision for the applicant.[2]

The courts are alive to the problem, and in *Re Canderton, Canderton* v. *Barclays Bank, Ltd.*[3] Ungoed-Thomas, J., divided the benefit between income and capital so that social security payments were affected to the least extent.

7. APPLICATIONS TO THE COURT

a. *Time for application*

As a general rule, an application must be made to the court within six months from the date when probate or letters of administration are first taken out.[4] For this purpose, a grant limited to settled land[5] is generally ignored.[6] Where a grant of administration is made because no will is found, but that grant is subsequently revoked because a will comes to light, and a grant of probate is made, the six month period runs from the date of the grant of probate.[7] Where, however, a will is proved in common form, and is subsequently proved in solemn form, the six month period runs from the original grant in common form.[8] The reason for the time limit is to enable the personal representatives to distribute the estate with reasonable expedition.

The rule can, however, cause hardship and the court has a discretion to allow an application to be made outside the six months period. Under the 1952 Act the grounds upon which the court could allow an application out of time were limited to where the subsequent discovery of a will or codicil involved a substantial

---

[1] [1967] 3 All E.R. 429; see p. 218, *ante*.
[2] *Re E., E.* v. *E.*, [1966] 2 All E.R. 44.
[3] (1970), 114 Sol. Jo. 208.
[4] 1938 Act, s. 2 (1), as amended.
[5] See *post*, p. 360.
[6] 1938 Act, s. 2 (1C), as amended.
[7] *Re Bidie, Bidie* v. *General Accident Fire and Life Assurance Corporation, Ltd.*, [1949] Ch. 121.
[8] *Re Miller, Miller* v. *de Courcey*, [1968] 3 All E.R. 844.

change in the disposition of the deceased's estate; where a question as to the nature of a beneficiary's interest had not been determined within the usual period; and where there was some other circumstance affecting the administration or distribution of the estate, such as the birth of a posthumous child shortly before the expiration of the six month period.[1] The court may be expected to exercise its discretion for similar reasons now, and for any other reason which it thinks fit. In principle, it will be prepared to extend the time if no hardship would be caused as a result.[2] There had been several decisions to the effect that the intending applicant's solicitor's mistake as to the time within which an application should be made was not sufficient to enable the court to extend the period.[3] It remains to be seen whether the court will now extend the period in these circumstances.[4]

b. *Position of personal representatives*

Sub-section 2 (1B) of s. 2 of the 1938 Act provides that personal representatives are not liable for distributing the estate after the six month period on the ground that they ought to have taken into account the possibility of an application to the court out of time. Of course, they ought not to make a distribution if proceedings are pending or are known to be imminent. The Act does not specifically provide that personal representatives should not distribute within the six months period, but where there is a person who could make an application, they will probably be liable for distributing within that period.[5]

c. *Variation of orders*

When an order has been made, an application to vary it may be made at any time. The grounds upon which a variation order may be made are:

---

[1] *Re Trott, Trott v. Miles*, [1958] 2 All E.R. 296.

[2] *Re Ruttie, Ruttie v. Saul*, [1969] 3 All E.R. 1633;

[3] *Re Greaves, Greaves v. Greaves*, [1954] 2 All E.R. 109; *Re Bone, Bone v. Midland Bank*, [1955] 2 All E.R. 555; *Re Trott, Trott v. Miles*, [1958] 2 All E.R. 296; *Re McNare, McNare v. McNare*, [1964] 3 All E.R. 373; *Re Kay, Kay v. West*, [1965] 3 All E.R. 724.

[4] See (1971), 121 N.L.J. 100.

[5] *Re Simson, Simson v. National Provincial Bank, Ltd.*, [1950] Ch. 38, at p. 43.

(i) that a material fact was not disclosed to the court on the prior application;[1]

(ii) that a substantial change has taken place in the circumstances of the applicant, or of a person beneficially interested under the will or on intestacy;[2] or

(iii) that an order should be made for the maintenance of another dependant of the deceased.[3]

Where a variation order is made, it may only affect property which at the date of the application for variation is available for the maintenance of any dependant of the deceased.[4]

d. *Interim orders*

Where the applicant is in immediate need of financial assistance the court may make an interim order, even though the merits of the application have not been ascertained. Upon making such an order, the court is entitled to impose such conditions as it thinks fit, for example requiring repayment to the estate if the merits of the application are subsequently rejected.

When an application is made under this legislation, the personal representatives may on their own authority make an interim payment,[5] but before doing so they will usually wish to obtain the consent either of the persons affected, or of the court.

e. *Courts having jurisdiction*

Where the net estate does not exceed £5,000, the application may be made to the Crown Court,[6] and if made in the High Court, it may be transferred to the Crown Court.[7] In other cases, the application should be made to the Chancery Division of the High Court.[8]

---

[1] 1938 Act, s. 4 (1) (a).

[2] *Ibid.*, s. 4 (1) (a).

[3] *Ibid.*, s. 4 (1) (b).

[4] *Re Dorgan, Dorgan* v. *Polley*, [1948] Ch. 366; *In the Estate of Gale*, [1966] Ch. 236.

[5] *Re Ralphs, Ralphs* v. *District Bank, Ltd.*, [1968] 3 All E.R. 285, *per* Cross, J., at p. 288.

[6] 1966 Act, s. 7 (1). The Lord Chancellor has power to extend the jurisdiction of the County Courts.

[7] *Ibid.*, s. 7 (3).

[8] Or the Courts of Chancery of the County Palatine of Lancaster, and of Durham.

f. *Effect of Order*

Once an Order is made it is deemed to have had effect from the deceased's death for all purposes.[1] A memorandum of the order is endorsed on the grant of representation under which the estate is being administered.[2]

8. THE COURT'S ORDER

a. *"Maintenance"*

The object of the courts is to provide for the "maintenance" of the applicant. "Maintenance" does not mean mere subsistence, but the appropriate standard is to be considered in the light of previous maintenance of the dependant.[3] This does not mean, however, that the previous standard of living will necessarily be material. In *Re Inns, Inns* v. *Wallace*[4] Wynn Parry, J., said[5] "What would be a reasonable provision for the widow of, for instance, a farm labourer would, in ordinary circumstances, be unreasonable provision for the widow of a wealthy man". In *Re Inns, Inns* v. *Wallace* the testator had an estate of £60,000, which produced an income of £18,000. He settled sufficient on his wife for life to produce £3,000 p.a. and in addition left her a life interest in a large house conditionally on her living in it and keeping it in good repair. The widow said that she needed another £500 p.a. to do this, and made an application accordingly. Wynn Parry, J., rejected her application on the basis that the will was unfortunate but not unreasonable. This reasoning may be unconvincing: it is an example of the reluctance with which the courts will interfere with a will.

The court can make an order up to the total income of the estate. This is the income which the capital of the estate would produce if invested, and not the larger amount which would be produced if it were sold to purchase annuities.

In the common case of a dispute between wife and mistress, or between first wife and second wife, the court is, of course, guided by the financial position of the parties, but shows a tendency to divide the estate down the middle, particularly where it is of

---

[1] 1938 Act, s. 3 (1).
[2] *Ibid.*, s. 3 (3).
[3] *Bosch* v. *Perpetual Trustee Co., Ltd.*, [1938] A.C. 463.
[4] [1947] Ch. 576.
[5] [1947] Ch. 576, at p. 581.

moderate size. This is so even though the ultimate financial positions of the parties will be unchanged. A good example is *Re Shanahan, De Winter* v. *Legal Personal Representatives of Shanahan*.[1] The applicant was the first wife of the deceased whom he married in 1927 and by whom he had four children. She obtained a divorce from him in 1956, with an order for maintenance. In 1965 the deceased married his second wife, and later made a will leaving her all his property. The first wife made an application, and was granted half the estate. Both first and second wives were at the end of their working lives. Wife no. 1 had no capital; wife no. 2 had £6,000. Wife no. 1 had a national insurance retirement pension of £250 p.a.; wife no. 2 had a pension from her job as a teacher and a national insurance pension of £1,100 p.a. Both as regards capital and income, wife no. 2 was better off, but the court divided the estate between them.

An unusual point arose in the case. The value of the estate had fallen between the date of death and the date of the hearing. The court, having followed the objective approach, held that it was not bound to look at the position from the point of view of the deceased, and therefore based its decision on the value of the estate at the date of the hearing.

In making an order the court may impose conditions or restrictions on the recipient. Thus, in *Re Lidington, Lidington* v. *Thomas*[2] the court made an order in favour of the deceased's widow on condition that she continued to maintain the deceased's infant children.[3]

b. *Lump sum payments*

It has been said that applications should not be made where the estate is too small to produce maintenance of a reasonable amount,[4] but even where the estate is small an application may be successful in that a lump sum may be ordered. The court has a general power to make an order for the payment of a lump sum either instead of, or in addition to, periodic payments.[5] This power will usually be exercised where the estate is small, and the income produced is negligible. No lump sum order can be made,

---

[1] [1971], 3 All E.R. 873.
[2] [1940] Ch. 927.
[3] See also *Re Pointer, Pointer and Shonfield* v. *Edwards*, [1941] Ch. 60.
[4] *Re Vrint, Vrint* v. *Swain*, [1940] Ch. 920.
[5] 1938 Act, s. 1 (4).

however, if it would necessitate an improvident realization of the assets of the estate.[1]

Lump sum payments will only be made for the maintenance of the applicant. There is no suggestion that the object of the provision is to enable the court to give legacies where it thinks this is appropriate.

c. *Time at which estate to be valued*

There is no doubt that the fact that the will has not made reasonable provision for the applicant must be established as at the date of death.[2] However, in deciding what order should be made, the court takes account of the value of the estate at the date of the hearing, and not at the date of death.[3] Thus, an applicant could be assisted if there was a material increase in the value of the estate between the date of death and the date of hearing.

d. *Date from which order takes effect*

The court has a complete discretion as to the date from which an order for the payment of maintenance will take effect. In many cases it will be backdated to the date of death, but where there has been a considerable delay before the hearing of the application, a later date is often taken. This is because where an order is backdated for a considerable time, the effect of an obligation to pay arrears is, in effect, to give a lump sum.[4]

9. APPLICATIONS UNDER THE MATRIMONIAL CAUSES ACT 1965

Section 26 of the Matrimonial Causes Act 1965, enables a former surviving husband or wife whose marriage to the deceased has been terminated by a decree of divorce or nullity, to make an application for maintenance from the estate of the deceased

---

[1] *Ibid.*, s. 1 (5).
[2] *Dun* v. *Dun*, [1959] A.C. 272.
[3] *Lusternik* v. *Lusternik*, [1972] 1 All E.R. 592.
[4] *Askew* v. *Askew*, [1961] 2 All E.R. 60; *Lusternik* v. *Lusternik*, [1972] 1 All E.R. 592.

provided the applicant has not remarried. Apart from having to prove the additional requirement that the applicant has not remarried, the position under this section is the same as under the 1966 Act, so that the applicant must prove a *locus standi*; that the deceased did not make reasonable provision for him; and that in the exercise of its discretion the court ought to make provision for the maintenance of the applicant out of the estate. In many cases an order will be made where the deceased was paying maintenance to the applicant but it has power to make an order even where an application for maintenance was made during the lifetime of the deceased and was dismissed.[1] An order for the maintenance of a former spouse of the deceased comes to an end on remarriage.[2]

The reason for having separate legislation, and more particularly for having applications under this Act made to the Family Division is that the court will often have on its file a substantial amount of information about the financial position of the deceased and of the applicant, and will always have information on its file as to the conduct of the parties. It is, therefore, convenient for the same court to consider the applications on death.

---

[1] *Re S.*, [1965] P. 165.
[2] Matrimonial Causes Act 1965, s. 26 (3), as amended by the Family Provision Act 1966, s. 4 (1).

CHAPTER 14

DEFEATING THE DEPENDANTS

The Family Provision legislation is surprisingly unsophisticated. It might be expected that there would be a provision which would enable the courts to upset devices which are designed to get round the power of the court to award income or capital to dependants. Yet there is no such anti-avoidance provision. A testator is, then, left considerable scope to defeat any likely application by his dependants. This chapter considers the main possibilities.

A. STATEMENT OF REASONS

In certain circumstances, a written statement[1] left by the deceased, which is accurate, may prevent a successful application. As well as being accurate in fact, it should be moderate and rational in tone. But the use of such a statement is very limited. In the first place it will probably not prevent the expense to the estate of an application, even if that application is unsuccessful. Secondly, its general importance is diminishing. While the test whether the deceased had made reasonable provision was subjective[2] a statement of his reasons was clearly important. Now that the test appears to be objective, the statement cannot in itself affect in any way the fact whether the provision was reasonable: it is now merely a way of ensuring that all facts which the deceased considered relevant are brought to the attention of the court in the event of an application being made.

B. ACQUIRE FOREIGN DOMICILE

The court does not have power to intervene if the deceased died domiciled outside England and Wales, even if he left property

---

[1] Inheritance (Family Provision) Act 1938, s. 1 (7); see *ante*, p. 211.

[2] See *ante*, p. 212.

here.[1] He may in any event wish to acquire a foreign domicile for tax reasons, but a distant journey is not necessary. Acquisition of a domicile in Jersey, the Isle of Man, or even Scotland[2] will be sufficient to oust the jurisdiction of the court.

C. REDUCTION OF NET ESTATE

1. THE "NET ESTATE"

The court can only make an order for payment out of the deceased's "net estate".[3] This is the property which the deceased had power to dispose of by his will (except property over which he had a special power of appointment), less the amount of his funeral and testamentary expenses, debts and liabilities.[4] It follows that the extent to which the court can operate can be restricted by reducing the size of the property which the deceased can dispose of by will; or by increasing his liabilities; or both.

2. GIFTS *INTER VIVOS*

A gift of assets *inter vivos* clearly reduces the size of the estate. The motive for, or the time of, the gift is irrelevant.[5] Even if the gift is made for the express purpose of defeating the dependants, and even if it is made very shortly before death, it will be effective.

3. TRUSTS

Just as an outright gift is effective to reduce the estate, so is the creation *inter vivos* of a trust. A trust can be a particularly useful instrument, because the testator can give to himself a life interest in the property. If he wants freedom of choice to determine the ultimate destination of his property, he can reserve to himself a power of appointment, provided this is a special and not a general power.[6] In principle, there is also no objection to

---

[1] Inheritance (Family Provision) Act 1938, s. 1 (1).

[2] *Ibid.*, s. 6 (3).

[3] *Ibid.*, s. 1 (1).

[4] *Ibid.*, s. 5 (1).

[5] Bogus transactions are considered *post*, at p. 232; but the court probably does not have power to order property which was disposed of *inter vivos* to be brought into the estate or made available for dependants, unless it uses a bastardised notion of a constructive trust.

[6] See definition of net estate in 1938 Act, s. 5 (1).

the testator reserving to himself the right to revoke the trust during his lifetime if he so wishes, and, in this way, he could alter the testamentary power of appointment in the light of changed circumstances. Provided the trust had come into existence by the date of death, the property would not form part of the estate and would not become subject to the Act.

4. CREATING LIABILITIES

The net estate can also be reduced by the creation of liabilities. The only criterion is that the liability should be legally enforceable. In principle, therefore, it is possible to covenant to pay a specified sum, roughly equal to or slightly in excess of, the size of the estate. If no payment is made under the covenant, the covenantee would have the right to sue the estate, and if the testator has done his mathematics correctly, the whole estate will be used up in the satisfaction of the claim. This is, however, subject to what is said below with regard to bogus transactions.[1]

D. COVENANTS TO MAKE A WILL

1. THE PROBLEM

Can a testator defeat his dependants by using the last principle just considered, that of creating liabilities? He may consider that if he enters into a contract or covenant to make a will, but does not make one, the promisee will have a claim in damages against the estate for breach of contract or covenant; and that if the will was to dispose of the whole estate, the claim for damages would extend to all his assets. The net estate would, therefore, be reduced to nil. How far is this device effective?

2. OBLIGATIONS TO MAKE A WILL

There is no doubt that a contract to make a will is capable of being valid.[2] So in *Synge* v. *Synge*[3] the court upheld a contract to make a will leaving property to a woman whom the promisor wished to marry. Likewise, a contract that the intending testator

---

[1] See *post*, p. 232.
[2] *Hammersley* v. *De Biel* (1845), 12 Cl. & Fin. 45; *Laver* v. *Fielder* (1862), 32 Beav. 1; *Coverdale* v. *Eastwood* (1872), L.R. 15 Eq. 121; *Re Fickus, Farina* v. *Fickus*, [1900] 1 Ch. 331; *Synge* v. *Synge*, [1894] 1 Q.B. 466; *Re Edwards, Macadam* v. *Wright*, [1958] Ch. 168; *Parker* v. *Clark*, [1960] 1 All E.R. 93.
[3] [1894] 1 Q.B. 466.

will leave his house to a woman if she will act as his housekeeper will also be valid. [1] If the will is made in performance of such a contract, or in performance of a covenant, it might be thought that the making of the will completely discharges the contract or covenant by performance; and that the contract or covenant ceases to have any effect. In this case the promisee would be in the same position as any other legatee. The gift could fail for lapse; or ademption; or be subject to abatement. Suppose that Martin contracts with Molly that he will leave her his house, known as The Nest, if she will act as his housekeeper. Even if she does so, and Martin makes a will accordingly, the gift will be adeemed if Martin sells The Nest and buys another house, so that Molly will get nothing. But at an even greater extreme, a contract merely to make a will could be discharged by making it, even if thereafter the testator revoked the will and made another. In view of these factors, and despite inconsistency in some of the cases[2] a contract or covenant to make a will is treated not merely as an obligation to make the will, but also to ensure that the promisee will take the property on death.

If the will is not made, the promisee can claim to be placed in the same position as if the will had been made, and the promisee may claim the amount promised as a liability of the estate.[3] If the testator makes a will, but it is ineffective because the estate is insolvent, the promisee is entitled to claim in the insolvency as a creditor.[4] So, the obligation continues to exist whether or not the will is made.

3. EFFECT OF OBLIGATION ON JURISDICTION OF COURT

Against this general background, it is now possible to consider the effect of the family provision legislation. Is a contract to make a will to be treated as an absolute obligation to see that the promisee takes the property; or is it an obligation to see that the promisee takes the property subject to the jurisdiction of the court under the family provision legislation?

Most of the litigation has taken place in Commonwealth juris-

---

[1] *Re Edwards, Macadam* v. *Wright*, [1958] Ch. 168; *Parker* v. *Clark*, [1960] 1 All E.R. 93.
[2] Lee, Contracts to make Wills (1971), 87 L.Q.R. 358.
[3] *Hammersley* v. *De Biel* (1845), 12 Cl. & Fin. 45.
[4] *Graham* v. *Wickham* (1863), 1 De G.J. & Sm. 474.

dictions[1,2] and it follows two inconsistent paths. One path comes from New Zealand, and the decision of the Privy Council in *Dillon* v. *Public Trustee of New Zealand*.[3] Henry Dillon was in dispute with his sons, and there was litigation between them. Eventually this was settled when he was 79, and as part of the settlement he agreed to leave land to his children. No doubt rejuvenated by the family peace, he married again at the age of 81, and made a will leaving the land to his children, and the remainder of his property to his new wife. After his death, the widow applied under the New Zealand family provision legislation.[4] The Privy Council held that, at least for the purposes of that legislation, Henry Dillon's obligation was completely discharged by the execution of the will, and that his children were in the same position as any other devisee. Thus, it was held that the court had power to give the whole or part of the land to the widow.

Dillon's case concerned a will which had actually been made, but, if this reasoning is followed, the position would be the same if the will had not been made. Indeed, the Privy Council opined, *obiter*, that if Henry Dillon had not made the will, his children would have had a right in damages, but that in the calculation of the damages the possibility of the court exercising its power under the legislation would have to be taken into account.

The other line of cases culminated recently in *Schaefer* v. *Schuhlmann*.[5] In a neat example of the combination of the old and new worlds, the testator lived at 124 Nuwarra Road, Chipping Norton. When he was in poor health, he engaged a housekeeper to look after him and his house, at a salary of $A12 a week. About two months later, he agreed with the housekeeper that she would cease to be paid, but would become entitled to the house on his death. The testator then executed a codicil to give effect

---

[1] In addition to cases discussed in text, see *Re Coffill's Settled Estates* (1920), 20 S.R.N.S.W. 278; *Re Syme, Union Trustee Co. of Australia, Ltd.* v. *Syme* [1933] V.L.R. 282; *Re Richardson's Estate* (1935), 29 Tas L.R. 149; *Re Morris* (1943), 43 S.R.N.S.W. 352; *Lieberman* v. *Morris* (1944), A.L.R. 150, *Re McNamara's Estate* (1943), 2 W.W.R. 344; *Re Foxe*, [1944] 2 D.L.R. 392; *Olin* v. *Perrin*, [1946] 2 D.L.R. 461; *Re Willan's Estate* (1951), 4 W.W.R. (N.S.) 114.

[2] See, however, *Re Brown* (1955), 105 L.Jo. 169.

[3] [1941] A.C. 294, P.C.

[4] Family Protection Act 1908, s. 33.

[5] [1972] A.C. 572, P.C.; [1972] 1 All E.R. 621.

to this agreement. When he died, his estate after the payment of debts and duties was $A14,500. Apart from the house, in his will he left $A2000 to each of his four daughters, and divided the residue equally between his sons. The daughters made an application under the New South Wales family provision legislation,[1] and the court was minded to increase their legacies. The question was whether this could only be done at the expense of the sons, or whether the increased legacies could be charged on the house. The Privy Council held that the legacies could not be charged on the house, and expressly refused to follow *Dillon's* case.

There can be no doubt that the decision in *Schaefer* v. *Schuhmann* follows the earlier authorities as to the effect of a contract to make a will, in that the promisee is regarded as being given an assurance that the property would pass to him or her on death. But those earlier authorities could have been distinguished. It would not be difficult to imply into any contract to make a will a term that the obligation is to be subject to the power of the court to intervene under the family provision legislation. But if *Schaefer* v. *Schuhmann* is to be followed, as Lord Simon observed in his dissenting opinion, the testator who wishes to defeat his dependants has now great scope for doing so easily. A common situation is that of the married man with children. In late middle age he wants to leave his wife and live with his mistress, and to ensure that his mistress has all his property. It seems that if he agrees with her that in return for her looking after him she will have the whole, or substantially the whole, of his property, that agreement will have priority over the dependants.

It may not be possible for the English courts to follow *Dillon*, because the New Zealand legislation gives the court power over the whole "estate", and not merely over the "net estate". But if it can be followed, it is surely desirable to do so, notwithstanding the criticisms that have been made.[2] If the obligation has been genuinely incurred, the testator will have incurred a moral obligation to the promisee, and that fact can be taken fully into account by the court in deciding whether, and, if so, to what extent, the contract should be overridden. One may support

---

[1] Testator's Family Maintenance and Guardianship of Infants Act 1916-1954.

[2] Gordon, "The Conflict between Limitations on Testamentary Power by Statute and Contract" (1941), 19 Can BR 603; (1942), 20 Can B.R. 72.

Lord Simon when he says[1] that the majority opinion in *Schaefer's* case hypnotically carries forward ancient authorities regardless of the social purpose of the modern legislation.

E. BOGUS TRANSACTIONS

At the beginning of this chapter it was pointed out that there is no anti-avoidance legislation. However, in reading the majority opinion in *Schaefer's* case, Lord Cross observed [2] that: "whether contracts made by a testator not with a view to excluding the jurisdiction of the court under the Act but in the normal course of arranging his affairs in his lifetime should be liable to be wholly or partially set aside by the court under legislation of this character is a question of social policy on which different people may reasonably take different views". The purport of this dictum may be incontrovertible, but Lord Cross slips in this distinction between contracts made with a view to excluding the jurisdiction of the court, and contracts made in the normal course of arranging one's affairs. But he gave no indication of how the distinction should be drawn, or operated. The testator who wishes to indulge in the entirely bogus transaction is now on notice that the courts will seek to find a loophole in favour of the dependants, and where this is likely to arise the testator will be advised to use one of the other methods of dealing with the problem, under which the property does not form part of the estate at all. It is ironic that, in rejecting *Dillon*, the Privy Council in *Schaefer's* case have taken away the best instrument for thwarting the bogus transaction. But if *Schaefer's* case is to be followed, there will be a great demand for coffins made of glass to show the contented smirk of the testator as he is carried to his grave knowing that he has made a monkey of the legislature; and possibly with a hole in the lid through which on that last journey an upstretched hand can gesticulate in the direction of Parliament and the dependants.

---

[1] [1972] A.C. 572, at p. 600; [1972] 1 All E.R. 621, at p. 639.
[2] *Ibid.*, at p. 592; *ibid.*, at p. 633.

Part V

PROBATE

CHAPTER 15

GRANTS OF
REPRESENTATION

A. INTRODUCTION

A grant of representation is an Order of the Court which confirms
or confers the authority of the personal representatives to administer the estate of the deceased, and which indicates the terms
on which the estate is to be administered. In every case the grant
issues under the Court seal and so takes effect as a Court order,
even though in most cases grants are obtainable by a quasi-
administrative process of lodging certain documents, described
later, at the offices of the Principal Registry of the Family Division
of the High Court[1] at Somerset House, or at the offices of the
District Registries of the High Court, or at Probate sub-
registries.

There are several types of grant, all of which are described in
detail later, but they fall into three broad categories:

a. Probate, which can be issued only where there is a will, and
   only to one or more of the executors named in the will;
b. Administration with will annexed (usually known as administration *cum testamento annexo*), which is issued where there
   is a will, but no proving executors;
c. Administration, which is issued where there is an intestacy.

Where an executor is appointed by the will, and subsequently
takes out probate, his authority dates from the death of the
testator, so that in his case the grant of probate confirms his
authority. In the other cases, the personal representative has no
authority prior to the grant, and derives his authority from the

---

[1] So named by Administration of Justice Act 1970, s. 1 (1).

grant itself. But in either case, the personal representative can only prove his authority by production of his grant.

As well as establishing the personal representative's authority, the grant of representation also indicates the terms on which the estate is to be administered. In the case of probate or letters of administration with will annexed, the court must be satisfied that the last effective will or wills of the deceased have been deposited with it, and when these types of grants are issued, a copy of the will is attached to the grant. In the case of a total intestacy, the court must be satisfied that the person applying for the grant is the person entitled to it under the Probate Rules.[1]

Where a copy of the will is attached to a grant, that copy is the only document on which the personal representatives and all others interested can rely. If, therefore, part of the will of the deceased was invalid because, for example, it did not comply with the formal requirements of the Wills Act 1837, or because it was the product of an insane delusion, that part will be omitted from the probate copy. Likewise, where a question of construction arises, the Chancery Division has regard not to the will as actually written by the deceased, but to the probate copy of the will.

Because any grant is an Order of the Court, both the personal representative named in it, and any purchaser from him, is fully protected, even if it should not have been issued. If, therefore, a later will is found, a grant of probate of the earlier will remains fully effective until it is revoked by a further order of the court.

A person to whom probate has been granted is known as the executor. A person acting under a grant of letters of administration with will annexed, or of letters of administration *simpliciter*, is known as an administrator. Both executors and administrators are known as personal representatives.

To conclude this general introduction, it may assist to give an illustration of a grant of probate and of a grant of letters of administration *simpliciter* (see pages 701 and 702 of the appendix). A copy of the will as proved is attached to the probate, for that is the executor's authority as to the manner in which the estate is to be distributed but the copy is not shown in the illustration. Examples of the oaths leading to these grants are shown in the appendix on pages 698 and 699.

---

[1] Non-contentious Probate Rules 1954, rr. 19 and 21. These Rules were made under the authority of the Judicature Act 1925.

B. HISTORICAL BACKGROUND

It was a natural extension of the jurisdiction of the church courts over the administration of wills of personal property that they should also deal with disputes as to the validity of wills. The origin of this jurisdiction cannot be traced with certainty, but by the late twelfth or early thirteenth centuries, the church courts are found pronouncing as to the validity of wills.[1] At the beginning of the fifteenth century, the jurisdiction of the church courts was accepted to the extent that the common law courts treated as conclusive a grant of probate, that is, the declaration that the will had been proved to the satisfaction of the bishop as being the last effective will of the deceased.[2] The Court of Chancery made an undetermined attempt to encroach upon the jurisdiction of the church courts, but fairly quickly concentrated on questions of interpretation, leaving the jurisdiction to grant probate firmly in the hands of the church courts. The only rivals to the church courts were certain local courts, such as the London Court of the Hustings, which had customary testamentary jurisdiction. A will was normally proved in the Court of the Ordinary, that is, the Bishop, of the place where the testator resided, but in certain circumstances grants were issued by the court of the Archbishop of the Province.

It first became possible to make a will of realty in 1540,[3] but the common law courts recognised only the will itself as evidence of the devise. There was no common law equivalent of probate for wills of realty. Where the same will governed both realty and personalty, the church courts granted probate, but the common law courts continued to pay regard in respect of the realty, only to the will itself.

By the Court of Probate Act 1857, the jurisdiction of the church courts and of such local courts as exercised testamentary jurisdiction was transferred to the newly created Court of Probate, which, thenceforth was the only court in which the validity of wills of personality could be challenged, or in which grants of probate could be obtained. The Court of Probate was not given juris-

---

[1] Holdsworth, H.E.L., Vol. I, 625-626, 640; Pollock & Maitland, H.E.L., Vol. II, 339, 340; Plucknett, Concise History of the Common Law, 8th ed., 740.
[2] Holdsworth, H.E.L., Vol. III, 539, 540.
[3] *Ante*, p. 205.

diction to grant probate of wills of realty only, though where probate of a will of realty and personalty was granted in solemn form[1] this was accepted as evidence of a devise of realty.

The jurisdiction of the Court of Probate was transferred by the Judicature Act 1873 to the Probate Divorce and Admiralty Division of the High Court. The position with regard to wills of realty was made the same as that with regard to personalty by the Land Transfer Act 1897, which required a grant of probate for wills of realty, and provided that such grant should be conclusive.

The relevant provisions of the Judicature Act 1873 and the Land Transfer Act 1897 were subsequently repealed and re-enacted, and now appear as ss. 4, 20 and 155 of the Judicature Act 1925.

The last change was effected by the Administration of Justice Act 1970, which renamed the Probate, Divorce and Admiralty Division as the Family Division. Logically, all probate business should be assigned to the Chancery Division, but this, apparently, would have caused too much administrative inconvenience. Thus, all non-contentious probate business continues to be dealt with in the Family Division, while contentious business is dealt with in the Chancery Division.[2]

---

[1] I.e., proved as a result of proceedings. See *post*, p. 297, for the distinction between proof in common form, and proof in solemn form.

[2] Administration of Justice Act 1970, s. 1 (4).

CHAPTER 16

THE APPOINTMENT OF EXECUTORS AND ADMINISTRATORS

This chapter is concerned with the persons who are entitled to one of the three basic types of grant of representation, namely, probate, letters of administration, or letters of administration with will annexed. The persons who are entitled to special types of grant are described in Chapter 18.

A. EXECUTORS

An executor is a person appointed by will to administer the property of the testator and to carry into effect the provisions of the will.[1] In the same way as a trustee, an executor should be appointed for his personal qualities, such as his knowledge of the deceased's family and affairs, his trustworthiness and business acumen, and his general common sense. As a result of the personal nature of the appointment, two rules emerge:

(i) in principle, an executor can be appointed only by the testator, in his will; and

(ii) the office is personal, and so can be exercised only by the person appointed by the will.

There are however, exceptions to both principles.

B. APPOINTMENT OF EXECUTORS OTHERWISE THAN BY THE TESTATOR

The exceptional circumstances in which an executor can be appointed otherwise than by the testator himself are now considered.

---

[1] This is the definition of Williams on Wills, 3rd ed., p. 124.

1. BY NOMINATED PERSON

A testator may, instead of appointing an executor himself, nominate some other person to make the appointment.[1] This power to nominate must be given in an instrument executed as a will. The power may indicate the persons who may or may not be nominated, but in the absence of any provision to the contrary in the power, the person who is given the power may nominate himself.[2] Although the power to appoint an executor can be delegated, the power to make a will cannot.

2. DURING MINORITY OR LIFE INTEREST

Although, as will be shown, where a minority or life interest arises a grant of letters of administration can be granted only to two or more administrators[3] there is no such rule affecting executors. Accordingly, a grant of probate can be made to a sole executor even if a minority or life interest arises under the will. However, in the case of a grant of probate in such circumstances, the person entitled to a life interest, or the guardian of a minor who is interested may apply to the court for the appointment of a co-executor, and the court has a discretion to make such an appointment.[4]

3. IN RESPECT OF SETTLED LAND

The curious provisions as to special personal representatives in respect of settled land are considered later.[5] In general terms, the testator may appoint as special personal representatives the persons who are the trustees for the purposes of the Settled Land Act, and if he does not do so, he is deemed to have appointed them.[6] This is the only statutory provision under which a person is ever "deemed" to be appointed an executor.

Special personal representatives, or any person entitled to a beneficial interest under the settlement, may apply to the court for the appointment of a special personal representative if there is

---

[1] *In the Goods of Cringan* (1828), 1 Hagl. Ecc. 548; *Jackson and Gill* v. *Paulet* (1851), 2 Rob. Eccl. 344.
[2] *In the Goods of Ryder* (1861), 2 Sw. & Tr. 127.
[3] Judicature Act 1925, s. 160 (1).
[4] *Ibid.*, s. 160 (2).
[5] *Post*, p. 358.
[6] Administration of Estates Act 1925, s. 22.

none, or an additional personal representative if there is only one, and the court has a discretion to make such appointment.[1]

4. CHAIN OF REPRESENTATION

Section 7 of the Administration of Estates Act 1925 provides[2] that an executor of a sole or last surviving executor of a testator is also the executor of that testator. Suppose that A and B take out a grant of probate of the will of X. On the death of A, B carries on as sole executor. If on B's death C takes out a grant of probate of B's will, C will be B's executor by virtue of the grant, and A's executor by virtue of s. 7. The result would be the same if B was from the outset X's sole executor.

The reasoning—which is specious—for this rule is that just as X had full confidence in his own choice of executors, so he ought to have like confidence in their choice of successor.

There are two aspects of this principle:

a. so long as the chain of representation is unbroken, the last executor in the chain is the executor of every preceding testator;[3] and

b. a proving executor automatically becomes executor by representation of every preceding testator, and he cannot accept one executorship and refuse any preceding executorship.[4] In the example just postulated, C must either renounce completely, or accept the executorship of both X and B.

An executor by representation is in the same position as the original executor. He thus has the same rights in respect of the estate of the original testator as the original executor would have had were he still living, and he is accountable to the same extent.[5]

The chain of representation applies only to a succession of proving executors. The chain is therefore broken by:

a. an intestacy; or

b. in the event of a testator making a will, his failure to appoint an executor under that will; or

---

[1] Administration of Estates Act 1925, s. 23 (2).

[2] In sub-s. (1).

[3] Administration of Estates Act 1925, s. 7 (2).

[4] *In the Goods of Perry* (1840), 2 Curt. 655; *Brooke* v. *Haymes* (1868), L.R. 6 Eq. 25.

[5] Administration of Estates Act 1925, s. 7 (4).

  c. the failure of a person appointed executor to prove the will,[1]
  unless there is another executor of that will who does prove;

  d. where there is *any* difference in the number of executors.

This last point may be illustrated by a further example. Suppose that Edward dies, appointing Fred and Frank to be his executors. Suppose also that only Frank proves the will, and that he dies leaving Gerald his proving executor. Gerald is the executor by representation of Edward. If Fred dies, or renounces probate Gerald's position is secure. If, however, Fred subsequently proves the will with Frank[2] the identity of representatives is broken at that time, and Gerald will then cease to be executor by representation of Edward's estate.

Where a person obtains a limited grant of probate[3] and he dies, appointing a full executor who proves, that executor is the executor by representation of the original testator.[4] On the other hand, if a person takes a limited grant to the estate of a full executor, he does not become the executor by representation of the original testator.[5]

Where a Scottish confirmation is obtained[6] that does not operate as a grant of probate for the purpose of this rule so that a Scottish grant will not cause the chain of representation to pass through it.[7] It appears, however, that a Northern Ireland grant of probate is treated as a grant of Probate.[8]

The rule is of considerable practical importance. If a person becomes executor by representation, he becomes so automatically, and no further formality is required. If a deceased's estate is not fully administered, and there is no executor by representation, the whole procedure of a new grant—in this case letters of administration *de bonis non*[9]—must be followed.

---

[1] Administration of Estates Act 1925, s. 7 (3).

[2] The original grant would have reserved him the power to prove at some subsequent time.

[3] *Post*, p. 283.

[4] *In the Goods of Beer* (1851), 2 Rob. Eccl. 349.

[5] *In the Goods of Bayne* (1858), 1 Sw. & Tr. 132; *In the Goods of Bridger* (1878), 4 P.D. 77.

[6] See *post*, p. 281.

[7] Administration of Estates Act 1971, s. 1 (3).

[8] *Ibid.*, s. 1 (4).

[9] See *post*, p. 285.

C. THE OFFICE OF EXECUTOR

1. PERSONAL NATURE

The general principle mentioned at the beginning of this chapter, that the office of executor is personal, is shown by the fact that it is non-assignable.[1] Even if the executor employs agents to carry out part of the work[2] he must always make the executive decisions.[3]

The general rule is broken by the operation of the chain of representation, which in effect causes a devolution of the office.

2. PERSONS WHO MAY BE APPOINTED

A testator may appoint whoever he likes to be his executor. Thus, he can appoint an infant, a person of unsound mind, a bankrupt[4] or an alien.[5] If the person under this incapacity is one of two or more executors probate is granted to the others, with power reserved[6] to the one under disability to prove when the disability ceases. If he is the sole executor, a grant of administration is made to his guardian or other person on his behalf. He may still apply for probate when the disability ceases.[7]

Special rules apply where the person appointed is an infant or person of unsound mind. So far as an infant is concerned, probate cannot be issued until he reaches the age of 18[8] and his appointment as executor by the will does not give him any interest in the deceased's property until probate is granted subsequent to him attaining 18.[9] Accordingly, he cannot even dispose of such items as personal chattels for which a grant is not normally required.[10]

Similarly, probate will not issue to a person of unsound mind

---

[1] *In the Goods of Galbraith*, [1951] P. 422; *Re Skinner*, [1958] 3 All E.R. 273.
[2] Under Trustee Act 1925, s. 23.
[3] Parker & Mellows, The Modern Law of Trusts, p. 200.
[4] *R.* v. *Raines* (1698), Carth. 457; *Hill* v. *Mills* (1691), 1 Show. 293. This is subject to Wills Act 1968, s. 1 (1).
[5] Status of Aliens Act 1914, s. 17, as amended.
[6] See *post*, p. 293.
[7] See *post*, p. 292.
[8] Judicature Act 1925, s. 165 (1).
[9] *Ibid.*, s. 165 (2).
[10] See *post*, Ch. 24.

or to a person suffering from some physical disability if the court is satisfied that he is incapable of managing his affairs.[1]

A corporation sole may be an executor.[2] Where a corporation aggregate which is a trust corporation is appointed, the grant of probate may be to that corporation in its own name and it may act as a sole executor, or jointly with an individual executor.[3] In the case of a corporation aggregate which is not a trust corporation, it cannot take a grant in its own name, but probate will be granted to its nominee.[4] However, before such grant is issued, it must be shown that the corporation has power under its constitution to act as personal representatives[5] and it is necessary to lodge with the court a copy of the resolution appointing the nominee.[6]

Where an unincorporated body is appointed, such as a firm of solicitors, in the absence of a contrary intention shown on the face of the will, the grant is made to members of the firm at the date of death.[7] This is usually inconvenient, and it is therefore important to express a contrary intention in the will itself.

3. NUMBERS OF EXECUTORS

A testator may appoint only one executor, and in that case that executor will have full power to deal with the estate. He may appoint any number of executors, but probate can only be granted to four executors in respect of the same property.[8] Subject to this principle, there is no restriction on numbers. So, four persons can be appointed executors in respect of personal property and four persons to deal with realty, or the assets can be split between them in any other way the testator wishes.

In *In the Estate of Holland*[9] a testator appointed four persons to be his general executors, and a fifth to be his literary executor. Bucknill, J., on appeal from the registrar, refused to grant probate

---

[1] Non-contentious Probate Rules 1954, r. 33; Non-contentious Probate (Amendment) Rules 1967, r. 2 (13).

[2] *Re Haynes* (1842), 3 Curt. 75.

[3] Judicature Act 1925, s. 161.

[4] *In the Goods of Hunt*, [1896] P. 288; Non-contentious Probate Rules 1954, r. 34 (3).

[5] *Practice Direction*, [1956] 1 W.L.R. 127.

[6] Non-contentious Probate Rules 1954, r. 34 (3).

[7] *In Re Horgan*, [1971] P. 50; cf. *In the Goods of Fernie* (1849), 6 Notes of Cases 657.

[8] Judicature Act 1925, s. 160 (1).

[9] [1936] 3 All E.R. 13.

save and except the literary works to the four, and to grant probate limited to literary works to the fifth, on the ground that under the will the general executors were appointed executors of the whole estate, so that in respect of the literary works there were in fact five executors.

Where more than one person is appointed executor, there need be no collaboration between them in obtaining a grant. Anyone can apply for probate without consulting the others. Probate will be granted to that one alone, with power reserved to the others to prove subsequently. Until such time as the others prove, the one who has probate has full authority.

D. MODES OF APPOINTMENT OF EXECUTORS

1. EXPRESS APPOINTMENT

In general, no problem arises with an express appointment. If, however, the appointment is not clear, the rules which apply to uncertainty of executor are:

a. where there is a person who fits exactly the name and description given in the will, the court will not admit extrinsic evidence to show that some other person was intended;[1]

b. the court will always have regard to the surrounding circumstances existing at the time when the will was made; in other words it will apply the armchair rule;[2]

c. extrinsic evidence of the testator's intention will be admitted to identify the executor where there is a latent ambiguity[3] but not where there is a patent ambiguity.[4] Thus in *In the Estate of Hubbock*[5] there was an appointment as executrix of "my granddaughter". There were in fact three granddaughters. This was a latent ambiguity, and evidence was admitted to identify the one intended by the testator. On the other hand, in *In the Goods of Blackwell*[6] where the executrix

---

[1] *In the Goods of Peel* (1870), L.R. 2 P. & D. 46.

[2] *Grant* v. *Grant* (1869), L.R. 2 P. & D. 8; *In the Goods of De Rosaz* (1877), 2 P.D. 66; *In the Goods of Twohill* (1879), 3 L.R. Ir. 21; *In the Goods of Brake* (1881), 6 P.D. 217.

[3] *In the Goods of Ashton*, [1892] P. 83.

[4] *In the Goods of Blackwell* (1877), 2 P.D. 72.

[5] [1905] P. 129.

[6] (1877), 2 P.D. 72.

was "one of my sisters" this was a patent ambiguity and evidence was not admitted.

If the executor is appointed by reference to his office, then in the absence of evidence to the contrary, probate will be granted to the holder of that office at the date of death, and not at the date of the will.[1]

2. IMPLIED APPOINTMENTS

An executor may be appointed by implication, in which case he is known as the "executor according to the tenor of the will". In order for a person to be appointed as executor according to the tenor, it must be shown that the testator intended him to discharge the major functions of an executor. In *In the Goods of Adamson*[2] the principal duties of an executor were stated to be:

a. getting in the assets of the deceased;

b. payment of funeral expenses and debts (including payment of estate duty[3]);

c. payment of legacies; and

d. accounting for the residuary estate.

What the testator envisaged that a person would do is a question of construction, but the following are examples of cases where a person has been held to be so appointed:

a. *In the Goods of Russell*[4] where the testator appointed trustees "to carry out my will";

b. *In the Goods of Baylis*[5] where a person was given all the testator's personalty, upon trust for sale and conversion, coupled with a direction to pay debts and funeral and testamentary expenses;

c. *In the Estate of Fawcett*[6] where the will contained the words "all else to be sold and proceeds after death . . . B will do this";

---

[1] *In the Estate of Jones* (1927), 43 T.L.R. 324.

[2] (1875), L.R. 3 P. & D. 253.

[3] In this case estate duty was not mentioned, as the present system is governed by the Finance Act 1894.

[4] [1892] P. 380.

[5] (1865), L.R. 1 P. & D. 21.

[6] [1941] P. 85.

d. *In the Goods of Cook*[1] where a person was appointed "to pay all my just debts". This must be carefully distinguished from the situation where a legatee is directed to pay debts, in which case the effect of the will may be only to make the legacies subject to the payment of debts.[2]

It is most important to note that a person is not appointed an executor according to the tenor merely because he is the universal or residuary beneficiary.[3] A man may, for example, wish his wife to take all his property, and yet regard her as being completely hopeless when it comes to administering financial matters.

Once it is clear that a person is appointed an executor according to the tenor, he is in exactly the same position as any other executor. Thus, where a person is expressly appointed executor, and another is appointed executor according to the tenor, probate will be granted to them both.[4]

3. CONDITIONAL APPOINTMENTS

An appointment may be made subject to a condition precedent or a condition subsequent. Thus, the appointment may be conditional upon a child attaining a specified age;[5] or upon another named person refusing to act as executor.[6] *In the Goods of Lane*[7] is an example of appointment subject to a condition subsequent. The will provided that if the executor should go abroad, his appointment should lapse, and another should take his place. The court gave effect to this provision.

4. LIMITED APPOINTMENTS

A testator may appoint executors to deal with property only of a special designation. There may be geographical limitation, such as an appointment to deal with "all my land in London", or "all my property in India". The appointment may be limited to "all my personalty".[8]

---

[1] [1902] P. 114.

[2] *In the Goods of Murphy* (1868), 18 L.T. 63.

[3] *In the Goods of Jones* (1861), 2 Sw. & Tr. 155; *Re Pryse*, [1904] P. 301.

[4] *In the Goods of Brown* (1877), 2 P.D. 110; *Re Lush* (1887), 13 P.D. 20; *In the Goods of Wright* (1908), 25 T.L.R. 15.

[5] *In the Goods of Langford* (1867), L.R. 1 P. & D. 458.

[6] *In the Goods of Betts* (1861), 30 L.J.P.M. & A. 167.

[7] (1864), 33 L.J.P. M. & A. 185; see also *In the Estate of Freeman* (1931), 146 L.T. 143.

[8] *In the Goods of Wallich* (1864), 3 Sw. & Tr. 423.

Special rules apply to settled land.[1]

An appointment may also be for a limited time. The usual examples are during the absence abroad of another person; during the minority of a child; or during the widowhood of the spouse. The appointment may, however, be limited as regards time in any way, so that it can commence in the future. Thus, an appointment of Simon if and when he shall qualify as a solicitor would be valid.

5. EXECUTOR DE SON TORT

An "executor de son tort" is a person who acts as if he had been appointed an executor although in fact he is not appointed as such, either expressly or by implication. He cannot obtain a grant of probate. The position of an executor de son tort is considered later.[2]

E. ACCEPTANCE AND RENUNCIATION

1. ACCEPTANCE

The normal way of accepting office is by applying for probate, but just as slight acts will be sufficient to make a person liable as an executor de son tort,[3] so slight acts will be sufficient to enable the court to find that an executor has accepted office. Examples of such acts are taking possession of some of the deceased's goods; collecting or releasing debts;[4] and advertising for claims against the estate under Trustee Act 1925, s. 27.[5] On the other hand, acts of mere humanity, such as arranging for the burial of the corpse[6] or feeding the deceased's children or cattle[7] will not be sufficient to show that a person has accepted office.

Apart from the case where he has actually accepted office, a person appointed in the will to be an executor cannot be compelled to take out a grant of probate. This is so even if during the lifetime of the testator he agreed to act as executor.[8]

---

[1] See *post*, p. 358.
[2] *Post*, p. 396.
[3] *Ibid.*
[4] *Stokes* v. *Porter* (1558), 2 Dyer 166b; *Pytt* v. *Fendall* (1754), 1 Lee 553.
[5] *Long and Feaver* v. *Symes and Hannan* (1832), 3 Hag. Ecc. 771.
[6] *Harrison* v. *Rowley* (1798), 4 Ves. 212.
[7] *Long and Feaver* v. *Symes and Hannan* (1832), 3 Hag. Ecc. 771.
[8] *Doyle* v. *Blake* (1804), 2 Sch. & Lef. 231; see Lord Redesdale at p. 239.

Where the person appointed as executor takes no action, and another person wishes to apply for a grant, a citation may issue against the executor to compel him to decide whether to accept or refuse. Where he has intermeddled a citation may be issued against him to compel him to take a grant,[1] failure to comply with which can lead to contempt of court.[2]

2. RENUNCIATION

Section 5 of the Administration of Estates Act 1925 provides, in effect, that a person who is appointed to be an executor may renounce probate, and that if he does so, he loses all his rights as executor and that as regards representation, the will is read as if he had never been appointed executor. A renunciation of the office of executor does not affect any other appointment which he is given in the will, so that where a person who is appointed executor and trustee renounces probate he is still entitled to act as trustee.[3]

With one exception the renunciation must be of the whole office. He cannot, therefore, renounce office as respects certain property only and, as has been shown, he cannot accept one executorship, and renounce other executorships which devolve with it under the chain of representation. In this case the executor may consider renouncing probate and applying for a grant of letters of administration. The position with regard to this is as follows. It will be shown[4] that if an administrator renounces his rights, he cannot without the leave of the court[5] obtain a grant of administration in a lower capacity.[6] By contrast, where an executor renounces probate he does not thereby renounce any right to apply for letters of administration.[7] Thus, in *In the Estate of Toscani*[8] the executor renounced, and letters of administration *cum testamento annexo* were granted to the residuary legatee.

---

[1] See, e.g. *In the Estate of Biggs*, [1966] P. 118.

[2] Contempt lies in failure to comply with an order to take a grant issued as a result of the citation.

[3] *Re Gordon, Roberts* v. *Gordon* (1877), 6 Ch.D. 531; *Re Clout and Frewer's Contract*, [1924] 2 Ch. 230.

[4] See *post*, p. 250.

[5] Non-contentious Probate Rules 1954, r. 35 (2).

[6] See *post*, p. 251.

[7] *In the Goods of Russell* (1869), L.R. 1 P. & D. 634.

[8] [1912] P. 1.

He died without fully administering the estate, and it was necessary to apply for a grant of letters of administration *cum testamento annexo et de bonis non.* The executor who had renounced was held entitled to such a grant as a creditor of the estate.

The exception to the principle that a person must renounce entirely or not at all applies to settled land. Under the Administration of Estates Act 1925, s. 23 (1), a person who is appointed general executor may renounce his office in respect of settled land without renouncing it in respect of other property.

For the purposes of the Administration of Estates Act 1925, s. 5 and the Non-contentious Probate Rules 1954, the term "renunciation" means a formal renunciation in writing, signed by the person who renounces, and lodged at the probate registry. Until that time the renunciation is ineffective and may be retracted at will.[1]

Once a formal renunciation has been made, it may be retracted only with the consent of the court.[2] The court has adopted the principle of allowing the retraction of a renunciation only if it can be shown to be for the benefit of the estate or of those interested under the will. In *In the Goods of Gill*[3] an executor who renounced received incorrect legal advice as to the effect of renunciation. He applied to retract, but was not allowed to do so, because it could not be shown that this would be for the benefit of the estate.[4] Where the court grants leave to retract, the retraction is made without prejudice to the previous acts and dealings of any other personal representatives who had taken out a grant of representation.

F. ADMINISTRATION WITH WILL

Where the deceased left a will, but there is no proving executor, a grant of administration *cum testamento annexo* is made. The long established principle is that the right to a grant of administration should follow the right of property.[5] In accordance with

---

[1] *In the Goods of Morant* (1874), L.R. 3 P. & D. 151.

[2] *Melville* v. *Ancketill* (1909), 25 T.L.R. 655.

[3] (1873), L.R. 3 P. & D. 113.

[4] See also *In the Goods of Stiles,* [1898] P. 12; *In the Estate of Heathcote,* [1913] P. 42.

[5] *In the Goods of Gill* (1828), 1 Hag. Ecc. 341; see also Judicature Act 1925, s. 162.

this principle, the order of priority of grants of administration with will annexed is[1]

(i) Trustees of the residuary estate (because their function is most nearly equated with that of the executor. They take no benefit as such, and occupy a fiduciary position.)

(ii) Persons having a life interest in the whole of the residue; or in the residuary realty or residuary personalty.

(iii) (a) ultimate residuary beneficiaries; or
   (b) where the residue is not wholly disposed of by will, the persons who take substantially the whole of the residue or who are entitled on intestacy, including the Treasury Solicitor acting on behalf of the Crown as the Person entitled to the assets as *bona vacantia* or, in either case the personal representative of any such person.[2] Thus, where the deceased leaves his estate to be divided into two equal shares, and one share lapses, the persons entitled to a grant will be equally the person entitled to the other share, and the person entitled on intestacy.

(iv) (a) specific legatees;
   (b) specific devisees;
   (c) creditors; or
   (d) the personal representative of any such person.

(v) (a) contingent beneficiaries;
   (b) persons who have no interest under the will, but who would be entitled on intestacy.

G. RIGHT TO GRANT WHERE TOTAL INTESTACY

Where there is no will, the following persons and in the following order are entitled to a grant of administration:

(i) The surviving spouse, or if he or she has not taken out a grant before death, his or her personal representative.

---

[1] Non-contentious Probate Rules 1954, r. 19.
[2] Subject to preference being given to living persons. See Non-contentious Probate Rules 1954, r. 25 (3), and *post*, p. 258.

Exceptionally, if the surviving spouse has died without taking a beneficial interest in the whole estate of the deceased, his or her personal representative has no prior right to apply for a grant.

(ii) The children of the deceased, or the issue of any child who died during the lifetime of the deceased.[1]

(iii) The father and mother of the deceased; or the mother alone of an illegitimate person.[2]

(iv) The brothers and sisters of the whole blood, or the issue of any brother or sister.[3]

If there is no person within these categories then any of the following may apply if they have a beneficial interest in the estate. This can only be the case where the deceased did not leave a surviving spouse:

(v) The brothers and sisters of the half blood, or the issue of any of them.[3]

(vi) Grandparents.

(vii) Uncles and aunts of the whole blood, or the issue of any of them[3]

(viii) Uncles and aunts of the half blood, or the issue of any of them.[3]

If there is no person in any of the above categories, or if they have all been cleared off, then a grant may issue to

(ix) The Treasury Solicitor, claiming *bona vacantia* on behalf of the Crown; or

(x) A creditor; or

(xi) Any person who has no immediate beneficial interest in the estate, but who may have such an interest in the event of an accretion to the estate. This will apply where the estate is so small that it is taken wholly by the spouse, but where, in the event of an increase in the size of the estate, others would then acquire a beneficial interest.

In each case it is for the applicant for the grant to prove his entitlement. A neat illustration of this arose in *Re Seaford,*

---

[1] Children includes illegitimate as well as legitimated and adopted children; Non-contentious Probate Rules 1954, r. 21 (4), substituted by Non-contentious Probate (Amendment) Rules 1969, Sched., para. 3.

[2] Non-contentious Probate (Amendment) Rules 1969.

[3] Non-contentious Probate Rules 1954, r. 21, substituted by Non-contentious Probate (Amendment) Rules 1969, Sched., para. 3.

Seaford v. *Seifert*.[1] In that case a wife obtained a decree nisi of divorce in March 1965, and in July 1965 her solicitors applied for the decree to be made absolute. It was found as a fact that the respondent husband took an overdose of sodium amytal tablets at some time between 9 p.m., 5th July and 4 a.m., 6th July. The decree was in fact made absolute at 10.00 a.m. on 6th July, but there is an old rule[2] that a judgment or order takes effect from the first moment of the day on which it was made. As the wife could not prove that the husband died before 00.01 a.m., Cairns, J., held that she had not discharged the burden of proof upon her, and refused to make a grant in her favour. However, the decision was reversed by the Court of Appeal[3] on the ground that as the deceased had undoubtedly died by 4 a.m., no effective application for a decree to be made absolute could be made, so that the doctrine of relation back did not apply.

H. GRANTS IN SPECIAL CIRCUMSTANCES

1. POWER TO DEPART FROM ORDER

The rules just considered, as to the persons entitled to grants of administration either with or without the will annexed, are subject to the overriding discretion of the court to make a grant of administration to such persons as it thinks fit. This power is conferred by Judicature Act 1925,[4] s. 162 (1) (b) which gives the court a discretion to depart from the normal order, and to make a grant of administration to such person as it considers expedient, in cases where it appears to be necessary or expedient by reason of the insolvency of the estate "or of any other special circumstance".

Section 162 of the Judicature Act 1925, as amended, replaced s. 73, Court of Probate Act 1857, and the scope of the section can be illustrated by cases under both Acts. The cases may be grouped into the following categories.

---

[1] [1967] 2 All E.R. 458 (first instance).
[2] *Ibid.*, at p. 461.
[3] [1968] 1 All E.R. 482.
[4] As amended by Administration of Justice Act 1928, s. 9.

a. *Person entitled incapable of acting*

Where the person entitled to a grant is incapable of acting, he will often be prepared to renounce, leaving the person next entitled in a position to obtain the grant. The person with the prior right may not be prepared to renounce, however, if he has no confidence in the person with the inferior right. In this case, he may appoint nominees to apply for a grant. In *In the Estate of Davis*[1] the person with the prior right was the sole executrix, and person entitled to the whole of the estate. Ill-health prevented her from acting, and her nominees were successful in obtaining a grant. The court will, however, probably be reluctant to exercise its discretion in such circumstances unless the unsuitability of the person next entitled can be proved, or unless, as in *In the Estate of Davis*, the person next entitled has no beneficial interest.

b. *Considerations of public policy*

Just as public policy demands that a person who has caused the death of a person by certain acts, such as murder and manslaughter, cannot take a benefit,[2] so by committing such an act the wrong-doer also may lose the right to a grant of representation. In *In the Estate of Crippen*[3] Crippen was convicted of murdering his wife, and was subsequently executed. His wife died intestate, and in normal circumstances her husband would have been entitled to a grant, and, as he was dead, that right would devolve on his personal representatives. In this case, however, a grant was made to the next of kin of the wife, and not to the personal representatives of the husband.

In the Estate of Crippen was followed in *Re S.*[4] where a husband made a will appointing his wife to be his sole executrix and beneficiary. The wife was convicted of the manslaughter of her husband and a grant was made to the deceased's daughters. Baker, J., appeared to place equal weight on the fact of the wife's conviction and the fact that because she was serving a term of life imprisonment it was "quite impossible"[5] for her to act as executrix.

---

[1] [1906] P. 330.
[2] See *post*, p. 470.
[3] [1911] P. 108.
[4] [1967] 2 All E.R. 150.
[5] [1967] 2 All E.R. 150 at p. 152. However, the judge appears to have overstated the position: the wife could have appointed agents, herself taking the basic decisions in prison.

c. *Person entitled refusing to act*

Where a person having a right to apply for a grant refuses to do so, but also refuses to renounce, the person next entitled may cite him to accept or refuse a grant,[1] or, where he has already intermeddled, he may be cited to accept a grant.[2] However, a citation to accept or refuse a grant may be issued only at the instance of a person having an inferior right to a grant, and a citation to accept a grant where the citee is an executor who has intermeddled[3] may also be issued at the instance of anyone interested in the estate. Where it is not possible to use this procedure, or in other cases where it is expedient to do so, an application may be made under s. 162. Thus, in *In the Goods of Knight*[4] where a person had a claim for damages for personal injuries, and was unable to proceed because the next of kin failed to apply for a grant, he successfully applied for the appointment of the Official Solicitor as administrator. The Official Solicitor, however, can be appointed only with his consent. Where he refuses consent, a grant may be made to the claimants' nominee.[5]

Special problems have arisen where a solicitor who is a sole practitioner dies, and no grant is taken out to his estate. In these circumstances, the court will entertain applications from a nominee of The Law Society for a grant.[6] Similar considerations would presumably apply in the case of the death of sole practitioners in other professions.

d. *Person entitled unsuitable*

The most frequent example of unsuitability to take a grant is mental or physical illness, but any other factor, such as a completely irrational approach to the estate will make the applicant unsuitable. A case which contained both aspects is *In the Estate of Biggs*.[7] The testator appointed by his will a husband and wife as joint executors. The estate was small, and the husband gave effect to the terms of the will, but without obtaining probate. Subsequently, it became necessary to obtain a grant, and the

---

[1] See *post*, p. 280.
[2] *Ibid.*
[3] Non-contentious Probate Rules 1954, r. 46 (3).
[4] [1939] 3 All E.R. 928.
[5] *In the Estate of Simpson*, [1936] P. 40.
[6] *Practice Direction*, [1965] 1 All E.R. 923.
[7] [1966] P. 118.

executor refused. As he had, by administering the estate, inter-meddled, a citation was issued to him to take a grant. He failed to appear to the citation, and an order was made that he should apply for and obtain a grant of probate. The executor ignored that order, and an application was made for his committal for contempt. When the hearing of the summons for committal was heard, it appeared that the executor was over 70 and seriously ill, but furthermore, that he had developed an overbearing sense of hostility to the estate, so that, according to Rees, J., he had "allowed his sense of grievance to overcome his judgment". This sense of hostility is illustrated by the executor's attitude towards the articled clerk who served the court order on him. In his affidavit, the articled clerk said: "I had made several visits to the citee's house without being able to meet him, and on June 14 I could get no reply except that a man whom I assumed was Mr. Glew (the citee) was standing behind the front door shouting abusive language and threats which were directed to me and a colleague who was with me, and I could not persuade him to open the door. Finally, I propelled the copy order . . . through the letter box, and I could see as I did so that it came into contact with Mr. Glew who was immediately behind the door. Mr. Glew at once opened the door picked up the copy order at the same time and he then proceeded to kick the copy order into the gutter of the road outside his house. I and my colleague retreated quickly down the road but Mr. Glew and his wife pursued us and it was only due to the intervention of a police constable that we were able to escape them." The court was therefore faced in this case with the situation where an executor had intermeddled, but it dis-charged its previous order and exercised its power under s. 162 to pass over the executor, and to make a grant to the applicant.

e. *Other cases*

It is not possible to give an exhaustive categorization of the "other special circumstances" for the purposes of s. 162. Other examples in which the power has been used are where, during wartime, the person entitled was an enemy alien,[1] and where,

---

[1] *In the Estate of Schiff*, [1915] P. 86; *In the Estate of Grundt*, [1915] P. 126; *In the Estate of Sanpietro*, [1941] P. 16.

following a dispute between the next of kin as to who should take a grant, a grant was made to their nominee.[1]

2. RESTRICTIONS ON SECTION 162

It seems that s. 162 governs only situations which are not otherwise specifically provided for, and that it cannot be used to override other statutory provisions. This was established in *Re Hall*.[2] Section 160 of the Judicature Act, requires that where a minority or life interest will arise, a grant of administration (but not of probate) must be made to two persons or to a trust corporation.[3] In *Re Hall* the deceased had died intestate at the age of 79, survived by several brothers and sisters. One of the brothers applied for a grant, and the other brothers and sisters all renounced. Over 40 years before his death he had entered into a deed of separation and his wife then went to Canada with their child. Nothing had been heard of either of them since. Willmer, J., held that as there was a possibility of the wife still being alive, and being entitled to a life interest, two administrators should be appointed. Accordingly, both the applicant and his wife were appointed.

Further, according to Willmer, J., in *In the Goods of Edwards-Taylor*[4] the expression "special circumstance" relates only to circumstances affecting the estate or its administration, not to circumstances affecting the beneficiary. While this dictum may go too far, it is clear that the court will not use s. 162 to interfere even indirectly with beneficial ownership. In *In the Goods of Edwards-Taylor* the beneficiary who was entitled to a considerable fortune under the will was said to be immature and unfitted to look after the money. An attempt was made to obtain a limited grant in favour of a trust corporation, but that was unsuccessful.

3. GENERAL DISCRETION OF THE COURT

In addition to the power under s. 162, the court has an inherent discretion to make a grant to whomsoever it wishes[5] but almost certainly it will now rely entirely upon s. 162.

---

[1] *Re Morgans* (1931), 47 T.L.R. 452.
[2] [1950] P. 156.
[3] See *post*, p. 259.
[4] [1951] P. 24, at p. 27.
[5] *Re Schwerdtfeger* (1876), 1 P.D. 424.

I. MORE THAN ONE PERSON ENTITLED

It is common for more than one person of the same degree to be entitled to a grant. For example, if there is no spouse but several children, all have an equal right. Any person so entitled may make an application without notice to the others, and may obtain a grant in his own name alone.[1] Where another person of the same degree wishes to prevent this happening, he may enter a caveat.[2]

1. DISAGREEMENT AS TO PERSON TO TAKE

Where there is a dispute between those entitled, the court adopts the following principles:

(i) The primary rule is that the grant is to be made to the person who is likely to deal with it best from the point of view of the creditors and beneficiaries.[3] Although usually expressed in this way, however, the result is that in effect all appointments will be regarded as likely to do equally as well for the beneficiaries and creditors unless there is a reason for *not* appointing a particular person. Examples of such reasons are the bankruptcy or insolvency of the applicant;[4] his general badness of character;[5] and, during wartime, his status as an enemy alien.[6]

(ii) Subject to that, the court will issue the grant to the person who has the largest beneficial interest; or the person whom the majority of members of the same degree favour.[7]

(iii) It used to be said that the eldest child would be preferred to the younger ones, unless the majority of them favoured another child,[8] and that subject to the same exception, sons would be preferred to daughters.[9] It is doubtful whether these considerations still operate.

(iv) "Live interests are preferred to dead." Rule 25 (3), Non-

---

[1] Non-contentious Probate Rules 1954, r. 25 (1).
[2] See *post*, p. 279.
[3] *Warwick* v. *Greville* (1809), 1 Phillim. 123, at p. 125.
[4] *Hill* v. *Mills* (1691), 1 Show. 293; *Bell* v. *Timiswood* (1812), 2 Phillim. 22; *Re Bowron* (1914), 84 L.J.P. 92.
[5] *In the Estate of Frost*, [1905] P. 140.
[6] *In the Estate of Sanpietro*, [1941] P. 16.
[7] *Budd* v. *Silver* (1813), 2 Phillim. 115.
[8] *Warwick* v. *Greville* (1809), 1 Phillim. 123.
[9] *Iredale* v. *Ford and Bramworth* (1859), 1 Sw. & Tr. 305.

contentious Probate Rules 1954, provides that as a general principle administration shall be granted to a living person rather than to the personal representative of a dead person entitled in the same degree. Thus, if a widower has two sons, one of whom predeceases him, administration will be granted to the son who survives in preference to the personal representative of the one who predeceases.

(v) If one applicant is of full capacity, and another is not, then the one of full age will be preferred to those representing the one who is not.[1]

2. NUMBER OF ADMINISTRATORS

When an application is made for a grant of administration, the applicant in his oath must swear whether, to the best of his knowledge and belief, a life interest or minority arises under the will or intestacy. The court acts on this oath, and where there is a minority or life interest, Judicature Act 1925, s. 160 (1) requires the grant to be made to two persons or to a trust corporation. This rule does not apply to probate. It seems that in such a case it is necessary to have two administrators, even if the estate is insolvent.[2]

Where there is only one administrator, either because the existence of a life interest or minority has subsequently become known, or because another administrator has died, then the court may appoint an additional administrator upon the application of any person interested.[3]

Section 160 (1) of the Judicature Act 1925, also provides that neither administration nor probate shall be granted to more than four persons in respect of the same property.[4]

J. GRANTS TO SPECIAL PERSONS

1. THE CROWN

Section 46 of the Administration of Estates Act 1925, limits the class of persons who can succeed to the property of an intestate to

---

[1] Non-contentious Probate Rules 1954, r. 25 (3).
[2] *Re White*, [1928] P. 75; cf. *Re Herbert*, [1926] P. 109 to the contrary.
[3] Judicature Act 1925, s. 160 (2).
[4] See *ante*, p. 244, for position as to probate.

those who are descended from one of his grandparents. Even in the absence of any relations within that class, more distant relations cannot take, and the Crown is entitled. In such circumstances the grant is made to the Treasury Solicitor. Where the deceased was resident in the Duchy of Lancaster or the Duchy of Cornwall, the grant is made to the solicitor to the appropriate Duchy.

2. CREDITORS

If no other person makes an application for a grant, a creditor may do so. The creditor's right is the lowest in priority, and he must therefore first cite everyone having a prior right (excluding the Crown where it has no beneficial interest) before he can take a grant himself. Where the creditor believes that the deceased left no relatives entitled to take, he is required to cite, in general terms, all persons claiming a right to share in the estate, and to serve that citation by means of advertisement. A copy of the advertisement must be delivered to the Treasury Solicitor.

Any creditor is entitled to apply, even if his debt is unenforceable as being barred by the Limitation Acts.[1] Creditors whose debts accrued after death or who took an assignment of the debt after death[2] are entitled to apply. A liquidator is entitled to apply for a grant to the estate of a contributory[3] on the winding up[4] and a trustee in bankruptcy of a creditor may obtain a grant.[5]

If there is a dispute between creditors, preference will generally be given to the one:

a. who has the greatest debts;[6] or
b. who is favoured by the majority of creditors.

3. PERSON HAVING A *spes successionis*

Under Non-contentious Probate Rules 1954, rule 27, a person having a *spes successionis* may apply for a grant. The rule provides that if the beneficial interest in the whole estate of the deceased is vested absolutely in a person who has renounced his right to a

---

[1] *Coombs* v. *Coombs* (1866), L.R. 1 P. & D. 288.
[2] *Newcombe* v. *Beloe* (1867), L.R. 1 P. & D. 314.
[3] A contributory is a member of the company liable to contribute towards its deficiency on winding up.
[4] Companies Act 1948, s. 245.
[5] *Downward* v. *Dickinson* (1864), 3 Sw. & Tr. 564.
[6] *Re Smith* (1892), 67 L.T. 503.

grant, then, if he consents, administration may be granted to the persons who would be entitled to the estate if he himself died intestate. Suppose that Howard is the sole person entitled to the estate of his brother George. Suppose also that Howard has a wife and two children, and that he himself renounces his right to the grant. If Howard consents his wife and children can jointly apply for a grant to the estate of George.

A surviving spouse is not entitled to apply by himself unless he or she would be entitled to the whole of the estate, whatever its value.[1]

4. ASSIGNEE

A *spes* grant is issued where the person beneficially entitled retains his beneficial interest, but renounces only his right to a grant. Where, however, the only person who is entitled to the beneficial interest in the estate assigns that interest, the assignee stands in the position of the assignor for the purpose of applying for a grant.[2] The same rule applies where there is more than one person entitled to the estate, and they all assign to the same assignee. Where there is more than one assignor, the assignee stands in the position of the assignor with the highest priority.

An assignee is only entitled to a grant where he is entitled to the whole beneficial interest. Where a person is entitled only to part of the beneficial interest, the assignee does not thereby become entitled to take a grant.

5. ATTESTING WITNESS

Where a beneficiary named in a will, or his spouse, attests the will, he is not entitled to take his beneficial interest.[3] By attesting the will, he also loses his right to a grant in the capacity as a beneficiary, although he can apply for a grant in some other capacity, such as a creditor.[4] Presumably where the will is executed by two other persons, so that Wills Act 1968, s. 1 (1), applies, the beneficiary will not lose his right to the grant.

---

[1] Non-contentious Probate Rules 1954, r. 27, proviso (substituted by Non-contentious Probate (Amendment) Rules 1967, r. 2 (8)).

[2] *Ibid.*, r. 22 amended by Non-contentious Probate (Amendment) Rules 1967, r. 2 (4).

[3] *Ante*, p. 62.

[4] Non-contentious Probate Rules 1954, r. 20.

6. COMMORIENTES

The terms of Law of Property Act 1925, s. 184, which provides that where two persons die in circumstances making it uncertain which of them survived the other, they are presumed to have died in the order of seniority as will be seen.[1] The effect of this has, however, been modified by Administration of Estates Act 1925, s. 46 (3), which was introduced by the Intestates Act 1952. Under this sub-section, which applies only to spouses, for the purpose of the devolution of the intestate's estate, the other spouse is deemed not to have survived the intestate.

7. WHERE DECEASED DOMICILED ABROAD

Where the deceased did not die domiciled in England, the court will grant administration either to the person who is actually entrusted with the administration of the estate by the law of the deceased's domicile, or to the person entitled to administer in accordance with that law.[2] The court will require an affidavit of law showing the entitlement of the applicant.

In special cases, an application may be made under s. 162 to enable a grant to be made to the person who would have been entitled had the deceased died domiciled in England.

K. WHY THE RUSH?

In some cases difficulty is caused because the person entitled to a grant refuses to apply for it.[3] However, far more difficulties are caused because there is a struggle between two or more persons to obtain a grant.

There are, in appropriate cases, sound practical reasons for this. Thus:

    a. Where the estate is large enough to pay all debts and legacies, the personal representative may pay himself his legacy forthwith, even if he is not in a position to pay the other legacies until some time later.

---

[1] *Post*, p. 459.

[2] Non-contentious Probate Rules 1954, r. 29; *In the Estate of Kaufman,* [1952] P. 325.

[3] E.g., *In the Estate of Biggs, ante,* p. 255.

b. He may by becoming a personal representative perfect a previously imperfect gift. The rule known as the Rule in *Strong* v. *Bird*[1] is to the effect that a previously incomplete gift will be completed when the donee becomes personal representative.[2] The rule applies both where the personal representative becomes executor[3] and where he becomes administrator.

c. He may have little confidence in the qualities of the other persons who may be entitled to a grant, and prefer to attend to the administration himself.

But the major reason is usually non-legal—it is the power lust which leads to the desire to gain control; or the opportunity which this gives to enable the personal representative to poke into other people's affairs; or the desire to be seen as the distributor of largesse—other people's. There need be little surprise, therefore, that there is a large number of reported decisions arising from contests to become personal representative.

---

[1] (1874), L.R. 18 Eq. 315.

[2] *Strong* v. *Bird* (1874), L.R. 18 Eq. 315; *Re Stewart, Stewart* v. *McLaughlin,* [1908] 2 Ch. 251.

[3] *Re James, James* v. *James,* [1935] Ch. 449.

CHAPTER 17

NON-CONTENTIOUS PROBATE

A. DEFINITION

The practice of probate, which for this purpose includes obtaining grants of administration, is divided into two categories, contentious and non-contentious. Contentious business involves a contested action, such as to prove the validity of an alleged will,[1] while in non-contentious business a grant is made upon the affidavit of the applicant, but without a formal hearing. The great majority of business is non-contentious.

B. DOCUMENTS ADMISSIBLE TO PROBATE

Every document which is executed in accordance with the formal requirements of the Wills Act 1837, as amended, is entitled to be admitted to probate if it has a testamentary character. A document has a testamentary character if:

1. it disposes of property; or
2. if it appoints an executor;

and perhaps:

3. if it revokes a will; or
4. it appoints a guardian.

In every case, however, it is necessary to show that there was adequate mental capacity on the part of the testator, and that he intended that the document should operate on death.

---

[1] See *post*, p. 296, for a full statement of the matters which are described as contentious business.

1. DISPOSAL OF PROPERTY

In general, a document may only be admitted to probate if it disposes of property in England or Wales. If the document does not dispose of such property, but disposes of property exclusively elsewhere, the general rule is that that document will not be admitted to probate. The rule is because probate or letters of administration operate as orders of the court, and in principle the court has no jurisdiction over property outside England.

There are, however, two exceptions to this rule:

a. Where there is a special reason for obtaining a grant. It is provided by s. 2 (1), Administration of Justice Act 1932, that notwithstanding the general rule, the court may issue a grant where no English property is involved. This will only be done where it is needed for a particular purpose, and that purpose must be recited in the affidavit leading to the grant. In *In the Estate of Wayland*[1] the facts of which were given at p. 87, the court admitted to probate the will disposing only of Belgian property, because the effect of this had been called into question by the revocation clause in the subsequent English will.

b. Where the will disposing of foreign property is referred to in another will dealing with English property, and it is necessary for both to be admitted to probate so that they can be read together.[2] Where the wills can be read separately, the foreign will is not admitted to probate.[3]

Examples of cases where probate is granted of wills dealing only with foreign property are where the grant is required for production to a foreign court, or where the personal representative wishes to commence proceedings in England. In *Carter and Crosts Case*[4] an executor who had obtained probate in Ireland was compelled to take out an English grant before he could sue in the English courts even to recover Irish assets.[5]

---

[1] [1951] 2 All E.R. 1041.

[2] *In the Goods of Howden* (1874), 43 L.J.P. 26; *In the Goods of Astor* (1876), 1 P.D. 150; *In the Goods of Bolton* (1887), 12 P.D. 202; *In the Goods of Callaway* (1890), 15 P.D. 147; *In the Goods of Seaman,* [1891] P. 253; *In the Goods of Fraser,* [1891] P. 285.

[3] *In the Goods of Murray,* [1896] P. 65; *In the Estate of White Todd,* [1926] P. 173.

[4] (1600), Godb. 33.

[5] See also *Whyte* v. *Rose* (1842), 3 Q.B. 493.

2. APPOINTMENT OF EXECUTORS

A document which merely appoints executors is admissible to probate. This frequently happens in the case of codicils which have no other function.

3. REVOCATION OF WILL

In *Re Durance*[1] considered above,[2] the testator in Canada sent an attested letter to his brother in England asking him to collect the will and destroy it. This was effective to revoke the will, and Lord Penzance made a grant of administration with the letter of revocation annexed. In *Toomer* v. *Sobinska*,[3] however, the court made a grant of letters of administration, without the revoking instrument annexed, but incorporating in the grant a note that it was made as a result of the revocation of the earlier will. The latter approach is better, and was followed in *Re Howard, Howard* v. *Treasury Solicitor*.[4]

Even if the document is not admissible to probate, it is an effective revocation.

4. APPOINTMENT OF GUARDIAN

The power to appoint a testamentary guardian is conferred by the Guardianship of Minors Act 1971. There is no decision whether a document which only appoints a guardian is admissible to probate, although, for evidential reasons, it would be most desirable to do so. Under the pre-1926 law, it is clear that a document only appointing a guardian was not admissible.[5]

5. NEED TO PROVE ALL TESTAMENTARY INSTRUMENTS

The executor is under a duty to propound all testamentary instruments unless there is any serious reason to doubt their validity. The problem often arises where there is a dispute over the will, and agreement is reached between the parties concerned that one document should be left out. In *In the Goods of Watts*[6]

---

[1] (1872), L.R. 2 P. & D. 406.
[2] *Ante*, p. 86.
[3] [1907] P. 106.
[4] [1944] Ch. 39.
[5] *In the Goods of Morton* (1864), 3 Sw. & Tr. 422; *In the Estate of Tollemache*, [1917] P. 246.
[6] (1837), 1 Curt. 594.

a testator made a will after he had been found lunatic by inquisition. Almost all the persons interested in the estate agreed that the will should be ignored, and an application was made for letters of administration. Sir Herbert Jenner refused the application on the basis[1] that: "The consent of parties interested proves nothing; no person's consent can make a will no will".

The rule has been followed. So, in *Re Muirhead*[2] the testator made a will appointing his wife to be the sole executrix, and giving her all his property. He then made what appeared to be a valid codicil giving his secretary half his estate. There were certain negotiations between widow and secretary, which are only hinted at in the report, but the widow tried to avoid proving the codicil by citing the secretary to prove the codicil. The secretary did not appear to the citation, and the widow sought probate of the will alone. This was refused. Cairns, J., decided that the will and codicil should both have been brought before the court in an application for probate in solemn form.

C. PROBATE OF PART OF A WILL

1. NO *animus testandi*

If a document or part of a document was not executed *animo testandi* it will not be admitted to probate. This has been held to apply where a clause has been inserted by fraud[3] or by forgery.[4]

Where a mistake has been made, it is necessary to draw a clear distinction between two situations. If the testator knew and approved of a particular word or phrase, then that cannot be omitted from probate, even though it produces a result contrary to the testator's intention. If, on the other hand, part of the will is included without the knowledge or instructions of the testator, that part will be omitted. An illustration of the former principle is *Collins* v. *Elstone*.[5] The testatrix was misinformed as to the effect of a revocation clause. It was held, however, that as she knew that

---

[1] (1837), 1 Curt. 594, at p. 595.
[2] [1971] 1 All E.R. 609.
[3] *Barton* v. *Robins* (1769), 3 Phillim. 455 n.; *Allen* v. *McPherson* (1847), 1 H.L.C. 191.
[4] *Plume* v. *Beale* (1717), 1 P. Wms. 388.
[5] [1893] P. 1.

that clause was in the will, it must stand.[1] The second principle is illustrated by *In the Goods of Boehm*[2] where the name of a legatee was wrongly inserted in a will, and the will was not read over to the testator before execution. The name was omitted from probate.[3]

A good recent illustration of the rule is *Re Morris*.[4] By clause 3 of her will the testatrix made provision for her housekeeper, and by clause 7 gave a total of twenty pecuniary legacies. Sub-clause 7(iv) was a pecuniary legacy to the housekeeper. The testatrix wrote to her solicitor saying that she wished to revoke the provisions in favour of her housekeeper, and to make new provisions for her. The codicil should have read: "I revoke clauses 3 and 7(iv)" but owing to an error in the solicitor's office it in fact read "I revoke clauses 3 and 7". Latey, J., admitted the codicil to probate, but omitting the "7" in the revocation clause, basing his decision on two grounds. First, the testatrix did not know and approve the contents of the codicil, and secondly that the testatrix was not to be bound by a mistake which the draftsman had made where the mind of the draftsman had never really been applied to the words introduced, and never adverted to their significance and effect.

The judge admitted that attempts to reconcile all the earlier cases had, in the past, "produced intellectual gymnastics, if not acrobatics". He followed the dictum of Sachs, J., in *Crerar* v. *Crerar*[5] that the court must "consider all the relevant evidence available and then, drawing such inferences as it can from the totality of that material, it has to come to a conclusion whether or not those propounding the will have discharged the burden of establishing that the testatrix knew and approved the contents of the document which is put forward as a valid testamentary disposition."

The general rule remains that "there is no difference between the words which a testator himself uses in drawing up his will,

---

[1] This was criticized in *Lowthorpe-Lutwidge* v. *Lowthorpe-Lutwidge*, [1935] P. 151. See *ante*, p. 88.

[2] [1891] P. 247.

[3] *In the Goods of Oswald* (1874), L.R. 3 P. & D. 162; *Morrell* v. *Morrell* (1882), 7 P.D. 68; *In the Goods of Moore*, [1892] P. 378; *In the Goods of Reade*, [1902] P. 75.

[4] [1971] P. 62.

[5] (1956) Unreported, but see (1956), 106 L.J. 674.

and the words which are *bona fide* used by one whom he trusts to draw it up for him".[1] If, therefore, a word is used intentionally, even though its significance is not appreciated, the testator will be bound by it. But it seems that the courts will now be reluctant to hold a testator bound by words which the draftsman clearly inserted contrary to the intention of the testator.

There is one qualification to the rule that a word or phrase may be omitted if inserted without the testator's knowledge or intention. The court will not make the omission if to do so would alter the meaning of what remains.[2]

The court can omit, but it cannot insert. Accordingly even in the most obvious case, the court cannot go further than to grant probate with a blank, leaving the court of construction to give meaning to the document in that form if it is able to do so.[3]

If a clause is invalid because of an insane delusion, that clause will be omitted, even though probate may be granted of the remainder of the document. So in *In the Estate of Bohrmann*[4] the facts of which were stated earlier,[5] probate was granted of the will and all codicils, except the part of the last codicil affected by the insane delusion.

2. OFFENSIVE MATERIAL

In certain circumstances, the court will omit from probate words which are of no testamentary effect, whose omission will not alter the meaning of the remainder of the will, and which are offensive. Thus, words have been omitted because they are libellous or scandalous.[6] In *In the Goods of Bowker*[7] Lord Merrivale, P., omitted words relating to the mode of disposal of the bodily remains of the deceased on the ground that they were "offensive and objectionable, and repugnant to the members of the deceased's family, and unless omitted would be broadcast in

---

[1] *Per* Lord Blackburn in *Rhodes* v. *Rhodes* (1882), 7 App. Cas. 192, at pp. 199, 200.

[2] *Re Horrocks, Taylor* v. *Kershaw,* [1939] P. 198; *Rhodes* v. *Rhodes* (1882), 7 App. Cas. 192.

[3] *In the Goods of Schott,* [1901] P. 190; cf. *Re Bushell* (1877), 13 P.D. 7.

[4] [1938] 1 All E.R. 271.

[5] *Ante,* p. 38.

[6] *In the Estate of White,* [1914] P. 153; *Re Maxwell* (1929), 140 L.T. 471; *In the Estate of Hall,* [1943] 2 All E.R. 159.

[7] [1932] P. 93.

the press and particularly in the locality where the deceased was well known and where the dependent and other members of the family lived". The court, will, however, be reluctant to exercise its power even where the words cause offence,[1] particularly where there is any suggestion that the excision of the offending words might affect the construction of what remains. In *In the Estate of Rawlings*[2] there was a gift on certain trusts with the direction: "do not in any way give, lend or have anything to do with that rascal her husband, or any of her family, except Cyril her son", and an application to omit the words "that rascal". Sir Boyd Merriman, P., took the view that those words might be relevant to the construction of what remained, and refused to omit them.

Words will also be omitted from the probate copy where it is in the interest of national security.[3] This may be expected to happen in particular where a soldier manages to make and send an uncensored formal or privileged will from a theatre of war.

3. IMPORTANCE OF PROBATE COPY

Once probate has been granted, questions of construction will, in principle, depend on the probate copy. In general, reference cannot be made to the original will[4] except to see whether the probate copy is correct.[5] Exceptionally, however, the court will look at the original will in order to determine questions of construction. So, in *Re Battie-Wrightson, Cecil v. Battie-Wrightson*[6] a clause which contained reference to a bank was omitted from probate. A later clause, which was included, referred to "the said bank". The court referred to the original will to determine the identity of the bank. In any case where the Chancery Division goes behind the probate copy, it is to some extent usurping the jurisdiction of the probate court, but that may be expected in view of Chancery's history of pinching jurisdiction where it can.

---

[1] *In the Goods of Honywood* (1871), L.R. 2 P. & D. 251; *In the Estate of Caie* (1927), 43 T.L.R. 697.

[2] (1934), 78 Sol. Jo. 338.

[3] *In the Estate of Heywood*, [1916] P. 47.

[4] *Havergal* v. *Harrison* (1843), 7 Beav. 49; cf. *Oppenheim* v. *Henry* (1853), 9 Hare. 802; *Gann* v. *Gregory* (1854), 3 De G.M. & G. 777.

[5] *Compton* v. *Bloxham* (1845), 2 Coll. 201; *Shea* v. *Boschetti* (1854), 18 Beav. 321.

[6] [1920] 2 Ch. 330.

D. TIME FOR OBTAINING A GRANT

A grant of probate or letters of administration with will annexed may be obtained at any time after seven days from the date of death, and a grant of letters of administration may be obtained at any time after fourteen days from death.[1] These time limits are intended to ensure that adequate time is given to look for any will, or any further will. The time limits may be waived if two registrars agree.[2]

The papers to lead to a grant may be lodged before these periods have expired, but the grant itself must not pass the court seal within the prescribed periods.

There is generally no limit on the time after death in which a grant may be obtained, and, indeed, in the case of certain types of grant, such as administration *de bonis non*[3] the application is often made several years after death. The one exception to this principle is that where a person who has intermeddled has, after citation, been ordered to take a grant within a certain period[4] if he fails to do so he is guilty of contempt.[5]

The penalties for acting without a grant are mentioned later.[6]

E. OBTAINING A GRANT IN COMMON FORM

It has already been explained that a grant of probate or letters of administration is an order of the court, and the decision whether to make a grant is accordingly a judicial act. But in most cases of the routine common form grants, the procedure, although theoretically a judicial act, is in fact far more administrative than judicial. The applicant for the grant, usually through his solicitor[7]

---

[1] Non-contentious Probate Rules 1954, r. 5 (3).

[2] *Ibid.*

[3] See *post*, p. 285. A grant *de bonis non* is made where an executor acting under a probate dies before the administration of the estate is complete, and a further grant is necessary so that another person can complete the administration.

[4] See *post*, p. 280.

[5] *In the Estate of Biggs*, [1966] P. 118.

[6] *Post*, p. 369.

[7] The papers can be lodged by the applicant personally.

lodges with the appropriate Probate Registry[1] or Probate sub-Registry[2] certain papers. These are considered by the registrar and his staff, and if they are in order, the applicant receives the grant through the post about ten days or a fortnight after the papers were lodged.

The documents required are:

1. IN ALL CASES

a. *Executor's or Administrator's Oath*

This is the basic document on which the grant is based. In it, the executor or administrator swears as to the date and place of death of the deceased; the domicile of the deceased (which is usually included but is not essential); whether the deceased held settled land under a settlement arising before his death and not terminating on death, so that any necessary reference to settled land may be made in the grant; and his own entitlement to take a grant. In common form business, the facts deposed to in the oath are taken as sufficient proof, so that no corroboration is required. It is not even necessary to support the fact of death by production of the death certificate (though as it is not necessary to produce a corpse in order to get a death certificate, this is perhaps not as surprising as it may seem).

As most readers of this book will be unfamiliar with such oaths, the two illustrations on pages 698 and 699 of the appendix may assist.[3]

b. *Inland Revenue Affidavit*

This document is prepared solely to determine whether, and if so, how much, estate duty is payable. It specifies each asset owned by the deceased, and shows its gross value, and any debts which are charged on it. It also gives details of general debts and liabilities, and funeral expenses. In the case of assets where the exact value is open to some doubt, such as the deceased's house, the personal representatives give their estimate of the value, usually on the low side, leaving adjustments to be made later.

---

[1] See *ante*, p. 235.

[2] Non-contentious Probate Rules 1954; r. 2A, added by Non-contentious Probate (Amendment) Rules 1968, r. 2 (1).

[3] Examples of the grants issued following these oaths are given on pages 701 and 702 of the appendix.

The present exemption limit for estate duty purposes is £15,000.[1] Where duty is payable, it must usually be paid before the papers are lodged for the grant.

In most cases some adjustment is necessary to the Inland Revenue Affidavit, either because further assets or liabilities come to light in the course of the administration, or because the value of an asset has to be altered. This is done by means of a Corrective Affidavit, which can be submitted to the Estate Duty Office at any time after grant.

2. IN CASES OF PROBATE, OR ADMINISTRATION WITH WILL
The will

The original will must be referred to in the Oath, and must be lodged when the application for the grant is made. Once lodged, the will is retained by the Registry. A photo-copy is available for public inspection at the Principal Registry, but not the original will.

There is some doubt whether the will, once lodged, can ever be released from the Registry. In *In the Estate of White Todd*[2] the applicant sought to prove the will abroad after it had been proved in England, and the court directed that the original could be released for this purpose provided a sealed copy was retained in the Registry. In *Re Greer*,[3] however, it was held that the court had no power to allow the will to be sent out of the jurisdiction for the purpose of proceedings abroad. Probably the court will only allow a will to be sent abroad if it is required to prove it abroad, and the English court is satisfied that the foreign court will not accept a sealed copy.

Where the will is held abroad, and cannot be brought here, as where it has been proved in a foreign court and that court will not release it, probate here can be granted of an authenticated copy of the foreign will.[4]

Sometimes the will, although not validly revoked, will not be in existence. It may, for example, have been destroyed without compliance with the provisions of the Wills Act as to revocation, or it may have been lost.[5] In this case, provided its contents can

---

[1] Finance Act 1972, s. 120.

[2] [1926] P. 173.

[3] (1929), 45 T.L.R. 362.

[4] Non-contentious Probate Rules 1954, r. 53 (1).

[5] There is, however, a presumption that in certain circumstances a will which has been lost has been destroyed *animo revocandi*; see *ante*, p. 98.

be reconstructed, probate will be granted of the best document available. So probate may be granted of a copy, or of a draft, or of a document which is a reconstruction from oral evidence.

Where the original will is in existence, it must be lodged at the registry, even if it is not in the custody of the applicant. Where the applicant cannot obtain the will he may obtain an Order requiring it to be lodged. It has been held that a solicitor cannot exercise a lien over a client's will to the extent of refusing to produce it until his costs are paid.[1]

3. PROBATE AND LETTERS OF ADMINISTRATION— SPECIAL CASES

The following documents are not generally required but will be required in the circumstances mentioned.

a. *Copy will*

When probate is granted, a photo-copy of the will is attached to the probate or letters of administration, and a further photo-copy is made available for public inspection. If the will is not suitable for photographic reproduction, an engrossment of the will suitable for photographing must be lodged.

If parts of the document are not admissible to probate, as in the case of inadmissible alterations or insertions, a copy of the will omitting these matters must be lodged.[2] Where the will contains pencil writing, a copy must be lodged in which the part in pencil on the original is underlined.[3]

b. *Translation of the will*

A will is valid even if written in a foreign language. Where the will is written in a language other than English, a translation must be lodged, together with an affidavit by the translator verifying the translation. The executor is sworn to the foreign will, but the photo-copy of the will attached to the probate is of the translation and not the original.

---

[1] *Re Wood ex parte Law* (1834), 2 Ad. & El. 45.
[2] Non-contentious Probate Rules 1954, r. 9 (1).
[3] Non-contentious Probate Rules 1954, r. 9 (4), amended by Non-contentious Probate Rules 1967, r. 2 (2).

c. *Affidavit as to due execution*

Where the will contains an attestation clause purporting to show that the formal requirements of the Wills Act have been complied with, then, in the absence of any other circumstances giving rise to doubt, that will be accepted as sufficient evidence that the will is formally valid.

Where, however, there is no, or a defective, attestation clause, or there are some circumstances leading to doubt, an affidavit of due execution is necessary.[1] This is an affidavit from one of the attesting witnesses, or from someone else who was present at the time, to the effect that the formal requirements were observed.

If it is not possible to trace anyone to make an affidavit, it may still be possible to satisfy the court under the rule *omnia praesumuntur rite esse acta.*[2]

d. *Affidavit of plight and condition*

In some circumstances an affidavit is required as to the condition of the will at the time when it was executed. In the first place this will be required where there is an alteration, obliteration or interlineation which is not authenticated by the signature or initials of the testator and witnesses in the margin.[3] The affidavit is required so that the registrar can decide whether to allow the will in that form to be admitted to probate. The usual evidence is an affidavit from someone who saw the will before or at the time of execution with those alterations.

An affidavit is also required where from the face of the will it appears that some other document may have been pinned to it. Pin marks, or the indentation made by a paper clip, are sufficient to require an affidavit of condition, because if the documents were attached at the time of execution, that might be sufficient to make both of them testamentary documents.[4] The registrar will usually require to see the documents which were attached. Thus solicitors should be careful to tell clients not to attach any covering letter to the will by means of a pin or paper clip.

If there is evidence of some attempt to tear or destroy the will, an affidavit of condition may also be required.[5]

---

[1] Non-contentious Probate Rules 1954, r. 10.
[2] See *post*, p. 277.
[3] Non-contentious Probate Rules 1954, r. 12 (1).
[4] See *ante*, p. 56.
[5] Non-contentious Probate Rules 1954, r. 13.

4. ADMINISTRATION, OR ADMINISTRATION WITH WILL

Guarantee

Section 167 of the Judicature Act 1925,[1] provides that before granting letters of administration, the court may require one or more persons to act as sureties. The sureties guarantee that they will make good any loss which any person interested in the administration of the estate may suffer in consequence of a breach by the administrator of his duties. At the time of requiring the guarantee to be given, the court fixes the limit of liability.

Once a guarantee is given, it automatically applies for the benefit of every person interested in the administration of the estate.[2] However, before any such person takes action against the sureties, he must obtain the leave of the court.

The section does not apply where the administration is granted to the Treasury Solicitor, and to certain other public or diplomatic officers.[3]

5. SPECIAL CASES

a. *Privileged wills*

Where an informal will is to be proved, it must be accompanied by an affidavit showing the circumstances in which it is alleged that the deceased was entitled to make a privileged will.[4]

b. *Affidavit of law*

An affidavit is sometimes required as to the law of a foreign country. Thus, where a person applies for the grant of administration to the estate of a person who died domiciled abroad on the ground that he is the person entitled by the law of domicile to administer, an affidavit of law is required to show that he is in fact so domiciled. Such an affidavit must be by a barrister or advocate who practices or has practised in that country, or by some other person who is able to satisfy the court that he has knowledge of the law of the country in question.[5]

---

[1] As amended by Administration of Estates Act 1971, s. 8.

[2] *Ibid.*, s. 167 (2).

[3] I.e., the Public Trustee, the Solicitor of the Duchy of Lancaster or of the Duchy of Cornwall; the Chief Crown Solicitor for Northern Ireland; and to certain consular officers where the Consular Conventions Act 1949, s. 1, applies.

[4] Non-contentious Probate Rules 1954, rr. 15, 16.

[5] Non-contentious Probate Rules 1954, r. 18.

6. SUMMARY

APPLICATION FOR:	WHEN REQUIRED:	WHAT REQUIRED:	SEE PAGE
Administration	All cases	Administrator's Oath	272
		Inland Revenue Affidavit	272
	Special cases	Guarantee	276
Probate	All cases	Executor's Oath	272
		Inland Revenue Affidavit	272
		Will	273
	Special cases	Copy will	274
		Translation of will	274
		Affidavit of due execution	275
		Affidavit of plight and condition	275
		Affidavit as to privilege	276
		Affidavit of law	276
Administration with will	All cases	Administrator's Oath	272
		Inland Revenue Affidavit	272
		Will	273
	Special cases	As appropriate for probate or administration in special cases	276

F. PRESUMPTION OF DUE EXECUTION

The court will in some circumstances apply the maxim *omnia praesumuntur rite esse acta* and admit a document to probate accordingly.[1] The classic statement of the doctrine is that of Lindley, L.J., in *Harris* v. *Knight*[2] where he said:[3] "The maxim expresses an inference which may reasonably be drawn when an intention to do some formal act is established; when the evidence is consistent with that intention having been carried into effect in a proper way; but when the actual observance of all due formalities can only be inferred as a matter of probability."

---

[1] Sims (1972), 116 S.J. 356.
[2] (1890), 15 P.D. 170.
[3] (1890), 15 P.D. 170, at p. 179.

When this dictum is analysed it may not be of very great assistance. The first part requires the establishment of an intention to do a formal act, that is to make a will. This intention will be presumed in the absence of evidence to the contrary if the document appears on its face to be a will. The second element in the dictum is that the evidence must be consistent with the intention having been carried into effect. The making of any will is consistent with an intention to make it. The final element is that the actual observance of all due formalities can only be inferred. One can therefore state rather more simply that the maxim will apply whenever there is a document which on its face appears to be a will and where its appearance is consistent with the formal requirements of the Act having been observed. The maxim is particularly useful where the only witnesses and other persons present at the time of execution are dead, or cannot be traced, or where their evidence is unreliable. Indeed, in *Rolleston* v. *Sinclair*,[1] an Irish case, it was said that the maxim can only be adopted in these circumstances.

The strength of the presumption was affirmed by Faulks, J., in *Re Webb, Smith* v. *Johnston*,[2] where he said: "The court will not allow defective memory alone to overturn a will which is upon the face of it duly executed; if the witnesses are utterly forgetful of the facts, the presumption *omnia praesumumtur rite esse acta* will prevail." In *Re Webb, Smith* v. *Johnston* an application was made to obtain probate of the draft of a will when the original had been lost. The original had probably been destroyed when the testatrix's solicitor's office was destroyed by a bomb in 1940. The draft showed that the will had been attested by a Mrs. Mackins, and by a solicitor, since deceased. No other person was found who was present when the will was made. Mrs. Mackins said in evidence that she did not remember the document at all, and that she remembered only having been called to the deceased's shop on one occasion and "that a little man in a Homburg hat was there". The judge accepted that this little man was the other solicitor, and admitted the will to probate.

Another example of the operation of the rule is *Re Denning, Harnett* v. *Elliott*.[3] That case was concerned with an application

---

[1] [1924] 2 I.R. 157.
[2] [1964] 2 All E.R. 91.
[3] [1958] 2 All E.R. 1.

for probate of a single sheet of paper, on one side of which was a dispositive part signed by the deceased, and on the reverse were the signatures of two unidentified persons without any attestation clause. In admitting the document to probate, Sachs, J., said that there was "no other practical reason why those names should be on the back of the document unless it was for the purpose of attesting the will".

The presumption can be used only where there is no evidence pointing to wrongful execution. So in *In the Estate of Bercovitz*[1] there was a signature of the testator and of two witnesses at the top of the document, and the signature of the testator alone at the bottom. This pointed to non-compliance with the provisions of the Wills Act, and the maxim did not apply to save the will. In this case Philimore, J., said[2] that the strength of the presumption varies with all the circumstances, it being strong where the document is in regular form, and weaker where it is unusual. *Re Denning, Harnett* v. *Elliott*,[3] however, shows the length to which the court will sometimes go in admitting a document to probate.

G. CAVEATS

A caveat is a notice to the registrar not to seal a grant without first giving notice to the person who lodged the caveat. A caveat may be lodged by any person. Once entered, it remains effective for six months, though it can then be renewed.[4]

If a caveat has been entered, the applicant for the grant will be notified of the caveat, and if he wishes to proceed he must seek to have the caveat removed by, in the curious expression, "warning" it. A warning to a caveat is issued by the registrar at the instigation of the applicant for the grant, and requires the caveator to enter an appearance to the warning within eight days of service. If the caveator does not enter an appearance, the caveat is removed and the grant will issue. If the caveator wishes to persist, the procedure depends on whether the caveator merely wishes to stop the applicant obtaining a grant, or whether he has some contrary interest. In the former case, he issues a summons for directions, which is heard by a registrar. In the latter case, he enters an

---

[1] [1961] 2 All E.R. 481; [1961] 1 W.L.R. 892.
[2] [1961] 2 All E.R. 481, at p. 485; [1961] 1 W.L.R. 892, at p. 894.
[3] [1958] 2 All E.R. 1.
[4] Non-contentious Probate Rules 1954, r. 44.

appearance which gives details of his interest. In either case, at that stage, contentious business begins.

A caveat may be withdrawn by the caveator.

The rules[1] provide that a caveat may be entered by any person. It is usually used:

a. where the caveator disputes the validity of a will which is about to be proved by another; *or*

b. where the caveator wishes to prevent one person entitled in the same degree as himself from obtaining a grant alone, as, for example, where there are two brothers both equally entitled to a grant; *or*

c. where the caveator wishes to show that the applicant is unfit to take a grant, or for some other reason a grant ought to be issued under s. 162; *or*

d. where the caveator just wishes to be notified of the grant, for such purposes as commencing proceedings against the estate, or for making an application under the Family Provision legislation.

H. CITATIONS

Citations are used both in contentious and non-contentious business, but for the sake of convenience, both are dealt with here. A citation is issued by the court at the instigation of a person interested for a variety of purposes. These are:

a. in the case of a person who has intermeddled, but, although entitled, has not applied for a grant. This is known as a citation to take a grant. Failure to take a grant once an order has been made following a citation is contempt, though the court may pass over the citee if it thinks fit;[2]

b. in the case of a person who has a prior right to a grant of administration, to compel him to accept or refuse a grant. If he fails to do so, he loses his right to a grant, and the person next entitled can apply;

---

[1] Non-contentious Probate Rules 1954, r. 44.
[2] *In the Estate of Biggs,* [1966] P. 118.

c. to set aside a will of which probate in common form has been granted. In this case, the executors and all persons interested are cited to propound the will. This merely requires the executors to prove the will in solemn form. It is not applicable where it is sought to have the grant revoked;[1]

d. to compel an executor or administrator to bring in a grant of representation so that it can be revoked, as, for example, where a will, or later will, is discovered; and

e. to persons "to see proceedings". This type of citation requires persons who are not made parties to a probate action to take notice of the proceedings so that they may be bound by the result as *res judicata*.

I. RE-SEALING

Where a person dies domiciled in Scotland, a confirmation (the Scottish equivalent of Probate) is treated in England and Wales as a grant of representation without further formality.[2] If the Scottish grant is made to persons who were not nominated by the deceased, it is treated as a grant of letters of administration.[3] Likewise a grant of probate or letters of administration made in Northern Ireland in respect of a person dying domiciled there is treated as valid in England and Wales without the need for re-sealing.[4]

Grants of representation issued in certain Colonial or former Colonial territories may be re-sealed in England.[5] Once the seal of the English court is impressed on the grant, it takes effect as if it were a grant of the English court, and has operation accordingly.

---

[1] *Re Jolley, Jolley* v. *Jarvis*, [1964] P. 262.
[2] Administration of Estates Act 1971, s. 1 (1), which came into force on 1 January 1972; Non-contentious Probate (Amendment) Rules 1971.
[3] Administration of Estates Act 1971, s. 1 (2).
[4] *Ibid.*, s. 1 (5). The converse is also true: *ibid.*, s. 2.
[5] Colonial Probates Act Application Order 1965.

CHAPTER 18

SPECIAL GRANTS

In the usual case, a grant of representation, whether of probate, letters of administration *simpliciter*, or letters of administration with will annexed are unlimited either as to property or to time. They therefore enable the personal representative to deal with the whole of the deceased's assets, and to complete fully the administration of his estate. In some cases, however, more restricted grants are issued. These may be divided into the following categories:

a. grants with a special purpose;
b. grants limited as to property;
c. grants limited as to time;
d. other special types of grant; and
e. grants relating to settled land.

A. GRANTS WITH A SPECIAL PURPOSE

1. GRANTS *ad colligenda bona*

Where the assets of the estate consist of perishables, or other assets which need quick attention, but no person applies for probate or administration, a grant *ad colligenda bona* may be obtained. This grant is intended to give the administrator power only to get in the estate of the deceased, and to do such acts as are necessary in order to preserve it, and it is usually limited in this way. A grant in these terms does not give a power to invest money collected in, nor to sell the assets, even where a sale is necessary because the asset is wasting. If it is anticipated that powers in this nature will be required, they may be expressly included in the grant upon application being made to the court.[1]

---

[1] The court has power to extend grants in this way under s. 162, Judicature Act 1925, *ante*, p. 253. For illustrations of the circumstances where such extended grants were made, see *In the Goods of Wyckoff* (1862), 32 L.J.P.M. & A. 214; *In the Goods of Schwerdtfeger* (1876), 1 P.D. 424; *In the Goods of Stewart* (1869), L.R. 1 P. & D. 727; *In the Goods of Bolton*, [1899] P. 186.

2. GRANTS *ad litem*

Two special types of grant may be issued in connexion with legal proceedings. The most usual is a grant of administration *pendente lite*, which gives the administrator full powers of administration, other than to distribute residue, except that his powers cease on the termination of the action. This type of grant is discussed at p. 288. The other type of grant in connexion with legal proceedings is a grant *ad litem*. Grants *ad litem* are made under Judicature Act 1925, s. 162[1] and the administrator *ad litem* merely has power to represent the estate in proceedings. He has no power over the assets of the estate. This type of grant is usually made only where it is necessary to make the estate a defendant to an action, but the persons, if any, entitled to a grant will not take one out. Thus, in *In the Goods of Knight*[2] where a person wished to bring a claim against the estate for personal injuries under the Law Reform (Miscellaneous Provisions) Act 1934, but was unable to do so because the next of kin refused to apply for a grant, a grant *ad litem* was made to the Official Solicitor.[3]

Where proceedings are in progress, and it is necessary to make the estate a party to the action, every Division of the High Court has power to appoint a person to represent the estate, and the acts of such a person bind the estate in the same way as if he had been a personal representative.[4] This procedure is, however, only applicable where the action is in progress, and the former procedure must be adopted where the estate is to be the defendant.

B. GRANTS LIMITED AS TO PROPERTY

1. LIMITED PROBATE

Although there may not be more than four executors or administrators in respect of the same item of property, a testator may appoint executors of only certain assets, or assets in a specified area.[5] Where this is done, the executors so appointed obtain

---

[1] See *In the Estate of Simpson*, [1936] P. 40.
[2] [1939] 3 All E.R. 928.
[3] The Official Solicitor can only be appointed with his consent, which was given in this case.
[4] R.S.C., O. 15, r. 15.
[5] *In the Estate of Falkner* (1913), 113 L.T. 927.

probate limited to that property. This type of grant is made usually in respect of literary works, where a special literary executor is appointed, and where the deceased left property both in England and elsewhere, and appoints separate executors of the English estate. Thus, in *In the Estate of Von Brentano*[1] the deceased, who was domiciled in Germany, made two wills, one dealing with English realty and appointing English executors, and the other dealing with the remaining assets in England and abroad. Limited probate was granted in respect of the English realty.

2. SECTION 155 GRANTS

Judicature Act 1925, s. 155, gives the Court power to grant probate or letters of administration of realty and personalty separately, and to limit in any way which it thinks fit a grant of realty. The section also gives a special power to make a grant in respect of a trust estate only. With the exception of the power in respect of trust estates, grants may not be issued separately under this section if the estate is insolvent.

Although the power to make separate grants exists, it will be exercised only where there is very good reason.[2] An example of the type of circumstances in which this power will be exercised is where a grant is needed only to complete title. Thus, in *In the Goods of Butler*[3] the testator died holding leasehold property, and title could only be made with the aid of a grant. A grant was made limited to that specified property.[4] The power may, but is not necessarily, used where a will is made exercising a power of appointment. Limited grants have been issued restricted to the property devolving under general powers of appointment.[5] Alternatively, a general grant may be issued but with probate of only so much of the will as related to the power of appointment.[6] The result is the same in either case.

The power to make a separate grant in respect of trust estates is useful. Where the deceased was the last surviving trustee of a

---

[1] [1911] P. 172.
[2] *In the Goods of Lady Somerset* (1867), L.R. 1 P. & D. 350.
[3] [1898] P. 9.
[4] See also *In the Goods of Baldwin*, [1903] P. 61; *In the Goods of Ratcliffe*, [1899] P. 110; *In the Goods of Agnese*, [1900] P. 60.
[5] *In the Goods of Russell* (1890), 15 P.D. 111.
[6] *In the Estate of Poole, Poole v. Poole*, [1919] P. 10.

trust fund the whole of the legal title to that fund would have been vested in him, and would normally pass to his general personal representatives, who would be bound to give effect to the terms of the trust. If a separate grant, limited to the trust fund, is taken out, the representative under that grant would be entitled to appoint a new trustee or new trustees of the trust under Trustee Act 1925, s. 36 (1). Representation limited to a trust fund may be granted to a beneficiary if the deceased sole trustee has no personal representatives, or if he has representatives and they agree.[1]

3. GRANTS "SAVE AND EXCEPT" AND *caeterorum*

Both of these grants are made where a limited grant either has been or will be made. If under the terms of a will an executor is appointed of a specified item of property, such as his literary works, as we have seen the executor is entitled to a grant limited to that property. Where the general executors wish to take out a grant before the limited grant is issued, they will take a grant Save and Except the literary works. If, however, the grant in respect of the literary works has already issued, they will take a grant *caeterorum*. The effect of these grants is exactly the same, and they differ only according to whether they precede or succeed the limited grant.

4. GRANTS *de bonis non*

A grant *de bonis non administratis* is made where following a grant of probate or letters of administration, the representative has not completed the administration of the estate, and there is no representative by the chain of representation. Under this type of grant, the administrator has full power to complete the administration of the estate.

Before a grant *de bonis non* can be issued it must be shown:

a. That a previous grant has been made to the deceased's estate. If part of the estate has been administered, but without a grant having been taken out, an original grant must be obtained, and not a grant *de bonis non*.

b. That there is no remaining personal representative.

c. That part of the estate is left unadministered.

---

[1] *In the Goods of Ratcliffe, ante*; *Pegg* v. *Chamberlain* (1860), 1 Sw. & Tr. 527.

The second requirement, that there must be no remaining personal representative, means that a grant *de bonis non* must not be issued where there is a surviving personal representative, or where there is an executor by representation.[1] If, therefore, there are two personal representatives, and one dies, the whole power will pass to the survivor, and there will be no case for a *de bonis non* grant. Again, if the whole or last surviving executor dies, and the executor appointed by his will proves, so that the chain of representation operates, there will be no case for a grant *de bonis non*.

Although *de bonis non* grants are usually issued following the death of the personal representative, they may also be issued where a previous grant is revoked. This has happened where the court revoked a grant of letters of administration because the administrator disappeared[2] and where the administrator permanently left the jurisdiction.[3]

When considering the third requirement, that some part of the estate must be left unadministered, it is important that the period of administration should not have come to an end, and in this connexion it is necessary to distinguish between the situation where a person holds as personal representative and where he holds as trustee. Suppose that Edward is appointed executor and trustee of a will, under which he is to pay £1,000 to the testator's son, Clarence, and that Clarence is aged 3 at the testator's death. Immediately after the death, Edward holds the £1,000 as executor, and not as trustee, but when the final estate accounts have been prepared, and all debts and other legacies have been paid[4] Edward will thereafter hold as trustee. The procedure to be followed on Edward's death will depend upon the time at which he dies. If he dies during the administration period, a grant *de bonis non* will be required. If he dies afterwards, *his* personal representatives will have power to appoint a new trustee of the £1,000 under Trustee Act 1925, s. 36 (1). Although in the case of personalty it appears that the capacity in which a person holds is one of fact, with regard to realty and leaseholds, it depends on whether a formal assent has been made.[5]

---

[1] *Ante*, p. 241.

[2] *In the Goods of Loveday*, [1900] P. 154.

[3] *In the Estate of Saker*, [1909] P. 233; *In the Estate of French*, [1910] P.169; *In the Estate of Thomas*, [1912] P. 177.

[4] See *post*, p. 320, for a more detailed statement of the position.

[5] *Re King's Will Trusts, Assheton* v. *Boyne*, [1964] Ch. 542.

A grant *de bonis non* involves the same full procedure as for obtaining any grant of administration, so that an Inland Revenue Affidavit of the whole of the estate (and not merely of the un-administered part) must be sworn, and a bond obtained. As it is usually far easier for an appointment of trustees to be made, an assent should be made at the earliest opportunity.[1]

Where the deceased personal representative was an executor, or administrator with will the grant will be of administration *cum testamento annexo et de bonis non administratis*, and if he was an administrator *simpliciter* he will be an administrator *de bonis non administratis*.

A grant *de bonis non* can only be made to the persons who would have been entitled to the original grant, either of administration or administration with will.[2]

C. GRANTS LIMITED AS TO TIME

1. LIMITED PROBATE, OR ADMINISTRATION WITH WILL

Just as a will may limit the property to which it is subject, so it may limit the time for which a person is to act as executor. Limited probate would be granted accordingly. The only situation where this is at all usual is where a person is appointed to act as executor during the minority of the testator's son.

2. WHERE WILL NOT AVAILABLE

Where the original will is in existence but it cannot be produced, as where it is held by a foreign court, and there is an urgent need to obtain a grant of representation, a grant of administration with will annexed may be issued, limited until the original or a more authentic copy of the will is brought into the registry.[3] Similarly, where a will is known to have been in existence after the date of the testator's death, but cannot subsequently be found, administration will be granted "till the will be found".[4] This situation must be carefully distinguished from that where the testator is

---

[1] *Post,* p. 320.

[2] I.e., the persons who would have been entitled to apply had no previous grant been made. See *ante,* p. 240.

[3] *In the Goods of Lemme,* [1892] P. 89; *In the Goods of Von Linden,* [1869] P. 148.

[4] *In the Goods of Wright,* [1893] P. 21.

known to have made a will, but it was not known to be in existence after his death. In this case, there is a presumption that it was revoked.[1]

3. ADMINISTRATION *durante absentia*

Judicature Act 1925, s. 164, provides that if at the expiration of twelve months from the death of the deceased the personal representative to whom a grant has been made is residing out of England and Wales[2] the court may grant administration *durante absentia* to a creditor or any person interested in the estate. Although the section refers to the personal representative being out of the jurisdiction "at" the expiration of twelve months from the death, this appears to mean "at or after".

There are two types of grant *durante absentia*. The earlier type, as the name shows, determines automatically upon the return to the jurisdiction of the original representative,[3] but for it now to have this effect, there must be a limitation to this effect included in the grant. The more common type of grant does not determine on the return of the original representative, nor on his death.[4] Where, however, a grant *durante absentia* has been made, and the representative under that grant is a party to proceedings, then in the event of the original representative returning to the jurisdiction he is also made a party to the proceedings.[5]

4. ADMINISTRATION *pendente lite*

The circumstances in which a grant *ad litem* will be made was explained at p. 296. Judicature Act 1925, s. 163, gives power to appoint an administrator *pendente lite* where there is any dispute as to the validity of a will[6] or as to the right to administer.[7]

Section 163 enables the court in these circumstances to appoint "an administrator". It has been held that this overrides the provisions of s. 160, which requires two administrators to be

---

[1] *Ante*, p. 92.

[2] The section applies even if the personal representative is in Scotland: *Taynton* v. *Hannay* (1802), 3 Bos. & P. 26.

[3] *Slaughter* v. *May* (1705), 1 Salk. 42.

[4] *Taynton* v. *Hannay* (1802), 3 Bos. & P. 26.

[5] Judicature Act 1925, s. 164 (3).

[6] See *Hewson* v. *Shelley*, [1914] 2 Ch. 13.

[7] *Frederick* v. *Hook* (1690), Carth. 153.

appointed in the case of a minority or life interest, so that in *Re Haslip*[1] appointment was made to only one administrator, even though there was a life interest.[2] Two administrators *pendente lite* may, of course, be appointed if it is so desired.

Administration *pendente lite* will only be granted where it can be shown that the appointment is necessary.[3] Thus, if there is an executor whose appointment is not in dispute, even if there is dispute as to the remainder of the will, probate will be granted to that executor and a grant *pendente lite* will not issue. Likewise, where only a codicil is in dispute, probate will issue to the executor named in the will. Thus, in *In the Estate of Day*[4] there was no dispute as to the validity of a will, but proceedings were brought as to the validity of a codicil. The codicil affected only a comparatively small part of the estate. The court refused to appoint an administrator *pendente lite*, but found in favour of the will, and granted probate to the executors upon their giving an undertaking not to administer the property the subject of the codicil, except in order to safeguard it. This left the validity of the codicil to be determined at a later date. A grant *pendente lite* can only issue where proceedings have actually been commenced, and the entry of a caveat, warning of a caveat, or entry of appearance to a warning[5] is not sufficient for this purpose.[6]

Although there is no theoretical restriction on appointing as administrator *pendente lite* a person who is a party to the action,[7] administration is in practice granted only to an independent person. This is usually a professional person with no interest in the outcome of the proceedings, or alternatively the joint nominee of the parties.[8]

Where an administrator *pendente lite* is appointed, the Chancery Division may still appoint a receiver, though it will seldom do so.[9]

---

[1] [1958] 2 All E.R. 275, n.; following *In the Estate of Lindley*, [1953] P. 203. However, in *Re Hall*, [1950] P. 156, a grant to a single administrator was refused under s. 162 (see *ante*, p. 257), so that the power to grant administration to only one person exists only under s. 163.

[2] *Ante*, p. 259.

[3] *Horrell* v. *Witts and Plumley* (1866), L.R. 1 P. & D. 103.

[4] [1940] 2 All E.R. 544.

[5] *Ante*, p. 279.

[6] *Salter* v. *Salter*, [1896] P. 291.

[7] *Re Griffin, Griffin* v. *Ackroyd*, [1925] P. 38.

[8] *Stratton* v. *Ford* (1754), 2 Lee. 49; *In the Goods of Shorter*, [1911] P. 184.

[9] *Re Oakes, Oakes* v. *Porcheron*, [1917] 1 Ch. 230.

The Probate Court, however, will, when deciding upon the appointment of an administrator *pendente lite* take into account the same considerations as the Chancery Division does when asked to appoint a receiver. These are the size and nature of the estate, and the fitness of the proposed administrator.[1]

Once an administrator *pendente lite* is appointed, he has all the powers of a general administrator, except that of distributing the residue. Although s. 163 provides that the only restriction on the administrator's power is on the distribution of residue, some of the older cases indicate that the administrator should not pay disputed debts or legacies.[2] It is not clear how far an administrator *pendente lite* is subject to these limitations after 1925. He may be sued by a creditor in the same way as an ordinary representative.[3]

The grant is limited to the duration of the proceedings, and the administrator's powers therefore come to an end on the termination of those proceedings. The person primarily entitled to the grant at that time then applies.

As an exception to the general position affecting personal representatives, an administrator *pendente lite* is entitled to remuneration, which is fixed by the court, and the account for his administration must be passed by the court.[4]

5. ADMINISTRATION *durante minore aetate*

By virtue of s. 160, Judicature Act 1925, an infant cannot take a grant, either of probate or of administration. Accordingly, s. 165 provides that where an infant is the sole executor of a will, administration with will annexed is granted to his guardian or such other person as the court thinks fit for his "use and benefit". Where the infant has no beneficial interest in the estate, administration will be granted to one administrator, but where he also has a beneficial interest, administration must be granted to two administrators, or a trust corporation.[5] Likewise, where an infant would be entitled to administration, administration *durante minore aetate* is made for the infant's use and benefit. As an infant can only be entitled to a

---

[1] *Re Bevan, Bevan* v. *Houldsworth*, [1948] 1 All E.R. 271.

[2] *Charlton* v. *Hindmarsh* (1860), 1 Sw. & Tr. 519; *Whittle* v. *Keats* (1866), 35 L.J.P. & M. 54.

[3] *Re Toleman, Westwood* v. *Booker*, [1897] 1 Ch. 866.

[4] Judicature Act 1925, s. 163 (2).

[5] Senior Registrar's Direction dated 23 May 1952.

grant of administration because he has a beneficial interest, the grant must be made to two individuals, or to a trust corporation.

The persons who are entitled to the grant are:

a. Where the infant is appointed sole executor, and has no interest in the residuary estate, the person entitled to the residue;[1]

b. Where the infant has a beneficial interest in the residue under a will, or is entitled on intestacy, his guardian and another. His guardian will be:

(i) if both his mother and father survive, both of them;[2]

(ii) if only one of his father and mother survive, that surviving parent;

(iii) the person appointed by a deceased parent as testamentary guardian.[3] Where the other parent is alive, they act together unless the surviving parent disagrees, then the matter can be resolved by the court.[4]

If there is no person in any of these classes:

(iv) if the infant is over 16, such person of his next of kin whom he nominates,[5] subject to the right of the court to refuse to accept such nomination;[6]

(v) if the infant is a married woman, her husband if nominated by her;[7] *or*

(vii) such person who is nominated as guardian by an order of the registrar.

The guardian as ascertained above may where two administrators are necessary nominate the other person to act with him. This again is subject to the right of the court to reject the person nominated.

A grant *durante minore aetate* is usually limited expressly until the infant attains the age of eighteen. On his attaining that age, the grant automatically ceases, and the infant may then apply for

---

[1] Non-contentious Probate Rules 1954, r. 31 (5).
[2] Non-contentious Probate Rules 1954, r. 31 (1) (a), substituted by Non-contentious Probate (Amendment) Rules 1967, r. 2 (12).
[3] Guardianship of Minors Act 1971, s. 4 (1).
[4] *Ibid.*, s. 4 (3), (4).
[5] Non-contentious Probate Rules 1954, r. 31 (1).
[6] *Fawkener* v. *Jordan* (1756), 2 Lee. 327.
[7] Non-contentious Probate Rules 1954, r. 31 (1).

probate. Where the infant does prove the will, the intervention of the *durante minore aetate* grant does not break the chain of representation.[1]

An administrator *durante minore aetate* has all the powers of an ordinary administrator, and he can therefore sell the estate in the course of administration, and complete the administration.[2] However, he exercises all his powers on behalf of the infant, and is accountable to the infant. The infant may, therefore, require the administrator to give him a full account of his administration, even if the infant has no beneficial interest in the estate.[3]

It is, of course, only appropriate to apply for a grant of this nature where the infant is the sole executor. Where he is the joint executor, the other executors are entitled to prove the will, with power to the infant to join in when he attains the age of 18. Provided he does prove at that time, again the chain of representation is not broken.[4]

6. ADMINISTRATION DURING MENTAL OR PHYSICAL INCAPACITY

The position where the person entitled to a grant is suffering from mental or physical incapacity is similar to that where the person entitled is an infant. Administration, either simple, or with will, as appropriate, will be granted for the use and benefit of the person under the incapacity. An application for a grant for the use and benefit of a person who is incapable of managing his affairs but is not resident in an institution must be accompanied by a certificate from his doctor showing, *inter alia*, that the patient is unlikely to become capable of managing his own affairs within three months.[5]

The persons entitled to the grant are:
a. in the case of mental incapacity, the person authorised by the Court of Protection;[6]

---

[1] Administration of Estates Act 1925, s. 7 (3).
[2] *Re Cope, Cope* v. *Cope* (1880), 16 Ch.D. 49.
[3] *Fotherby* v. *Pate* (1747), 3 Atk. 603; *Taylor* v. *Newton* (1752), 1 Lee. 15; *Harvell* v. *Foster*, [1954] 2 Q.B. 367.
[4] See *In the Goods of Reid*, [1896] P. 129.
[5] *Practice Direction*, [1969] 1 All E.R. 494.
[6] Non-contentious Probate Rules 1954, r. 33 (1).

b. in the case of mental incapacity where no person is authorised by the Court of Protection, and in the case of physical incapacity:

(i) if the person under the incapacity is entitled as executor, but has no interest in the residuary estate, the person who is in fact entitled to the residue;

(ii) if the person under the incapacity is entitled as administrator, or is an executor having an interest in the residuary estate, the person who would be entitled to a grant in respect of his estate if he had died intestate;[1] or

(iii) in either case, to such other person as the court thinks fit.

If more than one person is entitled to a grant, and only one is suffering from incapacity, the grant is made to the others, with power reserved to the one under incapacity to join in when the disability ceases.

Where the incapacity occurs after a grant has been made to a sole representative, the court will impound the grant, and make a grant to another limited to the period of the incapacity, and to the unadministered property.[2] Where the incapacity is of one of two or more representatives, the court will usually revoke the grant, making a new grant to the executor not under incapacity, with power to the other to join in when the disability ceases.[3]

In *In the Goods of Galbraith*[4] there were two executors, and both became incapable by reason of old age. On the application of a relative, the probate was revoked, and a new grant *de bonis non* was issued to another. A grant *de bonis non* will be issued only where the representatives will not recover from the incapacity.

D. MISCELLANEOUS GRANTS

1. DOUBLE PROBATE

It has been shown[5] that where in his will the testator appoints more than one executor, any of the executors may obtain a grant without notice to the others, and in this event power will be reserved to the others to apply for a grant later. Where that person

---

[1] Non-contentious Probate Rules 1954, r. 33 (1) (b), substituted by Non-contentious Probate (Amendment) Rules 1967, r. 2 (13).

[2] See Registrar's Direction dated 16 July 1956.

[3] *In the Estate of Shaw*, [1905] P. 92.

[4] [1951] P. 422.

[5] *Ante*, p. 245.

subsequently does apply for a grant, it will be called "double probate". The earlier grant is not called in.

2. CESSATE GRANT

Where a grant limited as to time has been made, and has ceased to have effect because that period has expired, the subsequent grant is known as a cessate grant. Thus, if a testator appoints one person to be his executor for, say, five years, and then appoints another, that other will, after the five year period has expired, obtain a cessate grant.

Theoretically, the cessate grant is a renewal of the whole original grant, whereas a grant *de bonis non* is a grant of only so much of the estate as is unadministered, but in practice cessate grants and grants *de bonis non* have the same effect.

3. GRANTS TO ATTORNEYS

If, and only if, the person entitled to the grant resides outside England, the grant may be made to his attorney.[1] The grant is usually limited for the use and benefit of the principal, and until such time as he himself shall apply for a grant.

While his grant is in force, the attorney has full power to administer the estate.[2] When he comes to distribute the residue, he may himself either distribute to the beneficiaries entitled, or, pay it over to the principal if, by the law of domicile of the principal the principal is obliged to perform the functions of executor or administrator.[3]

The grant will be revoked if and when the principal applies for a grant, or his principal dies.[4] However, where there are two principals, and they jointly appoint one attorney, the death of one only of the principals will not in itself revoke the grant, though it will be if the survivor appoints a different attorney.[5]

---

[1] *In the Goods of Burch* (1861), 2 Sw. & Tr. 139.

[2] *Re Rendell, Wood* v. *Rendell,* [1901] 1 Ch. 230.

[3] *Re Rendell, Wood* v. *Rendell; Re Achillopoulos, Johnson* v. *Mavromichali,* [1928] Ch. 433.

[4] *Pipon* v. *Wallis* (1753), 1 Lee. 402; *Re Cassidy* (1832), 4 Hag. Ecc. 360; *Suwerkrop* v. *Day* (1838), 8 Ad. & El. 624; and see *In the Goods of Dinshaw,* [1930] P. 180.

[5] *In the Goods of Dinshaw, supra.*

The usual provisions of the Powers of Attorney Act 1971 governing attorneys will apply to attorney administrators, and protection will be conferred thereby.

Where the principal was appointed executor, the attorney takes a grant of administration with will annexed, but nevertheless, for the purposes of the chain of representation, he is regarded as standing in the stead of the executor himself, so that the chain of representation is not broken by a grant of administration with will to an attorney administrator, even if his principal never himself proves the will.[1]

E. SETTLED LAND

Special rules apply to the persons entitled to a grant in respect of settled land, known as special personal representatives, and grants in respect of settled land are the most frequent types of grant which are made where there is a limitation to a particular type of property. It will however be more convenient to defer consideration of them until the devolution of settled land itself is discussed.[2]

---

[1] *In the Goods of Murguia* (1884), 9 P.D. 236.
[2] *Post*, p. 353.

CHAPTER 19

CONTENTIOUS BUSINESS

A. DEFINITION

There is no statutory definition of contentious business, although the expression is used in the same sense as the definition of a probate action in the Rules of the Supreme Court. This is:[1] "an action for the grant of probate of the will, or letters of administration of the estate, of a deceased person or for the revocation of such a grant, or for a decree pronouncing for or against the validity of an alleged will, not being an action which is non-contentious or common form probate business". It will be seen that care needs to be exercised in the use of the expression contentious business, because some aspects of the non-contentious procedure, particularly with regard to caveats and citations, may have an element of contention in them, although they are excluded from this definition. Contentious business is usually commenced by writ of summons, which is discretionary and is not issuable as of right. Contentious business is dealt with in the Chancery Division.[2]

Contentious business falls into three categories:

a. actions as to the validity of a will, which are actions to prove the will in solemn form;

b. actions between two or more applicants for the right to take a grant of representation; and

c. actions to revoke a grant, previously made in common form.

The same action may consist of any combination of these elements.

It is not proposed to consider here the procedure followed in a probate action, but to deal only with the entitlement to require a will to be proved in solemn form; evidence in contentious cases;

---

[1] R.S.C., O. 76, r. 1 (2).
[2] Administration of Justice Act 1970, s. 1.

and costs. Much of what is said with regard to the types of evidence which are admissible applies also to non-contentious business.

The use of citations in contentious business was referred to at p. 280.

B. PROOF OF WILL IN SOLEMN FORM

1. AT INSTANCE OF EXECUTOR

Probate in common form is an order of the court and therefore everyone acting under it is protected as long as those acts were done while it was in force. As will be seen, however, the executor can be required to prove the will in solemn form, and where this is anticipated it will be more convenient for the executor himself to apply for probate in solemn form at the outset. It is, therefore, advisable for the executor to seek probate in solemn form if there are doubts as to its validity, or as to the validity of a codicil, or if it is anticipated that there will be opposition to the will. As a general principle, the longer the time which elapses from the death, the more difficult will be the proof.

Apart from the more obvious case where the executor may apply for probate in solemn form, it may be noted that this procedure is often adopted where it is sought to obtain probate of a lost will, and the consent of persons having a contrary interest cannot be obtained. In these circumstances, it is open to the court to grant probate on motion, and it will do so where the issue is clear.[1] but if an attempt is made to obtain a grant on motion, the judge may well refuse to deal with the question on motion, and to require an action to be brought.[2]

2. AT INSTANCE OF OTHER PERSONS INTERESTED

Anyone who has a contrary beneficial interest to the will being propounded, that is, as being entitled on intestacy, or under an earlier will, or a person named as executor in another will may require the executor to prove the will in solemn form. Thus, the following classes of persons may require probate in solemn form:

   a. persons entitled to any share of the estate on intestacy. They are entitled to insist on this right even if they have

---

[1] See, e.g., *In the Estate of Penson,* [1960] C.L.Y. 1232.
[2] *In the Goods of Apted,* [1899] P. 272; c.f. *In the Goods of Pearson,* [1896] P. 289.

stood by while probate in common form was granted,[1] or even if they have received a legacy under the will.[2]

b. a beneficiary under the will. This is so that he can be sure of his own position, but as a condition of allowing him to take action to require probate in solemn form, he will be obliged to pay his legacy into court until the result of the action is known.[3]

c. a beneficiary under a previous will.

d. an executor under a previous will.

A creditor is not allowed to insist on solemn form probate, as he is concerned only to be paid his debt, which will be paid out of the estate irrespective of whether any will is valid.[4]

A person so interested may take action either before the will has been proved at all, or after it has been proved in common form.[5] The action is commenced by the person opposing the will, but the person propounding the will can insist that the opposer shows that he has some interest in the estate. This interest, however, may be very slight,[6] and the mere possibility of an interest is sufficient.[7]

An assignee of an interest under a will is in the same position as the assignor so far as being able to take action for probate in solemn form. So, in *Wintle* v. *Nye*,[8] Colonel Wintle was only able to take action against Mr. Nye by taking an assignment of a beneficial interest in a small part of the estate.

3. EFFECT OF PROBATE IN SOLEMN FORM

When proved in solemn form, the will becomes *res judicata* and will bind all those who had notice of it. In *Re Barraclough, Barraclough* v. *Young*[9] Payne, J., expressly approved the earlier dictum of Sir Cresswell Cresswell in *Young* v. *Holloway*[10] in the

---

[1] *Re Jolley, Jolley* v. *Jarvis*, [1964] P. 262.

[2] *Bell* v. *Armstrong* (1822), 1 Add. 365, at p. 374.

[3] *Braham* v. *Burchell* (1826), 3 Add. 243.

[4] *Burroughs* v. *Griffiths* (1754), 1 Lee. 544; *Menzies* v. *Pulbrook and Ker* (1841), 2 Curt. 845.

[5] *Re Jolley, Jolley* v. *Jarvis*, supra.

[6] *Hingeston* v. *Tucker* (1862), 2 Sw. & Tr. 596.

[7] *Kipping and Barlow* v. *Ash* (1845), 1 Rob. Eccl. 270.

[8] [1959] 1 All E.R. 552; see *ante*, p. 43.

[9] [1965] 2 All E.R. 311, at p. 316.

[10] [1895] P. 87.

following terms: "The general principle, as I collect it, is this, that where a party has had full notice, and has had the opportunity of availing himself of the contest, he will be bound by the decision." The principle applies if the party concerned has the opportunity to oppose the proceedings, whether or not he actually did so. *Re Barraclough, Barraclough* v. *Young*[1] was concerned with a will made in favour of a second wife, under which no reference was made to the child of the first marriage. The executrix under the will commenced proceedings to prove the will in solemn form, the daughter of the first marriage being a defendant to the action. She claimed that the deceased was not of sound mind, memory and understanding in that he was suffering from the insane delusion that she was not his lawful child. The defendant was of virtually no means, and obtained a legal aid certificate to enable her to be represented in the proceedings. In the usual way, the legal aid certificate was subject to a condition that at the close of pleadings the papers would be considered by counsel, who would advise as to merits. Counsel advised adversely to the defendant, and her legal aid certificate was discharged. Having been abandoned by the legal aid authority, a compromise was reached whereby she withdrew her opposition on the basis that the plaintiff executrix would not seek an order for costs against her. The action was dealt with on that basis, and probate in solemn form was granted. However some people never give up. The daughter subsequently obtained another opinion of counsel which was favourable to her, and sought to reopen the question. Payne, J., held that although he had jurisdiction[2] to set aside the proof in solemn form, as in the present case the action had been compromised, he would not do so. The daughter had had the opportunity of persisting in her opposition.[3]

Accordingly, probate in solemn form will only be set aside where it was obtained by fraud,[4] or a later will is discovered, or the party opposing has been prevented by some unavoidable accident from taking part in the proceedings.[5]

---

[1] [1965] 2 All E.R. 311.

[2] Under O. 36, r. 33.

[3] See also *Young* v. *Holloway*, [1895] P. 87; and *Re West, Tiger* v. *Handley*, [1948] W.N. 432.

[4] *Priestman* v. *Thomas* (1884), 9 P.D. 70; *Birch* v. *Birch*, [1902] P. 62.

[5] *Per* Payne, J., in *Re Barraclough, Barraclough* v. *Young*, [1965] 2 All E.R. 311, at p. 316. See also *In the Estate of Langton*, [1964] P. 163.

C. EVIDENCE IN PROBATE ACTIONS

1. ATTESTING WITNESSES

The best evidence which the court will accept of the due execution of a will is that of an attesting witness, so that a person propounding a will must call one of the attesting witnesses, unless they cannot be traced or are dead. This applies even if there is other evidence of due execution.

An attesting witness is regarded as a witness on behalf of the court, and not of either party.[1] Accordingly, if the executor calls one of the attesting witnesses, who gives evidence against proper execution, he may cross-examine that witness.[2] In *Oakes* v. *Uzzell*[3] where the executor called one witness who spoke against the will, he was then allowed to call the other. Probate may be granted in solemn form if one attesting witness speaks in favour of the will,[4] but if one speaks against the will, both must be called, if available.

Where neither of the attesting witnesses is available, the evidence of some other person who was also present at the time of execution may be admitted. The evidence of such a person is admissible, even if he takes a benefit under the will, and had for that reason refrained from attesting the will himself.[5]

2. OTHER EVIDENCE

If no attesting witness can be traced, and no other person can be found who was present at the time of execution, the court will admit the next best evidence that is available. Of this it is possible to give only examples. In *In the Estate of Phibbs*[6] the testator sent his will by registered post to his solicitor at Dublin, at the time of the civil disorder in Ireland. The letter never arrived and it was presumed to have been destroyed in a Post Office fire in Ireland. There was no record of who had witnessed the will. The testator's nephew, and the principal beneficiary who was a clerk

---

[1] *Oakes* v. *Uzzell*, [1932] P. 19.

[2] *Coles* v. *Coles and Brown* (1866), L.R. 1 P. & D. 70; *In the Estate of Fuld* (No. 2), [1965] P. 405.

[3] [1932] P. 19.

[4] *Bowman* v. *Hodgson* (1867), L.R. 1 P. & D. 362; *Owen* v. *Williams* (1863), 32 L.J.P. M. & A. 159.

[5] *Mackay* v. *Rawlinson* (1919), 35 T.L.R. 223.

[6] [1917] P. 93.

to a solicitor, had both read through the will after execution and were able to remember the contents. Probate was granted. In *Palin* v. *Ponting*[1] the will had first been proved in common form, and as part of that process, one of the attesting witnesses had sworn an affidavit of due execution. The witness was not available at the time of the application for probate in solemn form, and that previous affidavit of due execution was admitted in evidence. And in *In the Estate of Powe*[2] a solicitor who prepared the will was allowed to produce as a witness a note prepared by him at the same time.

3. DECLARATIONS BY THE TESTATOR
a. *Generally*

The general rule with regard to the construction of wills is that the intention of the testator must be deduced from the will itself, and extrinsic evidence is not admitted.[3] In accordance with this rule, declarations made by the testator, such as casual statements to friends, or remarks in letters, are likewise not admissible. In other circumstances, however, declarations made by the testator are admissible. These circumstances are:

a. Where the declaration is made by the testator in writing, and signed by him. In this case the declaration is within the terms of the Civil Evidence Act 1968, and is evidence of the statements contained in it.[4]

b. To show the state of mind of the testator. The type of situations in which this arises are:

(i) Where there is doubt whether a testamentary act has been done with the necessary *animus testandi* or *animus revocandi*. Thus evidence has been admitted to show whether the testator signed a will *animo testandi*;[5] whether he destroyed a will *animo revocandi*;[6] and whether the presumption that a will known to have existed cannot be

---

[1] [1930] P. 185.
[2] [1956] P. 110.
[3] *Ante*, p. 141.
[4] *In the Estate of Bridgewater*, [1965] 1 All E.R. 717, a decision on the Evidence Act 1938.
[5] *In the Goods of Slinn* (1890), 15 P.D. 156.
[6] *Giles* v. *Warren* (1872), L.R. 2 P. & D. 401.

found at death has been revoked *animo revocandi* could be rebutted.[1]

(ii) Whether a particular document is in fact intended to be a will, or some other type of instrument. Thus in *In the Goods of Slinn*[2] where an elderly widow executed a deed in which she granted her savings to her niece, and it was not apparent from the face of the document whether it was intended to operate as a deed *inter vivos* or a will, the court admitted evidence that the woman had said that she wanted to settle her affairs, to show that it was intended as a will.

(iii) Whether, in the case of an allegation of unsoundness of mind, the testator had mental capacity.

(iv) Whether, in the case of an allegation of fraud, the will was consistent with the testator's desires.[3]

c. Exceptionally, to show that a will or codicil has been made or revoked in accordance with the formal requirements of the Wills Act.

The last category causes difficulty. In general, declarations by the testator are not admissible to prove compliance with formal requirements. They are, however, admissible:

(i) where the declaration comes within the Civil Evidence Act 1968.

(ii) to support (and presumably, therefore, to rebut) a presumption of due execution. Thus, in *Clarke* v. *Clarke*[4] the testator made a holograph will which contained an attestation clause. He asked two illiterate farm hands to act as witnesses, and they signed the will with crosses. They died before the testator, and the court admitted in evidence a statement made by the testator to his wife at the time showing that he knew of the requirements for attestation.

A recent example of the application of two of these rules is *In the Estate of Bridgewater*.[5] The testator made two wills, one on

---

[1] *Keen* v. *Keen* (1873), L.R. 3 P. & D. 105.

[2] (1890), 15 P.D. 156; and see *ante*, p. 10.

[3] *Doe d. Ellis* v. *Hardy* (1836), 1 Mood. & R. 525; *Doe d. Shallcross* v. *Palmer* (1851), 16 Q.B. 747.

[4] (1880), 5 L.R. Ir. 47.

[5] [1965] 1 All E.R. 717.

27 March 1960 and the other on 29 March 1960, to which he referred as his "old will" and his "new will" respectively. In August 1960 his solicitor sent the new will to him, together with an accompanying letter, and the testator replied: "Thank you for your note with enclosure; you will find the old will has been deposited at the Municipal Bank, the new one having been destroyed." On his death in 1962, neither will was found. The applicant, who was named as executor in both wills claimed that notwithstanding the presumption that the new will was revoked because it could not be found, the testator had only destroyed the new will because he thought that the old will would thereby be revived, and that therefore the doctrine of dependent relative revocation would operate to save the new will. Scarman, J., held that the letter from the testator was evidence of the testator's intention to destroy the new will with a view to setting up the old one. He held that the letter was also admissible under the Evidence Act 1938 as evidence of actual destruction. On this basis, the applicant was successful, and probate was granted of the new will.[1]

b. *Where will lost or destroyed*

There is no doubt that where a will has been lost, or is destroyed without *animus revocandi*, and an attempt is being made to reconstruct it for probate purposes, declarations made by the testator before or at the time of making the will are admissible as evidence of its contents. As Sir J. P. Wilde said in *Johnson* v. *Lyford*[2]: "It would often be impracticable to judge of the quality and nature of acts done if the statements of the person doing them immediately preceding or accompanying those acts were excluded from view." There is, however, some doubt as to the admissibility of declarations made after the will was made.

The classic authority is *Sugden* v. *Lord St. Leonards*.[3] Lord St. Leonards was a former Lord Chancellor, and left an estate of over £300,000. Towards the end of his life he made numerous wills, the last being a will made in 1870, and eight codicils to it. On his death in 1875, the codicils were found, but not the will, and

---

[1] It had been held in *Powell* v. *Powell* (1866), L.R. 1 P. & D. 209, that the doctrine of dependent relative revocation could apply in circumstances such as this.

[2] (1868), L.R. 1 P. & D. 546.

[3] (1876), 1 P.D. 154.

an attempt was made to reconstruct the will. His daughter had acted as his secretary for a number of years, and she gave evidence that she had read the will and codicils on various occasions, and that she was able to write out from memory the main provisions of the will. She also gave evidence of conversations with Lord St. Leonards after the making of the will, which indicated the contents of the will. The court thought it inconceivable that he would have died intestate, and it accepted the daughter's evidence. In the Court of Appeal, the decision was upheld, but Mellish, L.J., dissented from the majority, and said that while he agreed with the result, the evidence of the conversations after the making of the will should not have been admitted.

The decision was doubted by the House of Lords in *Woodward* v. *Goulstone*[1] and it has been subsequently doubted by the Court of Appeal.[2] In the most recent decisions, *Sugden* v. *Lord St. Leonards* has been followed by the Court of Appeal,[3] and at first instance,[4] as well as being supported, *obiter*, by the Lord Chief Justice of Northern Ireland.[5]

Although the position cannot be regarded as settled, it seems that *Sugden* v. *Lord St. Leonards* remains binding, though it will not be extended.

D. COSTS

It is an implied term of the relationship between the executor and the estate that he is entitled to be paid out of the estate such costs as are incurred by him in establishing or maintaining his position. The position was summarized by Jessel, M.R., in *Turner* v. *Hancock*[6] who said that the right of an executor to his costs rests "substantially upon contract and [will] only be lost or curtailed by such inequitable conduct on the part of [the executor] as may amount to a violation or culpable neglect of his duty under the contract".[7]

---

[1] (1886), 11 App. Cas. 469.

[2] *Atkinson* v. *Morris*, [1897] P. 40, at p. 50; *Barkwell* v. *Barkwell*, [1928] P. 91, at p. 97.

[3] *In the Estate of MacGillivray*, [1946] 2 All E.R. 301.

[4] *In the Estate of Wipperman*, [1955] P. 59.

[5] *In the Goods of Gilliland*, [1940] N.I. 125.

[6] (1882), 20 Ch.D. 303, at p. 305.

[7] See also *In the Estate of Plant*, [1926] P. 139, especially at p. 146.

Accordingly, as long as an executor acts reasonably, his position with regard to costs is protected. *In the Estate of Speke, Speke* v. *Deakin*[1] is an example of a case where an order for costs was made against the executors. They had proved a will and two codicils in common form, and after the grant a third codicil was also found. The principal beneficiary under the third codicil asked the executors to prove that codicil, but they refused, saying that it had been made without the knowledge and approval of the testator. In some circumstances, where the evidence was abundantly clear, this attitude might have been proper, but in this case the judge described their attitude as "perfect folly". He condemned them to pay the costs personally.[2]

From one point of view the general rule is unsatisfactory. Although, in the absence of culpable behaviour, an established executor is entitled to his costs, where a will is being proved for the first time, the person propounding the will cannot know until the outcome of the case whether in fact he is the executor. A person who is nominated in the will is not automatically entitled to his costs if he fails to establish the validity of the will,[3] and in this case the costs are in the discretion of the court.[4]

So far as the costs of other parties are concerned, the position is:

a. in all cases, costs are in the discretion of the court;[5]

subject to this:

b. where the costs have been incurred through the fault of the testator, or of the persons interested in residue, the court will order the costs to be paid out of the estate;[6]

c. where a party is unsuccessful, but brought the proceedings reasonably, he may not have an order for costs made against him;[7]

d. in all other cases the court will usually award costs to the successful party.

---

[1] (1913), 109 L.T. 719.

[2] For another example, see *Thomas* v. *Jones*, [1928] P. 162.

[3] *In the Estate of Barlow*, [1919] P. 131.

[4] See R.S.C., O. 65, r. 1. See also *Davies* v. *Jones*, [1899] P. 161.

[5] *Mitchell and Mitchell* v. *Gard and Kingwell* (1863), 3 Sw. & Tr. 275, at p. 278; *Twist* v. *Tye*, [1902] P. 92, at p. 93; *Re Cutliffe, Le Duc* v. *Veness*, [1959] P. 6.

[6] *Spiers* v. *English*, [1907] P. 122.

[7] *Spiers* v. *English*, [1907] P. 122, at p. 123.

An example of a case where the costs are incurred through the fault of the testator would be where the will on its face is not clear, and judicial action is necessary to resolve the doubt. It does not include "fault" in a more general sense, such as failing to make provision for certain classes of beneficiary who may have a moral claim on the estate,[1] or by telling persons in his lifetime that he had made provision for them, whereas he had in fact not done so.[2]

---

[1] Subject to the right of an applicant to apply under the Family Provision legislation.

[2] *Re Cutliffe, Le Duc v. Veness*, [1959] P. 6, at p. 19.

CHAPTER 20

REVOCATION OF GRANTS

1. POWER TO REVOKE

Judicature Act 1925, s. 20, confers upon the High Court all the powers to revoke grants, as well as to make them, which were exercised under the now repealed Court of Probate Act 1857, and by the church courts prior to that Act. Section 20 itself is in general terms, and does not specify the circumstances in which a grant will be revoked, but a body of law has developed so that there is now little doubt as to when a grant will be revoked. The court also has power to amend a grant.[1]

2. WHEN GRANTS WILL BE REVOKED

There are two principles which the court applies in deciding whether to revoke a grant, namely:

a. the person truly entitled to a grant shall prevail; and

b. the court has regard to the interests of the beneficiaries under the will or on intestacy.[2]

By applying these principles, it appears that a grant will be revoked in the following circumstances:

1. Where the "deceased" is in fact alive;[3]

2. Where the grant has been made to the wrong person. Thus in *In the Goods of Bergman*[4] a grant was made to a person who claimed to be a relative, and who, had he in fact been a relative, would have been entitled to the grant. It was revoked when it was found that he was illegitimate. Again

---

[1] N.C.P.R. 1954, r. 42.

[2] See *In the Goods of Galbraith*, [1951] P. 422.

[3] *In the Goods of Napier* (1809), 1 Philim. 83; *In the Estate of Bloch* (1959), *Times*, July 2nd.

[4] (1842), 2 Notes of Cases 22.

in *Re Moore*¹ where a man and a woman had lived together as man and wife, and, upon the man's death, the woman obtained a grant of administration as his "widow", that grant was revoked upon it being shown that she had not been legally married;²

3. Where on the facts as known at the time of the grant it was properly made, but facts subsequently coming to light show it to have been improper. This will apply if after a will is proved, a codicil is discovered appointing a different executor, or if a completely new will is discovered. It will also apply if it subsequently appears that the deceased married after making the will;³

4. If the grant was obtained in contravention of the appropriate procedural requirements. This includes cases where a grant has been inadvertently issued after the entry of a caveat, but without notice to the caveator;⁴ where a person in a lower order of entitlement has obtained a grant of administration without citing all those with a higher right;⁵ and where a grant was mistakenly issued less than the prescribed time from the date of death;⁶

5. Where the grant was obtained through fraud on the court;⁷

6. Where, in the case of a grant in solemn form, a person having an opposing interest was, through unavoidable accident, precluded from taking part in the proceedings;⁸

7. Where, after a will has been proved in common form, the executors attempt to prove it in solemn form, but are unable to do so;

8. Where one of two representatives becomes incapable of acting, so that a new grant may be made to the other.⁹

---

¹ (1845), 3 Notes of Cases 601.
² See also *In the Goods of Langley* (1851), 2 Rob. Eccl. 407.
³ *Priestman* v. *Thomas* (1884), 9 P.D. 70, at p. 210.
⁴ *Trimlestown* v. *Trimlestown* (1830), 3 Hagg. Ecc. 243.
⁵ *Ravenscroft* v. *Ravenscroft* (1671), 1 Lev. 305.
⁶ *Trimlestown* v. *Trimlestown*, *ante*; *Blackborough* v. *Davis* (1700), 1 Salk. 38.
⁷ *Priestman* v. *Thomas* (1884), 9 P.D. 70; *Birch* v. *Birch*, [1902] P. 62; *Re Barraclough, Barraclough* v. *Young*, [1965] 2 All E.R. 311.
⁸ See *Re Barraclough, Barraclough* v. *Young*, [1965] 2 All E.R. 311, at p. 316.
⁹ *In the Goods of Phillips* (1824), 2 Addams 335; *In the Estate of Shaw*, [1905] P. 92; see *ante*, p. 292.

Where, however, a sole representative becomes incapable, the grant will usually be impounded during the period of incapacity, and not revoked.[1]

9. Where the representative has permanently left the jurisdiction, or otherwise cannot be found.[2]

The first seven of these grounds are within the first principle, namely proper entitlement, and the other two are within the second principle, of the court acting to safeguard the interests of the beneficiaries.

3. PROCEDURE ON REVOCATION

The Non-Contentious Probate Rules[3] envisage that in most cases an application for revocation will be made by the party to whom the grant was made, and they provide that a grant is to be revoked on the application of some other party only in exceptional circumstances. This, however, applies only to non-contentious business. Where an application is made to compel revocation, and the person to whom the grant was made actively resists, the matter will be contested, and will come within the definition of contentious business.[4]

In general, the court will not make a new grant until the old grant has been revoked.[5] Where the application for revocation is made by some person other than the person to whom the grant was issued, he may issue a citation to the grantee requiring him to bring in his grant to the registry.[6] However, Administration of Justice Act 1956, s. 17, enables the court to call in a grant on its own initiative, and to revoke a grant without it being called in, if it cannot be obtained.[7] Further, a personal representative is always under an obligation to deliver up his grant when called upon to do by the court.[8] A theoretical distinction is drawn between the

---

[1] *In the Goods of Cooke*, [1895] P. 68; see *ante*, p. 292.
[2] *Re Bradshaw* (1887), 13 P.D. 18; *In the Estate of French*, [1910] P. 169; *In the Estate of Thomas*, [1912] P. 177.
[3] N.C.P.R. 1954, r. 42, proviso.
[4] See *ante*, p. 296.
[5] *Re Hornbuckle* (1890), 15 P.D. 149.
[6] See *ante*, p. 280.
[7] E.g., if it has been lost, or cannot be traced.
[8] Administration of Estates Act 1925, s. 25 (c), substituted by Administration of Estates Act 1971, s. 9.

situation where a grant is called in and cancelled, and one where, because it cannot be produced, it is revoked but not cancelled.[1] No practical difference results from this distinction.

4. AMENDMENT

The court has power to amend a grant,[2] but this power will only be exercised where a non-substantial error has been made on the grant, such as a mistake in the date or place of death of the deceased, or in the name or address of the grantee. All questions of substance must be dealt with by revocation, and the issue of a new grant.

It should be noted, however, that the court will not revoke a grant if there is any other way of achieving a proper result. If, therefore, after a grant has been made of a will, a codicil is discovered, a separate grant will be made of that codicil, without disturbing the existing grant in respect of the will, unless the codicil appoints different executors.[3]

5. MISCONDUCT ON PART OF GRANTEE

It will be noted that in the list of circumstances given above in which the court will revoke a grant, no reference was made to revocation on the ground of the representative's misconduct. This is because the beneficiaries will usually be protected by some other means. In particular, the representatives can be compelled to make on oath an inventory and account under Administration of Estates Act 1925, s. 25, and an action will lie against them at the instance of the beneficiaries in the case of default.[4]

The provisions of Judicature Act 1925, s. 20, are, however, wide enough to enable the court to revoke in the case of misconduct, but presumably it will do so only where there is no other remedy available which will give adequate protection to those interested in the estate.

6. EFFECT OF REVOCATION

A grant of probate or administration, being an order of the court, confers full protection on those acting under it while it

---

[1] *In the Estate of Thomas*, [1912] P. 177.
[2] N.C.P.R. 1954, r. 42.
[3] In this case the grant will be revoked.
[4] *Hill* v. *Bird* (1648), Sty. 102; *In the Estate of Cope*, [1954] 1 All E.R. 698.

remains in force, and it is specifically provided that even if it was improperly issued, a purchaser acting under it will be protected, even if he had knowledge of the impropriety.[1] This is particularly important with regard to settled land. Where it appears on the face of the will that a grant of special representation should have been made to the trustees for the purposes of the Settled Land Act,[2] but in fact a general grant is issued, the purchaser from the general personal representatives is protected, and obtains a good title.[3]

There is no single provision which protects persons who have relied upon a grant which is subsequently revoked, but a series of separate provisions which go a long way towards having the same effect. These are:

a. *Administration of Estates Act* 1925, *section* 27

Sub-s. (2) provides that if a payment has been made to a personal representative, and his grant is subsequently revoked, the receipt of the personal representative at that time is a good discharge. This sub-section also enables a representative, upon revocation of his grant, and upon his accounting to the new personal representative, to reimburse himself for those payments which he made while the grant was in force, and which were proper to be made in the administration of the estate.

b. *Administration of Estates Act* 1925, *section* 37

Under this section, a "conveyance" of either realty or personalty to a "purchaser" is declared to be valid, notwithstanding the subsequent revocation of the grant. The word "conveyance" is used in a very wide sense, and is defined[4] to "include" a mortgage, lease, vesting instrument and every other assurance "by any instrument". It is not clear whether the handing over of chattels, where no instrument is involved, would be within the section. The section clearly contemplates a written means of transferring title, but as the definition is stated to "include" such instruments, it may well be that the definition is wide enough to embrace the physical handing over.

---

[1] Law of Property Act 1925, s. 204.
[2] *Post*, p. 353.
[3] *Re Bridgett and Hayes' Contract*, [1928] Ch. 163; *In the Estate of Taylor*, [1929] P. 260, at p. 263.
[4] Administration of Estates Act 1925, s. 55 (1).

c. *Law of Property Act* 1925, *section* 204

The protection conferred upon a purchaser, even where he knows of the irregularity, has already been mentioned.

d. *Administration of Estates Act* 1925, *section* 39 (1) (iii)

This sub-section confers upon personal representatives the statutory powers given to trustees for sale. It provides that all contracts entered into by personal representatives within these powers as trustees for sale are enforceable by and against the personal representatives for the time being, so that a contract entered into by a personal representative whose grant is revoked will be binding upon the new representative.

e. *Administration of Estates Act* 1925, *section* 17

This section applies only to the revocation of temporary grants, and not to the revocation of permanent ones. Under it, the court may direct that proceedings pending by or against a temporary representative whose grant is revoked may be continued by or against the new representative. This power is, however, within the discretion of the court.

The effect of these provisions is to confer adequate protection upon purchasers, which means any person who acquires an interest in property for valuable consideration.[1] Unfortunately, the provisions do not deal expressly with the position of a person who receives property without consideration, as, for example, the person entitled under a will. What is the position of a person to whom an assent is made in accordance with the terms of the will, and upon a new will being discovered the grant is revoked?

The principle in *Hewson* v. *Shelley*[2] assists. In that case letters of administration had been granted to the widow of a man who was thought to have died intestate. The administratrix in the course of administration sold part of the estate. Subsequently, a will was discovered, the grant of administration revoked, and probate of the will granted to the executors named in it. They instituted an action against the purchaser to recover the land on the ground that the original grant was void *ab initio*, and they were successful at first instance. The decision was reversed by the Court of Appeal,

---

[1] Administration of Estates Act 1925, s. 55 (1).
[2] [1914] 2 Ch. 13, C.A.

who held that the grant was not void *ab initio* but that the revocation took effect only from the date of revocation. Although the case is concerned with the position of a purchaser, and its result has now been given statutory authority, the principle would appear to apply to any disposal. The transferee would obtain a good title, but it seems that upon the grant being revoked, an action would lie at the instance of the new representatives for the recovery of that asset.[1]

---

[1] *Re Diplock's Estate, Diplock* v. *Wintle,* [1948] Ch. 465.

Part VI

THE POSITION OF THE PERSONAL REPRESENTATIVES

CHAPTER 21

THE PERSONAL REPRESENTATIVE'S OFFICE

1. FUNCTIONS OF PERSONAL REPRESENTATIVES

At the outset of this section of the book, on the administration of estates, it may be useful to outline the functions of a personal representative. Broadly following the usual chronological order, a personal representative must:

(i) ascertain the assets and liabilities of the deceased;

(ii) pay the estate duty, if any,[1] on the net value of the assets, as so ascertained;

(iii) obtain a grant of probate or letters of administration, where it is proposed to take out a grant;[2]

(iv) collect in the assets, including in some cases, such as stocks and shares, the registration of those assets in the name of the personal representative;

(v) realize at least sufficient of the assets to pay all debts and liabilities of the estate, and, where assets are not to be transferred *in specie*, to pay pecuniary legacies;

(vi) examine each of the debts and liabilities, and to pay such of them as are properly payable. This will include agreement of the deceased's liability for income tax and capital gains tax up to the date of death;

(vii) pay the pecuniary and specific legacies;

(viii) make any adjustment necessary to the Inland Revenue Affidavit of the deceased's estate which may become necessary in

---

[1] At present (1973), there is no liability for estate duty where the net estate does not exceed £15,000: Finance Act 1972, s. 120.

[2] See *post*, p. 366, for a discussion of the circumstances in which a personal representative need not apply for a grant.

view of further assets or liabilities coming to light, and pay any additional estate duty which is exigible. Upon payment of all duty on the estate as finally agreed, the personal representative will apply for and obtain an estate duty clearance certificate, being a certificate that the Commissioners of Inland Revenue are satisfied that all duty properly payable in respect of the assets declared has been paid;[1]

(ix) agree and discharge all liabilities of the administration itself (as distinct from the liabilities of the deceased which were dealt with under (iv)). These will include payment of the funeral account; reimbursement of any expenses to which the personal representative has been put; payment of his remuneration, if by virtue of a charging clause he is entitled to make a charge for his services; payment of legal and any other professional fees incurred during the course of the administration; and the payment of any income tax and capital gains tax which is payable in respect of events occurring since the death of the deceased;

(x) prepare the estate accounts, giving details of all assets received, payments made, and the balance due to the residuary beneficiaries;

(xi) transfer the residue to the residuary beneficiaries, or, if the personal representative is to hold that residue on trust, assent to the vesting of that property in himself as trustee.

There are many possible variations in this order, but this list will serve as a sufficient outline. Other chapters of this book deal with obtaining the grant of probate or letters of administration,[2] and the management of assets prior to the grant.[3] It is not proposed to discuss here the incidence of estate duty, or the personal representative's liability therefor, but the remainder of the items mentioned above are considered in the following chapters.

2. THE ADMINISTRATION PERIOD

Generally speaking, a personal representative holds office during the administration period. There is, however, no statutory

---

[1] The certificate is given pursuant to Finance Act 1894, s. 11.
[2] See *ante*, p. 239.
[3] See *post*, p. 366.

definition of the administration period for general purposes. Some assistance may be derived from Income and Corporation Taxes Act 1970, s. 433, which is considered later. It will be seen that the definition in this section stops at item (x) in the list given above, and would not include (xi). It is thought, however, that while special considerations which apply to income tax which would justify this interpretation, for general purposes the administration period would include item (xi).

The general statement that a personal representative holds office during the administration period is subject to these qualifications:

a. a personal representative may be sued after he has ceased to function as such for acts committed during the period of administration;[1]

b. in special cases grants may be obtained many years after the completion of the administration period; and

c. in many cases it is more appropriate to ask whether a person is a personal representative in respect of a particular asset or in respect of a particular liability than to ask the question in a more general sense.

The last two points need elaboration.

We have seen that in some cases a further grant of representation can be obtained after the completion of the administration period in the sense given above. Thus, if an infant is entitled to a grant, administration may be entrusted to a person for his use and benefit, leaving the infant to obtain a grant upon attaining the age of 18.[2] If the administration is complete by that time, this will involve the administrator in the liability only to give to the former infant an account of his administration. Likewise, where, for example, an asset falls into the estate, and the original representatives are no longer alive, a grant *de bonis non* may be necessary. Suppose, therefore, that Albert makes a will leaving his house to his nephew Basil for life, with remainder to Clarence. Suppose also that Albert dies in 1940, Clarence in 1950 and Basil in 1960. The administration of Clarence's estate may have been completed within a year or so after his death, without his personal representatives having any knowledge of the reversionary interest to

---

[1] See *post*, p. 433.
[2] See *ante*, p. 290.

which his estate would be entitled. If one or more of his personal representatives was alive at the date of death of Basil, then he could deal with the house at that time in accordance with Clarence's will, but if no personal representative was then alive a grant *de bonis non* to the estate of Clarence would be necessary, unless there was an executor acting under the chain of representation.

On these considerations alone, therefore, it indicates that it is often better to consider in respect of a particular asset whether a person is acting as personal representative.

3. PERSONAL REPRESENTATIVE OR TRUSTEE?

The function of a personal representative is essentially to wind up an estate and distribute assets, whereas the function of a trustee is essentially to hold assets until a specified event happens. In many cases the same persons are appointed by will to be executors and trustees, either because a trust is expressly created by will, or because a trust will arise by operation of law in that one or more of the beneficiaries may be under 18, and so unable to give a good discharge. In this type of case there will be a normal progression from acting as personal representative to acting as a trustee. There is, however, considerable doubt as to the point of time at which the transition takes place, and whether formalities are necessary to mark the transfer in status.

a. *Importance of distinction*

It is important to know whether a person is acting as personal representative or as trustee because:

(i) In respect of personal property, personal representatives have several authority, while trustees only have joint authority.[1] Thus *Attenborough* v. *Solomon*,[2] was concerned with the dealing by one of two persons with silver plate. One executor alone would have had power to sell the plate in the course of the administration of the estate, but it was held that as the dealing occurred over ten years after the administration had ceased, the personal representative had by then become a trustee, so that he alone could give no title to it.[3] This distinction applies only to

---

[1] *Jacomb* v. *Harwood* (1751), 2 Ves. Sen. 266.
[2] [1913] A.C. 76.
[3] This case is discussed further, *post*, p. 323.

pure personalty: in respect of realty, and leaseholds,[1] the authority of both personal representatives and trustees is joint.

(ii) A sale by a sole, or sole surviving, personal representative will be sufficient to overreach equitable interests, whereas a sale by a sole trustee will not be sufficient for this purpose.[2] Where, therefore, title is proposed to be made by a sole trustee, the purchaser must insist on the appointment of a co-trustee, to enable him to obtain a title free of overreachable equities.[3]

(iii) A new trustee can be appointed of an existing trust by the existing trustees, or, if there are none, by the personal representatives of the last surviving trustee.[4] There is no similar provision in respect of executors and administrators, so that if the only or last surviving personal representative dies, and there is no executor by representation, then if the estate is not fully administered, a new grant *de bonis non* must be obtained.

(iv) Certain rights and liabilities may be exercised only in respect of the deceased's estate, and not in respect of trust property. For example, where a guarantee is given by a surety, it makes him liable only in respect of acts done during the administration of the estate.[5]

(v) Actions against personal representatives in respect of personal estate may be brought within twelve years from the cause of action arising,[6] whereas actions by beneficiaries to recover trust property or in respect of breach of trust cannot be brought later than six years from the accruer of the right of action.[7] These limitations apply in neither case where there is fraud, or retention by the trustee or personal representative of the property.[8]

b. *Principles*

Before examining the cases, it may assist to formulate the conclusions which it is suggested can be drawn from them. These are:

---

[1] Administration of Estates Act 1925, s. 23(1), 54.

[2] Unless the sole trustee is a trust corporation. See Law of Property Act 1925, s. 27(2), and Settled Land Act 1925, s. 18(1).

[3] Subject to the provisions of the Law of Property (Joint Tenants) Act 1964.

[4] Trustee Act 1925, s. 36.

[5] See on the position of an administration bond, which was replaced by the guarantee, *Harvell* v. *Foster*, *post*, p. 324.

[6] Except in respect of actions to recover arrears of interest on legacies, when the period is six years.

[7] Limitation Act 1939, s. 19(2), 20.

[8] Limitation Act 1939, s. 20.

(i) It is necessary to draw a distinction between the office of a personal representative and the functions which attach to that office:

    a. where the grant is limited as to time, the office of personal representative will terminate at the expiration of that period. It will also terminate if the grant is revoked by the court, unless, presumably, it is replaced by another grant to the same person but in a different capacity. In all other cases, the office of personal representative will last for the duration of the life of the executor or administrator, although, as it terminates on his death, it will not devolve to his estate. There is, therefore, a distinction between the time during which the personal representative holds his office, and the administration period.

    b. the functions which attach to that office are those comprised in the list with which this chapter began.

(ii) A person may be both personal representative and trustee at the same time, although he cannot hold the same item of property in both capacities simultaneously. Accordingly, after the administration of the estate has been completed the person holds property as trustee, but he nevertheless retains his office of personal representative, and so he can act if, for example, further property falls into the estate.

(iii) In respect of any item of property, a personal representative will cease to hold as such and will thereafter hold as trustee:

    a. in the case of land, if, and only if, he executes an assent in his favour in the capacity of trustee;

    b. in the case of pure personalty,

        1. if he executes an assent in his favour as trustee; or

        2. upon the completion of the administration, whichever occurs first.

(iv) For the purposes of the last rule, it is a question of fact in all cases whether the administration has been completed, although there will probably be a presumption that when all the items listed at the beginning of this chapter have been dealt with, the administration is complete.

We can now turn to the cases which either support these principles, or are at least consistent with them. *Attenborough* v.

Solomon[1] is clear authority that provided a person does hold as trustee, then he has authority over assets jointly with trustees, and not individually. In that case the testator appointed his two sons to be his executors and trustees. He left to them part of the estate beneficially, in respect of which no question arose, and part to be held upon trust for his daughter. The testator died in March 1878, and the residuary account was prepared in March 1879, all debts and legacies having been paid before that time. One of the assets forming part of the residue which was to be held upon trust for the daughter consisted of silver plate, which had always been in the sole custody of one of the sons.[2] In March 1892 he pledged the plate to secure a loan, the lender having no notice that it consisted of trust property. The son who pledged the plate subsequently died, and the other son brought an action against the lender to recover the plate, on the basis that he had no title to it. If the sons had had several authority, the action could not have succeeded, because each could have made title, and the lender took without notice of the rights of the beneficiaries. The plaintiff did, however, succeed, both in the Court of Appeal and in the House of Lords. Viscount Haldane, L.C. found as a fact that "the executors considered that they had done all that was due from them as executors by 1879, and were content when the residuary account was passed that the dispositions of the will should take effect. That is the inference I draw from the form of the residuary account; and the inference is strengthened when I consider the lapse of time since then, and that in the interval nothing was done by them purporting to be an exercise of power as executors . . . It follows that under these dispositions the residuary estate, including the chattels in question, became vested in the trustees as trustees."

It will be noted that Lord Haldane took into account, when making his decision on the facts, that a residuary account had been prepared; the interval of time since then; and the attitude of the personal representatives themselves.

The next case is *Re Ponder, Ponder v. Ponder*.[3] In that case, a widow was granted letters of administration to her late husband's

---

[1] [1913]. A.C. 76.
[2] It was the duty of the other son to see that the asset was brought under joint control, and an action would have been brought against him for failing to do so.
[3] [1921] 2 Ch. 59.

estate. She had discharged the debts and had ascertained the residue, and had divided it into the separate funds which were required under the pre-1926 Statutes of Distribution. Sargant, J. held that she had assumed the character of trustee in respect of that property, and so advantage could be taken of the statutory powers[1] for appointing new trustees.[2]

Re Ponder, Ponder v. *Ponder* was called into question in *Harvell* v. *Foster*.[3] In that case the testator's daughter was appointed the sole executrix of his will. She was married but under 21, and so could not take probate.[4] Accordingly, a grant of letters of administration with will annexed was granted to her husband for her use and benefit during her minority.[5] An administration bond was given. The husband received the net residue of almost £1,000, which under the terms of the will belonged to the daughter, his wife. He gave her £300, turned her out of the matrimonial home, and disappeared. When she attained the age of 21, the daughter had the bond assigned to her, and, her husband not being traceable, she brought action on the bond against the sureties. The terms of the bond required the husband "well and truly to administer the estate according to law" and "to make or cause to be made a just and true account of the administration of the estate".

At first instance Lord Goddard, C.J.,[6] dismissed the action. Relying upon *Re Ponder, Ponder* v. *Ponder*[7] he held that once the net residue was in the husband's hands, he became a trustee of it, and as the sureties to the bond were liable only in respect of acts done by the husband *qua* administrator, they were not liable. The decision was reversed on appeal. The exact ground of the decision is uncertain. In the first place considerable importance was attached to the wording of the bond itself. Lord Evershed, M.R., said, "upon the failure . . . of her husband to account for the proceeds of the realisation of the testator's estate, having in fact misappropriated it to his own use, the latter was shown not to have 'well and truly administered' the estate 'according to law'

---

[1] At that time, under the Trustee Act 1893.

[2] The appointment then had to be made with the assistance of the court. It can now be made without the intervention of the court under Trustee Act 1925, s. 36.

[3] Under the rules then in force.

[4] [1954] 2 Q.B. 367.

[5] As to this type of grant, see *ante*, p. 290.

[6] [1954] 1 Q.B. 591.

[7] [1921] 2 Ch. 59.

within the true meaning and interest of the bond".[1] It may be that the Court regarded the expression "well and truly administer" for the purposes of the bond as being rather different than administration for more general purposes. Secondly, the Court was clearly influenced by the fact that the grant was for a limited time only. In this connexion, Lord Evershed observed that "the present is not an 'ordinary' case, for the husband, by the terms of his appointment as administrator, ceased altogether to have that character" when the daughter attained 21. It is difficult to see the theoretical justification for any reliance being placed on this point.

Thirdly, Lord Evershed drew a distinction between the office as such, which, where the grant is not limited as to time, "the personal representative, once appointed, retains for all time" and the duties of functions of office which will be exhausted.

He then said that a personal representative may retain that office and nevertheless hold assets *qua* trustee. Indeed, accepting that the widow in *Re Ponder*, *Ponder* v. *Ponder* had become a trustee, Lord Evershed said that "it does not necessarily follow that she had therefore altogether cast off her duties and capacity as administratrix". But difficulty is caused by the application of this distinction to the facts in question. There would have been no difficulty in saying that after the residue had been ascertained, the husband held as trustee, although he could still be sued as personal representative for acts done during the period leading up to the ascertainment of the residue. But Lord Evershed went much further. He said, in an important passage, "we are unable to accept the view . . . that because a personal representative who has cleared the estate becomes a trustee of the net residue for the persons beneficially interested, the clearing of the estate necessarily and automatically discharges him from his obligations as personal representative and, in particular, from the obligation of any bond he may have entered into for the due administration of the estate. We would add that, in our view, the duty of an administrator as such must at least extend to paying the funeral and testamentary expenses and debts and legacies (if any) and where, as here, immediate distribution is impossible owing to the infancy of the person beneficially entitled, retaining the net residue in trust for the infant". Lord Evershed recognised the

[1] Emphasis supplied.

possibility that an express appointment of trustees of the fund *could* be made under Administration of Estates Act 1925, s. 42, but subject to this the personal representative would hold as such until the infant reached majority.

For present purposes, the most important aspect of *Harvell* v. *Foster* is the remarks made upon the decision in *Re Ponder*, *Ponder* v. *Ponder*. "If Sargant, J. in *Re Ponder*, *Ponder* v. *Ponder* is to be taken to have decided that once a personal representative, by clearing the estate, has discharged all his functions other than those of a trustee for the persons beneficially interested in the net residue, and has thus become a trustee for those persons, he must be regarded, merely by virtue of such clearance, to have discharged himself from all his obligations as personal representative, because the capacities of personal representative and trustee are mutually exclusive, then we think the proposition too widely stated." The Court of Appeal refused to say whether they thought *Re Ponder*, *Ponder* v. *Ponder*, was correctly decided on its own facts, and also refused to define exactly the moment at which the personal representative would become trustee.

If *Harvell* v. *Foster* is to be regarded as authority that a personal representative can be sued as such while holding property as trustee, then it may be unobjectionable, for this merely recognises the distinction made above. But the clear doubt which it casts on *Re Ponder* is objectionable, not so much in itself, but more because the court refused to substitute what the proper test was.

In *Re Cockburn's Will Trusts*[1] Danckwerts, J. was asked to decide whether an administrator who had cleared the estate and a period of about ten years had elapsed therefrom, could exercise the statutory power of appointing new trustees. He was firm. "I feel no doubt about the matter at all. Whether persons are executors or administrators, once they have completed the administration in due course, they become trustees holding for the beneficiaries either on an intestacy or under the terms of the will, and are bound to carry out the duties of trustees." He then dealt with *Harvell* v. *Foster*. "My attention has been called to the observations made in *Harvell* v. *Foster* which are *obiter* so far as they cast any doubt on the decision of Sargant, J. and which, with all respect, I should have thought were not justified." But were they *obiter*? Perhaps one cannot be quite so certain.

---

[1] [1957] Ch. 438.

The most important recent case is *Re King's Will Trusts*,[1]
where, ironically, the plaintiff and the defendant were both
partners in the same firm of solicitors. The testatrix died in 1939,
and her will was proved by Henry and Cecil, two of the executors
named in it. The administration account was finalised in 1951,
but Henry and Cecil did not execute an assent of land in their
favour as trustees. Cecil died in 1953, leaving Henry as the sole
surviving executor and trustee and in the same year Henry
appointed Basil to be a co-trustee. Henry died in 1958, and his
will was proved by the defendant, who thereby also became the
executor by representation[2] of the will of the testatrix. In 1959
Basil appointed the plaintiff to be a trustee of the will, and Basil
thereafter died. The question was whether the legal estate was
held by the plaintiff or the defendant. Previously, the practice of
many conveyancers had been to follow *Re Ponder*, and to accept
a personal representative as having power to appoint trustees if
he was in fact acting in the capacity of a trustee. In *Re King*,
however, Pennycuick, J., regarded himself as bound by s. 36(4),
Administration of Estates Act 1925. This provides that "An
assent to the vesting of a legal estate shall be in writing, signed
by the personal representative, and shall name the person in
whose favour it is given, and shall operate to vest in that person
the legal estate to which it relates; and *an assent not in writing* or
not in favour of a named person *shall not be effectual* to pass a
legal estate . . ."[3] It was argued that because the appointments
of trustees had been by deed, there would be an implied vesting
of the legal estate in the new trustees under Trustee Act 1925,
s. 40. Pennycuick, J., said, however, that s. 40 operated only
where the person making the appointment held the property
in his capacity as a trustee. In this case, at the time of the 1953
deed of appointment, the legal estate was held by Henry as
personal representative, although he held as trustee, and could
confer upon himself and the new trustee, the right to insist on a
transfer of the legal estate.[4] Thus, it was held that the legal estate
remained with the defendant.

---

[1] [1964] Ch. 542.
[2] See *ante*, p. 241.
[3] Emphasis supplied.
[4] [1964] Ch. 542, at p. 545.

The decision in *Re King's Will Trusts* has been criticised,[1] particularly because it has rendered defective many titles which were previously thought to be good. The decision is, however, comprehensible.

It will be appreciated that *Harvell* v. *Foster* is the decision which makes it difficult to give a coherent statement of the law. Subject to this, and with the other cases in mind, it is thought that the cases are at least consistent with the principles suggested at p. 322.

4. NATURE OF THE PERSONAL REPRESENTATIVE'S ESTATE

a. *Distinct from personal estate*

For most purposes the position of a person as personal representative is kept quite distinct from his position in his personal capacity, and it is almost as if the "personal representative" is constituted by law as a separate legal entity. For example, if the personal representative becomes bankrupt, the property which he holds as personal representative cannot be touched by the trustee in bankruptcy.[2] If the personal representative is sued in his personal capacity, the judgment creditor generally has no right against the assets of the estate. The only major circumstance in which this distinction is broken is where the personal representative has been guilty of some improper act or inaction, and he is sued on that ground, his personal effects can be taken in execution.

It would perhaps be more accurate to speak of the personal representatives for most purposes constituting a separate legal entity, with the entity unchanged despite alterations in the persons comprising them. Thus, where two executors are appointed, and one dies, the survivor is bound by the acts of both of them. One aspect of this is dealt with in Administration of Estates Act 1925, s. 39 (1) (iii), which provides that when a contract is entered into by personal representatives, then their successors as personal representatives are fully bound by that contract.[3]

The most general statement of the rule is in fact contained in Finance Act 1965, s. 24(6), which deals with the liability of the estate to capital gains tax. It provides that "in relation to property

---

[1] See e.g., Walker (1964), 80 L.Q.R. 328; Garner (1964), 28 Conv. (N.S.) 298.
[2] Bankruptcy Act 1914, s. 38.
[3] See *ante*, p. 312, for other circumstances where changes in personal representatives do not affect obligations.

forming part of the estate of a deceased person the personal representatives shall for the purposes of this Part of this Act be treated as being a single and continuing body of persons (distinct from the persons who may from time to time be the personal representatives) . . .".

These twin principles, that:

(i) capacity as personal representative is generally kept entirely distinct from personal capacity; and

(ii) generally, account is not taken of changes in the persons who are from time to time personal representatives

lead to several other more detailed rules.

b. *No merger of estates*

The Law of Property Act has an infuriating habit of frequently only saying what it means indirectly, when direct expression would be quite easy. Section 185 of the Law of Property Act, re-enacting a provision of the Judicature Act 1873, provides that "there is no merger by operation of law only of an estate the beneficial interest in which would not be deemed to be merged or extinguished in equity". The situation here contemplated is where the personal representative owns an interest in land in his personal capacity and then acquires a further interest in the same land in his representative capacity. The common law rule was that where a freeholder subsequently acquired a lease, that lease became automatically merged in the freehold. The section considered here modifies that rule.

The approach of equity was that merger was not presumed where it was not in the interest of the party that it should take place, or even where it was only consistent with the duty of the party that it should not take place.[1] Accordingly, merger does not take place where there are the different capacities of personal and representative entitlement.[2]

Although merger does not take place at first, if the personal representative is also beneficially entitled, and he acquires

---

[1] *Chambers* v. *Kingham* (1878), 10 Ch. D. 743; *Capital and Counties Bank* v. *Rhodes*, [1903] 1 Ch. 631, at p. 653; cf. *Manks* v. *Whiteley*, [1912] 1 Ch. 735 (overruled *sub nom. Whiteley* v. *Delaney*, [1914] A.C. 132; *Re Radcliffe Radcliffe* v. *Bewes*, [1892] 1 Ch. 227, at p. 231.

[2] *Re French-Brewster*, [1904] 1 Ch. 713; *Re Hodge, Hodge* v. *Griffiths*, [1940] Ch. 260, at p. 265.

beneficially the estate's interest in the property then merger may take place.[1]

c. *Bankruptcy of Personal Representative*

It is expressly provided that where the personal representative becomes bankrupt, the trustee in bankruptcy cannot take the property, belonging to the estate, provided that it is distinguishable from the debtor's own property. Accordingly, even if the property belonging to the estate is taken by the trustee in bankruptcy, the court will order it to be returned.[2]

There is, however, possible scope for confusion, having regard to the provisions of Bankruptcy Act 1914, s. 38(2) (c), which enables the trustee in bankruptcy to take goods which at the commencement of the bankruptcy are in the possession, order or disposition of the bankrupt in his trade or business, by the consent or permission of the true owner. The section applies only to "goods", which exclude choses in action other than debts, and it applies only to goods used in the trade or business. Subject to that, assets of the estate may be taken. Thus, in *Fox* v. *Fisher*[3] the person entitled to take out letters of administration failed to do so, but remained in possession of the deceased's goods for twelve years. He then became bankrupt, and a grant of administration was then made to another. On the facts it was held that the goods were in the possession, order, or disposition of the bankrupt, with the consent of the true owner, so that they could be taken. This exception to the general rule is clearly of only limited application.

d. *Personal debts of personal representative*

Generally, the assets of the estate cannot be taken in satisfaction of a debt due from the personal representative personally.[4] In one case, where an administrator took possession of the deceased's chattels, and used them for three months, it was held that they could not be taken in execution for the administrator's own debt.[5]

---

[1] Bankruptcy Act 1914, s. 38.
[2] *Re Condon, Ex parte James* (1874), 9 Ch. App. 609; *Re Simmons* (1885), 16 Q.B.D. 348.
[3] (1819), 3 B. & Ald. 135.
[4] *Farr* v. *Newman* (1792), 4 Term Rep. 621, at p. 645.
[5] *Gaskell* v. *Marshall* (1831), 1 Mood. & R. 132.

However, it seems that where a substantial period has elapsed in which the assets have been in the hands of the personal representative, equity will not intervene to prevent those goods being taken in satisfaction of the representatives' personal debts.[1]

The general rule applies even where the debt is incurred by the personal representative in his personal capacity while acting on behalf of the estate. In *Re Morgan, Pillgrem* v. *Pillgrem*,[2] an executor carried on a business previously carried on by the testator, the will giving a power for this to be done.[3] The executor carried on the business in his own name, and the assets used in it appeared to be those of the executor personally, but even so the judgment creditor was held not entitled to take the assets on a warrant of execution.

There is no exception to the converse rule, that a personal representative is not *ipso facto* liable to have his own goods taken in satisfaction of the debts of the estate.

e. *No disposition by will*

On the death of a personal representative, others may remain, and whether or not they do, the personal representative cannot leave the deceased's assets by will, even if they are left upon the same trusts as are declared by the deceased's will.[4] Powers of disposition will therefore pass to the next person to be appointed personal representative either by a further grant, or by an executor being entitled by virtue of the chain of representation.

f. *Dispositions* inter vivos

The personal representative has full power of disposition *inter vivos*, save that in the case of freehold and leasehold land, this power must be exercised jointly.[5] It is, however, established, that where the personal representative acting in his personal capacity makes a disposition of property, and the extent of the

---

[1] *Ray* v. *Ray* (1815), Coop. G. 264; though this case may be explicable on the basis that the facts raised an inference of a gift by the testator's creditor to the executor—see Fry, J. in *Re Morgan, Pillgrem* v. *Pillgrem*, (1881), 18 Ch. D. 93, at p. 101.

[2] (1881), 18 Ch. D. 93.

[3] As to the general position where the personal representative carries on the deceased's business, see *post*, p. 417.

[4] *Bransby* v. *Grantham* (1557), 2 Plowd. 525.

[5] See *ante*, p. 321.

property passed is not clear, there will be a presumption against it including property of which he is personal representative. Thus, in *Knight* v. *Cole*[1] Holt, C.J., held that where an executor who executed a deed of release by which he released all actions and rights of action "which he had for any cause whatever", he had in fact only released actions which were personal to him, and not actions which he had on behalf of the estate.

g. *Taxation*

The provision of Finance Act 1965, s. 24(6), in respect of capital gains tax has already been mentioned, and the effect is that the personal representative's liability for capital gains tax is kept quite distinct from his personal liability, so that his personal liability cannot be affected in any way by the fact that he also becomes liable *qua* personal representative. This, however, is subject to the qualification that if he is beneficially entitled under the will, his representative capacity is ignored from the time when he becomes absolutely entitled beneficially.[2]

Likewise for the purposes of income tax, the income of the estate is taxed quite separately from that of the representative, whose personal liability is unaffected by his representative capacity.

---

[1] (1690), 1 Show. 150.
[2] Finance Act 1965, s. 22 (5).

CHAPTER 22

REALISING ASSETS

A. DEVOLUTION OF ASSETS

As their name suggests, personal representatives originally held only personal estate, and, indeed, since the time when the office of executor became recognised only the personal estate automatically devolved upon him. At common law realty devolved directly to the devisee named in the will, or, if there was no will, to the heir upon intestacy. The position was altered by the Land Transfer Act 1897, but this has been repealed and the position is now governed by Administration of Estates Act 1925, s. 1.

Sub-section 1(3) lays down the general principle that "the personal representatives shall be the representative of the deceased in regard to his real estate to which he was entitled for an interest not ceasing on his death as well as in regard to his personal estate". Logically, therefore, executors and administrators should be, but are not, called real and personal representatives.

The devolution of realty is governed by sub-s. 1(1) of the Administration of Estates Act 1925, by which real estate devolves on the personal representative "in like manner as before the commencement of this Act chattels real devolved on the personal representative from time to time of a deceased person". This is another piece of legislative obscurity. Its general meaning is clear enough, but there is no definition of chattels real. They clearly include leaseholds[1] but otherwise one is thrown back on the somewhat loose definition of Coke, who described them as such chattels as concern or savour of the realty.[2]

Fortunately, the point is not important. All assets to which the deceased was entitled at his death, other than for an interest

---

[1] See Administration of Estates Act 1925, s. 55 (1) (xxiv), and Law of Property Act 1925, s. 205 (1) (xxvii).
[2] Co. Litt 118 b.

ceasing on his death, now devolve on the personal representative, either by virtue of the common law or by virtue of the statute.

There are two riders to this general statement. First, the extract from sub-s. 1(1) given above contains the phrase "personal representative from time to time", which indicates that where there is a change in personal representatives, such as upon the revocation of a grant and the issue of a new one, then the assets held by the old personal representative automatically vest in the new one.

Secondly, the provisions of s. 1 and the general rule as to the devolution of personal estate must be read subject to s. 9. Under this section, where the deceased dies intestate, all his property, both real and personal, vests in the President of the Family Division until a grant of administration is made, whereupon it automatically vests in the administrator. This section is considered later.[1]

B. SPECIAL TYPES OF PROPERTY AND PERSON

1. TRUST PROPERTY

Where the deceased was one of two or more trustees the trust property will be held by the trustees as joint tenants, so that on the death of the deceased, the *ius accrescendi* will apply to vest the whole title in the surviving trustees. If, however, the deceased was the sole, or sole surviving trustee, the property will devolve upon his personal representatives. This has always been the case so far as personalty is concerned, and is declared to be so so far as realty is concerned by Administration of Estates Act 1925, s. 3.[2]

The *ius accrescendi* will also apply where the deceased was himself one of two or more personal representatives. However, where he was the sole or sole surviving personal representative, the property of the estate will not devolve upon his personal representatives, so that a new grant will be required.[3]

---

[1] *Post*, p. 372.
[2] Sub-section 3 (1) (ii).
[3] *Ante*, p. 285.

2. JOINT PROPERTY

a. *Joint tenancy*

The *ius accrescendi* was recognised as an incident of a joint tenancy of the goods in the same way as a joint tenancy of the legal estate,[1] and in this case the whole title passes upon the death of one to the survivor.

Where the asset owned jointly is land, it must be held upon a legal joint tenancy, whether or not the equitable interests are also joint, so that the legal title will automatically accrue to the survivor.[2] For this reason, Administration of Estates Act 1925, s. 3 (4), provides that "the interest of a deceased person under a joint tenancy where another tenant survives the deceased is an interest ceasing on his death and shall devolve to his successor".

There is no similar requirement, however, that chattels must be held upon a joint tenancy. Where the joint owners are tenants in common, either because that was their express intention, or because in the circumstances equity presumes[3] a tenancy in common, the personal representatives of the deceased tenant in common will themselves stand in the same position as the deceased.

In this connexion the decision in *Young* v. *Sealey*[4] should be noted. This illustrates that even where equity raises a presumption of a tenancy in common, that presumption may be rebutted by contrary evidence. In that case a woman held a joint account with her nephew. During her lifetime, she alone made payments into the account, and withdrawals from it. Evidence was admitted to rebut the presumption which equity would raise that the woman and her nephew held upon trust for the woman alone, and it was shown that the woman intended the whole beneficial interest to pass to her nephew on her death.

Evidence will always be admitted to show that an apparent beneficial joint tenancy was intended to be a beneficial tenancy in common.

b. *Joint mortgages*

Where two or more persons lend money on mortgage, there is

---

[1] See Co. Litt 182 a; Swinb. Pt. 3, s. 6, pl. 1; *Harris* v. *Fergusson* (1848), 16 Sim. 308; *Crossfield* v. *Such* (1853), 8 Exch. 825.

[2] Litt 280; Co. Litt 181 a.

[3] For the circumstances in which Equity presumes a tenancy in common, reference must be made to the standard text-books on Equity.

[4] [1949] Ch. 278.

an equitable presumption that they are to hold as tenants in common.[1] Accordingly, when one of the lenders dies, it is *prima facie* necessary for his personal representatives to join with the other lenders in giving a discharge when the loan is repaid.[2] To overcome this difficulty, it became the practice in mortgage deeds to include a "joint account clause", which was a clause declaring that the money being lent belonged to the lenders as joint tenants beneficially. So far as the mortgagor was concerned, he could rely on this clause, and in the event of the death of one of the lenders, he could presume that the *ius accrescendi* applied, and so take a good discharge from the survivor alone. Such a clause is now unnecessary in a mortgage of land, for it is deemed to be included by statute.[3] The joint account clause, either express or deemed to be incorporated by statute, operates only as between mortgagor and mortgagees, and does not affect the rights of mortgagees *inter se*. As a result, although the survivor can give the mortgagor a good discharge, the survivor is then bound to account to the estate of the deceased lender for his share.[4]

c. *Husband and wife*

There are no special rules affecting the devolution of the property of married persons dying on or after 2 August 1935. This arises from the Law Reform (Married Women and Tortfeasors) Act 1935, which enables a married woman to acquire, hold and dispose of both *inter vivos* and by will all property as if she were a *femme sole*.[5]

Complex questions arise as to the ownership of property by husband and wife *inter vivos*, and for these reference should be made to the standard textbooks on Equity.

3. PARTNERSHIP PROPERTY

Where land is held by partners, they must hold as joint tenants at law, and the *ius accrescendi* will apply to vest the legal estate in

---

[1] *Petty* v. *Styward* (1632), 1 Rep. Ch.57; *Rigden* v. *Vallier* (1751), 2 Ves. Sen. 252, at p. 258; *Morley* v. *Bird* (1798), 3 Ves. 628, at p. 631; *Vickers* v. *Cowell* (1839), 1 Beav. 529.

[2] *Petty* v. *Styward, ante; Vickers* v. *Cowell, supra.*

[3] Law of Property Act 1925, s. III.

[4] *Re Jackson, Smith* v. *Sibthorpe* (1887), 34 Ch. D. 732.
Repealing Married Women's Property Act 1882, ss. 1 to 5.

the survivors upon the death of one of the partners.[1] The survivors will therefore hold the legal estate upon trust to give effect to the beneficial interests of the partners, including the estate of the deceased[2].

So far as partnership chattels are concerned, these are regarded both at common law and in equity as being held by the partners in common, so that the *ius accrescendi* does not apply. However, the surviving partner or partners have the right to realise the assets of the partnership for the purpose of paying the partnership debts. Once the debts of the partnership have been ascertained, the executors of the deceased partner have a lien over the surplus assets for the proportion due to the estate.[3]

Where the deceased was one of only two partners, his death will *ipso facto* bring the partnership to an end. Even where there were more than two partners, *prima facie* the death of one will bring the partnership to an end. This, however, leads to complications, and partnership agreements often provide that where there are more than two partners, the partnership will continue notwithstanding the death of one of them, and such agreements are binding on the personal representatives. The partnership agreement may specify the rights and liabilities of the deceased's estate. In the absence of such provision, if the other partners continue to trade, the surviving partner may deduct a "salary"[4] but subject thereto the personal representatives of the deceased partner have the option either to take the deceased's share of profits as if he were still alive, or to charge the surviving partners interest on the capital belonging to the deceased and used by them for partnership purposes.

If the partnership continues, for income tax purposes the trade is regarded as having ceased on the death of the deceased partner, and a new trade as having been commenced the day after.[5] This effect can be avoided if the surviving partners, and the personal representatives of the deceased partner give notice to the Inspector of Taxes within twelve months from the date of death that they require the trade to be regarded as having continued throughout.[6]

---

[1] Law of Property Act 1925, s. 34.
[2] Law of Property Act 1925, ss. 34 to 36; Partnership Act 1890, s. 22.
[3] *Re Bourne, Bourne* v. *Bourne*, [1906] 2 Ch. 427.
[4] Partnership Act 1890, s. 42 (1).
[5] Income and Corporation Taxes Act 1970, s. 154.
[6] *Ibid.*, s. 154 (6).

The personal representatives of the deceased partner must, however, be satisfied that in giving such a notice, the estate will be benefited[1] or at least that it does not suffer. Failure to do this will render them personally liable in an action for breach of trust.

4. PROPERTY SUBJECT TO POWER OF APPOINTMENT

Section 3 (2) of the Administration of Estates Act 1925, provides that where the deceased exercised by will a general power of appointment over realty, then for the purposes of devolution that property shall pass on his death to his personal representatives, who take it to give effect to the terms of the appointment. A similar provision makes property which was entailed, and is disposed of in accordance with Law of Property Act 1925, s. 176,[2] devolve upon the deceased's personal representatives.

Section 3(2) applies only to realty. At common law personal property over which the deceased had a power of appointment did not devolve upon the personal representatives of the appointor, and there is no statutory provision to alter this position.[3]

5. CORPORATOR SOLE

On the death of a corporator sole, such as a bishop, his interest in the corporation's property, both real and personal, is regarded as an interest ceasing on death. Accordingly, it does not pass to his personal representatives, but devolves to his successor.[4]

6. OPTIONS AND POWERS OF SELECTION

Where the deceased held an option, this may, according to its true construction, be either personal to the deceased, or transmissible to his personal representatives.[5] In many instances the option is regarded as being transmissible. So, in *Re Adams and Kensington Vestry*[6] the deceased's executor was held entitled to exercise an option to purchase the freehold of land of which the deceased held the lease.[7]

---

[1] See, Mellows, Taxation for Executors and Trustees, 3rd ed., p. 13.

[2] This is the section by which a person of full age may bar an entail by will, and so dispose of it.

[3] *O'Grady* v. *Wilmot*, [1916] 2 A.C. 231.

[4] Administration of Estates Act 1925, s. 3 (5).

[5] *Skelton* v. *Younghouse*, [1942] A.C. 571; *Re Avard, Hook* v. *Parker*, [1948] Ch. 43; cf. *Belshaw* v. *Rollins* (1904), 1 I. R. 284.

[6] (1883), 24 Ch. D. 199; on appeal (1884), 27 Ch. D. 394.

[7] The executor has also been held entitled to exercise an option in respect of stocks and shares: *James* v. *Buena Nitrate Grounds Syndicate, Ltd.*, [1896] 1 Ch. 456.

The rules governing the exercise of a power of selection given to the deceased are more stringent. The basic situation is that the deceased is given, usually under the will of another, a power to select articles and dies before exercising the power of selection. The rules are:

a. where the power of selection was as to the articles themselves, and no selection was made in the deceased's lifetime, then there is no property to pass to his personal representatives, who accordingly cannot exercise the power.[1] So in *Re Madge, Pridle v. Bellamy*,[3] a testator left to his widow such articles of a specified character as she should select within two months of his death. She died within two months of his death, and her personal representatives were held not entitled to exercise the power, even within the two month period.

b. (i) Where the power is not as to the article itself, but is only as to the degree of the gift, this can usually be exercised by the personal representatives. So in *Jones v. Cherney*[3] a person was granted by will a lease of either 40 or 60 years as he should elect. Upon his death before election, his personal representatives were held entitled to choose.

(ii) This is subject to the general rule that where selection must be made within a specified time, or on a specified occasion, it must then be made, and personal representatives cannot make the selection later.[4]

7. LEASEHOLDS

Leaseholds will devolve upon the personal representatives in the usual way.[5] Likewise, weekly, monthly, or yearly tenancies will also devolve on the personal representatives.[6] Accordingly, before possession can be recovered by the landlord, a notice to quit must be served either on the personal representatives, or, in the case of an intestate prior to the issue of letters of administration, upon the President of the Family Division.[7]

---

[1] *Morris v. Levesay* (1594), 1 Roll. Abr. 725.

[2] (1928), 44 T.L.R. 372.

[3] (1680), Freem. K.B. 530.

[4] Co. Litt 145 a.

[5] See *ante*, p. 333; Administration of Estates Act 1925, s. 1 (1).

[6] *Doe d. Shore v. Porter* (1789), 3 Term Rep. 13; *Rees d. Mears v. Perrot* (1830), 4 C. & P. 230; *Abbey v. Barnstyn*, [1930] 1 K.B. 660.

[7] Under Administration of Estates Act 1925, s. 9; see *post*, p. 372.

The position is similar with regard to agricultural holdings. These too devolve upon the personal representatives[1] though notice to quit may be given within three months from death. In the event of determination of the tenancy by notice to quit served on the personal representatives, they may obtain rights of compensation.[2]

Statutory tenancies

On the death of a statutory tenant, the tenancy may be transmitted on two occasions only,[3] and on the second transmission the tenancy automatically ceases to be statutory, and becomes a regulated tenancy subject to the Rent Act 1965.[4] However, the transmission is not to the personal representatives as such, but is to the tenant's widow,[5] or, where the tenant has no widow, to a member of his family who resided with him for not less than six months before his death.[6]

C. REGISTRATION AND NOTICE

1. REGISTERED LAND

Section 41 of the Land Registration Act 1925 provides that registered land is within the expression "real estate" for the purposes of s. 1 of the Administration of Estates Act 1925, so that although the legal estate devolves upon the personal representative, he cannot deal with it until he becomes the registered proprietor.

One of two courses are open to a personal representative in respect of registered land:

a. he may lodge with the Land Registry the land certificate together with the probate or letters of administration, whereupon the land certificate and register will be altered to show the personal representative as registered proprietor.[7] As that

---

[1] See the definition of "tenant": Agricultural Holdings Act 1948, s. 94 (1).

[2] Agricultural Holdings Act 1948, s. 25 (1); Agriculture Act 1958, s. 8.

[3] Increase of Rent and Mortgage Interest (Restrictions) Act 1920, s. 12 (1) (g); Rent Act 1965, s. 13.

[4] Unless, the tenancy is a business tenancy subject to Part II of the Landlord and Tenant Act 1954: see Rent Act 1965, s. 13 (5).

[5] Landlord and Tenant Act 1954, s. 42 (2).

[6] Increase of Rent and Mortgage Interest (Restrictions) Act 1920, s. 12 (1) (g). Rent and Mortgage Interest Restrictions (Amendment) Act 1933, s. 13.

[7] Land Registration Act 1925, s. 41 (1).

transaction will not be for value, the registrar will also note on the title that until the property is sold, it remains liable for the payment of any estate duty outstanding, although this note will not be made if a clearance certificate relating to that land is also lodged;[1] or

b. he may wait until the property is sold, or until it is to be transferred to the person entitled either in accordance with the terms of the will or on intestacy.[2] In the case of sale, the purchaser will be registered as proprietor upon lodging with the registry the land certificate (still showing the deceased as registered proprietor), the grant of representation, and the transfer executed by the personal representative. In the case of a transfer to the beneficiary, an assent will be used instead of a transfer, but otherwise the procedure is the same. In the latter case the same note that the land is subject to the payment of any estate duty will be made on the register unless a clearance certificate is lodged.

Where the deceased was a joint registered proprietor, the registrar will delete his name from the register upon proof of death being given, either by production of a death certificate, or by production of the grant of representation.[3]

2. STOCKS AND SHARES

The position is similar where the deceased held stocks and shares. These will devolve on death upon the personal representatives who may deal with them in one of two ways:

a. register themselves as owners, by production of the grant of representation, together with the share certificate. Where the company has notice of the death, it will usually not make any further payment of dividends until the personal representatives are registered, although dividends held back pending registration will be paid to the personal representatives upon registration; or

---

[1] Finance Act 1894, s. 11 (1); now in practice superseded by Law of Property Act 1925, s. 16 (7).

[2] Land Registration Act 1925, ss. 37 (1), (2).

[3] Land Registration Rules 1925, r. 172.

b. execute forms of transfer in favour of a purchaser or beneficiary, which will be registered upon the share certificate being lodged with the company and production of the grant. Unless the articles of association otherwise provide, the personal representatives may transfer the stocks or shares without first being registered as owners;[1] or

c. where the personal representative is beneficially entitled, instead of executing a transfer in favour of himself, he may procure his beneficial registration by completing a document known as a Letter of Request and lodging this with the certificate and grant.[2]

There is no provision for notice of any outstanding liability for estate duty to be endorsed on a share certificate or upon the register of members of the company.

3. LEASEHOLD PROPERTY

If there is no provision to the contrary in the lease, the personal representatives are not required to notify the landlord of the devolution of the title to them, nor are they required to obtain the landlord's consent for the transfer of the lease to the person entitled under the will or on intestacy, or upon sale.[3] Nevertheless, the landlord will usually wish to know where the legal estate in the lease lies, so that he can take any action for arrears of rent and serve any notices[4] required to be served in accordance with the terms of the lease. Furthermore, in most cases, the landlord will wish to control the person who will be occupying the property. Two clauses will therefore frequently be found among the lessee's covenants in the lease, namely:

a. that the tenant shall not assign underlet or part with the possession of the premises; or that he shall not do so without the consent of the lessor; and

---

[1] Companies Act 1948, s. 76; *Re Greene, Greene v. Greene*, [1949] Ch. 333.

[2] A Letter of Request is exempt from Stamp Duty. Forms of transfer, even to the personal representatives in their beneficial capacity, will attract stamp duty of 50p. each.

[3] *Doe d. Mitchinson v. Carter* (1798), 8 Term Rep. 57, at p. 60.

[4] The lease may contain provision for the landlord to determine the term upon giving notice; or he may wish to serve notice for repairs to be carried out.

b. that following any permitted assignment, or other devolution, notice must be given of that assignment or devolution within a prescribed time.

The first type of covenant applies only to voluntary dispositions, so that it does not prevent the lease vesting in the personal representatives on death.[1] However, the landlord's consent is probably required before the personal representatives can give effect to the terms of the will.[2]

The second type of clause does require notice of devolution of death to be given to the landlord, provided that the clause in the lease requiring notice to be given is not confined on its terms to dispositions *inter vivos*.

4. CHOSES IN ACTION

Where the deceased was owed a debt, or had the benefit of some other chose in action, the personal representatives must protect their position by giving notice of the devolution to the debtor or other person under obligation.[3]

D. DEVOLUTION ON SEPARATE REPRESENTATIVES

Where the testator appointed different personal representatives in respect of different types of property, the relevant property will devolve automatically on the appropriate representative. This is most likely to arise where there are different representatives of settled land, and this is considered in the next chapter. The other situations in which this may be met are where the testator appoints a separate literary executor, and where he appoints separate representatives in respect of realty and personalty.

In the latter case, care needs to be taken where one of the assets was a mortgage. Section 3 (1) (ii) of the Administration of Estates Act 1925, provides that for the purposes of that part of the Act the expression "real estate" includes land held by way of mortgage, so that it devolves to the personal representatives under s. 1 (1).

---

[1] *Fox* v. *Swann* (1655), Sty. 482; *Doe d. Goodbehere* v. *Bevan* (1815), 3 M. & S. 353.
[2] *Re Wright, Exparte Landau* v. *Trustee*, [1949] Ch. 729.
[3] *Loveridge* v. *Cooper* (1823), 3 Russ. 1; *Dearle* v. *Hall* (1823), 3 Russ. 1.

The provision is unnecessary, because a mortgage can only take effect as a mortgage by demise, subject to provision for cesser on redemption,[1] or as a charge by deed by way of legal mortgage,[2] in both of which cases the mortgage would devolve as a chattel real upon the personal representatives under the general law.

However, s. 3 applies only to devolution, and not to the nature of the property devolved. The mortgage will devolve upon the personal representative entitled to personalty[3] unless the mortgagor's right of redemption was barred at the date of death of the deceased, when it will devolve as realty.[4]

E. CONTRACTUAL RIGHTS

a. *Personal and non-personal contracts*

We are concerned here with rights of action which had accrued to the deceased prior to his death. It is necessary first to draw a distinction between personal contracts, which terminated on the death of the deceased, and non-personal contracts which accrue to the benefit of the estate. The more common examples of personal contracts are contracts between employer and employee,[5] principal and agent,[6] and artist and the person commissioning him.[7] Where the contract is personal, it will be discharged by death unless there is an express provision to the contrary.[8] It may be necessary for adjustments to be made under the Law Reform (Frustrated Contracts) Act 1943.

A contract which is not of its nature personal may be brought to an end by the death of one of the parties, if there is an express or implied agreement to that effect. So in *Neal* v. *Hanbury*[9] Thomas Neal had the right to receive an annuity of £5. He was described as being "a very lewd, dissolute man", and the annuity was made conditional upon Thomas Neal behaving civilly to the payer's wife. It was held that this annuity was personal to him, and therefore died with him.

---

[1] Law of Property Act 1925, s. 85 (1).
[2] *Ibid.*
[3] See Coote on *Mortgages*, 9th ed., pp. 870 *et seq.*
[4] Law of Property Act 1925, ss. 88, 153 (3).
[5] *Farrow* v. *Wilson* (1869), L.R. 4 C.P. 744, esp. at p. 746.
[6] *Ibid.*; and *Graves* v. *Cohen* (1929), 46 T.L.R. 121.
[7] *Robinson* v. *Davison* (1871), L.R. 6 Exch. 269.
[8] *Farrow* v. *Wilson, supra.*
[9] (1700), Prec.Ch. 173.

Where a contract which is not of a personal nature is not discharged by death, the position depends on whether it was broken in the deceased's lifetime.

b. *Contract broken in deceased's lifetime*

At common law the rule was *actio personalis moritur cum persona*[1] so that where a personal contract had been broken in the lifetime of the deceased, although the deceased himself could have sued, his personal representatives could not. This rule was altered by Law Reform (Miscellaneous Provisions) Act 1934, s. 1 (1). The essential words of this section are that "on the death of any person after (25 July, 1934) all causes of action[2] . . . vested in him shall survive . . . for the benefit of his estate". The terms of this section are wide enough to include actions for breach of personal contracts.

There are two qualifications to this principle.

  (i) exemplary damages may not be awarded;[3] and

  (ii) the general rule of public policy that personal representatives cannot sue where money arises from the felonious act of the deceased. So in *Beresford* v. *Royal Insurance Co., Ltd.*[4] the personal representatives of an assured were held not entitled to sue for moneys under a life policy on his life because his death was caused by his own suicide.

c. *Representative's position*

Where the contract was broken before the death of the deceased, or where it was not personal and remained in force at his death, personal representatives stand in the position of the deceased, even though they are not mentioned in the contract. There are numerous examples of this. To give but one, in *Beswick* v. *Beswick*[5] the widow was entitled to enforce the contract even though on its face it referred just to the parties themselves, no mention being made of their personal representatives.

---

[1] *Raymond* v. *Fitch* (1835), 2 Cr.M. & R. 588.
[2] See *Sugden* v. *Sugden*, [1957] P. 120.
[3] Law Reform (Miscellaneous Provisions) Act 1934, s. 1 (2).
[4] [1938] A.C. 586.
[5] [1966] Ch. 538.

F. RIGHTS OF ACTION IN TORT

1. GENERALLY

a. *Survival of actions*

Section 1 (1) of the Law Reform (Miscellaneous Provisions) Act 1934 also saves rights of action in tort, and declares that all causes of action[1] subsisting in the deceased at the time of his death survive for the benefit of his estate. This applies whether or not action was commenced by the deceased himself.

Where proceedings were not commenced by the deceased, they may be commenced by the personal representatives. The normal rules apply, but where the action is for negligence, nuisance, or breach of duty, and the claim is for damages for personal injury, whether or not any other relief is sought, proceedings must be commenced within three years from the date when the cause of action arose.[2] If, however, none of the personal representatives had actual or constructive notice of a cause of action, proceedings may be commenced within three years of such knowledge being acquired.[3] The position relating to proceedings against the estate is considered at p. 381.

All causes of action in tort survive the deceased except actions for defamation.[4]

b. *Damages*

The normal rules as to remoteness and quantum of damages apply, with few exceptions. Damages are recoverable for the pain and suffering of the deceased between the wrong and the date of death,[5] and damages are also recoverable for loss of expectation of life.[6]

---

[1] See *Kelly* v. *Kelly and Brown*, [1961] P. 94.

[2] Law Reform (Miscellaneous Provisions) Act 1934, s. 1 (2), as amended by Law Reform (Limitation of Actions) Act 1954, s. 4.

[3] Law Reform (Miscellaneous Provisions) Act 1971, s. 3.

[4] Law Reform (Miscellaneous Provisions) Act 1934, s. 1.

[5] *Rose* v. *Ford*, [1937] A.C. 826.

[6] *Ibid.*; see also *Wise* v. *Kaye*, [1962] 1 Q.B. 638; *Andrews* v. *Freeborough*, [1967] 1 Q.B. 1.

There are two qualifications to the normal rules. First exemplary damages cannot be awarded.[1] Secondly, apart from funeral expenses, which can be awarded,[2] damages are to be calculated without reference to any loss or gain to the estate as a result of the death. On this basis, payments received under insurance policies do not reduce the amount of damages awarded, but on the other hand, where the deceased had an interest ceasing on his death, such as the usual type of life interest, no damages are awarded for the reduction in the period for which he has enjoyed that interest.

2. FATAL ACCIDENTS

a. *Right of action*

The Fatal Accidents Act 1846, provides that where the death of a person is caused by the wrongful act of another, then an action will lie against the person causing the death if the deceased could himself have brought an action against him had he survived.[3]

The action must normally be brought by the personal representatives,[4] who must have a grant before proceedings are instituted,[5] but this is only a device of convenience. Whereas other tortious (and contractual) actions are brought or continued for the benefit of the estate, actions brought by the personal representatives under the Fatal Accidents Acts are not brought for the benefit of the estate, but for a prescribed class of dependants of the deceased. The dependants are the wife, husband, parent grandparent, child, grandchild;[6] or brother, sister, uncle aunt, or their issue, of the deceased.[7] Illegitimate and adopted relatives within these descriptions can also take.[8] It is interesting to compare this list with the much narrower list of dependants who may make an application under the Family Provision legislation.[9]

---

[1] Law Reform (Miscellaneous Provisions) Act 1934, s. 1.
[2] *Ibid.*, s. 2 (3).
[3] Fatal Accidents Act 1846, s. 1.
[4] *Ibid.*, s. 5.
[5] See *post*, p. 370.
[6] Law Reform (Miscellaneous Provisions) Act 1934, s. 5.
[7] Fatal Accidents Act 1959, s. 1, (1).
[8] *Ibid.*, s. 1 (2), (3).
[9] See *ante*, p. 207.

b. *Damages*

The fundamental principle of the Acts is *"to compensate the recipient on a balance of gains and losses for the injury sustained by the death"*.[1] For this purpose "injury" means pecuniary loss only,[2] and in order to succeed, it is necessary for the plaintiffs to show actual pecuniary loss, or the loss of a reasonable possibility of pecuniary advantage.[3]

Payments under private and various State insurance schemes are ignored[4] but otherwise pecuniary advantages or disadvantages to the dependants as a result of the death are taken into account. In particular, where action is brought both under the Law Reform Act and under the Fatal Accidents Acts, then if the persons entitled to the estate are the same persons as those entitled as dependents, the amount of an award under the Fatal Accidents Acts will be reduced by the award under the Law Reform Act.[5]

G. GENERAL POWERS OF PERSONAL REPRESENTATIVES

Personal representatives have very wide powers to get in the assets of the deceased; preserve and maintain them pending distribution or disposal; and to dispose of them. In most cases it will be found that the personal representatives have the power to take the action which they wish to take in connexion with the administration of the estate, but where the power does not exist, the court nevertheless has jurisdiction to confer the power in a special case.[6]

1. POWERS TO GET IN ASSETS

a. *To take proceedings*

Where the assets of the deceased are not in the possession of the personal representatives, the person having custody of them will

---

[1] *Per* Lord Wright, *Davies* v. *Powell Duffryn Associated Collieries, Ltd.,* [1942] A.C. 601, at p. 617.

[2] *Blake* v. *Midland Rail. Co.* (1852), 18 Q.B. 93.

[3] *Duckworth* v. *Johnson* (1859), 4 H. & N. 653; *Barnett* v. *Cohen,* [1921] 2 K.B. 461.

[4] Fatal Accidents (Damages) Act 1908; Fatal Accidents Act 1959, s. 2.

[5] *Davies* v. *Powell Duffryn Collieries, Ltd., supra.*

[6] Trustee Act 1925, s. 57.

usually be prepared to hand them to the personal representative upon production of evidence of his authority, namely the grant of representation, or, in some cases, of the will itself. Where the personal representatives cannot obtain the assets upon request, they have the right to take proceedings.

There are two types of proceedings which the personal representatives may wish to take:

(i) where rights of action have devolved upon them, but in respect of which the deceased himself did not commence proceedings. Subject to the exceptions noted above,[1] all rights of action of the deceased devolve to his representatives; and

(ii) where it is necessary for them to take proceedings to recover assets. They have a general power to sue to recover assets.[2]

Before proceedings of either type are commenced, personal representatives, to safeguard their own position, will usually be advised to apply to the court at the outset for directions.[3] It will be remembered that an asset of the estate is the right to recover void or voidable dispositions made by the deceased, such as gifts *inter vivos* made by the deceased while under undue influence. *Re Craig, Meneces* v. *Middleton*,[4] which has been discussed above,[5] is an example of this, even though in that case the proceedings were taken by a residuary beneficiary and not by the executors themselves.

b. *To levy distress*

Ordinary actions in respect of arrears of rent expressly come within the general power to sue just considered. There is a special statutory power to levy distress. Section 26 (4), Administration of Estates Act 1925, confers upon personal representatives the right to distrain for arrears of rent due to the deceased in the same way as he might have done had he been living. This sub-section confers a special right to distrain, for it is not necessary for the

---

[1] *Ante*, pp. 344 and 347.

[2] *Cobbett* v. *Clutton* (1826), 2 C. & P. 471.

[3] If they do not do so, they may not be able to obtain their costs from the estate.

[4] [1971] Ch. 95; [1970] 2 All E.R. 390.

[5] See *ante*, p. 46.

personal representatives themselves to be the reversioners. Thus, it appears that a deceased's general personal representatives may levy distress even if the reversion devolves upon his special representatives.

Provided the tenant is still in possession, the personal representatives can exercise this power even within six months after the determination of the term.[1]

c. *To give receipts*

In general, personal representatives each have entire authority over the whole of the estate,[2] and a receipt or release given by one personal representative will be good.[3] In respect of land, if there is only one personal representative he can give a valid receipt for capital money, although if there are two or more proving executors, they will both have to join in.[4]

2. POWERS OF MANAGEMENT

The principal powers of management are:

a. to invest in authorised securities[5] or in accordance with the terms of the will, whichever is wider;

b. to operate a bank account;[6]

c. to deposit money in a deposit account[7] and to deposit documents with a banker or depositary.[8] There is no express power to enable him to deposit articles of value, but it is doubtful whether, if he exercised reasonable care, he would be liable for any loss which resulted;

d. to insure any building or other property to three-quarters of its full value against damage by fire.[9] The statutory power is unsatisfactory. In the first place it is often desirable to insure to the full re-instatement value. Secondly, it is often desirable to insure against other risks as well. Thirdly, the statutory power

---

[1] Administration of Estates Act 1925, s. 26 (4).
[2] *Ex parte Rigby* (1815), 19 Ves. 463; *Owen* v. *Owen* (1738), 1 Atk. 494.
[3] *Jacomb* v. *Harwood* (1751), 2 Ves. Sen. 266.
[4] Law of Property Act 1925, s. 27 (2).
[5] Under the Trustee Investments Act 1961.
[6] Trustee Act 1925, s. 11 (1).
[7] *Ibid.*, s. 11 (1).
[8] *Ibid.*, s. 21.
[9] *Ibid.*, s. 19.

does not extend to any property which the personal representative is bound to transfer forthwith to a beneficiary.[1] Accordingly, it is better practice to include wider powers of insurance in the will;

e. to pay calls on shares;[2] to take up rights issues of shares, or to renounce the rights;[3] and to concur in schemes for the amalgamation or reconstruction of a company, or for the modification of the rights attaching to shares;[4]

f. in respect of land, all the powers of trustees for sale of land.[5]

g. in respect of debts and disputes very wide powers to compromise or abandon, provided such action is taken in good faith.[6]

Personal representatives also have the general power of trustees to appoint agents.[7]

3. POWERS IN CONNEXION WITH DISPOSAL

The main powers are:

a. to raise money on mortgage, for the payment of the debts and liabilities of the deceased, and the administration expenses.[8] Where this is done, the appropriate adjustment has to be made between the various beneficiaries so that there is no alteration in the incidence of liabilities.

b. to sell

(i) personal representatives have a wide power to sell assets if the proceeds are required for the purpose of administration, even if the assets are specifically bequeathed;[9]

(ii) they have a power to sell assets in order to raise capital for the payment of legacies;[10]

(iii) where there is a total or partial intestacy, the undisposed of property is held upon a trust for sale[11] with full power to

---

[1] Trustee Act 1925, s. 19 (1).
[2] *Ibid.*, s. 11 (2).
[3] *Ibid.*, s. 10 (4).
[4] *Ibid.*, s. 10 (3); *Re Walker's Settlement*, [1935] Ch. 567; Trustee Investment Act 1961, s. 9 (1).
[5] Administration of Estates Act 1925, s. 39 (1), (ii).
[6] Trustee Act 1925, s. 15.
[7] *Ibid.*, s. 23.
[8] Administration of Estates Act 1925, s. 40.
[9] *Re Cohen*, [1960] Ch. 179, at p 188.
[10] Trustee Act 1925, s. 16 (1).
[11] Administration of Estates Act 1925, s. 33.

postpone. However, personal representatives are directed not to sell reversionary interests or personal chattels unless there is some special reason for doing so;

(iv) in respect of land, personal representatives have all the powers of trustees for sale;[1]

(v) personal representatives have a wide discretion as to the method of sale. They can sell assets separately or together; subject to or free from charges and incumbrances; and by private contract or by auction.[2]

Personal representatives are under the same restriction as trustees with regard to purchasing the property of the estate.

The use of assets to effect a sale, and the protection conferred upon purchasers from personal representatives is considered later.[3]

4. OTHER POWERS OF TRUSTEES

Section 69 of the Trustee Act 1925, provides that the provisions of the Trustee Act, except where there is an express statement to the contrary, apply to executorships and administratorships, and accordingly the other powers conferred by the Trustee Act will apply to personal representatives. These will include the statutory powers of maintenance and advancement.[4]

---

[1] Administration of Estates Act 1925, s. 39 (1) (ii).
[2] Trustee Act 1925, s. 12.
[3] *Post*, p. 555.
[4] Trustee Act 1925, ss. 31, 32,

CHAPTER 23

DEVOLUTION OF SETTLED LAND

1. THE PROBLEM

The concept of settled land should have been scrapped long ago. The complexity which it produces in property law is out of all proportion to its practical advantages,[1] and some of this complexity has affected the law of succession. Before stating the legal position, however, it will be as well to identify the problem. Suppose that land is settled upon trust for Victoria for life, with remainder to Edward for life, with remainder to George absolutely, and suppose also that Victoria has just died. The law must establish machinery whereby:

a. estate duty payable upon Victoria's death is paid, or provision is made for its payment;

b. the legal estate becomes vested in Edward; and

c. the transfer of the legal estate to Edward is effected without breach of the fundamental Settled Land Act principle of keeping matters affecting the legal estate distinct from those affecting equitable interests.

For estate duty purposes, the value of the settled land itself, and not merely the value of Victoria's life interest in it, will be aggregated with her "free", that is, non-settled, property.[2] The rate of estate duty increases on a sliding scale and the effect of aggregation to increase the duty payable in respect of the settled property and of the free property.[3] Thus, if:

---

[1] This is not to argue for the simple abolition of the Settled Land Act settlement, but for a new type of settlement based largely, but not entirely, on the trust for sale.

[2] Unless the free estate does not exceed £15,000; Finance Act 1896, s.16; Finance Act 1972, s. 120.

[3] Finance Act 1969, sched. 17.

The value of the settled land is—   £30,000
And the value of the free estate is—   £20,000

The aggregate is—   £50,000
On which the total duty payable is—   £11,750
So that the portion attributable to the settled land is—

whereas: $\dfrac{30,000}{50,000} \times 11,750 =$ £7,050

If the settled land had not been aggregable, the maximum rate would
have been based on—   £30,000
For which the appropriate duty is—   £4,250

It will, therefore, be appreciated that the amount of duty payable on settled land cannot be ascertained until the total size of the
settled land and free estate is known. So far as free estate is concerned, there is every inducement for the duty to be paid, because,
as was shown earlier,[1] it has to be paid before probate or letters
of administration can be obtained. This is subject to an option
which exists in the case of realty[2] and leaseholds[3] for the duty to
be paid by eight yearly or sixteen half yearly instalments, but
whether or not the option is exercised, in respect of free estate
the duty has either been paid or definite arrangements for payment by instalments have been made. The Revenue clearly seek
some similar provision in respect of settled land so that it is in
fact frozen until duty is paid or arranged.

It may seem that, apart from the Revenue considerations, the
simplest procedure would be for the legal estate to vest automatically following the death of a tenant for life in the next person
entitled. This would not, however, provide a satisfactory solution,
for on the death of a life tenant it would be necessary to refer to
the trust instrument to see who in fact was next entitled. The
principle of separation between legal estate and equitable interests
would thereby be smashed.

From considerations both of the collection of estate duty, and
keeping the devolution of the legal estate separate from equitable
interests it is, therefore, necessary to interpose another person

---

[1] *Ante*, p. 273. This ensues from Finance Act 1894, s. 6 (20).
[2] Finance Act 1894, s. 6 (8). Where the option is exercised, interest is also
payable on the duty.
[3] Finance Act 1971, s. 62 (2).

between the deceased tenant for life and the person next entitled under the settlement. It is on this basis that the Administration of Estates Act makes provision for a special personal representative, whose function is to discharge the estate duty and to transfer the legal estate to the person next entitled.

The scheme of the Act is:

a. to distinguish between land which ceases to be settled on the death of a life tenant, and land which will remain settled after his death;

b. in respect of land which ceases to be settled on the death:

(i) to provide that the land vests in the deceased's *general* personal representatives; who

(ii) vest it in the person absolutely entitled under the settlement;

c. in respect of land which remains settled after the death of the life tenant;

(i) to provide that the land vests in the *special* personal representatives; who

(ii) vest it in the person next entitled under the settlement.

These principles now require elaboration.

2. LAND CEASING TO BE SETTLED LAND

a. *Following death of life tenant*

It is essential to distinguish between land which ceases to be settled on the death of a tenant for life, and land which remains settled. In order to decide this, it is necessary to look at the position not at the time while the tenant for life was alive, but at the moment immediately after his death. If immediately after the death the land is not settled land, within the terms of Settled Land Act 1925, s. 1,[1] of which the the most common example is land limited for persons in succession[2] then it will cease to be settled. This is so even though the person ultimately entitled is entitled because of the terms of the settlement. Again consider the example of land settled upon trust for Victoria for life, with remainder to Edward

---

[1] In general terms, Settled Land Act 1925, s. 1, defines "settled land" as land limited in trust for any persons by way of succession; or limited in trust for any person in possession for an entailed or similar interest; or limited in trust for any person contingently on the happening of any event; or land charged by way of family arrangement. The Schedule to the Law of Property (Amendment) Act 1926, excludes land held upon trust for sale.

[2] Settled Land Act 1925, s. 1 (1) (i).

for life, with remainder to George absolutely. Upon the death of Victoria the land remains settled. If the position is considered immediately after Victoria's death, the land is still limited for persons in succession, namely Edward for life, with remainder to George. However, on the death of Edward, the land ceases to be settled. Considered immediately after his death, the land is no longer limited in succession, but is held for George absolutely.

This principle was established by the important decision in *Re Bridgett and Hayes Contract*.[1] In that case, land was held, in essence, upon trust for A for life, with a direction for it to be sold on the death of A and the proceeds of sale held for specified beneficiaries. It was held that the land ceased to be settled land on the death of A, so that the legal estate vested in his general personal representatives.[2]

Land which was settled will cease to be settled following the death of a tenant for life if the remainderman then becomes fully entitled. This is subject to two exceptions and where these apply the land will remain settled. They are:

(i) if any charge exists under the settlement, or any power of charging is still capable of being exercised;[3]

(ii) if the person who is absolutely and beneficially entitled is an infant,[4] in which case the land will continue to be settled until the infant attains the age of 18.[5]

If the remainderman, during the lifetime of the tenant for life, himself created a settlement of his remainder, that will cause the land to remain settled, even though the original settlement would then come to an end.[6]

b. *Where trust for sale arises*

Express trust for sale

If following the death of a tenant for life the land becomes subject to an express trust for sale, the land ceases to be settled land and should be conveyed to the trustees of the settlement as

---

[1] [1928] 1 Ch. 163.

[2] See also *In the Estate of Bordass*, [1929] P. 107; *In the Estate of Birch*, [1929] P. 164.

[3] Settled Land Act 1925, s. 3 (a).

[4] Settled Land Act 1925, s. 3 (b).

[5] Settled Land Act 1925, s. 1 (1) (ii) (d) and s. 2.

[6] *In the Estate of Taylor*, [1929] P. 260.

trustees for sale. This is the result of the unhappy Settled Land Act 1925, s. 36 (1). This provides that "if and when . . . settled land is held in trust for persons entitled in possession under a trust instrument in undivided shares, the trustees of the settlement (if the settled land is not already vested in them) may require the estate owner in whom the settled land is vested . . . to convey the land to them . . . as joint tenants". The use of the expression "settled land" in the opening part of the section is unfortunate, for the definition of settled land is restricted to "land not held upon trust for sale".[1] However, it has been held that the effect of the trust for sale in putting an end to the settlement is ignored for the purposes of s. 36,[2] so that the section can be interpreted as if it read "land which was previously settled land".

Suppose, therefore, that land is limited upon trust for Peter for life, and thereafter for Queenie and Quince in undivided shares, for general purposes the land will cease to be settled on the death of Peter, although it will remain settled for the purpose only of s. 36.

In such circumstances, the land will only cease to be settled for the purposes of the Administration of Estates Act if there is no outstanding charge taking priority over the trust for sale. So, in *Re Norton, Pinney* v. *Beauchamp*,[3] land was held upon trust for A for life, and then, subject to certain rent charges and portions charged on the land, upon trust for sale. Romer, J. held that upon the death of A, the land remained settled land.

A further difficulty arises under Settled Land Act 1925, s. 36. Section 36 (2) provides that when land is vested in the trustees of the settlement, they hold upon a statutory trust for sale.[4] This subsection refers to "settled land", but, as in the case of sub-s. 36 (1), it seems that this means "land which was previously settled". In *Re Cugny's Will Trusts*,[5] in essence, land was settled upon trust for A for life, with remainder to B and C in undivided shares. It was held that following the death of A, s. 36 (2) applied, and that the trustees of the settlement were entitled to have the legal estate vested in them as trustees for sale. However, it was

---

[1] Schedule, Law of Property (Amendment) Act 1926.
[2] *Re Cugny's Will Trusts, Smith* v. *Freeman*, [1931] 1 Ch. 305, at p. 309.
[3] [1929] 1 Ch. 84.
[4] Settled Land Act 1925, s. 36 (6).
[5] [1931] 1 Ch. 305.

also held that, in accordance with the principle in *Re Bridgett and Hayes Contract*[1] the land had ceased to be settled on the death of A, for the purposes of the Administration of Estates Act, with the result that it devolved first on the general personal representatives of A. To put it at its lowest, there is the highly inelegant result that at the same time the land was not settled land, so that it devolved on the general personal representatives, but that it was settled land, so that s. 36 (2) applied. It is only possible to reconcile this by saying that the expression "settled land" means "settled land" for the Administration of Estates Act, but that it means "land which was previously settled land" for the purposes of Settled Land Act, s. 36. In any event, in *Re Cugny's Will Trusts* the land was regarded as settled land only for the purposes of s. 36, and for no other.

It should be noted that whereas generally land remains settled land if there are any charges outstanding, s. 36 (2) operates even if there are any such charges, and that the trustees for sale take subject to them.

The position may therefore be summarized as follows:

a. For the purposes of the Administration of Estates Act, land will cease to be settled if the person entitled following the death of the tenant of life is

   (i) entitled absolutely and beneficially;

   (ii) is of full age;

   (iii) there are no outstanding charges, or powers of creating charges; and

   (iv) there are no derivative interests.

b. Even where land ceases to be settled for the purposes of the Administration of Estates Act, it may remain settled for the purposes of, and only for the purposes of, Settled Land Act, s. 36.

3. SPECIAL PERSONAL REPRESENTATIVES

a. *Special probate*

Administration of Estates Act 1925, s. 22 (1), provides that a testator may appoint as his special executors the persons who are the trustees of the settlement at the date of his death. If he does not make that appointment, they are nevertheless deemed to be

---

[1] [1928] Ch. 163; see *ante*, p. 356.

his special executors. Accordingly, where the deceased left a will, and there are trustees of the settlement in existence at the date of his death, they will be his special executors, either by virtue of the express, or alternatively because of the deemed, appointment.

Settled Land Act 1925, s. 30 (3), is another section in that Act which causes difficulty. It applies to settlements made by will, and provides that where there are no trustees of the settlement, then the personal representatives of the deceased settlor shall be deemed to be the trustees of the settlement until others are appointed. From this section, it would be expected that where the settlement arose by will, and there are no express trustees of the settlement at the date of death of the tenant for life, then the personal representatives of the deceased settlor would be the special executors of the deceased tenant for life. This, indeed, was the decision in *In the Estate of Gibbings*.[1] In that case, a settlor died in 1890, appointing his wife and son to be his executors, and devising land upon trust for his wife for life, and, in the events which happened, thereafter for his children equally. On the death of the wife, after 1925, it was held that the deceased's son, as surviving executor of his will, was the special executor of the wife.

Notwithstanding this decision, the Probate Registry draws a distinction between cases where the personal representatives of the deceased settlor have expressly appointed themselves as trustees of the settlement, and where they have not. It is only in the former case that special probate will be granted: in the latter case it is only possible to obtain a grant of special administration with will annexed. The only possible justification for this silly distinction is the argument that s. 30 applies for the purposes of the Settled Land Act only, so that it cannot also apply for the purposes of s. 22, Administration of Estate Act. There would seem to be no merit in this argument at all.

Administration of Estates Act 1925, s. 22, refers to "the persons, if any, who are at his death the trustees of the settlement". Accordingly, if there are no trustees of the settlement at that time, but some are appointed after the death but before the application for the grant, they will not be special executors, though they can apply for special administration with will annexed.

---

[1] [1928] P. 28.

b. *Special administration*

Section 162 of the Judicature Act 1925, directs, *inter alia*, that where a deceased life tenant died wholly intestate, then special administration shall be granted to the trustees of the settlement, if they are willing to act. Rule 28[1] amplifies this, and prescribes the following order of priority for a grant of special administration:

   (i) the trustees of the settlement at the time of application for the grant;

  (ii) if there are no such trustees, and the settlement arises under a will or intestacy, the personal representative of the settlor; and

 (iii) the general personal representative of the deceased.

Although special probate can be granted only where the trustees are in existence at the date of the death of the life tenant, special administrators can be appointed where they are appointed trustees after the death but before the application for the grant.

c. *Type of grant*

It will have been seen that there may be a grant of special probate, special administration with will annexed, or special administration *simpliciter*, but, although there are these different types of grant, the position of the special personal representative under them is exactly the same.

Whatever the basic type of grant, it will usually be the normal type of grant limited to particular property, namely, settled land.[2] Accordingly, the general personal representatives will obtain a grant "save and except settled land", or a grant "caeterorum", depending on whether the general grant precedes or succeeds the limited grant.[3]

Where the same persons are both general personal representatives and also entitled to special representation, they may take separate grants,[4] or they may take one grant expressly including settled land.[5]

---

[1] Non Contentious Probate Rules, 1954.
[2] *Ante*, p. 283.
[3] *Ante*, p. 285.
[4] Non-Contentious Probate Rules 1954; r. 28 (4).
[5] Non-Contentious Probate Rules 1954; r. 28 (5).

4. DEVOLUTION OF SETTLED LAND
a. *Land ceasing to be settled*

Where land ceases to be settled land, for the purposes of s. 22, Administration of Estates Act, it will vest in the general personal representatives of the deceased. This is the principle of *Re Bridgett and Hayes Contract*.[1]

There will be no need for a special grant, but although it is rarely used in these circumstances, the court nevertheless has a power to grant representation limited to settled land, under Judicature Act 1925, s. 155. Thus, in *In the Estate of Mortifee*[2] the tenant for life died intestate, and upon his death the remainder-man became absolutely entitled. The tenant for life had no known kin. A grant of letters of administration save and except settled land was made to the Treasury Solicitor, and a grant limited to the settled land was made to the remainderman.

Where the land for most purposes ceases to be settled, but remains settled for the purposes of s. 36, Settled Land Act, the land will vest in the general personal representatives, but they will be required to transfer it to the trustees of the settlement as trustees for sale, if they do not require it for the purposes of administration.[3]

b. *Land remaining settled*

If the land was settled previous to the death of the deceased, and remains settled thereafter, the legal estate will vest automatically on his death in his special executors, if he had any. If he has none, the legal estate will vest in the usual way in the President of the Family Division[4] until a grant of representation with or without will is made, when it will vest in the special administrators.

If the land is not required for the purposes of administration by the special administrators, they will execute a vesting assent in favour of the next person entitled under the settlement.

5. POWERS OF SPECIAL PERSONAL REPRESENTATIVES

The provisions of Part III of the Administration of Estates Act 1925, which apply generally to the administration of assets,

---

[1] [1928] Ch. 163.
[2] [1948] P. 274.
[3] Settled Land Act 1925, s. 36 (1), (2).
[4] See *post*, p. 372.

apply to special personal representatives. They may, therefore, sell the settled land, or mortgage it for the purposes of raising money for the payment of estate duty in respect of the settled land itself, or for the costs of the administration of that land.[1]

Special personal representatives have an express power to dispose of the settled land without the concurrence of the general representatives, and likewise the general representatives may dispose without the concurrence of the special representatives.[2]

Where a person is entitled to a grant of administration, and he is not a trustee of the settlement, he may renounce his right to special administration, without renouncing his right to general administration.[3] This is contrary to the normal rule that where there is a renunciation, it must be renunciation of the whole entitlement to a grant. Likewise, where a grant has been made including settled land, then the administrator may apply for the revocation of the grant in respect of settled land without revoking it in respect of other property.[4]

These provisions are designed to encourage the trustees of the settlement to take special administration. Further to this end, it is also provided that the trustees of the settlement or any person beneficially interested under the settlement may apply to the court for the appointment of a special or additional personal representative in respect of the settled land. In the absence of special circumstances, the court must appoint such persons as will secure that the representatives after the appointment are the same as the trustees of the settlement.[5] This provision is also contrary to another general rule, namely that additional personal representatives cannot usually be appointed.[6]

6. THE POSITION OF PURCHASERS

As the provisions affecting special personal representatives are somewhat complicated, purchasers may in some circumstances encounter difficulty. This difficulty is usually connected with the fact that a grant of representation does not specify the land in respect of which it is made.

---

[1] Administration of Estates Act 1925, s. 36.
[2] Administration of Estates Act 1925, s. 24 (1).
[3] Administration of Estates Act 1925, s. 23 (1) (a).
[4] *Ante*, p. 309.
[5] Administration of Estates Act 1925, s. 23 (1) (b).
[6] *Ante*, p. 240.

In the first place, suppose that a grant of special representation ought to have been made, but was not made. For example, if land was limited to A for life, with remainder to B for life, and with remainder to C absolutely, and on the death of A, a general grant was obtained to A's estate. There should, of course, have been either a general grant save and except settled land, together with a special grant limited to settled land, or alternatively a general grant expressly including settled land. But if neither of these courses was followed, perhaps because at the time of application for the grant the general personal representatives did not know of the existence of the settled land, and a general grant was issued without reference to settled land, would a purchaser be safe in accepting title from them? On these facts it is clear that a special grant should have been obtained, and if the existence of the settled land was only discovered after the grant, then advantage should have been taken of Administration of Estates Act 1925, s. 23 (1) (b), and the grant revoked to the extent only that it concerned settled land. On the other hand, any grant is an order of the court, and a person is entitled to rely upon it. The latter is generally assumed to be correct, and the purchaser is thought to be protected. This was said in *Re Bridgett and Hayes*,[1] although because in that case the land had ceased to be settled land, the statement was *obiter*.[2]

The second difficulty is more substantial. Suppose that a person is the life tenant under two settlements, one of which comes to an end on his death, and the other of which continues. A special grant should be taken out in respect of the land comprised in the settlement which continues, and a general grant to the remainder. Suppose on these facts that a general grant save and except settled land is granted to A and B, and a grant limited to settled land is made to C and D. Then suppose that through some confusion the immediate title to the land which remains settled is:

    vesting deed in favour of deceased;

    general grant in favour of A and B,

what is the position of a purchaser from A and B? Conversely, suppose that title to the land which ceased to be settled is deduced as:

---

[1] [1928] Ch. 163.
[2] See also *In the Estate of Taylor*, [1929] P. 260, at p. 263.

vesting deed in favour of deceased;
special grant in favour of C and D,

what is the position of a purchaser from C and D?

In these two cases A and B on the one hand, and C and D on the other, are purporting to sell land which is not vested in them. Can the purchaser be protected? It seems that he can properly protect himself only by examining the equitable interests, to confirm that the correct grant has been made, but this would breach the principle of separation of legal estate and equitable interests. On the other hand it is just possible that the situation is saved by Administration of Estates Act, s. 36. This provides that "a personal representative may assent to the vesting in any person who . . . may be entitled thereto",[1] and that an assent by the personal representatives "shall operate to vest in that person the estate or interest to which the assent relates".[2] One might suppose that these sections can only apply if the property is vested in the personal representatives in the first place, but if in fact they enable personal representatives to transfer a title which they do not have, the difficulty just postulated would be resolved (although greater difficulties would arise in its place).

There is no satisfactory answer to this problem, and if and until it is resolved, the purchaser is at risk.

7. A BETTER SOLUTION?

At the outset of this chapter the problem was posed. On the assumption that Settled Land Act settlements are to continue, a system is needed whereby estate duty is collected efficiently, and the legal estate is transferred to the next person entitled without the purchaser having to enquire into the equitable interests. The succeeding discussion has illustrated other more particular difficulties which have arisen. It may be thought that it would have been far better not to have had special personal representatives at all, but only general representatives, in whom all property, both free and settled, would vest. All assets would be under their control for the ascertainment of estate duty, and they could vest in the person next entitled. If there was only one grant, it would

---

[1] Sub-s. (1).
[2] Sub-s. (2).

not matter whether the land ceased to be settled, or remained settled so far as the devolution of the title, or so far as the type of grant was concerned.

This is open to the objection that the general representatives, being persons other than the trustees of the settlement, would not have first hand information as to who was next entitled. But this is really no objection, for this is exactly the position which general representatives are in when the principle in *Re Bridgett and Hayes* operates. At least, if there were only general personal representatives, this chapter would not have been necessary.

CHAPTER 24

POSITION OF PERSONAL REPRESENTATIVES WITHOUT A GRANT

A. WHERE NO GRANT IS REQUIRED

In general a grant of probate or letters of administration is necessary to enable the personal representatives to administer the estate. In particular cases, however, assets can be dealt with without the need for a grant. The assets about to be discussed can be, and usually are, dealt with under the terms of a grant, so that advantage is taken of the special provisions only where it is not proposed to take out a grant. The special provisions are:

1. ADMINISTRATION OF ESTATES (SMALL PAYMENTS) ACT 1965

In order to enable small estates to be administered with little expense and formality, numerous statutes have enabled statutory and similar authorities to pay over to persons beneficially entitled assets in their hands, usually provided that the value of the asset did not exceed £100. These statutes have been amended by the Administration of Estates (Small Payments) Act 1965, to increase the financial limit to £500 in respect of deaths occurring on or after 4 September 1965.

The most important cases where this applies are:

a. *National Savings Bank, and Trustee Savings Banks*

By the combined effect of the Post Office Savings Bank Act 1954,[1] the Trustee Savings Bank Act 1954,[2] the 1965 Act, and the

---

[1] Section 7 (2).
[2] Section 21 (5).

National Savings Bank Act 1971, investments in the hands of the National Savings Bank and Trustee Savings Banks up to £500 may be dealt with without grant. This power includes savings certificates and premium bonds as well as deposits. The limit of £500 may be increased from time to time by order under the 1965 Act.

b. *Government stocks*

Section 1 (2) of the 1965 Act gives power for regulations to be made enabling the transfer to the persons beneficially entitled of certain holdings of Government stock.[1]

c. *Building Societies and Friendly Societies*

Investments in a building society[2] and in a Loan Society[3] may be dealt with without grant up to a maximum of £500. Likewise, shares in an Industrial or Provident Society[4] and in a Friendly Society[5] can be dealt with without grant. Prior to the passing of the Administration of Estates Act 1965, not only was the limit reduced to various figures below £50 and £100, but the Act applied only where there was an intestacy, and, in some cases, where there was a nomination. By virtue of the 1965 Act, the power is extended to all cases, even where there is a will.

d. *Members of H.M. Forces, and the public services*

Where sums of money or assets not exceeding £500 in value are held by the Ministry of Defence on behalf of deceased members or former members of H.M. Forces, they may be handed over to the persons beneficially entitled without grant. The sums will usually consist of arrears of pay and allowances, or of arrears of pension, but the Act also applies to the personal effects of deceased servicemen.[6]

Similar provisions relate to amounts held on behalf of deceased

---

[1] Thus amending National Debt Act 1958, s. 5 (1).
[2] Building Societies Act 1962, s. 46.
[3] Loan Societies Act 1840, s. 11.
[4] Industrial and Provident Societies Act 1965, ss. 23 to 25.
[5] Friendly Societies Act 1896, ss. 56, 58; Friendly Societies Act 1955, s. 5.
[6] Army Pensions Act 1830, s. 5; Navy and Marines (Property of Deceased) Act 1865, ss. 3, 6, 11 and 15; Pensions and Yeomanry Pay Act 1884, s. 4; Regimental Debts Act 1893, s. 9; Naval Prize Act 1918, s. 4.

civil servants and public servants such as policemen and, in some cases, teachers.[1]

e. *Merchant seamen*

Amounts up to £500 held by the Board of Trade for merchant seamen and apprentices may be dealt with without grant.[2] Again, such payments will usually consist of arrears of pay, or war pensions, or to the personal effects of seamen killed at sea.

2. NOMINATIONS

A nomination is a direction by a person who holds certain types of investments to the authority in which that investment is made requiring payment to be made on the death of the investor to the person nominated.[3] Payment is made to the nominee on proof of death only. A nomination may be made by an infant once he has attained the age of 16, and by any adult. It may be revoked or varied by a subsequent nomination, and is revoked on marriage. A nomination is not, however, revoked by will. In every case a nomination must be in writing, and in most cases an attesting witness is required. The form of nomination is usually held by the authority in which the investment is made, and so its existence will come to light when an application is made by the personal representative to deal with the asset after grant, even if he previously did not know of its existence.

Nominations are the only method of testamentary disposition available to infants who are not entitled to make a privileged will, and are a cheap method of testamentary disposition for poorer members of the community. There is often a danger, however, that the existence of the nomination is forgotten by the investor, and this disadvantage is particularly serious because a nomination is not revoked by a subsequent will.

There are two broad types of nominations, the distinction depending on the financial limits:

---

[1] E.g., Police Pensions Act 1948; Teachers (Superannuation) Acts 1925 and 1927; Superannuation (Miscellaneous Provisions) Act 1948.

[2] Merchant Shipping Act 1894, s. 176; Pensions (Navy, Army and Air Force and Mercantile Marine) Act 1939, s. 6 (3).

[3] See *ante*, p. 12.

a. Nominations in the Post Office Savings Department, including national savings certificates, where there is no financial limit;[1] and

b. Nominations in Trustee Savings Banks;[2] Friendly Societies;[3] and Industrial and Provident Societies[4] where the limit is £500.

If a nomination is for an amount above the prescribed limit, it is valid to the extent of the limit. Further, if it complies with the requirements of the Wills Act 1837, a nomination may be proved as a will.[5]

3. PERSONS DOMICILED ABROAD—INSURANCE POLICIES

The general requirement as to a grant of representation applies to any assets situate in England and Wales, even if the deceased died domiciled abroad. As an exception to this principle[6] a grant is not required for the payment of the proceeds of a policy of assurance on the life of a person domiciled abroad.[7] This does not, however, exempt the policy moneys from estate duty, which may still be payable.[8]

4. OTHER CASES

Stamp Act 1815, s. 37, provides that any person who takes possession of the deceased's personal estate and does not take out a grant of representation within six months from death, or two months from the termination of any dispute affecting the will or right to take administration, whichever is the later, is liable to a penalty of £100 and 10% of the duty payable on the grant. Furthermore, s. 40, Customs and Inland Revenue Act 1881 gives the Commissioners of Inland Revenue the alternative of charging double the duty which is payable although this may be multiplied if they so wish.[9]

In fact the 1815 Act is now obsolete, and any action is taken

---

[1] Post Office Savings Bank Act 1954, s. 7.
[2] Trustee Savings Bank Act 1954, s. 21 (3).
[3] Friendly Societies Act 1896, ss. 56, 57; Friendly Societies Act 1955, s. 5.
[4] Industrial and Provident Societies Act 1965, ss. 23, 24.
[5] *In the Goods of Baxter*, [1903] P. 12.
[6] Under Revenue Act 1884, s. 11.
[7] Revenue Act 1889, s. 19.
[8] *Haas* v. *Atlas Assurance Co., Ltd.*, [1913] 2 K.B. 209.
[9] Inland Revenue Regulation Act 1890, s. 35.

under the 1881 Act. It follows that where the total value of the estate is below the limit for duty, the personal representative has nothing to fear from this legislation. Accordingly, in this case he will be free to proceed without a grant in respect of any asset for which formal evidence of title is not required, such as personal chattels, and any other asset where the person entitled agrees to dispense with the grant. So that in the case of an ordinary bank account which is only a small amount in credit, the bank may be prepared to agree to transfer that balance to the person beneficially entitled, even although it is entitled to insist on a grant.

B. EXECUTOR'S AUTHORITY PRIOR TO GRANT

The executor derives his authority from the will, and the probate merely confirms his rights. Generally, however, the executor can only prove his right by taking a grant of probate. The result is that he can do any act without a grant except:

a. sue to judgment where it is necessary to show his title as executor; and

b. in practice, make title.

Thus, it has been held that an executor without a grant may levy distress for unpaid rent,[1] pay and release debts, receive payments, sell chattels, and pay legacies.[2] On the other hand, before he has taken out a grant he may be sued by a creditor of the testator.[3]

Although the probate is only evidence of the executor's authority an unproved will can be admitted in evidence to prove that the testator had made a will. In *Whitmore* v. *Lambert*[4] a contractual tenant of a dwelling-house died leaving a will naming his widow as sole beneficiary and executrix. She did not prove the will and the question arose whether she could put the unproved will in evidence to show her entitlement to remain in possession of the

---

[1] *Whitehead* v. *Taylor* (1839), 10 A. & E. 210.
[2] *Wankford* v. *Wankford* (1699), 1 Salk. 299; *Woolley* v. *Clark* (1822), 5 B. & Ald. 744.
[3] *Mohamidu Mohideen Hadjiar* v. *Pitchey*, [1894] A.C. 437.
[4] [1955] 2 All E.R. 147; [1955] 1 W.L.R. 495.

premises.[1] In holding that she could do, Evershed, M.R., said[2] that "a person appointed executor or executrix by will can do a number of things, and justify doing them, in relation to the property which was in the possession of the deceased, by virtue of the will before that will is proved: even though, because the executor or executrix dies, it never is proved, or capable of being proved by virtue of s. 5 of the Administration of Estates Act. One such thing which the executor may do or justify doing is entering upon property which was in the ownership and occupation, or in the occupation only, of the deceased". Unfortunately, the Master of the Rolls did not classify further the other things which could and could not be done.

The first of the two situations in which the executor needs a grant is to sue to judgment. Any executor before grant can begin any action, and he can continue any action commenced by the deceased, provided it does not lapse on death.[3] He must obtain probate before judgment, if the action depends on his title as executor, but probate is not needed in any other case. If, therefore, it is necessary only to show possession and not title, as an action for trespass, the action can be completed without a grant.[4]

The second situation where the grant is needed is to make title. So far as land is concerned, on the death of the testator, the legal estate vests in the executor, and if he executes a conveyance of it, that will vest the legal estate in the purchaser. But, the purchaser will, as a matter of practice, insist on proof of title, which can be provided only by the probate. Accordingly, in *Re Stevens, Cooke* v. *Stevens*[5] a purchaser was held entitled to refuse to complete until probate was obtained. Further, s. 36 (5), Administration of Estates Act 1925, provides that where a personal representative makes an assent or conveyance of a legal estate, the person in whose favour it is made is entitled to demand that a notice of that assent or conveyance is endorsed on the grant. A purchaser may well not complete before he is able to secure the endorsement of

---

[1] The question was relevant for the purposes of a provision of the Rent Acts then in force.

[2] [1955] 2 All E.R. 147, at p. 151; [1955] 1 W.L.R. 495, at p. 501.

[3] *Meyappa Chetty* v. *Supramanian Chetty*, [1916] 1 A.C. 603; *Biles* v. *Caesar*, [1957] 1 All E.R. 151.

[4] *Oughton* v. *Seppings* (1830), 1 B. & Ad. 241.

[5] [1897] 1 Ch. 422.

that notice, and to examine the probate to see that no endorsement has been made on it in favour of any other person.[1]

Even where he does not need to sue, or to make title, and even where s. 40, Customs and Inland Revenue Act 1881, does not induce him to take out a grant, a personal representative will usually wish to do so. This is because although he may think that he has the last will, and that he is appointed executor under it, he cannot know that this is so until probate has been granted. In most cases, therefore, the executor will wish to obtain protection for distributing the estate in the manner provided for by the will which a grant gives.

C. ADMINISTRATOR'S AUTHORITY BEFORE GRANT

Although the executor's authority stems from the will, in general an administrator—whether an administrator *simpliciter* or an administrator with will annexed—has no authority before the grant is issued. Between the date of death and the date of grant, the legal title to all the assets of the deceased vests in the President of the Family Division[2]—for want of a better repository of the legal estate.

Perhaps the most striking illustration of the position prior to grant is provided by *Ingall* v. *Moran*.[3] The deceased was killed during the war by the negligence of an Army lorry driver. The limitation legislation then in force required any action to be commenced within one year of death.[4] The deceased was killed on 19 September 1941, and the action was commenced by the deceased's father, claiming as administrator, on 17 September 1942. He did not in fact take out a grant until November 1942. The action was dismissed, because the father had no authority to bring the action prior to grant, and this defect was not cured by the subsequent grant. Further, it was then too late for him to start another action. In *Finnegan* v. *Cementation Co., Ltd.*[5] a

---

[1] *Re Miller and Pickersgill's Contract*, [1931] 1 Ch. 511.
[2] Administration of Estates Act 1925, s. 9, there called the Probate Judge.
[3] [1944] K.B. 160.
[4] Public Authorities Protection Act 1893, as amended by Limitation Act 1939, s. 21.
[5] [1953] 1 Q.B. 688.

widow brought an action under the Fatal Accidents Act arising out of the death of her husband. The death occurred in Eire and the widow took out a grant in Eire. It appeared, however, that the head office of the defendants was in England and that the action should be here. No grant of administration had been taken out in England and the writ was set aside. Again, in *Burns* v. *Campbell*[1] where an administrator who had obtained a Northern Ireland grant issued a writ in England before the Northern Ireland grant had been resealed here.[2] It was held that the subsequent re-sealing did not have any retroactive validity, so that the writ was defective. A final example is provided by *Long* v. *Burgess*[3] where a widow, who was a contractual tenant, died. The landlord served notice to quit on the President of the Probate Divorce and Admiralty Division[4] and immediately that expired, he commenced proceedings for possession against the widow's two sons who were in occupation. When the case was heard, the sons had no grant of administration, and the case was adjourned to enable them to apply for it. The Court of Appeal, however, held that even by obtaining the grant the sons were not helped because the notice to quit had expired before the grant was issued.

Long v. *Burgess*[5] shows that where an interest has been lawfully determined prior to the grant, no action can be taken when the grant has been obtained. There is, however, a limited doctrine of relation back, to enable the administrator to take action on behalf of the estate in respect of wrongful acts done before the grant. So, after he has obtained the grant, the administrator can sue a person who wrongfully appropriates the assets of the estate between date of death and the date of grant.[6]

It follows from what has been said that an administrator has no power whatever to execute an assent or conveyance before obtaining his grant[7] although where a recital of entitlement was

---

[1] [1952] 1 K.B. 15.

[2] Re-sealing is not now necessary; see *ante,* p. 281.

[3] [1950] 1 K.B. 115.

[4] The predecessor in this respect of the Family Division.

[5] [1950] 1 K.B. 115.

[6] *Foster* v. *Bates* (1843), 12 M. & W. 226; *Tharpe* v. *Stallwood* (1843), 5 Man. & Gr. 760; *Re Pryse,* [1940] P. 301.

[7] *Morgan* v. *Thomas* (1853), 8 Exch. 302.

contained in the assent or conveyance, the purchaser would presumably in due course obtain the legal estate under the doctrine of "feeding the estoppel".[1]

---

[1] See e.g., *Rawlin's Case* (1587), Jenk. 254; *Mackley* v. *Nutting*, [1949] 2 K.B. 55; *Universal Permanent Building Society* v. *Cooke*, [1952] Ch. 95.

CHAPTER 25

DISCHARGE OF DEBTS
AND LIABILITIES

A. ASSETS

As well as bearing its colloquial meaning of any item of property, the word "assets" is used in the technical sense of the property which is liable for the payment of the deceased's debts and liabilities.

1. WHAT PROPERTY IS ASSETS?

Administration of Estates Act 1925, s. 32 (1), provides that the following items of real and personal estate are available as assets:

a. property of the deceased, to the extent of his beneficial interest in it;

b. property which is subject to a general power which the deceased exercised by will. This property will usually be that subject to a power of appointment; and

c. entailed property held by the deceased and which he disposed of under the power contained in Law of Property Act 1925, s. 176.

The section provides that these items are assets for the payment of debts and liabilities, but it appears that the liabilities must arise out of obligations entered into by the deceased during his lifetime, and not obligations incurred by the personal representatives.[1]

Section 32 is not, however, comprehensive, and the following other items of property are available:

---

[1] *Hamer's Devisees' Case* (1852), 2 De G.M. & G. 366.

375

a. Property acquired after death

If by virtue of Wills Act 1837, s. 33[1] a deceased son was held to have outlived his parent, and to take under the parent's will, the property received in that way would be available. Likewise, income which arises after the death is available.[2]

b. Property appointed

Although s. 32 refers to property subject to a general power being disposed of by will, it is necessary to consider this further. There are in each case two questions to be asked: does the property devolve upon the personal representative; and is it available for the payment of debts. The possible permutations are:

(i) *real property appointed by will.* A testator is deemed to have been entitled at his death to an interest in any realty which is subject to a power of appointment where his will operates as an appointment of that property.[3] Accordingly, it is within the terms of Administration of Estates Act 1925, s. 1 (1), and devolves upon the personal representative. It is available for the payment of debts under s. 32.

(ii) *personalty appointed by will.* At common law personalty appointed by will did not devolve upon the personal representatives of the appointor, but upon the appointee.[4] There is no provision of the Administration of Estates Act which alters this position. However, it has been held that the personal representative can give a valid receipt for it[5] and can use it for the payment of debts under s. 32. If the personal representatives do not take it, the creditors, as they could before 1926, can still take action

---

[1] *Post*, p. 454.

[2] *Re Tong, Hilton* v. *Bradbury*, [1931] 1 Ch. 202. See also *Bromfield* v. *Chichester* (1773), 2 Dick. 480; *James* v. *Dean* (1805), 11 Ves. 383; *Randall* v. *Russell* (1817), 3 Mer. 190; *Fitzroy* v. *Howard* (1828), 3 Russ. 225; *Giddings* v. *Giddings* (1827), 3 Russ. 241; *Fosbrooke* v. *Balguy* (1833), 1 My. & K. 226; *Bevan* v. *Webb*, [1905] 1 Ch. 620; *Re Thomson, Thomson* v. *Allen*, [1930] 1 Ch. 203.

[3] Administration of Estates Act 1925, s. 3 (2).

[4] *O'Grady* v. *Wilmot*, [1916] 2 A.C. 231.

[5] *Re Hoskin's Trusts* (1877), 5 Ch.D. 229; *on appeal* 6 Ch.D. 281; *Re Peacock's Settlement, Kelcey* v. *Harrison*, [1902] 1 Ch. 552; *O'Grady* v. *Wilmot, supra.*

to satisfy their claims out of the appointed property.[1] This rule is based on the notion that as it was a general power, the testator could have exercised it in favour of the creditors, and it would be inequitable for the testator to give a benefit to volunteers while his creditors remained unsatisfied.[2] This reasoning is taken to its logical conclusion in *Beyfus* v. *Lawley*[3] where it was held that the testator cannot prefer creditors by appointing in favour of one of them. The appointment under the will operates as a legacy, even though made in favour of a person who is a creditor, and the other creditors may intervene.

(iii) *property appointed by deed.* The scope of the rule allowing creditors to intervene was extended under the pre-1926 rules to allow them to claim property which was appointed by deed.[4] In *Townshend* v. *Windham*[5] Lord Hardwicke said that the rules had to be the same for appointment by will and by deed. If not "the justice intended by the court in these cases would be avoided in every instance; as then it would be putting it barely on the form of the conveyance". It is uncertain, however, how far this rule applies, but the general view is that it applies only to an appointment by deed which operates on death and not during the testator's lifetime. This is because the creditor's action is to "intercept" the fund *in transitu*[6] and in the case of an appointment which is operative *inter vivos* the transfer is complete. The 1925 legislation has not altered this position.[7]

(iv) *property not appointed.* Property which is subject to a general power of appointment is available for the payment of creditors if the testator did not exercise the power and if he is entitled in

---

[1] *Thompson* v. *Towne* (1694), 2 Vern. 319; *Hinton* v. *Toye* (1739), 1 Atk. 465; *Bainton* v. *Ward* (1741), 2 Atk. 172; *Townshend* v. *Windham* (1706), 2 Ves Sen. 1, at p. 9; *Jenney* v. *Andrews* (1822), 6 Madd. 264; *Williams* v. *Lomas* (1852), 16. Beav. 1; *Platt* v *Routh* (1840), 6 M. & W. 756; *Fleming* v. *Buchanan* (1853), 3 De G.M. & G. 976, at p. 979; *Re Hadley, Johnson* v. *Hadley*, [1909] 1 Ch. 20; *Re Pryce, Lawford* v. *Pryce*, [1911] 2 Ch. 286.

[2] *Townshend* v. *Windham, supra; Re Phillips, Lawrence* v. *Huxtable*, [1931] 1 Ch. 347.

[3] [1903] A.C. 411.

[4] *Townshend* v. *Windham, supra; George* v. *Milbanke* (1803), 9 Ves. 190; *Pack* v. *Bathurst* (1745), 3 Atk. 269; *Troughton* v. *Troughton* (1747), 3 Atk. 656.

[5] (1706), 2 Ves. Sen. 1.

[6] *O'Grady* v. *Wilmot*, [1916] 2 A.C. 231, at pp. 248, 273 and 279.

[7] *Re Phillips, Lawrence* v. *Huxtable, supra.*

default of appointment. The property is not available if he is not entitled in default.[1]

(v) *property subject to a special power*. This is not available for creditors[2] unless, presumably, the deceased was entitled in default of appointment and no appointment was made.

c. *Donationes mortis causa*

Property which is the subject of a *donatio mortis causa* has been held to be liable for the payment of debts if all other property has been exhausted.[3]

2. PROPERTY NOT AVAILABLE

a. *Property not in hands of executor*

There is a theoretical distinction between property which is available for the payment of debts, and property for which the personal representative is liable. All property within s. 32 is available for the payment of debts, but a personal representative is responsible only to take reasonable care to safeguard the assets.[4] Accordingly if the assets are stolen through no fault of his, or if being perishable, they cease to exist through no fault of his, the personal representative is not liable.[5] In practice this has the result of making the assets unavailable.

b. *Trust property*

Section 32 makes property liable for the payment of debts to the extent of the deceased's beneficial interest. Trust property, therefore, is not available. In *Re Webb, Barclays Bank, Ltd.* v. *Webb*,[6] for example, the deceased effected a policy of assurance on his own life. The beneficiary of the policy, according to its terms, was his infant son. The deceased paid the premiums, but it was held that as he held the policy on trust for his son, the proceeds did not form part of his estate.[7]

---

[1] *Holmes* v. *Coghill* (1802-06), 7 Ves. 499; on appeal (1806), 12 Ves. 206.

[2] *Per* Lord Hardwicke in *Townshend* v. *Windham* (1706), 2 Ves. Sen. 1, at p. 9.

[3] *Smith* v. *Casen* (1718), 1 P. Wms. App. 406; *Ward* v. *Turner* (1751), 2 Ves. Sen. 431; *Re Korvine's Trust*, [1921] 1 Ch. 343.

[4] *Post*, p. 426.

[5] *Jenkins* v. *Plombe* (1705), 6 Mod. 181.

[6] [1941] Ch. 225.

[7] See also *Re Gordon*, [1940] Ch. 851, which turned on the rules of a friendly society; *Re Sinclair's Life Policy*, [1938] Ch. 799.

c. *Foreign property*

The general rule is that "assets in any part of the world shall be assets in every part of the world".[1] All assets, wherever situated, are therefore liable for the payment of debts. But a similar distinction must be drawn to that with regard to assets not in the hands of the executor: a personal representative is liable only to the extent of assets which he has or ought to have under his control as the English personal representative. The ability of the personal representative to use foreign assets for the payment of English debts will depend on whether, by the law of the country in which the assets are situated, they can be used for the discharge of English liabilities.

B. DEBTS AND LIABILITIES

1. POWER TO SETTLE AND COMPROMISE

Trustee Act 1925, s. 15, confers upon personal representatives wide powers in respects of debts. These are:

a. to allow any debt or claim on any evidence which they think sufficient;

b. to allow time for payment of any debt;

c. to agree to the settlement of any debt by compromise, compounding, or in any other way; and

d. to abandon any debt or claim.

So long as the personal representative exercises these powers in good faith, he is not responsible for any loss which arises as a result.

2. ADMISSIBLE DEBTS

Subject to the general provisions of Trustee Act 1925, s. 15, the personal representative is responsible for paying funeral expenses; expenses incurred in the administration of the estate; debts which were outstanding at the date of death; and liabilities which arose as a result of actions of the deceased in his lifetime.

---

[1] *Per* Lord Lyndhurst in *A.-G.* v. *Dimond* (1831), 1 Cr. & J. 356.

a. *Funeral expenses*

Funeral expenses are payable out of the estate before any other debt.[1] Even in the case of an insolvent estate, the necessary funeral expenses take first priority.[2]

Where the estate is insolvent, the personal representative is allowed to incur only those expenses which are absolutely necessary.[3] In *Shelly's Case*[4] these were said by Lord Holt to be the cost of the coffin, ringing the church bell, and the fees of the parson clerk and undertaker, but they also include the cost of digging the grave. Where the estate is solvent, the personal representative will be allowed all expenses which are reasonable having regard to the circumstances and quality of the deceased. In one case[5] £600 was allowed in 1692 on the funeral of a wealthy local celebrity.

In all cases the extent of the allowable expenses depends on the facts, and it is difficult to extract a clear principle. The cost of a tombstone has been disallowed.[6] In *Paice* v. *Archbishop of Canterbury*[7] Lord Eldon allowed the cost of mourning rings distributed among the deceased's relations and friends, and in *Pitt* v. *Pitt*[8] a widow was allowed her mourning expenses, although a contrary result was reached in *Johnson* v. *Baker*.[9]

b. *Debts*

In general all debts due from the deceased are payable by his personal representatives. If a debt has been held in an action to be statute barred, then it may not be paid,[10] but in other cases the personal representatives may pay a statute barred debt.[11] They are not entitled, however, to pay a debt which is unenforceable due to non-compliance with the requirements of the Statute of Frauds, where they still exist, or Law of Property Act 1925, s. 40.[12]

---

[1] *R.* v. *Wade* (1818), 5 Price 621, at p. 627.
[2] *Re Walter, Slocock* v. *Official Receiver*, [1929] 1 Ch. 647.
[3] *Re Wester Wemyss, Tilley* v. *Wester Wemyss*, [1940] Ch. 1.
[4] (1693), 1 Salk. 296.
[5] *Offley* v. *Offley* (1691). Prec. Chanc. 26.
[6] *Bridge* v. *Brown* (1843), 2 Y. & C.C.C. 181.
[7] (1807), 14 Ves. 364.
[8] (1758), 2 Lee 508.
[9] (1825), 2 C. & P. 207.
[10] *Re Midgley, Midgley* v. *Midgley*, [1893] 3 Ch. 282.
[11] *Norton* v. *Frecker* (1737). 1 Atk. 524, at p. 526; *Stahlschmidt* v. *Lett* (1853), 1 Sm. & G. 415.
[12] *Re Rownson, Field* v. *White* (1885), 29 Ch.D. 358.

c. *Contractual obligations*

Personal contracts are frustrated by death and accordingly do not bind the personal representatives.[1] If, however, the deceased had broken a personal contract during his lifetime, and judgment had been given against him, that judgment is binding on the estate.[2] Other contracts are binding upon the personal representatives. If, for example, the deceased had contracted to redecorate a house, the personal representatives must arrange for this to be done at the expense of the estate, or for the contract to be terminated by consent.[3]

The obligations under a lease[4] and in respect of a business carried on by the deceased[5] are considered later.

d. *Liability in tort*

In general all causes of action subsisting against the deceased survive his death subject to two qualifications. Actions for defamation[6] do not survive.

Previously, if proceedings had not been commenced before the death of the deceased, they had to be commenced within six months of a grant of representation being made.[7] This rule was, however, abolished by the Proceedings Against Estates Act 1970.[8]

e. *Liabilities for tax*

Most obligations of the deceased can be ascertained within a short time of death, but this does not apply to liabilities for income tax and capital gains tax. The amount of the liability for income tax depends on the total income of the deceased for the period from the preceding 5th April to the date of death. This has

---

[1] *Farrow* v. *Wilson* (1869), L.R. 4 C.P. 744, at p. 746; *Robinson* v. *Davison* (1871), L.R. 6 Exch. 269; *Graves* v. *Cohen* (1929), 46 T.L.R. 121.

[2] *Phillips* v. *Homfray* (1883), 24 Ch.D. 439.

[3] *Quick and Harris* v. *Ludborrow* (1615), 3 Bulst. 29; *Re Rushbrook's Will Trusts*, [1948] Ch. 421.

[4] *Post*, p. 423.

[5] *Post*, p. 417.

[6] Law Reform (Miscellaneous Provisions) Act 1934, s. 1.

[7] The proceedings would have been commenced with this six-month period even if they had become statute-barred in the deceased's lifetime: *Airey* v. *Airey*, [1958] 2 All. E.R. 571.

[8] See Ogus (1969), 32 M.L.R. 551.

to be agreed with the Inspector of Taxes, as well as any liability outstanding in respect of previous fiscal years. Although it may well take several months for this liability to be ascertained and discharged, it is regarded as an obligation existing at the date of death.[1]

f. *Estate duty*

Although estate duty arises on death and not before it, it is paid from the estate as a first charge, after only the funeral and testamentary expenses.

3. TIME FOR PAYMENT

The rule governing the time for payment of debts was stated by Uthwatt, J. in *Re Tankard, Tankard* v. *Midland Bank Executor and Trustee Co., Ltd.*[2] in the following terms: "it is the duty of executors, as a matter of the due administration of the estate, to pay the debts of their testator with due diligence having regard to the assets in their hands which are properly applicable for that purpose, and in determining whether due diligence has been shown regard must be had to all the circumstances of the case". Personal representatives should, when acting with due diligence, give special attention to debts which carry interest, and threats by creditors to sue for payment. If the cost of the estate is increased without cause, for example, by interest accruing when there were ample funds from which the debt could be discharged, or by an order for costs being made against the estate unnecessarily, the personal representative will be liable to make good that loss out of his own pocket.[3] It does not follow, of course, merely because interest accrues or costs are incurred that the personal representative has not acted with due diligence. He may have had insufficient assets to make earlier payment, or he may have been waiting until all liabilities were known so that he could see whether the estate was solvent.

Subject to this "due diligence" rule, it appears that the normal rule applies that the personal representatives cannot be called upon to make payment within one year from death. This rule is discussed in connexion with legacies at p. 496.

---

[1] See further, Mellows, Taxation for Executors and Trustees, 3rd ed., p. 1
[2] [1942] Ch. 69.
[3] *Post*, p. 424.

C. SOLVENT ESTATES

An estate is solvent if there are sufficient assets for the payment of the funeral, testamentary and administration expenses, and for the payment of the creditors in full.[1] Where the estate is subject to the payment of an annuity[2] the annuitant may insist that the annuity is valued, and the capital value treated as a debt due from the estate.[3]

If the estate is solvent, the creditors are not concerned with the source of the funds from which they are paid, as they will all be paid in full. The beneficiaries may well be affected, however, particularly where debts are charged on assets, and this topic is accordingly dealt with in connexion with the distribution of the estate to the beneficiaries.[4]

It is prudent to distribute the assets among creditors on the basis that the estate is insolvent—that is, to follow the statutory order for payment—until it becomes quite clear that the assets are more than sufficient to discharge all liabilities.[5]

D. INSOLVENT ESTATES

1. METHODS OF ADMINISTRATION

An insolvent estate may be administered in any one of three ways:

a. by the personal representatives in the usual way, without the intervention of the court;

b. under an administration order, which can be obtained from the court either by personal representatives or creditors, or other persons interested;[6] or

c. following an order for the administration of the estate in

---

[1] *Re Leng, Tarn v. Emmerson*, [1895] 1 Ch. 652, at p. 658.
[2] That is, where the annuity was given in the deceased's lifetime, and does not arise under the will.
[3] *Re Pink, Elvin v. Nightingale*, [1927] 1 Ch. 237, at p. 241.
[4] *Post*, p. 517.
[5] *Re Milan Tramways Co., Ex parte Theys* (1884), 25 Ch.D. 587, *Re Pink, Elvin v. Nightingale, ante; Re McMurdo, Penfield v. McMurdo*, [1902] 2 Ch. 684.
[6] In accordance with R.S.C., O. 85.

bankruptcy.[1] The petition may be either by the personal representatives, or by any creditor whose debt would have been sufficient to support a bankruptcy petition against the deceased if he had remained alive.[2] The effect of an administration order in bankruptcy is that the deceased's estate vests in the Official Receiver until a trustee in bankruptcy is appointed.[3]

2. PRIORITY OF DEBTS

The priority of debts is governed by Administration of Estates Act 1925, s. 34 (1), which provides that where the estate is insolvent, it shall be administered in accordance with Part I of the First Schedule. This Schedule has the following effect:

(i) Funeral, testamentary and administration expenses have priority.

(ii) Subject to this, the same rules apply as they do to the administration of the assets of persons who have been adjudicated bankrupt.

There is no statutory definition of testamentary and administration expenses. They include the expense of obtaining a grant of representation; costs incurred in the collection, maintenance or disposal of the deceased's assets; costs of obtaining legal advice as to the construction of any will and the administration of the estate; payments of other liabilities arising since the date of death, such as rent; and other expenses to which the personal representatives are put in carrying out their functions as such.[4]

3. THE STATUTORY ORDER

The effect of the Bankruptcy Act 1914, and of certain other acts is to create four classes of debts. These are:

a. *Specially preferred debts*

(i) Money or property belonging to any friendly society which came into the possession of the deceased in his capacity as an

---

[1] Under Bankruptcy Act 1914, s. 130.

[2] *Ibid*, s. 130 (1).

[3] *Ibid*, s. 130 (4).

[4] *Sharp* v. *Lush* (1879), 10 Ch.D. 468, at p. 470; cf. *Re Rooke, Jeans* v. *Gatehouse*, [1933] Ch. 970.

officer of the society,[1] even if he had ceased to be an officer of the society by the time of his death.[2]

(ii) Money or property belonging to any trustee savings bank which at the date of death of the deceased was held by him in his capacity as an officer or employee of the bank.[3]

(iii) Where the deceased was at the date of his death subject to military law, and he had in his possession money or property subject to the Regimental Debts Act 1893.

b. *Preferred debts*

(i) All local rates due from the deceased at the date of his death which had become due and payable at any time within twelve months before his death.[4] This priority applies even if the assessment is made after death.[5]

(ii) Arrears of tax for one year.[1] The Crown has the right to select as its preferential debt the tax outstanding for any year[6] of assessment, even if that was not the last year before the deceased's death.[7]

(iii) Arrears of wages to employees for services rendered to the deceased during four months before his death, subject to a limit of £200 for each employee.[8] This includes arrears of holiday pay.[9]

(iv) Arrears of National Insurance contributions in respect of the twelve months ending with the date of death.[10] This includes the deceased's own contributions where he was self-employed or non-employed, and contributions for his employees where he was the employer.

(v) Arrears of tax deducted by the deceased from his employees' remuneration under the P.A.Y.E. scheme, and not remitted to the Revenue,[11] for the period of twelve months ending with the date of death.

---

[1] Friendly Societies Act 1896, s. 35.
[2] *Re Eilbeck*, [1910] 1 K.B. 136.
[3] Trustee Savings Bank Act 1954, s. 61.
[4] Bankruptcy Act 1914, s. 33 (9).
[5] *Gowers* v. *Walker*, [1930] 1 Ch. 262.
[6] Bankruptcy Act 1914, s. 33 (9).
[7] *Re Pratt, Ex parte Inland Revenue Commissioners* v. *Phillips*, [1951] Ch. 225.
[8] Companies Act 1948, s. 319 (1) (b).
[9] *Ibid*, s. 319 (1) (d).
[10] Bankruptcy Act 1914, s. 33 (1), as amended by National Insurance (Industrial Injuries) Act, 1965.
[11] Finance Act 1952, s. 30 (1).

(vi) Arrears of purchase tax due from the deceased which had become due within twelve months before death.[1]

(vii) Any sum, not exceeding £200, ordered to be paid by the deceased for failing to reinstate a former employee in his civil employment following military service, provided the deceased himself had been at fault with regard to such failure to re-instate at some time prior to his death.[2]

(viii) Payments in lieu of contributions which are payable on the termination of a person's employment in certain circumstances.[3]

c. *Ordinary debts*

These are all debts which do not fall into any other class.

d. *Deferred debts*

(i) Loans made to a person who is either engaged in or is about to be engaged in a business if the lender is to receive interest varying with the profits of a business;[4]

(ii) Payment due for the price of the goodwill of a business, where the price is payable in the form of a share of the profits;[5]

(iii) Money or other property lent by a husband to his wife for the purposes of her trade or business; and money or property lent by a wife to her husband for any purpose;[6]

(iv) Claims under a covenant or contract made by the deceased in consideration of marriage to settle after acquired property for the benefit of his spouse or children.[7]

Where the relationship of husband and wife does not exist for the purposes of the last two heads, the loan may still be deferred within category (i). Thus, in *Re Meade, Ex parte Humber* v. *Palmer*,[8] a woman lent the deceased £7,000 which he used in his riding academy. This sum was intended to provide benefit for

---

[1] Purchase Tax Act 1963, s. 30 (1).
[2] Under Reinstatement in Civil Employment Act 1944, s. 18 (1), or National Service Act 1948, s. 48.
[3] Under National Insurance Act 1965, s. 61.
[4] Partnership Act 1890, s. 3; Bankruptcy Act 1914, s. 33 (9).
[5] *Ibid.*
[6] Bankruptcy Act 1914, s. 36 (1), (2).
[7] *Ibid.*, s. 42.
[8] [1951] Ch. 774.

both of them, and the Court of Appeal held that the debt came within the first category, and was therefore deferred.

The personal representatives must pay the debts in each class *pari passu.*

This order for the payment of debts is statutory, and applies before any effect is given to the terms of the will. Accordingly, the testator cannot alter the priorities by any direction contained in his will.[1]

4. FURTHER PROVISIONS

a. *Interest*

Where the debt carries interest, interest is to be calculated at the rate of not more than £5% in the first instance. Where the estate is being administered in bankruptcy following an order under Bankruptcy Act 1914, s. 130, the interest is calculated to the date of the receiving order.[2] Where the estate is being administered under an Administration Order, interest is calculated to the date of the order.[3] There is no clear rule as to the date to which interest is to be calculated where the estate is being administered by the personal representatives out of court, but this should presumably be the date of death.[4]

If there is any surplus after the payment of all creditors in full, and interest calculated on this basis, moneylenders are entitled to be paid the difference between the rate of interest provided for in the moneylending contract and the rate of £5%.[5] Other creditors are entitled to be paid from the surplus interest at £4% from the date of death on the amount of the admitted debts.[6]

b. *Contingent liabilities*

Contingent liabilities are provable.[7] In this case an estimate is made of the value of the liability, and the debt is provable at that figure. Appeal lies to the court.[8]

---

[1] *Turner* v. *Cox* (1853), 8 Moo P.C.C. 288; *Re Rothermere, Mellors Basden & Co.* v. *Coutts & Co.*, [1943] 1 All E.R. 307.

[2] Bankruptcy Act 1914, s. 66.

[3] *Re Sagor, Russian Commercial and Industrial Bank* v. *Kogan*, [1930] W.N. 149.

[4] By analogy with Bankruptcy Act 1914, s. 33 (5).

[5] Moneylenders Act 1927, s. 9 (1).

[6] Bankruptcy Act 1914, s. 33 (5), (8).

[7] *Ibid.*, s. 30 (4), (5), (6).

[8] *Ibid.*

c. *Exclusion of certain bankruptcy rules*

Normally, when a person becomes bankrupt, certain rules are applied to increase the size of his estate available for the payment of his creditors. These include the reputed ownership clause,[1] the fraudulent preference clause[2] and certain other provisions which defeat settlements.[3] These do not apply where an estate of a deceased person is being administered in bankruptcy.[4]

5. LANDLORD'S POWER OF DISTRESS

Section 35 (1) of the Bankruptcy Act 1914, provides that where an order for the administration of the estate of a deceased has been made under s. 130, the landlord can use his power of distress only for six months' rent accrued due before the date of the administration order. It is uncertain whether this applies where the estate is being administered under an administration order. In *Re Wells*[5] Romer, J. said that it did not apply, whereas in *Re Bush, Lipton, Ltd.* v. *Macintosh*[6] Luxmoore, J. said that it did. *Re Bush, Lipton, Ltd.* v. *Macintosh* is generally thought to be correct.

If distress is levied within the period of three months preceding the death, the specially preferred and preferred debts are a first charge on the goods taken.[7] If the landlord is forced to give up the goods taken, he is then subrogated to the creditor.[8]

E. POSITION OF SECURED CREDITORS

A creditor who has security for his debt in the form of a mortgage, charge or lien[9] over property of the deceased is in an advantageous position. The fact that he is secured in this way gives him certain rights over the property charged. Depending on the nature of the charge, he may have a power of sale,[10] or the

---

[1] Bankruptcy Act 1914, s. 38 (c).

[2] *Ibid*, s. 44.

[3] *Ibid*, s. 42. See also Law of Property Act 1925, s. 172.

[4] *Re Leng, Tarn* v. *Emmerson*, [1895] 1 Ch. 652.

[5] [1929] 2 Ch. 269.

[6] [1930] 2 Ch. 202; see also *Re Fryman's Estate, Fryman* v. *Fryman* (1888), 38 Ch. D.468.

[7] Bankruptcy Act 1914, s. 33 (4).

[8] *Re Caidan, Ex parte Official Receiver* v. *Regis Property Co., Ltd.*, [1942] Ch. 90.

[9] Bankruptcy Act 1914, s. 167.

[10] See, e.g., Law of Property Act 1925, s. 101.

power to appoint a receiver and to apply to the court for an order for sale.[1] These powers may be exercised notwithstanding the death of the deceased, and they apply irrespective of the provisions of the will.

Where the value of the security is more than adequate to cover the amount of the debt, the creditor is adequately protected, whether or not the estate is insolvent. If, for example, a lender has a mortgage over the deceased's property, he may exercise his power of sale, assuming it has arisen, and thus repay himself in full. He is therefore unaffected by the statutory order for the payment of debts. To give an extreme case, if the lender took a legal mortgage to secure a debt which would rank as a deferred debt, then subject to the security being of sufficient value to satisfy the debt, the creditor will be paid in full, even if there are no assets for the preferred creditors.

If the estate is insolvent, and the value of the security is not sufficient to cover the whole of the debt the creditor has the choice of:

   (i) realising his security, and proving for the balance of his claim;[2]

   (ii) valuing his security and proving for the balance;[3] or

   (iii) surrendering his security and proving for the whole debt.[4] It is difficult to envisage anyone in his senses doing this.

In most cases only the first course will be desirable. If the second course is adopted, the personal representative or trustee in bankruptcy, depending on the type of administration, has the right to have the security redeemed at the value placed on it by the creditor, or sold, but this right can only be exercised for six months from being required by the creditor to make his election.[5] The creditor will thus be restricted in the action which he can take and will usually wish to sell outright, where he has the power to do so.

The existence of security in the case of a solvent estate will affect the rights of beneficiaries, and this aspect is considered later.[6]

---

[1] Law of Property Act 1925, s. 91.

[2] Bankruptcy Act 1914, s. 7 (2), and Sched. II, para. 10.

[3] Bankruptcy Act 1914, Sched. II, paras. 12-17.

[4] *Ibid*, para. 11.

[5] *Ibid*, paras. 12-17.

[6] *Post*, p. 517 *et seq*.

F. RIGHTS OF RETAINER AND PREFERENCE

A personal representative previously had rights of retainer and preference. The former was a right to retain debts due to him in preference to paying other creditors of the same degree. The latter was a right to pay one creditor in preference to other creditors of the same class. These rights were abolished in respect of deaths occurring after 1971.[1]

G. CONTINGENT LIABILITIES

1. THE PROBLEM
a. *Generally*

Contingent liabilities may present considerable difficulties to the personal representative. There is no general rule of law that a personal representative is liable only for those debts of which he knows, or for those liabilities which have crystallised.[2] In principle, whenever a liability becomes apparent, then, provided it is still not statute barred, the personal representative is liable to satisfy the claim to the extent of the assets which have passed through his hands.

The deceased may have given a guarantee in respect of the payment of a debt by another, or a bond for the performance by another of some obligation, and at the date of death there may be no indication at all that the principal debtor may default. The deceased may have been the holder of shares in a company which were not paid up in full. In this case, if the company goes into liquidation the shareholders will be called upon to pay the difference between the amount actually paid up on the shares and the full amount due. At the date of death the company may be flourishing and show no signs of going into liquidation.[3]

Again, the deceased may have taken a lease of certain property, and as such remain liable throughout the length of term for the lessee's covenants, notwithstanding that the lease has been

---

[1] Administration of Estates Act 1971, ss. 10, 14 (2).

[2] Although certain protection is conferred by Trustee Act 1925, ss. 26, 27, *post*, pp. 391, 393.

[3] See e.g. *Taylor* v. *Taylor* (1870), L.R. 10 Eq. 477; *Knatchbull* v. *Fearnhead* (1837), 3 My. & Cr. 122; *Newcastle Banking Co.* v. *Hymers* (1856), 22 Beav. 367; *Re Bewley's Estate, Jefferys* v. *Jefferys* (1871), 24 L.T. 177.

assigned.[1] These are just some of the many circumstances in which at the time of death and during the administration period there may be contingent liabilities which have not actually become debts.

The general rule is that the personal representative is liable for the satisfaction of all such liabilities as and when, if at all, they crystallise into debts.[2] He may have rights to recover assets from legatees, but if the legatees have parted with the assets, or disappeared, this right may be worthless. Is, then, the cautious personal representative bound to retain a large part of the estate, almost indefinitely, to satisfy any claims if and when they are made?

Special provisions apply to leases, which will be examined first, and then the general position considered further.

b. *Leases*

It is necessary to consider separately the position of the personal representative who is liable as such because he is an assignee by operation of law of the lease; and his position where he enters into possession of the demised property and so also becomes liable by virtue of the doctrine of privity of estate.

(i) Liability as assignee.

Trustee Act 1925, s. 26, deals with the position where a personal representative, or trustee, is liable in his capacity as such for any rent or other covenant in a lease; for any rent or other covenant arising out of a rentcharge; or any covenant for indemnity given in respect of rent or other obligation under a lease or rentcharge. The section provides that where the personal representative discharges all liability which has accrued and been claimed to the date of distribution, and sets aside any fixed sum which the deceased agreed to lay out, even if it is to be paid at some time in the future, then he may pass on the property to the beneficiary entitled, or sell it, without making any further provision for liabilities to arise. Where the property is passed on in this way, the personal representative is not personally liable under any subsequent claim, although the lessor or grantor has the right to

---

[1] As to leases, see *infra*.
[2] *Nector and Sharp* v. *Gennet* (1590), Cro. Eliz. 466; *Eeles* v. *Lambert* (1648), St. 37; *Hawkins* v. *Day* (1753), Amb. 160; *Pearson* v. *Archdeaken* (1831), 1 Alcock & Nap. 23.

follow assets into the hands of the beneficiaries where any further liability does arise.[1]

The section only protects personal representatives who discharge all liabilities which accrue due, and make provision for any further fixed sum to be paid while the lease is still vested in them.[2]

It will be seen that the section provides adequate protection for personal representatives as assignees by operation of law.

(ii) Liability after entry into possession.

By entering into possession of the property the personal representatives become liable under the terms of the lease in their personal capacity by virtue of the doctrine of privity of estate, and the protection of Trustee Act, s. 26, does not assist them.[3] Where they incur liability in this way, they should set aside a fund to meet any further liability.[4] This fund belongs to the residuary beneficiaries (assuming it was taken from residue) subject to such claims, and the residuary beneficiaries are entitled to have it transferred to them when any claims are statute barred.[5]

This can work hardly, however, on the residuary beneficiaries where the lease is the subject of a specific gift, or is sold. While another person enjoys the benefit of the lease, they suffer the retention out of the funds due to them of the contingency fund.

c. *Other liabilities*

In the case of liabilities under leases or rentcharges outside Trustee Act, s. 26, and in the case of other contingent liabilities, the personal representative can adopt one of several possible courses:

(i) Obtain indemnity and distribute. Administration of Estates Act, s. 26 (10), expressly empowers a personal representative as a condition of making any assent in favour of a beneficiary to require security for the discharge of outstanding debts and liabilities. Unless an indemnity is secured in some way, such as by a mortgage or bond, the personal representative always runs some risk in proceeding in this way, as the beneficiary himself may be

---

[1] Trustee Act 1925, s. 26 (2).
[2] *Re Bennett, Midland Bank Executor and Trustee Co., Ltd.* v. *Fletcher*, [1943] 1 All E.R. 467; *Re Owers, Public Trustee* v. *Death*, [1941] Ch. 389.
[3] *Re Owers, Public Trustee* v. *Death, supra.*
[4] *Re Lewis, Jennings* v. *Hemsley*, [1939] Ch. 232.
[5] *Re Lewis, supra.*

lost to trace or become bankrupt. The personal representative would still be liable, and the indemnity worthless. The personal representative must clearly be guided by the character of the indemnifier and the nature of the liability.

If an unconditional assent has been made, the right to demand an indemnity is then lost.[1]

(ii) Distribute under order of court. Where the estate is administered under an order of the court, then, provided the court has been given full knowledge of all relevant facts known to the personal representative, he will be fully protected.[2] Such an order can only be made in the course of an administration action, but this can be commenced at any time, even when most of the estate is distributed.

(iii) Retain fund. Where the fund is retained to meet possible liabilities, it can work hardship on the residuary beneficiaries, as mentioned above.[3]

H. UNKNOWN DEBTS AND LIABILITIES

The general principle is that a personal representative is liable to pay any debts to the extent of the assets which have passed through his hands, even if acting in good faith and without notice of the debts he has distributed the whole of the assets to the beneficiaries.[4] This remains the position where the personal representative does not advertise for liabilities, but he can obtain statutory protection against claims by advertising.

Section 27 of the Trustee Act 1925[5] applies both to personal

---

[1] *Re Bennett, Midland Bank Executor Trustee Co., Ltd.* v. *Fletcher*, [1943] 1 All E.R. 467.

[2] *Dean* v. *Allen* (1855), 20 Beav. 1; *Smith* v. *Smith* (1861), 1 Drew & Sm. 384; *Dodson* v. *Sammell* (1861), 1 Drew & Sm. 575; *Waller* v. *Barrett* (1857), 24 Beav. 413; *Re Sanford's Trust, Bennett* v. *Lytton* (1860), 2 John & H. 155; *Addams* v. *Ferick* (1859), 26 Beav. 384; *Williams* v. *Headland* (1864), 4 Giff. 505; *England* v. *Lord Tredegar* (1866), L.R. 1 Eq. 344; *Re King, Mellor* v. *South Australian Land Mortgage and Agency, Co.*, [1907] 1 Ch. 72; *Re Johnson* v. *King Edward Hospital Fund for London*, [1940] W.N. 195.

[3] *Ante*, p. 391.

[4] *Chelsea Water Works Co.* v. *Cowper* (1795). 1 Esp. N.P.C. 275; *Norman* v. *Baldry* (1834), 6 Sim. 621; *Smith* v. *Day* (1837), 2 M. & W. 684; *Knatchbull* v. *Fearnhead* (1837), 3 My & Cr. 122; *Hill* v. *Gomme* (1839), 1 Beav. 540.

[5] As amended by the Law of Property (Amendment) Act 1926.

representatives and trustees. It provides that they may obtain
protection by:

a. in the case of land giving notice of the intended distribution
   in the London Gazette[1] and in a newspaper circulating in the
   district in which the land is situate; and

b. in the case of personalty, by giving notice only in the
   Gazette;[2] and

c. in either case by giving in special cases such further notices
   as the court would have directed in an administration action.

The notices must require any person interested to send to the
personal representatives particulars of their claim within the
time specified in the notice, which must not be less than two
months from its publication.

Where a special case does arise, the personal representative
will only be safe in applying to the court for directions as to the
notices which it requires.[3]

A personal representative may then distribute the estate taking
into account:

a. claims of which he has, apart from the advertisement, actual
   or constructive notice,[4] irrespective of whether the claimant
   replies to the advertisement; and

b. claims which appear as a result of the advertisement.

The personal representative is not liable for any other claim,
although the section does not prevent any other claimant from
following the assets into the hands of the beneficiaries. By following the statutory procedure, the personal representative is given
the same protection as if he had administered the estate under an
order of the court.[5]

There is a curious proviso to the section, which provides that
the section does not free the personal representative "from any

---

[1] Trustee Act 1925, s. 68 (4).

[2] The section does not expressly say that this single notice is sufficient, but
this seems to follow from the wording of the section.

[3] *Re Bracken, Doughty* v. *Townson* (1889), 43 Ch. D. 1; *Re Letherbrow,
Hopp* v. *Dean*, [1935] W.N. 34; *Re Holden, Isaacson* v. *Holden*, [1935] W.N. 52.

[4] *Re Land Credit Co. of Ireland, Markwell's Case* (1872), 21 W.R. 135; Law
of Property Act 1925, s. 199.

[5] *Clegg* v. *Rowland* (1866), L.R. 3 Eq. 368; *Hunter* v. *Young* (1879), 4 Ex. D.
256.

obligation to make searches . . . which an intending purchaser would be advised to make". This will involve the personal representative in making all the searches which would normally be made at any stage of a routine purchase. These will be:[1]

a. *in the case of unregistered land:*
  (i) in the land charges register against the names of all estate owners since 1 January 1926, including the deceased and himself, for land charges which have been registered;
  (ii) in the land charges register against the beneficiary to whom it is to be assented, to ensure that he is not bankrupt; and
  (iii) in the local land charges registers, for local land charges.

b. *in the case of registered land:*
  (i) in the Land Registry;
  (ii) in the land charges register against the beneficiary, and in the local land charges registers, as above.

c. *in the case of an equitable interest in registered land*
  (i) in the minor interests index maintained by the Land Registry;
  (ii) in the land charges register against the beneficiary.

d. *in the case of personalty*
  (i) in the land charges register against the beneficiary.

It will be seen that in each case it is probably wise to make a search in the land charges register, because this will show whether the beneficiary is bankrupt.

See further, Mellows, Conveyancing Searches.

CHAPTER 26

EXECUTOR *DE SON TORT*

A. DEFINITION

The expression "executor *de son tort*" is occasionally used in the sense of a personal representative who improperly administers the assets of the estate,[1] but the usual meaning is that of a person who is not the personal representative of the deceased but who acts in one or more respects as if he were.[2] This is frequently described as intermeddling with the property of the deceased, and, indeed, this definition has been adopted by the Administration of Estates Act 1925,[3] where it provides that, in respect to liability for the payment of estate duty, the term personal representative "includes any person who takes possession of or intermeddles with the property of a deceased person without the authority of the personal representatives or of the court".

It is not, however, every act with regard to the deceased's property which will make a person executor *de son tort*, for a distinction is drawn between, on the one hand, intermeddling, and on the other hand acts of necessity or humanity. The acts of humanity are generally confined to feeding the deceased's cattle or wife,[4] and arranging for his funeral in a manner suitable to the estate.[5] The acts of necessity are likely to be acts of preservation, such as locking up the deceased's valuables, and maintaining his property.[6]

Other acts will constitute a person executor *de son tort*, even if they are very slight. The mere act of taking a Bible or bedstead,[7]

---

[1] See, e.g., Lord Dyer in *Stokes* v. *Porter* (1558), Dyer 167a.
[2] *Peters* v. *Leeder* (1878), 47 L.J.Q.B. 573.
[3] Section 55 (1) (ix).
[4] *Long* v. *Symes* (1832), 3 Hagg. Ecc. 771—but not necessarily in that order.
[5] *Harrison* v. *Rowley* (1798), 4 Ves. 212.
[6] *Laury* v. *Aldred* (1612), 2 Brownl. & Golds. 182.
[7] *Robin's Case* (1601), Noy. 69.

or of taking only sufficient of the deceased's goods to satisfy a debt[1] have been held to be sufficient.[2]

It seems that the mental state of the executor *de son tort* is irrelevant, provided he has full mental capacity. Accordingly, he may still be liable however innocently he may have acted.[3]

A person who is entitled to a grant of probate or letters of administration and who does acts prior to the grant can be cited to take a grant,[4] but once there is a properly constituted personal representative, in most circumstances there cannot also be an executor *de son tort*. As an exception to this, however, if a person is in possession of assets which he received from the deceased in his lifetime as a result of a fraudulent disposition, and he disposes of those assets, he thereby makes himself liable as executor *de son tort*.[5]

Although liability as an executor *de son tort* usually arises as a result of physical interference with chattels, it need not do so. Thus, in *New York Breweries Co., Ltd.* v. *A.-G.*[6] the deceased, who died domiciled in America, owned shares in an English company. The American executors did not obtain a grant of probate in England, as they could have done, and the English company knew that they had not obtained a grant, and had no intention of doing so. Nevertheless the company, at their request, registered the deceased's shares in the American executors' names, and paid dividends to them. In so doing the English company was held to have acted as executors *de son tort*. At first instance Wills, J. having regard to the nature of the property, had said that the company had not intermeddled. Commenting on this in the House of Lords, Lord Halsbury said: "In what way could a person, dealing with this particular class of property, otherwise intermeddle with the estate? The appellants have done that which, as I say, has created a new title in somebody else . . . they have done a legal act, and by virtue of that legal act they have enabled

---

[1] *Read's Case* (1604), 5 Co. Rep. 33b; *Serle* v. *Waterworth* (1838), 4 M. & W. 9.
[2] See also *Stokes* v. *Porter* (1558), 2 Dyer 166b; *Stamford's Case* (1574). 2 Leon. 223.
[3] *Per* Lord Halsbury in *New York Breweries Co., Ltd.* v. *A.-G.*, [1899] A.C. 62.
[4] *Ante*, p. 280; see also *post*, p. 399.
[5] *Stamford's Case, ante; Hawes* v. *Leader* (1610), Cro. Jac. 271; *Edwards* v. *Harben* (1788), 2 Term Rep. 587.
[6] [1899] A.C. 62.

it to be dealt with by somebody else, and made available by him for any purpose he desires". Although the result of the case avoids an unduly fine distinction between choses in action and other property, the act of the company has to be regarded as the equivalent of physically taking possession.[1]

B. EFFECT OF ACTS

1. CREDITORS

Section 28 of the Administration of Estates Act 1925, governs the position of anyone who, in defraud of creditors, or without valuable consideration, obtains any assets of the deceased. It provides that he is liable to account for those assets, after deducting any debt properly due to him from the deceased at the time of his death, and any payment made by him which might properly be made by a personal representative. Accordingly, where the executor *de son tort* uses the assets of the deceased's estate to pay debts and liabilities, the creditors will be properly paid, and will not be liable to refund the sums received. Likewise, the executor *de son tort* receives credit for those payments. It follows that where the executor *de son tort* applies all the deceased's assets in the discharge, in proper order, of the debts, he will not be liable beyond the scope of those assets.[2]

2. RIGHTFUL REPRESENTATIVES

Where a person has intermeddled, and has therefore made himself liable as executor *de son tort*, and subsequently a grant of probate or letters of administration is made to another person, some of his acts will bind the true representatives. It seems that in order to bind the true representatives, the acts done must either:

    (i) involve making payments or disposing of assets to a third party who reasonably believes that the executor *de son tort* has lawful authority to act as executor;[3] or

---

[1] As was recognised by Lord Halsbury in this case.
[2] *Hooper* v. *Summersett* (1810), Wight. 16; *Yardley* v. *Arnold* (1842), Car. & M. 434.
[3] *Mountford* v. *Gibson* (1804), 4 East. 441; *Thomson* v. *Harding* (1853), 2 E. & B. 630.

(ii) be acts which the rightful representative was bound to do, and not merely be acts which he was entitled to do.[1]

An illustration of the first situation is given in *Mountford* v. *Gibson*.[2] In that case the deceased had purchased, but not paid for, goods which had been delivered to him. The vendor asked the deceased's widow, shortly following his death, for the return of the goods, and she returned them accordingly. In so doing, the widow made herself liable as executrix *de son tort*. Letters of administration were subsequently granted to another person, who sued the vendor. The vendor claimed that the goods had been handed over by the widow, whom he was entitled to regard as executrix *de son tort*. It was held that because the return of the goods by the widow was an isolated act, and that she had done no other act which would make her liable, the vendor had no sufficient cause for believing that she had authority to act, and the administrator succeeded.

With regard to the second category of acts mentioned above, it is necessary to draw a distinction between payments and other acts. Under Administration of Estates Act 1925, s. 28, the executor *de son tort* is entitled to credit for all payments which the personal representatives might properly have made, even if they were not obliged to do so. So far as other acts are concerned, it seems that only those which the personal representatives were bound to do will bind them.[3]

C. LIABILITY

1. TO TAKE GRANT

Where the executor *de son tort* is entitled to a grant of probate or letters of administration, the acts which he has done will probably amount to an acceptance of office by conduct, so that he cannot thereafter renounce his right. Accordingly, if he is an executor he may be cited to take a grant, or if he is entitled to letters of administration he may be cited to accept or refuse a grant.[4] Where, however, he is not entitled to a grant, he cannot be compelled to apply for one.[5]

---

[1] *Buckley* v. *Barber* (1851), 6 Exch. 164.
[2] (1804), 4 East. 441.
[3] *Buckley* v. *Barber, supra.*
[4] *Ante*, p. 280.
[5] *Re Davis* (1860), 4 Sw. & Tr. 213.

2. TO ACCOUNT

His primary liability is to render an account for assets which he has received. His liability here is less than in the case of a properly constituted representative. The properly constituted representative is liable to account both for assets which he has received, and for which he ought to have received,[1] whereas the liability of an executor *de son tort* is restricted by s. 28 "to the extent of the real and personal estate received or coming to his hands, or the debt or liability released".[2]

It is, in fact, only by accounting to the rightful executor, and handing the balance of the assets to him, that the executor *de son tort* can obtain his discharge.[3]

The liability to account is both to the rightful representatives and the creditors of the estate.[4] *New York Breweries Co., Ltd.* v. *A.-G.*[5] is an example of an action by a creditor, in that case the Crown, for penalties against those who administer the estate without a grant.[6]

---

[1] *Post*, p. 424.

[2] This was the position even before the 1925 Act: *Coote* v. *Whittington* (1873), L.R. 16 Eq. 534.

[3] *Curtis* v. *Vernon* (1790), 3 Term Rep. 587.

[4] *Fyson* v. *Chambers* (1842), 9 M. & W. 460.

[5] [1899] A.C. 62.

[6] For details of these penalties, see *ante*, p. 369.

CHAPTER 27

TAXATION DURING THE ADMINISTRATION PERIOD

At appropriate places in the preceding chapters references have been made to some of the tax implications of transactions, and it may now be useful to give a general statement of the taxation position during the administration of the estate.

In this chapter the liability of personal representatives to income tax and capital gains tax is considered. Where they own land, personal representatives can also be liable for rates.

A. THE ADMINISTRATION PERIOD

Certain special provisions apply for income tax purposes to the "administration period", which is defined in Income and Corporation Taxes Act 1970, s. 426 (1), to be the period from the date of death to the completion of the administration of the estate. There is, however, no legislative rule to determine when the administration of an estate is complete although, curiously, s. 433, which applies only to Scotland and Northern Ireland, provides that any reference to the completion of the administration of an estate is to be construed as a reference to the date at which "after discharge of, or provision for, liabilities falling to be met out of the deceased's estate (including, without prejudice to the aforesaid generality, debts, legacies immediately payable and legal rights of surviving spouse or children[1] the free balance held in trust for behoof of the residuary legatees has been ascertained". By using this section as an analogy, and by applying the general principles of law, it appears that the administration is complete

---

[1] These are rights under Scottish law to a fixed proportion of the deceased's assets, and the reference here is not to legacies.

401

when the residue is ascertained, and is available for distribution or appropriation to the residuary beneficiaries.[1]

This chapter is confined to the administration period. Thereafter the rules applicable to private individuals or trustees, according to whether the residuary estate was distributed or continues to be held in trust, will operate.

B. GENERAL PRINCIPLES OF INCOME TAXATION

There are four general principles which govern income taxation during the administration period.

1. TAXABLE RECEIPTS

The fundamental principle is that only the same type of receipt is taxable in the hands of personal representatives as would be taxable in the hands of a private individual taxpayer. Accordingly, if it can be shown that a receipt would not normally be taxable, then it will not be taxable in the hands of the personal representatives. The types of taxable income which personal representatives will be concerned with most frequently are bank deposit interest; dividends and interest from stock exchange and similar securities; the profits of any business which they carry on prior to disposal; and profits from any land which is let.

2. A SEPARATE AND CONTINUING BODY

The law, in effect, constitutes the personal representatives together as a single continuing body of persons,[2] separate from the individuals themselves. Assessments are therefore made on the personal representatives as such. Any changes in their number are irrelevant for taxation purposes, and any assessment made on them as personal representatives has no effect whatever on their personal tax position. The only circumstance in which their representative capacity overlaps with their private one is that if, having had funds to meet an assessment raised on them as

---

[1] *Ante*, p. 319.

[2] Income and Corporation Taxes Act 1970, s. 432; see also in relation to capital gains tax, Finance Act 1965, s. 24 (6).

personal representatives, they distribute all the assets of the estate, they can be made personally liable for the amount of that assessment.

3. ALL INCOME TAXABLE AT BASIC RATE

The normal income tax structure is for tax to be payable on a sliding scale. A private individual is entitled to a personal allowance with the result that the first part of his income is tax free; the second part is taxable at the basic rate and providing his income is sufficiently large higher rates of income tax are payable. In the case of personal representatives, however, all income is taxable at the basic rate. There are no personal allowances or personal reliefs, and no higher rates of tax are payable.

With regard to reliefs, a distinction must be drawn between personal allowances and other allowances or reliefs. Although the personal representatives cannot claim in respect of the income of the estate any personal allowance and although where they carry on the deceased's business any profits are not treated as earned income, they may claim non-personal reliefs. These are loss relief, in which case a loss may be set off against other profits,[1] and relief for interest paid.[2]

It was established in *Inland Revenue Commissioners* v. *Countess of Longford*[3] that personal representatives are not liable for higher rates of income tax however high the income of the estate may be. It is, therefore, sometimes wise to disclaim interest on a legacy or on a statutory entitlement, if the recipient would personally be liable to tax at higher rates.[4]

4. NET INCOME PAID TO BENEFICIARIES

Personal representatives must make payments of an income nature to the beneficiaries subject to deduction of tax. These payments will include the income from a fund in which the beneficiary has a life interest; payments of an annuity from the

---

[1] Either by carrying it forward against future profits from the same source under Income and Corporation Taxes Act 1970, s. 171 or by setting it off against other profits at the same time under s. 168.

[2] Subject to the provisions of Income and Corporation Taxes Act 1970, ss. 57-64.

[3] [1928] A.C. 252.

[4] See *post*, p. 452.

estate; and the actual income from assets specifically devised or bequeathed. At the same time the personal representative issues to the beneficiary a certificate that the payment has been made subject to deduction of tax. On the other hand, interest on legacies, where payable, is paid gross.[1]

The income received by the personal representatives will itself either have been taxed at source, or have been received by them gross. Other types of income will have been received subject to deduction of tax at the basic rate, so that the personal representatives will be under no further liability for that. If they let property, or carry on a business, the profits made will be gross. The personal representatives must, therefore, make a return showing all income received by them, and the amount of the tax suffered by them in respect of sums received subject to deduction of tax. The balance of tax due, being the tax at the basic rate on the income received by them gross, is payable by the personal representatives to the Revenue, so that in the result all the income in their hands will have been taxed, and they are left with a net sum. It is this net sum, less expenses attributable to income, which is paid to the beneficiaries.[2]

The procedure whereby payments are made to the beneficiaries subject to deduction of tax cannot work to their overall disadvantage. If they are liable to pay tax at the basic rate, they will have no further tax to pay on the amounts received from the estate. If, on the other hand, their total income is sufficiently low for them not to have to pay at the basic rate, they can obtain a refund of tax by production of the certificate of deduction of tax issued by the personal representatives when making the payment.

In order to ascertain whether a payment to be made to a beneficiary is to be made subject to deduction of tax, it is necessary to consider the character of the receipt in his hands. If in his hands the receipt is taxable, it is necessary for the personal representatives to deduct tax when paying, and this is so even if the total income of the estate is not large enough to support the payment. The serious effects of this are considered later, at p. 509, in respect of annuity payments, and the same principle

---

[1] Income and Corporation Taxes Act 1970, s. 54.
[2] *Ibid.*, s. 52.

applies wherever the income payments due from the estate exceed its actual income.

It will be seen from that discussion that where a payment has to be made good from capital, a much larger sum—the actual sum depending on the basic rate at the time when payment is made—must be taken from capital. The loser is the estate, with the Revenue being the only person to gain. Accordingly, it is now unwise to include in a will a provision that a deficiency of income should be made good from capital.[1]

C. DISTRIBUTION OF RESIDUARY INCOME

Payments of interest on legacies, annuities, and the actual income from assets specifically devised or bequeathed follow the principles just discussed, and present no other problems. The position is different where a distribution is made of residuary income, the difference arising from the fact that in general payments are made to residuary beneficiaries during the course of the administration of the estate generally on account of the amount due to them, so that as each interim payment is made, it may not be possible to show how much represents income, and how much capital, or, where it clearly does represent income, in respect of of what period it accrued.

Accordingly, a distinction is drawn between a residuary beneficiary who has a "limited" interest, that is, a right only to income from the property,[2] and a beneficiary who has an "absolute" interest, which is a right to the residuary capital when ascertained, together with the right to income from it until ascertainment.[3]

The rules governing a residuary beneficiary with a "limited" interest are:

a. all sums paid to the beneficiary during the administration period are treated at first as part of his total income for the year of assessment in which they are actually paid. These sums will have been paid subject to deduction of tax at

---

[1] Income and Corporation Taxes Act 1970, s. 53. The disadvantage can sometimes be overcome by giving the personal representatives power to advance a capital sum.

[2] *Ibid.*, s. 432 (3).

[3] *Ibid.*, s. 432 (2).

source, so that their grossed up equivalent will form part of the beneficiary's total income.

b. **on** completion of the administration, the sums actually paid **are** added to those which remain due to the beneficiary. The **total** is then deemed to have accrued from day to day.

c. **a** final computation is made, and revised assessments, if necessary, are issued to cover each of the years of assessment during the administration period.

The total income paid to the residuary beneficiary will therefore be the total income of the estate, less income paid to others, and less management expenses, but spread out equally over the whole period of the administration.

An example may illustrate these rules. Harriet died on 5 January 1970, having left her residuary estate to Rupert for life, with remainder to Lavinia. The executors make to Rupert the following payments:

1 January 1971	£500
1 January 1972	£2,000
1 January 1973	£400.

On completion of the administration of the estate, on 5 October 1973, they are holding a further £1,975 for Rupert. Provisional assessments are raised on Rupert as follows:

1969/70[1]	nil
1970/71	£500
1971/72	£2,000
1972/73	£400.

In this case no provisional assessment is made for 1973/74, as it will then be possible to calculate the amended assessments.

In 1973/74 it is possible to make the recalculation. The total income produced and available for Rupert is £4,875. and the administration period has lasted three and three quarter years. On an even day to day basis, therefore, income has accrued at the rate of £1,300 p.a. It is now possible to make the revised assessments as follows:

---

[1] A year of assessment runs from 6 April to the following 5 April.

	PROVISIONAL ASSESSMENT	INCOME AS FINALLY APPORTIONED	ADJUSTMENT TO PROVISIONAL ASSESSMENT
1969/70 (administration period only occupied three months: ¼ × £1,300)	nil	£325	+£325
1970/71	£500	£1,300	+£825
1971/72	£2,000	£1,300	− £700
1972/73	£400	£1,300	+£900
1973/74 (administration period only occupied six months: ½ × £1,300)	nil	£650	+£650.

Different rules govern the position of the beneficiary with an "absolute" interest. During the administration of the estate, various sums might be paid to the residuary beneficiary generally on account of the amount due to him and without distinguishing between capital and income. In order to distinguish between capital and income, the following process is adopted:

a. the "residuary income" of the estate is calculated for each year of assessment or part of a year of assessment during the administration period. "Residuary income" for a period is the total income received by the personal representatives during that period, less interest paid on legacies, annuity payments and management expenses relating to income.

b. the payments actually made to the residuary beneficiary in each of the years of assessment are then regarded as having been payments of income up to the total of the residuary income for that year, the balance being treated as capital.

c. on completion of the administration of the estate, the whole of the residuary income is deemed to have been paid to the beneficiary, and any necessary revised assessment will be made.

Again an example may help. Martin dies on 6 April 1971, leaving a legacy of £1,000 to his son, and the remainder to his widow absolutely. The total net estate is about £21,000. On 5 April 1972 the executors pay the legacy to the son, together with interest at 5 per cent from the date of death, and they also pay to the widow £500 generally on account. They pay the widow a further £10,000 generally on account on 5 April 1973, and complete the administration of the estate and pay her the balance in July 1973. The expenses of the administration attributable to income amount to £50 p.a. The residuary income for the various years of assessment is:

1971/72	Actual gross income from estate	£1,260
	Less:	
	Management expenses attributable to income	50
		1,210
	Interest on legacy paid to son	50
		£1,160
1972/73	Actual gross income from balance of estate	1,120
	Less:	
	Management expenses attributable to income	50
		£1,070
1973/74	Actual gross income to completion of administration of estate	£300
	Less:	
	Management expenses attributable to income	30
		£270

For 1971/72, because the amount of the residuary income is greater than the amount paid to the residuary beneficiary, the residuary beneficiary is treated as having received the whole £500 as income subject to deduction of tax. For 1972/73, she is treated as having received the whole of the residuary income, subject to deduction of tax, and the balance of £8,930 would be regarded as capital. For 1973/74 she would be treated as having received income of £270, and the balance of whatever was paid to her is regarded as capital.

On completion of the administration of the estate, it would then appear that although the whole of the residuary income for the years 1972/73 and 1973/74 would have been deemed to have been paid to the widow, only £500 gross of the £1,160 gross available for distribution would have been paid to her for 1971/72. A revised assessment for that balance of £660 would then be raised on her for 1971/72.[1]

---

[1] Income and Corporation Taxes Act 1970, ss. 427, 428.

D. SUBSIDIARY RULES

1. TAX ON APPORTIONMENTS

It will be recalled that the rule in *Re Earl of Chesterfield's Trusts*[1] requires an apportionment to be made between life tenant and remainderman when a reversionary interest falls into possession. Suppose that a reversionary interest of £300 is received two years after the inception of a trust. The rule of apportionment directs the personal representatives to ascertain what sum would, if invested at the date of death at £4 per cent compound interest with yearly rests, less income tax for the time being in force, have produced £300 at the time when it was in fact received. If the basic rate of tax were 50 per cent for each of the two years, the amount would be £288·35. This sum would be added to capital, and the remaining £11·65 paid to the life tenant as compensation for the loss of income from the asset over the previous two years. The object of the rule is to compensate the life tenant for loss of income, and income tax is deducted when making the calculations because if the asset had been in hand at the date of death, the life tenant would have suffered tax on the income. The apportionment rules require tax to be taken into account, but this is solely for the purpose of determining the exact loss of the life tenant. The apportionment itself is of a capital sum, and by applying the rule, no part of the sum is actually converted into income. Accordingly, it is not necessary for the executors or beneficiary to include the figures in their tax returns.

2. TAX ON DISCLAIMED INTEREST

The general rule is[2] that although tax is usually charged on the amount to which a person is entitled, in the case of interest on legacies tax is charged only on what is received, so that where interest is disclaimed, no tax will, in principle, be chargeable on it. This principle was established in *Dewar* v. *Inland Revenue Commissioners*.[3] This only applies, however, so long as the interest to which the legatee is entitled is not set aside for him. *Spens* v. *Inland Revenue Commissioners*[4] was concerned with the liability

---

[1] (1883), 24 Ch.D. 643.
[2] *Post*, p. 452.
[3] [1935] 2 K.B. 351.
[4] [1970] 3 All E.R. 295.

of a life tenant to surtax on income from the trust to which he was entitled but which he did not receive. Megarry, J., drew the distinction between the two situations in these words: In *Dewar's case* the true point was that no identifiable income had come into existence. No income had been segregated by the executors as being the interest which the legatee could claim. On the other hand, where a trustee who receives income from investments holds those investments on trust for a life tenant, each sum received by the trustee is for surtax purposes the income of the life tenant as soon as it is received, for it is forthwith under the life tenant's control."

E. LONG-TERM CAPITAL GAINS

1. BASIC PRINCIPLES

The capital gains tax imposes a charge to tax on the difference between the price at which an asset is acquired, and the value at which it is disposed of. A person is deemed to dispose of all his assets on death, and, where they devolve upon the personal representatives, they acquire the assets at their value at the date of death.[1] Although the deceased is treated as having disposed of his assets on death, no charge to duty arises as a result of that disposal.[2] If the assets devolve on someone other than the personal representatives, that person is deemed to have acquired them on the death of the deceased for their market value at that time.

Where personal representatives are assessable to capital gains tax, the rate of charge is 30 per cent of the gain.[3] There is an alternative basis of charge open to a private individual but this does not apply to personal representatives.[4]

The liability for capital gains tax following the death of the deceased depends on whether the personal representatives sell the asset, or transfer it to a beneficiary.

---

[1] Finance Act 1965, s. 24 (1) (a), substituted by Finance Act 1971, Sched. 12.
[2] *Ibid.,* s. 24 (1) (b), as so substituted.
[3] *Ibid.,* s. 20 (3).
[4] *Ibid.,* s. 21.

2. ASSETS SOLD BY PERSONAL REPRESENTATIVES

Where the personal representatives sell the assets in order to pay the estate duty or administration expenses, or to provide a fund for the payment of legacies, and they sell for a figure in excess of that at which they are deemed to have acquired the asset at the date of death, the estate will be liable to tax. Again there are various exceptions from the charge to tax, including chattels where the disposal value does not exceed £1,000.[1]

3. ASSETS TRANSFERRED TO BENEFICIARIES

Where an asset is transferred to a beneficiary in accordance with the terms of the will, or in accordance with the provisions relating to total or partial intestacy, that beneficiary is treated, retrospectively, as having acquired the asset at the date of death of the deceased. This provision applies whether the transferee takes beneficially or as a trustee. As a result, the personal representatives are not themselves liable for capital gains tax on any of the assets transferred to the beneficiaries in respect of any increase in the value of those assets between the date of death and the date of transfer.[2] The transferee is deemed to acquire the assets at their market value at the date of death.

Finance Act 1965, s. 22 (5), provides that in relation to assets held by a person as nominee or trustee for another person "absolutely entitled as against the trustee, or for any person who would be so entitled but for being an infant or other person under disability", the property in the hands of the trustee or nominee is regarded as being in the hands of the beneficiary. Accordingly, no charge to capital gains tax can arise when the trustee or

---

[1] The others are private motor cars (1965 Act, s. 27 (1)); national savings certificates, premium bonds, defence bonds and national development bonds (1965 Act, s.27 (4)); gains on the disposal of foreign currency acquired for personal expenditure abroad (1965 Act, s.27 (5)); betting winnings and winnings from prizes (1965 Act, s. 27 (7)); in some cases moneys received under life policies (1965 Act, s. 28); disposal of only or main private residence of the deceased together with appropriate grounds (1965 Act, s. 29); works of art bequeathed for national purposes (1965 Act, s. 31); land given to the public (1965 Act, s. 32); interests under trusts, unless acquired by purchase (1965 Act, sched. 7, para. 13); decorations for valour, unless purchased (1965 Act, s. 27 (6)).

[2] Finance Act 1965, s. 24 (7).

nominee in fact transfers the asset to the beneficiary. Therefore, when the personal representatives hold an asset absolutely for a beneficiary, and transfer it to him, no charge to tax can arise.[1]

The meaning of s. 22 (5) was considered by the Court of Appeal in *Tomlinson* v. *Glyns Executor and Trustee Co.*[2] In that case trustees of a settlement held property "in trust for such of the beneficiaries as shall attain the age of 21 years or marry under that age". There were four infant beneficiaries so entitled. The Court held that the words "absolutely entitled . . . as against the trustee" in s. 22 (5) referred to a person who was able to direct the trustee how to deal with the property, and to give him a good receipt for anything with which he parted. Accordingly, an infant contingent beneficiary was not within the terms of s. 22 (5), and the trustees were themselves liable to be assessed. Where personal representatives hold assets upon trust for persons with a contingent interest, or with only a discretionary interest, they will be assessable on gains made by them as trustees.[3]

4. DEEDS OF ARRANGEMENT

If the terms of the will are varied by a document such as a deed of family arrangement, for capital gains tax purposes the variations are treated as if they formed part of the will, provided the deed is executed within two years of death.[4] Accordingly, the person entitled under the deed of arrangement would be regarded as having acquired the asset at the date of death, so that no charge would arise on the transfer by the personal representatives to the beneficiary during the course of the administration. If, however, the deed is not completed within the period of two years from the date of death, when the personal representatives transfer the asset to the beneficiary, they would themselves be regarded as disposing of the asset, and the estate would be assessable accordingly. In this case, the beneficiary would be deemed to have acquired the asset at its market value at the date when he became entitled under the deed of arrangement, and not at its market value at the date of death.

---

[1] Finance Act 1965, s. 24 (7).
[2] [1970] Ch. 112; [1970] 1 All E.R. 381.
[3] Finance Act 1965, s. 25.
[4] *Ibid.*, s. 24 (11).

5. EXPENSES OF SALE OR TRANSFER

Where an asset is sold, and the personal representatives are liable for capital gains tax, they may deduct from the gain accruing on disposal the expenses of putting themselves in a position to sell and also the expenses of sale. So, a proportion of the solicitor's costs of obtaining probate, and of making a valuation for probate may be deducted.[1] Where an asset is transferred to a beneficiary entitled under the will or under the intestacy rules, the personal representatives may deduct the cost of the transfer from the gain accruing on the death of the deceased, and thereby reduce the assessment on death. Alternatively, they may transfer the benefit of the expense to the beneficiary. In this case, the beneficiary can add the expense of transfer to the market value at which he is deemed to acquire the asset, and by thus increasing his acquisition value, he reduces the gain which he will ultimately make when he disposes.[2]

The expenses which can be treated in this way include the actual cost of transfer, together with the costs reasonably incurred in making any valuation or apportionment for capital gains tax purposes, including particularly the expenses of ascertaining the market value of the asset.[3]

---

[1] *Inland Revenue Commissioners* v. *Richards' Executors*, [1971] 1 All E.R. 785, H.L.

[2] Finance Act 1965, sched. 6, para. 16.

[3] Finance Act 1966, sched. 10, para. 5.

CHAPTER 28

THE LIABILITY OF PERSONAL REPRESENTATIVES

The chest may puff out with pride when the executor learns with gratification of his appointment. In other situations, his appointment may have come only after a long struggle.[1] Yet caution, not enthusiasm, is to be counselled. In general, unless there is some contrary provision in the will, the personal representative may be liable to make good out of his own pocket any loss which arises as a result of his unauthorised acts, even if they were done honestly. Further, again unless there is some contrary provision in the will, the personal representative may not derive any benefit[2] from acting as such. Gratification of his power lust may be his only reward.

This chapter indicates the extent of the personal representative's personal liability. He may become liable:

1. In contract, for contracts made by him during the administration of the estate.

2. Under the doctrine of privity of estate for lessee's covenants under a lease.

3. In *devastavit*, if he
   a. misappropriates assets of the estate;
   b. maladministers the estate; or
   c. fails to safeguard the assets.

4. In breach of trust.

A. LIABILITY IN CONTRACT

1. CONTRACT CARRYING PERSONAL LIABILITY

A personal representative may in the course of the administration of the estate enter into two types of contract, namely

---

[1] *Ante,* p. 262.

[2] Although the office of personal representative can confer certain advantages: see *ante,* pp. 262, 263.

contracts made on the basis that his liability is to be limited to the net assets of the estate, and contracts made without any such limitation.

In order to limit the liability to the assets of the estate, two conditions must be satisfied:

a. the fact that the liability is to be limited must be established; and

b. the contract must be an authorised contract.

a. *Limitation of liability*

The liability of the personal representative may be limited by an express limitation, in which case no problem arises, by contracting "as executor" of the deceased, or "as personal representative" of the deceased, or by expressly contracting in pursuance of the statutory power conferred by Administration of Estates Act 1925, s. 39.

Most of the reported decisions relate to contracts which the personal representative entered into as a result of some transaction of the deceased. Indeed, Mellish, L.J. in *Farhall* v. *Farhall*[1] referred to them as all having in common that "the consideration for the promise of the executor was a contract or transaction with the testator". In *Powell* v. *Graham*,[2] for example, the testator had contracted with a woman that if she entered his employment as his nurse, and was still serving in that capacity at the date of his death, he would pay her £20. The woman became his nurse, and was still so acting when he died. The payment was not made on death, but the deceased's executor promised that whenever he, in his capacity as executor, was asked for the £20, he would pay it to her. The executor was held to be not personally liable on the contract, but only to the extent of the assets of the deceased.[3]

Although most of the reported decisions relate to contracts following transactions with the deceased, there is no reason in principle why the rule should be so restricted.

b. *Authorised contracts*

The liability of the personal representative is only limited where the contract which he makes is authorised. It is, therefore,

---

[1] (1871), 7 Ch. App. 123 at p. 127.
[2] (1817), 7 Taunt. 580.
[3] See also *Dowse* v. *Coxe* (1825), 3 Bing. 20.

important to know what contracts are authorised, but it is impossible to give a comprehensive list. The position is stated in Administration of Estates Act 1925, s. 39, which provides that:

(i) personal representatives have all the powers which personal representatives had before the Act came into force;[1] and

(ii) all the powers conferred upon trustees for sale.[2]

To these must be added:

(iii) powers conferred by the Trustee Act 1925;[3] and

(iv) powers conferred by the will itself.

The effect of making these contracts a charge upon the estate—which is the effect of making an authorised contract—is that they are considered to be either necessary for the purposes of administration, or otherwise for the general benefit of the estate.

It follows that where an executor effectively limits his liability in this way, and the estate has no assets, there is no asset or fund to which the party contracting with the executor can have recourse.

A personal representative cannot restrict his liability by contracting as executor if the contract is unauthorised. This is because he must not involve the estate in unauthorised contracts,[4] which will often be burdensome, or to its disadvantage. A strict view is taken so far as contracts by a personal representative to borrow money are involved. In some cases, for example, to raise money to pay estate duty prior to grant, and so before realisation of assets, contracts to borrow money are authorised, but in most cases they are not. Thus, in *Farhall* v. *Farhall*[5] where the personal representative borrowed money "as executrix", James, L.J. held that this was not a charge on the estate, but only on the representative. He maintained that to hold otherwise would be to give executors the power to charge debts on the estate to an unlimited extent. This decision must, however, be treated with caution: whether or not a contract to borrow is authorised will depend on the circumstances of each case.

---

[1] Subs. (1) (i).

[2] Subs. (1) (ii).

[3] Trustee Act 1925, s. 69 (1), provides that except where otherwise expressly provided, the provisions of the Act applicable to trusts apply also to executorships and administratorships.

[4] *Farhall* v. *Farhall* (1871), L.R. 7 Ch. 123; *Owen* v. *Delamere* (1872), L.R. 15 Eq. 134.

[5] (1871), 7 Ch. App. 123.

2. FUNERAL EXPENSES

It is necessary to mention separately funeral expenses. There is a rule that if no other person is liable, an executor is liable for funeral expenses to the extent of the assets in his hands by virtue of an implied contract with the undertaker for the provision of a funeral in accordance with the circumstances and station in life[1] of the deceased.[2]

Where the order for the funeral is given by someone other than the personal representative, the person giving the order to the undertaker will generally become liable, but he will have a right of indemnity against the estate. Taking these principles together, the position is:

a. If the personal representative gives the order for the funeral, in his capacity as such, he will be liable only to the extent of the assets.

b. If the personal representative gives the order without restricting his liability, he will be personally liable to the undertaker for the whole funeral account[3] but will have a right of recourse against the estate to the extent of the assets.[4]

c. If someone else gives the order, he is liable to the undertaker. Unless he paid the account gratuitously, he can recover against the executor to the extent of the assets of the estate.

d. If someone else arranges the funeral, but upon the basis that he accepts no liability for it, the executor will be liable on the implied contract to the extent of a funeral appropriate to the circumstances of the deceased, and to the extent of the assets of the deceased.

3. TRADING CONTRACTS

a. *Generally*

Where the deceased carried on a business in his personal capacity—and the rules now to be discussed have no application if he carried on business by means of an incorporated company—

---

[1] If a deceased can have a station in life.

[2] *Tugwell* v. *Heyman* (1812), 3 Camp. 298; *Rogers* v. *Price* (1829), 3 Y. & J. 28; *Corner* v. *Shaw* (1838), 3 M. & W. 350; *Rees* v. *Hughes*, [1946] 1 K.B. 517 at p. 524.

[3] *Brice* v. *Wilson* (1834), 8 Ad. & El. 349; *Walker* v. *Taylor* (1834), 6 Car. & P. 752; *Corner* v. *Shew* (1838), 3 M. & W. 350.

[4] See *post*, p. 421, as to this right of recourse.

then if it was carried on at a profit, or is capable of being carried on at a profit, the business may well have some goodwill. For this purpose, goodwill may be regarded as little more than the likelihood that customers will continue to resort to the business, and will depend on such matters as the location of the business, the personality of the deceased, and the length of time for which the business has been established. It is by no means unusual for the value of the goodwill to be the only asset of any size of a business.

In most cases the goodwill will be lost completely if the business is closed down for more than a few days. It is, therefore, usually important for the business to be continued after the testator's death. On the other hand, the function of personal representatives is to distribute assets, and not primarily to carry on a trade.

The general rule of law, which applies both to testate and intestate estates, is that personal representatives are entitled to carry on the deceased's business:

(i) if the business, which here means the goodwill, is of value; and

(ii) to such extent only as will enable the business to be sold to the best advantage of the estate.

Where these conditions are satisfied, and the personal representative carries on the business, the expenses of so doing are an administration expense, and along with, for example, funeral expenses[1] rank in priority to other liabilities. The personal representative is liable to trade creditors, but may, therefore, obtain a full indemnity from the assets of the estate.

If the business is carried on for longer than the time needed to dispose of the business, it is necessary to consider the position of the creditors and of the personal representative.

b. *Position of creditors—pre-death debts*

Where the debts arose before the death of the deceased, they become liabilities of the estate in the normal way. The executor will be entitled to recover the administration expenses from the estate as a first charge, and these will include expenses of carrying

---

[1] Although funeral expenses are payable in priority to other administration expenses.

on the business with a view to its disposal as a going concern, but the trade creditors will rank with other creditors in taking priority next.

In general, and subject to one exception, if the personal representative prolongs the trading, and is entitled to an indemnity from the estate, his right of indemnity is postponed to rights of the trade creditors existing at the date of death. The one exception to this principle is where the creditors at the date of death expressly sanction the continuance of the business at their risk. This exception was established in *Dowse* v. *Gorton*[1] and was summarised by Buckley, L.J. in *Re Oxley*,[2] where he said: "In order to introduce the principle of *Dowse* v. *Gorton* it must I think be established that the old creditor has so acted, either by claiming (as he did in that case) the assets of the continued business or by affirmative acts by which he so adopts the action of the executors in carrying on the business, as to shew that he has abandoned that which is *prima facie* his right . . . and that he has assented to another course, namely, that the fund to which he is entitled to look shall be risked in trade with the result that there may be loss or there may be further additions made for his benefit. It is necessary I think to shew an active affirmative assent. Mere standing by with knowledge and doing nothing is not sufficient".

c. *Creditors' post-death debts*

A personal representative who carries on the deceased's trade, whether for the purpose of speedy realisation, or upon a longer term, and whether or not he is authorised by the will, makes himself personally liable to the creditors, who may sue him. There are several reported cases in which the personal representative has been made bankrupt as a result.[3] It seems that this is so even if the personal representative holds himself out as carrying on the business *qua* personal representative.[4]

The primary right of the creditor in respect of post-death contracts is, therefore, to sue the personal representative personally and not as personal representative. In some circumstances, how-

---

[1] [1891] A.C. 190.
[2] [1914] 1 Ch. 604.
[3] *Ex p. Garland* (1803), 10 Ves. 110; *Owen* v. *Delamere* (1872), L.R. 15 Eq. 134; *Fairland* v. *Percy* (1875), L.R. 3; P. & D. 217.
[4] *Labouchere* v. *Tupper* (1857), 11 Moo. P.C.C. 198.

ever, he will also have a right against the estate under the principle of subrogation. This is considered later.[1]

d. *Position of beneficiaries*

The pre-death debts will always be liabilities of the estate, and the beneficiaries will always take subject thereto.[2] The same rule applies in respect of post death debts incurred for the purpose of realisation. In respect of other post death debts, the position varies according to the terms of the will.

(i) AUTHORITY IN WILL. Where the will authorises the personal representative to carry on the business longer than for mere realisation, or without restriction as to length of time, the personal representative will have a right of indemnity against the assets of the estate which must be satisfied before the beneficiaries can take. It is necessary to deduce from the will clear authority in that respect[3] and a restrictive interpretation is usually made. Thus, in *McNeillie* v. *Acton*,[4] where there was a simple direction to the personal representative to carry on the testator's business, it was held that that provision authorised the employment only of the capital which was in the business at the date of death, and that the personal representative had no right of recourse to other assets.[5]

As well as by explicit authority, a power to continue the business may be given where there is a trust for sale and conversion of the deceased's assets, coupled with a power to postpone sale. This is sufficient to enable the personal representative to continue the business indefinitely[6] unless there is a provision requiring sale within a specified time.[7]

(ii) INTESTACY. It will be recalled that Administration of Estates Act 1925, s. 33 (1), provides that where any property devolves as on intestacy, the personal representatives hold that property upon trust for sale and conversion "with power to postpone such sale and conversion for such a period as the personal representatives, without being liable to account, may think

---

[1] *Post*, p. 421.

[2] Provisions of the will can alter the incidence of liability.

[3] *Kirkman* v. *Booth* (1848), 11 Beav. 273 at p. 280.

[4] (1853), 4 De G.M. & G. 744.

[5] See also *Cutbush* v. *Cutbush* (1839), 1 Beav. 184; *Thompson* v. *Andrews* (1832), 1 M. & K. 116.

[6] *Re Crowther*, [1895] 2 Ch. 56; *Re Ball*, [1930] W.N. 111.

[7] *Re Smith*, [1896] 1 Ch. 171.

proper". The effect of this provision is to give personal representatives power to carry on a business longer than for mere realisation,[1] but probably only until the estate is distributable. In the case of an express trust for sale under a will, where there was a power to postpone, it was held that that power ceased to operate when the estate was divisible,[2] and there seems to be no reason why the same rule should not apply on intestacy.[3]

It has been suggested[4] that the power to postpone in the case of intestacy only authorises the personal representatives to use assets employed by the deceased in carrying on his business at the date of death, but there is no authority as to this.

e. *Indemnity and subrogation*

If the personal representative carries on the business longer than is necessary for realisation, and if he does so with the authority either of the will or of Administration of Estates Act, s. 33 (1), he has a right of indemnity from the estate which ranks after the liabilities as at the date of death but before the beneficiaries have been paid. If the assets are insufficient, the personal representative bears the difference from his own pocket.

Where the testator authorised the personal representative to carry on the business, but the authority is limited to assets employed by the deceased in the business at the date of death, the personal representative's right of indemnity is likewise confined.

In those cases where the personal representative has a right of indemnity, creditors in respect of post-death debts have a claim against the estate by subrogation. This right, however, only extends to the assets in respect of which the personal representative could exercise his right[5] and with the same degree of priority.[6]

It follows that the only circumstance in which the post-death creditors can proceed against the estate and take priority over the pre-death creditors is where the latter expressly authorised the personal representatives to continue to trade.

---

[1] *Re Crowther*, [1895] 2 Ch. 56.

[2] *Re Crowther*, [1895] 2 Ch. 56; *Re Ball*, [1930] W.N. 111.

[3] *Re Ball*, [1930] W.N. 111.

[4] *Re Crowther*, [1895] 2 Ch. 56.

[5] Ex p. *Garland* (1803), 10 Ves. 110; *Re Beater*, Ex p. *Edmonds* (1862), 4 De G. F. & J. 488.

[6] *Cutbush* v. *Cutbush* (1839), 1 Bear. 184; *Thompson* v. *Andrews* (1832), 1 M. & K. 116; *Strickland* v. *Symons* (1884), 22 Ch.D. 666; *Moore* v. *M'Glynn*, [1904] 1 Ir. R. 334.

f. *Trading profit*

It will be shown later in this chapter that a personal representative is for most purposes in the same position as a trustee. As a result, the personal representative cannot make any profit from his office unless, generally, he is authorised to do so in the will itself. The general rule is that a trustee could spend the whole of his waking hours in carrying on the business, without being entitled to be paid a penny.[1] A personal representative is, therefore, often faced with the choice either of carrying on the business—for the profit of the beneficiaries if he is successful, or at his personal expense if he is not—or of abandoning the business. He can, however, be protected, or be entitled to remuneration for his services, if all the beneficiaries are *sui iuris* and he is able to make an agreement with them to this effect.

g. *Action to be taken*

Where the personal representative is faced with the possibility of personal loss, and he is unable to obtain an agreement for indemnity from the beneficiaries, it will probably be in his interest to form a limited company, and use that as a vehicle for carrying on the business. This may not be authorised in the will, but it will be an effective means of saving the personal representative from personal liability for post-death debts.

h. *Summary of order for payment of debts*

The order in which assets of the estate will be applied in the discharge of trading debts is:

(i) Debts incurred by the personal representatives in carrying on the business only until such time as it can be realised. This ranks first, as it is an administration expense.

(ii) Pre-death debts, unless the personal representatives have been given an express authority from the creditors to continue to use the assets for trading.

(iii) The amount required to indemnify the personal representatives for the business carried on for longer than is necessary

---

[1] *Robinson* v. *Pett* (1734), 3 P. Wms. 249; *Williams* v. *Barton*, [1927] 2 Ch. 9; *Dale* v. *Inland Revenue Commissioners*, [1954] A.C. 11.

for realisation, where this has been done with authority. The amount will be paid either to the personal representatives, or to creditors who exercise a right of subrogation.

(iv) Pre-death debts where the pre-death creditors expressly authorised the personal representatives to carry on the business at their risk.

It will be seen that personal representatives will suffer:

a. under (i) above, to the extent that the assets of the estate are insufficient to meet the debts;

b. under (iii) above, to the extent that the assets of the estate are insufficient to meet the debts, unless the personal representatives have protected themselves by trading by means of a limited company; and

c. to the total extent of unauthorised trading, unless they have an effective right of recourse against the beneficiaries under an indemnity agreement.

B. LIABILITY UNDER A LEASE

A personal representative can only limit his liability, by express agreement, if that liability is purely contractual. Special considerations arise in the case of a lease, where the relationship will be by virtue of contract and of estate. The lease vests in the executor upon the death of the deceased, and in an administrator upon the making of a grant.[1] If the personal representative does nothing more, he can only be liable as an assignee to the extent of the assets of the estate.[2]

The personal representative does, however, become liable by virtue of the doctrine of privity of estate if he enters upon the demised premises. In this case his liability is not limited, and he may be sued in his personal capacity both in respect of rent for the period from when he entered[3] and for breach of covenant.[4]

---

[1] See *ante*, p. 339.
[2] *Rendall* v. *Andreae* (1892), 61 L.J.Q.B. 630; *Whitehead* v. *Palmer*, [1908] 1 K.B. 151.
[3] *Re Owers*, [1941] Ch. 17 and Ch. 389.
[4] *Buckley* v. *Pirk* (1695), 1 Salk. 316; *Tilney* v. *Norris* (1700), 1 Ld. Raym. 553.

It follows that where the personal representative has entered into possession, the lessor may sue him:

(i) *as executor*, in which case the claim is limited to the assets of the estate; or

(ii) *personally*, in which case, generally, there is no limit to the liability.

There is a curious exception to the general rule that where an executor enters into the demised premises he is personally liable for the future rent under the covenants of the lease.

Where the executor is sued for the rent, he may limit his liability to the value of the premises if that is less than the rent.[1] If the executor seeks to limit his liability in this way, he is accountable not only for the amount actually received, but also for the amount which he might have received by the exercise of reasonable diligence.[2] Therefore, if the letting value of the premises is decreased because the executor fails to comply with the repairing covenants in the lease, his liability will be for the letting value which would have been produced if the premises had been kept in a good state of repair.[3]

C. *DEVASTAVIT*

A personal representative must preserve, protect, and properly administer the assets of the estate with due diligence.[4] Further, he is under a general statutory obligation to administer the estate of the deceased in accordance with law.[5] Any failure to do so amounts to *devastavit*, or a wasting of the assets[6] and an action will lie against the personal representative personally.

There are three types of *devastavit*:

1. misappropriation of assets by the personal representative;
2. maladministration; and
3. failure to safeguard assets.

---

[1] *Helier* v. *Casebert* (1665), 1 Lev. 127; *Rendall* v. *Andreae* (1892), 61 L.J. Q.B. 630.

[2] *Re Bowes, Earl Strathmore* v. *Vane* (1887), 37 Ch.D. 128; *Whitehead* v. *Palmer*, [1908] 1 K.B. 151.

[3] *Hornidge* v. *Wilson* (1840), 11 Ad. & E. 645.

[4] *Re Tankard*, [1942] Ch. 69.

[5] Administration of Estates Act 1925, s. 25 (a), substituted by Administration of Estates 1971, s. 9.

[6] Bac. Abr. Exors I. 1.

1. MISAPPROPRIATION

Little explanation of this is necessary. The most obvious example is where the personal representative uses the assets of the estate in the payment of his personal liabilities.[1] Other examples are the fraudulent disposal of the assets, such as the collusive sale of part of the estate at an undervalue,[2] or putting part of the assets into his own pocket.

2. MALADMINISTRATION

a. *Misapplication*

Maladministration for this purpose means applying the assets, albeit in good faith, otherwise than in the order provided by statute and any will. Accordingly, if the personal representative uses all the assets of the estate in the payment of ordinary creditors, and fails to discharge a preferential debt, that creditor has an action against him.[3] The same principle applies if the personal representative pays legacies, leaving insufficient for creditors or paying residuary beneficiaries leaving insufficient for specific legatees.

b. *Unjustified expenses*

Expenses incurred in the course of the administration must in all the circumstances be reasonable. If legal advice is required, it may be reasonable to consult a solicitor, but not to take the opinion of silk. The personal representatives should, for example, incur funeral expenses only to a standard suitable to the estate and quality of the deceased, and greater expense will constitute *devastavit*.[4] In each case it is for the personal representative to be able to show that the expenses which he incurred were reasonably necessary.

c. *Wasting the assets*

It is also *devastavit* for a personal representative to give away an asset of value, or, within certain limits, to pay debts which he is not bound to pay. *Thompson* v. *Thompson*[5] is an example of the

---

[1] *Re Morgan* (1881), 18 Ch.D. 93; *Ricketts* v. *Lewis* (1882), 20 Ch.D. 745.
[2] *Rice* v. *Gordon* (1848), 11 Beav. 265.
[3] *Wheatley* v. *Lane* (1669), 1 Wms. Saund. 216.
[4] *Shelly's Case* (1693), 1 Salk. 296; *Stag* v. *Punter* (1744), 3 Atk. 119.
[5] (1821), 9 Price 464.

former situation. In that case the deceased held leasehold property which had a greater value than the rent payable under it. In those circumstances the lease could have been sold at a premium, but the personal representative surrendered the lease without consideration. He was held liable. Where the converse applies, that is, where the rent exceeds the value, the personal representative will also be liable in devastavit if he fails to take steps so far and as quickly as possible, to surrender or assign the lease.[1]

As has been shown[2] the position with regard to the payment of debts is governed by Trustee Act 1925, s. 15. That gives power to trustees and personal representatives[3] to pay or allow any debt or claim on such evidence as they think fit, and this will be a good defence provided the power is exercised in good faith. He is entitled to pay statute barred debts[4] and he is not obliged to plead the Limitation Act in the case of actions brought by creditors against the estate.[5] However, a debt must not be paid where a court has declared it to be barred.[6]

3. FAILURE TO SAFEGUARD ASSETS

The personal representative must take reasonable steps to maintain the value of the estate, and of its assets. At one time a personal representative was liable for the loss of assets once they had come into his hands, even if they were lost without fault.[7] The modern rule, however, was stated by Jessel, M.R. in *Job* v. *Job*[8] as follows: "An executor or administrator is in the position of a gratuitous bailee who cannot be charged with the loss of his testator's assets without wilful default".[9] In *Job* v. *Job*[10] the testator was a watchmaker, and the executor's son was also a watchmaker. The executor had to dispose of the testator's stock in trade, and

---

[1] *Rowley* v. *Adams* (1839), 4 Myl. & Cr. 534.

[2] *Ante*, p. 379.

[3] Trustee Act 1925, s. 69.

[4] *Midgley* v. *Midgley*, [1893] 3 Ch. 282.

[5] *Williamson* v. *Naylor* (1838), 3 Y. & C. Ex. 208; *Lowis* v. *Rumney* (1867), L.R. 4 Eq. 451.

[6] *Re Midgley, Midgley* v. *Midgley*, [1893] 3 Ch. 282; *Re Rownson* (1885), 29 Ch.D. 358.

[7] *Crosse* v. *Smith* (1806), 7 East 246.

[8] (1877), 6 Ch. 562.

[9] As to the meaning of "wilful default", see *Re Leeds City Brewery*, [1925] Ch. 532; *Re City Equitable Fire Insurance Co.*, [1925] Ch. 407; *Re Vickery*, [1931] 1 Ch. 572.

[10] (1877), 6 Ch.D. 562.

handed it to his son for disposal in the ordinary course of trade. The executor was held not be guilty of wilful default, so that he was not liable when the son became bankrupt.

Further examples of this type of *devastavit* are failure to pay debts when the personal representative is able to do so, with the result that the creditor involves the estate in expense when he sues;[1] failure to get in assets until they are irrecoverable, as where the personal representative fails to sue until the debt becomes statute barred[2] unless he had reasonable grounds for thinking that the debt would not be recovered even if he did sue;[3] and loss caused by failure to sell an asset at the proper time.[4]

D. LIABILITY FOR BREACH OF TRUST

1. LIABILITY

The object of the rules relating to *devastavit* is to keep the value of the estate, after payment of proper debts and administration expenses, as high as possible, for the benefit both of creditors and beneficiaries. But by accepting office as personal representative, a person also becomes liable as a trustee. There is an overlap between liability for *devastavit* and liability for breach of trust. For example, paying the wrong beneficiaries, and failing to take reasonable care of assets would be both *devastavit* and breach of trust. Liability for breach of trust is, however, wider than for *devastavit*, so that an executor will be liable for breach of trust if, for example, he makes a profit from his office which is not authorised by the will, even if the estate itself does not lose[5] or if he makes an unauthorised investment of the assets of the estate.[6]

Again the executor will be liable for breach of trust if he fails to observe the terms of the will. Thus, if he is directed by the will to sell and convert the assets into authorised investments, he will be liable for any loss which results from failure to do so, unless he

---

[1] *Seaman* v. *Everard* (1680), 2 Lev. 40; *Hancocke* v. *Prowd* (1810), 1 Wms. Saund. 328.

[2] *Hayward* v. *Kinsey* (1701), 12 Mod. 573.

[3] *Clack* v. *Holland* (1854), 19 Beav. 262; *Re Brogden* (1888), 38 Ch.D. 546.

[4] *Phillips* v. *Phillips* (1676), 2 Freem. 11; *Fry* v. *Fry* (1859), 27 Beav. 144.

[5] *Williams* v. *Barton*, [1927] 2 Ch. 9.

[6] *Re Salmon* (1889), 42 Ch.D. 351; *Re Emmet* (1881), 17 Ch.D. 142

had a power to postpone, and genuinely exercised his discretion to postpone.[1] It is not possible to give an exhaustive statement of the circumstances in which a breach of trust will be committed, and for a more comprehensive statement reference should be made to standard books on Trusts.

In one respect there is an important difference between the liability of executors and the liability of other trustees. A trustee of a trust created *inter vivos* is under an obligation to inform the beneficiary of his interest under the trust[2] but where the trusts arise under a will or on intestacy, there is no similar duty.[3] This is because a will, together with the probate, and a grant of administration are public documents open to public inspection.

2. BENEFIT FROM OFFICE

As in the case of other trusts, the general rule is that a personal representative is entitled to be refunded from the estate the expenses to which he has been put, but that he is entitled to no remuneration.

To be allowable the expenses must in the circumstances be reasonable[4] and must not arise from his own default.[5] Where the personal representative is involved in court proceedings the personal representative has a choice. He may participate in the proceedings, when, upon the conclusion of the matter the court may make such order as to costs as it thinks fit. Alternatively, and preferably, he can at the outset apply to the court for directions. If he does so, then whatever the outcome, he will be allowed an indemnity from the estate.[6]

The most usual way in which a personal representative is entitled to remuneration is by virtue of a charging clause included in the will. The normal form of charging clause enables a professional person acting as a trustee to make a charge for the time and services incurred and rendered by him in connexion with the administration, whether or not it was necessary for a professional person to attend to those matters. However, a charging clause ranks as a legacy, and it will be ineffective if the executor witnessed

---

[1] *Marsden* v. *Kent* (1877), 5 Ch.D. 598.

[2] *Hawkesley* v. *May*, [1956] 1 Q.B. 304.

[3] *Re Lewis*, [1904] 2 Ch. 656.

[4] *Potts* v. *Leighton* (1808), 15 Ves. 273; *Hyde* v. *Haywood* (1740), 2 Atk. 126.

[5] *Field* v. *Peckett* (1861), 29 Beav. 576.

[6] See Lord Radcliffe, *Chettiar* v. *Chettiar* (*No. 2*), [1962] 2 All E.R. 238, at p. 245.

the will,[1] or if there are insufficient assets in the estate to enable any legacies to be paid.

The court has a general power to authorise remuneration, but it will only exercise this power where the personal representative is able to render exceptional services in the discharge of his duties,[2] or otherwise it is for the benefit of the estate.

If the will contains no charging clause, and no order is obtained from the court authorising payment, the personal representative may reach agreement with the beneficiaries with regard to his remuneration. If all the beneficiaries are ascertained, and are *sui iuris*, and they all agree, they can together authorise the personal representative to be paid out of the estate. In any other case, an individual beneficiary can himself agree to pay the personal representative out of his share, but he cannot authorise remuneration to be taken out of the estate itself before appropriation.

3. LIABILITY FOR ACTS OF CO-REPRESENTATIVES AND AGENTS

Personal representatives are given an express power to appoint agents by Trustee Act 1925, s. 23, which provides that "Trustees or personal representatives may, instead of acting personally, employ and pay an agent, whether a solictior, banker, stockbroker, or other person, to transact any business or do any act required to be transacted or done in the execution of the trust, or the administration of the testator's or intestate's estate, including the receipt and payment of money, and shall be entitled to be allowed and paid all charges and expenses so incurred, and shall not be responsible for the default of any such agent if employed in good faith". This power is wide enough to allow personal representatives to appoint agents to do acts which they themselves could have done, and the section represents a marked change in the pre-1926 position, when an agent could only be appointed if it was reasonably necessary to do so, or a man of ordinary prudence would have appointed an agent had he been dealing with his own affairs.[3]

Although s. 23 is clear in allowing the appointment of agents,

---

[1] See *ante*, p. 62.
[2] *Boardman* v. *Phipps*, [1967] 2 A.C. 46.
[3] *Re Weall* (1889), 42 Ch.D. 674; *Re Belchier* (1754), Amb. 218; *Re Speight, Speight* v. *Gaunt* (1883), 22 Ch.D. 727.

the extent of the personal representative's liability for the acts of the agent is less clear. It will be recalled that s. 23 (1) concludes with the words that the person employing the agent "shall not be responsible for the default of any such agent if employed in good faith". On the other hand, s. 30 of the same Act provides that a trustee—and this includes a personal representative[1]—shall be chargeable only for money and securities actually received by him, and shall not be responsible for any other loss "unless the same happens through his wilful default".[2] On the one hand it would appear that the person appointing the agent is absolved from liability if the appointment is made in good faith, while on the other hand it might appear that failure to exercise firm control over the agent may in itself amount to "wilful default", such as to make the personal representative liable. The inconsistency may be reconciled on the basis that a personal representative will be responsible for any loss arising through the fault of an agent who is not appointed in good faith, but that if he is appointed in good faith, the personal representative will remain liable if he is guilty of wilful default in failing to exercise reasonable supervision over the agent.[3]

Rather different considerations apply where loss arises through the default not of an agent but of a co-representative. Where the loss arises through the act of a co-representative alone, the position appears to be governed by s. 30, which will usually absolve the others. The others may themselves be liable, however, if they have been guilty of wilful default in failing to procure that assets were brought under their joint control, or in failing to take account of the acts of their co-executor. In this case they will be jointly liable.

The beneficiary or creditor who loses as a result may sue all the personal representatives jointly, or any of them individually. In the latter case there will be rights of contribution so that the ultimate position of the personal representatives *inter se* is that they each contribute to the liability. There is, however, no right of contribution where the fault occurs solely through the act of

---

[1] Trustee Act 1925, s. 69.

[2] As to the meaning of "wilful default", see cases cited *ante*, at p. 426, footnote 9.

[3] See further discussion Parker & Mellows, The Modern Law of Trusts, 2nd ed., p. 243.

the one who is sued, and the others have not been guilty of wilful default, or where there has been fraud;[1] where one of the personal representatives was a solicitor and the wrongful act was done on his advice and under his influence;[2] where one personal representative alone benefits from the breach;[3] and to a limited extent where one personal representative is also a beneficiary.[4] Again reference should be made to the books on Trusts for a detailed statement of the position in these cases.

E. RELIEF FROM LIABILITY

Where a personal representative would otherwise be liable to beneficiaries or creditors, he may in certain circumstances be relieved from liability. These circumstances are:

1. where there is a relieving clause in the will;
2. where the court makes a relieving order;
3. where there is agreement with the beneficiaries.

1. CLAUSE IN WILL

The testator can restrict the liability of his personal representatives by including in the will a provision to this effect. The usual form of clause used to this effect restricts liability to wilful and individual fraud or wrongdoing on the part of the person to be made liable, and relieves him from liability for mistakes made in good faith or for the acts or defaults of co-representatives or agents. The effect of such a clause is to restrict liability so far as beneficiaries are concerned, but it cannot affect the position of creditors of the estate at the date of death. They have a right to be paid irrespective of any provisions of the will.

2. ORDER OF COURT

Trustee Act 1925, s. 61, enables the Court to grant relief to a trustee or personal representative,[5] either wholly or in part, where he has acted:

   a. honestly, that is, in good faith;

---

[1] *Bahin* v. *Hughes* (1886), 31 Ch.D. 390.

[2] *Lockhart* v. *Reilly* (1856), 25 L.J. Ch. 697; *Head* v. *Gould*, [1898] 2 Ch. 250; *Re Partington* (1887), 57 L.T. 654.

[3] *Bahin* v. *Hughes* (1886), 31 Ch.D. 390.

[4] *Chillingworth* v. *Chambers*, [1896] 1 Ch. 685.

[5] Trustee Act 1925, s. 69.

b. reasonably; and
c. ought fairly to be excused.

When these conditions are satisfied the court has a power, but not a duty, to relieve from liability, and in this case the relief may be against both beneficiaries and creditors. Each case depends on its own circumstances, and the courts refuse to lay down any rules to govern the situations in which the power will be exercised.[1] A good example, however, is *Re Kay*[2] where the personal representative of the will of the testator who died leaving an estate of over £22,000, and had apparent claims of only about £100, paid a legacy of £300, and only thereafter learned of liabilities which exceeded the value of the estate. In the circumstances of the case it was held reasonable for him to assume that with an estate of this size liabilities would not approach the value of the estate, so that he could safely pay the legacy. The court therefore granted him relief.

In general it is more difficult for a personal representative who is entitled to take the benefit of a charging clause, or who is a professional trustee, to obtain relief than one who is unpaid. So, in *Re Rosenthal, Schwarz* v. *Bernstein*[3] the executors paid from residue part of the estate duty in respect of realty. Estate duty on realty is, in principle, payable by the donee,[4] but in this case the property had been transferred to the donee without provision being made for the duty. The residuary beneficiary objected to the payment being made from residue and one of the executors, who was a solicitor, sought relief under s. 61. Plowman, J., held that although he had acted honestly, he had not shown that he had acted reasonably, or that he ought fairly to be excused. Had relief been granted, the residuary beneficiary, who was the deceased's widow, would have suffered.

3. AGREEMENT OF BENEFICIARIES

Where a beneficiary has agreed to or concurred in a breach of trust, he cannot afterwards bring an action in respect of it.[5] The

---

[1] See Byrne, J. in *Re Turner*, [1897] 1 Ch. 536; and Romer, J. in *Re Kay*, [1897] 2 Ch., at p. 524.
[2] [1897] 2 Ch. 518.
[3] [1972] 3 All E.R. 552.
[4] Finance Act 1894, s. 9 (1).
[5] *Nail* v. *Punter* (1832), 5 Sim. 555.

agreement of concurrence must be at a time when the beneficiary was *sui iuris*, and had full knowledge of the relevant facts, and was not acting under any undue influence.[1] Likewise the beneficiaries will not be able to take action if, after having learned of a wrongful act on the part of the personal representative, acquiesce in it, or give the personal representative a release.[2]

Similarly, where the beneficiary instigated[3] or requested the personal representative to do a wrongful act with the intention of obtaining a personal benefit from it, or if he concurred in a breach of trust and actually derived a personal benefit from it, not only is that beneficiary stopped from suing the personal representative, but the personal representative may be able to claim an indemnity from the beneficiary.[4] Further, the court has power under Trustee Act 1925, s. 62, to impound a beneficiary's interest if he instigates or concurs in a wrongful act, whether or not with a view to obtaining personal benefit.

F. LIMITATION OF ACTIONS

1. CLAIMS BY CREDITORS

The limitation rules so far as creditors are concerned are entirely statutory. In respect of causes of action outstanding at the death of the deceased, proceedings in simple contract or tort must be commenced, in the usual way, within six years from the date when the cause of action arose,[5] and proceedings on a covenant within twelve years.[6]

The usual rule as to acknowledgement of debts applies, so that a creditor may rely upon an acknowledgement of the debt made by

---

[1] *Thomson* v. *Eastwood* (1877), 2 App. Cas. 215.

[2] *Ghost* v. *Waller* (1846), 9 Beav. 497.

[3] *Trafford* v. *Boehm* (1746), 3 Atk. 440.

[4] *Montford* v. *Cadogan* (1816), 19 Ves. 635; *Fuller* v. *Knight* (1843), 6 Beav. 205.

[5] Limitation Act 1939, s. 2 (1).

[6] *Ibid.*, s. 2 (3). Formerly, proceedings in tort had to be commenced within six months from the grant of representation, but this rule was abolished by the Proceedings Against Estates Act 1970.

the deceased or his personal representatives within the period of six or twelve years, as the case may be.[1] To be effective the acknowledgement must be in writing, and signed by the person making it, and it must be made to the person who is making the claim. Accordingly, the inclusion of the debt in the Inland Revenue Affidavit, or in an affidavit of assets and liabilities made for probate purposes, does not amount to an acknowledgement.[2]

An acknowledgement by one only of several personal representatives is sufficient.[3]

2. CLAIMS BY BENEFICIARIES

A beneficiary who wishes to claim either personalty[4] or realty of which the deceased was possessed when he died[5] must bring his action within twelve years from the date on which he became entitled, and to recover arrears of interest the action must be brought within six years.[6] Where the existence of the right of action is concealed by fraud the period is extended until the beneficiary has discovered it, or could with reasonable diligence have discovered it.[7] The period is also extended where the beneficiary's interest is a future interest only.[8]

These statutory periods do not apply, however, if the action is based on the fraud of the personal representative,[9] or if the action is for the recovery of property or the proceeds of property which the personal representative still has in his possession or has converted to his own use. In these cases there is no statutory period, though, no doubt, the equitable doctrine of laches would prevent action by a beneficiary if he delayed unreasonably in bringing proceedings once he learned of the facts.[10]

---

[1] Limitation Act 1939, s. 23 (4).

[2] *Bowring-Hanbury's Trustee* v. *Bowring-Hanbury*, [1943] Ch. 104; *Howard* v. *Hennessey*, [1947] Ir. R. 336.

[3] *Re Macdonald*, [1897] 2 Ch. 181; see, however, *Astbury* v. *Astbury*, [1898] 2 Ch. 111.

[4] Limitation Act 1939, s. 20.

[5] *Ibid.*, s. 4 (3), 5 (2).

[6] *Ibid.*, s. 20.

[7] *Ibid.*, s. 26. See also *G. L. Baker Ltd.* v. *Medway Building and Supplies, Ltd.*, [1958] 2 All E.R. 532.

[8] Or where the beneficiary is under a disability. See Limitation Act 1939, ss. 6, 20, 22, 31 (2).

[9] Limitation Act 1939, s. 19.

[10] An attempt was made to raise this defence in *Re Howlett*, [1949] Ch. 767.

One of the differences between the position of a personal representative and the position of a trustee is that in the latter case the normal period of limitation is six years and not twelve from when the right of action arose.[1] It can, therefore, be important to know whether the proposed defendant was acting as a personal representative or as a trustee at the relevant time. Accordingly, it is beneficial for the personal representative to assent to the vesting of assets in himself as trustee at as early a stage as possible if there is any possibility of proceedings subsequently being taken against him.

---

[1] Limitation Act 1939, s. 19.

Part VII

THE POSITION OF
THE BENEFICIARIES

CHAPTER 29

RIGHTS OF BENEFICIARY DURING ADMINISTRATION

A. A BENEFICIAL INTEREST?

In general terms it is customary to regard the legal title and equitable interest in the deceased's property as devolving separately on his death. According to this view, the legal title passes to the personal representatives, and the beneficial interest to the beneficiaries, subject to the right of the personal representatives to sell the assets for the purposes of the administration of the estate. While it is permissible to think in these terms so far as concerns the deceased's property considered as a whole, it is not accurate to regard each asset in a similar way. So far as each asset is concerned it is necessary to distinguish between the period before the residue is ascertained, and the period thereafter.

1. BEFORE RESIDUE ASCERTAINED

For many purposes a personal representative is regarded as a trustee, in that he is made liable in the same way as a trustee. Thus, in *Re Marsden, Bowden* v. *Layland*,[1] Kay, J. said: "An executor is personally liable in equity for all breaches of the ordinary trusts which in Courts of Equity are considered to arise from his office". The position of a trustee need not be the exact corollary of that of the beneficiary[2] but there is this sense in which a personal representative may be regarded as a trustee.

---

[1] (1884), 26 Ch.D. 783, at p. 789.
[2] As in the case of calling a vendor a trustee of the property for a purchaser, following exchange of contracts. The vendor does indeed owe the purchaser fiduciary duties, but the normal trustee-beneficiary relationship certainly does not exist.

However, to call a person a trustee can lead to confusion, for in any particular case it is necessary to know the duties which arise from the alleged trusteeship. Thus, although a personal representative is subject to the trusts of the office, those trusts "might just as well have been termed 'duties in respect of the assets' as trusts".[1]

If the phrase "duties in respect of the assets" is substituted for trusts, it becomes easier to understand the attitude of equity. It was that equity did not recognise the residuary beneficiary as having any beneficial interest in the assets during the administration of the estate, although the personal representatives could be compelled to discharge their duties in respect of those assets. In the eyes of equity the whole property devolved upon the personal representatives without distinction between legal and equitable interests. In this way, it was possible for equity to impose duties on the personal representative without creating or recognising a separate equitable interest.

The position was reviewed by the Privy Council in *Stamp Duties Commissioner (Queensland)* v. *Livingston*,[2] which was heard on appeal from the High Court of Australia. A testator had died domiciled in the State of New South Wales, leaving property in Queensland. Under the terms of his will, the testator's widow was entitled to a share of the residue which included the Queensland property. The widow herself died before the estate was administered. If the widow held a beneficial interest in the Queensland property at the date of her death, duties would have been payable on her death, but not otherwise. The Privy Council held that because the estate was not administered by the time of her death, and the residue not ascertained, she did not have a beneficial interest in that property. All she had was the right to secure the proper administration of the estate. Accordingly no duty was payable.[3]

Equity could have treated the assets of the estate as a present, though fluctuating, trust fund held for the benefit of those

---

[1] *Per* Lord Radcliffe, *Commissioner of Stamp Duties (Queensland)* v. *Livingston*, [1965] A.C. 694.

[2] [1965] A.C. 694.

[3] See also *Lord Sudeley* v. *A.-G.*, [1897] A.C. 11; and article by S. J. Bailey, 1965 C.L.J. 44.

interested in the estate. It did not do so, although this would, perhaps, have been logical.

Part of the difficulty with the *Livingston* decision is to know where the beneficial interest in the property lies during the administration period. The decision shows that it is not with the beneficiaries: and presumably, because they can derive no benefit from it, it is not with the personal representatives. The difficulty was recognised. In *Livingston* Lord Radcliffe said: "Where, it is asked, is the beneficial interest in those assets during the period of administration? It is not, ex hypothesi, in the executor: where else can it be but in the residuary legatee? This dilemma is founded on a fallacy, for it assumes mistakenly that for all purposes and at every moment of time the law requires the separate existence of two different kinds of estate or interest in property, the legal and the equitable. There is no need to make this assumption. When the whole right of property is in a person, as it is in an executor, there is no need to distinguish between the legal and equitable interest in that property, any more than there is for the property of a full beneficial owner."

Lord Radcliffe's argument does not convince. Although there is no *need* to distinguish between the legal estate and equitable interest in the case of a full beneficial owner, it is possible to regard such a person as having both the legal estate and equitable interest. So long as the personal representatives can obtain no benefit from their office, the same reasoning does not apply to them. The question remains: where can the beneficial interest be regarded as being during the administration period?

The failure to regard the beneficiary as having any proprietary interest in the residuary estate was to the advantage of the beneficiary in *Livingston*, but it is more likely to work to disadvantage.

Eastbourne Mutual Building Society v. *Hastings Corporation*[1] was concerned with the position of a person entitled under the intestacy rules before completion of the administration. Under the relevant compulsory purchase legislation then in force[2] when a local authority declared an area to be a clearance area, they were entitled to purchase the land in that clearance area at site value compensation only, that is, making no payment for the

---

[1] [1965] 1 All E.R. 779.
[2] Housing Act 1957, s. 61.

house or other building erected on the land. Where, however, the house was occupied by a person who acquired it between certain specified dates "or by a member of his family [who] was entitled to an interest in the house"[1] full market value compensation was payable. In this case a woman acquired the property during the specified dates and died intestate. The value of the estate was small, and her husband became entitled to the whole of it, but no grant of representation was ever made. However, the husband continued to occupy the house. Relying on *Livingston*, and without further explanation, Plowman, J. held that the husband did not have an "interest" in the house, with the result that only site value compensation was payable, and not full compensation. The decision is particularly hard because had the husband applied for a grant, and assented to the property in his favour, full compensation would have been payable.

Related considerations arose in *Lall* v. *Lall.*[2] A son was the registered owner of a house. He claimed that he was the beneficial owner, whereas his mother claimed that he held the house as trustee for his late father. If the mother's contention was correct, the beneficial interest in the house would form part of the husband's estate, and she would be entitled to have the house appropriated to her as part of her statutory share.[3] No grant of representation had been made. The mother was in occupation of the house and the son commenced proceedings for possession. Buckley, J. held that although the mother had the right to claim the house as part of her statutory share if it formed part of her husband's estate, nevertheless she had no *locus standi* to defend the son's action for possession. She had no interest in the property recognisable by law.

A somewhat similar situation to *Lall* v. *Lall*, although raising different issues, arose in *Barclay* v. *Barclay.*[4] The testator gave express directions for the sale of his bungalow, and for the division of the proceeds in five equal shares between his sons and daughters in law. One of the sons lived in the bungalow, and refused to move out. The plaintiff, who was a daughter-in-law, took out letters of administration, and wished to sell with vacant posses-

---

[1] See Housing Act 1957, para 4 (2), Part 2, Schedule 2.
[2] [1965] 3 All E.R. 330.
[3] See *ante*, p. 180.
[4] [1970] 2 All E.R. 676, C.A.

sion. The Court of Appeal held that none of the beneficiaries had any right in the bungalow itself, but only in the proceeds of sale. Accordingly, the plaintiff was entitled to an order for possession. However, in the course of his judgment, Lord Denning, M.R., said:[1] "An equitable tenancy in common arises wherever two or more persons become entitled to the possession of property (or the rents and profits thereof) in undivided shares. They may become so entitled by grant, or under a will . . . ." Lord Denning suggests, therefore, that an equitable interest in the property itself could arise under the will if it is appropriately worded. Much will depend on the object of the provision in the will.

These cases, and the present position, cannot be regarded as satisfactory. It would be far better if the beneficiary was regarded as having a defeasible equitable interest in the assets of the estate. Although this would cause, perhaps, some difficulty, it would avoid the hardship in the *Eastbourne Mutual Building Society case*, and *Lall* v. *Lall* and it would also accord more with the other rights of the beneficiary to be considered later.

2. AFTER RESIDUE ASCERTAINED

It seems that once the residue has been ascertained, the personal representatives will hold the property on trust for the beneficiary, even if there has been no formal assent either to themselves or others *qua* trustees. Although there appears to be no authority for this proposition, it is the converse of *Livingston* and the other cases. In *Livingston* Lord Radcliffe quoted two extracts from the House of Lords decision in *Barnardo's Homes* v. *Special Income Tax Commissioners*.[2] In that case, Viscount Finlay said: "the legatee of a share in the residue has no interest in any of the property of the testator *until the residue has been ascertained*.[3] His right is to have the estate properly administered and applied for his benefit when the administration is complete". In the same case, Viscount Cave said: "When the personal estate of a testator has been fully administered by his executors, and the net residue ascertained, the residuary legatee is entitled to have the residue, as so ascertained, with any accrued income, transferred and paid

---

[1] [1970] 2 All E.R. 676, C.A., at p. 678.
[2] [1921] 2 A.C. 1.
[3] Author's italics.

18

to him; but until that time he has no property in any specific investment forming part of the estate or in the income from any such investment, and both corpus and income are the property of the executors and are applicable by them as a mixed fund for the purposes of administration."

There is no rule of law to determine when the residue is ascertained: this is a question of fact.[1] It is not necessary for all liabilities of the estate to have been discharged, provided funds have been set aside to meet those liabilities.[2] The essential point is whether the exact amount due to the residuary beneficiaries is known.

B. AN INCHOATE RIGHT

Although during the administration period the beneficiary does not have, until the residue is ascertained, an interest in the assets, he has more than a mere right to compel proper administration. He has an inchoate right. The results from this are as follows:

1. ESTATE DUTY ON GIFT

For estate duty purposes, the general rule is that duty is payable on the property passing on the death on each occasion on which it passes. If, therefore, John dies leaving all his property to Mary, and then Mary dies leaving all her property to her daughter Lavinia, estate duty is payable both on the death of John and on the death of Mary.[3] There is, however, a "surviving spouse" exemption[4] which applies if duty was paid on the death of the first spouse to die, and the second only had a life interest in the property, without a power to dispose of the capital. If, therefore, John had given all his property to Mary for life, with remainder to Lavinia, duty would have been payable in the normal way on the death of John, but no duty would have been payable in respect of that property on the death of Mary.

An ingenious but unsuccessful attempt was made to take

---

[1] *Inland Revenue Commissioners v. Smith*, [1930] 1 K.B. 713; *Corbett v. Inland Revenue Commissioners*, [1938] 1 K.B. 567.

[2] *Inland Revenue Commissioners v. Smith, supra.*

[3] Finance Act 1894, s. 2 (1). (a).

[4] Finance Act 1894, s. 5 (2); Finance Act 1898, s. 13; Finance (1909-10) Act 1910, s. 55; Finance Act 1914, s. 14.

advantage of these rules in *Re Parsons, Parsons* v. *A.-G.*[1] The wife bequeathed to her husband a holding of £10,000 £2½ per cent Consols absolutely, and a life interest in her residuary estate. The surviving spouse exemption applied to the residue, but not to the legacy of Consols. During the executor's year, and before the residue was ascertained, the husband disclaimed the legacy of Consols. The Consols therefore fell into residue, and he hoped that in this way the surviving spouse exemption would apply to that property also. It was held, however, that the husband had been "competent to dispose" of the Consols during the period between the date of the wife's death and the date of disclaimer, with the result that the surviving spouse exemption did not apply.

It would seem that where an interest under a will is surrendered and another person thereby benefits, the person making the surrender will be regarded as making a gift, both for estate duty[2] and capital gains tax[3] purposes.

2. TRANSMISSIBLE INTEREST

As long as the beneficiary survives the deceased, he will acquire a transmissible interest, and the doctrine of lapse will not apply.[4] Accordingly, if George dies on 1 January, leaving a legacy of £500 to Harry; if Harry dies on 2 January; and the estate is administered by 1 September, the £500 given to Harry will devolve to his estate. Accordingly, the benefit under the will of George can be left by will, or disposed of *inter vivos*.

A recent example of the transmission of the right is *Re Leigh's Will Trusts,*[5] *Handyside* v. *Durbridge.* The testatrix made a will leaving "all shares which I hold and any other interest or assets which I may have in Sheet Metal Prefabricators (Battersea), Limited". She had never owned any shares or interest in that company, but her husband had owned 51 per cent. of the shares in that company, and he also had the benefit of a loan account with it. The husband died intestate, and at the date of her death the testatrix was the sole administratrix and beneficiary under the unadministered estate. Buckley, J., held that the words used

---

[1] [1943] Ch. 12.
[2] Finance Act 1894, s. 2 (1) (c); but there is a concession where only a life interest is surrendered.
[3] Finance Act 1965, s. 22 (4).
[4] See *post*, p. 453.
[5] [1970] Ch. 277.

were sufficient to pass to the legatee under the will of the testatrix the chose in action in respect of the husband's estate.[1]

There is, therefore, the rather absurd result that although during the period of administration the beneficiary has no "interest" in the assets, he nevertheless has rights in them which he can dispose of *inter vivos* or by will.

3. POSSESSION WITH CONSENT

The provisions of Administration of Estates Act 1925, s. 43, are noted later.[2] Section 36 (10) of the Act requires a personal representative to give an assent in favour of a beneficiary, in effect, as soon as is convenient, and without necessarily waiting for the discharge of liabilities if other provision has been made for them. Section 43 provides that before giving an assent in favour of any person "entitled", the personal representative may permit that person to take possession without prejudice to the right of the personal representative to retake possession if he needs to do so for the purpose of the administration of the estate.

On a broad view, the beneficiary is therefore entitled to take possession of the land with the consent of the personal representative. On the narrow view, what does "entitled" mean in this section? This may come near to going beyond the recognition of a mere inchoate right.

4. EFFECT OF ASSENT

It is also significant that Administration of Estates Act 1925, s. 36 (2), provides that an "assent shall relate back to the death of of the deceased" unless a contrary intention appears. It seems, however, that this section, applying the common law rule to the same effect,[3] does not apply to an assent of the residuary estate.[4]

C. OTHER RIGHTS

1. TO COMPEL DUE ADMINISTRATION

The beneficiary has an undisputed right to compel due admin-

---

[1] The decision has its difficulties: see (1970), 86 L.Q.R. 20 (Baker).

[2] *Post*, p. 555. The assets can be bequeathed separately: *Re Leigh's Will Trusts*, [1969] 3 All E.R. 432.

[3] *Inland Revenue Commissioners* v. *Hawley*, [1928] 1 K.B. 578.

[4] *Barnardo's Homes* v. *Special Income Tax Commissioners*, [1921] 2 A.C.1; *Corbett* v. *Inland Revenue Commissioners*, [1938] 1 K.B. 567.

istration of the estate. This in effect gives him three possible courses of action:

a. to apply by originating summons for the determination of certain questions which the court will deal with without ordering full administration. These include:

(i) the ascertainment of any class of creditors or beneficiaries;
(ii) the ascertainment of the rights or interests of creditors or beneficiaries;
(iii) the furnishing by the personal representatives of accounts, and the vouching of those accounts;
(iv) directing the personal representatives to do or abstain from doing any particular act;
(v) the determination of any question arising in the administration of the estate.[1]

This power is also available to the personal representatives themselves.

b. to apply for the administration of the estate. Again this application may be made either by beneficiary or personal representative. In fact, an administration order is often made at the request of the personal representative, as a means of securing his own protection, but the court will also act at the request of a beneficiary if it considers it necessary in order to protect the interests of the beneficiaries generally or of creditors. The personal representatives act under responsibility to and supervision of the Court.

c. to sue the personal representatives for *devastavit*. This was considered at p. 424.

2. INFORMATION AND ACCOUNTS

It is considered that a beneficiary under a will or upon intestacy has the same rights to information and accounts as does the beneficiary under a trust, except that a personal representative is under no obligation to inform the beneficiary of his entitlement.[2]

In general, all knowledge or information coming to personal representatives is held by them in their fiduciary capacity. They can only use it for the benefit of the estate and the beneficiaries are

[1] R.S.C., O. r. 2.
[2] *Re Lewis, Lewis* v. *Lewis*, [1904] 2 Ch. 656.

entitled to it.[1] In *O'Rourke* v. *Darbishire*,[2] a case on trusts, Lord Wrenbury said: "a beneficiary has a right of access to the documents which he desires to inspect upon what has been called in the judgments in this case a proprietary right. The beneficiary is entitled to see all trust documents, because they are trust documents and because he is a beneficiary". The same would seem to apply to a beneficiary under a will. As an exception to the general principle, the beneficiary is not entitled to inspect those parts of trust documents which give reasons for the exercise of a discretion,[3] nor may they in general question the exercise of a discretion where it has been exercised in good faith.[4]

In the same way, the beneficiaries are entitled to production of accounts.[5] Strictly, their right is to be able to inspect accounts, and they are only entitled to have copies prepared for them at their own expense.[6] Nevertheless the better and more satisfactory practice is for copies of accounts to be prepared by the personal representatives, and supplied to the residuary beneficiaries.

D. INCOME TAX

The actual decision in the *Dr Barnardo's* case is no longer good law. Under the Income and Corporation Taxes Act 1970, a distinction is drawn between the position of a residuary beneficiary who has only a limited interest, that is, a right only to the income of the residue, and a residuary beneficiary who has an absolute interest, that is, a right to the capital.[7] The general effect of the rules, which were considered in greater detail in chapter 27, is that so far as a residuary beneficiary with a limited interest is concerned, the whole of the residuary income is regarded as being part of the total income of the beneficiary calculated on a day to day basis from the date of death to the date of ascertainment of the residue. The different rules are necessary in the

---

[1] *Phipps* v. *Boardman*, [1965] Ch. 992.

[2] [1920] A.C. 581.

[3] *Re Londonderry's Settlement, Peat* v. *Walsh*, [1965] Ch. 918

[4] *Re Beloved Wilkes's Charity* (1851), 3 Mac. & G. 440; *R.* v. *Archbishop of Canterbury and Bishop of London* (1812), 15 East 117.

[5] *Kemp* v. *Burn* (1863), 4 Giff. 348; *Re Cowin, Cowin* v. *Gravett* (1886), 33 Ch.D. 179; *Re Tillott, Lee* v. *Wilson*, [1892] 1 Ch. 86; *Re Page, Jones* v. *Morgan*, [1893] 1 Ch. 304, at p. 309.

[6] *Ottley* v. *Gilby* (1845), 8 Beav. 602.

[7] Income and Corporation Taxes Act 1970, s. 432 (2), (3).

case of a residuary beneficiary with an absolute interest, to distinguish between income and payments, but he too is regarded as having had all the income of the residue, less administration expenses paid from income.[1]

The current income tax position is, in effect, to strengthen the notion that the beneficiary has almost an interest in the property. This is also the position with regard to capital gains tax introduced by the Finance Act 1965. Where an asset is transferred to a beneficiary in accordance with the terms of the will, or in accordance with the intestacy rules, the beneficiary is treated, retrospectively, as having acquired the asset at the date of death of the deceased, and the personal representatives are then not regarded as having had any chargeable interest in the asset.[2]

The result of all these provisions is that a beneficiary has most of the rights of the owner of an equitable interest in property, although *Livingston* constitutes a formidable barrier to the final logical step being taken.

---

[1] See further, Mellows, Taxation for Executors and Trustees, 3rd ed., p. 75.
[2] Finance Act 1965, s. 24 (7).

CHAPTER 30

FAILURE OF BENEFIT

In this chapter it is proposed to consider the various circumstances in which a beneficiary will not receive the benefit to which at first sight he appears to be entitled under the will or under the intestacy rules.

A. DISCLAIMER

1. RIGHT TO DISCLAIM

A beneficiary cannot be forced to accept a gift under a will or part of the estate of an intestate. If authority for this obvious proposition is needed, it is provided by Abbott, C.J. in *Townson* v. *Tickell*[1] where he said: "The law is not so absurd as to force a man to take an estate against his will". Disclaimer may be made by deed, writing under hand only, or even as a result of contract,[2] though any document is admissible so that evidence of the disclaimer is available.

A disclaimer once made is usually retro-active to the date of death of the deceased.[3] Until the disclaimer has been made, however, the beneficiary has a right to have the asset transferred to him.[4] If he does disclaim, he will be treated for estate duty purposes as making a gift, and a liability to duty may arise if he dies within seven years of the disclaimer.[5] By concession, estate duty is not claimed on the disclaimer of statutory legacies on intestacy.

---

[1] (1819), 3 B. & Ald. 31.

[2] *Begbie* v. *Crook* (1835), 2 Bing N.C. 70; *Re Birchall, Birchall* v. *Ashton* (1889), 40 Ch.D. 436; *Re Clout and Frewer's Contract*, [1924] 2 Ch. 230.

[3] *Re Parsons, Parsons* v. *A.-G.*, [1943] Ch. 12.

[4] Unless it is required in the course of the administration of the estate.

[5] Customs and Inland Revenue Act 1881, s. 38 (2)(a), and Finance Act 1894, s. 2 (3), as amended by Finance Act 1968, s. 35. See also *Re Stratton's Deed of Disclaimer*, [1958] Ch. 42.

A disclaimer may be made at any time before the asset is vested in or transferred to the beneficiary.

2. RETRACTION OF DISCLAIMER

A disclaimer made without consideration may be retracted where it has not been acted upon by the personal representatives, or the other parties have not altered their position in reliance upon it.[1] In *Re Young*,[2] for example, a tenant for life had refused to accept the income from the property for some time, but then changed his mind. He was held entitled to receive the income from the time when he changed his mind, but not before.

In all other circumstances, a disclaimer once given is final and cannot be retracted.

3. REASONS FOR DISCLAIMING

A beneficiary who does not want an asset to which he is entitled will usually accept it, and then give it away or sell it. A gift is rarely disclaimed, therefore, merely because the beneficiary does not like it. There are better reasons for disclaiming:

a. *Unacceptable conditions*

A gift by will may be subject to conditions. In general, a person may not accept a conditional gift without becoming subject to the condition, and this may make the gift in that form unacceptable. As will be seen, in some circumstances, where the beneficiary disclaims the gift, he might be entitled to the property on intestacy, in which case he will take free from any conditions.

b. *Onerous property*

The most usual reason for disclaiming a gift is because it is onerous, that is, subject to liabilities which more than outweigh the value of the property. An example is property held on a lease which will expire shortly, and under which the tenant is responsible for substantial delapidations.

Sometimes it is difficult to know whether a beneficiary can disclaim one of two gifts. The principle is easy to state. If upon a true construction of the will two assets are intended to be taken

---

[1] *Re Young, Fraser* v. *Young*, [1913] 1 Ch. 272; *Re Cranstoun's Will Trusts*, [1949] Ch. 523.
[2] [1913] 1 Ch. 272.

together or not at all, then one of them alone cannot be disclaimed, and where several assets are given under one heading, then some of those assets alone cannot be disclaimed. Thus, where there is a gift of residue, the whole of the assets comprising the residue must be taken or none at all.[1] In other cases, the beneficiary may disclaim one asset and accept another. In *Guthrie* v. *Walrond*[2] Fry, L.J., said:[3] "It appears to me plain that when two distinct legacies or gifts are made by will to one person, he is, as a general rule, entitled to take one and disclaim the other, but that his right to do so may be rebutted if there is anything in the will to show that it was the testator's intention that that option should not exist".

Although these principles are clearly established, difficulty may be experienced in applying them. In *Re Lysons, Beck* v. *Lysons*,[4] for example, a gift of a leasehold house and its furniture was held to constitute two independent gifts, so that the beneficiary could accept the furniture and disclaim the lease, but in *Re Joel, Rogerson* v. *Joel*[5] there was a contrary result on similar facts. It is a question of construction in each case.

c. *Income tax saving*

Interest on legacies is regarded as separate from the legacies themselves, so that the interest may be waived without affecting the right to the legacy itself. In *Dewar* v. *Inland Revenue Commissioners*[6] a beneficiary was entitled to a legacy of £1 million. This was not paid by the end of the executor's year, and he therefore became entitled to interest from that time. He refused to accept the interest, and was held not to be assessable on it. The principle applies, however, only while no identifiable income for the legatee has come into existence.[7]

d. *To take on intestacy*

If the beneficiary is entitled both to a specific legacy, and also

---

[1] *A.-G.* v. *Brackenbury* (1863), 1 H. & C. 782, at p. 791; *Re Hawkins, Hawkins* v. *Hawkins* (1880), 13 Ch.D. 470; *Parnell* v. *Boyd*, [1896] 2 I.R. 571.

[2] (1883), 22 Ch.D. 573.

[3] (1883), 22 Ch.D. 573, at p. 577.

[4] (1912), 107 L.T. 146.

[5] [1943] Ch. 311.

[6] [1935] 2 K.B. 351.

[7] See *Spens* v. *Inland Revenue Commissioners*, [1970] 3 All E.R. 295, discussed *ante*, p. 409.

to the residue, or on intestacy, it is sometimes in his interest to disclaim the specific legacy and to take under the residuary gift or the intestacy rules. This can be a particularly useful way of obtaining free of conditions property which is left in the will subject to conditions. It is clear that the beneficiary may disclaim where he intends to take in this way.

B. LAPSE

1. THE GENERAL PRINCIPLE

Until the testator dies, his will has no effect.[1] If the beneficiary is no longer alive at the date of the testator's death, the beneficiary's estate will not in general take any benefit under the will, and the gift in the will is of no effect. Although the will may contain alternative provisions providing what is to happen on the predecease of a beneficiary[2] a mere declaration against lapse will be of no effect.[3]

Where a legacy other than a gift of residue lapses, the property which is the subject of that gift falls into residue, and where a gift of residue lapses, the property devolves as on intestacy.[4]

To the general rule as to lapse there are the following exceptions:

a. in respect of gifts of entails;
b. in respect of gifts to the child or other issue of the testator;
c. in respect of gifts in satisfaction of a moral obligation;
d. in respect of certain gifts to charity;
e. where there are substitutory provisions in the will.

2. GIFT OF ENTAILS

Section 32 of the Wills Act 1837 provides that if an entail of realty is devised to a person who predeceases the testator but who leaves issue who would take under the entail, then the gift does not fail. In this case the devise takes effect as if the death of the devisee occurred immediately after the death of the testator. The general provision of Law of Property Act 1925, s. 130 (1),[5] applies statutory

---

[1] Except in the case of mutual wills.
[2] See *post*, p. 458.
[3] *Re Ladd, Henderson v. Porter*, [1932] 2 Ch. 219; see also article at 78 L.Q.R. 90.
[4] *Re Pugh's Will Trusts, Marten v. Pugh*, [1967] 3 All E.R. 337.
[5] By this sub-section, personal property was for the first time made entailable.

provisions relating to entails of realty to entailed interests in personalty, with the result that s. 32 now applies to all entailed gifts whether of realty or personalty.

The provisions of s. 32 are clearly sensible. If a testator leaves an entailed interest he clearly intends to benefit not only the immediate beneficiary but his heirs. Section 32 may be displaced by a contrary direction on the part of the testator.

The effect of a gift saved from lapse under this section is the same as in the case of gift saved under s. 33: this section is now to be considered, and it is better to consider the effect at that stage.

3. GIFTS TO CHILDREN AND ISSUE

a. *Scope of section 33*

Section 33 provides that where a testator makes a gift in favour of his child or remoter issue, and that child or issue predeceases him, then the gift will be saved from lapse if the beneficiary named in the will himself left issue living at the date of death of the testator. The section does not apply if the gift to the beneficiary named in the will was only of an interest, such as a life interest, determinable on the death of the beneficiary.

The words of the section, referring to the entitlement of the beneficiary to "any estate or interest not determinable at or before the death of" the beneficiary have a wider application than might seem at first sight. In *Re Wolson, Wolson* v. *Jackson*[1] the testator made a bequest to his daughter contingently on her attaining the age of 25. In fact, she predeceased him dying at the age of 24, but leaving issue. It was held that her interest was "determinable at her death", in the circumstances which happened, so that the gift was not saved from lapse.[2]

It is necessary for the issue of the beneficiary named in the will to be "living" at the date of death of the testator, so that the birth of a posthumous child does not save the gift from lapse.[3] An

---

[1] [1939] Ch. 780.

[2] Cf. *Re Wilson, Lothian* v. *Wilson* (1920), 89 L.J. Ch. 216, where the beneficiary did attain the specified age.

[3] *Elliot* v. *Joicey*, [1935] A.C. 209; *Re Griffiths' Settlement, Griffiths* v. *Waghorne*, [1911] 1 Ch. 246.

illegitimate child or issue is treated for all purposes of s. 33 as a legitimate child or issue.[1]

b. *Relation to class closing rules*

Suppose that a testator leaves his property to his children. He has three children, one of whom predeceases him leaving issue who survive him. If the gift is a class gift, then the rules relating to class gifts[2] will operate, and the property will be divided between the two children who survive the testator.[3]

The section will apply, however, where the testator has identified his children as individuals. If he names them, the section will apply[4] and it will also apply if he designates them in some other way. In *Re Stansfield, Stansfield* v. *Stansfield*,[5] for example, there was a gift to "my nine children". This was held to be the equivalent of naming the children, so that the gift could be saved from lapse.[6]

The general rule applies, however, that a gift will only be saved from lapse where there is no expression of contrary intention.

c. *Effect of the section*

The intention of the legislature is clear. To take the basic case, if Angela makes a will leaving £1,000 to her son Bertram, and Bertram predeceases her, leaving his daughter Clarissa living, then Clarissa is to take the gift which Bertram would have taken had he survived. That was the intention, but the words of the section do not necessarily lead to that result. The section provides that the gift shall not lapse "but shall take effect as if the death of such person (i.e. the beneficiary) happened immediately after the death of the testator". Suppose, on this example that Bertram made a will leaving all his property to his friend Ethel, then because Clarissa is alive at the date of the death of Angela, the gift is saved from lapse, but the property will form part of Ber-

---

[1] Family Law Reform Act 1969, s. 16.
[2] *Ante*, p. 159.
[3] *Viner* v. *Francis* (1789), 2 Cox Eq. Cas. 190.
[4] *Re Wilson, ante.*
[5] (1880), 15 Ch.D. 84.
[6] *Re Morris, Corfield* v. *Waller* (1916), 86 L.J. Ch. 456.

tram's estate and so will pass under Bertram's will to Ethel.[1]
Likewise, if Bertram's estate is insolvent, the property can be
taken for his debtors.[2]

There have been two approaches to s. 33, the so-called wide
and narrow approaches. The wide approach is illustrated by *Re
Allen's Trusts*.[3] In that case the testator gave a legacy to his
married daughter. She predeceased him leaving a husband and
two children. The husband died before the death of the testator,
so that the actual order of deaths was: daughter—husband—
testator. The narrow approach would be to allow the section to
save the gift from lapse, but to have no other effect. On this basis,
because the daughter left no will, the property would have gone
to her husband, and so to his estate, because he in fact survived
her. The wide approach was to regard the daughter as having
survived the testator for all testamentary purposes. On this basis,
the deemed order of deaths would be: husband—testator—
daughter. The daughter would, therefore, have been regarded as
having died a widow, and under the intestacy rules, the property
would have devolved on her children. In *Re Allen*, in fact, the
wider view prevailed.[4]

Re Allen was not cited to Farwell, J., during the hearing of *Re
Hurd, Stott v. Stott*.[5] In that case the testatrix left a gift to her
daughter Sarah. The daughter predeceased her mother, leaving
three daughters. One of the daughters was legitimated under the
Legitimacy Act 1926, with effect from 1 January 1926. The
daughter Sarah actually died in 1923, and her mother in 1939.
On the narrow view Sarah must be regarded as dying in 1923,
that is before her daughter became legitimated, and on the wider
view Sarah would be regarded as dying in 1939. Farwell, J., took
the narrow view, and founded his decision on the basis that s. 33
should not be construed so as to alter the persons who would be
entitled to benefit having regard to the actual circumstances at the
beneficiary's death.[6]

---

[1] *Johnson* v. *Johnson* (1843), 3 Hare. 157; *Eager* v. *Furnivall* (1881), 17 Ch.D.
115, at p. 118.
[2] *Re Pearson, Smith* v. *Pearson*, [1920] 1 Ch. 247.
[3] [1909] W.N. 181.
[4] See also *In the Goods of Councell* (1871), L.R. 2 P. & D. 314.
[5] [1941] Ch. 196.
[6] *Ibid.*, at p. 199.

The difficulty inherent in the wider view can be shown from the facts of *Re Hurd, Stott* v. *Stott* itself. Sarah's estate (without taking into account the benefit to be derived under her mother's will) would have been distributed in accordance with the law prevailing in 1923. In so far as the gift under her mother's will was concerned, the estate was to be administered under the 1939 law, the rather extraordinary result would ensue that different persons would be entitled.

Re Allen's Trusts and the wider view have now been finally rejected, although only at first instance, by the decision of Upjohn, J., in *Re Basioli*.[1] In that case the testatrix left property to her daughter, Mrs. Basioli. Mrs. Basioli died before her mother, leaving a husband and a son. The actual order of deaths was:

1929   daughter,
1939   daughter's husband,
1940   testatrix.

Upjohn, J., held that the gift under the testatrix's will was saved from lapse, but that in all other respects regard was to be had to the facts which actually happened. Thus all the property of the daughter, under the gift, was distributable as at 1929, and her husband's estate therefore benefited under the intestacy rules.

Application of the section may lead to a circuitous argument from which there is no logical escape. This was illustrated by *Re Hensler, Jones* v. *Hensler*.[2] A father made a will leaving his house to his son. The son predeceased him, leaving issue who survived the father. The son had also made a will, under which he left all his property to his father. The process is as follows. Because of the survival of the issue, the gift to the son is saved from lapse. The house therefore forms part of the son's estate. Section 33 applies only to save the gift from lapse[3] and for all other purposes the actual events prevail. As in fact the father survived the son, the gift in the son's will in favour of the father was valid, and there was no question of lapse in respect of the son's will. Thus, the house, having come into the son's estate, would then pass to the father's estate under the son's will. The father's personal representatives would deal with it under his will, that is,

---

[1] [1953] Ch. 367.
[2] (1881), 19 Ch.D. 612.
[3] The narrow view was adopted: see explanation of Upjohn, J., in *Re Basioli*.

pass it to the son, and the whole process would never stop. To prevent this result Hall, V.C., apparently on no authority,[1] held that when the house had passed into the son's estate, it should be dealt with in accordance with the intestacy rules. Even if there was no authority for this, the result is sensible.

4. GIFTS IN SATISFACTION OF MORAL OBLIGATION

The principle was laid down in some early cases that where the gift was made with the intention of discharging a moral obligation, then it would not lapse. As long as there is a moral obligation existing at the testator's death, the rule applies even though there is no legally enforceable obligation. The rule has been held to apply to statute barred debts[2] and debts barred by a discharge in bankruptcy.[3] There is no statutory authority for the principle, and its extent is uncertain.[4]

5. GENERAL CHARITABLE GIFTS

Where a gift is made to a charitable institution which ceases to exist in the testator's lifetime, that gift may take effect as a gift of general charitable intent, and be applicable *cy-pres*.[5]

6. SUBSTITUTORY PROVISIONS

Gifts are most frequently prevented from lapsing not by the application of any of the foregoing rules, but because the testator has expressly provided what is to happen in the event of predecease of the beneficiary. To obviate the difficulties which may arise, it is always advisable for the testator to say expressly what he wishes to happen. Thus, in many cases he will wish to provide "£500 to my daughter Wendy, but if she shall predecease me, to her son Winkle". By making this type of substitutory provision, the testator is not, of course, restricted by the scope of ss. 32 and 33, and he will prevent the unexpected results which sometimes flow from the application of these sections.

---

[1] See (1941) Law Journal, p. 252.

[2] *Williamson* v. *Naylor* (1838), 3 Y. & C. Ex. 208; *Philips* v. *Philips* (1844), 3 Hare. 281.

[3] *Re Sowerby's Trusts* (1856), 2 K. & J. 630; *Turner* v. *Martin* (1857), 7 De G.M. & G. 429.

[4] *Stevens* v. *King*, [1904] 2 Ch. 30; see also article at 78 L.Q.R. 88/89.

[5] This doctrine is not explained in this book, and readers are referred to the text-books on trusts.

C. COMMORIENTES

1. THE RULE

It is for every person who claims to be entitled to a part or the whole of the testator's estate to prove that entitlement, and as part of that burden he must, as a general principle, prove that he survived the testator. As has been shown[1] if the beneficiary did not survive the testator, the gift will lapse. This caused difficulty where the deaths of testator and beneficiary were virtually simultaneous. In some pre-1926 cases, the personal representatives of a deceased beneficiary were held to be unable to succeed if they could not prove that the beneficiary outlived the testator.[2] At common law there was no presumption as to who died first. The court firmly declared in *Wright* v. *Netherwood*[3] that it was more reasonable to consider the parties as all dying at the same time rather than "to resort to some fanciful supposition of survivorship on account of degrees of robustness".

This position was altered by Law of Property Act 1925, s. 184, which provides that where after 1925 "two or more persons have died in circumstances rendering it uncertain which of them survived the other or others, such deaths shall for all purposes affecting the title to property, be presumed to have occurred in order of seniority, and accordingly the younger shall be deemed to have survived the elder".

The scope of this section was clarified in *Hickman* v. *Peacey*.[4] In this case two brothers were killed while in a house which was destroyed by a high-explosive bomb during an enemy air attack. They had each made a will leaving a legacy to the other. It was argued that the evidence indicated that both brothers died simultaneously, so that the circumstances did not render it "uncertain" which of them died first. If this had been accepted, s. 184 would have had no application. The House of Lords, by a majority, and reversing the Court of Appeal, held that s. 184 did apply. Lord Macmillan said:[5] "All that is necessary in order to invoke

---

[1] *Ante*, p. 453.

[2] *Underwood* v. *Wing* (1855), 24 L.J. Ch. 293; *Wing* v. *Angrave* (1860), 8 H.L. Cas. 183; *Re Nightingale, Hargreaves* v. *Shuttleworth* (1927), 71 Sol. Jo. 542.

[3] (1793), 2 Salk. 593, n.

[4] [1945] A.C. 304.

[5] *Ibid.*, at p. 325.

the statutory presumption is the presence in the circumstances of an element of uncertainty as to which of the deceased survived." The House of Lords held that although the evidence suggested that the deaths were simultaneous, there was still an element of uncertainty as to the exact moment when each brother died, and this was sufficient to operate the section.

Hickman v. *Peacey* does not expressly say that s. 184 applies where death is simultaneous. It seems that if it could be proved conclusively that both deaths were simultaneous, to the very moment, then the section would not apply, but the effect of *Hickman* v. *Peacey* is that for all practical purposes it will never be possible to prove simultaneity of death to the very moment.[1]

2. EXCEPTIONS TO THE RULE

a. *Order of the Court*

Section 184 itself incorporates the words "subject to any order of the Court". It is doubtful, however, whether those words have any meaning. In *Re Lindop, Lee-Barber* v. *Reynolds*[2] Bennett, J., said that they did not give the court a discretion not to operate the section because it might be unfair. Subsequently it has been said that the words are obscure, if not meaningless.[3]

b. *Finance Act 1958, s. 29 (1)*

The effect of s. 184 is to cause the property to pass from elder to younger, and then from younger to the person entitled under his will or upon intestacy. There is, therefore, a double passing, and estate duty is normally charged upon each "passing". However, s. 29 (1) Finance Act 1958, provides that for estate duty purposes only, both people are deemed to have died at the same instant.

c. *Intestate spouses*

Under the intestacy rules, where a married person dies his or her spouse becomes entitled to certain benefits.[4] The effect of

---

[1] *Re Bate, Chillingworth* v. *Bate*, [1947] 2 All E.R. 418.
[2] [1942] Ch. 377.
[3] See *Hickman* v. *Peacey*, [1945] A.C. 304, at p. 314; *Re Bate, Chillingworth* v. *Bate*, [1947] 2 All E.R. 418.
[4] *Ante*, p. 190.

s. 184 in the event of virtually simultaneous deaths was—assuming the husband to be the elder—to cause his property to pass to his wife, and for it then, in the absence of children, to pass to her family. By virtue of Intestates Estates Act 1952, s. 1 (4)[1] in the case of post 1952 deaths, where it is uncertain which of intestate husband and wife survives the other, each is regarded as having survived the other.[2]

D. ADEMPTION

The expression ademption is used in several situations. Its common use, and that with which this chapter is concerned, is where an asset bequeathed or devised by will ceases to be subject to the testator's power of disposition, or ceases to conform to the description given in the will. In the simplest case, if the testator makes a gift of "my red double-deck omnibus", and between making the will and dying he sells that 'bus, then the beneficiary receives nothing. Or, if the 'bus, having been taken out of service through old age, is then crushed into a small metal block by a scrapping machine, the words of the will are not sufficient to pass the block, even though its ingredients are the same as the 'bus

1. DOCTRINE APPLIES TO SPECIFIC GIFTS

Ademption operates on specific legacies only, and not on general legacies. It will be shown[3] that generally a gift of money is not specific, though it may be if a particular sum—e.g., "my £100 which I keep under the bed"—is indicated. If there is no estate, or the estate is insolvent, then even in the case of general legacies the beneficiary will receive nothing, but that is termed abatement and not ademption.

Because of this distinction between general and specific legacies the courts have often shown a reluctance to find that a gift is specific. Where there is room for any doubt, if the asset can be replaced, and there is no inevitable description pointing to the testator, the gift will usually be regarded as general. This is illustrated by *Re Gage, Crozier* v. *Gutheridge*.[4] In that case the

---

[1] And 1st Schedule.
[2] See *ante*, p. 183.
[3] *Post*, p. 491.
[4] [1934] Ch. 536.

testator bequeathed to his niece "the sum of £1,150 Five per Cent
War Loan 1929-47 Stock and to M.G. the sum of £500 New
South Wales Five per Cent Stock now standing in my name".
At the time of making the will the testator held £1,150 of this
War Loan Stock, but had disposed of it before his death. Clauson,
J., held that the two parts of the clause were disjunctive, so that
the words "now standing in my name" applied only to the New
South Wales Stock. Accordingly, while the gift of New South
Wales Stock was specific, the gift of War Loan was held to be
general, so that the executors were directed to purchase £1,150
of this stock for the beneficiary.

A warning has, however, been given in *Re Rose, Midland Bank
Executor and Trustee Co.* v. *Rose*[1] that in each case the will as a
whole must be construed, so that where there is evidence of an
intention to make a specific gift, that will of course prevail.

2. CHANGES IN NATURE OF ASSET

a. *Generally*

Once it is established that a gift is specific, there is usually
no doubt whether it has been adeemed or not: either the asset
exists and forms part of the estate, or it does not. Difficulty does,
however, arise where the asset changes its nature. The test was
stated by Cozens-Hardy, M.R., in *Re Slater, Slater* v. *Slater*[2] in
these words: "You have to ask yourself, where is the thing which
is given? If you cannot find it at the testator's death, it is no use
trying to trace it unless you can trace it in this sense, that you find
something which has been changed in name or form only, but
which is substantially the same thing." Whether the change is of
form only is in all cases a question of fact.[3]

The application of the doctrine may be illustrated by reference
to stocks and shares. Where after a reorganization of the capital
structure of a company the testator continues to hold stocks and
shares in that company, even if the new securities carry different
rights and are of different quantity, the gift will not be adeemed.
Thus, it has been held that there is no ademption if bonds are
converted into shares[4] or if shares are sub-divided, as, for example,

---

[1] [1949] Ch. 78.
[2] [1907] 1 Ch. 665.
[3] *Re Bridle* (1879), 4 C.P.D. 336, at p. 341.
[4] *Re Pilkington's Trusts* (1865), 6 New Rep. 246.

where four 25p. shares are issued to shareholders in place of each
£1 share,[1] or if shares in a reconstituted company are issued to
replace the holding in the previous company.[2] In these cases there
has been:

  a. a unity of the company issuing the security, in the sense that
     it has either been the same company, or a new company
     formed just to take over the old;
  b. a similarity in the nature of the security itself;[3] and
  c. a similarity in the quantity of the holding before and after
     the change.

It seems that if any of these three unities is missing, the gift will
be adeemed. Thus, where the company is not merely reconstructed,
but is amalgamated with a larger organization, whether or not as
a result of a take over bid, ademption will take place. In *Re
Slater, Slater* v. *Slater*[4] a gift of shares in a private water company
was adeemed when the company was taken over by the Metro-
politan Water Board. A gift of stock is also adeemed when it is
converted into cash. So in *Harrison* v. *Jackson*[5] a gift of stock was
adeemed, when the holding was redeemed by the company by
repayment in cash to the stockholders.

Where there is some element of increment, such as the issue of
additional shares as part of the reorganization the additional shares
will not pass under the gift, though the gift of the other shares
will not be adeemed.[6]

b. *Changes by Act of Parliament*

The principle of ademption applies even to changes which are
forced upon the testator. Some, but not all, of the company
changes just described may in effect be forced upon the testator,
but compulsory changes are more usually effected by Act of
Parliament. These changes are of two broad types: changes of
substance, and changes in the legal nature of the asset without
affecting any physical change.

---

[1] *Re Greenberry, Hops* v. *Daniell* (1911), 55 Sol. Jo. 633; *Re Clifford, Mallam*
v. *McFie*, [1912] 1 Ch. 29.
[2] *Re Leeming*, [1912] 1 Ch. 828.
[3] Although admittedly this to some extent begs the question.
[4] [1907] 1 Ch. 665.
[5] (1877), 7 Ch.D. 339.
[6] *Re Kuypers, Kuypers* v. *Kuypers*, [1925] Ch. 244.

An example of the first type of case is provided by *Re Anderson, Public Trustee* v. *Bielby*.[1] The testator owned shares in one of the local railway companies, and by the Railways Act 1921, the undertaking of this company was transferred to one of the national railway companies. A specific gift of the shares in the local company was adeemed. However, the legislation may, and it might be thought, always should, include a provision to prevent ademption. *Re Jenkins, Jenkins* v. *Davies*,[2] for example, was concerned with the gift of a holding in the Swansea Harbour Trust. This holding was converted by the Great Western Railway Act 1923, into G.W.R. stock, which would normally have adeemed the gift. There was, however, a general section in the 1923 Act by which reference to the Swansea Harbour Trust in, *inter alia*, wills and codicils were to be construed as references to the G.W.R. stock substituted for it.

The operation of the doctrine of ademption is important having regard to the various nationalization measures. An early example is provided by an Act in 1833 for the abolition of slavery in Jamaica. Upon abolition, the owners of the slaves were entitled to payment from a compensation fund. In *Richards* v. *A.-G. of Jamaica*[3] a former owner made a specific gift of his share in the compensation fund. By the law of Jamaica, slaves had been regarded as realty, and could only be devised as such, and at the time there were different formalities for wills of realty and wills of personalty. In this case, if the share in the compensation fund was regarded as representing the slaves, and so as realty, then the will would not be effective, but if as a gift of personalty, it would be effective. It was treated as personalty.[4]

A more recent example arises under the Coal Act 1938. By virtue of this Act, coal and coal mines vested in the Coal Commission, and the owner received compensation money. In *Re Viscount Galway's Wills Trusts*[5] Harman, J., held that a gift of property, which would have included the coal, did not pass the compensation money, which accordingly went to the residuary legatee.

---

[1] (1928), 44 T.L.R. 295.
[2] [1931] 2 Ch. 218.
[3] (1848), 6 Moo. P.C.C. 381.
[4] See also *Frewen* v. *Frewen* (1875), 10 Ch. App. 610.
[5] [1950] Ch. 1.

In general, therefore, nationalization will either involve the issue of new stock, or monetary compensation. In the former case, unless there is some excepting provision, or in any case in the latter, the gift will be adeemed, subject to what is said below[1] about contrary intention.

c. *Ademption following conversion*

Considerable difficulty has arisen from s. 35, Law of Property Act 1925. Before 1 January 1926, it was possible for two or more persons to own land concurrently. A share in land was realty. By s. 35, whenever more than one person holds land concurrently, there is a trust for sale, under which the interest of the owner is in the proceeds of sale. The owner's interest is therefore converted into personalty. If, then, there was a pre-1926 will leaving in terms applicable to realty a share in land, and the testator dies after 1925, what is the effect of s. 35 on the will. Of course, the answer ought to be: None! In fact the position is considerably more complicated.

The principle was expressed by Farwell, J., in *Re Newman, Slater* v. *Newman*:[2] "If the testator uses language that can only be construed as a devise of real estate, and, notwithstanding the imposition of the statutory trusts, he dies without altering or confirming his will, the conversion effected by the statutory trusts adeems the devise, because there is nothing left for that devise to operate on. If, on the other hand, the testator uses language wide enough to carry any interest in the property, whether it be in law real or personal property, the conversion is immaterial."

Four rules may be deduced from the cases:

(i) In general, a gift of an undivided share in realty in a pre-1926 will is converted into personalty, and passes as personalty. In *Re Kempthorne, Charles* v. *Kempthorne*[3] the testator who owned an undivided share in land, made a will in 1911 leaving a general gift of realty to A and a general gift of personalty to B. The share in land passed to B.

---

[1] *Post*, p. 467.
[2] [1930] 2 Ch. 409.
[3] [1930] 1 Ch. 268.

(ii) This is so, even if there is a specific gift of the property. So, in *Re Newman, Slater* v. *Newman*[1] the gift was not, as in *Re Kempthorne, Charles* v. *Kempthorne*, a general gift of realty, but a gift of "all my share in Blackacre". This share was held to have been converted into personalty on 1 January 1926, and to pass as such. The words were "not apt to pass anything but a moiety of real estate".

(iii) Ademption will not take place if the words of the gift are wide enough to pass personalty. So in *Re Mellish*[2] Eve, J., held that where the testator gave all his "interest" in Blackacre, that was wide enough to pass personalty, so that the gift was not adeemed.

(iv) Ademption will also not take place if a post-1925 codicil confirms the will. If, by this means, the will can be treated as being post-1925, and the words used are applicable to realty, the words are treated as an example of misdescription, not of ademption.[3] In this case, even if the post-1925 codicil does not confirm the will, ademption will nevertheless be prevented.[4]

The result is, therefore, that if the words of the will are so narrow that they can only apply to realty, then the courts regard themselves as bound. They will, however, strive to find some way round the difficulty.

3. REPUBLICATION FOLLOWING ADEMPTION

From the cases just considered, it may be thought that if ademption occurs through operation of law, a subsequent codicil will be sufficient to prevent ademption. On the other hand in *Re Viscount Galway's Wills Trusts*[5] as has been seen, a codicil made after the coming into effect of the Coal Act 1938, was held by Harman, J., not to give the beneficiary named a right to compensation. *Re Viscount Galway's Wills Trusts* is quoted as authority for the proposition that republication by codicil cannot operate

---

[1] [1930] 2 Ch. 409.

[2] Not reported, but see *Re Wheeler*, [1929] 2 K.B. 81; *Re Warren, Warren* v. *Warren*, [1932] 1 Ch. 42, at p. 47.

[3] *Re Warren, Warren* v. *Warren*, *supra*; *Re Lowman, Devenish* v. *Pester*, [1895] 2 Ch. 348, as explained in *Re Newman, Slater* v. *Newman*.

[4] *Re Harvey, Public Trustee* v. *Hosken*, [1947] Ch. 285.

[5] [1950] Ch. 1.

to make good a legacy once adeemed,[1] but this does not seem to be entirely correct. It is necessary to distinguish between three situations:

a. if the testator has ceased to own the asset before the date of republication, then republication will generally not confer a right to compensation. This is the *Re Viscount Galway's Wills Trusts* position;

b. exceptionally, if the codicil not only republishes, but also indicates an intention to pass the compensation, then it will be effective to do so;

c. if the testator retains the asset, but it undergoes a change in its legal nature, and the will is republished after that legal change, ademption will be prevented. This is the *Re Harvey, Public Trustee* v. *Hosken* situation.

4. CONTRARY INTENTION

The courts will apply the doctrine of ademption subject to any indication of the testator's intention expressed in the will. Where the asset ceases to exist, the most that the testator can do is either to treat the gift as general and not specific, or perhaps to provide for the possibility that the asset may no longer be owned. If, therefore, the testator wishes to give his house to his wife, he may give her "my house, The Nook, or such other house as may be my principal residence at the date of my death".

There is little that a testator can do in advance of nationalization or statutory conversion, and he must remember to alter his will after such measure has come into force.

The account of the decisions arising from the 1925 legislation has been purposely simplified. Even so, the spectacle of intellectual gymnastics by the judges is hardly edifying. The primary fault is that of the legislature. It is regrettable that the various legislation which has caused ademption, either by nationalization, or confiscation, does not expressly provide against ademption. This is surely what would most accord with the wishes of the majority of testators.

---

[1] E.g., Parry, 6th ed., p. 101.

E. ABATEMENT

1. THE PRINCIPLES

Where there is insufficient in the estate after the payment of debts and liabilities to pay all legacies in full, they will abate in the following order:

a. residue;

b. general legacies;

c. specific and demonstrative legacies.

This is, however, subject to any contrary intention shown in the will, and to the discussion in chapter 32 on the effect of the First Schedule to the Administration of Estates Act 1925.

2. CATEGORIES OF GIFT FOR ABATEMENT

a. **Residue.** In strict principle, the residue can only be ascertained after all other legacies have been paid, and if there is insufficient to meet them, the residuary beneficiary will take no benefit.[1] As will be seen, however,[2] this is subject to any expression of contrary intention on the part of the testator.

b. **General legacies.** The classification of legacies is considered elsewhere,[3] but for present purposes a general legacy is any legacy other than a specific legacy, and other than a demonstrative legacy to the extent indicated below. General legacies abate entirely before the specific legacies are touched,[4] but again this is subject to any contrary intention.[5]

c. **Specific and demonstrative legacies.** The last category to abate is specific legacies.[6] A demonstrative legacy is treated as a specific legacy so long as the asset out of which it is to be paid remains in existence.[7] When, however, the asset out of which it was to be paid is exhausted, the legacy is

---

[1] *Purse* v. *Snaplin* (1738), 1 Atk. 414; *Fonnereau* v. *Poyntz* (1785), 1 Bro. C.C. 472; *Harley* v. *Moon* (1861), 1 Drew. & Sm. 623; *Baker* v. *Farmer* (1868), 3 Ch. App. 537.

[2] *Post*, p. 469.

[3] *Post*, p. 491.

[4] *Clifton* v. *Burt* (1720), 1 P. Wms. 678.

[5] *Infra.*

[6] *Barton* v. *Cooke* (1800), 5 Ves. 461.

[7] *Roberts* v. *Pocock* (1798), 4 Ves. 150; *Creed* v. *Creed* (1844), 11 Cl. & F. 491; *Robinson* v. *Geldard* (1851), 3 Mac. & G. 735.

then treated as a general legacy, and abates with the other general legacies.[1]

d. Contrary intention.

These rules are all subject to the testator's intention A good example is the old decision in *Sayer* v. *Sayer*.[2] There was a gift both of pecuniary legacies and specific legacies, but a direction that the pecuniary legacies should be taken out of the whole personalty. The effect was that the pecuniary legacies were taken first, causing the specific legacies to abate.

3. ABATEMENT WITHIN EACH CATEGORY

The general principle is that all legacies within each category abate rateably.[3] Where the legacy is of an asset which has a fluctuating value, such as stock exchange securities, the asset is valued at the end of one year from the testator's death.[4] Again, however, the testator can indicate that legacies within each class shall abate in some other way. In *Marsh* v. *Evans*[5] the testator gave legacies to his two sons and his daughter, but he provided that if the estate was not large enough for the three legacies to be paid in full, the legacy to his daughter should be fully satisfied, and the legacies to his sons should abate.[6]

Unless such a contrary intention can be shown, a legacy given for a specific purpose will abate rateably with all other legacies in the same category. So, a legacy to the executor as a recompense for his trouble,[7] or a charging clause for a solicitor-executor[8]

---

[1] *Paget* v. *Huish* (1863), 1 H. & M. 663.

[2] (1714), Prec. Ch. 392.

[3] *Clifton* v. *Burt* (1720), 1 P. Wms. 678; *Duke of Devon* v. *Atkins* (1726), 2 P. Wms. 381; *Sleech* v. *Thorington* (1754), 2 Ves. Sen. 561; *Fielding* v. *Preston* (1857), 1 De G. & J. 438; *Re Cohen, National Provincial Bank* v. *Katz*, [1960] Ch. 179.

[4] *Blackshaw* v. *Rogers*, cited in *Simmons* v. *Vallance* (1793), 4 Bro. C.C. 349; *Auther* v. *Auther* (1843), 13 Sim. 422. See also *Re Hollins*, [1918] 1 Ch. 503.

[5] (1720), 1 P. Wms. 668.

[6] See also *A-G* v. *Robins* (1722), 2 P. Wms. 24; *Lewin* v. *Lewin* (1752), 2 Ves. Sen. 415; *Beeston* v. *Booth* (1819), 4 Madd. 161; *Brown* v. *Brown* (1836), 1 Keen 275; *Pepper* v. *Blomfield* (1843), 3 Dr. & War. 499; *Haynes* v. *Haynes* (1853), 3 De G.M. & G. 590; *Gyett* v. *Williams* (1862), 2 Johns. & H. 429.

[7] *Re White, Pennell* v. *Franklin*, [1898] 2 Ch. 217.

[8] *Re Brown, Wace* v. *Smith*, [1918] W.N. 118; *O'Higgins* v. *Walsh*, [1918] 1 I.R. 126.

which ranks as a legacy[1] will abate rateably with legacies not given for a specific purpose.

4. INTEREST ON LEGACIES

Interest on legacies, where it is payable,[2] is payable in full. It is not treated as an additional legacy, and so does not abate with the legacy itself.[3]

RULES OF STATUTE AND PUBLIC POLICY

This section deals with those rules of statute or public policy which prevent a gift in a will having the effect which it appears to have on its face. The rule which in many cases prevents an attesting witness from taking a benefit was considered earlier.[4]

F. SLAYING THE TESTATOR

1. THE RULE

It is a rule of public policy that a person shall not be allowed to benefit from his crime. If, therefore, A makes a will in favour of B, and B shoots A dead, B is not allowed to claim the property to which he would otherwise be entitled under the will. Likewise, he is not entitled to claim under an intestacy.

Although the principle can be readily appreciated, the scope of the rule is uncertain. The reported cases are concerned both with murder[5] and manslaughter.[6] It is uncertain whether the rule extends beyond this. For example, if the testator is killed as a result of dangerous driving on the part of the beneficiary, will that be sufficient to deprive the beneficiary? There is Australian authority that the motive and degree of moral guilt is irrelevant[7] and if this is so, presumably death by dangerous driving would prevent the beneficiary from taking under the will.

---

[1] See *ante*, p. 62.
[2] See *post*, p. 498.
[3] *Re Wyles, Foster* v. *Wyles*, [1938] Ch. 313.
[4] *Ante*, p. 62.
[5] *Cleaver* v. *Mutual Reserve Fund Life Association*, [1892] 1 Q.B. 147; *In the Estate of Crippen*, [1911] P. 108.
[6] *In the Estate of Hall*, [1914] P. 1.
[7] *McKinnon* v. *Lundy* (1894), 21 A.R. 560.

The English court has recently decided that where the killing is by manslaughter, the question of moral blame is irrelevant. In *Re Giles, Giles* v. *Giles*[1] a wife killed her husband by hitting him with what is described as a "bedroom utensil". Under the terms of the will she would have taken the entire estate. She was found guilty of manslaughter by reason of diminished responsibility, and was ordered to be detained in Broadmoor Hospital. Penny-cuick, V.-C., held that she could not take either under the will or under the intestacy rules. The judge professed some sympathy for the woman, but he appears to have been influenced in his decision by the thought that the relaxation of the rule in other cases of diminished responsibility could be harmful and dangerous. The case is unsatisfactory. At the criminal trial, the court accepted medical evidence that the woman should be detained in Broad-moor without limit of time. On the other hand, if the medical illness was so great that the verdict was "not guilty by reason of insanity" the rule would have had no application.[2] Penny-cuick, V.-C., followed the approach of Hamilton, L.J., in *In the Estate of Hall, Hall* v. *Knight and Baxter*[3] where he refused to consider degrees of guilt on the ground[4] that it would "encourage what, I am sure, would be very noxious—a sentimental specula-tion as to the motives and degree of moral guilt of a person who has been justly convicted". The cold, unfeeling hand of the law is laid upon us.

The rule is of comparatively recent origin. Before the Forfeiture Act 1870, where a felon was a beneficiary under the will of the person whom he murdered, the murderer's interest was forfeit to the Crown. Since 1870, the basis of the rule appears to have altered. In its early formulation in *Cleaver* v. *Mutual Reserve Fund Life Association*[5] Fry, L.J., said: "It appears to me that no system of jurisprudence can with reason include among the rights which it enforces rights directly resulting to the person asserting them from the crime of that person. If no action can arise from fraud, it seems impossible to suppose that it can arise from felony or

---

[1] [1972] Ch. 544.
[2] *Re Houghton, Houghton* v. *Houghton*, [1915] 2 Ch. 173; *Re Pitts, Cox* v. *Kilsby*, [1931] 1 Ch. 546; *Re Batten* (1961), 105 Sol. Jo. 529.
[3] [1914] P. 1.
[4] *Ibid.*, at p. 9.
[5] [1892] 1 Q.B. 147.

misdemeanour." In other words, the rule is expressed in terms that the law will not lend its aid to assist a criminal to recover. It left open the question whether the executors could nevertheless pay.[1] However, in *Re Callaway, Callaway* v. *Treasury Solicitor*[2] Vaisey, J., said: "Now this rule, based on public policy, is that no person is allowed to take any benefit arising out of a death brought about by the agency of that person acting feloniously, whether it be a case of murder or manslaughter." Accordingly, the personal representatives should not make the payment, even if they are minded to do so.

2. EFFECT OF THE RULE

To apply the rule, it is necessary to see what claim the slayer can establish, and then, when it is established, to use the rule as a personal bar. The effect is, therefore, the same as if a beneficiary had witnessed the will.[3] Accordingly, in *Re Callaway, Callaway* v. *Treasury Solicitor*[4] Mrs. C, a widow, died leaving a son A.F.C. and a daughter Mrs. S. Mrs. C left a will leaving all her property to her daughter Mrs. S. Mrs. S killed her mother. Mrs. S could not take under the will, and the property was therefore undisposed of, and so fell to be dealt with in accordance with the rules of intestacy. Under the intestacy rules, the son and daughter would have normally taken half of the estate each, but the daughter was prevented from taking, so the son took all. By applying this rule, the normal rules of distribution are disturbed as little as possible. The other possibilities in this case would have been for the Crown to have stepped into the shoes of Mrs. S under the will, and taken all, or to have taken her place under the intestacy, and taken one half, but Vaisey, J., somewhat reluctantly rejected this. It will be appreciated that *someone* always benefits—in this case the son— and that the rule only precludes the killer from benefiting.

In *Cleaver* v. *Mutual Reserve Fund Life Association*[5] Fry, J., drew a distinction between the rights of the criminal on the one hand, and "alternative or independent" rights on the other hand. Thus, where A leaves property to B for life with remainder to C

---

[1] Cf. *Pullan* v. *Koe*, [1913] 1 Ch. 9.
[2] [1956] Ch. 559.
[3] *Ante*, p. 62.
[4] [1956] Ch. 559.
[5] [1892] 1 Q.B. 147.

and B kills A, C will become entitled at once. Although C's right followed B's, they were not dependent on this. By contrast, if A leaves property to B absolutely, and B kills A, then not only is B precluded from benefiting, but also those claiming under B's estate. Thus, in *In the Estate of Crippen*[1] Crippen's wife died intestate, and by the intestacy rules, all her property passed to Crippen. Crippen made a will in favour of his mistress. After his execution, it was held that his mistress could not take.

G. WITNESSING

The circumstances in which an attesting witness is barred from taking a benefit under the will were considered earlier.[2]

H. FRAUD

Although there has been very little litigation on the point, it is clear that a person is not entitled to benefit under a will if it was induced by fraud.[3] It has been suggested[4] that if a person, being already married, goes through a bigamous ceremony of marriage with the testator, and he then makes a gift to "my wife", that gift might be void for fraud.

I. ILLEGAL AND IMMORAL PURPOSES

If the object of the will, or of a part of it, is to advance an illegal purpose, or a purpose which is against public policy, then no effect will be given to that object. Whether a purpose is illegal or against public policy will be decided in the same way as in the case of trusts.[5]

---

[1] [1911] P. 108.
[2] See *ante*, p. 62.
[3] *Lord Donegal's Case* (1751), 2 Ves. Sen. 408.
[4] Bailey, Law of Wills, 6th ed., p. 202.
[5] Examples are *Thrupp* v. *Collett* (1858), 26 Beav. 125 where there was a trust to apply money to discharge persons committed to prison for non-payment of fines under the game laws; *Brown* v. *Burdett* (1882), 21 Ch.D. 667, which was a direction to board up property so that it could not be used for twenty years.

Special consideration must be given to gifts to illegitimate children. In respect of wills made before 1970, whenever there is a gift to an illegitimate child, it is always necessary to show:

a. that on a true construction of the gift, an illegitimate person is to take;[1] and

b. that the gift is not against public policy.

The basis of the rule of public policy is that no gift will be valid if it is an encouragement to future immorality. The aim of this rule may be laudable: its formulation and application is both naive and absurd. In general, a gift to an illegitimate child not in existence at the date of the will will be void. It is as if the law solemnly imagines a man bargaining with a woman: "if you want me to make a will . . ."

Accordingly, no question of public policy arises if the child was alive or *en ventre sa mere* at the date of the will. If, however, the child was not alive or *en ventre sa mere* at that date, the gift will be void unless:

a. by the date of death of the testator it can be proved that paternity had been acknowledged, or that it is a matter of general repute.[2] This test demands objective proof: it is not sufficient for the will to refer to the child in general terms of paternity—e.g., to the children of A by B;[3] or

b. the child is described by reference to maternity alone—e.g., to the children of Winnie.[4]

Because the first exception depends on reputation or acknowledgement of paternity, it is difficult to prove acknowledgement in the case of a child *en ventre sa mere* at the date of the father's death. It is sometimes stated that in the case of such a child he cannot come within this exception, but this probably puts it too strongly.

---

[1] That has been dealt with, *ante*, p. 153.

[2] *Occleston* v. *Fullalove* (1874), 9 Ch. App. 147; *Re Hyde, Smith* v. *Jack,* [1932] 1 Ch. 95.

[3] *Re Bolton, Brown* v. *Bolton* (1886), 31 Ch.D. 542; *Re Shaw, Robinson* v. *Shaw,* [1894] 2 Ch. 573; *Re Du Bochet, Mansell* v. *Allen,* [1901] 2 Ch. 441; *Re Pearce, Alliance Assurance Co., Ltd.* v. *Francis,* [1914] 1 Ch. 254; *Re Homer, Cowlishaw* v. *Rendell* (1916), 86 L.J. Ch. 324.

[4] *In the Estate of Frogley,* [1905] P. 137.

The position has been altered in respect of wills made on or after January 1970. The Family Law Reform Act 1969, s. 15 (7) has simply abolished the rule that a disposition for future illegitimate children is void for public policy. With the blessing of the Legislature, one may now bargain: "if you want me to make a will . . ."

J. PERPETUITY AND ACCUMULATIONS

A gift in a will does not take effect if it contravenes the perpetuity and accumulations rules. These are not considered in this book, and readers are referred to the standard books on property and trusts.

K. UNCERTAINTY

It is convenient to mention here that if a gift is to take effect, both the subject matter of the gift, and the objects, must be stated with sufficient certainty to enable the court to enforce its terms.

The courts go to great lengths in order to save gifts which appear to be too vague. Thus, in *Re Lewis, Goronwy* v. *Richards*[1] a gift to X and/or Y was upheld as a gift to X and Y as joint tenants, and in *Makeown* v. *Ardagh*[2] a bequest of " . . . hundred pounds" has been upheld as a gift of one hundred pounds.

In some cases, however, the courts are unable to give any effect to the words used. A good example occurred in *Asten* v. *Asten*.[3] In his will the testator included a gift of "all that newly-built house being No. . . . Sudeley Place" to A, and gifts in

---

[1] [1942] Ch. 424.
[2] (1876), I.R. 10 Eq. 445.
[3] [1894] 3 Ch. 260

identical terms to B, C and D. He clearly intended to complete these gifts himself, but did not do so. They were all held to be invalid, as the subject matter of the gifts had not been sufficiently identified.

Other examples of gifts which have failed for uncertainty are "some of my best linen";[1] "a handsome gratuity to each of my executors";[2] a devise to "one of my sons" (without naming him).[3]

Where beneficiaries have a right to select articles, but the order in which they are to select is not stated, then they are to select in the order in which their names appear in the will. If they are described as members of a class and if they cannot agree among themselves, their order of choice is by lot. Both of these rules were illustrated by *Re Knapton, Knapton v. Hindle*[4] where a testatrix had given "one house to each of my nephews and nieces and one to N.H. One to F.K. One to my sister. One to my brother". The nephews and nieces were held entitled to choose first, then N.H., F.K., and then the sister and the brother. The nephews and nieces chose by lot between themselves.

In many respects "charity" is regarded by the law as an entity itself,[5] so that a gift with a general charitable intention can never fail for uncertainty. The Charity Commissioners or the Court will prescribe the way in which the fund is to be applied if it is insufficiently identified in the will.

EQUITABLE DOCTRINES

L. SATISFACTION

Equity has established certain presumptions which apply to the situation where a person is under an obligation to do an act, and then does some other act which may be regarded as fulfilling that obligation. The presumption is that the latter act is to be taken as being done in substitution for, and not in addition to, the existing obligation.

---

[1] *Peck* v. *Halsey* (1726), 2 P. Wms. 387.
[2] *Jubber* v. *Jubber* (1839), 9 Sim. 503.
[3] *Strode* v. *Lady Russel* (1708), 2 Vern. 620.
[4] [1941] Ch. 428.
[5] See Parker and Mellows, The Modern Law of Trusts, 2nd ed., pp. 170 *et seq.*

The doctrine of satisfaction applies in three situations:

1. Satisfaction of debts by legacies. Suppose A owes B £1,000 and then in his will A leaves B £1,000. Is B entitled to both the debt and the legacy?

2. Satisfaction of portion debts by legacies. A portion may at this stage be described as a substantial gift for a child or other person to whom the testator stands *in loco parentis*. Suppose that in a marriage settlement C covenants to pay £5,000 for his child, and subsequently makes a will leaving that child £5,000. Can the child claim both?

3. Satisfaction (otherwise called ademption) of legacies by portions or portion debts. This is the converse of 2. C here makes a will leaving his child D a legacy of £5,000, and subsequently either pays D £5,000 or enters into a covenant to pay £5,000. Is D entitled to both?

Reference is also sometimes made to:

4. Satisfaction of legacies by legacies. The situation here envisaged is a gift in a will of £5,000 to A and a further gift of £5,000 to A later in the will. Does A take both?

1. SATISFACTION OF DEBTS BY LEGACIES

a. *The rule*

There is a presumption that a debt is to be satisfied by a legacy if all the following factors are present:

   (i) the debt must precede the will;
  (ii) the amount of the legacy must equal or exceed the amount of the debt;
 (iii) the legacy must be as advantageous to the creditor as the debt;
 (iv) the nature of the debt must be the same as that of the legacy;
  (v) there is no contrary intention in the will.

(i) The debt must precede the will. Because the doctrine is based on the presumed intention of the testator, he can only be presumed to have intended to satisfy a debt if it was in existence at the date of the will.[1] The testator's presumed intention is con-

---

[1] *Cranmer's Case* (1702), 2 Salk. 508; *Thomas* v. *Bennet* (1725), 2 P. Wms. 341; *Fowler* v. *Fowler* (1735), 3 P. Wms. 353; *Crichton* v. *Crichton*, [1896] 1 Ch. 870; *Horlock* v. *Wiggins* (1888), 39 Ch.D. 142.

sidered as at the date of the will, so that the presumption still applies if the debt is paid off in the testator's lifetime, and the legacy will not take effect.

(ii) The legacy must equal or exceed the debt. Although ther is a presumption of satisfaction if the legacy is equal to or exceeds the value of the debt, there is no presumption of even partial satisfaction if the legacy is less than the debt.[1] The only reported exception to this is *Hammond* v. *Smith*[2] where the testator informed the creditor that the legacy was to be taken in part payment of the debt, and he did not object.

(iii) The legacy must be as advantageous as the debt. It must be shown on the face of the will that the legacy will be as advantageous as the debt. The presumption does not therefore apply where the amount of the legacy, as in the case of a share of residue, does not appear from the will itself.[3] This is so even if the legacy does in fact turn out to be more beneficial. An example of a case where a legacy is not as advantageous as the debt is where the debt is secured, whereas the legacy is not.[4]

There is doubt as to the position where there is no special provision as to the date of payment. The general rule is that legacies are payable by the end of the executor's year,[5] and it is probably true that even if the will directs earlier payment, it cannot be enforced before the end of the executor's year.[6] In *Re Horlock, Calham* v. *Smith*[7] the testator owed £300, payable within three months of death, and left the creditor £400, without expressing time for payment. Stirling, J., held that the legacy was not as advantageous, so that there was no satisfaction. The logic of this view was overcome by Swinfen Eady, J., in *Re Rattenberry, Ray* v. *Grant*.[8] In general, a legacy does not carry interest[9] but Lord

---

[1] *Minuel* v. *Sarazine* (1730), Mos. 295; *Eastwood* v. *Vinke* (1731), 2 P. Wms. 613; *Gee* v. *Liddell* (1866), 35 Beav. 621.

[2] (1864), 33 Beav. 452.

[3] *Crompton* v. *Sale* (1729), 2 P. Wms. 553; *Barret* v. *Bechford* (1750), 1 Ves. Sen. 519; *Lady Thynne* v. *Earl of Glengall* (1848), 2 H.L. Cas. 131.

[4] *Re Stibbe, Cleverley* v. *Stibbe* (1946), 175 L.T. 198; cf. *Re Haves, Haves* v. *Haves*, [1951] 2 All. E.R. 928.

[5] See *post*, p. 496.

[6] *Pearson* v. *Pearson* (1802), 1 Sch. & Lef. 10; *Wood* v. *Penoyre* (1807), 13 Ves. 325; *Benson* v. *Maude* (1821), 6 Madd. 15; *Brooke* v. *Lewis* (1822), 6 Madd. 358.

[7] [1895] 1 Ch. 516.

[8] [1906] 1 Ch. 667.

[9] See *post*, p. 498.

Hardwicke had held in *Clark* v. *Sewell*[1] that a legacy in satisfaction of a debt carries interest from the date of death. This rule enabled Swinfen Eady, J., in *Re Rattenberry*, *Ray* v. *Grant* to hold that the legacy was as advantageous as the debt, and that therefore the debt was satisfied. This decision is clearly to be preferred; to follow *Re Horlock*, *Calham* v. *Smith* would, in effect, be virtually to destroy the rule.

If the debt itself carries interest under the agreement by which it was created, there will usually be some arrears of interest at the date of death. Suppose a debt of £1,000 carries interest at £10% payable half yearly in arrear on 1st January and 1st July in each year. Suppose also that the testator paid the interest due on 1st January and died on 1st April. He will then owe £25 interest. Does a legacy of £1,000 satisfy this debt? In *Fitzgerald* v. *National Bank, Ltd.*[2] it was held that for the purposes of the rule the "debt" was to be taken as the capital sum outstanding, so that provided the legacy was equal to the amount of the debt, the debt itself would be satisfied. A separate action would lie for the arrears of interest. The reasoning for this decision lacks conviction: it is based on the fact that at the time of the decision in *Talbot* v. *Duke of Shrewsbury*[3] which is often regarded, erroneously, as having established the doctrine, interest had to be sued for separately. But while the reasoning may not convince, the result is surely in accordance with common sense.

(iv) *Nature of debt and legacy.* Where there is a substantial difference in the nature of the debt and the legacy, there will be no satisfaction. So in *Eastwood* v. *Vinke*[4] a gift of land by will did not satisfy a debt of money. On somewhat similar reasoning, it was held in *Carr* v. *Eastabrooke*[5] that a legacy did not satisfy the amount outstanding on a negotiable instrument, for the latter may have come into the hands of a third party.

(v) *Contrary intention.* The rule will only operate in the absence of a contrary intention. Such a contrary intention may be expressed or implied. An example of the latter would be if the motive for

---

[1] (1744), 3 Atk. 96.
[2] [1929] 1 K.B. 394.
[3] (1714), Prec. Ch. 394.
[4] (1731), 2 P. Wms. 613.
[5] (1797), 3 Ves. 561.

making the gift could be construed, and that motive was other than to satisfy the debt.

A direction to pay debts, or to pay debts and legacies, will show a contrary intention sufficient to rebut the rule.[1] This must be borne in mind when drafting a will with this type of direction.

2. SATISFACTION OF PORTION DEBTS BY LEGACIES

a. *Nature of a portion*

A "portion" is a substantial provision for the child of the testator, or some other person to whom he stands *in loco parentis* made with the object of establishing the child in life. There are, therefore, two aspects:

    (i) relationship between donor and donee; and

    (ii) object of the gift.

The donee must be either the child of the testator, or the testator must stand *in loco parentis* to him. For this purpose, it is not necessary for the testator to adopt the child, or even necessarily to undertake all the obligations of parenthood. If the object of the gift satisfied the rule, a gift from a father will be presumed to be a portion. A gift from a mother would not previously have carried that presumption, but it is possible that in view of the altered social conditions, this may not now be the case.[2]

The object of the gift was described by Jessel, M.R., in *Taylor* v. *Taylor*[3] in these words: "I have always understood that an advancement by way of portion is something given by the parent to establish the child in life, or to make what is called a provision for him. . . . You may make the provision by way of marriage portion on the marriage of the child. You may make it on putting him into a profession or business in a variety of ways . . . or by a father giving a large sum to a child in one payment."

The occasion of making the gift is also important. Unless it is made on marriage, *prima facie* an advancement must be made in

---

[1] *Chancey's Case* (1717), 1 P. Wms. 408; *Horlock* v. *Wiggins* (1888), 39 Ch.D. 142; *Re Manners, Public Trustee* v. *Manners*, [1949] 2 All E.R. 201, at p. 204.

[2] See *Loades-Carter* v. *Loades-Carter*, unreported, but discussed in article at (1966), 110 Sol. 3, 683; the traditional view is stated in *Re Ashton, Ingram* v. *Papillon*, [1897] 2 Ch. 574.

[3] (1875), L.R. 20 Eq. 155, at pp. 157, 158.

early life.[1] The gift must be substantial, having regard both to the purpose for which it was intended and the size of the testator's estate.[2]

A portion debt is an obligation created by the testator, as under a covenant, with the same object as giving a portion.

b. *The rule*

There is a presumption that a portion debt will be satisfied by a legacy if the following conditions are present:

(i) the portion debt precedes the will;
(ii) there is no substantial difference between the nature of the debt and of the legacy; and
(iii) there is no contrary intention in the will.

The operation of the doctrine, which applies only where there is the relationship of parent to child, could in principle work to the advantage of strangers. Suppose, therefore, that the testator leaves £10,000 to be divided between his three children A, B and C and his nephew D. Suppose also that he had incurred a portion debt to B of £2,000. The *prima facie* effect of the doctrine is to satisfy B's entitlement by £2,000, so that A, C and D would each receive £3,000 and B £1,000. It was held, however, in *Meinertzagen* v. *Walters*[3] that where the residue is to be divided between children and strangers, the operation of the rule is not to increase the share of the stranger. Thus, on the same facts as in the example just given, the nephew D would receive his *prima facie* entitlement of £2,500, and the remaining £7,500 would be distributable as to £3,167 to each of A and C, and £1,166 to B.

In contradistinction to the satisfaction of ordinary debts by legacies, a portion debt can be satisfied *pro tanto* by a legacy of a smaller amount than the debt.[4] Where the will creates successive interests, the interest of the tenant for life can be satisfied, while the interest of the remainderman is unaffected. Thus, in *Lord Chichester* v. *Earl of Coventry*[5] Lord Romilly said[6] that if a father

---

[1] *Ibid.*, at p. 155.
[2] *Re Scott, Langton* v. *Scott*, [1903] 1 Ch. 1; *Re Hayward, Kerrod* v. *Hayward*, [1957] Ch. 528.
[3] (1872), 7 Ch. App. 670.
[4] *Warren* v. *Warren* (1783), 1 Bro. C.C. 305.
[5] (1867), L.R. 2 H.L. 71.
[6] *Ibid.*, at p. 91.

covenanted to settle £10,000 on his daughter for her life, with remainder to the children of the marriage, this would be satisfied so far as the daughter was concerned by a legacy of £10,000, although the interests of the children would be unaffected.

The differences between the nature of the portion debt and of the legacy sufficient to exclude the presumption may be either as to the nature of the asset, or the nature of the interest. In *Grave* v. *Earl of Salisbury*[1] it was held that where the portion debt is a covenant to pay money, and the will contains a devise of land, that will not give rise to the presumption, so that the child takes both.[2] Likewise, if one gift is absolute, and the other contingent this difference will be sufficient to rebut the presumption, unless the contingency was so remote that the testator thought that it should not be taken into account.[3]

c. *Effect of operation of rule*

Where the portion debt is still outstanding at the date of death, the beneficiary has the option either to take what is due to him in respect of the debt, or to take the gift under the will. Unless the benefit given by the will is greater, the beneficiary will usually wish to rely on the debt, for this will rank as a liability of the estate, and so not be subject to abatement in the event of insufficiency of assets to pay the creditors in full[4] or to the diminution in the size of the legacy by virtue of an order made under the Family Provision legislation.[5]

3. SATISFACTION OF LEGACIES BY PORTIONS

This rule is the corollary of the previous one: in this case the legacy comes first, and it is followed by the portion. If a portion is given before the will, the child takes both, for this must have been the intention of the testator in making a will in favour of the child after making that gift. This is not so, however, where the testator merely incurs a portion debt before making the will. Although the general position is the same as has just been discussed, there are certain differences.

---

[1] (1784), 1 Bro. C.C. 425.

[2] See also *Bellasis* v. *Uthwatt* (1737), 1 Atk. 426, at p. 428.

[3] *Powys* v. *Mansfield* (1837), 3 My. & Cr. 359, *per* Lord Cottenham at pp. 374, 375.

[4] See *ante*, p. 468.

[5] See *ante*, p. 206.

The general rule applies that if there is a substantial difference between the gift and the legacy, there is no satisfaction. An example of this difference occurs with subsequent marriage settlements. Suppose that a father gives a substantial benefit to his child by will, and that subsequently the child marries. If on the marriage of that child the father gives a portion to the child for life, with remainders over for his spouse or children, the legacy is adeemed. It was decided in *Earl of Durham* v. *Wharton*,[1] however, that if the will contains not an absolute gift, but a life interest, and on the subsequent marriage, the portion is given to the child for life, with different remainders over, the differences between the two are too great to permit the rule to apply.

Likewise the rule is prevented from operating for the benefit of strangers. Under the rule in *Re Heather*, *Pumfrey* v. *Fryer*,[2] the same type of calculation has to be made as was mentioned in connexion with *Meinertzagen* v. *Walters*.[3] Suppose, therefore, that the testator leaves his estate to be divided between his children A and B and X a stranger. Suppose also that he gives a portion of £3,000 to A and dies leaving a residuary estate of £12,000. X receives his one third share of £4,000. The basis of the calculation as between A and B is:

Total apparent shares of A and B		£8,000
Portion of A, to be brought into account		£3,000
		£11,000
A's one half share	£5,500	
Less: portion	£3,000	£2,500
B's one half share		£5,500
		£8,000

Although, therefore, the general position of the beneficiary is the same whether the will was made before or after the portion or portion debt, there is one important difference. Where the portion debt is incurred first, the beneficiary is, as has been said, entitled to exercise an option whether to rely on the debt, or to take under

---

[1] (1836), 10 Bli. N.S. 526.

[2] [1906] 2 Ch. 230.

[3] (1872), 7 Ch. App. 670; *ante*, p. 481.

the will. Where the will comes first, and the portion or portion debt comes later, the beneficiary has no such option: the effect of giving the portion has been to extinguish the legacy. In this type of case, therefore, it is more appropriate to speak of ademption of legacies by portions.

M. DOUBLE LEGACIES

Certain presumptions have been established to deal with the situation where the testator bequeaths two legacies to the same person, either by the same will, or by a will and codicil. The rules are:

a. where the testator says expressly or by implication that both legacies are to be payable, that intention prevails.[1]

b. where the legacies are

    (i) of unequal amounts;[2] *or*

    (ii) of a different nature, such as a pecuniary legacy and a share of residue;[3] *or*

    (iii) are expressed to be given for different reasons;[4] *or*

    (iv) are given by separate instruments, such as will and codicil,[5]

both are payable.

c. the only cases in which there is a presumption that only one legacy is payable are:

    (i) where they are of the same amount and are given by the same instrument; or

    (ii) where they are of the same amount and are given in different instruments but for the same motive.[6]

---

[1] *Re Silverston, Westminster Bank, Ltd.* v. *Kohler,* [1949] Ch. 270.
[2] *Re Davies, Davies* v. *Mackintosh,* [1957] 1 W.L.R. 922, at p. 925.
[3] *Kirkpatrick* v. *Bedford* (1878), 4 App. Cas. 96.
[4] *Hurst* v. *Beach* (1821), 5 Madd. 351.
[5] *Hurst* v. *Beach, supra; Re Davies, supra.*
[6] *Hurst* v. *Beach, supra.*

N. THE DOCTRINE OF ELECTION

1. THE RULE

Occasionally, either by accident or design, a testator gives his own property to a beneficiary, and purports to give some of the beneficiary's property to a third party. In this case, the beneficiary becomes subject to a general principle that a person cannot take under a will without conforming to all its provisions.[1] If, therefore, he is to take the testator's property left to him, he must also hand over his property which the testator has purported to dispose of by will, or he must compensate the third party to the value of the property that that third party would have received. But the beneficiary named in the will cannot be compelled to take any action under it, and he may disclaim his legacy.

Suppose, therefore, that Edward makes a will leaving £5,000 to Frank, and Frank's car, worth £2,000 to Geraldine. In this case, there are three possibilities open to Frank:

a. he may *disclaim the legacy under the will*. In this case he derives no benefit whatever from that gift[2] and keeps his car;

b. he may *"take under the will"*, namely accept the legacy of £5,000 and transfer the car to Geraldine; or

c. he may *"take against the will"*, namely accept the legacy of £5,000, retain the car, but pay to Geraldine £2,000 to compensate her for not receiving the car.

In both the second and third cases Frank is a net sum of £3,000 better off, and Geraldine receives either the asset or cash to the value of £2,000.

2. BASIS OF THE DOCTRINE

There have been three suggestions as to the basis of the rule.

a. *Implied condition*

The earliest view was that the testator gave his property to the recipient on the implied condition that the recipient would give

---

[1] *Codrington* v. *Codrington* (1875), L.R. 7 H.L. 854. See especially Lord Cairns at pp. 861, 862.

[2] With the result that it is usually only prudent to disclaim where the value of the gift under the will does not exceed the value of the property to be given to the third party.

his property to the third party.[1] While this may be a satisfactory explanation of the situation where the recipient elects to take under the instrument, the inadequacy of this view is seen where he elects to take against it. If the testator expressly imposes a condition that the recipient must give his property to the third party, then if the recipient does not do so, he is entitled to no benefit under the will. The example just given, however, shows that the recipient can insist on keeping his own property, merely compensating the third party for the value which he would have received.

b. *Presumed intention of the testator*

While in some cases the testator may actually intend to put the recipient to his election, the doctrine of election applies irrespective of the testator's actual intention, save that it will not apply where there is a clear contrary intention. In *Cooper* v. *Cooper*[2] Lord Cairns expressly said that the rule was not based either on the testator's intention as expressed or on his presumed intention. This view, that the doctrine is based on intenton, cannot therefore stand.

c. *"Equity"*

The most recent, and most satisfactory explanation is that it is a rule of Equity imposed as a matter of conscience in order to achieve a just result in the circumstances of the case. It was expressed by Buckley, J. in *Re Mengel's Will Trusts*[3] as "a doctrine by which equity fastens on the conscience of the person who is put to his election and refuses to allow him to take the benefit of a disposition contained in the will, the validity of which is not in question, except on certain conditions".[4]

3. WHEN THE DOCTRINE APPLIES

In order for the doctrine to apply, it must be shown that all of the following conditions are satisfied:

---

[1] *Noys* v. *Mordaunt* (1706), 2 Vern. 581; *Streatfield* v. *Streatfield* (1735), Cas. *temp.* Tabl. 176; *Ker* v. *Wauchope* (1819), 1 Bli. 1.

[2] (1874), L.R. 7 H.L. 53.

[3] [1962] Ch. 791.

[4] See also Lord Cairns in *Cooper* v. *Cooper* (1874), L.R. 7 H.L. 53, at p. 67; *Brown* v. *Gregson*, [1920] A.C. 860.

a. *The donor must give his own property to the recipient*

In *Bristow* v. *Warde*[1] a father had a power to appoint stock in favour of his children, the trust instrument providing that in default of his appointment the children were entitled equally. By his will the father purported to appoint part of the fund to persons who were not objects of the power. As he had not given any of his own property to the children, there was no case for election, with the result that they took under the appointment the part of the fund that had been appointed to them, and they took in default of appointment that part of the fund which had been invalidly appointed to the non-objects. On the other hand, in *Whistler* v. *Webster*[2] where the facts were essentially the same except that the testator also gave his own property to the children, the children were put to their election, whether to take the father's own property under the will, and allow the appointment to the non-object to stand.[3]

b. *The recipient's property must be freely alienable*

No case for election arises where the recipient is not able to dispose of his property which the testator has purported to leave. In *Re Lord Chesham, Cavendish* v. *Dacre*[4], Lord Chesham was the tenant for life of certain chattels subject to a settlement. The testator left his own property to Lord Chesham, his eldest son, and the chattels to his younger sons. Chitty, J. held that because Lord Chesham could not dispose of the chattels, he was entitled to take the benefit under the will and to keep the chattels. Where, however, the recipient does not own the whole of an asset, but does own absolutely a share in that asset, he can be made to elect to the extent of that share. Thus, in *Re Dicey, Julian* v. *Dicey*,[5] the defendant was entitled to a beneficial one half share in realty. The testatrix gave her own property to the defendant, and that realty to the plaintiff. The court held that the defendant had to elect, as she could assign to the plaintiff her one half share in the realty.

---

[1] (1794), 2 Ves. 336; see also *Re Fowler's Trust* (1859), 27 Beav. 362; *Fox* v. *Charlton* (1862), 6 L.T. 743.

[2] (1794), 2 Ves. 367.

[3] See also *Reid* v. *Reid* (1858), 25 Beav. 469; *Re Fletcher's Settlement Trusts*, [1936] 2 All E.R. 236.

[4] (1886), 31 Ch.D. 466.

[5] [1957] Ch. 145.

c. *Both gifts must be in the same instrument*

The testator must give his own property to the recipient and the recipient's property to a third party in the same instrument. Otherwise, the recipient could take the benefit under one instrument, and ignore or disclaim under the other.

d. *The testator must intend to dispose of what he does not own*

There is a strong presumption that a man has only intended to dispose of what he himself owns.[1] If, therefore, he owns an interest in property, and uses words which are capable of being construed either as leaving that interest only, or the whole property, they will carry the narrower meaning.[2] It will, then, rarely be possible to show that the doctrine should operate where the testator does in fact own some interest in the property given to the third party. An example of a case where the doctrine did apply, however, is *Padbury* v. *Clark*.[3] In that case the testator owned a moiety of a freehold house. In his will he gave some of his own property to the owner of the other moiety, and the whole house to a third person. The owner of the other moiety was put to his election.

Although the testator must intend to dispose of the property, it is not necessary for him to be aware that he does not own it.

e. *Must the claim be outside the will?*

In *Wollaston* v. *King*[4] James, V.-C. said that the rule of election "is to be applied as between a gift under a will and a claim *dehors* the will, and adverse to it, and is not to be applied as between one clause in a will and another clause in the same will". This is because where there are two gifts in the same will, any inconsistency between them will usually be resolved by the principles of construction.

The facts of *Wollaston* v. *King*[5] were that the testatrix had a power of appointment over property in favour of her children,

---

[1] See e.g., Turner, L.J. in *Evans* v. *Evans* (1863), 2 New Rep. 408, at p. 401. Also *Re Harris, Leacroft* v. *Harris*, [1909] 2 Ch. 206; *Re Booker, Booker* v. *Booker* (1886), 54 L.T. 239.

[2] Lord Eldon in *Lord Rancliffe* v. *Lady Parkyns* (1818), 6 Dow. 149, at p. 185; Page Wood, V.C. in *Howells* v. *Jenkins* (1863), 2 J. & H. 706, at p. 713.

[3] (1850), 2 Mac. & G. 298. See also *Miller* v. *Thurgood* (1864), 33 Beav. 496; *Wilkinson* v. *Dent* (1871), 6 Ch. App. 339.

[4] (1869), L.R. 8 Eq. 165, p. 174.

[5] (1869), L.R. 8 Eq. 165.

who were also entitled in default of appointment. She appointed £5,000 to her son on certain trusts, and the remainder of the fund to her daughters. She also gave her own property to her daughters. The gift to the son was void for perpetuity, so that the whole fund passed to the daughters under the residuary appointment. James, V.-C. said: "It would seem a very strange thing that in construing the same instrument the Court, dealing with a clause in which a fund is expressed to be given partly to A. and partly to B., should hold that the gift to A., being void, the testator's intention is that B. should take the whole; and then coming to another clause in which another fund is given to B., and no mention of A. at all, it should hold that there is an implied intention that he should take."

Doubt as to the extent of the principle has been thrown by the difficult decision in *Re Macartney, MacFarlane* v. *Macartney*.[3] The testator held 95 per cent of the issued shares in a company, Macartney McElroy, Ltd. That company held 90 per cent of the issued shares in Malta Tramways, Ltd. The only asset of Malta Tramways Ltd. of any value was a holding of £3,000 colonial stock, which was registered in the name of the testator as nominee for Malta Tramways. By his will the testator bequeathed the holding of colonial stock to his daughter Maggie, and gave his shares in Macartney McElroy, Ltd. to his seven children, including Maggie. As the stock belonged to Malta Tramways she could not take it, and Maggie sought compensation from the other children. If the testator had left the shares in Macartney McElroy, Ltd. to Malta Tramways, Ltd., and the stock to Maggie, Malta Tramways would clearly have been put to their election. Because of the similarity of shareholdings, Neville, J. appears to have ignored the existence of the companies, regarding the children as being in the same position as Malta Tramways. On this basis he required the children to elect, and, in the event, to compensate Maggie for the stock which she did not receive.

If the case is viewed in this way, there appears to be no conflict with *Wollaston* v. *King*, but the case can also be seen, and with less ingenuity, as a case where both claims arose under the will. Whichever way the case is regarded, its difficulties are apparent. It is difficult to justify the equation of the position of the children

---

[1] [1918] 1 Ch. 300.

with Malta Tramways, both because of the separate existence of the companies, and because of the fact that the shareholders in Macartney McElroy, Ltd. held only 95 per cent of 90 per cent of the colonial stock. *Re Macartney, MacFarlane* v. *Macartney*[1] has been criticised[2] but the result does seem to accord with what the testator intended, namely that Maggie should have the stock and that the children generally should have the shares less the value of the stock represented in them. The decision shows that the doctrine will be extended beyond its normal limits where it is necessary in order to achieve a just result.[3]

4. METHOD AND TIME OF ELECTION

Election may be express or by implication. In order to be held to have elected by implication, however, it must be shown that the beneficiary was in possession of all the relevant facts.[4] Where he has knowledge of these facts, acts such as receiving the income, or dealing with the property given under the will, may show an implied intention to take under the will.[5]

Where election is made against the will, the amount of compensation which has to be paid is ascertained according to the value of the asset at the date of death of the testator.[6] If the will prescribes the time by which the election must be made, and person does not elect within that time, he is deemed to have elected against the instrument.[7]

---

[1] [1918] 1 Ch. 300.

[2] See e.g. Pettit, Equity and the Law of Trusts, 2nd ed., pp. 511, 512.

[3] For a further example of its extension, see *Re Allen's Estate*, [1945] 2 All E.R. 264.

[4] *Pusey* v. *Desbouverie* (1734), 3 P. Wms. 315; *Kidney* v. *Coussmaker* (1806), 12 Ves. 136.

[5] *Dewar* v. *Maitland* (1886), L.R. 2 Eq. 834; *Re Shepherd, Harris* v. *Shepherd*, [1943] Ch. 8.

[6] *Re Hancock, Hancock* v. *Pawson*, [1905] 1 Ch. 16.

[7] *Dillon* v. *Parker* (1818), 1 Swan 359, at p. 381.

CHAPTER 31

EXTENT OF BENEFIT

A. LEGACIES AND DEVISES

1. TYPES OF LEGACY

It is customary to divide legacies into five categories, and it is proposed first to explain these categories and then to indicate the importance of the distinctions between them.

The categories of legacy are:

a. *specific legacy*, namely a gift of an asset which forms part of the testator's estate at the date of death, and is distinguished from the totality of the testator's assets, or from the totality of the residue. The will must show an intention that it should pass *in specie*. The subject matter of the gift may be either of one or more specified assets, or such assets as come within a description sufficient to include fluctuating items.[1] Examples of specific legacies are "my book to Andrew", "the money in my bag to Basil",[2] "my books to Clarence",[3] and "my 3,000 I.C.I. shares to Deborah".[4]

b. *demonstrative legacy*, which is gift of a general, that is, non-specific nature, directed to be paid from a particular fund.[5] Thus, a gift of "£1,000 out of my account with Coutts Bank"[6] is a demonstrative legacy. The essential distinction between a specific legacy and a demonstrative legacy is one of intention: in the case of a specific legacy the testator shows an intention that the beneficiary shall receive only the specified asset, so

---

[1] *Castle* v. *Fox* (1871), L.R. 11 Eq. 542. See especially at p. 552.

[2] *Lawson* v. *Stitch* (1738), 1 Atk. 507.

[3] See *Castle* v. *Fox*, *supra*.

[4] This is specific because of the inclusion of the word "my". See *post*, p. 492, and *Re Tetsall, Foyster* v. *Tetsall*, [1961] 2 All E.R. 801.

[5] *Kirby* v. *Potter* (1799), 4 Ves. 748; *Re Webster, Goss* v. *Webster*, [1937] 1 All E.R. 602.

[6] *Fowler* v. *Willoughby* (1825), 2 Sim. & St. 354.

that if it ceases to exist at the date of death, he receives nothing.[1] In the case of a demonstrative legacy, the testator indicates an intention that the gift shall be taken *primarily* from the specified fund, but that any balance can be taken from the residue in the event of deficiency. In *Re Webster, Goss* v. *Webster*,[2] for example, there was a gift of £3,000 from a specified business. At the testator's death the business was worth less than £3,000. Had the gift been specific, the beneficiary would have received only the value of the business, but in this case, as it was held on a true construction to be a demonstrative legacy, the beneficiary received the value of the business, and the deficiency was then made good to him from the remainder of the estate.

c. *general legacy*, which is a gift of an item irrespective of whether the testator owned such an item at the date of his death, or at the date when the will is made. Thus, a gift of "a Rolls Royce motor car to Edwina" will be a general legacy. The testator may never have owned such a motor car, but the effect of the will is to require his executors to purchase a motor car of this description for the beneficiary. Gifts of stocks and shares are *prima facie* general and not specific gifts, although they may be specific if they are described as "*my* shares in I.C.I.".

d. *pecuniary legacy*, which is basically a gift of money. A gift of money may alternatively be a specific legacy or a demonstrative legacy. Thus "£1,000 to Frederick" is an example of a pecuniary legacy; "£1,000 out of my National Savings Certificates to Georgina" is a demonstrative legacy; and "the £1,000 which William owes to me to Harriet" is a specific legacy. It follows that where a gift of money is not specific or demonstrative, it is general.

For the purposes of the Administration of Estates Act 1925, however, the expression "pecuniary legacy" has a much wider significance. It is defined[3] to include a general legacy, an annuity, and a demonstrative legacy in so far as the gift is not discharged out of the designated property.

e. *residuary gift*, is what remains after the payment of all debts, liabilities, expenses and other legacies.

---

[1] See *ante*, p. 461.
[2] [1937] 1 All E.R. 602.
[3] Administration of Estates Act 1925, s. 55 (1) (ix).

With regard to devises, it used to be said that all devises are specific.[1] This is no longer the case and devises are now specific "my freehold cottage The Nest, Swaffham, Suffolk to Isobel"; or general "all my freehold land to Julie"; or residuary "all my houses not otherwise disposed of by this my will to Kenneth".

2. IMPORTANCE OF CLASSIFICATION

The difficulty with this topic is that different classifications are relevant for different purposes, and it may be useful to summarise the position here in general terms. It is stressed that this summary is only in general terms and in many cases the rules themselves admit of certain exceptions.

PURPOSE	TYPE OF LEGACY	SEE
1. Definition under will	Any, according to terms of will	below
2. Ademption	Doctrine applies to specific legacies only	p. 461
3. Abatement	Order for abatement is: a. residuary gifts b. pecuniary gifts (in wide A.E.A. sense) c. specific gifts	p. 468
4. Interest	Generally payable from death on specific legacies but not on pecuniary legacies	p. 498
5. Right of beneficiary to demand payment in lieu	a. general gifts; and b. annuities in case of capital deficiency	below p. 507

It is necessary here to deal only with the first and last of these items. In the first case, the testator may himself give a definition, expressly or impliedly, in the will, and if he does, that will prevail. Thus, in *Re Compton, Vaughan* v. *Smith*[2] the testator gave a gift of shares in a form which was clearly specific. He then included that legacy in the expression "as general and not as specific legacies". It was held that the legacy was, by virtue of these words, to be treated as general.

In the case of a general gift, the personal representatives are, in the absence of a contrary direction in the will, under an obliga-

---

[1] *Giles* v. *Melsom* (1873), L.R. 6 H.L. 24, at p. 30; *Re Ridley, Nicholson* v. *Nicholson*, [1950] Ch. 415, at p. 421.

[2] [1914] 2 Ch. 119.

tion either to purchase such item as is included in the gift if there is no article of that description in the estate, or to pay to the beneficiary that amount in lieu. In this case, the beneficiary is also entitled to interest on that sum at the rate of £4% from the expiration of the executor's year.[1]

B. ACCELERATION

1. THE GENERAL RULE

The doctrine of acceleration applies to the case where interests are conferred in succession—such as, to husband for life, with remainder to his brother—and for some reason the gift to the first person entitled determines before the time envisaged by the testator. This may be because the first person entitled dies, or because he disclaims his life interest, or because he witnessed the will, or because it was revoked by codicil, or for any other reason. The principle of acceleration regards the interest of the next person entitled as being the whole interest in the asset or property subject to the prior right of the first person entitled so that when it appears that the first person cannot take, the next person's interest is at once accelerated. So in *Re Davies, Davies* v. *Mackintosh*[2] there was a gift to A for life with remainder to his issue. When A disclaimed, Vaisey, J., held that the gift to the issue was accelerated. Likewise, in *Jull* v. *Jacobs*[3] where there was a gift to A for life, with remainder to the children of A, and A could not take because she witnessed the will, Malins, V.C., held that the children's interest was accelerated.

In some circumstances the interest of the remainderman may not be vested absolutely, but vested subject to divesting, e.g., to A for life, with remainder to B, but if C shall have a child, then to that child. If A is unable to take, the interest of B will be accelerated, and he will be entitled to the income, but distribution of the capital must be delayed until it is known whether C will have a child.[4]

---

[1] See *post*, p. 499.
[2] [1957] 3 All E.R. 52.
[3] (1876), 3 Ch.D. 703.
[4] *Re Taylor, Lloyds Bank* v. *Jones*, [1957] 3 All E.R. 56.

2. ACCELERATION PREVENTED

The words of the will may suggest that the interest of the remainderman is to take effect at a specified time in the future. If, on a true construction, this is what the testator intended, acceleration will be prevented. Thus, if the testator makes a gift to A until 1980, and in 1980 to B, this will probably be construed as meaning that B can take no benefit until 1980. If A cannot take, the income of the property will belong to the residuary beneficiary until 1980.

The courts are, however, very reluctant to adopt a construction which prevents the acceleration of the remainderman's interest. If, therefore, there is a gift to A for life and after A's death to B, the words "after A's death" will be treated, in the absence of a clear contrary expression, as meaning "after the termination of A's interest". So that if, for example, A disclaims, B's interest is accelerated.[1] This approach is an exception to the general rule of construction that words carry their natural meaning.

3. ACCELERATION AND CLASS GIFTS

Suppose the gift is to A for life with remainder to such of his children who attain the age of 21. If A enjoys the property until his death, the class will then close, to admit all children then alive who do in fact attain 21.[2] But now suppose that in his lifetime A disclaims and has children after the disclaimer: are those after-born children excluded from the class?

In *Re Davies, Davies* v. *Mackintosh*[3] Vaisey, J., held, on similar facts, that the interest of the class was accelerated, and the closing rules should be applied as at the date of disclaimer to exclude after-born children.[4] However, in *Re Kebty-Fletcher's Will Trusts*[5] Stamp, J., doubted whether *Re Davies, Davies* v. *Mackintosh* was correctly decided, and refused to follow it in the case of a disclaimer of the prior interest. Children born during the lifetime of A were held entitled to be members of the class.

---

[1] *Re Flower's Settlement Trusts*, [1957] 1 All E.R. 462.
[2] See *ante*, p. 159.
[3] [1957] 3 All E.R. 52.
[4] See also *Jull* v. *Jacobs* (1876), 3 Ch.D. 703; *Re Townsend's Estate* (1886), 34 Ch.D. 357.
[5] [1969] 1 Ch. 339.

The doubts expressed as to the correctness of *Re Davies* were reinforced when, in *Re Harker's Will Trusts, Kean* v. *Harker*,[1] Goff, J., refused to follow *Re Davies*. A fund was held upon trust for a father for life, with remainder to the children who should attain 21. During his lifetime he surrendered his interest in the fund to his children. At that time, he had one son over 21 and two under that age. The eldest son claimed that the class closing rule applied as soon as the father's interest was surrendered, so that his share of the fund could be distributed forthwith. Goff, J., rejected this, and held that the class remained open until the death of the father. The basis of his decision[2] is that it would be wrong to allow one person by his unilateral act to defeat the interest of others, or, applied to these facts, that the father by the deed of release should be able to defeat the interest of children born after the execution of the deed.

C. TIME FOR PAYMENT

1. LEGACIES

The period of one year from the testator's death is known as the executor's year. During this year the executor must ascertain the assets and liabilities of the deceased, so that he can make arrangements for the discharge of liabilities and the distribution of the remainder of the estate.[3] Although this does not mean that the estate must be fully administered by the end of that year— this may be impossible because of complications affecting the assets, or difficulty in the construction of the will—the converse is true, namely that a beneficiary cannot compel the representative to make payment before the end of that year. Accordingly, any direction for payment at any time before the end of the year takes effect as if it were a direction to pay at the end of the year. So, in *Brooke* v. *Lewis*[4] the testator directed certain legacies to be

---

[1] [1969] 3 All E.R. 1.
[2] *Ibid.*, at p. 4.
[3] *Garthshore* v. *Chalie* (1804), 10 Ves. 1; *Re Tankard, Tankard* v. *Midland Bank Executor and Trustee Co., Ltd.*, [1942] Ch. 69.
[4] (1882), 6 Madd. 358.

paid within six months from his death, and directed the residue to be divided among such of certain named persons who were living at the time of distribution. If the obligation to distribute arose at the expiration of six months from death, the persons living at that time would have taken the residue. It was held, however, that only those living at the end of the year from death were entitled, as that was the time when the obligation came into force.[1]

This rule is expressed in Administration of Estates Act 1925, s. 44, which provides that "a personal representative is not bound to distribute the estate of the deceased before the expiration of one year from the death". This is, however, subject to sub-s. 36 (10). It is explained towards the end of this chapter that a personal representative may transfer to a beneficiary real and leasehold property by means of an assent, and that he may require the beneficiary to give security for outstanding liabilities before giving the assent. Sub-section 36 (10), however, provides that a personal representative must not delay in giving an assent to the person entitled where reasonable arrangements have been made for discharging the liabilities.

Subject to this exception, personal representatives cannot be compelled to make payment before the end of the executor's year, although they may do so if they so wish.[2] Where the estate is being administered by solicitors, it is often a very good advertisement for the firm to make payment of the pecuniary legacies, or at least a payment on account, as soon as possible after the grant is obtained. Where, however, a claim may be made under the Family Provision legislation,[3] it may well be inadvisable to distribute much of the estate too early.[4]

2. ANNUITIES

The general rule applies to annuities left by will, so that the first sum becomes payable at the end of the executor's year.[5] Some problems can arise with regard to the calculation of the first payment. The rules are:

(i) in the absence of a contrary direction in the will, annuities

---

[1] See also *Benson* v. *Maude* (1821), 6 Madd. 15.
[2] *Pearson* v. *Pearson* (1802), 1 Sch. & Lef. 10; *Angerstein* v. *Martin* (1823), Turn. & R. 232; *Garthshore* v. *Chalie* (1804), 10 Ves. 1.
[3] See *ante*, p. 206.
[4] *Re Simson, Simson* v. *National Provincial Bank, Ltd.*, [1950] Ch. 38.
[5] *Re Friend, Friend* v. *Young* (No. 2) (1898), 78 L.T. 222.

commence at death and are payable yearly in arrear. Accordingly, the first payment made at the end of the executor's year is in respect of the year from the testator's death.

(ii) Accordingly, if without further direction there is a gift in the will of an annuity of £52 p.a. to Alfred, the first payment he receives is of £52 at the end of one year.

(iii) If the annuity is directed to commence at some date within the executor's year, the calculation is made from the date directed, although payment need not be made until the end of the year. Thus, if there is a gift by will of a testator dying on 1 January of an annuity of £52 to Bertie, to be payable three-monthly to commence three months after death, the first payment which becomes due is in respect of the period 1 April to 30 June. The executors may pay then, or they may defer payment until 1 January in the following year, when a total of £39 will be due.[1]

D. INTEREST AND INCOME

1. DISTINCTION

This section is concerned with the extent to which a beneficiary is entitled to receive income from an asset between the date of death and the date when it is actually transferred to him; and the extent to which a pecuniary legatee is entitled to receive interest on his legacy during that period. Interest is a calculation, usually at 4%, on the amount of the legacy, and, where the legatee is entitled to interest, it is payable whether or not the estate actually receives any income. Income is the actual income produced by an asset, and is payable only to the extent that it is so earned.

The rules are complicated, and it is necessary to consider each type of gift.

2. GIFTS OF REALTY

The testator can make a gift of the income produced by any asset, including realty, from the date of death to the date of transfer. He could, for example, give land to Angela, but direct

---

[1] *Houghton* v. *Franklin* (1823), 1 Sim. & St. 390; *Byrne* v. *Healy* (1828), 2 Mol. 94; *Irvin* v. *Ironmonger* (1831), 2 Russ. & M. 531; *Williams* v. *Wilson* (1865), 5 New Rep. 267.

that the income derived from it during the course of administration should belong to the residuary beneficiary. Subject to this, and to any other contrary direction in the will, the person entitled to realty is entitled also to the income which it produces from the date of death. This applies whether the gift is specific or residuary,[1] and whether the gift is vested or contingent.[2]

3. SPECIFIC GIFTS OF PERSONALTY

A specific gift of personalty also carries with it the income which the asset produces, subject to any direction in the will to the contrary. This is so whether the gift is vested[3] or contingent,[4] and whether it is a present or future gift.[5] The rule is not confined to income in the accounting sense, and includes any accretion derived from the asset. Thus, if there is a specific gift of shares, the beneficiary is entitled not only to the shares themselves, and to the dividends,[6] but also to any bonus and rights issues.[7]

4. GENERAL AND DEMONSTRATIVE LEGACIES

a. *The principle*

It is necessary to draw a distinction between two periods of time. The first is the period of one year from the date of death, when, generally, interest is not payable on general and demonstrative legacies.[8] The second period is that following the first year from the death, in which interest is generally payable. A legacy is normally payable at the end of the executor's year[9] and interest becomes due from the end of that year in order to compensate the beneficiary for failure to pay him the legacy by

---

[1] Law of Property Act 1925, s. 175 (1).

[2] *Ibid.*

[3] *Barrington* v. *Tristam* (1801), 6 Ves. 345; *Bristow* v. *Bristow* (1842), 5 Beav. 289; *Re Marten, Shaw* v. *Marten*, [1901] 1 Ch. 370; *Re Jacob, M'Coy* v. *Jacob*, [1919] 1 I.R. 134.

[4] Law of Property Act 1925, s. 175 (1); *Sleech* v. *Thorington* (1754), 2 Ves. Sen. 561; *Clive* v. *Clive* (1854), Kay 600.

[5] L.P.A., 1925, s. 175 (1).

[6] *Re Joel, Johnson* v. *Joel*, [1936] 2 All E.R. 962.

[7] *Re Edwards, Newbery* v. *Edwards*, [1918] 1 Ch. 142; *Re Bate, Public Trustee* v. *Bate*, [1938] 4 All E.R. 218.

[8] *Webster* v. *Hale* (1803), 8 Ves. 410; *Bourke* v. *Ricketts* (1804), 10 Ves. 330; *Wood* v. *Penoyre* (1807), 13 Ves. 325; *Marquis of Hertford* v. *Lord Lowther* (1846), 9 Beav. 266; *Re Lord's Estate, Lord* v. *Lord* (1867), 2 Ch. App. 782.

[9] See *ante*, p. 496.

the due date. The right to interest is, therefore, not treated as an example of the testator's bounty, but as a question of fairness.[1]

To this general principle there are numerous exceptions.

b. *Exceptions*

Interest is payable from death in the following cases:

(i) Legacy to child of testator

Where the testator gives a legacy to his child, then, if certain conditions are satisfied, the law assumes that the legacy was intended for the maintenance of the child, and it will carry interest from the date of death. The conditions are:

a. the legacy is given to the child of the testator, or to some other child to whom he stood *in loco parentis*;[2]

b. the child is an infant;[3]

c. the child is entitled to the legacy either upon attaining the age of 18, or marrying under that age;[4]

d. the legacy is expressed to be payable to the child, and not to others, such as trustees, on his behalf;[5]

e. the will contains no other provision for his maintenance.

Subject to these conditions being satisfied, the legacy will carry interest from death, even if it is contingent.

(ii) Legacy for maintenance of other children

Where the testator gives a legacy to children not coming within the head just dealt with, and he shows an intention that it shall be used for the maintenance of that child, the legacy will carry interest from the date of death. Thus it may be used for the maintenance of strangers. Where a legacy comes within the former category, the law will presume an intention that it is to be used for maintenance, so that it will carry interest, but in the latter case it is necessary to show an intention to use the legacy for maintenance.

---

[1] *Re Wyles, Foster v. Wyles*, [1938] Ch. 313; see *post*, p. 505.

[2] *Wilson v. Maddison* (1843), 2 Y. & C. Ch. Cas. 372.

[3] *Raven v. Waite* (1818), 1 Swan. 553; *Wall v. Wall* (1847), 15 Sim. 513.

[4] *Re Pollock, Rugsley v. Pollock*, [1943] Ch. 338.

[5] *Re Medlock, Ruffle v. Medlock* (1886), 55 L.J. Ch. 738; *Re Pollock, Pugsley v. Pollock*, [1943] Ch. 338.

(iii) Legacy in satisfaction of debt

It was said in *Clark* v. *Sewell*[1] that where the legacy is in satisfaction of a debt, interest is always allowed from death. While this is clearly fair if the debt was payable at death, the rule may not apply if the debt itself was interest free and not payable until some time after death.

(iv) Legacy charged on realty

This exception applies only where the legacy is charged on realty, and not merely on land which is regarded as converted into personalty under a trust for sale.[2] The legacy bears interest from death.

c. *Future legacies*

A legacy might not be payable until some future date, either because the will is worded to that effect, or because the nature of the property makes it impracticable to make the payment earlier. Where the will expressly provides that the legacy is not to be payable until some future date, interest runs only from that date. This is so whether a particular date is specified,[3] or whether the legacy is only to be payable if an event occurs.[4] It is generally considered that if the will specifies that the legacy is to be payable only upon the happening of an event, and that event actually occurs before the death of the testator, then the legacy is treated as an ordinary legacy, and interest is payable from the end of the executor's year.[5]

Where payment is delayed because of the nature of the assets, different considerations apply. Suppose, for example, that the only asset out of which the legacy can be paid is a reversionary interest, and that it is not practicable to realise the asset before it falls into possession. In general, the ordinary rule applies, so

---

[1] (1744), 3 Atk. 96.

[2] *Pearson* v. *Pearson* (1802), 1 Sch. & Lef. 10; c.f. *Turner* v. *Buck* (1874), L.R. 18 Eq. 301.

[3] *Thomas* v. *A.-G.* (1837), 2 Y. & C. Ex. 525; *Donovan* v. *Needham* (1846), 9 Beav. 164; *Re Gyles, Gibbon* v. *Chaytor*, [1907] 1 I.R. 65; *Re White, White* v. *Shenton* (1909), 101 L.T. 780.

[4] *Holmes* v. *Crispe* (1849), 18 L.J. Ch. 439; *Re Lord's Estate, Lord* v. *Lord* (1867), 2 Ch. App. 782.

[5] *Re Palfreeman, Public Trustee* v. *Palfreeman*, [1914] 1 Ch. 877; cf. *Pickwick* v. *Gibbes* (1839), 1 Beav. 271; *Coventry* v. *Higgins* (1844), 14 Sim. 30.

that the interest is payable from the end of the executor's year.[1] The beneficiary is not to suffer because of the form of the assets. However, this is subject to the rule that the testator may show a contrary intention, and if in fact he indicates that the legacy is not to be payable until the asset falls in, interest only runs from that date.[2]

d. *Contingent legacies*

It has been shown[3] that in the case of *specific* bequests, the rules are the same whether the gift is vested or contingent. This is not so with general legacies. In general, a contingent general legacy does not carry interest until the contingency has happened.[4] This is, however, subject to a contrary intention on the part of the testator, and such a contrary intention will be assumed if the testator directs the legacy to be set aside for the benefit of the legatee. In that case, the general rule applies.[5]

e. *Vested legacies subject to divesting*

Where a legacy is vested, but is subject to divesting, the legatee is entitled to interest in accordance with the ordinary rules until the defeasance occurs.[6]

f. *Contrary intention*

The rules so far discussed are subject to contrary directions by the testator. So, if the testator directs that a legacy shall be paid on a specific date, even although it is in the executor's year, interest runs from that date.[7] But very clear evidence of intention that interest should run from a date earlier than the end of

---

[1] *Re Blachford, Blachford v. Worsley* (1884), 27 Ch.D. 676.

[2] *Holmes v. Crispe* (1849), 18 L.J. Ch. 439; *Re Lord's Estate, Lord v. Lord* (1867), 2 Ch. App. 782.

[3] See *ante*, p. 499.

[4] *Wyndham v. Wyndham* (1789), 3 Bro. C.C. 58; *Rawlins v. Rawlins* (1796), 2 Cox Eq. Cas. 425; *Re George* (1877), 5 Ch.C. 837; *Re Dickson, Hill v. Grant* (1885), 29 Ch.D. 331; *Re Inman, Inman v. Rolls*, [1893] 3 Ch. 518.

[5] *Kidman v. Kidman* (1871), 40 L.J. Ch. 359; *Re Medlock, Ruffle v. Medlock* (1886), 55 L.J. Ch. 738; *Re Inman, Inman v. Rolls*, [1893] 3 Ch. 518; *Re Clements, Clements v. Pearsall*, [1894] 1 Ch. 665; *Re Snaith, Snaith v. Snaith* (1894), 71 L.T. 318; *Re Woodin, Woodin v. Glass*, [1895] 2 Ch. 309.

[6] *Re Buckley's Trusts* (1883), 22 Ch.D. 583.

[7] *Harrison v. Rhodes* (1753), 1 Lee 197; *Lord Londesborough v. Somerville* (1854), 19 Beav. 295; *Re Pollock, Rugsley v. Pollock*, [1943] Ch. 338.

the executor's year is required. Thus, interest will only run from the end of that year even if the legacy is directed to be paid "as soon as possible", and there are funds available to pay it.[1]

5. RESIDUARY GIFTS OF PERSONALTY

a. *Vested gifts*

A residuary beneficiary with a vested interest is not entitled to interest, but he is entitled to the actual income produced by the estate, to which no other legatee is entitled.

b. *Contingent gifts*

In general, a contingent gift of personalty, or of realty and personalty, carries the intermediate income,[2] and it has been shown that this is also the case where there is a contingent residuary gift of realty.[3] However, the residuary beneficiary is not entitled to the income arising after the expiration of a trust for accumulation.[4] In this case, the income is undisposed of, and devolves as on intestacy.

c. *Future gifts*

A future gift of residue does not, in principle, carry the intermediate income,[5] so that, unless the income is disposed of by the will, it is undisposed of, and passes as on intestacy.[6]

6. ANNUITIES

In principle, an annuity is a series of legacies,[7] and as interest is paid on legacies which are overdue, it would appear that it ought to be paid on overdue annuity payments. However, in *Re Hiscoe, Hiscoe* v. *Waite*,[8] Kekewich, J., after reviewing the

---

[1] *Webster* v. *Hale* (1803), 8 Ves. 410; *Benson* v. *Maude* (1821), 6 Madd. 15.

[2] *Re Dumble, Williams* v. *Murrell* (1883), 23 Ch.D. 360; *Re Burton's Will, Bank* v. *Heaven*, [1892] 2 Ch. 38; *Re Taylor, Smart* v. *Taylor*, [1901] 2 Ch. 134; *Re Mellor, Alvarez* v. *Dodgson*, [1922] 1 Ch. 312.

[3] See *ante*, p. 499.

[4] *Re Ransome's Will Trusts, Moberley* v. *Ransome*, [1957] Ch. 348.

[5] *Bective* v. *Hodgson* (1864), 10 H.L. Cas. 656.

[6] *Re Gillett's Will Trusts, Barclays Bank, Ltd.* v. *Gillett*, [1950] Ch. 102; *Re Geering, Gulliver* v. *Geering*, [1964] Ch. 136.

[7] Per Cross, J., in *Re Berkeley, Inglis* v. *Countess of Berkeley*, [1967] 3 All E.R. 170 at p. 176.

[8] (1902), 71 L.J. Ch. 347; see at pp. 349-351.

authorities, held that interest on annuity payments was only to be paid in exceptional circumstances, and this was followed by the Court of Appeal in *Re Berkeley, Inglis v. Countess of Berkeley*,[1] although at first instance Cross, J., observed[2] that whatever the reason may have been for preventing the payment of interest, "it no longer obtains, and the rule is one that I at least would be glad to see swept away by the Law Commission in some tidying up operation". An example of an exceptional circumstance in which interest is payable is where the non-payment of the annuity is due to the fault of the person entitled to the surplus income.[3]

7. ANCILLARY ASPECTS

a. *Rate of interest*

Where interest is payable, it is normally calculated at the rate of £4 per cent.[4] Where, however, the testator is the parent of the beneficiary, or stands *in loco parentis* to him, the rate of interest is £5 per cent. This is absurdly low, particularly in times when it is possible to lay out funds on security to show a return in excess of 12%. Fairly recently, the Privy Council[5] has shown a change of approach, by indicating that no fixed rates should be laid down, and that the proper criterion is the rate which could have been obtained by the beneficiary had the funds been in his hands. While, however, the courts can adopt a flexible approach, it is necessary for a rate to be prescribed which all executors can apply without recourse to the courts. The objection is not, therefore, to having a fixed rate, but to having an artificially low rate. The interest rate ought to be made to vary with the cost of money, as by linking it to the Bank of England Minimum Lending Rate for the time being.

b. *The nature of the right to interest*

In *Re Wyles, Foster v. Wyles*,[6] Farwell, J., was concerned with the nature of the right to interest. In that case the testator gave various legacies, including legacies to two nephews, but he included in his will a provision that if the estate should not be

---

[1] [1968] Ch. 744; [1968] 3 All E.R. 364.

[2] [1967] 3 All E.R. 170, at p. 177.

[3] *Ibid.*

[4] *Re Campbell, Campbell v. Campbell,* [1893] 3 Ch. 468, at p. 472; *Re Davy, Hollingsworth v. Davy,* [1908] 1 Ch. 61.

[5] *Wentworth v. Wentworth,* [1900] A.C. 163, at p. 171.

[6] [1938] Ch. 313.

sufficient, the legacies to the nephews should abate before the other legacies. The judge said[1] that interest "is a sum given in the course of administration to the legatee because justice requires that owing to the failure to pay his legacy in due time he should be put in the position which he would have been had it been so paid". He therefore held that while the legacies themselves abated, the interest did not. The result is, however, curious. Interest is intended to compensate the legatee for late payment. The effect of *Re Wyles* is that the legatee is compensated at a rate appropriate to a larger sum than that to which, in the circumstances, he is entitled.

c. *Treatment of payments on account*

Subject to any direction in the will, where a payment is made to a beneficiary on account of his entitlement to a legacy and to interest on it, the beneficiary may treat the sum paid as interest, to the extent of his entitlement to interest, leaving the whole or part of the legacy itself outstanding.[2] Or, he may treat it, *pro tanto*, as satisfying the legacy, leaving the claim for interest outstanding. He will largely be guided by income tax considerations in making his choice, for he will be taxable on the interest, but not on the legacy itself.[3]

d. *Expenses of property specifically given*

Just as a specific beneficiary is entitled, generally, to the actual income produced from the asset, so he must suffer the expenses in respect of it. This is considered later.[4]

E. ANNUITIES

1. NATURE

An annuity is a periodic payment. It may either be secured on land, in which case it is known as a rentcharge, or secured on other property or unsecured, in which case it is known as an annuity. Administration of Estates Act 1925, s. 55 (1) (ix), defines "pecuniary legacy" to include an annuity, so that the general rules previously mentioned with regard to pecuniary legacies apply also to annuities.

---

[1] [1938] Ch. 313, at p. 316.
[2] *Re Prince, Hardman* v. *Willis* (1935), 51 T.L.R. 526; *Re Morley's Estate, Hollenden* v. *Morley*, [1937] Ch. 491.
[3] See *ante*, p. 452.
[4] See *post*, p. 515.

Two special problems, however, arise with regard to annuities:

a. The circumstances in which the annuitant is entitled to payment of a capital sum in lieu of the annuity;

b. The extent to which annuities abate for the payment of debts.

2. CAPITAL SUM IN LIEU

In general, an annuitant is not entitled to a capital sum in lieu of his annuity.[1] He is, however, entitled to a capital sum in three circumstances:

a. Where the will gives him the right to take a capital sum;

b. Where the will directs the personal representatives to purchase an annuity for him; and

c. Where there is insufficient capital, after payment of other legacies, to secure his annuity.

The first of these possibilities needs no explanation.

a. *Direction in will to purchase*

If the will sets aside a capital sum to be used for the purchase of an annuity, the beneficiary has the option either to take that sum[2] or to have it applied in the purchase of an annuity, usually from an insurance company.[3] Although in many cases annuities purchased from an insurance company have taxation advantages, in that part of the payment is regarded as capital, and so is received by the annuitant free of tax,[4] this advantage does not apply in the case of an annuity purchased pursuant to a direction in a will.[5] Accordingly, where a will is being prepared, it is preferable from the tax point of view to leave the annuitant a lump sum. If he chooses to purchase an annuity with it, he will then obtain the tax relief just described.

If the testator gives a sum for the purchase of an annuity, and

---

[1] This is because the testator intended that he should receive annual payments.

[2] *Re Robbins, Robbins* v. *Legge*, [1907] 2 Ch. 8; *Re Brunning, Gammon* v. *Dale*. [1909] 1 Ch. 276.

[3] Formerly where there was a direction to purchase an annuity, without giving the personal representatives power to purchase from a public company, they were compelled to purchase an annuity from the Government. Since 1962 it has not been possible to purchase Government annuities, but the tables are still used for the purposes of s. 47A.

[4] *Inland Revenue Commissioners* v. *Lady Castlemaine*, [1943] 2 All E.R. 471.

[5] Income and Corporation Taxes Act 1970, s. 230.

then adds to it a direction that an annuity must be purchased, and the annuitant is not entitled to its value, it seems that not-withstanding that provision the annuitant is entitled to the capital sum.[1] The explanation given is that the subsequent restriction is inconsistent with the gift itself.[2] On the other hand, where another person is entitled to the annuity upon the happening of a particular event, the annuitant is not entitled to the capital sum. For example, if the will provides that the annuity shall go to another if the annuitant assigns or charges his annuity, that provision is effective to prevent him claiming the capital sum.[3] The distinction between these two situations is very fine.

It has even been held that if the annuitant dies before the annuity has been purchased, then the capital sum forms part of the annuitant's estate.[4]

b. *Insufficient capital to secure*

An annuitant is entitled to demand that his interest is protected.[5] This is done by setting aside a sufficient part of the capital of the estate to provide adequate income to meet the annuity. There can, of course, be no absolute assurance that the capital set aside will be sufficient, and if there is a deficiency, the annuitant would be entitled to have recourse to the remainder of the residue.[6] In general, therefore, the personal representatives should not dis-tribute the whole of the remainder of the residue even where a fund has been set aside for the payment of the annuity. If they wish to distribute, the personal representatives must either rely upon a provision in the will that upon a sum being set aside the residue is exonerated,[7] a clause which many well drawn wills contain, or alternatively make an application to the court.

---

[1] *Stokes* v. *Cheek* (1860), 28 Beav. 620; *Re Nunn's Trusts* (1875), L.R. 19 Eq. 331; *Hunt-Foulston* v. *Furber* (1876), 3 Ch.D. 285.

[2] *Re Mabbett, Pitman* v. *Holborrow*, [1891] 1 Ch. 707, at p. 713.

[3] *Power* v. *Hayne* (1869), L.R. 8 Eq. 262; *Re Draper* (1888), 57 L.J. Ch. 942; *Roper* v. *Roper* (1876), 3 Ch. D. 714; *Re Thomas, Public Trustee* v. *Falconer*, [1946] Ch. 36.

[4] *Re Draper* (1888), 57 L.J. Ch. 942.

[5] *May* v. *Bennett* (1826), 1 Russ. 370; *Boyd* v. *Buckle* (1840), 10 Sim. 595.

[6] *May* v. *Bennett* (1826), 1 Russ. 370; *Mills* v. *Drewitt* (1855), 20 Beav. 632; *Ingleman* v. *Worthington* (1855), 25 L.J. Ch. 46; *Carmichael* v. *Gee* (1880), 5 App. Cas. 588.

[7] *Baker* v. *Baker* (1858), 6 H.L. Cas. 616; *Michell* v. *Wilton* (1875), L.R. 20 Eq. 269.

The rule that the annuitant may require part of the capital to be set aside is one of convenience only. It must be remembered that unless there is a direction in the will to the contrary, an annuitant is entitled to have any deficiency of income made up from capital, though this has taxation disadvantages.[1] The position was reviewed by the Court of Appeal in *Re Hill, Westminster Bank, Ltd.* v. *Wilson*.[2] In that case a number of pecuniary legacies were given, together with several annuities. At the outset there was insufficient capital for all pecuniary legacies to be paid in full and for sums to be set aside for the annuities, although there was no commercial risk that the annuities would not be paid in full. As soon as even the smallest of the annuities ceased to be payable, the income of the residue would have been sufficient to meet all the annuities. In the meantime, it was possible to resort to capital to the small degree necessary. At first instance Uthwatt, J. thought that the annuitants had a right to the capital sum, the rule[3] being a rule of law. This was reversed on appeal. In the Court of Appeal Lord Greene, M.R. said that the rule "has obviously no application to a case like the present where it is plain that the available estate is more than sufficient to provide for the payment in full of the annuities out of income and capital as directed by the testator unless a series of events should transpire entirely outside the scope of human expectation, namely, the joint survival of all the annuitants for a period of time of impossible length having regard to their respective ages at the time when the matter is to be considered".

Where it cannot be said that there is no commercial risk of any insufficiency, the rule applies. The valuation of the annuity is made actuarially, disregarding risks which attach to the annuitant's occupation.[4] The capital value of an annuity will always be less than the capital sum needed to pay the annuity out of income. (£100 invested at £5 per cent will produce £5 p.a.; but to purchase an annuity of £5 p.a. the amount will depend on the age of the

---

[1] See *ante*, p. 405; *post*, p. 510.

[2] [1944] Ch. 270.

[3] The rule that the annuitant is entitled to have a capital sum set aside. See *Re Cox, Public Trustee* v. *Eve*, [1938] Ch. 556; See also *Wroughton* v. *Colquhoun* (1847), 1 De G. & Sm. 357; *Re Cottrell, Buckland* v. *Bedingfield*, [1910] 1 Ch. 402.

[4] *Re Bradberry, National Provincial Bank, Ltd.* v. *Bradberry* and *Re Fry, Tasker* v. *Gulliford*, both reported at [1943] Ch. 35.

annuitant. It may be possible to purchase for, say, £40 an annuity of £5 p.a. if the annuitant is old.) It may be, then, that the capitalised value of the annuity, taken with the amount of the legacies, does not exceed the total value of the estate. In this case, legatees and annuitants are paid in full by capital sums, unless the will attaches conditions to the annuity, such as for its payment to another upon the happening of certain events, in which case another annuity will have to be purchased with the capitalised value. If the capitalised value of the annuity, and the amount of the legacies, exceeds the value of the estate, they abate rateably.

c. *Capital sum by agreement*

It is possible for the annuitant to take a capital sum if he can reach agreement with the residuary beneficiaries under the rule in *Saunders* v. *Vautier*.[1] If all the residuary beneficiaries are not ascertained or are not *sui iuris*, and the amount at issue is large enough, an application can be made to the Court under the Variation of Trusts Act 1958. The advantage of taking a capital sum is explained at p. 405.

3. ANNUITIES PAID FROM CAPITAL

Periodic payments of income are subject to special rules of income tax. The person making the payment is in all cases obliged to pay or suffer tax on the fund from which the payment is made, and to make the payment to the recipient out of that taxed fund.[2] Suppose that £1,000 is invested at £5 per cent p.a. interest. The personal respresentatives receive each year £50 interest. They will pay tax on that at the basic rate of income tax for the time being in force. If this is 50% they are left with a net sum of £25. Now suppose that they have to pay an annuity of £50 p.a. In all cases they must pay the annuity subject to deduction of tax. In this case they pay over £25 to the annuitant. As this has come from a taxed fund, there are no further tax complications. Suppose however the facts are the same, but that the annuity is £150 p.a. The net sum to be paid to the annuitant is £75, of which £25 will come from taxed income. In order to make up the difference of £50, they must take £100 from capital.

---

[1] (1841), Cr. & Ph. 240.
[2] See *ante*, p. 403.

£50 is used to pay the annuitant, and the remaining £50 has to be paid to the Revenue by way of tax.[1] Accordingly, where the basic rate of tax is 50%, the capital of the residue is used at exactly double the rate needed to make up the deficiency in income for the annuitant. For this reason, testators should be reluctant to include in their wills provisions directing any deficiency of income for an annuitant to be made up from capital.[2] The taxation liability on payments from capital must be taken into account when deciding whether there is any commercial risk of insufficiency for the purposes of *Re Hill, Westminster Bank, Ltd.* v. *Wilson*.[3]

4. RETENTION TO COVER FUTURE INSUFFICIENCY

Where the testator makes provision for an annuity, he will usually charge that income on a particular fund, or on the residuary estate, leaving the surplus income elsewhere. In this case a problem arises where the personal representatives wish to accumulate the surplus income, and hold it against future deficits of capital. The personal representatives are entitled to retain the surplus income where they foresee a future deficiency. In doing so they will be accumulating that income, but as the accumulation is necessitated by the administration of the estate, it is not within the legislation regulating accumulations, so that there is no limit to the time for which it may be accumulated.[4]

5. ANNUITIES "TAX-FREE"

When considering leaving an annuity, the testator may approach the problem from the size of the income of his estate, or from the needs of the beneficiary. If he adopts the former approach, and leaves an annuity of, say, £50 p.a., income tax will be deducted from that sum at the basic rate in force for each year for which the annuity is paid. As the basic rate of tax fluctuates, the annuitant does not know the actual net amount which he will receive year by year. To counter this, the testator may wish to leave an annuity of, say, £50 p.a. "free of tax", so that however the basic

---

[1] Income and Corporation Taxes Act 1970, s. 53.

[2] In some cases it is possible to prevent hardship to the annuitant by using the power of advancement where there is an income deficiency.

[3] [1944] Ch. 270.

[4] *Re Berkeley, Inglis* v. *Countess of Berkeley*, [1968] Ch. 744; [1968] 3 All E.R. 364.

rate of tax might fluctuate, the annuitant is left with the net sum of £50. Generally, one may not make an agreement to make payments free of tax[1] but there is no objection to directing in a will or settlement that they shall be free of tax. The result is the same as if the testator had directed his personal representatives to pay an annuity of such sum as after the deduction of tax will amount to the specified amount. In this case the annuitant receives the payment free of tax at the basic rate, and if he pays higher rate income tax, he is entitled to recover from the personal representatives the tax at the higher rate which he has paid on the annuity. This increases still further the burden on the estate. If, however, the beneficiary is entitled to a repayment of income tax, perhaps because his total income is low, he must pay back to the personal representatives so much of that repayment as relates to the annuity.[2]

The result is different if the testator expressly says that the annuity shall be of such a sum as after the deduction of income tax at the basic rate for the time being in force shall leave the specified sum. In this case the annuitant cannot claim his higher rate income tax from the estate, but on the other hand is not obliged to account for any repayment of tax which he receives.[3]

6. ADVANTAGES OF CAPITAL SUM

From the point of view of the annuitant, it will almost always be in his interest to take a capital sum. In the first place, the amount which he receives is free of income tax,[4] whereas, as has just been shown, if he receives an annuity, the whole of the payments will be subject to tax. Furthermore, provided the annuitant receives the actuarial value of his annuity, he may himself purchase an annuity of the equivalent amount mentioned in the will, but if he purchases it, as distinct from the personal representatives purchasing it for him, he will be entitled to the special tax advantage under Income and Corporation Taxes Act 1970, s. 230.[5]

It will also often be in the interest of the residuary beneficiaries

---

[1] Taxes Management Act 1970, s. 106 (2).
[2] *Re Pettit, Le Fevre v. Pettit*, [1922] 2 Ch. 765; *Re Kingcome, Hickley v. Kingcome*, [1936] Ch. 566.
[3] *Re Bates, Selmes v. Bates*, [1925] Ch. 157.
[4] *Inland Revenue Commissioners v. Lady Castlemaine*, [1941] 2 All E.R. 471.
[5] See *ante*, p. 506.

for the annuitant to be paid a capital sum. Suppose that the annuitant is entitled to an annuity of £50 p.a., and that the actuarial valuation of the annuity is £300. If the annuity is to be met from capital, £1,000 will have to be set aside, and subject to what was said above[1] the residue will have to be retained to meet any income deficiency. If the annuitant is paid a capital sum, he will receive £300. The balance of £700 can be paid forthwith to the residuary beneficiaries, and the remainder of the residue distributed. This may more than compensate for the ultimate loss of the £300—for on the death of the annuitant there will now be no payment due to them—and in any case, this premature determination of the annuity will probably also have estate duty advantages.[2]

F. OPTIONS

The testator may during his lifetime have granted to another an option to purchase a particular asset which is exercisable after his death, or he may in his will grant an option to a person to purchase an asset at less than its true value. Different considerations arise in these cases.

1. OPTION GRANTED DURING TESTATOR'S LIFETIME

When a binding contract for the sale of an asset is made, in the view of equity the asset in the hands of the vendor is converted into money.[3] The same principle applies where a binding contract comes into force following the exercise of an option. For general purposes, the vendor becomes under a binding obligation to sell at the time when the option is exercised[4] but for the purpose of the administration of estates, the conversion is regarded, illogically, as being retroactive to the date of the grant of the option.

Suppose therefore, that the testator during his lifetime grants an option to Andrew to purchase his house for £1,000, and dies having made a will leaving his realty to Brendon and his personalty to Clarissa. If the option is exercised in the lifetime of Andrew, the house will be converted into personalty at that time, and the proceeds of sale will accrue to Clarissa even if the sale is not

---

[1] See *ante*, p. 510.
[2] Provided he lives for at least four, and preferably seven years: Finance Act 1968, s. 35.
[3] *Lady Foliamb's Case* (1651), cited in *Daire* v. *Beversham* (1661), Nels. 76.
[4] *Edwards* v. *West* (1878), 7 Ch.D. 858.

completed until after death. Where the option is exercised after death one would expect that as the house was not converted at the date of death, it would belong to Brendon, so that in the event of the exercise of the option, he would be entitled to the proceeds of sale. The rule is, however, firmly established that for the purpose of deciding between respective beneficiaries the option, once exercised, is deemed to have caused conversion at the date of the grant of the option, that is, in the testator's lifetime, so that the proceeds of sale belong to the beneficiary entitled to personalty.

The rule was established in the leading case of *Lawes* v. *Bennett*.[1] The testator granted to his lessee in 1758 an option to purchase the freehold reversion at any time before 29 September, 1765. The testator died in 1763, leaving his realty to Bennett, and his personalty to Bennett and Lawes in equal shares. The option was exercised in February, 1765. Kenyon, M.R. held that when exercised, the option related back to the original agreement so that Lawes was entitled to half the proceeds of sale. The rule applies even where the option cannot be exercised before the death of the testator.[2]

Until the option is exercised, the person *prima facie* entitled to the asset under the will is entitled to the rents and profits.[3] Thus, on the facts of *Lawes* v. *Bennett*[4] Bennett, being entitled to the realty, would have been entitled to the rent from the date of death to the date of the exercise of the option.[5] The illogical result is that for the purpose of determining devolution of capital, the asset is deemed to be converted at the date of grant of the option, whereas for the purposes of determining entitlement to income, the asset is converted at the date of exercise of the option.

The rule in *Lawes* v. *Bennett*[6] operates only to carry into effect the presumed intention of the testator, so that it will be excluded by contrary evidence in the will.[7] Although the rule applies in principle whether the option is granted before or after the making of the will, if the option was granted before the will, and the will contains a specific devise, that will point to an intention on the

---

[1] (1785), 1 Cox Eq. Cas. 167.
[2] *Re Isaacs, Isaacs* v. *Reginall*, [1894] 3 Ch. 506.
[3] *Re Adams and Kensington Vestry* (1884), 27 Ch.D. 394.
[4] (1785), 1 Cox Eq. Cas. 167.
[5] In fact this point was not decided in *Lawes* v. *Bennett* itself.
[6] (1785), 1 Cox Eq. Cas. 167.
[7] *Re Pyle, Pyle* v. *Pyle*, [1895] 1 Ch. 724.

part of the testator that the devisee shall take either the property itself or its proceeds.[1] The rule will also be excluded where the will preceeds the option, but contains a specific devise and is republished after the grant of the option.[2]

The operation of the rule is not restricted to contests between the person entitled to realty on the one hand and the person entitled to personalty on the other hand, but it extends to contests between persons entitled to different types of personalty. In *Re Carrington, Ralphs* v. *Swithenbank*[3] the testator bequeathed a holding of preference shares to A., and left his residuary personalty to B. Subsequently he granted an option to C. to purchase those shares, the option to be exercised within one month of his death. The Court of Appeal applied the rule in *Lawes* v. *Bennett* to hold that when exercised, the option became retroactive to the date of grant, so that B. was entitled to the proceeds of sale. The decision is unpopular because the illogicality of the rule in *Lawes* v. *Bennett* led to a general feeling that it should be restricted to options for the purchase of freeholds, and because the equitable doctrine of conversion is properly concerned with conversion between realty and personalty, and not with conversion of one class of personalty into another.[4] The decision has, however, been followed.

2. OPTIONS GRANTED BY WILL

Where the option is granted by the will itself, no problem arises as long as the size of the estate is sufficient to pay all debts and legacies. In this case, the person entitled to the asset under the will takes it subject to the option, and if the option is exercised, that person becomes entitled to the proceeds of sale.

A problem does arise where the estate is not sufficiently large for the payment of all debts and legacies. Where the option is to purchase at less than the market value, the difference between the market value and the option price can be regarded as a gift. Nevertheless it was held in *Re Eve*[5] that this gift was not a specific gift, and, indeed, that it did not come within any of the paragraphs 1 to 6 in the First Schedule to the Administration of Estates Act.

---

[1] *Drant* v. *Vause* (1842), 1 Y. & C. Ch. Cas. 580.
[2] *Emuss* v. *Smith* (1848), 2 De G. & Sm. 722.
[3] [1932] 1 Ch. 1.
[4] Hanbury (1933), 49 L.Q.R. 173.
[5] [1956] Ch. 479.

The asset itself is available for the payment of debts, but only after all classes of assets within the Schedule have been exhausted. It was pointed out above that it has not yet been decided how the various types of assets available for the payment of debts which are not within the Schedule rank between themselves.

It follows that to ascertain whether the estate is solvent, it is necessary to consider whether the purchase price payable under the option, and not the value of the asset itself, together with the other assets, is capable of meeting all the debts.

If the testator grants an option by will, he may instead of fixing the price at which the option is to be exercised, prescribe that the beneficiary shall have the option of purchasing at a "reasonable valuation", or some similar expression. In this case the valuation will be made as at death if no other time for valuation is specified in the will, but in making this valuation account may also be taken of subsequent events. So, in *Talbot* v. *Talbot*[1] Harman, L.J. said:[2] "that does not mean . . . that the valuers are to draw blinkers over their eyes or to shut their eyes to the fact that . . . the lands have very much increased in value since (the date of death): they are entitled to say what, today, knowing what they do, and discounting back for the three years (since death), is the proper market value". In any case, the person who is given the option is entitled to have the property valued before deciding whether to exercise the option. Harman, L.J., expressed the memorable principle "before we buy the pig, take it out of the poke".

It also follows that because of the rules as to abatement, it can be more advantageous to have an option at a fairly low price than to have a legacy.

G. ADMINISTRATION EXPENSES IN RESPECT OF SPECIFIC ASSETS

It has been shown that where an asset is specifically bequeathed, and produces income, the beneficiary is entitled to the income produced from the date of death of testator, unless there is a provision in the will to the contrary.[3] The corollary to this is that where expenditure is incurred on the preservation and upkeep of property specifically bequeathed, those expenses are payable

---

[1] [1968] Ch. 1.
[2] *Ibid*, at p. 13.
[3] See *ante*, p. 499.

by the beneficiary, and not out of the general residue.[1] This principle, which applies whether or not the property is income producing, would cover expenditure for items such as storage and insurance.

If, however, the beneficiary only becomes specifically entitled at some time later than the death of the testator, he is responsible for bearing the expenses only from the date when he becomes specifically entitled.[2] So, if an asset is appropriated by way of a share of residue, the liability for expenses would commence at the date of appropriation. And if there is a power to select items from the estate, the liability arises at the time of selection.

H. REFUNDING LEGACIES

In certain circumstances, a legatee may be compelled to refund his legacy, or a part of it, if further liabilities of the estate appear. These circumstances are:

a. where the payment was made by the executor under the threat of proceedings;[3] and

b. where the payment was made voluntarily, and at the time of payment the personal representatives had no notice of the debt.[4]

If the personal representatives pay the legacy with clear notice of the debt, they cannot recover from the legatee, and will be required to make good the deficiency from their own pockets.[5] Personal representatives are not prevented from recovering, however, if the liability was at the date of payment only a remote possibility.

Where the personal representatives honestly make an overpayment, and they subsequently become due to make further payments, the overpayment may be adjusted from those further payments.[6]

Unsatisfied creditors, and non-paid or under-paid legatees or next of kin also have rights against the legatees, but these rights are not considered in this book.[7]

---

[1] *Re Rooke, Jeans* v. *Gatehouse*, [1933] Ch. 970.

[2] *Re Collins' Settlement Trusts, Donne* v. *Hewetson*, [1971] 1 All E.R. 283.

[3] *Newman* v. *Barton* (1690), 2 Vern. 205.

[4] *Jervis* v. *Wolferstan* (1874), L.R. 18 Eq. 18, at p. 25; *Re Kershaw, Whittaker* v. *Kershaw* (1890), 45 Ch.D. 320, at p. 325.

[5] *Jervis* v. *Wolferstan* (1874), L.R. 18 Eq. 18.

[6] *Livesey* v. *Livesey* (1827), 3 Russ. 287; *Dibbs* v. *Goren* (1849), 11 Beav. 483; *Re Horne, Wilson* v. *Cox Sinclair*, [1905] 1 Ch. 76; *Re Ainsworth, Finch* v. *Smith*, [1915] 2 Ch. 96.

[7] Reference should be made to the standard books on Equity.

CHAPTER 32

THE INCIDENCE OF DEBTS AND LEGACIES

A. INTRODUCTION

This chapter is concerned with problems which arise in the course of the administration of a solvent estate. Suppose that the deceased bought a house on mortgage, and that the mortgage was outstanding at the date of his death. Is the person who takes the house under the will entitled to have the mortgage discharged out of the general estate, or does he have to take the property subject to the mortgage? Suppose again that the testator gave various legacies and left his residuary personalty to Andrew and his realty to Bernard. Are the legacies to be paid from the personalty only; or from both realty and personalty; and if from both, in what proportions? These questions most frequently affect the size of the benefit which the persons entitled to residue, or entitled to property which is undisposed of take under the intestacy rules. It is convenient first to consider the position with regard to the payment of debts, and then to consider problems with regard to legacies.

At the outset, however, the reader is warned. The relevant parts of the Administration of Estates Act are drafted extremely badly, and the problems are legion. To describe the position as "tortuous"[1] or "notoriously obscure"[2] is to express it mildly. No part of this branch of the laws warrants more the use of the cold towel.

B. DEBTS CHARGED ON PROPERTY

1. WHEN THE CHARGE ARISES

In certain circumstances, debts can, prior to the death of the deceased, be charged on specific assets, and the general principle

---

[1] Per Harman, J., in Re Midgley, Barclays Bank Ltd. v. Midgley, [1955] Ch. 576; [1955] 2 All E.R. 625.

[2] Per Salt, Q.C., Ch., in Re Taylor's Estate and Will Trusts, [1969] 2 Ch. 245.

is that where this is so, the beneficiary takes the asset subject to the liability to discharge the debt.

The debt may be charged on the property in one of three situations:

a. where it was charged under the old law, and that law still prevails;

b. where the liability is an incident of the property itself; and

c. where s. 35 of the Administration of Estates Act applies.

a. *Provisions of the old law*

Before Locke King's Acts of 1854, 1867 and 1877, a devisee of land could generally require a mortgage debt to be paid off out of the general personal estate. However, this right applied only to mortgage debts which the testator had himself created[1] or which, if created by others, he had adopted, as by paying the interest, or making repayments of capital. Where the testator had not created or adopted the debt the devisee took the property subject to that liability,[2] and the devisee still takes such property subject to the liabilities. He does so as a result of the old general principle, and not as a result of s. 35 of the Administration of Estates Act which is considered below, but the circumstances in which this arises in practice are rare indeed. In certain other unusual circumstances, the general personal estate was not liable for the debts, and in these cases also the beneficiary under the will takes the assets subject to the burden of the debts.[3]

b. *Incidents of the property*

A legatee of leasehold property takes the property subject to the burdens of the lease itself, which includes the liability to pay the rent.[4] This applies to all liabilities which arise from the

---

[1] *Ibbetson* v. *Ibbetson* (1841), 12 Sim. 206; *Jenkinson* v. *Harcourt* (1854), Kay 688; *Field* v. *Moore* (1855), 7 De G.M. & G. 691; *Re Anthony, Anthony* v. *Anthony*, [1893] 3 Ch. 498.

[2] *Perkins* v. *Baynton* (1784), 1 Bro. C.C. 375; *Noel* v. *Lord Henley* (1819), 7 Price 241; *Scott* v. *Beecher* (1820), 5 Madd. 96; *Swainson* v. *Swainson* (1856), 6 De G.M. & G. 648; *Re Leeming* (1861), 3 De G.F. & J. 43; *Hepworth* v. *Hill* (1862), 30 Beav. 476.

[3] *Edwards* v. *Freeman* (1727), 2 P. Wms. 435; *Lanoy* v. *Athol* (1742), 2 Atk. 444; *Graves* v. *Hicks* (1833), 6 Sim. 391; *Loosemore* v. *Knapman* (1853), Kay 123.

[4] *Eccles* v. *Mills*, [1898] A.C. 360; *Re Hughes, Ellis* v. *Hughes*, [1913] 2 Ch. 491; *Re Day*, [1962] 1 W.L.R. 1419.

relationship of landlord and tenant. But the executors may themselves also be liable to the landlord, and, as will be seen,[1] they are entitled to insist on indemnities before transferring the property to the beneficiary.

c. *Under Administration of Estates Act 1925, s. 35*

Section 35 of the 1925 Act, which replaces Locke King's Acts, applies to all property which at the time of the death of the deceased is charged with the payment of money. It provides that so far as beneficiaries claiming through the deceased are concerned, the property charged is primarily liable for the payment of the debt. The section affects only the ultimate burden of the debt and it does not affect the position of the creditors, who are entitled to payment in any event.[2] If the amount of the debt is greater than the value of the asset, the beneficiary will take no benefit under the will, and the creditor will have a right of recourse against uncharged assets of the estate. The section does not affect the position of any beneficiary who takes otherwise than through the deceased: it does not, for example, affect the beneficiary who takes the property on the death of the deceased under a pre-existing trust.[3] And even where it does affect the beneficiary, it does not impose upon him any personal liability to discharge the debt.[4]

2. EXTENT OF CHARGE UNDER S. 35

The section applies to any form of specific charge, whether legal or equitable. As well as a charge by way of legal mortgage, it applies to a rentcharge,[5] a local land charge which is registered,[6] and a charge which is registered in order to secure the payment of estate duty.[7] An equitable mortgage is included,[8] as is any other

---

[1] See *ante*, p. 423.

[2] Administration of Estates Act 1925, s. 35 (2).

[3] *Re Anthony, Anthony v. Anthony*, [1893] 3 Ch. 498; *Re Ritson, Ritson v. Ritson*, [1899] 1 Ch. 128; *Re Fison's Will Trusts, Fison v. Fison*, [1950] Ch. 394.

[4] *Syer v. Gladstone* (1885), 30 Ch.D. 614.

[5] *Re Fraser, Lowther v. Fraser*, [1904] 1 Ch. 111, 726.

[6] *Re Hesketh, Saunders v. Bibby Hesketh* (1900), 45 Sol. Jo. 11 (decided prior to the Land Charges Act 1925).

[7] *Re Bowerman, Porter v. Bowerman*, [1908] 2 Ch. 340.

[8] *Pembroke v. Friend* (1860), 1 Johns. & H. 132; *Coleby v. Coleby* (1866), L.R. 2 Eq. 803; *Davis v. Davis* (1876), 24 W.R. 962; *Re Hawkes, Reeves v. Hawks*, [1912] 2 Ch. 251.

form of equitable charge or lien.[1] It is probable, however, that
the charge must be specific, and that a general charge, such as a
banker's lien, is outside the scope of the section.[2]

The section only applies to the extent that the debt is charged
on the property, even if other debts have been incurred in respect
of the asset. The distinction is illustrated by *Re Birmingham*,
Savage v. *Stannard*.[3] The testatrix had contracted to purchase
a house, but died before completing the purchase, and before
paying the balance of the purchase money. Her estate therefore
owned the equitable interest in the property, subject to the vendor's
lien for unpaid purchase money. Shortly before her death, the
testatrix executed a codicil giving the house to one person, and
the residue of her estate to others. The person claiming the house
had to discharge the vendor's lien, but the legal costs in connexion
with the purchase, which were only a simple contract debt, and
not a charge on the property, were payable out of residue.

3. SPECIAL CIRCUMSTANCES

a. *More than one beneficiary*

If more than one person is entitled to the property subject to
the charge, each is responsible for discharging the charge according to the value of his benefit.[4]

b. *More than one security*

More than one asset may be charged to secure the same debt.
Suppose, for example, that the deceased purchased a house with
the aid of a mortgage, but that the lender required additional
security in the form of a charge over, say, another property or a
life policy. In such cases it is necessary to establish whether
both assets charged together constitute the primary security, or
whether only one is the primary security and the other is secondary.
This is a question of fact, and is not resolved by the description
which the parties give to the deed of charge.[5] If both properties

---

[1] *Re Cockcroft, Broadbent* v. *Groves* (1883), 24 Ch.D. 94; *Re Kidd, Brooman*
v. *Kidd*, [1894] 3 Ch. 558; *Re Turner, Tennant* v. *Turner*, [1938] Ch. 593.

[2] *Re Dunlop, Dunlop* v. *Dunlop* (1882), 21 Ch.D. 583.

[3] [1959] Ch. 523.

[4] *Evans* v. *Wyatt* (1862), 31 Beav. 217; *Trestrail* v. *Mason* (1878), 7 Ch.D.
665; *Re Newmarch, Newmarch* v. *Storr* (1878), 9 Ch.D. 12; *Leonino* v. *Leonino*
(1879), 10 Ch.D. 460; *Re Major, Taylor* v. *Major*, [1914] 1 Ch. 278.

[5] *Re Athill, Athill* v. *Athill* (1880), 16 Ch.D. 211.

are given to the same person, then, subject to what is said below, that person must discharge the total liability. If the properties are given to separate persons, those persons will bear the liability rateably if both properties were primary securities.[1]

If, however, only one property is the primary security the beneficiary of that property bears the whole of the debt, to the extent of its value, and the beneficiary of the secondary security is responsible only to the extent that the primary security is insufficient.[2]

c. *More than one property given to same beneficiary*

The testator may give to the same beneficiary two or more assets each subject to separate liabilities. If the assets are given separately, the beneficiary can treat them as being unrelated. Thus, if the debt on one asset exceeds its value, the undischarged balance is payable out of the general residue, and not out of the other properties.[3] If, however, the assets were given as one composite gift, the beneficiary takes subject to the obligation to discharge the total liabilities attaching to them and he does not have recourse to the general estate.[4]

4. "CONTRARY OR OTHER INTENTION"

The operation of the section may be negatived by a contrary intention expressed in the will, or in any other deed or document.[5] However, sub-s. 35 (2) provides that a contrary intention is not shown merely by

    a. a general direction to pay debts out of the personal estate;[6]

    b. a direction to pay debts out of the residuary real and personal estate, or the residuary realty;[7] or

    c. a charge of debts upon any such property.[8]

---

[1] *Re Athill, Athill* v. *Athill* (1880), 16 Ch.D. 211.

[2] *Marquis of Bute* v. *Cunynghame* (1826), 2 Russ. 275; *Re Athill, supra*; *Re Ritson, Ritson* v. *Ritson*, [1899] 1 Ch. 128.

[3] *Re Holt, Holt* v. *Holt* (1916), 85 L.J. Ch. 779.

[4] *Re Baron Kensington*, [1902] 1 Ch. 203.

[5] Administration of Estates Act 1925, s. 35 (1) expressly declares its operation to be subject to any contrary intention.

[6] Administration of Estates Act 1925, s. 35 (2) (a).

[7] *Ibid.*

[8] *Ibid.*, s. 35 (2) (b).

It is not even sufficient to direct that all sums "secured on mortgage" are to be paid.[1] But the contrary intention can be shown by implication. In *Re Valpy, Valpy* v. *Valpy*[2] there was a direction to pay all debts, except a mortgage debt on a particular property, and this was held to show an intention that all other mortgage debts should be paid from residue. Generally it is necessary to show that the testator intended that a particular debt should be paid from residue.

5. POSITION WHERE CONTRARY INTENTION SHOWN

The section refers to a contrary "or other" intention because the testator might intend that the debts should be dealt with in one of two ways. He might indicate that the debts should be paid from a particular fund. If he does so, s. 35 is displaced only to the extent that the fund is adequate.[3] So, in *Re Fegan, Fegan* v. *Fegan*[4] the testator left to his children insurance policies worth about £4,000, but which were subject to charges of £2,000. He left another fund to be used to pay his debts. It was held that the children were entitled to have the debts on the policies discharged from the other fund so far as was possible, but that they were responsible for discharging the balance of the policy debt which could not be discharged from the fund.

On the other hand, the testator may merely displace s. 35 without making provision for the payment from any other fund. In this event, the position is as if the section had not been enacted. Property in the first two categories specified at the beginning of this chapter, which bear their own charges independently of the statute, continue to do so, unless the will shows an intention that these debts also should be discharged from residue. Other debts are treated in the same manner as uncharged debts, shortly to be considered.

C. ACCEPTANCE OF LIABILITY TO PAY DEBTS

The testator may give a legacy to a beneficiary on condition that the beneficiary pays all the debts. The legatee can disclaim

---

[1] *Re Beirnstein, Barnett* v. *Beirnstein*, [1925] Ch. 12.

[2] [1906] 1 Ch. 531.

[3] *Re Birch, Hunt* v. *Thorn*, [1909] 1 Ch. 787; *Re Major, Taylor* v. *Major*, [1914] 1 Ch. 278; *Re Fegan, Fegan* v. *Fegan*, [1928] 1 Ch. 45.

[4] [1928] 1 Ch. 45.

the legacy,[1] but, if he accepts it, he is responsible for paying all the debts, even if they exceed the value of the property given to him.[2] Where this occurs, there is no call for the application of any other principles as to the incidence of debts.

D. INCIDENCE OF UNCHARGED DEBTS

1. THE STATUTORY SCHEDULE

The Administration of Estates Act 1925, s. 34 (3) provides that a deceased person's real and personal estate "shall be applicable towards the discharge of the funeral, testamentary and administration expenses, debts and liabilities payable thereout in the order mentioned in Part II of the First Schedule" of the Act. The Schedule is as follows:

Order of Application of Assets where the Estate is Solvent

1. Property of the deceased undisposed of by will, subject to the retention thereout of a fund sufficient to meet any pecuniary legacies.

2. Property of the deceased not specifically devised or bequeathed but included (either by a specific or general description) in a residuary gift, subject to the retention out of such property of a fund sufficient to meet any pecuniary legacies, so far as not provided for as aforesaid.

3. Property of the deceased specifically appropriated or devised or bequeathed (either by a specific or general description) for the payment of debts.

4. Property of the deceased charged with, or devised or bequeathed (either by a specific or general description) subject to a charge for the payment of debts.

5. The fund, if any, retained to meet pecuniary legacies.

6. Property specifically devised or bequeathed, rateably according to value.

7. Property appointed by will under a general power, including the statutory power to dispose of entailed interests, rateably according to value.

8. The following provisions shall also apply—

---

[1] See *ante*, p. 450.

[2] *Messenger* v. *Andrews* (1828), 4 Russ. 478; *Dover* v. *Gregory* (1839), 10 Sim. 393. Cf. *Henvell* v. *Whitaker* (1827), 3 Russ. 343.

(a) The order of application may be varied by the will of the deceased.

(b) This part of this Schedule does not affect the liability of land to answer the death duty imposed thereon in exoneration of other assets."

2. ASSETS OUTSIDE THE SCHEDULE

It is curious that the seven classes of assets given in the Schedule are not comprehensive, and that other assets are available for the payment of creditors. They are:

   (i) funds payable to the estate upon the exercise of an option;[1]

   (ii) property subject to a *donatio mortis causa;* and

   (iii) property subject to a general power of appointment exercisable by deed if it had been exercised.[2]

With regard to the former category, in *Re Eve, National Provincial Bank* v. *Eve*,[3] a beneficiary was granted by will an option to purchase certain shares from the estate. Roxburgh, J., held that this did not amount to a specific gift of the shares, within category 6 of the Schedule, and that so long as the purchase price payable under the option, and the remainder of the assets were together sufficient for the payment of debts, the purchase price was to be used for creditors, and not the shares themselves.

3. VARIATION OF THE STATUTORY ORDER

Paragraph 8 (a) of the Schedule provides that the statutory order "may be varied by the will of the deceased". There is nothing remarkable in this, for, by varying the order, the testator is merely adjusting the manner of distribution among the beneficiaries. However, difficulty is caused as to the relationship between paragraph 8 on the one hand and paragraphs 2, 3 and 4 on the other hand. Paragraph 2 deals with the payment of debts from residue; and paragraphs 3 and 4 deal with the payment of debts from property appropriated or charged by the deceased for this purpose. Suppose that by his will the testator leaves £1,000 to Andrew subject to the payment of debts, and the residue to Belinda. If the statutory order is applied, the debts are paid from residue

---

[1] *Re Eve, National Provincial Bank* v. *Eve*, [1956] Ch. 479.

[2] *Re Phillips, Lawrence* v. *Huxtable*, [1931] 1 Ch. 347.

[3] [1956] Ch. 479.

(para. 2) before the legacy (para. 4). But property can only be brought within paragraphs 3 and 4 by a provision in the will: does not any such provision indicate an intention that debts should be paid from that property before the residue."

In the example, did not the testator, by charging the debts on the legacy, show that Belinda was to take the residue free from deduction? Is it not impossible to bring property within paragraphs 3 and 4 without thereby altering the statutory order?

In logic this may be so, but to give some effect to both provisions, the courts have accepted that there are two possible types of provision in a will:

(i) a mere appropriation or charging of property, which does not displace the statutory order; and

(ii) a direction to pay debts from specified property, coupled with an intention to exonerate other property. This direction takes effect in priority to the Schedule.

An example of the first type of provision is *Re Gordon, Watts* v. *Rationalist Press Association, Ltd.*[1] In that case a testatrix gave by her will a specific legacy, and a legacy of £50, with a direction to pay from it her debts, and to pay over the balance to another. Her residue was undisposed of. It was held that the statutory order was not displaced, with the result that the debts were paid from the undisposed of residue, rather than from the legacy set aside for this purpose. It could not be said that there was any intention to exonerate the residue.[2]

There are several cases where the intention to exonerate has been shown. For example, in *Re James, Lloyds Bank, Ltd.* v. *Atkins*,[3] the testator directed payment of his debts from a particular fund, and left the residue to his wife. Roxburgh, J., said: "I should hold that the direction to pay debts out of a particular fund necessarily involved an intention to exonerate some other fund which the testator disposed of in some other part of his will —in other words, necessarily involved an intention to exonerate the residue of his estate which he devised and bequeathed to his wife absolutely." The judge was asking himself not in general terms whether there was a contrary intention, but whether there

---

[1] [1940] Ch. 769.
[2] See also *Re Kempthorne, Charles* v. *Kempthorne*, [1930] 1 Ch. 268.
[3] [1947] Ch. 256.

was an intention to exonerate other property. This intention appeared to come automatically from the gift of residue.

This was followed in *Re Meldrum's Will Trusts*.[1] The testator bequeathed to his daughter the residue of a bank account after the payment of legacies and debts, and left the residue of his property between his son and daughter. Upjohn, J., expressly approved the dictum of Roxburgh, J., quoted above, and held that the direction to pay debts from the bank account showed an intention to exonerate the residue.

Whether or not the courts will hold that the statutory order has been displaced has in these cases been influenced very largely by the existence or otherwise of a gift to another person of the residue, but in all cases it is a question of construction of the will.

4. OVERLAP BETWEEN CATEGORIES

The legislature does not appear to have realised that property could fall within more than one category. Paragraphs 3 and 4 deal with property charged with or appropriated for the payment of debts. The paragraphs envisage that specific property will be charged or appropriated, but it is also possible for residue to be so charged. If residue charged with the payment of debts were regarded as being within paragraph 4 an absurd result would ensue. Suppose that a testator left his residue to be divided equally between Edward and George, but charged George's share with the payment of debts. The strict application of the schedule would mean that Edward's uncharged share, in para. 2, would be taken before George's charged share, in para. 4.

In many cases this situation will not in fact arise because a contrary intention will be shown. In the example just considered, it might well be possible to show an intention to exonerate Edward's share. Where this is not the case, it is necessary to rely upon the reasoning in *Re Kempthorne, Charles* v. *Kempthorne*[2] to the effect that if property comes within one class, it cannot be regarded as coming also within a later class.

5. PAYMENT FROM UNDISPOSED OF SHARE OF RESIDUE

The courts have been concerned in several cases with the situation where a share of residue lapses. Suppose that the testator

---

[1] [1952] Ch. 208.
[2] [1930] 1 Ch. 268.

leaves all his property, worth £50,000, to be divided between his two brothers, Frank and George, and that Frank predeceases him. Suppose also that the debts amount to £10,000. There are two possible solutions. First, the debts can be deducted from the entire estate, to reduce it to £40,000. The net estate is divided into shares, so that George takes £20,000, and the remaining £20,000 devolves as on intestacy. This would have been the position before 1926. Alternatively, there can first be a division into shares, so that George takes £25,000. The remaining £25,000 is then applied first in the discharge of the debts, and the balance of £15,000 devolves as on intestacy.

If the testator has not contemplated the possibility of lapse, and so has not made alternative provision in the event of lapse, it may be thought that in most cases he would wish to benefit those named in the will, who are the conscious objects of his bounty, rather than those entitled on intestacy, whoever they may be. Thus, approaching the problem *de novo*, it seems appropriate to divide the entire estate, or the entire residue, into shares before discharging the debts. While this is a reversal of the pre-1926 position, it is suggested that it is now the basic rule. Thus, in *Re Sanger, Taylor* v. *North*[1] there was a direction to pay debts, followed by a gift of residue. The debts were not charged on the residue, and Simonds, J., held that the division should be made before the debts were discharged, and that they should be discharged from the undisposed of share.

This basic approach, however, is clearly subject to a contrary intention on the part of the testator, and it can be shown in one of two ways. The will itself may direct that the debts are to be paid before the residue is ascertained; or it may charge the debts on the whole of the residue.

An example of this first situation is *Re Kempthorne, Charles* v. *Kempthorne*.[2]

In that case the testator left all his property, after payment of debts and legacies, to be divided among his brothers and sisters. Two predeceased him. At first instance Maugham, J., held that the mere fact that the testator had directed debts to be paid did not vary the statutory order. Accordingly, he made his division first, and then directed the debts to be paid from the undis-

---

[1] [1939] Ch. 238.
[2] [1930] 1 Ch. 268.

posed of share. This was reversed on appeal: in the opinion of the Court of Appeal the wording of the will, which left the residue "after" payment of expenses, debts and legacies, showed that the testator intended that the debts should be paid before the residue could be ascertained, and so before it could be divided.[1]

Re Harland-Peck, Hercy v. *Mayglothing,*[2] is an example of the other situation in which a contrary intention can be shown, namely where the debts are charged on the whole of the residue. In that case the testator left his property "subject to the payment of funeral and testamentary expenses and debts" to two persons. The Court of Appeal held that these words charged the debts on the whole residue, and that they had to be discharged before the division was made. The Court drew a distinction between a gift which is made subject to the payment of debts; and a direction to pay debts followed by a gift of residue. In the first case, but not the second, there is a charge on the property given.

The distinction between these types of case is easy to state in principle but very difficult to decide in practice. Yet there seems to be no other satisfactory solution. In most cases, it is more convenient to divide first, so that the debts can be paid from property undisposed of, but on the other hand, the testator must retain his right to vary the order if he so wishes.

6. AVAILABILITY OF REALTY

The Act is suspiciously silent as to the extent to which realty is liable for the payment of debts, and it is, therefore, necessary to consider the pre-1926 rules, and then to see whether they have been modified.

a. *Pre-1926 rules*

Before 1926, the extent to which realty could be taken for the payment of debts was clear. The rules were:

(i) debts were payable primarily out of the general personal estate;[3]

---

[1] See also *Re Petty, Holliday* v. *Petty*, [1929] 1 Ch. 726; *Re Atkinson, Webster* v. *Walter*, [1930] Ch. 47.

[2] [1941] Ch. 182.

[3] *Manning* v. *Spooner* (1796), 3 Ves. 114; *Harmood* v. *Oglander* (1803), 8 Ves. 106.

(ii) liability for debts could be shifted from the general personalty to a specific fund of personalty by charging them on the specific fund;[1]

(iii) liability for debts could be shifted from personalty to realty, but in order to do so, it was necessary not only to charge the debts on the realty, but also to show an intention to exonerate the personalty.[2] A charge of the debts on realty, unaccompanied by an intention to exonerate the personalty, merely made the realty liable after the personalty had been exhausted.[3]

b. *Post-1925 position: realty in prior class*

Two situations are to be considered. The first is where there is realty in one category, and personalty in a later category. The second is where there is both realty and personalty in the same category. It is clear beyond doubt that realty in one category can be taken before personalty in a subsequent category. The Schedule uses the word "property", and the definition section[4] shows that "property" includes any interest in real or personal property. Thus, debts should be paid from undisposed of property, even if it is all realty, before residuary property, even if it is all personalty.

c. *Post-1925 position: realty and personalty in same class*

Where realty and personalty are in the same class, the position is not clear. On the one hand it has been said that the personalty must be used in its entirety before any part of the realty can be taken. On the other hand, it has been said that the realty and personalty should be taken rateably.

A case which suggests that the old rules may still apply, or apply in a modified form, is *Re Anstead, Gurney* v. *Anstead*.[5] That case was in fact one on the incidence of legacies, not debts, but the reasoning would appear to apply to debts. The testator's estate consisted of realty worth about £15,000 and personalty

---

[1] *Webb* v. *De Beauvoisin* (1862), 31 Beav. 573; *Vernon* v. *Earl Manvers* (1862), 31 Beav. 623; *Coventry* v. *Coventry* (1865), 2 Dr. & Sm. 470; *Trott* v. *Buchanan* (1885), 28 Ch.D. 446.

[2] *Bootle* v. *Blundell* (1815), 1 Mer. 193; *Bickham* v. *Cruttwell* (1838), 3 My. & Cr. 763; *Collis* v. *Robins* (1847), 1 De G. & Sm. 131; *Trott* v. *Buchanan*, (1885), 28 Ch.D. 446.

[3] *Rhodes* v. *Rudge* (1826), 1 Sim. 79; *Walker* v. *Hardwick* (1833), 1 My. & K. 396; *Forrest* v. *Prescott* (1870), L.R. 10 Eq. 545; *Poole* v. *Heron* (1873), 42 L.J. Ch. 348; *Re Ovey* (1885), 31 Ch.D. 113.

[4] Administration of Estates Act 1925, s. 55 (1) (xvii).

[5] [1943] Ch. 161.

worth about £95,000. He left various legacies, as well as gifts of residue. Utthwatt, J., directed the executors to set aside from the personalty a fund sufficient to satisfy the pecuniary legacies, leaving the realty and residuary personalty available for debts. Paragraphs 1 and 2 of the Schedule, however, while requiring a fund to be set aside to meet pecuniary legacies, do not indicate that the fund to be used is only the personalty. Utthwatt, J., was in fact applying the pre-1926 rules. If they are applicable to legacies, it is possible to argue that the old rules are also applicable to debts.

The other view is that the old rules do not apply, and that the fund for debts should be taken rateably from realty and personalty. There are two arguments in favour of this view. First, this was the view of Luxmoore, L.J., in *Re Harland-Peck, Hercy* v. *Mayglothing*,[1] based on Administration of Estates Act, s. 32. That section provides that "the real and personal estate . . . of a deceased person . . . are assets for the payment of his debts", without distinction being drawn between realty and personalty. Secondly, the Schedule itself uses the word "property", and, as has been mentioned, the definition section of the Act shows that "property" includes any interest in real or personal property.

In the light of this judicial conflict, which approach is to be preferred? On a narrow, if not blinkered, view of the law, the personalty is taken first. It would be argued that the pre-1926 rules, which were not expressly altered, are to continue to apply to the extent that they are not inconsistent with the terms of the Act. But, on a wider view, land has now lost the magic of former centuries, and the whole approach of the Act is to treat realty and personalty alike. It is suggested that the view of Luxmoore, L.J., in *Re Harland-Peck* should be followed, and that realty and personalty should be taken rateably.

7. APPLICATION OF THE STATUTORY ORDER TO DEBTS

It is now possible to consider the application of the statutory schedule upon the basis that the testator has not shown any intention to vary it. It is thought that the administration should proceed according to the following steps.

Step 1. Identify the property which is undisposed of

Strictly, property which is undisposed of is that which remains after the discharge of all debts and legacies. However, it is now

---

[1] [1941] Ch. 182.

clear that where a share of residue lapses, it can be treated as property undisposed of, even though debts have not been taken into account. It has been suggested earlier[1] that the division should be made into shares as the first stage unless there is a provision in the will to the contrary.

Step 2. Set aside a fund from property undisposed of sufficient to meet pecuniary legacies

Paragraph 1 of the Schedule provides that the debts are to be paid from undisposed of property "subject to the retention thereout of a fund sufficient to meet any pecuniary legacies". There is doubt, which is discussed later, whether this imposes on the executors a duty to take pecuniary legacies from the undisposed of property or whether it merely gives them power to do so.[2]

In setting aside a fund for the payment of legacies, it would be more satisfactory to regard property without distinction, or to take the fund from realty and personalty rateably. It has been mentioned, however, that in *Re Anstead, Gurney* v. *Anstead*[3] the fund was taken from personalty alone, and more recently this approach has been followed in *Re Wilson, Wilson* v. *Mackay*.[4] The testatrix died leaving net personalty of about £16,500, and net realty of about £7,000. She gave pecuniary legacies totalling £27,000, and "all my real estate and the residue of my personal estate" to my daughter. There was a clear indication that all the realty was to go to the daughter, and, if necessary, that indication was sufficient under paragraph 8 to displace the statutory order. Pennycuick, J., held that a fund was to be set aside from the personalty to meet the legacies. As the amount of the legacies exceeded the value of the personalty, the whole of the personalty was earmarked for them. However, as the testatrix had shown a clear intention that none of the realty was available for the legacies, no part of them was charged on the realty. The decision depends on the particular wording of the will, but Pennycuick, J., observed[5] that "it may well be that if the incidence of legacies were not covered by express provision in the will the result would be the same under paragraph 2 of Part 2 of Schedule 1". The judge then held that the realty came within paragraph 2 of the Schedule, and the debts were taken from that.

---

[1] See *ante*, p. 527.
[2] See *post*, p. 541.
[3] [1943] Ch. 161.
[4] [1967] Ch. 53.
[5] *Ibid.*, at p. 67.

Step 3. Use remainder of property undisposed of

If any property remains after setting aside the fund for pecuniary legacies, that is to be used for the debts. It seems that if all the property undisposed of is not required for legacies, the amount needed for the debts is taken from realty and personalty rateably after the fund for the legacies has been set aside.

Step 4. Identify the residue

The problems here are to calculate the residue where there is property undisposed of—which was considered in step 1—and to know what gifts of land are residuary. Before 1926 all gifts of freehold land were treated as specific, even though residuary in form.[1] Now, it is clear that a gift of realty can be residuary. The apparent result of the cases is that a gift of realty will be residuary if it is so either objectively, or was intended to be residuary by the testator. Thus, if there is a gift of my house in London to Margaret, and all my other freehold land to Rose, the latter is a gift of residue, just as is a gift of all my freehold land to Rose, even if there is no prior specific gift of realty to Margaret.[2] In *Re Ridley, Nicholson* v. *Nicholson*,[3] however, there was, in effect, a gift of all my land to Margaret, and the residue of my property to Rose. Harman, J., held that the gift of the land was specific, because the wording used in the will showed that the testatrix regarded all her property together, with the land taken out first. It was only her personalty that she thought of as residue.

Step 5. Set aside from residuary property a fund to meet legacies, so far as not provided for in step 2

This would follow step 2, so that, on the reasoning suggested earlier, the residuary personalty will be used first for the pecuniary legacies fund.

Step 6. Use remainder of residue

The remainder of the residue after setting aside a fund for the legacies will be available for debts, taking realty and personalty rateably.

Step 7. Identify the property appropriated for, or charged with, the payment of debts

---

[1] *Hensman* v. *Fryer* (1867), 3 Ch. App. 420; *Lancefield* v. *Iggulden* (1874), 10 Ch. App. 136.

[2] *Re Rowe, Bennetts* v. *Eddy*, [1941] Ch. 343, at p. 348.

[3] [1950] Ch. 415.

This is necessary in order to apply paragraphs 3 and 4 of the Schedule. Property is appropriated where a fund is set aside for the payment of debts, the testator envisaging that it would all be required for that purpose. Property is charged with the payment of debts if it is given to a beneficiary or to the executors subject to an obligation to pay debts.

Step 8. Discharge debts from the property appropriated and the property charged, in so far as they have not been discharged under steps 3 and 6

Step 9. Discharge debts from the pecuniary legacies fund, so far as they have not been discharged in steps 3, 6 and 8

Step 10. Discharge any balance of debts from any property specifically devised or bequeathed

The statute provides that the property in this category shall be subject to the payment of debts "rateably according to value", so that there is no question of personalty being taken before realty.

Step 11. Discharge any balance of debts from property appointed under a general power of appointment

Here also the property is subject to the payment of debts rateably according to value.

Step 12. Discharge debts from property not within the Schedule

It is not clear in which order these types of property will be taken.

E. THE INCIDENCE OF LEGACIES: THE PROBLEMS

It has been seen that the position with regard to the incidence of debts has been altered substantially by the 1925 Act: it has been the subject of much discussion whether the pre-1926 rules as to legacies were also changed by the same legislation, so that the present rules as to the incidence of debts also apply to the incidence of legacies.[1] On this fundamental point there are irreconcilable differences of judicial approach. As an example of one view, in *Re Worthington, Nichols* v. *Hart*[2] Lord Hanworth, M.R., said: "The provisions of the statute indicate that unless

---

[1] See Ryder, "The Incidence of General Pecuniary Legacies" [1956] C.L.J. 80
[2] [1933] Ch. 771.

there is some provision in the will which negatives the prescribed order of administration, that order of administration must apply both to legacies and to debts." The statement would have been more convincing if Lord Hanworth had indicated which provisions he had in mind, or, more importantly, if there were in fact any provisions which gave that indication. In fact, Lord Hanworth was inventing a new rule, although, as will be seen, he has been followed in so doing.[1] On the other hand, *Re Thompson, Public Trustee* v. *Husband*[2] is an example of the other view. In that case, Clauson, J., said: "It is suggested that the effect of that provision (s. 34 (3)) is to alter the law (to equate the incidence of debts and legacies) . . . The provision does not say so, and the provision is not concerned with any such matter. The provision is concerned with the way in which funeral, testamentary and administration expenses, debts and liabilities are to be met. There is no indication that there is any intention of altering the law in respect of the rights of the legatees as against those interested in the residuary personalty and residuary real estate, or in respect of the rights *inter se* of those interested in the residuary realty and personalty respectively, as regards bearing the charge of legacies, and I can see no foundation for the suggestion that that provision has in any way altered 'the law' as previously laid down."

As a result of this complete conflict of judicial approach it is too dangerous to ask the simple question whether the post-1925 rules as to the incidence of debts applies also to legacies. Rather, it is necessary to identify three subsidiary questions which are concealed by the broad simple one, and to ask:

1. Do the pre-1926 rules still operate to identify what property has lapsed, and what forms part of residue?

2. Does the statutory order apply where no point arises as to the nature of the property, such as where it is all personalty?

3. Where the property consists of both realty and personalty, to what extent is realty available for legacies?

In order to answer these questions it is necessary to state the pre-1926 position; and the post-1925 position as to debts; and then to consider the post-1925 position as to legacies.

---

[1] E.g. *Re Lamb, Vipond* v. *Lamb*, [1929] 1 Ch. 722; *Re Gillett's Will Trusts*, [1950] Ch. 102.

[2] [1936] Ch. 676.

F. LEGACIES FROM LAPSED SHARE OF RESIDUE

1. THE PROBLEM

The problem is the same as that considered at p. 526 for debts. Suppose that a testator makes a will leaving £1,000 to his secretary, and directing that his residue is to be divided between his three children. Suppose also that one of the children predeceases him (and that the gift is not saved from lapse[1]). Is the estate divided into three parts, and the legacy taken from the lapsed share? Or is the legacy taken from the estate first, and the residue then divided into three parts?

In essence, the problem consists not in applying the statutory schedule, but in deciding how to ascertain the size of the lapsed share. If the estate in the example just considered is £10,000, and the former solution is adopted the lapsed share is £3,333, and the legacy is taken from that. If the latter solution is adopted, the lapsed share is £3,000.

2. PRE-1926 POSITION

Before 1926, the legacies were paid from the entire estate, and the residue was only ascertained when that had been done. Consequently, legacies were not taken from the lapsed share.

3. POST-1925 POSITION AS TO DEBTS

It has been suggested above[2] that the general rule after 1925 in respect of debts is that the estate is divided into shares first, and that debts are to be taken so far as is possible from the lapsed share; but that this is subject to a contrary intention shown either by an expression that the debts are to be paid before division; or a charging of the debts on the whole of the residue.

4. POST-1925 POSITION AS TO LEGACIES

a. *Statutory trust for sale*

The decisions in the various cases seem often to have depended on the nature of the trust for sale which arises in respect of the lapsed property, although, at least in some of the cases, this factor does not appear to have been in the forefront of the judges'

---

[1] See *ante*, p. 454.
[2] See *ante*, p. 527.

minds. It will be appreciated that usually there will be either an express or a statutory trust for sale.[1] If the will does not contain an express trust for sale, the statutory trust for sale applicable to a total or partial intestacy under s. 33 will apply. This section does not indicate how the undisposed of property is to be calculated, but s. 33 (2) appears to envisage that debts and legacies will be treated in the same way. In the case of a statutory trust for sale, then, it may be expected that the rules as to debts and legacies will be the same, and this does indeed appear to be the case.

Thus, in *Re Worthington, Nichols* v. *Hart*[2] the testatrix left certain legacies and her residue to be divided between two persons, one of whom predeceased her, and the question was whether the legacies should be taken before or after the division of the residue into shares. At first instance, Bennett, J., held that the old law applied, and that the legacies were payable out of the general estate before the residue was ascertained, although he applied the new law to the payment of debts, which were taken from the lapsed share. In so far as it related to legacies, the decision was reversed in the Court of Appeal, and it was held that the residue should be divided first, and the legacies taken from the lapsed share after division.

Re Worthington was followed in *Re Gillett's Will Trusts, Barclays Bank, Ltd.* v. *Gillett*.[3] In that case, the testator had given certain legacies, and then left his residue to provide annuities for four people. On the death of the last of the annuitants, the balance of the fund was then to be held on trust for others. The testator made no provision for the income from the fund which would arise between the deaths of the first and fourth annuitants, and this surplus income was therefore property undisposed of. Roxburgh, J., held that the legacies were to be paid from the property undisposed of, rather than from the residue of the general estate.

b. *Express trust for sale*

Different considerations apply where there is an express trust for sale, for the testator may give his own answer to the problem. It may be clear from the words which he uses that the legacies are

---

[1] There cannot be both an express and a statutory trust for conversion: *Re McKee, Public Trustee* v. *McKee*, [1931] 2 Ch. 145 (*per* Maughan, J., at p. 149); *Re Taylor's Estate and Will Trusts*, [1969] 1 All E.R. 113, at p. 117.
[2] [1933] Ch. 771.
[3] [1950] Ch. 102.

to be paid before the residue can be ascertained, and so before the division into shares can be made. Where this is so, it is not a question whether the old law or the new law applies, but merely what the testator intended. Where, however, no indication is given, the authorities leave the question open. In *Re Midgley, Barclays Bank, Ltd.* v. *Midgley*[1] the testatrix left certain legacies, and then gave her residue upon an express trust for sale for the benefit of six people. She revoked the gift to one of the six, without making any substitutory provision, so that it was undisposed of. Harman, J., held that the division should take place first, and the legacies should be taken primarily from the undisposed of share of residue. On the other hand, the opposite result was reached in *Re Beaumont's Will Trusts, Walker* v. *Lawson*[2] and in the recent decision in *Re Taylor's Estate and Will Trusts*.[3] In the latter case the testatrix left five pecuniary legacies of £100 each, and subject thereto her residuary estate upon trust for sale, and thereafter for division among certain persons, one of whom predeceased the testatrix. The judge found that there was no indication of how the legacies should be borne, and then held that the old law continued to apply.

5. THE SOLUTION

Quite apart from the inconsistency among the express trust for sale cases themselves, it is absurd that the result should depend on whether or not there is an express, as contrasted with a statutory, trust for sale. For the reasoning given in respect of debts,[4] it is suggested that the decisions in *Re Beaumont* and *Re Taylor* are wrong[5] and that the position should be the same as that for debts, whether the trust for sale is statutory or express. It is suggested, therefore, that the rule *should* be that the residue should be divided first, and the legacies taken from the lapsed share, unless there is some provision to the contrary in the will.

---

[1] [1955] Ch. 576.
[2] [1950] Ch. 462.
[3] [1969] 2 Ch. 245.
[4] See *ante*, p. 527.
[5] See Albery (1969), 85 L.Q.R. 464.

G. DOES THE STATUTORY SCHEDULE APPLY TO LEGACIES?

1. THE PROBLEM

The problem just considered involves the application of the statutory schedule, but it is really a preliminary to it: the rules just considered identify the size of the property undisposed of, and the Schedule can then apply, unless in the very process of the ascertainment of the property undisposed of, the legacies have been paid. The true nature of the problem is seen by taking situations where there is no property undisposed of. Suppose, for example, that a testator gives a fund of £5,000 to Vanessa, subject to the payment thereout of a legacy of £300 to her grandson, and the residue to Matilda. Is the legacy to be taken from the property charged with the payment of the legacy which would be the position under the pre-1926 law; or are they to be taken from residue applying paragraph 2 of the Schedule, in priority to the legacy to Vanessa (para. 4)?

2. POST-1925 RULES AS TO LEGACIES

There is a good deal of superficial attraction in suggesting that the Schedule does not apply. The Schedule is governed by s. 34 (3) which provides that "debts and liabilities" shall be payable in the order mentioned in the Schedule. It would not normally even be suggested that the word "liabilities" includes legacies. There is no express provision that the Schedule shall apply to legacies. Further, the wording of the Schedule itself contains surprising omissions if it is to govern legacies. For example, it would be expected that paragraphs 3 and 4 would also deal with legacies. It seems, therefore, fairly likely that the legislature did not intend legacies to be affected by the Schedule.

But the position is open. There is, as yet, no authority to determine the solution to the problem posed above affecting Vanessa and Matilda. And the inconsistency of judicial approach mentioned earlier shows that the basis for the solution has not been established in any way.

3. THE SOLUTION

In these circumstances one is free to suggest the solution. Again, it is suggested that the rules as to debts and legacies should be equated, as in the case of the suggestion made above[1] as to the

---

[1] See *ante*, p. 537.

incidence of legacies where there is a lapsed share. But it is stressed that this is only a suggestion: the actual position is open.

H. AVAILABILITY OF REALTY TO SATISFY LEGACIES

1. THE PROBLEM

The problem here does not specifically involve the Schedule. Suppose that the testator leaves a legacy of £5,000 to his wife, and the residue of his property between his brothers Peter and Paul. Suppose also that the estate consists of personalty worth £4,000 and realty worth £6,000. Is the legacy to be paid as to £2,000 from personalty and as to £3,000 from realty? Or is it to be paid so far as possible from personalty, so that the whole of the personalty is taken, and only £1,000 from realty? Or, even, is it to be paid only to the extent that personalty is available, so that while the whole of the personalty is taken, no part of the realty is available, and the legacy therefore abates to £4,000?

The problem is important from three points of view. The legatee is concerned to know whether the legacy will be paid in full. The position of the residuary beneficiaries is affected if there is a gift of realty to one person and personalty to another. And the incidence of estate duty can also be affected.

2. PRE-1926 POSITION

The position before 1926 was:

a. in the absence of a contrary intention in the will, pecuniary legacies were payable only out of residuary personalty. If that was not sufficient, the legacies abated proportionately;[1]

b. where there was a gift of residuary realty and personalty together, the testator was presumed to have intended that the residuary realty could be taken after the personalty was exhausted.[2] Thus, all the residuary personalty would be taken first, and then resort could be made to the realty;

c. where there was a gift of personalty and realty together, and the testator expressly directed that the legacies were to be paid from it, the realty and personalty were proportionately liable to satisfy the legacies;[3]

---

[1] *Robertson* v. *Broadbent* (1883), 8 App. Cas. 812.
[2] *Greville* v. *Browne* (1859), 7 H.L.C. 689.
[3] *Roberts* v. *Walker* (1830), 1 Russ & M. 152.

d. legacies could be paid from realty in priority to personalty if, and only if, the testator both charged the realty with payment of legacies, and also showed an intention to exonerate the personalty.[1]

3. POST-1925 POSITION AS TO DEBTS

It was suggested above[2] that realty and personalty should be treated without distinction, but that the authorities, particularly *Re Anstead*[3] and *Re Wilson*[4], show that personalty is to be used first.

4. POST-1925 POSITION AS TO LEGACIES

There is a strong indication that the pre-1926 rules still apply. *Re Thompson, Public Trustee* v. *Husband*[5] has already been mentioned.[6] The testator's estate consisted of, in very general figures, personalty worth about £2,000 and net realty worth about £10,000. He left legacies of £3,000, and gifts of residue. Clauson, J., rejected a suggestion that about £500 should be taken from personalty, and £2,500 from realty. He directed that the £2,000 personalty should be taken in full, and the balance made up from realty. *Re Wilson*[7] strongly suggests that this approach will be followed.

It is against this general approach that two specific situations can be considered:

a. *Realty and personalty in same class*

The pre-1926 law has been applied to show that where realty and personalty are in the same class, generally legacies can only be paid from personalty, and that they will abate to the extent that the personalty is not sufficient.[8] Realty can, however, be used to make up a shortfall where there is insufficient personalty if both are given in one mass;[9] and, presumably, realty and personalty will be taken rateably where there is a direction to

---

[1] *Elliott* v. *Dearsley* (1881), 16 Ch.D. 322.
[2] See *ante*, p. 531.
[3] [1943] Ch. 161.
[4] [1967] Ch. 53.
[5] [1936] Ch. 676.
[6] See *ante*, p. 534.
[7] [1967] Ch. 53.
[8] *Re Rowe, Bennetts* v. *Eddy*, [1941] Ch. 343.
[9] *Re Anstead, Gurney* v. *Anstead*, [1943] Ch. 161; *Re Timson, Harper* v. *Timson*, [1953] 2 All E.R. 1252.

pay the legacies from a fund of realty and personalty given in one mass.[1]

b. *Realty and personalty in different classes*

It seems clear that where there is a statutory trust for sale, the realty ceases to exist as such, and what was realty is available for legacies. Thus, in *Re Martin, Midland Bank Executor and Trustee Co., Ltd.*[2] a gift of realty which lapsed, and was undisposed of, but which was subject to the statutory trust for sale, was held to be available for the payment of legacies in priority to residuary personalty.[3] In the absence of authority, the same would appear to be the approach in the case of an express trust for sale.

5. THE SOLUTION

The general approach of preserving the pre-1926 law, and thus giving priority to personalty, accords with the general position in respect of debts, and thus is consistent with the view maintained here that the rules as to debts ought to be equated with those governing legacies. On the other hand, it is now distinctly archaic to treat land in this special way, and the ideal solution will be to treat land in the same way as personalty both as regards debts and as regards legacies.

I. THE PECUNIARY LEGACIES FUND

It will be recalled that paragraph 1 of the Schedule deals with property undisposed of "subject to the retention thereout of a fund sufficient to meet any pecuniary legacies". Paragraph 2 deals with residuary property "subject to the retention out of such property of a fund sufficient to meet any pecuniary legacies, so far as not provided for (under paragraph 1)". It is suggested that these words mean what they say, and that personal representatives are under an obligation to set aside a pecuniary legacies fund from

---

[1] See, on the pre-1926 law, *Re Boards, Knight* v. *Knight*, [1895] 1 Ch. 499.
[2] [1955] Ch. 699.
[3] See also *Re Berrey's Will Trusts, Greening* v. *Walters*, [1959] 1 W.L.R. 30; and (1959), 23 Conv. (N.S.) 139.

undisposed of property, and, if necessary, from residue.[1] In *Re Taylor's Estate and Will Trusts*,[2] however, Salt, Q.C., Ch., came to the opposite conclusion, and held that the words did not impose a mandatory obligation, but were to be read subject to words such as "if appropriate" or "at the discretion of the personal representatives". The judge gave four reasons in support of his view:

1. In respect of property undisposed of, an inconsistency arises with s. 33 (2). This sub-section, which imposes a statutory trust to convert property which devolves on a total or partial intestacy in accordance with the intestacy rules, provides that the personal representatives must pay the debts, and that out of the residue of the converted property they must set aside a fund to provide for pecuniary legacies. Thus, s. 33 envisages that the pecuniary legacies fund is not to be established until after the debts have been paid: and this would be inconsistent with an obligation in paragraphs 1 and 2 to establish a pecuniary legacies fund before the debts have been paid. The judge maintained that the clearly mandatory provisions of s. 33 (2) are not to be modified by the less strong words of the Schedule. Yet the expressions in paragraphs 1 and 2 must be intended to have the same meaning whenever they apply; and there can be no inconsistency with s. 33 in the case of property undisposed of where there is an express trust for sale[3] nor where the gift is of residue. The inconsistency is, therefore, confined to the case of a total or partial intestacy where there is no express trust for sale. In order to preserve consistency within the Schedule, it seems better to modify the apparent effect of s. 33. The apparent effect of one or the other must be modified.

2. Paragraph 5 of the Schedule deals with "The fund, if any, retained to meet pecuniary legacies". The judge considered that this wording indicated that there may be a gift of pecuniary legacies, where no fund has been set aside to answer them. Had this not been so, he suggested that the Schedule would have been worded

---

[1] See *ante*, pp. 531 and 532.

[2] [1969] 1 All E.R. 113.

[3] Because there cannot be both a subsisting express trust for sale and a statutory trust for sale: *Re McKee, Public Trustee* v. *McKee*, [1931] 2 Ch. 145, *per* Maugham, J., at p. 149. In *Re Taylor*, Salt, Q.C., Ch., accepted this principle (at p. 117).

"The fund retained to meet pecuniary legacies, if any". To this it may be answered that in a Schedule where there has been so much imprecision in other respects—which have occupied most of this chapter—such precision would be surprising. Surely the more obvious meaning of the paragraph is any fund which has been retained in accordance with the previous provisions, without indicating whether or not there was an obligation under those previous to set such a fund aside.

3. The words "subject to the retention . . ." are a curious formula if the legislature had intended to impose (as in s. 33 (2)) a clear obligation on the personal representatives to retain a fund to meet pecuniary legacies"[1] This may be so, but it is hardly a sufficient ground for going in the face of what is suggested to be their obvious meaning.

4. If the words were read in a mandatory sense, they would, as has been seen,[2] reverse the pre-1926 rules. It is here that one comes back to the basic problem: was this the intention?

The judge's reasons are hardly convincing—even though, individually, they may not be capable of convincing reply.[3] But the words "subject to the retention . . ." must be intended to have some meaning, if Parliament has made a solemn act, and not a solemn farce. It would lead to an absurd result to read the words, as the judge suggested, as being subject to the personal representatives' discretion: clearly beneficial entitlement cannot be allowed to depend on the personal representatives' discretion without the very clearest words. It is suggested that the decision is wrong, and that the words do impose a statutory duty.

---

[1] [1969] 1 All E.R. 113, at p. 118.
[2] See *ante*, p. 539.
[3] But see Albery (1969), 85 L.Q.R. 464.

CHAPTER 33

DONATIONES MORTIS CAUSA

A *donatio mortis causa* is a type of gift which is mid way between a gift *inter vivos* and a testamentary gift. As there are special rules governing the devolution of property comprised in a *donatio mortis causa*, its liability for the debts of the deceased, and incidence of estate duty, it will be convenient to deal with the whole subject here.

A. REQUIREMENTS FOR *DONATIO MORTIS CAUSA*

1. MEANING

A *donatio mortis causa* is a gift made by a person in his lifetime with the intention that it shall take effect only on that person's death. The gift is therefore conditional upon death, but once the condition is satisfied it takes effect retroactively, from the date of the gift.[1] It follows that the donor must have intended that the gift should be absolute upon the condition being fulfilled.[2]

The institution of *donatio mortis causa* is derived from Roman law, and was introduced into English law through the church courts. The reason for recognising it was given by Lord Cowper in *Hedges* v. *Hedges*[3] in these terms: "Where a man lies in extremity, or being surprised with sickness, and not having an opportunity of making his will; but lest he should die before he could make it, he gives with his own hands his goods to his friends about him: this, if he dies, shall operate as a legacy; but if he recovers, then does the property thereof revert to him".

---

[1] *Rigden* v. *Vallier* (1751), 2 Ves. Sen. 252; *Kelly* v. *O'Connor*, [1917] 1 I.R. 312.

[2] *Re Beaumont, Beaumont* v. *Ewbank*, [1902] 1 Ch. 889, at p. 892.

[3] (1708), Prec. Ch. 269.

2. CHARACTERISTICS

A valid *donatio mortis causa* must fulfil the following three conditions:

a. the gift must be made in contemplation of the donor's death;
b. the donor must intend it to be conditional upon his death, but subject thereto, to be unconditional; and
c. the donor must have parted with dominion over the asset.

a. *Made in contemplation of death*

It follows from the statement by Lord Cowper given above that a *donatio mortis causa* is usually made during an illness of the donor. In this case, the donor must contemplate the possibility of his death from that illness, or from surgery as a result of that illness.[1] It is not sufficient therefore, for the donor to contemplate death in a general way, and at no particular time, but he must contemplate his death within the near future, and from some reason which he believes to be impending.[2]

The donor may make the gift conditional upon death from a specified cause, and if he does so, that condition will be effective.[3] If, however, it is not made conditional upon a particular cause of death, the *donatio* will be valid even if death occurs from another cause. Accordingly, if the donor makes a gift in contemplation of death from an illness from which he is suffering, without the gift being conditional on death actually occurring from that cause, and he is killed in an accident while being taken to hospital in an ambulance, the gift will be valid.[4]

b. *Conditional on death*

The gift must be intended to be conditional on the death of the donor. If, therefore, the gift is intended to be unconditional, and so to take effect *inter vivos*, it cannot amount to a valid *donatio mortis causa*.[5] In this case it will depend for its validity

---

[1] *Agnew* v. *Belfast Banking Co.*, [1896] 2 I.R. 204, at p. 221.
[2] *Re Craven's Estate*, [1937] Ch. 423, at p. 426; see also *Wilkes* v. *Allington*, [1931] 2 Ch. 104, at p. 110.
[3] *Wilkes* v. *Allington, ante; Mills* v. *Shields* and *Kelly*, [1948] I.R. 367.
[4] *Agnew* v. *Belfast Banking Co., supra.*
[5] *Walter* v. *Hodge* (1818), 2 Swan. 92; *Edwards* v. *Jones* (1836), 1 My. & Cr. 226; *Re Lillingston, Pembery* v. *Pembery*, [1952] 2 All E.R. 184.

on whether it complies with the formalities for an *inter vivos* gift, or where the donee subsequently acquires the legal title by becoming personal representative, whether it is saved by the rule in *Strong* v. *Bird*.[1]

Although, strictly, the donee ought to prove that the gift was to take effect only on death,[2] the courts will infer this, at least where the gift is made during the donor's last illness.[3] In *Gardner* v. *Parker*[4] for example, two days before his death, and when already confined to his bed, the donor gave a bond for £1,800 to the donee with the words: "There, take that, and keep it". Leach, V.C., found in favour of the donee, and inferred the necessary condition that the gift was to take effect only upon death from the illness from which the donor was then suffering.

c. *Parting with dominion*

The basic rule is that the property to be disposed of must actually be handed over to the donee,[5] or to someone else as trustee for the donee.[6] Where the subject matter of the gift is a small item of personal property, such as a watch, this is clearly possible, but other rules have had to be established to deal with the situation where the item is too bulky to be handed over in this way, or where it is an item of property, such as a debt, which is not capable of manual delivery.

Where the article is too bulky to be physically handed over, it is sufficient for the donor to hand over the means whereby the donee can take possession. In a number of cases[7] the delivery of a key to, for example, a trunk or a warehouse, has been regarded as a valid delivery of the goods in the trunk or warehouse. It is important to note that the donor is not handing over a mere

---

[1] (1874), L.R. 18 Eq. 315; and see *post* p. 550.

[2] *Irons* v. *Smallpiece* (1819), 2 B. & Ald. 551; *Tate* v. *Leithead* (1854), Kay 658; *Staniland* v. *Willot* (1851), 3 Mac. & G. 664, at p. 675.

[3] *Wilkes* v. *Allington, supra.*

[4] (1818), 3 Madd. 184.

[5] *Ward* v. *Turner* (1751), 2 Ves. Sen. 431; *Irons* v. *Smallpiece, supra; Powell* v. *Hellicar* (1858), 26 Beav. 261; *Re Johnson, Sandy* v. *Reilly* (1905), 92 L.T. 357; *Re Craven's Estate, ante.*

[6] *Drury* v. *Smith* (1717), 1 P. Wms. 404; *Re Korvine's Trust*, [1921] 1 Ch. 343.

[7] *Jones* v. *Selby* (1710), Prec. Ch. 300; *Ward* v. *Turner, supra; Smith* v. *Smith* (1740), 2 Stra. 955; *Re Wasserberg, Union of London and Smiths Bank, Ltd.* v. *Wasserberg*, [1915] 1 Ch. 195; *Re Lillingston, Pembery* v. *Pembery*, [1952] 2 All E.R. 184.

symbol of possession, for that is not sufficient, but the very means by which possession can be obtained.[1]

The position is clearly illustrated by *Reddel* v. *Dobree*.[2] The donor gave to the donee a locked cash box, telling her that it contained money for her to use when he had died, and that on his death she should obtain the key from his son. The donor required the donee to produce the box to him at three monthly intervals for the remainder of his life. This was done on two occasions, but after each production the box was returned to the donee. The donor kept the key throughout. Shadwell, V.C., held that this did not amount to a valid *donatio* because the donee had not been put in full possession of the box, and the donor had retained throughout his life full power over it.[3]

Gifts of the balances in bank accounts cause difficulty. The basic principle applies, that the donor must hand over to the donee not merely a symbol of ownership, but the instrument which entitles the donee to payment. A cheque drawn in favour of the donor, and endorsed in favour of the donee may when handed over, be a valid *donatio*,[4] and likewise bank notes can be the subject matter of a gift.[5] A cheque drawn by the donor in favour of the donee cannot be the subject matter of a *donatio* because it is regarded only as an order by the donor to his bankers.[6]

A bank statement, or a pass-book of a current account is regarded only as a symbol of ownership, and is not sufficient to constitute a *donatio* nor is the passbook of a deposit account which is operated by the donor in the same way as a current account.[7] Deposit account passbooks, where the deposit account is operated as a deposit account and not as a current account, give more difficulty. The position was considered in *Birch* v. *Treasury Solicitor*.[8] The deceased had made a gift of a Trustee Savings Bank book, and of the deposit pass books of two joint stock banks.

---

[1] *Ward* v. *Turner, supra; Bunn* v. *Markham* (1816), 7 Taunt. 224.

[2] (1839), 10 Sim. 244.

[3] See also *Treasury Solicitor* v. *Lewis*, [1900] 2 Ch. 812.

[4] *Clement* v. *Cheesman* (1884), 27 Ch.D. 631.

[5] *Miller* v. *Miller* (1735), 3 P. Wms. 356; *Re Hawkins*, [1924] 2 Ch. 47

[6] *Re Beaumont, Beaumont* v. *Ewbank*, [1902] 1 Ch. 889.

[7] *Delgoffe* v. *Fader*, [1939] Ch. 922, as explained in *Birch* v. *Treasury Solicitor*, [1951] Ch. 298.

[8] [1951] Ch. 298.

In *Ward* v. *Turner*[1] Lord Hardwicke had said that a *donatio mortis causa* could not be made "without a transfer or something amounting to that". The Court of Appeal attempted to apply this test. As Lord Evershed, M.R. said: "The question then is, where actual transfer does not or cannot take place, what will 'amount to that'?" He then said: "we think that the real test is whether the instrument 'amounts to a transfer' as being the essential indicia or evidence of title, possession or production of which entitled the possessor to the money or property purported to be given". On this basis, the Court of Appeal held that the deceased had made a valid *donatio mortis causa*. Although the decision is in accord with common sense, it is by no means clear in any particular case what will amount to the essential indicia of title.[2] Although a deposit passbook is the nearest that may be obtained, the donee cannot obtain the money merely by production of the passbook: the signature of the donee on a withdrawal form is also required. It follows that whereas for personal chattels the donee must be able to obtain actual possession of the chattels during the donor's lifetime, in the case of a chose in action, it is sufficient that he has the essential indicia of title, without actually being able to obtain the money due within the deceased's lifetime.

It is in accord with *Birch* v. *Treasury Solicitor* that it has been held that a bond, and a mortgage deed can be the subject of a *donatio*.[3] However, there can be no valid *donatio* of land.[4]

B. DEVOLUTION OF PROPERTY

It has already been stated that once the gift has become unconditional by virtue of the death of the deceased, it takes effect retroactively to the date of the gift. The ownership in the property therefore passes by the gift, and does not devolve on the personal representatives.[5] This was so before 1925, and there is no provision in the Administration of Estates Act to alter the position.

---

[1] (1752), 2 Ves. Sen. 431.

[2] See note by R.E.M., 81 L.Q.R. 21.

[3] *Duffield* v. *Elwes* (1827), 1 Bli. N.S. 497; see also *Snellgrove* v. *Baily* (1744), 3 Atk. 214; *Ward* v. *Turner, ante; Gardner* v. *Parker, ante; Re Dillon, Duffin* v. *Duffin* (1890), 44 Ch.D. 76; *Re Richards, Jones* v. *Rebbeck*, [1921] 1 Ch. 513.

[4] *Duffield* v. *Hicks* (1827), 1 Bli. N.S. 497.

[5] *Rigden* v. *Vallier* (1751), 2 Ves. Sen. 252; *Kelly* v. *O'Connor*, [1917] 1 I.R. 312.

Where, however, some further act is necessary to complete the title of the donee, for example, where there is a gift of a mortgage, and a transfer of mortgage to the donee is necessary before the mortgagor can obtain a good receipt for the redemption monies, the personal representatives can be compelled to perfect the gift.[1]

Although for general purposes the property in the subject matter of the gift does not devolve on death, for estate duty purposes, it is regarded as "passing" on death, so that duty is payable.[2]

It follows from the fact that the property in the subject matter of the gift does not pass to the personal representatives that they are not liable for the estate duty on the gift, and that that estate duty is not a testamentary expense of the estate.[3] The donee is, therefore, responsible for the payment of duty. If the personal representatives pay the duty on the gift at the request of the donee, they automatically obtain a charge over the property comprised in the gift for their reimbursement.[4]

C. AVAILABILITY FOR DEBTS

Although the property in the gift passes to the donee in the donor's lifetime, it has been held that where the deceased's estate is not sufficient for the payment of all his debts and liabilities, then property given by a *donatio* may be used for this purpose, but only after all the assets of the estate have been exhausted completely.[5]

D. DEFECTIVE *DONATIONES MORTIS CAUSA*

Where the deceased has attempted to make a *donatio mortis causa*, but has done so ineffectively, then the personal representatives will not be compelled to complete the gift. It is an illustration of the rule that equity will not assist a volunteer.[6]

---

[1] *Duffield* v. *Elwes, ante; Re Wasserberg, Union of London and Smiths Bank Ltd.* v. *Wasserberg*, [1915] 1 Ch. 195, at p. 202.

[2] Customs and Inland Revenue Act 1881, s. 38 (2) (a); Finance Act 1894, s. 2 (1) (c); *Re Hudson, Spencer* v. *Turner*, [1911] 1 Ch. 206.

[3] *Re Hudson, Spencer* v. *Turner, supra.*

[4] Finance Act 1894, ss. 6 (2), 9.

[5] *Smith* v. *Casen*, not reported, but mentioned in *Drury* v. *Smith* (1717), 1 P. Wms. 404; *Re Korvine's Trusts*, [1921] 1 Ch. 343.

[6] *Per* Lord Eldon, L.C. in *Duffield* v. *Elwes* (1827), 1 Bl. N.S. 497.

Nevertheless, it may be possible for the gift to be saved under the rule in *Strong* v. *Bird*.[1] The principle in this case is that where the deceased intended to make a gift to the donee, but attempted to do so ineffectively, then if the donee subsequently acquires the legal title to that property, the gift will be completed. This is because there are two elements in a complete gift: an intention to make the gift, and the transfer of the legal title. Accordingly, where the intention continued to the date of death,[2] and the legal title is then transferred to the donee, the two elements are present, albeit perhaps not concurrently. The legal title is usually acquired by a grant of probate[3] or letters of administration,[4] but it may be acquired in any other way.[5]

In theory, there is a difference between the element of intention required for the rule in *Strong* v. *Bird* to operate, on the one hand, and for there to be a valid *donatio mortis causa* on the other hand. The intention in the former case is to make an *inter vivos* gift, whereas in the latter case it is to make a gift conditional on death. Despite this theoretical difference, however, it may well be possible in practice to establish sufficient evidence for *Strong* v. *Bird* to apply where it is not possible to establish a valid *donatio mortis causa*.

---

[1] (1874), L.R. 18 Eq. 315; *Re Stewart Stewart* v. *McLaughlin*, [1908] 2 Ch. 251.

[2] *Re Freeland, Jackson* v. *Rodgers*, [1952] Ch. 110; see also *Re Innes, Innes* v. *Innes*, [1910] 1 Ch. 188.

[3] As in *Strong* v. *Bird* itself.

[4] *Re James, James* v. *James*, [1935] Ch. 449.

[5] *Re Ralli's Will Trusts*, [1964] Ch. 288.

CHAPTER 34

DISTRIBUTION AMONG BENEFICIARIES

A. POWER OF APPROPRIATION

It is realised that a beneficiary who is left, say, a pecuniary legacy might prefer to take articles of similar value belonging to the estate. Administration of Estates Act 1925, s. 41 which applies to both testate and intestate estates[1] accordingly confers a power of appropriation on the personal representatives.

The power may be exercised in favour of legatees, or in favour of persons entitled to a share in residue.[2] It may not be exercised in respect of property which is subject to a specific devise or bequest[3] without the consent of the specific beneficiary, but subject to that, the power applies in respect of all property of any description forming part of the estate.

Property which is appropriated is taken in the actual condition or state of investment which it has at the time of appropriation[4] and it is likewise valued at that time.[5]

The statutory power can only be exercised subject to certain consents. If the beneficiary is absolutely entitled, he must consent, or, if he is not *sui iuris*, his parent or person having control over his property may consent on his behalf.[6] Where an appropriation is being made in respect of an interest under the will which is settled, the consent required is that of the tenant for life,[7] or of

---

[1] Administration of Estates Act 1925, s. 41 (9).
[2] *Ibid.*, s. 41 (1).
[3] *Ibid*, s. 41 (1) proviso (i).
[4] *Ibid*, s. 41 (1).
[5] *Re Lepine, Dowsett* v. *Culver*, [1892] 1 Ch. 210; *Re Brooks, Coles* v. *Davis* (1897), 76 L.T. 771; *Re Nickels, Nickels* v. *Nickels*, [1898] 1 Ch. 630; *Re Charteris, Charteris* v. *Biddulph*, [1917] 2 Ch. 379.
[6] Administration of Estates Act 1925, s. 41 (1) proviso (ii) (b).
[7] *Ibid.*

the trustee if he is a person different from the personal representative.[1]

The section expressly authorises the setting apart of a fund to answer an annuity by means of the income of that fund, or in some other way, but it is unclear whether, following such an appropriation, the annuitant loses his right of recourse to other parts of residue in the event of deficiency.[2]

Once an appropriation has been made it binds all persons who have consented, by virtue of their consent, and all persons who are interested in the property but whose consent is not required by virtue of the section.[3]

The statutory power is important. Once made, the beneficiary to whom property is appropriated suffers any subsequent loss of the property, and obtains the benefit of any accretions. But it has one disadvantage. Except where the appropriation is in favour of a residuary beneficiary[4] or where it consists of the matrimonial home appropriated to the surviving spouse,[5] or where it consists of the total estate of an intestate payable to the surviving spouse,[6] the instrument by which the appropriation is made will be subject to stamp duty at the rate of £1 per £100 of the value of the article.[7] For this reason, many wills contain an express power of appropriation incorporating the statutory power, but declaring it to be exercisable without any of the consents required by s. 41. Where this power is given, no stamp duty is payable, as the contractual element has been removed.

B. TRANSFER SUBJECT TO EXISTING LIABILITIES

Items of property may automatically be subject to two types of liability. Where during the lifetime of the deceased incumbrances

---

[1] Administration of Estates Act 1925, s. 41 (9).

[2] But on principle he should lose it: *Baker* v. *Farmer* (1867), L.R. 4 Eq. 382; *Ballard* v. *Marsden* (1880), 14 Ch.D. 374; *Fraser* v. *Murdoch* (1881), 6 App. Cas. 855.

[3] Administration of Estates Act 1925, s. 41 (4).

[4] This is generally acepted as being so, although there are *dicta* to the contrary in *Re Beverley, Watson* v. *Watson*, [1901] 1 Ch. 681.

[5] Intestates' Estates Act 1952, s. 6 and Schedule I.

[6] According to Revenue practice.

[7] *Re Beverley, Watson* v. *Watson*, [1901] Ch. 681; *Dawson* v. *Inland Revenue Commissioners*, [1905] 2 Ir. R. 69; *Jopling* v. *Inland Revenue Commissioners*, [1940] 2 K.B. 282.

were charged on them, then the personal representatives may transfer the property to the beneficiary entitled subject to that charge. Where there is no danger that the creditor will not be paid there is no objection to this course. Thus, if a house worth £6,000 is subject to a mortgage of £2,000, as was pointed out earlier,[1] in the absence of contrary intention in the will, the devisee takes subject to that mortgage. The personal representatives will, however, be liable if the creditor is not paid, perhaps because of the subsequent diminution in value of the asset transferred. They must, therefore, require payment to be made prior to transfer to the beneficiary if there is any doubt.

Secondly, property may be transferred to a beneficiary subject to estate duty. Estate duty is dealt with in two ways. In respect of property which on the death of the deceased passed to the personal representative "as such", that is, by virtue of his office in accordance with the law prevailing at that time, the estate duty becomes a charge on the estate, and ranks as an administration expense.[2] In general terms, this will include all English personalty. Real property did not pass to the executor as such, and together with certain other types of property[3] remains subject to the provisions of Finance Act 1894, s. 9 (1). Under this section, the property is said to "carry its own duty", that is, the duty is a first charge on the property itself. Accordingly, the beneficiary will take subject to the charge for duty if it has not been paid in pursuance of a direction in the will out of the general estate, and also, in the absence of a registered charge, a purchaser is not affected by any outstanding claim for duty.[4]

In other cases, the assets will be transferred to the beneficiaries free of incumbrances.

C. MODE OF TRANSFER

1. ASSENT

a. *Use*

Both executors and administrators[5] may transfer an estate or

---

[1] See *ante*, p. 519.

[2] *Re Clemow, Yeo* v. *Clemow*, [1900] 2 Ch. 182.

[3] Other types of asset which do not pass to the personal representative as such are foreign property, property included in gifts and settlements, and the share of a deceased joint tenant.

[4] Land Charges Act 1972, s. 4 (6).

[5] Administration of Estates Act 1925, s. 36 (1).

interest in realty and in leaseholds[1] by means of an assent.[2] Assents differ from the general rule that a document transferring a legal estate must be under seal in that by virtue of Administration of Estates Act 1925, s. 6 (4), they need only be in writing. That sub-section also requires an assent to be signed by the personal representatives, and to name the person in whose favour it is given. The power to make an assent is restricted to personal representatives, and cannot be used by trustees.

There is some doubt as to the circumstances in which an assent may be used. Section 36 (1) confers upon personal representatives the power to use an assent to vest a legal estate in "any person who (whether by devise, bequest, devolution, appropriation or otherwise) may be entitled thereto". The doubt relates to whether an assent may be used in favour of a purchaser. The nearest decision appears to be *G.H.R. Co., Ltd.* v. *Inland Revenue Commissioners*.[3] In his lifetime the testator had sold his property, and had received the purchase money for it, but he had not executed a conveyance in favour of the purchaser. His executor had to make title, and did so by means of an assent. This was upheld. There is no decision where the purchase price is payable upon the handing over of the sale deed, as is the normal case, although there is little advantage in using an assent. Although it is a shorter document than a conveyance, the stamp duty payable is the same.[4]

Where a personal representative is expressed to assent "as personal representative" he will thereby give the same covenants for title as if he were executing a conveyance.[5]

b. *Effect*

When an assent is made, it is that document which vests the legal estate in the person in whose favour it is made.[6] Under the will, or the intestacy rules, he only acquires an equitable interest.[7] However, when the assent is made, it relates back to the death of the deceased unless it contains an expression of intention to the contrary.[8]

---

[1] Administration of Estates Act 1923, s. 36 (1).
[2] *Ibid.*
[3] [1943] K.B. 303.
[4] See cases cited in footnote 7, *ante*, p. 552.
[5] Administration of Estates Act 1925, s. 36 (3).
[6] *Ibid*, s. 36 (2).
[7] See *ante*, pp. 439 *et seq*.
[8] Administration of Estates Act 1925, s. 36 (2).

It has already been pointed out that the personal representative will not wish to distribute the estate until provision has been made for all outstanding liabilities. He is given power to require a beneficiary to give security for outstanding liabilities as a condition of giving an assent, and an assent may be subject to any legal mortgage.[1] The personal representative may not, however, delay giving an assent because of outstanding liabilities if reasonable arrangements have been made for them.[2]

Where he wishes to defer giving an assent, the personal representative may take advantage of Administration of Estates Act, s. 43. Under that section, he may allow a person who appears to be entitled to an assent to enter into possession of the property prior to giving the assent. That permission does not prevent him subsequently retaking possession, and disposing of the property if this is necessary in the course of the administration of the estate. By using s. 43 the beneficiary can be given possession at an early date, leaving the assent to follow when all liabilities have been dealt with.

Protection of purchasers and others

A beneficiary in whose favour an assent is made is entitled to insist that a notice of the assent is endorsed on the probate or letters of administration at the cost of the estate. He may also require the personal representatives at any future time to produce the grant to prove that the notice has been endorsed.[3] As will now be shown, the endorsement of this notice protects the beneficiary against a disposition in favour of a purchaser.

A purchaser will normally insist that the conveyance to him contains a statement by the personal representatives that they have not previously given or made any assent or conveyance in respect of the legal estate.[4] If this statement is incorrect, it does not prejudice the title of any previous purchaser, but if the personal representatives have previously made an assent in favour of a beneficiary, the execution of the conveyance with this statement operates to shift the legal estate from that beneficiary to the purchaser.[5] The conveyance only has this effect, however, if the

---

[1] Administration of Estates Act 1925, s. 36 (10).
[2] *Ibid.*
[3] *Ibid*, s. 36 (5).
[4] *Ibid*, s. 36 (6).
[5] *Ibid*, s. 36 (6) (2nd paragraph).

purchaser accepted the conveyance on the faith of this statement, and if there was no notice of a previous assent endorsed on the grant of representation.

There is little advantage in including in an assent to a beneficiary a statement that the personal representative has not previously given any assent or made any conveyance because the statutory protection applies only in favour of purchasers. Conversely, although purchasers are entitled to have a notice of their conveyance endorsed on the grant[1] they will not be prejudiced if they fail to do so.

It is a principle of the 1925 legislation that equitable interests are kept off the title, and a will can since 1925 affect only the equitable interests. Accordingly, a purchaser is never concerned to look at the will when investigating title from personal representatives. As a result he does not know that the assent or conveyance is made in favour of the person properly entitled. Section 36 (7) confers a large measure of protection. It provides that in favour of a purchaser, the fact that an assent or conveyance is made by a personal representative is "sufficient evidence that the person in whose favour [it] is given is the person entitled to have the legal estate conveyed to him". This will usually be adequate protection for the purchaser, but it should be noted that "sufficient evidence" is not "conclusive evidence". Almost certainly a purchaser is not required to examine the will to ensure that the assent is made in favour of the correct person, but he will be affected by notice received during the proper investigation of title of the fact that the assent or conveyance should have been made in favour of another. Thus, in *Re Duce and Boots Cash Chemists (Southern), Ltd.'s Contract*[2] a recital in the assent showed that the land was prior to the death of the deceased settled, and that it remained settled notwithstanding his death. Accordingly it should have been vested in the next tenant for life. In fact the assent was in favour of the remainderman, and the purchaser's objection to the title was upheld.

2. OTHER INSTRUMENTS

Apart from assents, the formalities normally observed upon the transfer of the legal title in an asset must be followed. Where the

---

[1] Administration of Estates Act 1925, s. 36 (5).
[2] [1937] Ch. 642.

transfer is effected by instrument which would normally be subject to ad valorem stamp duty, it attracts only a fixed duty of 50p.,[1] unless one of the circumstances mentioned above,[2] where an appropriation attracts ad valorem duty, applies.

In the case of land which remains settled notwithstanding the death of the deceased, the legal estate is vested in the next person entitled by means of a vesting assent. Where a settlement arises under the will, the will constitutes the trust instrument, and a separate vesting instrument is required.

3. SUMMARY OF FORMALITIES FOR TRANSFER OF ASSETS

ASSET	METHOD OF TRANSFER
1. Unregistered land.	
a. transfer to beneficiary absolutely entitled.	Assent.
b. transfer to purchaser.	Conveyance (or perhaps assent).
c. transfer to tenant for life in case of settlement.	Vesting assent.
2. Registered land.	
a. transfer to beneficiary.	Land Registry form of assent, to be accompanied by Land Certificate.*
b. transfer to purchaser.	Transfer.*
c. transfer to tenant for life in case of settlement.	Land Registry form of vesting assent, to be accompanied by Land Certificate.*
3. Stock exchange securities.	Transfer accompanied by stock or share certificate.*
4. Choses in action; choses in equity.	Assignment, with notice to debtor.
5. Mortgage of land.	
a. unregistered title.	Transfer of mortgage.
b. registered title.	Land Registry form of Transfer of Mortgage, accompanied by Charge Certificate.*
6. Bank Account.	Written instructions to transfer from personal representatives, accompanied by copy of grant of representation. If already registered, by cheque.
7. Post Office Savings Bank account, Trustee Savings Bank account, National Savings Certificates, etc.	Withdrawal or transfer forms, following registration of grant of representation.

[1] Stamp Act 1891, s. 62; Finance (1909-10) Act 1910, s. 62.
[2] *Ante*, p. 552.

8. Chattels.   (i) Manual delivery; or
                                     (ii) Assent, which may be by deed
                                          or only under hand.

*Note: if the personal representatives are not themselves registered as proprietors of the land,[1] a copy of the grant of representation is also required.

D. CURRENCY OF PECUNIARY LEGACIES

In general, it is presumed that where the testator was domiciled in one country, and a beneficiary is resident elsewhere, legacies are to be paid in the currency of the country in which the testator died domiciled.[2] This is subject to any contrary intention on the part of the testator, and a contrary intention will be presumed where:

1. the legacy is expressed in a foreign currency, such as a gift of $US 100;[3]

2. a specific, immovable property abroad is charged with the payment of a legacy, in which case the legacy is payable in the currency of the country of the property.[4] If, however, all the testator's immovable property abroad, in several countries, is charged generally with the payment of legacies, they are payable in the currency of the country of the testator's domicile.[5]

Subject to any direction in the will to the contrary, where a legacy is payable to a beneficiary in another country, the rate of exchange is that prevailing on the first anniversary of the testator's death.[6] No deduction is made for the cost of remitting.[7] If, however,

---

[1] The personal representatives may have registered themselves by production to H.M. Land Registry of the grant of representation.

[2] *Saunders* v. *Drake* (1742), 2 Atk. 465; *Pierson* v. *Garnet* (1786), 2 Bro. C.C., 38; *Malcolm* v. *Martin* (1790), 3 Bro. C.C. 50; *Marchioness of Lansdowne* v. *Marquis Lansdowne* (1820), 2 Bligh 60; *Yates* v. *Maddan* (1849), 16 Sim. 613.

[3] *Raymond* v. *Brodbelt* (1800), 5 Ves. 199.

[4] *Saunders* v. *Drake* (1742), 2 Atk. 465; *Pierson* v. *Garnet* (1786), 2 Bro. C.C., 38.

[5] *Phipps* v. *Earl of Anglesea* (1721), 5 Vin. Abr. 209; *Wallis* v. *Brightwell* (1722), 2 Pl. Wms. 88; *Marchioness of Lansdowne* v. *Marquis of Lansdowne* (1820), 2 Bligh 60.

[6] *Re Eighmie, Colbourne* v. *Wilks*, [1935] Ch. 524.

[7] *Cockerell* v. *Barber* (1810), 16 Ves. 461; *Re Schnapper, Westminster Bank Ltd.* v. *Schnapper*, [1936] 1 All E.R. 322.

payment is made to a beneficiary from assets situated in the country of the beneficiary, the value of the legacy is calculated according to the official exchange rate, and not according to the sum which would actually be required to purchase that currency.[1]

E. COSTS OF TRANSFER

It has been shown[2] that a beneficiary is responsible for the cost of upkeep of an asset from the time when he becomes specifically entitled to it. He is also responsible for all costs incurred in connexion with the transfer of the asset from the executors to him.[3] Thus, in *Re Fitzpatrick, Bennett* v. *Bennett*[4] the testator left assets in Monaco to a beneficiary living in England. It was held that the beneficiary had to pay the cost of carriage and insurance.

This rule is often contrary to what the testator would intend, and some well drawn wills include express provisions for the costs of transfer to be paid from residue.

Whether the costs of transfer are paid by the beneficiary or by the personal representatives, the beneficiary is entitled to bring into account that cost in the computation of his ultimate capital gains tax liability.[5]

---

[1] *Campbell* v. *Graham* (1831), 1 Russ. & M. 453.
[2] See *ante*, p. 515.
[3] For earlier decisions against this principle, see *Perry* v. *Meddowcroft* (1841), 4 Beav. 197, *Re De Sommery, Coelenbier* v. *De Sommery*, [1912] 2 Ch. 622; *Re Scott, Scott* v. *Scott*, [1915] 1 Ch. 592; *Re Hewett, Eldridge* v. *Hewett*, [1920] W.N. 366.
[4] [1952] Ch. 86.
[5] See *ante*, p. 413.

payment is made to a beneficiary in another country is the cost ... of transfer incurred, will, of course, at least usually be, not the official exchange rate, and not, therefore, the sum which would actually be required to buy those francs, francs.

4. COSTS OF TRANSFER

It has been shown that a benefit is compensation for the loss of ability to translate from the ... should be compensated, is entitled to his reparation for any loss sustained ... loss, in connexion with the intrusive of the ascertain of the cost ... the injured, i.e. the injured etc. if done so ... ought to take costs in Mexico or to transmit money to be calculated if necessary, to the injured ... and if not any transaction of exchange rate, and, it seems, that ...

This ... that sterling, to all his creditor would ... and hence will ... not with ... of those private, it is ... the cost of transfer is to be paid from ...

Whether the costs of transfer should be ... into account where ... so, it is only ... personal injury cases ... to compensation is entitled to be ... into account where cost as compensation ... the injured, with ... pecuniary liability.

APPENDIX

APPENDIX

STATUTES

WILLS ACT 1837
(7 Will. 4 & 1 Vict., c. 26)

Meaning of certain words in this Act.

1. The words and expressions hereinafter mentioned, which in their ordinary signification have a more confined or a different meaning, shall in this Act, except where the nature of the provision or the context of the Act shall exclude such construction, be interpreted as follows: (that is to say), the word "will" shall extend to a testament, and to a codicil, and to an appointment by will or by writing in the nature of a will in exercise of a power, and also to a disposition by will and testament or devise of the custody and tuition of any child, by virtue of an Act passed in the Twelfth year of the reign of King Charles the Second, intituled *An Act for taking away the courts of wards and liveries, and tenures in capite and by Knights service, and purveyance, and for settling a Revenue upon His Majesty in lieu thereof* (*Tenures Abolition Act 1660*), or by virtue of an Act passed in the Parliament of Ireland in the fourteenth and fifteenth years of the reign of King Charles the Second, intituled *An Act for taking away the court of ward and Liveries, and Tenures in capite and by Knight's Service* (*Tenures Abolition Act* (*Ireland*) *1662*) and to any other testamentary disposition; and the words "real estate" shall extend to manors, advowsons, messuages, lands, tithes, rents, and hereditaments, whether freehold, customary freehold, tenant right, customary or copyhold, or of any other tenure, and whether corporeal, incorporeal, or personal, and to any undivided share thereof, and to any estate, right, or interest (other than a chattel interest) therein; and the words "personal estate" shall extend to leasehold estates and other chattels real, and also to monies, shares of government and other funds, securities for money (not being real estates), debts, choses in action, rights, credits, goods, and all other property whatsoever, which by law devolves upon the executor or administrator, and to any share or interest therein; and every word importing the singluar number only shall extend and be applied to several persons or things as well as one person

563

or thing; and every word importing the masculine gender only shall extend and be applied to a female as well as a male.

2. [Repealed by Statute Law Revision Act 1874, s. 45]

All property may be disposed of by will.

3. It shall be lawful for every person to devise, bequeath, or dispose of, by his will executed in manner hereinafter required, all real estate, and all personal estate which he shall be entitled to, either at law or in equity, at the time of his death, and which, if not so devised, bequeathed or disposed of would devolve upon the heir at law, or customary heir of him, or if he became entitled by descent, of his ancestor, or upon his executor or administrator; and the power hereby given shall extend to all real estate of the nature of customary freehold or tenant right, or customary or copyhold, notwithstanding that the testator may not have surrendered the same to the use of his will, or notwithstanding that, being entitled as heir, devisee, or otherwise to be admitted thereto, he shall not have been admitted thereto; or notwithstanding that the same, in consequence of the want of a custom to devise or surrender to the use of a will or otherwise, could not at law have been disposed of by will if this Act had not been made, or notwithstanding that the same, in consequence of there being a custom that a will or a surrender to the use of a will should continue in force for a limited time only, or any other special custom, could not have been disposed of by will according to the power contained in this Act, if this Act had not been made: and also to estates *pur autre vie*, whether there shall or shall not be any special occupant thereof, and whether the same shall be freehold, customary freehold, tenant right, customary or copyhold, or of any other tenure, and whether the same shall be a coporeal or an incorporeal hereditament; and also to all contingent, executory, or other future interests in any real or personal estate, whether the testator may or may not be ascertained as the person or one of the persons in whom the same respectively may become vested, and whether he may be entitled thereto under the instrument by which the same respectively were created, or under any disposition thereof by deed or will; and also to all rights of entry for conditions broken, and other rights of entry; and also to such of the same estates, interests, and rights respectively, and other real and personal estate, as the testator may be entitled to at the time of his death, notwithstanding that he may become entitled to the same subsequently to the execution of his will.

[See also Law of Property Act 1925, s. 178:

"Section three of the Wills Act 1837 shall (without prejudice to the rights and interests of a personal representative) authorise and be deemed always to have authorised any person to dispose of real property or chattels real by will notwithstanding that by reason of illegitimacy or otherwise he did not leave an heir or next of kin surviving him."

See also Law of Property Act 1925, s. 176 in respect of estates tail.]

4 to 6. [Repealed by Statute Law (Repeals) Act 1969]

No will of a minor valid.

7. No will made by any person under the age of eighteen years shall be valid.

[As amended by Family Law Reform Act 1969, s. 3 (1) (a).]

8. [Repealed by Statute Law (Repeals) Act 1969].

Every will to be in writing, and signed in the presence of two witnesses.

9. No will shall be valid unless it shall be in writing, and executed in manner hereinafter mentioned; (that is to say,) it shall be signed at the foot or end thereof by the testator or by some other person in his presence and by his direction; and such signature shall be made or acknowledged by the testator in the presence of two or more witnesses present at the same time, and such witnesses shall attest and shall subscribe the will in the presence of the testator, but no form of attestation shall be necessary.

[See also Wills Act Amendment Act 1852, s. 1:

Position of the testator's signature: Where by the Wills Act 1837, it is enacted, that no will shall be valid unless it shall be signed at the foot or end thereof by the testator, or by some other person in his presence, and by his direction: Every will shall, so far only as regards the position of the signature of the testator, or of the person signing for him as aforesaid, be deemed to be valid within the said enactment, as explained by this Act, if the signature shall be so placed at or after, or following or under, or beside, or opposite to the end of the will, that it shall be apparent on the face of the will that the testator intended to give effect by such his signature to the writing signed as his will; and no such will shall be affected by the circumstance that the signature shall not follow or be immediately after the foot or end of the will, or by the circumstance that a blank space shall intervene between the concluding words of the will and the signature, or by the circumstance that the signature shall be placed among the words of the testimonium clause or the clause of attestation, or shall follow or be after or under the clause of attestation, either with or without a blank space intervening, or shall follow or be after, or under, or beside the names or one of the names of the subscribing witnesses, or by the circumstance that the signature shall be on a side page or other portion of the paper or papers containing the will whereon no clause or paragraph or disposing part of the will shall be written above the signature, or by the circumstance that there shall appear to be sufficient space on or at the bottom of the preceding side or page or other portion of the same paper on which the will is written to contain the signature; and the enumeration of the above circumstances shall not restrict the generality of the above enactment; but no signature under the said Act or this Act shall be operative to give effect to any disposition or direction which is underneath or which follows it, nor shall it give effect to any disposition or direction inserted after the signature shall be made.

Section 2: (This Act extends to wills already made of which probate not granted because of defective execution).]

Appointments by will to be executed like other wills.

10. No appointment made by will, in exercise of any power, shall be valid, unless the same be executed in manner hereinbefore required; and every will executed in manner hereinbefore required shall, so far as respects the execution and attestation thereof, be a valid execution of a power of appointment by will, notwithstanding it shall have been expressly required that a will made in exercise of such power should be executed with some additional or other form of execution or solemnity.

Soldiers and mariners wills excepted.

11. Provided always . . . that any soldier being in actual military service, or any mariner or seaman being at sea, may dispose of his personal estate as he might have done before the making of this Act.

12. [Repealed by the Admiralty Powers Act 1865, s.1.]

Publication not to be requisite.

13. Every will executed in manner hereinbefore required shall be valid without any other publication thereof.

Will not void by incompetency of witnesses.

14. If any person who shall attest the execution of a will shall at the time of the execution thereof or at any time afterwards be incompetent to be admitted a witness to prove the execution thereof, such will shall not on that account be invalid.

Gifts to an attesting witness to be void.

15. If any person shall attest the execution of any will to whom or to whose wife of husband any beneficial devise, legacy, estate, interest, gift or appointment, of or affecting and real or personal estate (other than and except charges and directions for the payment of any debt or debts), shall be thereby given or made, such devise, legacy, estate, interest, gift, or appointment, shall, so far only as concerns such person attesting the execution of such will, or the wife or husband of such person, or any person claiming under such person or wife, or husband, be utterly null and void, and such person so attesting shall be admitted as witness to prove the execution of such will, or to prove the validity or invalidity thereof, notwithstanding such devise, legacy, estate, interest, gift, or appointment mentioned in such will.

[See now Wills Act 1968.

1. (1) For the purposes of section 15 of the Wills Act 1837 (avoidance of gifts to attesting witnesses and their spouses) the attestation of a will by a person to whom or to whose spouse there is given or made any such disposition as is described in that section shall be disregarded if the will is duly executed without his attestation and without that of any other such person.

(2) This section applies to the will of any person dying after the passing of this Act, whether executed before or after the passing of this Act.

2. (1) This Act may be cited as the Wills Act 1968.

(2) This Act does not extend to Scotland or Northern Ireland.

Creditor attesting to be admitted a witness.

16. In case by any will any real or personal estate shall be charged with any debt or debts, and any creditor, or the wife or husband, of any creditor whose debt is so charged, shall attest the execution of such will, such creditor notwithstanding such charge shall be admitted a witness to prove the execution of such will, or to prove the validity or invalidity thereof.

Executor to be admitted a witness.

17. No person shall, on account of his being an executor of a will, be incompetent to be admitted a witness to prove the execution of such will, or a witness to prove the validity or invalidity thereof.

Will to be revoked by marriage.

18. Every will made by a man or woman shall be revoked by his or her marriage (except a will made in exercise of a power of appointment, when the real or personal estate thereby appointed would not in default of such appointment pass to his or her *heir*, customary heir, executor, or administrator, or the person entitled as his or her *next of kin*, under the Statute of Distributions 1670.

[See now Law of Property Act 1925 (15 Geo. 5, c. 20) s. 177:

(1) A will expressed to be made in contemplation of a marriage shall, notwithstanding anything in section eighteen of the Wills Act 1837, or any other statutory provision or rule of law to the contrary, not be revoked by the solemnisation of the marriage contemplated.

(2) This section only applies to wills made after the commencement of this Act.

See also Administration of Estates Act 1925, s. 50 (1).]

No will to be revoked by presumption.

19. No will shall be revoked by any presumption of an intention on the ground of an alteration in circumstances.

In what cases wills may be revoked.

20. No will or codicil, or any part thereof, shall be revoked otherwise than as aforesaid, or by another will or codicil executed in manner hereinbefore required, or by some writing declaring an intention to revoke the same, and executed in the manner in which a will is hereinbefore required to be executed, or by the burning, tearing, or otherwise destroying the same by the testator, or by some person in his presence and by his direction, with the intention of revoking the same.

No alteration in a will shall have any effect unless executed as a will.

21. No obliteration, interlineation, or other alteration made in any will after the execution thereof shall be valid or have any effect, except so far as the words or effect of the will before such alteration shall not be apparent, unless such alteration shall be executed in like manner as herein before is required for the execution of the will; but the will, with such alteration as part thereof, shall be deemed to be duly executed if the signature of the testator and the subscription of the witnesses be made in the margin or on some other part of the will opposite or near to such alteration, or at the foot or end of or opposite to a memorandum referring to such alteration, and written at the end or some other part of the will.

How revoked will shall be revived.

22. No will or codicil, or any part thereof, which shall be in any manner revoked, shall be revived otherwise than by the re-execution thereof, or by a codicil executed in manner hereinbefore required, and showing an intention to revive the same; and when any will or codicil which shall be partly revoked, and afterwards wholly revoked, shall be revived, such revival shall not extend to so much thereof as shall have been revoked before the revocation of the whole thereof, unless an intention to the contrary shall be shown.

When a devise not to be rendered inoperative.

23. No conveyance or other act made or done subsequently to the execution of a will of or relating to any real or personal estate therein comprised, except an act by which such will shall be revoked as aforesaid, shall prevent the operation of the will with respect to such estate or interest in such real or personal estate as the testator shall have power to dispose of by will at the time of his death.

A will to speak from the death of the testator.

24. Every will shall be construed, with reference to the real estate and personal estate comprised in it, to speak and take effect as if it had been executed immediately before the death of the testator, unless a contrary intention shall appear by the will.

What a residuary devise shall include.

25. Unless a contrary intention shall appear by the will, such real estate or interest therein as shall be comprised or intended to be comprised in any devise in such will contained, which shall fail or be void by reason of the death of the devisee in the lifetime of the testator, or by reason of such devise being contrary to law or otherwise incapable of taking effect, shall be included in the residuary devise (if any) contained in such will.

What a general devise shall include.

26. A devise of the land of the testator, or of the land of the testator in any place or in the occupation of any person mentioned in his will, or otherwise described in a general manner and any other general devise which would describe a customary, copyhold, or leasehold estate if the testator had no freehold estate which could be described by it, shall be construed to include the customary, copyhold and leasehold estates of the testator, or his customary, copyhold, and leasehold estates, or any of them, to which such description shall extend, as the case may be, as well as freehold estates, unless a contrary intention shall appear by the will.

What a general gift shall include.

27. A general devise of the real estate of the testator, or of the real estate of the testator in any place or in the occupation of any person mentioned in his will, or otherwise described in a general manner, shall be construed to include any real estate, or any real estate to which such description shall extend (as the case may be), which he may have power to appoint in any manner he may think proper, and shall operate as an execution of such power, unless a contrary intention shall appear by the will; and in like manner a bequest of the personal estate of the testator, or any bequest of personal property described in a general manner, shall be construed to include any personal estate, or any personal estate to which such description shall extend (as the case may be), which he may have power to appoint in any manner he may think proper, and shall operate as an execution of such power, unless a contrary intention shall appear by the will.

How a devise without words of limitation shall be construed.

28. Where any real estate shall be devised to any person without any words of limitation, such devise shall be construed to pass the fee simple, or other the whole estate or interest which the testator had power to dispose of by will in such real estate, unless a contrary intention shall appear by the will.

How the words "die without issue" shall be construed.

29. In any devise or bequest of real or personal estate the words "die without issue" or "die without leaving issue", or "have no issue", or any other words which may import either a want or failure of issue of any person in his lifetime, or at the time of his death, or an indefinite failure of his issue, shall be construed to mean a want or failure of issue in the lifetime or at the time of the death of such person, and not an indefinite failure of his issue, unless a contrary intention shall appear by the will, by reason of such person having a prior estate tail or of a preceding gift, being, without any implication arising from such words, a limitation of an estate tail to such person or issue, or otherwise; Provided that this Act shall not extend to cases where such words as aforesaid import if no issue described in a preceding gift shall be born, or if there shall be no issue who shall live to attain the age or otherwise answer the description required for obtaining a vested estate by a preceding gift to such issue.

2 2

No devise to trustees or executors, except in certain cases, shall pass a chattel interest.

30. Where any real estate (other than or not being a presentation to a church) shall be devised to any trustee or executor, such devise shall be construed to pass the fee simple or other the whole estate or interest which the testator had power to dispose of by will in such real estate, unless a definite term of years, absolute or determinable or an estate of freehold, shall thereby be given to him expressly or by implication.

Trustees under an unlimited devise, etc. to take the fee.

31. Where any real estate shall be devised to a trustee, without any express limitation of the estate to be taken by such trustee, and the beneficial interest in such real estate, or in the surplus rents and profits thereof, shall not be given to any person for life, but the purposes of the trust may continue beyond the life of such person, such devise shall be construed to vest in such trustee the fee simple, or other the whole legal estate which the testator had power to dispose of by will in such real estate, and not an estate determinable when the purposes of the trust shall be satisfied.

Devises of estates tail shall not lapse.

32. Where any person to whom any real estate shall be devised for an estate tail or an estate in quasi entail shall die in the lifetime of the testator leaving issue who would be inheritable under such entail, and any such issue shall be living at the time of the death of the testator, such devise or bequest shall not lapse, but shall take effect as if the death of such person had happened immediately after the death of the testator, unless a contrary intention shall appear by the will.

Gifts to children or other issue who leave issue living at the testator's death shall not lapse.

33. Where any person being a child or other issue of the testator to whom any real or personal estate shall be devised or bequeathed for any estate or interest not determinable at or before the death of such person shall die in the lifetime of the testator leaving issue, and any such issue of such person shall be living at the time of the death of the testator, such devise or bequest shall not lapse, but shall take effect as if the death of such person had happened immediately after the death of the testator, unless a contrary intention shall appear by the will.

[See Family Law Reform Act 1969, s. 16 (1) in respect of post-1969 wills.]

To what wills and estates this Act shall extend.

34. This Act shall not extend to any will made before the first day of January, one thousand eight hundred and thirty-eight, and every will re-executed or republished, or revived by any codicil, shall for the purposes of this Act be deemed to have been made at the time at which the same shall be so re-executed, republished, or revived; and this Act shall not extend to any estate *pur autre vie* of any person who shall die before the first day of January, one thousand eight hundred and thirty-eight.

Extent.

35. This Act shall not extend to Scotland.

36. [Repealed by Statute Law Revision Act 1874].

WILLS ACT AMENDMENT ACT 1852
(15 & 16 Vict., c. 24)

See annotation to Wills Act 1837, s. 9. (*ante*, p. 565).

WILLS (SOLDIERS AND SAILORS) ACT 1918
(7 & 8 Geo. 5, c. 58)

Explanation of s. 11 of 7 Will. 4 & 1 Vict. c. 26.

1. In order to remove doubts as to the construction of the Wills Act 1837, it is hereby declared and enacted that section eleven of that Act authorises and always has authorised any soldier being in actual military service, or any mariner or seaman being at sea, to dispose of his personal estate as he might have done before the passing of the Act, though under the age of eighteen years.

[As amended by Family Law Reform Act 1969, s. 3 (1) (b).]

Extension of s. 11 of Wills Act 1837.

2. Section eleven of the Wills Act 1837, shall extend to any member of His Majesty's naval or marine forces not only when he is at sea but also when he is so circumstanced that if he were a soldier he would be in actual military service within the meaning of that section.

Validity of testamentary dispositions of real property made by soldiers and sailors.

3. (1) A testamentary disposition of any real estate in England or Ireland made by a person to whom section eleven of the Wills Act 1837, applies, and who dies after the passing of this Act, shall, notwithstanding that the person making the disposition was at the time of making it under eighteen years of age or that the disposition has not been made in such manner or form as was at the passing of the Act required by law, be valid in any case where the person making the disposition was of such age and the disposition has been made in such manner and form that if the disposition had been a disposition of personal estate made by such a person domiciled in England or Ireland it would have been valid.

[As amended by Family Law Reform Act 1969, s. 3 (1) (b).]

(2) [Repealed by Succession (Scotland) Act 1964.]

Power to appoint testamentary guardians.

4. Where any person dies after the passing of this Act having made a will which is, or which, if it had been a disposition of property, would have been rendered valid by section eleven of the Wills Act 1837, any appointment contained in that will of any person as guardian of the infant children of the testator shall be of full force and effect.

Short title and interpretation.

5. (1) This Act may be cited as the Wills (Soldiers and Sailors) Act 1918.

(2) For the purposes of section eleven of the Wills Act 1837, and this Act the expression "soldier" includes a member of the Air Force, and references in this Act to the said section eleven include a reference to that section as explained and extended by this Act.

LAW OF PROPERTY ACT 1925
(15 Geo. 5, c. 20)

177. (See annotation to Wills Act 1837, s. 18; *ante*, p. 568.)

184. In all cases where, after the commencement of this Act, two or more persons have died in circumstances rendering it uncertain which of them survived the other or others, such deaths shall (subject to any order of the court), for all purposes affecting the title to property, be presumed to have occurred in order of seniority, and accordingly the younger shall be deemed to have survived the elder.

ADMINISTRATION OF ESTATES ACT 1925
(15 Geo. 5, c. 23)

[As amended by Intestates' Estates Act 1952 and Family Provision Act 1966].

PART I.

DEVOLUTION OF REAL ESTATE.

Devolution of real estate on personal representative.

1. (1) Real estate to which a deceased person was entitled for an interest not ceasing on his death shall on his death, and notwithstanding any testamentary disposition thereof, devolve from time to time on the personal representative of the deceased, in like manner as before the commencement of this Act chattels real devolved on the personal representative from time to time of a deceased person.

(2) The personal representatives for the time being of a deceased person are deemed in law his heirs and assigns within the meaning of all trusts and powers.

(3) The personal representatives shall be the representative of the deceased in regard to his real estate to which he was entitled for an interest not ceasing on his death as well as in regard to his personal estate.

Application to real estate of law affecting chattels real.

2. (1) Subject to the provisions of this Act, all enactments and rules of law, and all jurisdiction of any court with respect to the appointment of administrators or to probate or letters of administration, or to dealings before probate in the case of chattles real, and with respect to costs and other matters in the administration of personal estate, in force before the commencement of this Act, and all powers, duties, rights, equities, obligations, and liabilities of a personal representative in force at the commencement of this Act with respect to chattels real, shall apply and attach to the personal representative and shall have effect with respect to real estate vested in him, and in particular all such powers of disposition and dealing as were before the commencement of this Act exercisable as respects chattels real by the survivor or survivors of two or more personal representatives, as well as by a single personal representative, or by all the personal representatives together, shall be exercisable by the personal representatives or representative of the deceased with respect to his real estate.

(2) Where as respects real estate there are two or more personal representatives, a conveyance of real estate devolving under this Part of this Act shall not, save as otherwise provided as respects trust estates including settled land, be made without the concurrence therein of all such representatives or an order of the court, but where probate is granted to one or some of two or more persons named as executors, whether or not power is reserved to the other or others to prove, any conveyance of the real estate may be made by the proving executor or executors for the time being, without an order of the court, and shall be as effectual as if all the persons named as executors had concurred therein.

(3) Without prejudice to the rights and powers of a personal representative, the appointment of a personal representative in regard to real estate shall not, save as hereinafter provided, affect—

(a) any rule as to marshalling or as to administration of assets;
(b) the beneficial interest in real estate under any testamentary disposition;
(c) any mode of dealing with any beneficial interest in real estate, or the proceeds of sale thereof;
(d) the right of any person claiming to be interested in the real

estate to take proceedings for the protection or recovery thereof against any person other than the personal representative.

Interpretation of Part I.

3. (1) In this Part of this Act "real estate" includes—

(i) Chattels real, and land in possession, remainder, or reversion, and every interest in or over land to which a deceased person was entitled at the time of his death; and

(ii) Real estate held on trust (including settled land) or by way of mortgage or security, but not money to arise under a trust for sale of land, nor money secured or charged on land.

(2) A testator shall be deemed to have been entitled at his death to any interest in real estate passing under any gift contained in his will which operates as an appointment under a general power to appoint by will, or operates under the testamentary power conferred by statute to dispose of an entailed interest.

(3) An entailed interest of a deceased person shall (unless disposed of under the testamentary power conferred by statute) be deemed an interest ceasing on his death, but any further or other interest of the deceased in the same property in remainder or reversion which is capable of being disposed of by his will shall not be deemed to be an interest so ceasing.

(4) The interest of a deceased person under a joint tenancy where another tenant survives the deceased is an interest ceasing on his death.

(5) On the death of a corporator sole his interest in the corporation's real and personal estate shall be deemed to be an interest ceasing on his death and shall devolve to his successor.

This subsection applies on the demise of the Crown as respects all property, real and personal, vested in the Crown as a corporation sole.

PART II.

EXECUTORS AND ADMINISTRATORS.

General Provisions

4. [Repealed by Judicature Act 1925, s. 226:—see now s. 159 Judicature Act 1925.]

Cesser of right of executor to prove.

5. Where a person appointed executor by a will—

    (i) survives the testator but dies without having taken out probate of the will; or

    (ii) is cited to take out probate of the will and does not appear to the citation; or

    (iii) renounces probate of the will;

his rights in respect of the executorship shall wholly cease, and the representation to the testator and the administration of his real and personal estate shall devolve and be committed in like manner as if that person had not been appointed executor.

Withdrawal of renunciation.

6. (1) Where an executor who has renounced probate has been permitted, whether before or after the commencement of this Act, to withdraw the renunciation and prove the will, the probate shall take effect and be deemed always to have taken effect without prejudice to the previous acts and dealings of and notices to any other personal representative who has previously proved the will or taken out letters of administration, and a memorandum of the subsequent probate shall be endorsed on the original probate or letters of administration.

(2) This section applies whether the testator died before or after the commencement of this Act.

Executor of executor represents original testator.

7. (1) An executor of a sole or last surviving executor of a testator is the executor of that testator.

This provision shall not apply to an executor who does not prove the will of his testator, and, in the case of an executor who on his death leaves surviving him some other executor of his testator who afterwards proves the will of that testator, it shall cease to apply on such probate being granted.

(2) So long as the chain of such representation is unbroken, the last executor in the chain is the executor of every preceding testator.

(3) The chain of such representation is broken by—

    (a) an intestacy; or

(b) the failure of a testator to appoint an executor; or

(c) the failure to obtain probate of a will;

but is not broken by a temporary grant of administration if probate is subsequently granted.

(4) Every person in the chain of representation to a testator—

(a) has the same rights in respect of the real and personal estate of that testator as the original executor would have had if living; and

(b) is, to the extent to which the estate whether real or personal of that testator has come to his hands, answerable as if he were an original executor.

Right of proving executors to exercise powers.

8. (1) Where probate is granted to one or some of two or more persons named as executors, whether or not power is reserved to the others or other to prove, all the powers which are by law conferred on the personal representative may be exercised by the proving executor or executors for the time being and shall be as effectual as if all the persons named as executors had concurred therein.

(2) This section applies whether the testator died before or after the commencement of this Act.

Vesting of estate of intestate between death and grant of administration.

9. Where a person dies intestate, his real and personal estate, until administration is granted in respect thereof, shall vest in the Probate Judge in the same manner and to the same extent as formerly in the case of personal estate it vested in the ordinary.

Discretion of court as to persons to whom administration is to be granted.

10.–14. [Repealed by Judicature Act 1925, s. 226. See now ss. 162, 167 (2), 160, 155 and 161, respectively, of the Judicature Act 1925].

Executor not to act while administration is in force.

15. Where administration has been granted in respect of any real or personal estate of a deceased person, no person shall have power to bring any action or otherwise act as executor of the deceased person in respect of the estate comprised in or affected by the grant until the grant has been recalled or revoked.

Administration pending litigation.

16. [Repealed by Judicature Act 1925, s. 226. See now Judicature Act 1925, s. 163].

Continuance of legal proceedings.

17. If, while any legal proceeding is pending in any court by or against an administrator to whom a temporary administration has been granted, that administration is revoked, that court may order that the proceeding be continued by or against the new personal representative in like manner as if the same had been originally commenced by or against him, but subject to such conditions and variations, if any, as that court directs.

18.–20. [Repealed by Judicature Act 1925, s. 226. See now ss. 164, 166, and 165, respectively, of the Judicature Act 1925.]

Rights and liabilities of administrator.

21. Every person to whom administration of the real and personal estate of a deceased person is granted, shall, subject to the limitations contained in the grant, have the same rights and liabilities and be accountable in like manner as if he were the executor of the deceased.

Special Provisions as to Settled Land

Special executors as respects settled land.

22. (1) A testator may appoint, and in default of such express appointment shall be deemed to have appointed, as his special executors in regard to settled land, the persons, if any, who are at his death the trustees of the settlement thereof, and probate may be granted to such trustees specially limited to the settled land.

In this subsection "settled land" means land vested in the testator which was settled previously to his death and not by his will.

(2) A testator may appoint other persons either with or without such trustees as aforesaid or any of them to be his general executors in regard to his other property and assets.

Where representation is not granted to trustees of settlement.

23. (1) Where settled land becomes vested in a personal representative, not being a trustee of the settlement, upon trust to convey the land to or assent to the vesting thereof in the tenant for life or statutory owner in order to give effect to a settlement created before the death of the deceased and not by his will, or would, on the grant of representation to him, have become so vested, such representative may—

(a) before representation has been granted, renounce his office in regard only to such settled land without renouncing it in regard to other property;

(b) after representation has been granted, apply to the court for revocation of the grant in regard to the settled land without applying in regard to other property.

(2) Whether such renunciation or revocation is made or not, the trustees of the settlement, or any person beneficially interested thereunder, may apply to the High Court for an order appointing a special or additional personal representative in respect of the settled land, and a special or additional personal representative, if and when appointed under the order, shall be in the same position as if representation had originally been granted to him alone in place of the original personal representative, if any, or to him jointly with the original personal representative, as the case may be, limited to the settled land, but without prejudice to the previous acts and dealings, if any, of the personal representative originally constituted or the effect of notices given to such personal representative.

(3) The court may make such order as aforesaid subject to such security, if any, being given by or on behalf of the special or additional personal representative, as the court may direct, and shall, unless the court considers that special considerations apply, appoint such persons as may be necessary to secure that the persons to act as representatives in respect of the settled land shall, if willing to act, be the same persons as are the trustees of the settlement, and an office copy of the order when made shall be

furnished to the principal registry of the Family Division of the High Court for entry, and a memorandum of the order shall be endorsed on the probate or administration.

(4) The person applying for the appointment of a special or additional personal representative shall give notice of the application to the principal registry of the Family Division of the High Court in the manner prescribed.

(5) Rules of court may be made for prescribing for all matters required for giving effect to the provisions of this section, and in particular—

(a) for notice of any application being given to the proper officer;

(b) for production of orders, probates, and administration to the registry;

(c) for the endorsement on a probate or administration of a memorandum of an order, subject or not to any exceptions;

(d) for the manner in which the costs are to be borne;

(e) for protecting purchasers and trustees and other persons in a fiduciary position, dealing in good faith with or giving notices to a personal representative before notice of any order has been endorsed on the probate or administration or a pending action has been registered in respect of the proceedings.

[As amended by Administration of Justice Act 1970, s. 54 (3) and Sched. 11.]

Power for special personal representatives.

24. (1) The special personal representatives may dispose of the settled land without the concurrence of the general personal representatives, who may likewise dispose of the other property and assets of the deceased without the concurrence of the special personal representatives.

(2) In this section the expression "special personal representatives" means the representatives appointed to act for the purposes of settled land and includes any original personal representative who is to act with an additional personal representative for those purposes.

Duties, Rights, and Obligations.

Duty of personal representatives

25. The personal representatives of a deceased person shall be under a duty to—

(a) collect and get in the real and personal estate of the deceased and administer it according to law;

(b) when required to do so by the court, exhibit on oath in court a full inventory of the estate and when so required render an account of the administration of the estate to the court;

(c) when required to do so by the High Court, deliver up the grant of probate or administration to that court.

[Substituted by Administration of Estates Act 1971, s. 9.]

Rights of action by and against personal representative.

26. (1)–(2) [Repealed by Law Reform (Miscellaneous Provisions) Act 1934, s. 1 (7)].

(3) A personal representative may distrain for arrears of a rentcharge due or accruing to the deceased in his lifetime on the land affected or charged therewith, so long as the land remains in the possession of the person liable to pay the rentcharge or of the persons deriving title under him, and in like manner as the deceased might have done had he been living.

(4) A personal representative may distrain upon land for arrears of rent due or accruing to the deceased in like manner as the deceased might have done had he been living.

Such arrears may be distrained for after the termination of the lease or tenancy as if the term or interest had not determined, if the distress is made—

(a) within six months after the termination of the lease or tenancy;

(b) during the continuance of the possession of the lessee or tenant from whom the arrears were due.

The statutory enactments relating to distress for rent apply to any distress made pursuant to this subsection.

(5)–(6) [Repealed by Law Reform (Miscellaneous Provisions) Act 1934, s. 1 (7)].

Protection of persons acting on probate or administration.

27. (1) Every person making or permitting to be made any payment or disposition in good faith under a representation shall be indemnified and protected in so doing, notwithstanding any defect or circumstance whatsoever affecting the validity of the representation.

(2) Where a representation is revoked, all payments and dispositions made in good faith to a personal representative under the representation before the revocation thereof are a valid discharge to the person making the same; and the personal representative who acted under the revoked representation may retain and reimburse himself in respect of any payments or dispositions made by him which the person to whom representation is afterwards granted might have properly made.

Liability for fraud.

28. If any person, to the defrauding of creditors or without full valuable consideration, obtains, receives or holds any real or personal estate of a deceased person or effects the release of any debt or liability due to the estate of the deceased, he shall be charged as executor in his own wrong to the extent of the real and personal estate received or coming to his hands, or the debt or liability released, after deducting—

(a) any debt for valuable consideration and without fraud due to him from the deceased person at the time of his death; and

(b) any payment made by him which might properly be made by a personal representative.

Liability of estate of personal representative.

29. Where a person as personal representative of a deceased person (including an executor in his own wrong) wastes or converts to his own use any part of the real or personal estate of the deceased, and dies, his personal representative shall to the extent of the available assets of the defaulter be liable and chargeable in respect of such waste or conversion in the same manner as the defaulter would have been if living.

Provisions applicable where administration granted to nominee of the Crown.

30. (1) Where the administration of the real and personal estate of any deceased person is granted to a nominee of the Crown (whether the Treasury Solicitor, or a person nominated by the Treasury Solicitor, or any other person), any legal proceeding by or against that nominee for the recovery of the real or personal estate, or any part or share thereof, shall be of the same character, and be instituted and carried on in the same manner, and be subject to the same rules of law and equity (including, except as otherwise provided by this Act, the rules of limitation under the statutes of limitation or otherwise), in all respects as if the administration had been granted to such nominee as one of the persons interested under this Act in the estate of the deceased.

(2) An information or other proceeding on the part of His Majesty shall not be filed or instituted, and a petition of right shall not be presented, in respect of the real or personal estate of any deceased person or any part or share thereof, or any claim thereon, except subject to the same rules of law and equity within and subject to which a proceeding for the like purposes might be instituted by or against a subject.

(3) The Treasury Solicitor shall not be required, when applying for or obtaining administration of the estate of a deceased person for the use or benefit of His Majesty, to deliver, nor shall the High Court or the Commissioners of Inland Revenue be entitled to receive in connexion with any such application or grant of administration, any affidavit, statutory declaration, account, certificate, or other statement verified on oath; but the Treasury Solicitor shall deliver and the said Division and Commissioners respectively shall accept, in lieu thereof, an account or particulars of the estate of the deceased signed by or on behalf of the Treasury Solicitor.

(4) References in sections two, four, six and seven of the Treasury Solicitor Act 1876, and in subsection (3) of section three of the Duchy of Lancaster Act 1920, to "personal estate" shall include real estate.

[As amended by Limitation Act 1939, Sched.; and Administration of Justice Act 1970, s. 54 (3) and Sched. 11.]

Power to make rules.

31. Provision may be made by rules of court for giving effect to the provisions of this Part of this Act so far as relates to real estate and in particular for adapting the procedure and practice on the grant of letters of administration to the case of real estate.

PART III.

ADMINISTRATION OF ASSETS.

Real and personal estate and payment of debts.

32. (1) The real and personal estate, whether legal or equitable, of a deceased person, to the extent of his beneficial interest therein, and the real and personal estate of which a deceased person in pursuance of any general power (including the statutory power to dispose of entailed interests) disposes by his will, are assets for payment of his debts (whether by specialty or simple contract) and liabilities, and any disposition by will inconsistent with this enactment is void as against the creditors, and the court shall, if necessary, administer the property for the purpose of the payment of the debts and liabilities.

This subsection takes effect without prejudice to the rights of incumbrancers.

(2) If any person to whom any such beneficial interest devolves or is given, or in whom any such interest vests, disposes thereof in good faith before an action is brought or process is sued out against him, he shall be personally liable for the value of the interest so disposed of by him, but that interest shall not be liable to be taken in execution in the action or under the process.

Trust for sale.

33. (1) On the death of a person intestate as to any real or personal estate, such estate shall be held by his personal representatives—

(a) as to the real estate upon trust to sell the same; and
(b) as to the personal estate upon trust to call in sell and convert into money such part thereof as may not consist of money,

with power to postpone such sale and conversion for such a period as the personal representatives, without being liable to account, may think proper, and so that any reversionary interest be not sold until it falls into possession, unless the personal representatives see special reason for sale, and so also that, unless required for purposes of administration owing to want of other assets, personal chattels be not sold except for special reason.

(2) Out of the net money to arise from the sale and conversion

of such real and personal estate (after payment of costs), and out of the ready money of the deceased (so far as not disposed of by his will, if any), the personal representative shall pay all such funeral, testamentary and administration expenses, debts and other liabilities as are properly payable thereout having regard to the rules of administration contained in this Part of this Act, and out of the residue of the said money the personal representative shall set aside a fund sufficient to provide for any pecuniary legacies bequeathed by the will (if any) of the deceased.

(3) During the minority of any beneficiary or the subsistence of any life interest and pending the distribution of the whole or any part of the estate of the deceased, the personal representatives may invest the residue of the said money, or so much thereof as may not have been distributed, in any investments for the time being authorised by statute for the investment of trust money, with power, at the discretion of the personal representatives, to change such investments for others of a like nature.

(4) The residue of the said money and any investments for the time being representing the same, including (but without prejudice to the trust for sale) any part of the estate of the deceased which may be retained unsold and is not required for the administration purposes aforesaid, is in this Act referred to as "the residuary estate of the intestate."

(5) The income (including net rents and profits of real estate and chattels real after payment of rates, taxes, rent, costs of insurance, repairs and other outgoings properly attributable to income) of so much of the real and personal estate of the deceased as may not be disposed of by his will, if any, or may not be required for the administration purposes aforesaid, may, however such estate is invested, as from the death of the deceased, be treated and applied as income, and for that purpose any necessary apportionment may be made between tenant for life and remainderman.

(6) Nothing in this section affects the rights of any creditor of the deceased or the rights of the Crown in respect of death duties.

(7) Where the deceased leaves a will, this section has effect subject to the provisions contained in the will.

Administration of assets.

34. (1) Where the estate of a deceased person is insolvent, his real and personal estate shall be administered in accordance with the rules set out in Part I of the First Schedule to this Act.

(2) [Repealed by Administration of Estates Act 1971, s. 12 and Sched. 2, Pt. II.]

(3) Where the estate of a deceased person is solvent his real and personal estate shall, subject to rules of court and the provisions hereinafter contained as to charges on property of the deceased, and to the provisions, if any, contained in his will, be applicable towards the discharge of the funeral, testamentary and administration expenses, debts and liabilities payable thereout in the order mentioned in Part II of the First Schedule to this Act.

Charges on property of deceased to be paid primarily out of the property charged.

35. (1) Where a person dies possessed of, or entitled to, or, under a general power of appointment (including the statutory power to dispose of entailed interests) by his will disposes of, an interest in property, which at the time of his death is charged with the payment of money, whether by way of legal mortgage, equitable charge or otherwise (including a lien for unpaid purchase money), and the deceased has not by will deed or other document signified a contrary or other intention, the interest so charged shall, as between the different persons claiming through the deceased, be primarily liable for the payment of the charge; and every part of the said interest, according to its value, shall bear a proportionate part of the charge on the whole thereof.

(2) Such contrary or other intention shall not be deemed to be signified—

(a) by a general direction for the payment of debts or of all the debts of the testator out of his personal estate, or his residuary real and personal estate, or his residuary real estate; or

(b) by a charge of debts upon any such estate;

unless such intention is further signified by words expressly or by necessary implication referring to all or some part of the charge.

(3) Nothing in this section affects the right of a person entitled to the charge to obtain payment or satisfaction thereof either out of the other assets of the deceased or otherwise.

Effect of assent or conveyance by personal representative.

36. (1) A personal representative may assent to the vesting, in any person who (whether by devise, bequest, devolution, appropriation or otherwise) may be entitled thereto, either beneficially or as a trustee or personal representative, of any estate or interest in real estate to which the testator or intestate was entitled or over which he exercised a general power of appointment by his will, including the statutory power to dispose of entailed interests, and which devolved upon the personal representative.

(2) The assent shall operate to vest in that person the estate or interest to which the assent relates, and, unless a contrary intention appears, the assent shall relate back to the death of the deceased.

(3) The statutory covenants implied by a person being expressed to convey as personal representative, may be implied in an assent in like manner as in a conveyance by deed.

(4) An assent to the vesting of a legal estate shall be in writing, signed by the personal representative, and shall name the person in whose favour it is given and shall operate to vest in that person the legal estate to which it relates; and an assent not in writing or not in favour of a named person shall not be effectual to pass a legal estate.

(5) Any person in whose favour an assent or conveyance of a legal estate is made by a personal representative may require that notice of the assent or conveyance be written or endorsed on or permanently annexed to the probate or letters of administration, at the cost of the estate of the deceased, and that the probate or letters of administration be produced, at the like cost, to prove that the notice has been placed thereon or annexed thereto.

(6) A statement in writing by a personal representative that he has not given or made an assent or conveyance in respect of a legal estate, shall, in favour of a purchaser, but without prejudice to any previous disposition made in favour of another purchaser deriving title mediately, or immediately under the personal representative, be sufficient evidence that an assent or conveyance has not been given or made in respect of the legal estate to which the statement relates, unless notice of a previous assent or conveyance affecting that estate has been placed on or annexed to the probate or administration.

A conveyance by a personal representative of a legal estate to a purchaser accepted on the faith of such a statement shall (without prejudice as aforesaid and unless notice of a previous assent or conveyance affecting that estate has been placed on or annexed to the probate or administration) operate to transfer or create the legal estate expressed to be conveyed in like manner as if no previous assent or conveyance had been made by the personal representative.

A personal representative making a false statement, in regard to any such matter, shall be liable in like manner as if the statement had been contained in a statutory declaration.

(7) An assent or conveyance by a personal representative in respect of a legal estate shall, in favour of a purchaser, unless notice of a previous assent or conveyance affecting that legal estate has been placed on or annexed to the probate or administration, be taken as sufficient evidence that the person in whose favour the assent or conveyance is given or made is the person entitled to have the legal estate conveyed to him, and upon the proper trusts, if any, but shall not otherwise prejudicially affect the claim of any person rightfully entitled to the estate vested or conveyed or any charge thereon.

(8) A conveyance of a legal estate by a personal representative to a purchaser shall not be invalidated by reason only that the purchaser may have notice that all the debts, liabilities, funeral, and testamentary or administration expenses, duties, and legacies of the deceased have been discharged or provided for.

(9) An assent or conveyance given or made by a personal representative shall not, except in favour of a purchaser of a legal estate, prejudice the right of the personal representative or any other person to recover the estate or interest to which the assent or conveyance relates, or to be indemnified out of such estate or interest against any duties, debt, or liability to which such estate or interest would have been subject if there had not been any assent or conveyance.

(10) A personal representative may, as a condition of giving an assent or making a conveyance, require security for the discharge of any such duties, debt, or liability, but shall not be entitled to postpone the giving of an assent merely by reason of the subsistence of any such duties, debt or liability if reasonable arrangements have been made for discharging the same; and an assent

may be given subject to any legal estate or charge by way of legal mortgage.

(11) This section shall not operate to impose any stamp duty in respect of an assent, and in this section "purchaser" means a purchaser for money or money's worth.

(12) This section applies to assents and conveyances made after the commencement of this Act, whether the testator or intestate died before or after such commencement.

Validity of conveyance not affected by revocation of representation.

37. (1) All conveyances of any interest in real or personal estate made to a purchaser either before or after the commencement of this Act by a person to whom probate or letters of administration have been granted are valid, notwithstanding any subsequent revocation or variation, either before or after the commencement of this Act, of the probate or administration.

(2) This section takes effect without prejudice to any order of the court made before the commencement of this Act, and applies whether the testator or intestate died before or after such commencement.

Right to follow property and powers of the court in relation thereto.

38. (1) An assent or conveyance by a personal representative to a person other than a purchaser does not prejudice the rights of any person to follow the property to which the assent or conveyance relates, or any property representing the same, into the hands of the person in whom it is vested by the assent or conveyance, or of any other person (not being a purchaser) who may have received the same or in whom it may be vested.

(2) Notwithstanding any such assent or conveyance the court may, on the application of any creditor or other person interested,—

(a) order a sale, exchange, mortgage, charge, lease, payment, transfer or other transaction to be carried out which the court considers requisite for the purpose of giving effect to the rights of the persons interested;

(b) declare that the person, not being a purchaser, in whom the property is vested is a trustee for those purposes;

(c) give directions respecting the preparation and execution of any conveyance or other instrument or as to any other matter required for giving effect to the order;

(d) make any vesting order, or appoint a person to convey in accordance with the provisions of the Trustee Act 1925.

(3) This section does not prejudice the rights of a purchaser or a person deriving title under him, but applies whether the testator or intestate died before or after the commencement of this Act.

Powers of management.

39. (1) In dealing with the real and personal estate of the deceased his personal representatives shall, for purposes of administration, or during a minority of any beneficiary or the subsistence of any life interest, or until the period of distribution arrives, have—

(i) the same powers and discretions, including power to raise money by mortgage or charge (whether or not by deposit of documents), as a personal representative had before the commencement of this Act, with respect to personal estate vested in him, and such power of raising money by mortgage may in the case of land be exercised by way of legal mortgage; and

(ii) all the powers, discretions and duties conferred or imposed by law on trustees holding land upon an effectual trust for sale (including power to overreach equitable interests and powers as if the same affected the proceeds of sale); and

(iii) all the powers conferred by statute on trustees for sale, and so that every contract entered into by a personal representative shall be binding on and be enforceable against and by the personal representative for the time being of the deceased, and may be carried into effect, or be varied or rescinded by him, and, in the case of a contract entered into by a predecessor, as if it had been entered into by himself.

(2) Nothing in this section shall affect the right of any person to require an assent or conveyance to be made.

(3) This section applies whether the testator or intestate died before or after the commencement of this Act.

Powers of personal representative for raising money, etc.

40. (1) For giving effect to beneficial interests the personal representative may limit or demise land for a term of years absolute, with or without impeachment for waste, to trustees on usual trusts for raising or securing any principal sum and the interest thereon for which the land, or any part thereof, is liable, and may limit or grant a rentcharge for giving effect to any annual or periodical sum for which the land or the income thereof or any part thereof is liable.

(2) This section applies whether the testator or intestate died before or after the commencement of this Act.

Powers of personal representative as to appropriation.

41. (1) The personal representative may appropriate any part of the real or personal estate, including things in action, of the deceased in the actual condition or state of investment thereof at the time of appropriation in or towards satisfaction of any legacy bequeathed by the deceased, or of any other interest or share in his property, whether settled or not, as to the personal representative may seem just and reasonable, according to the respective rights of the persons interested in the property of the deceased:

Provided that—

    (i) an appropriation shall not be made under this section so as to affect prejudicially any specific devise or bequest;

    (ii) an appropriation of property, whether or not being an investment authorised by law or by the will, if any, of the deceased for the investment of money subject to the trust, shall not (save as hereinafter mentioned) be made under this section except with the following consents:—

        (*a*) when made for the benefit of a person absolutely and beneficially entitled in possession, the consent of that person;

        (*b*) when made in respect of any settled legacy share or interest, the consent of either the trustee thereof, if any (not being also the personal representative), or the person who may for the time being be entitled to the income:

        If the person whose consent is so required as aforesaid is an infant or is incapable, by reason of mental disorder within the meaning of the Mental Health Act 1959 of managing and administering his property and affairs; the consent shall be given on his behalf by his parents or parent, testamentary or other guardian, receiver, or if, in the case of an infant, there is no such parent or guardian, by the court on the application of his next friend;

(iii) no consent (save of such trustee as aforesaid) shall be required on behalf of a person who may come into existence after the time of appropriation, or who cannot be found or ascertained at that time;

(iv) if no receiver is acting for a person suffering from mental disorder then, if the appropriation is of an investment authorised by law or by the will, if any, of the deceased for the investment of money subject to the trust, no consent shall be required on behalf of the said person;

(v) if, independently of the personal representative, there is no trustee of a settled legacy share or interest, and no person of full age and capacity entitled to the income thereof, no consent shall be required to an appropriation in respect of such legacy share or interest, provided that the appropriation is of an investment authorised as aforesaid.

[As amended by Mental Health Act 1959, s. 149 (1) and Sched. 7, Pt. II].

(2) Any property duly appropriated under the powers conferred by this section shall thereafter be treated as an authorised investment, and may be retained or dealt with accordingly.

(3) For the purposes of such appropriation, the personal representative may ascertain and fix the value of the respective parts of the real and personal estate and the liabilities of the deceased as he may think fit, and shall for that purpose employ a duly qualified valuer in any case where such employment may be necessary; and may make any conveyance (including an assent) which may be requisite for giving effect to the appropriation.

(4) An appropriation made pursuant to this section shall bind all persons interested in the property of the deceased whose consent is not hereby made requisite.

(5) The personal representative shall, in making the appropriation, have regard to the rights of any person who may thereafter

come into existence, or who cannot be found or ascertained at the time of appropriation, and of any other person whose consent is not required by this section.

(6) This section does not prejudice any other power of appropriation conferred by law or by the will (if any) of the deceased, and takes effect with any extended powers conferred by the will (if any) of the deceased, and where an appropriation is made under this section, in respect of a settled legacy, share or interest, the property appropriated shall remain subject to all trusts for sale and powers of leasing, disposition, and management or varying investments which would have been applicable thereto or to the legacy, share or interest in respect of which the appropriation is made, if no such appropriation had been made.

(7) If after any real estate has been appropriated in purported exercise of the powers conferred by this section, the person to whom it was conveyed disposes of it or any interest therein, then, in favour of a purchaser, the appropriation shall be deemed to have been made in accordance with the requirements of this section and after all requisite consents, if any, had been given.

(8) In this section, a settled legacy, share or interest includes any legacy, share or interest to which a person is not absolutely entitled in possession at the date of the appropriation, also an annuity, and "purchaser" means a purchaser for money or money's worth.

(9) This section applies whether the deceased died intestate or not, and whether before or after the commencement of this Act, and extends to property over which a testator exercises a general power of appointment, including the statutory power to dispose of entailed interests, and authorises the setting apart of a fund to answer an annuity by means of the income of that fund or otherwise.

Power to appoint trustees of infants' property.

42. (1) Where an infant is absolutely entitled under the will or on the intestacy of a person dying before or after the commencement of this Act (in this subsection called "the deceased") to a devise or legacy, or to the residue of the estate of the deceased, or any share therein, and such devise, legacy, residue or share is not under the will, if any, of the deceased, devised or bequeathed to trustees for the infant, the personal representatives of the deceased may appoint a trust corporation or two or more individuals not exceeding four (whether or not including the personal representatives or one or more of the personal representatives), to be the trustee or trustees of such devise, legacy, residue or share for the infant, and to be trustees of any land devised or any land being or forming part of such residue or share for the purposes of the Settled Land Act 1925, and of the statutory provisions relating to the management of land during a minority, and may execute or do any assurance or thing requisite for vesting such devise, legacy, residue or share in the trustee or trustees so appointed.

On such appointment the personal representatives, as such, shall be discharged from all further liability in respect of such devise, legacy, residue, or share, and the same may be retained in its existing condition or state of investment, or may be converted into money, and such money may be invested in any authorised investment.

(2) Where a personal representative has before the commencement of this Act retained or sold any such devise, legacy, residue or share, and invested the same or the proceeds thereof in any investments in which he was authorised to invest money subject to the trust, then, subject to any order of the court made before such commencement, he shall not be deemed to have incurred any liability on that account, or by reason of not having paid or transferred the money or property into court.

Obligations of personal representative as to giving possession of land and powers of the court.

43. (1) A personal representative, before giving an assent or making a conveyance in favour of any person entitled, may permit that person to take possession of the land, and such possession shall not prejudicially affect the right of the personal representative to take or resume possession nor his power to convey the land as if he were in possession thereof, but subject to the interest of any lessee, tenant or occupier in possession or in actual occupation of the land.

(2) Any person who as against the personal representative claims possession of real estate, or the appointment of a receiver thereof, or a conveyance thereof, or an assent to the vesting thereof, or to be registered as proprietor thereof under the Land Registration

Act 1925, may apply to the court for directions with reference thereto, and the court may make such vesting or other order as may be deemed proper, and the provisions of the Trustee Act 1925, relating to vesting orders and to the appointment of a person to convey, shall apply.

(3) This section applies whether the testator or intestate died before or after the commencement of this Act.

Power to postpone distribution.

44. Subject to the foregoing provisions of this Act, a personal representative is not bound to distribute the estate of the deceased before the expiration of one year from the death.

PART IV.

DISTRIBUTION OF RESIDUARY ESTATE.

Abolition of descent to heir, curtesy dower and escheat.

45. (1) With regard to the real estate and personal inheritance of every person dying after the commencement of this Act, there shall be abolished—

(a) All existing modes rules and canons of descent, and of devolution by special occupancy or otherwise, of real estate, or of a personal inheritance, whether operating by the general law or by the custom of gavelkind or borough english or by any other custom of any county, locality, or manor, or otherwise howsoever; and

(b) Tenancy by the curtesy and every other estate and interest of a husband in real estate as to which his wife dies intestate, whether arising under the general law or by custom or otherwise; and

(c) Dower and freebench and every other estate and interest of a wife in real estate as to which her husband dies intestate, whether arising under the general law or by custom or otherwise: Provided that where a right (if any) to freebench or other like right has attached before the commencement of this Act which cannot be barred by a testamentary or other disposition made by the husband, such right shall, unless released, remain in force as an equitable interest; and

(d) Escheat to the Crown or the Duchy of Lancaster or the Duke of Cornwall or to a mesne lord for want of heirs.

(2) Nothing in this section affects the descent or devolution of an entailed interest.

Succession to real and personal estate on intestacy.

46. (1) The residuary estate of an intestate shall be distributed in the manner or be held on the trusts mentioned in this section, namely:—

 (i) If the intestate leaves a husband or wife, then in accordance with the following table:

TABLE

If the intestate—

(1) leaves—	the residuary estate shall be held in trust for the surviving husband or wife absolutely.
(a) no issue, and	
(b) no parent, or brother or sister of the whole blood, or issue of a brother or sister of the whole blood.	
(2) leaves issue (whether or not persons mentioned in sub-paragraph (b) above also survive)	the surviving husband or wife shall take the personal chattels absolutely and, in addition, the residuary estate of the intestate (other than the personal chattels) shall stand charged with the payment of a fixed net sum free of death duties and costs, to the surviving husband or wife with interest thereon from the date of the death at the rate of four pounds per cent. per annum until paid or appropriated, and, subject to providing for that sum and the interest thereon, the residuary estate (other than the personal chattels) shall be held—

(a) as to one half upon trust for the surviving husband or wife during his or her life, and, subject to such life interest, on the statutory trusts for the issue of the intestate, and

(b) as to the other half, on the statutory trusts for the issue of the intestate.

(3) leaves one or more of the following, that is to say, a parent, a brother or sister of the whole blood, or issue of a brother or sister of the whole blood, but leaves no issue

the surviving husband or wife shall take the personal chattels absolutely and, in addition, the residuary estate of the intestate (other than the personal chattels) shall stand charged with the payment of a fixed net sum, free of death duties and costs, to the surviving husband or wife with interest thereon from the date of the death at the rate of four pounds per cent. per annum until paid or appropriated, and, subject to providing for that sum and the interest thereon, the residuary estate (other than the personal chattels) shall be held—

(a) as to one half in trust for the surviving husband or wife absolutely, and

(b) as to the other half—

(i) where the intestate leaves one parent or both parents (whether or not brothers or sisters of the intestate or their issue also survive) in trust for the parent absolutely or, as the case may be, for the two parents in equal shares absolutely,

(ii) where the intestate leaves no parent, on the statutory trusts for the brothers and sisters of the whole blood of the intestate.

[The fixed net sums referred to in paragraphs (2) and (3) of this Table shall be of the amounts provided by or under section 1, of the Family Provision Act 1966, *post*, p. 640.]

(ii) If the intestate leaves issue but no husband or wife the residuary estate of the intestate shall be held on the statutory trusts for the issue of the intestate;

(iii) If the intestate leaves no husband or wife and no issue but both parents, then the residuary estate of the intestate shall be held in trust for the father and mother in equal shares absolutely;

(iv) If the intestate leaves no husband or wife and no issue but one parent, then the residuary estate of the intestate shall be held in trust for the surviving father or mother absolutely;

(v) If the intestate leaves no husband or wife and no issue and no parent, then the residuary estate of the intestate shall be held in trust for the following persons living at the death of the intestate, and in the following order and manner, namely:—

First, on the statutory trusts for the brothers and sisters of the whole blood of the intestate; but if no person takes an absolutely vested interest under such trusts; then

Secondly, on the statutory trusts for the brothers and sisters of the half blood of the intestate; but if no person takes an absolutely vested interest under such trusts; then

Thirdly, for the grandparents of the intestate and, if more than one survive the intestate, in equal shares; but if there is no member of this class; then

Fourthly, on the statutory trusts for the uncles and aunts of the intestate (being brothers or sisters of the whole blood of a parent of the intestate); but if no person

takes an absolutely vested interest under such trusts;
then

Fifthly, on the statutory trusts for the uncles and aunts
of the intestate (being brothers or sisters of the half
blood of a parent of the intestate);

(vi) In default of any person taking an absolute interest under
the foregoing provisions, the residuary estate of the intestate
shall belong to the Crown or to the Duchy of Lancaster
or to the Duke of Cornwall for the time being, as the case
may be, as bona vacantia, and in lieu of any right to escheat.

The Crown or the said Duchy or the said Duke may
(without prejudice to the powers reserved by section nine
of the Civil List Act 1910, or any other powers), out of
the whole or any part of the property devolving on them
respectively, provide, in accordance with the existing
practice, for dependants, whether kindred or not, of the
intestate, and other persons for whom the intestate might
reasonably have been expected to make provision.

(2) A husband and wife shall for all purposes of distribution or
division under the foregoing provisions of this section be treated as
two persons.

(3) Where the intestate and the intestate's husband or wife have
died in circumstances rendering it uncertain which of them
survived the other and the intestate's husband or wife is by virtue
of section one hundred and eighty-four of the Law of Property Act
1925, deemed to have survived the intestate, this section shall,
nevertheless, have effect as respects the intestate as if the husband
or wife had not survived the intestate.

(4) The interest payable on the fixed net sum, payable to a
surviving husband or wife shall be primarily payable out of income.

[For details of the amounts of the "fixed net sum" see Family
Provision Act 1966, s. 1, *post*, pp. 640,697.]

*Statutory trusts in favour of issue and other classes of relatives of
intestate.*

47. (1) Where under this Part of this Act the residuary estate
of an intestate, or any part thereof, is directed to be held on the
statutory trusts for the issue of the intestate, the same shall be held
upon the following trusts, namely:—

(i) In trust, in equal shares if more than one, for all or any the children or child or the intestate, living at the death of the intestate, who attain the age of eighteen years or marry under that age, and for all or any of the issue living at the death of the intestate who attain the age of eighteen years or marry under that age of any child of the intestate who predeceases the intestate, such issue to take through all degrees, according to their stocks, in equal shares if more than one, the share which their parent would have taken if living at the death of the intestate, and so that no issue shall take whose parent is living at the death of the intestate and so capable of taking;

[As amended by Family Law Reform Act 1969, s. 3 (2).]

(ii) The statutory power of advancement, and the statutory provisions which relate to maintenance and accumulation of surplus income, shall apply, but when an infant marries such infant shall be entitled to give valid receipts for the income of the infant's share or interest;

(iii) Where the property held on the statutory trusts for issue is divisible into shares, then any money or property which, by way of advancement or on the marriage of a child of the intestate, has been paid to such child by the intestate or settled by the intestate for the benefit or such child (including any life or less interest and including property covenanted to be paid or settled) shall, subject to any contrary intention expressed or appearing from the circumstances of the case, be taken as being so paid or settled in or towards satisfaction of the share of such child or the share which such child would have taken if living at the death of the intestate, and shall be brought into account, at a valuation (the value to be reckoned as at the death of the intestate), in accordance with the requirements of the personal representatives;

(iv) The personal representatives may permit any infant contingently interested to have the use and enjoyment of any personal chattels in such manner and subject to such conditions (if any) as the personal representatives may consider reasonable, and without being liable to account for any consequential loss.

(2) If the trusts in favour of the issue of the intestate fail by reason of no child or other issue attaining an absolutely vested interest—

(a) the residuary estate of the intestate and the income thereof and all statutory accumulations, if any, of the income thereof, or so much thereof as may not have been paid or applied under any power affecting the same, shall go, devolve and be held under the provisions of this Part of this Act as if the intestate had died without leaving issue living at the death of the intestate;

(b) references in this Part of this Act to the intestate "leaving no issue" shall be construed as "leaving no issue who attain an absolutely vested interest";

(c) references in this Part of this Act to the intestate "leaving issue" or "leaving a child or other issue" shall be construed as "leaving issue who attain an absolutely vested interest".

(3) Where under this Part of this Act the residuary estate of an intestate or any part thereof is directed to be held on the statutory trusts for any class of relatives of the intestate, other than issue of the intestate, the same shall be held on trusts corresponding to the statutory trusts for the issue of the intestate (other than the provision for bringing any money or property into account) as if such trusts (other than as aforesaid) were repeated with the substitution of references to the members or member of that class for references to the children or child of the intestate.

(4) References in paragraph (i) of subsection (1) of the last foregoing section to the intestate leaving, or not leaving, a member of the class consisting of brothers or sisters of the whole blood of the intestate and issue of brothers or sisters of the whole blood of the intestate shall be construed as references to the intestate leaving, or not leaving, a member of that class who attains an absolutely vested interest.

(5) [Repealed by Family Provision Act 1966, s. 9].

Right of surviving spouse to have own life interest redeemed.

47A. (1) Where a surviving husband or wife is entitled to a life interest in part of the residuary estate, and so elects, the personal representative shall purchase or redeem the life interest by paying

2 3

the capital value thereof to the tenant for life, or the persons deriving title under the tenant for life, and the costs of the transaction; and thereupon the residuary estate of the intestate may be dealt with and distributed free from the life interest.

(2) The said capital value shall be reckoned in accordance with the rules set out in this subsection:—

    1. There shall be ascertained the annual value of the life interest to which the surviving husband or wife would be entitled if the said part of the residuary estate (whether or not yielding income) were on the date of redemption of the life interest reinvested in the two-and-a-half per cent consolidated stock referred to in section two of the National Debt (Conversion) Act 1888.

    2. There shall be ascertained the amount which if invested on the said date in the purchase under the Government Annuities Act 1929 of an immediate savings bank annuity, would purchase an annuity for the tenant for life of the annual value ascertained under rule 1.

    3. The said capital value shall, subject to rule 4, be the amount ascertained under rule 2 diminished by five per cent. thereof.

    4. If the age of the tenant for life on the said date exceeds eighty years, a further deduction shall be made equal to five per cent. of the amount ascertained under rule 2 for each complete year by which the age exceeds eighty:

    Provided that, if the effect of this rule would otherwise be that the said capital value was less than one-and-a-half times the annual value ascertained under rule 1, the said capital value shall be one-and-a-half times that annual value.

(3) An election under this section shall only be exercisable if at the time of the election the whole of the said part of the residuary estate consists of property in possession, but, for the purposes of this section, a life interest in property partly in possession and partly not in possession may be treated as consisting of two separate life interests in those respective parts of the property.

(4) If the tenant for life dies after the exercise of the election under this section but before effect is given to that election, the date of redemption shall be taken for the purposes of subsection

(2) of this section to be the date immediately before the death of the tenant for life.

(5) An election under this section shall be exercisable only within the period of twelve months from the date on which representation with respect to the estate of the intestate is first taken out:

Provided that if the surviving husband or wife satisfies the court that the limitation to the said period of twelve months will operate unfairly—

(a) in consequence of the representation first taken out being probate of a will subsequently revoked on the ground that the will was invalid or,

(b) in consequence of a question whether a person had an interest in the estate, or as to the nature of an interest in the estate, not having been determined at the time when representation was first taken out, or

(c) in consequence of some other circumstances affecting the administration or distribution of the estate,

the court may extend the said period.

(6) An election under this section shall be exercisable, except where the tenant for life is the sole personal representative, by notifying the personal representative (or, where there are two or more personal representatives of whom one is the tenant for life all of them except the tenant for life) in writing; and a notification in writing under this subsection shall not be revocable except with the consent of the personal representative.

(7) Where the tenant for life is the sole personal representative an election under this section shall not be effective unless written notice thereof is given to the principal registrar of the Family Division of the High Court within the period within which it must be made; and provision may be made by probate rules for keeping a record of such notices and making that record available to the public.

In this subsection the expression "probate rules" means rules made under section one hundred of the Supreme Court of Judicature (Consolidation) Act 1925.

(8) An election under this section by a tenant for life who is an infant shall be as valid and binding as it would be if the tenant for life were of age; but the personal representative shall, instead of

paying the capital value of the life interest to the tenant for life, deal with it in the same manner as with any other part of the residuary estate to which the tenant for life is absolutely entitled.

(9) In considering for the purposes of the foregoing provisions of this section the question when representation was first taken out, a grant limited to settled land or to trust property shall be left out of account and a grant limited to real estate or to personal estate shall be left out of account unless a grant limited to the remainder of the estate has previously been made or is made at the same time.]

[As amended by Post Office Act 1969, s. 94 and Sched. 6, Pt. III; and Administration of Justice Act 1970, s. 1 (6) and Sched. 2, para. 4.]

Powers of personal representative in respect of interests of surviving spouse.

48. (1) [Repealed by Intestates Estates Act 1952, s. 2 (a).]

(2) The personal representatives may raise—

(a) The fixed net sum or any part thereof and the interest thereon payable to the surviving husband or wife of the intestate on the security of the whole or any part of the residuary estate of the intestate (other than the personal chattels), so far as that estate may be sufficient for the purpose or the said sum and interest may not have been satisfied by an appropriation under the statutory power available in that behalf; and

(b) in like manner the capital sum, if any, required for the purchase or redemption of the life interest of the surviving husband or wife of the intestate, or any part thereof not satisfied by the application for that purpose of any part of the residuary estate of the intestate;

and in either case the amount, if any, properly required for the payment of the costs of the transaction.

Application to cases of partial intestacy.

49. (1) Where any person dies leaving a will effectively disposing of part of his property, this Part of this Act shall have effect as respects the part of his property not so disposed of subject to the provisions contained in the will and subject to the following modifications:—

(aa) where the deceased leaves a husband or wife who acquires any beneficial interests under the will of the deceased (other than personal chattels specifically bequeathed) the references in this Part of this Act to the fixed net sum, payable to a surviving husband or wife, and to interest on that sum, shall be taken as references to the said sum diminished by the value at the date of death of the said beneficial interests, and to interest on that sum as so diminished and, accordingly, where the said value exceeds the said sum, this Part of this Act shall have effect as if references to the said sum, and interest thereon, were omitted,

(a) the requirements of section forty-seven of this Act as to bringing property into account shall apply to any beneficial interests acquired by any issue of the deceased under the will of the deceased, but not to beneficial interests so acquired by any other persons;

(b) the personal representative shall, subject to his rights and powers for the purposes of administration, be a trustee for the persons entitled under this Part of this Act in respect of the part of the estate not expressly disposed of unless it appears by the will that the personal representative is intended to take such part beneficially.

(2) References in the foregoing provisions of this section to beneficial interests acquired under a will shall be construed as including a reference to a beneficial interest acquired by virtue of the exercise by the will of a general power of appointment (including the statutory power to dispose of entailed interests), but not of a special power of appointment.

(3) For the purposes of paragraph (aa) in the foregoing provisions of this section the personal representative shall employ a duly qualified valuer in any case where such employment may be necessary.

(4) The references in subsection (3) of section forty-seven A of this Act to property are references to property comprised in the residuary estate and, accordingly, where a will of the deceased creates a life interest in property in possession, and the remaining

interest in that property forms part of the residuary estate, the said references are references to that remaining interest (which, until the life interest determines, is property not in possession).

Construction of documents.

50. (1) References to any Statutes of Distribution in an instrument inter vivos made or in a will coming into operation after the commencement of this Act, shall be construed as references to this Part of this Act; and references in such an instrument or will to statutory next of kin shall be construed, unless the context otherwise requires, as referring to the persons who would take beneficially on an intestacy under the foregoing provisions of this Part of this Act.

(2) Trusts declared in an instrument inter vivos made, or in a will coming into operation, before the commencement of this Act by reference to the Statutes of Distribution, shall, unless the contrary thereby appears, be construed as referring to the enactments (other than the Intestates' Estates Act 1890) relating to the distribution of effects of intestates which were in force immediately before the commencement of this Act.

Savings.

51. (1) Nothing in this Part of this Act affects the right of any person to take beneficially, by purchase, as heir either general or special.

(2) The foregoing provisions of this Part of this Act do not apply to any beneficial interest in real estate (not including chattels real) to which a lunatic or defective living and of full age at the commencement of this Act, and unable, by reason of his incapacity, to make a will, who thereafter dies intestate in respect of such interest without having recovered his testamentary capacity, was entitled at his death, and any such beneficial interest (not being an interest ceasing on his death) shall, without prejudice to any will of the deceased, devolve in accordance with the general law in force before the commencement of this Act applicable to freehold land, and that law shall, notwithstanding any repeal, apply to the case.

For the purposes of this subsection, a lunatic or defective who dies intestate as respects any beneficial interest in real estate shall not be deemed to have recovered his testamentary capacity unless his receiver has been discharged.

[As amended by Mental Health Act 1959, s. 149 (2).]

(3) Where an infant dies after the commencement of this Act without having been married, and independently of this sub-section he would, at his death, have been equitably entitled under a settlement (including a will) to a vested estate in fee simple or absolute interest in freehold land, or in any property settled to devolve therewith or as freehold land, such infant shall be deemed to have had an entailed interest, and the settlement shall be construed accordingly.

(4) This Part of this Act does not affect the devolution of an entailed interest as an equitable interest.

Interpretation of Part IV.

52. In this Part of this Act "real and personal estate" means every beneficial interest (including rights of entry and reverter) of the intestate in real and personal estate which (otherwise than in right of a power of appointment or of the testamentary power conferred by statute to dispose of entailed interests) he could, if of full age and capacity, have disposed of by his will.

PART V.

SUPPLEMENTAL.

General savings.

53. (1) Nothing in this Act shall derogate from the powers of the High Court which exist independently of this Act or alter the distribution of business between the several divisions of the High Court, or operate to transfer any jurisdiction from the High Court to any other court.

(2) Nothing in this Act shall affect any unrepealed enactment in a public general Act dispensing with probate or administration as respects personal estate not including chattels real.

(3) Nothing in this Act shall—

(a) alter any death duty payable in respect of real estate or impose any new duty thereon:

(b) render any real estate liable to legacy duty or exempt it from succession duty:

(c) alter the incidence of any death duties.

Application of Act.

54. Save as otherwise expressly provided, this Act does not apply in any case where the death occurred before the commencement of this Act.

Definitions.

55. In this Act, unless the context otherwise requires, the following expressions have the meanings hereby assigned to them respectively, that is to say:—

(1) (i) "Administration" means, with reference to the real and personal estate of a deceased person, letters of administration, whether general or limited, or with the will annexed or otherwise:

(ii) "Administrator" means a person to whom administration is granted:

(iii) "Conveyance" includes a mortgage, charge by way of legal mortgage, lease, assent, vesting, declaration vesting instrument, disclaimer, release and every other assurance of property or of an interest therein by any instrument, except a will, and "convey" has a corresponding meaning, and "disposition" includes a "conveyance" also a devise bequest and an appointment of property contained in a will, and "dispose of" has a corresponding meaning:

(iv) "the Court" means the High Court, and also the county court, where that court has jurisdiction.
[As amended by the Courts Act 1971, s. 56 and Sched. II, Pt. II.]

(v) "Income" includes rents and profits:

(vi) "Intestate" includes a person who leaves a will but dies intestate as to some beneficial interest in his real or personal estate:

(vii) "Legal estates" mean the estates charges and interests in or over land (subsisting or created at law) which are by statute authorised to subsist or to be created at law; and "equitable interests" mean all other interests and charges in or over land or in the proceeds of sale thereof:

(viii) "Lunatic" includes a lunatic whether so found or not, and in relation to a lunatic not so found; and "defective" includes every person affected by the provisions of section one hundred and sixteen of the Lunacy Act 1890, as extended by section sixty-four of the Mental Deficiency Act 1913, and for whose benefit a receiver has been appointed:

[As amended by Mental Health Act 1959, s. 149 (2)].

(ix) "Pecuniary legacy" includes an annuity, a general legacy, a demonstrative legacy so far as it is not discharged out of the designated property, and any other general direction by a testator for the payment of money, including all death duties free from which any devise, bequest, or payment is made to take effect:

(x) "Personal chattels" mean carriages, horses, stable furniture and effects (not used for business purposes), motor cars and accessories (not used for business purposes), garden effects, domestic animals, plate, plated articles, linen, china, glass, books, pictures, prints, furniture, jewellery, articles of household or personal use or ornament, musical and scientific instruments and apparatus, wines, liquors and consumable stores, but do not include any chattels used at the death of the intestate for business purposes nor money or securities for money:

(xi) "Personal representative" means the executor, original or by representation, or administrator for the time being of a deceased person, and as regards any liability for the payment of death duties includes any person who takes possession of or intermeddles with the property of a deceased person without the authority of the personal representatives or the court, and "executor" includes a person deemed to be appointed executor as respects settled land:

(xii) "Possession" includes the receipt of rents and profits or the right to receive the same, if any:

(xiii) "Prescribed" means prescribed by rules of court or by probate rules made pursuant to this Act:

(xiv) "Probate" means the probate of a will:

(xv) "Probate judge" means the President of the Family Division of the High Court:

[As amended by Administration of Justice Act 1970, s. 1 (6) and Sched. 2, para. 5.]

(xvi) "Probate rules" mean rules and orders made by the Probate Judge for regulating the procedure and practice of the High Court in regard to non-contentious or common form probate business:

(xvii) "Property" includes a thing in action and any interest in real or personal property:

(xviii) "Purchaser" means a lessee, mortgagee or other person who in good faith acquires an interest in property for valuable consideration, also an intending purchaser and "valuable consideration" includes marriage, but does not include a nominal consideration in money:

(xix) "Real estate" save as provided in Part IV. of this Act means real estate, including chattels real, which by virtue of Part I. of this Act devolves on the personal representative of a deceased person:

(xx) "Representation" means the probate of a will and administration, and the expression "taking out representation" refers to the obtaining of the probate of a will or of the grant of administration:

(xxi) "Rent" includes a rent service or a rentcharge, or other rent, toll, duty, or annual or periodical payment in money or money's worth, issuing out of or charged upon land, but does not include mortgage interest; and "rentcharge" includes a fee farm rent:

(xxii) "Rules of Court" include, in relation to non-contentious or common form probate business, probate rules.

(xxiii) "Securities" include stocks, funds, or shares:

(xxiv) "Tenant for life," "statutory owner," "land," "settled land," "settlement," "trustees of the settlement," "term of years absolute," "death duties," and "legal mortgage," have the same meanings as in the Settled Land Act 1925, and "entailed interest" and "charge by way of legal "mortgage" have the same meanings as in the Law of Property Act 1925:

(xxv) "Treasury solicitor" means the solicitor for the affairs of His Majesty's Treasury, and includes the solicitor for the affairs of the Duchy of Lancaster:

(xxvi) "Trust corporation" means the public trustee or a corporation either appointed by the court in any particular case to be a trustee or entitled by rules made under subsection (3) of section four of the Public Trustee Act 1906, to act as custodian trustee:

(xxvii) "Trust for sale," in relation to land, means an immediate binding trust for sale, whether or not exercisable at the request or with the consent of any person, and with or without a power at discretion to postpone the sale; and "power to postpone a sale" means power to postpone in the exercise of a discretion:

(xxviii) "Will" includes codicil.

(2) References to a child or issue living at the death of any person include a child or issue en ventre sa mere at the death.

(3) References to the estate of a deceased person include property over which the deceased exercises a general power of appointment (including the statutory power to dispose of entailed interests) by his will.

Repeal.

56. The Acts mentioned in the Second Schedule to this Act are hereby repealed to the extent specified in the third column of that Schedule, but as respects the Acts mentioned in Part I. of that Schedule only so far as they apply to deaths occurring after the commencement of this Act.

Application to Crown.

57. (1) The provisions of this Act bind the Crown and the Duchy of Lancaster, and the Duke of Cornwall for the time being, as respects the estates of persons dying after the commencement of this Act, but not so as to affect the time within which proceedings for the recovery of real or personal estate vesting in or devolving on His Majesty in right of His Crown, or His Duchy of Lancaster, or on the Duke of Cornwall, may be instituted.

(2) Nothing in this Act in any manner affects or alters the descent or devolution of any property for the time being vested in His Majesty either in right of the Crown or of the Duchy of Lancaster or of any property for the time being belonging to the Duchy of Cornwall.

Short title, commencement and extent.

58. (1) This Act may be cited as the Administration of Estates Act 1925.

(2) [Repealed by Statute Law Revision Act 1950].

(3) This Act extends to England and Wales only.

SCHEDULES.

FIRST SCHEDULE.

Part I.

Rules as to Payment of Debts where the Estate is Insolvent.

1. The funeral, testamentary, and administration expenses have priority.

2. Subject as aforesaid, the same rules shall prevail and be observed as to the respective rights of secured and unsecured creditors and as to debts and liabilities provable and as to the valuation of annuities and future and contingent liabilities respectively, and as to the prorities of debts and liabilities as may be in force for the time being under the law of bankruptcy with respect to the assets of persons adjudged bankrupt.

Part II.

Order of Application of Assets where the Estate is Solvent.

1. Property of the deceased undisposed of by will, subject to the retention thereout of a fund sufficient to meet any pecuniary legacies.

2. Property of the deceased not specifically devised or bequeathed but included (either by a specific or general description) in a residuary gift, subject to the retention out of such property of a fund sufficient to meet any pecuniary legacies, so far as not provided for as aforesaid.

3. Property of the deceased specifically appropriated or devised or bequeathed (either by a specific or general description) for the payment of debts.

4. Property of the deceased charged with, or devised or bequeathed (either by a specific or general description) subject to a charge for the payment of debts.

5. The fund, if any, retained to meet pecuniary legacies.

6. Property specifically devised or bequeathed, rateably according to value.

7. Property appointed by will under a general power, including the statutory power to dispose of entailed interests, rateably according to value.

8. The following provisions shall also apply—

(a) The order of application may be varied by the will of the deceased.

(b) This part of this Schedule does not affect the liability of land to answer the death duty imposed thereon in exoneration of other assets.

[Second Schedule repealed by Statute Law Revision Act 1950].

SUPREME COURT OF JUDICATURE (CONSOLIDATION) ACT 1925

(15 & 16 Geo. 5, c. 49)

4. (1) For the more convenient despatch of business in the High Court there shall be in the High Court three Divisions, namely:

(i) The Chancery Division, consisting of the Lord Chancellor, who shall be president thereof, and not less than five puisne judges;

(ii) The King's Bench Division, consisting of the Lord Chief Justice, who shall be president thereof, and not less than seventeen puisne judges;

(iii) The Probate, Divorce and Admiralty Division consisting of a president and not less than three puisne judges.

* * * * *

(4) Without prejudice to the provisions of this Act relating to the distribution of business in the High Court, all jurisdiction vested in the High Court under this Act shall belong to all the Divisions alike.

[As amended by Administration of Justice Act 1928, s. 6; and Supreme Court of Judicature (Amendment) Act 1944, s. 1].

Probate jurisdiction of High Court.

20. Subject to the provisions of this Act the High Court shall, in relation to probates and letters of administration, have the following jurisdiction (in this Act referred to as "probate jurisdiction"), that is to say:—

(a) all such voluntary and contentious jurisdiction and authority in relation to the granting or revoking of probate and administration of the effects of deceased persons as was at the commencement of the Court of Probate Act, 1857, vested in or exercisable by any court or person in England, together with full authority to hear and determine all questions relating to testamentary causes and matters:

(b) all such powers throughout England in relation to the personal estate in England of deceased persons as the Prerogative Court of Canterbury had immediately before the commencement of the Court of Probate Act 1857, in the Province of Canterbury or in the parts thereof within its jurisdiction in relation to those testamentary causes and matters and those effects of deceased persons which were at that date within the jurisdiction of that court;

(c) such like jurisdiction and powers with respect to the real estate of deceased persons as are herein before conferred with respect to the personal estate of deceased persons;

(d) all probate jurisdiction which, under or by virtue of any enactment which came into force after the commencement of the Act of 1873 and is not repealed by this Act, was immediately before the commencement of this Act vested in or capable of being exercised by the High Court constituted by the Act of 1873;

and the court shall, in the exercise of the probate jurisdiction perform all such like duties with respect to the estates of deceased persons as were immediately before the commencement of the Court of Probate Act 1857, to be performed by ordinaries generally or by the Prerogative Court of Canterbury in respect of probates, administrations and testamentary causes and matters which were at that date within their respective jurisdictions.

PART VII.—PROBATE CAUSES AND MATTERS

Grants of Probate and Administration

Application for grants.

150. An application for the grant or revocation of probate or administration may be made through the principal probate registry:

Provided that—

(a) Where, in any contentious matter arising out of the application, the court is satisfied that the state of the property and the place of abode of the deceased were such as to give jurisdiction in the matter to a county court, the court may remit the matter to that county court and the judge thereof shall proceed in the matter as if the application had been made to the county court in the first instance;

(b) Where a registrar of the principal probate registry is satisfied by affidavit that the personal estate of the person in respect of whose estate the application for the grant or revocation is made exclusive of what he was possessed of or entitled to as a trustee and not beneficially, but without any deduction on account of his debts, was at the time of his death under the value of two hundred pounds, and that at that time he was not seised or entitled beneficially of or to any real estate of the value of three hundred pounds or upwards, the judge of the county court having jurisdiction in the place of abode of the deceased shall have the jurisdiction of the High Court in respect of any

contentious matter arising in connection with the said grant or revocation.
[Repealed by County Courts Act 1934, but re-enacted by County Courts Act 1959].

151. and 152. [Relate to *grants in District Registries*].

Second and subsequent grants.

153. Second and subsequent grants shall be made in the principal probate registry or in the district probate registry where the original will is registered or the original grant was made, or to which the original will or a registered copy thereof or the record of the original grant has been transmitted in pursuance of section eighty-nine of the Court of Probate Act 1857, or of this Part of this Act.

Caveats

154. (1) A caveat against a grant of probate or administration may be entered in the principal registry or in any district probate registry.

(2) On a caveat being entered in a district registry, the district probate registrar shall immediately send a copy thereof to the principal probate registry to be entered among the caveats in that registry.

Power to grant representation of real and personal estate separately or together.

155. (1) Probate or administration in respect of the real estate of a deceased person, or any part thereof, may be granted either separately or together with probate or administration of his personal estate, and may also be granted in respect of real estate only where there is no personal estate, or in respect of a trust estate only, and a grant of administration to real estate may be limited in any way the court thinks proper:

Provided that where the estate of the deceased is known to be insolvent, the grant of representation to the estate shall not be severed except as regards a trust estate.

(2) Provision may be made by probate rules and orders for adapting to the case of real estate the procedure and practice on the grant of administration.

Provisions as to Executors and Administrators

Summons of executor to prove or renounce.

159. The High Court shall have power to summon any person named as executor in a will to prove or renounce probate of the will, and to do such other things concerning the will as were customary before the commencement of this Act.

Provisions as to the number of personal representatives.

160. (1) Probate or administration shall not be granted to more than four persons in respect of the same property, and administration shall, if there is a minority or if a life interest arises under the will or intestacy, be granted either to a trust corporation, with or without an individual, or to not less than two individuals:

Provided that the court in granting administration may act on such prima facie evidence, furnished by the applicant or any other person, as to whether or not there is a minority or life interest, as may be prescribed by probate rules and orders.

(2) If there is only one personal representative (not being a trust corporation) then, during the minority of a beneficiary or the subsistence of a life interest and until the estate is fully administered, the court may, on the application of any person interested or of the guardian, committee or receiver of any such person, appoint one or more personal representatives in addition to the original personal representative in accordance with probate rules and orders.

(3) This section shall apply to grants made after the date of the commencement of this Act, whether the testator or intestate dies before or after that date.

Power to grant representation to a trust corporation.

161. (1) The High Court may—

(a) Where a trust corporation is named in a will as executor, whether alone or jointly with another person, grant probate to the corporation either solely or jointly with another person, as the case may require; and

(b) grant administration to a trust corporation, either solely or jointly with another person,

and the corporation may act accordingly as executor or administrator, as the case may be.

(2) Probate or administration shall not be granted to a syndic or nominee on behalf of a trust corporation.

(3) Any officer authorised for the purpose by a trust corporation or the directors or governing body thereof may, on behalf of the corporation, swear affidavits, give security and do any other act or thing which the court may require with a view to the grant to the corporation of probate or administration, and the acts of an officer so authorised shall be binding on the corporation.

(4) Where, at the commencement of this Act, any interest in any estate is vested in a syndic on behalf of a trust corporation acting as the personal representatives of a deceased person, the said interest shall, by virtue of this Act, vest in the corporation, and the syndic shall be kept indemnified by the corporation in respect of the said interest.

This subsection shall not apply to securities registered or inscribed in the name of a syndic or to land or a charge registered under the Land Registration Act 1925, in the name of a syndic, but any such securities, land or charge, shall be transferred by the syndic to the corporation or as the corporation may direct.

(5) This section shall have effect whether the testator or the intestate died before or after the commencement of this Act, and no such vesting or transfer as aforesaid shall operate as a breach of a covenant or condition against alienation or give rise to a forfeiture.

Discretion of court as to persons to whom administration is to be granted.

162. (1) In granting administration the High Court shall have regard to the rights of all persons interested in the estate of the deceased person or the proceeds of sale thereof, and, in particular, administration with the will annexed may be granted to a devisee or legatee, and in regard to land settled previously to the death of the deceased and not by his will, may be granted to the trustees of the settlement, and any such administration may be limited in any way the court thinks fit:

Provided that—

(a) where the deceased died wholly intestate as to his estate, administration shall be granted to some one or more persons interested in the residuary estate of the deceased, if they make an application for the purpose, and as regards lands settled previously to the death of the deceased be granted to the trustees, if any, of the settlement, if willing to act; and

(b) if, by reason of the insolvency of the estate of the deceased or of any other special circumstances, it appears to the court to be necessary or expedient to appoint as administrator some person other than the person who, but for this provision, would by law have been entitled to the grant of administration, the court may in its discretion, notwithstanding anything in this Act, appoint as administrator such person as it thinks expedient, and any administration granted under this provision may be limited in any way the court thinks fit.

(2) This section shall apply only in the case of persons dying after the date of the commencement of this Act, and the High Court in granting administration in the case of persons dying at any time before that date shall act in accordance with the principles and rules in accordance with which it would have acted if this Act had not passed.

Administration pendente lite.

163. (1) Where any legal proceedings touching the validity of the will of a deceased person, or for obtaining, recalling or revoking any grant, are pending, the High Court may grant administration of the estate of the deceased to an administrator, who shall have all the rights and powers of a general administrator, other than the right of distributing the residue of the estate, and every such administrator shall be subject to the immediate control of the court and act under its direction.

(2) The court may, out of the estate of the deceased, assign to an administrator appointed under this section such reasonable remuneration as the court thinks fit.

Grant of special administration where personal representative is abroad.

164. (1) If at the expiration of twelve months from the death of a person any personal representative of the deceased to whom a grant has been made is residing out of the jurisdiction of High

Court, the court may, on the application of any creditor or person interested in the estate of the deceased, grant to him in the prescribed form special administration of the estate of the deceased.

(2) The court may, for the purpose of any legal proceedings to which the administrator under the special administration is a party, order the transfer into court of any money or securities belonging to the estate of the deceased person, and all persons shall obey any such order.

(3) If the personal representative capable of acting as such returns to and resides within the jurisdiction of the High Court while any legal proceedings to which a special administrator is a party are pending, that personal representative shall be made a party to the legal proceedings, and the costs of and incidental to the special administration and the legal proceedings shall be paid by such person and out of such funds as the court in which the proceedings are pending may direct.

Administration during minority of executor.

165. (1) Where an infant is sole executor of a will, administration with the will annexed shall be granted to his guardian, or to such other person as the court thinks fit, until the infant attains the age of twenty-one years, and on his attaining that age, and not before, probate of the will may be granted to him.

(2) Where a testator by his will appoints an infant to be an executor, the appointment shall not operate to transfer any interest in the property of the deceased to the infant or to constitute him a personal representative for any purpose unless and until probate is granted to him under this section.

Administration with will annexed.

166. Subject to the provisions of any enactment relating to special executors in the case of settled land, administration with the will annexed shall continue to be granted in every case where such a grant was customary before the commencement of this Act, and in such case the will of the deceased shall be performed and observed in like manner as if probate thereof had been granted to an executor.

Power to require administrators to produce sureties

167. (1) As a condition of granting administration to any person the High Court may, subject to the following provisions of this section and subject to and in accordance with probate rules and orders, require one or more sureties to guarantee that they will make good, within any limit imposed by the court on the total liability of the surety or sureties, any loss which any person interested in the administration of the estate of the deceased may suffer in consequence of a breach by the administrator of his duties as such.

(2) A guarantee given in pursuance of any such requirement shall ensure for the benefit of every person interested in the administration of the estate of the deceased as if contained in a contract under seal made by the surety or sureties with every such person and where there are two or more sureties, as if they had bound themselves jointly and severally.

(3) No action shall be brought on any such guarantee without the leave of the High Court.

(4) Stamp duty shall not be chargeable on any such guarantee.

(5) This section does not apply where administration is granted to the Treasury Solicitor, the Public Trustee, the Solicitor for the affairs of the Duchy of Lancaster or the Duchy of Cornwall or the Chief Crown Solicitor for Northern Ireland, or to the consular officer of a foreign state to which section 1 of the Consular Conventions Act 1949 applies, or in such other cases as may be prescribed by probate rules and orders.

[Substituted by Administration of Estates Act 1971, s. 8.]

Depositories of wills of living persons.

172. There shall, under the control and direction of the High Court, be provided safe and convenient depositories for the custody of the wills of living persons, and any person may depsit his will therein on payment of such fees and subject to such regulations as may from time to time be prescribed by the President of the Probate Division.

LEGITIMACY ACT 1926
(16 & 17 Geo. 5, c. 60.)

Legitimation by subsequent marriage of parents

1. (1) Subject to the provisions of this section, where the parents of an illegitimate person marry or have married one another, whether before or after the commencement of this Act, the marriage shall, if the father of the illegitimate person was or is at the date of the marriage domiciled in England or Wales, render that person, if living, legitimate from the commencement of this Act, or from the date of the marriage, whichever last happens, [or from October 29 1959 if his father or mother was married to someone else when he was born: Legitimacy Act 1959, ss. 1, 6 (3).]

(2) [*Repealed by the Legitimacy Act* 1959 (*c.* 73), *s.* 1 (1).]

(3) The legitimation of a person under this Act does not enable him or his spouse, children or remoter issue to take any interest in real or personal property save as is hereinafter in this Act expressly provided.

Rights of legitimated persons, etc., to take interests in property

3. (1) Subject to the provisions of this Act, a legitimated person and his spouse, children or more remote issue shall be entitled to take any interest—

(a) in the estate of an intestate dying after the date of legitimation;

(b) under any disposition coming into operation after the date of legitimation;

(c) by descent under an entailed interest created after the date of legitimation;

in like manner as if the legitimated person had been born legitimate.

(2) Where the right to any property, real or personal, depends on the relative seniority of the children of any person, and those children include one or more legitimated persons, the legitimated person or persons shall rank as if he or they had been born on the day when he or they became legitimated by virtue of this Act,

and if more than one such legitimated person became legitimated at the same time, they shall rank as between themselves in order of seniority.

(3) Where property real or personal or any interest therein is limited in such a way that, if this Act had not been passed, it would (subject or not to any preceding limitations or charges) have devolved (as nearly as the law permits) along with a dignity or title of honour, then nothing in this Act shall operate to sever the property or any interest therein from such dignity, but the same shall go and devolve (without prejudice to the preceding limitations or charges aforesaid) in like manner as if this Act had not been passed. This subsection applies, whether or not there is any express reference to the dignity or title of honour and notwithstanding that in some events the property, or some interest therein, may become severed therefrom.

(4) This section applies only if and so far as a contrary intention is not expressed in the disposition, and shall have effect subject to the terms of the disposition and to the provisions therein contained.

Succession on intestacy of legitimated persons and their issue

4. Where a legitimated person or a child or remoter issue of a legitimated person dies intestate in respect of all or any of his real or personal property, the same persons shall be entitled to take the same interests therein as they would have been entitled to take if the legitimated person had been born legitimate.

Application to illegitimate person dying before marriage of parents

5. Where an illegitimate person dies after the commencement of this Act and before the marriage of his parents leaving any spouse, children or remoter issue living at the date of such marriage, then, if that person would, if living at the time of the marriage of his parents, have become a legitimated person, the provisions of this Act with respect to the taking of interests in property by, or in succession to, the spouse, children and remoter issue of a legitimated person (including those relating to the rate of death duties) shall apply as if such person as aforesaid had been a legitimated person and the date of the marriage of his parents had been the date of legitimation.

Right of illegitimate child and mother of illegitimate child to succeed on intestacy of the other

9. [*Repealed by the Family Law Reform Act 1969.*]

Savings

10. (1) Nothing in this Act shall affect the succession to any dignity or title of honour or render any person capable of succeeding to or transmitting a right to succeed to any such dignity or title.

(2) Nothing in this Act shall affect the operation or construction of any disposition coming into operation before the commencement of this Act, or affect any rights under the intestacy of a person dying before the commencement of this Act.

INHERITANCE (FAMILY PROVISION) ACT 1938

(1 & 2 Geo. 6, c. 45)

[As amended by Intestates' Estates Act 1952,
Family Provision Act 1966, Family Law Reform Act 1969, and
Administration of Justice Act 1970

Power for court to order payment out of net estate of deceased for benefit of surviving spouse or child.

1. (1) Where, after the commencement of this Act, a person dies domiciled in England leaving—

(a) a wife or husband,

(b) a daughter who has not been married, or who is, by reason of some mental or physical disability, incapable of maintaining herself,

(c) a son who has not attained the age of twenty-one years,

(d) a son who is, by reason of some mental or physical disability, incapable of maintaining himself,

then, if the court on application by or on behalf of any such wife, husband, daughter or son as aforesaid (in this Act referred to as a "dependant" of the deceased) is of opinion that the disposition of the deceased's estate effected by his will, or the law relating to intestacy, or the combination of his will and that law, is not such as to make reasonable provision for the maintenance of that dependant, the court may order that such reasonable provision as the court thinks fit shall, subject to such conditions or restrictions, if any, as the court may impose, be made out of the deceased's net estate for the maintenance of that dependant.

(2) The provision for maintenance to be made by an order shall, subject to the provisions of subsection (4) of this section, be by way of periodical payments and the order shall provide for their termination not later than—

(a) in the case of a wife or husband, her or his re-marriage;

(b) in the case of a daughter who has not been married, or who is under disability, her marriage or the cesser of her disability, whichever is the later;

(c) in the case of a son who has not attained the age of twenty-one years, his attaining that age;

(d) in the case of a son under disability, the cesser of his disability;

or, in any case, his or her earlier death.

(4) The court shall have power, if it sees fit, to make an order providing for maintenance, in whole or in part, by way of a lump sum payment.

(5) In determining whether, and in what way, and as from what date, provision for maintenance ought to be made by an order, the court shall have regard to the nature of the property representing the deceased's net estate and shall not order any such provision to be made as would necessitate a realisation that would be improvident having regard to the interests of the deceased's dependants and of the person who, apart from the order, would be entitled to that property.

(6) The court shall, on any application made under this Act, have regard to any past, present or future capital or income from any source of the dependant of the deceased to whom the application relates, to the conduct of that dependant in relation to the deceased and otherwise, and to any other matter or thing which in the circumstances of the case the court may consider relevant or material in relation to that dependant, to persons interested in the estate of the deceased, or otherwise.

(7) The court shall also, on any such application, have regard to the deceased's reasons, so far as ascertainable, for making the dispositions made by his will (if any), or for refraining from disposing by will of his estate or part of his estate, or for not

making any provision, or any further provision, as the case may be, for a dependant, and the court may accept such evidence of those reasons as it considers sufficient including any statement in writing signed by the deceased and dated, so, however, that in estimating the weight, if any, to be attached to any such statement the court shall have regard to all the circumstances from which any inference can reasonably be drawn as to the accuracy or otherwise of the statement.

(8) The court in considering for the purposes of subsection (1) of this section whether the disposition of the deceased's estate effected by the law relating to intestacy, or by the combination of the deceased's will and that law, makes reasonable provision for the maintenance of a dependant shall not be bound to assume that the law relating to intestacy makes reasonable provision in all cases.

Time within which application must be made.

2. (1) Except as provided by section 4 of this Act, an application under this Act shall not, without the permission of the court, be made after the end of the period of six months from the date on which representation in regard to the estate of the deceased is first taken out.

(1B) The provisions of this Act shall not render the personal representatives of the deceased liable for having distributed any part of the estate of the deceased after the expiration of the said period of six months on the ground that they ought to have taken into account the possibility that the court might permit an application under this Act after the end of that period, but this subsection shall be without prejudice to any power to recover any part of the estate so distributed arising by virtue of the making of an order under this Act.

(1C) In considering under the foregoing subsections the question when representation was first taken out, a grant limited to settled land or to trust property shall be left out of account and a grant limited to real estate or to personal estate shall be left out of account unless a grant limited to the remainder of the estate has previously been made or is made at the same time.

(2) For the purpose of section 162(1) of the Supreme Court of

Judicature (Consolidation) Act 1925 which relates to the discretion of the court as to the persons to whom administration is to be granted) a dependant of a deceased person by whom or on whose behalf an application under this Act is proposed to be made shall be deemed to be a person interested in his estate.

Effect and form of order.

3. (1) Where an order is made under this Act then for all purposes including the purposes of the enactments relating to death duties the will or the law relating to intestacy or both the will and the law relating to intestacy, as the case may be, shall have effect, and shall be deemed to have had effect as from the deceased's death, subject to such variations as may be specified in the order for the purpose of giving effect to the provision for maintenance thereby made.

(1A) Any order under this Act providing for maintenance by way of periodical payments may provide for payments of a specified amount, or for payments equal to the whole or part of the income of the net estate or of the income of any part to be set aside or appropriated under this Act of the net estate, or may provide for the amount of the payments or any of them to be determined in any other way which the court thinks fit.

(2) The court may give such consequential directions as it thinks fit for the purpose of giving effect to an order made under this Act, but no larger part of the net estate shall be set aside or appropriated to answer by the income thereof the provision for maintenance thereby made than such a part as, at the date of the order, is sufficient to produce by the income thereof the amount of the said provision.

(3) A copy of every order made under this Act shall be sent to the principal registry of the Family Division for entry and filing, and a memorandum of the order shall be endorsed on, or permanently annexed to, the probate or letters of administration under which the estate is being administered.

Variation of orders.

4. (1) On an application made at a date after the expiration of the period specified in section 2(1) of this Act the court may make such an order as is hereinafter mentioned, but only as respects property the income of which is at that date applicable for the maintenance of a dependant of the deceased, that is to say,

   (a) an order for varying the previous order on the ground that any material fact was not disclosed to the court when the order was made, or that any substantial change has taken place in the circumstances of the dependant or of a person beneficially interested in the property under the will or, as the case may be, under the law relating to intestacy, or

   (b) an order for making provision for the maintenance of another dependant of the deceased.

(2) An application to the court for an order under paragraph (a) of the preceding subsection may be made by or on behalf of a dependant of the deceased or by the trustees of the property or by or on behalf of a person beneficially interested therein under the will or, as the case may be, under the law relating to intestacy.

Interim orders.

4A. (1) Where on an application for maintenance under this Act it appears to the court—

   (a) that the applicant is in immediate need of financial assistance, but it is not yet possible to determine what order (if any) should be made on the application for the provision of maintenance for the applicant; and

   (b) that property forming part of the net estate of the deceased is or can be made available to meet the need of the applicant;

the court may order that, subject to such conditions or restrictions, if any, as the court may impose and to any further order of the court, there shall be paid to or for the benefit of the applicant out of the deceased's net estate such sum or sums and (if more than one) at such intervals as the court thinks reasonable.

(2) In determining what order, if any, should be made under this section the court shall, so far as the urgency of the case admits, take account of the same considerations as would be relevant in determining what order should be made on the application for the provision of maintenance for the applicant; and any subsequent order for the provision of maintenance may provide that sums

paid to or for the benefit of the applicant by virtue of this section shall be treated to such extent, if any, and in such manner as may be provided by that order as having been paid on account of the maintenance provided for by that order.

(3) Subject to subsection (2) above, section 3 of this Act shall apply in relation to an order under this section as it applies in relation to an order providing for maintenance.

(4) Where the deceased's personal representative pays any sum directed by an order under this section to be paid out of the deceased's net estate, he shall not be under any liability by reason of that estate not being sufficient to make the payment, unless at the time of making the payment he has reasonable cause to believe that the estate is not sufficient.

Interpretation.

5. (1) In this Act, unless the context otherwise requires, the following expressions shall have the meanings hereby respectively assigned to them, that is to say—

"the court" means the High Court and also the Court of Chancery of the County Palatine of Lancaster or the Court of Chancery of the County Palatine of Durham or a county court where those courts respectively have jurisdiction;

"death duties" means estate duty and every other duty leviable or payable on death;

"net estate" means all the property of which a deceased person had power to dispose by his will (otherwise than by virtue of a special power of appointment) less the amount of his funeral, testamentary and administration expenses, debts and liabilities and estate duty payable out of his estate on his death;

"will" includes codicil;

"son" and "daughter" respectively include an illegitimate son or daughter of the deceased, a male or female child adopted by the deceased in pursuance of adoption proceedings taken in any part of the United Kingdom, the Isle of Man and the Channel Islands, and also the son or daughter of the deceased en ventre sa mere at the date of the death of the deceased.

(2) References in this Act to any enactment or any provision of

any enactment shall, unless the context otherwise requires, be construed as references to that enactment or provision as amended by any subsequent enactment including this Act.

Short title and extent.

6. (1) This Act may be cited as the Inheritance (Family Provision) Act 1938.

(2) This Act shall not extent to Scotland or to Northern Ireland.

INTESTATES' ESTATES ACT 1952
(15 & 16 Geo 6 & 1 Eliz. 2, c. 64)

* * * *

5. The Second Schedule to this Act shall have effect for enabling the surviving husband or wife of a person dying intestate after the commencement of this Act to acquire the matrimonial home.

* * * *

SECOND SCHEDULE
RIGHTS OF SURVIVING SPOUSE AS RESPECTS THE MATRIMONIAL HOME

1. (1) Subject to the provisions of this Schedule, where the residuary estate of the intestate comprises an interest in a dwelling-house in which the surviving husband or wife was resident at the time of the intestate's death, the surviving husband or wife may require the personal representative, in exercise of the power conferred by section forty-one of the principal Act (and with due regard to the requirements of that section as to valuation) to appropriate the said interest in the dwelling-house in or towards satisfaction of any absolute interest of the surviving husband or wife in the real and personal estate of the intestate.

(2) The right conferred by this paragraph shall not be exercisable where the interest is—

> (a) a tenancy which at the date of the death of the intestate was a tenancy which would determine within the period of two years from that date; or

(b) a tenancy which the landlord by notice given after that date could determine within the remainder of that period.

[See, however, Leasehold Reform Act 1967, s. 7 (8): *post*, p. 642.]

(3) Nothing in subsection (5) of section forty-one of the principal Act (which requires the personal representative, in making an appropriation to any person under that section, to have regard to the rights of others) shall prevent the personal representative from giving effect to the right conferred by this paragraph.

(4) The reference in this paragraph to an absolute interest in the real and personal estate of the intestate includes a reference to the capital value of a life interest which the surviving husband or wife has under this Act elected to have redeemed.

(5) Where part of a building was, at the date of the death of the intestate, occupied as a separate dwelling, that dwelling shall for the purposes of this Schedule be treated as a dwelling-house.

2. Where—

(a) the dwelling-house forms part of a building and an interest in the whole of the building is comprised in the residuary estate; or

(b) the dwelling-house is held with agricultural land and an interest in the agricultural land is comprised in the residuary estate; or

(c) the whole or a part of the dwelling-house was at the time of the intestate's death used as a hotel or lodging house; or

(d) a part of the dwelling-house was at the time of the intestate's death used for purposes other than domestic purposes,

the right conferred by paragraph 1 of this Schedule shall not be exercisable unless the court, on being satisfied that the exercise of that right is not likely to diminish the value of assets in the residuary estate (other than the said interest in the dwelling-house) or make them more difficult to dispose of, so orders.

3. (1) The right conferred by paragraph 1 of this Schedule—

(a) shall not be exercisable after the expiration of twelve

months from the first taking out of representation with respect to the intestate's estate;

(b) shall not be exercisable after the death of the surviving husband or wife;

(c) shall be exercisable, except where the surviving husband or wife is the sole personal representative, by notifying the personal representative (or, where there are two or more personal representatives of whom one is the surviving husband or wife, all of them except the surviving husband or wife) in writing.

(2) A notification in writing under paragraph (c) of the foregoing sub-paragraph shall not be revocable except with the consent of the personal representative; but the surviving husband or wife may require the personal representative to have the said interest in the dwelling-house valued in accordance with section forty-one of the principal Act and to inform him or her of the result of that valuation before he or she decides whether to exercise the right.

(3) Subsection (9) of the section forty-seven A added to the principal Act by section two of this Act shall apply for the purposes of the construction of the reference in this paragraph to the first taking out of representation, and the proviso to subsection (5) of that section shall apply for the purpose of enabling the surviving husband or wife to apply for an extension of the period of twelve months mentioned in this paragraph.

4. (1) During the period of twelve months mentioned in paragraph 3 of this Schedule the personal representative shall not without the written consent of the surviving husband or wife sell or otherwise dispose of the said interest in the dwelling-house except in the course of administration owing to want of other assets.

(2) An application to the court under paragraph 2 of this Schedule may be made by the personal representative as well as by the surviving husband or wife, and if, on application under that paragraph, the court does not order that the right conferred by paragraph 1 of this Schedule shall be exercisable by the surviving husband or wife, the court may authorise the personal representative to dispose of the said interest in the dwelling-house within the said period of twelve months.

(3) Where the court under sub-paragraph (3) of paragraph 3 of this Schedule extends the said period of twelve months, the court may direct that this paragraph shall apply in relation to the extended period as it applied in relation to the original period of twelve months.

(4) This paragraph shall not apply where the surviving husband or wife is the sole personal representative or one of two or more personal representatives.

(5) Nothing in this paragraph shall confer any right on the surviving husband or wife as against a purchaser from the personal representative.

5. (1) Where the surviving husband or wife is one of two or more personal representatives, the rule that a trustee may not be a purchaser of trust property shall not prevent the surviving husband or wife from purchasing out of the estate of the intestate an interest in a dwelling-house in which the surviving husband or wife was resident at the time of the intestate's death.

(2) The power of appropriation under section forty-one of the principal Act shall include power to appropriate an interest in a dwelling-house in which the surviving husband or wife was resident at the time of the intestate's death partly in satisfaction of an interest of the surviving husband or wife in the real and personal estate of the intestate and partly in return for a payment of money by the surviving husband or wife to the personal representative.

6. (1) Where the surviving husband or wife is a person of unsound mind or a defective, a requirement or consent under this Schedule may be made or given on his or her behalf by the committee or receiver, if any, or, where there is no committee or receiver, by the court.

(2) A requirement or consent made or given under this Schedule by a surviving husband or wife who is an infant shall be as valid and binding as it would be if he or she were of age; and, as respects an appropriation in pursuance of paragraph 1 of this Schedule, the provisions of section forty-one of the principal Act as to obtaining the consent of the infant's parent or guardian, or of the court on behalf of the infant, shall not apply.

2 4

7. (1) Except where the context otherwise requires, references in this Schedule to a dwelling-house include references to any garden or portion of ground attached to and usually occupied with the dwelling-house or otherwise required for the amenity or convenience of the dwelling-house.

(2) This Schedule shall be construed as one with Part IV of the principal Act.

ADOPTION ACT 1958
(7 Eliz. 2, c. 5)

English intestacies, wills and settlements

16. (1) Where, at any time after the making of an adoption order, the adopter or the adopted person or any other person dies intestate in respect of any real or personal property (other than property subject to an entailed interest under a disposition to which subsection (2) of this section does not apply), that property shall devolve in all respects as if the adopted person were the child of the adopter born in lawful wedlock and were not the child of any other person.

(2) In any disposition of real or personal property made, whether by instrument inter vivos or by will (including codicil) after the date of an adoption order—

    (a) any reference (whether express or implied) to the child or children of the adopter shall, unless the contrary intention appears, be construed as, or as including, a reference to the adopted person;

    (b) any reference (whether express or implied) to the child or children of the adopted person's natural parents or either of them shall, unless the contrary intention appears, be construed as not being, or as not including, a reference to the adopted person; and

    (c) any reference (whether express or implied) to a person related to the adopted person in any degree shall, unless the contrary intention appears, be construed as a reference to the person who would be related to him in that degree if he were the child of the adopter born in lawful wedlock and were not the child of any other person.

(3) Where under any disposition any real or personal property or any interest in such property is limited (whether subject to any preceding limitation or charge or not) in such a way that it would, apart from this section, devolve (as nearly as the law permits) along with a dignity or title of honour, then, whether or not the disposition contains an express reference to the dignity or title of honour, and whether or not the property or some interest in the property may in some event become severed therefrom, nothing in this section shall operate to sever the property or any interest therein from the dignity, but the property or interest shall devolve in all respects as if this section had not been enacted.

(4) The references in this section to an adoption order include references to an order authorising an adoption made under the Adoption of Children Act (Northern Ireland) 1950, or any enactment of the Parliament of Northern Ireland for the time being in force.

Provisions supplementary to s. 16

17. (1) For the purposes of the application of the Administration of Estates Act 1925 to the devolution of any property in accordance with the provisions of the last foregoing section, and for the purposes of the construction of any such disposition as is mentioned in that section, an adopted person shall be deemed to be related to any other person being the child or adopted child of the adopter or (in the case of a joint adoption) of either of the adopters—

(a) where he or she was adopted by two spouses jointly, and that other person is the child or adopted child of both of them, as brother or sister of the whole blood;

(b) in any other case, as brother or sister of the half-blood.

(2) For the purposes of subsection (2) of the last foregoing section, a disposition made by will or codicil shall be treated as made on the date of the death of the testator.

(3) Notwithstanding anything in the last foregoing section, trustees or personal representatives may convey or distribute any real or personal property to or among the persons entitled thereto without having ascertained that no adoption order has been made by virtue of which any person is or may be entitled to any interest therein, and shall not be liable to any such person of whose claim

they have not had notice at the time of the conveyance or distribution; but nothing in this subsection shall prejudice the right of any such person to follow the property, or any property representing it, into the hands of any person, other than a purchaser, who may have received it.

(4) Where an adoption order is made in respect of a person who has been previously adopted, the previous adoption shall be disregarded for the purposes of the last foregoing section in relation to the devolution of any property on the death of a person dying intestate after the date of the subsequent adoption order, and in relation to any disposition of property made, or taking effect on the death of a person dying, after that date.

(5) The references in this section to an adoption order shall be construed in accordance with subsection (4) of the last foregoing section.

WILLS ACT 1963
(Elizabeth II, 1963, c. 44)

General rule as to formal validity.

1. A will shall be treated as properly executed if its execution conformed to the internal law in force in the territory where it was executed, or in the territory where, at the time of its execution or of the testator's death, he was domiciled or had his habitual residence, or in a state of which, at either of those times, he was a national.

Additional rules.

2. (1) Without prejudice to the preceding section, the following shall be treated as properly executed—

    (a) a will executed on board a vessel or aircraft of any description, if the execution of the will conformed to the internal law in force in the territory with which, having regard to its registration (if any) and other relevant circumstances, the vessel or aircraft may be taken to have been most closely connected;

    (b) a will so far as it disposes of immovable property, if its execution conformed to the internal law in force in the territory where the property was situated;

(c) a will so far as it revokes a will which under this Act would be treated as properly executed or revokes a provision which under this Act would be treated as comprised in a properly executed will, if the execution of the later will conformed to any law by reference to which the revoked will or provision would be so treated;

(d) a will so far as it exercises a power of appointment, if the execution of the will conformed to the law governing the essential validity of the power.

(2) A will so far as it exercises a power of appointment shall not be treated as improperly executed by reason only that its execution was not in accordance with any formal requirements contained in the instrument creating the power.

Certain requirements to be treated as formal.

3. Where (whether in pursuance of this Act or not) a law in force outside the United Kingdom falls to be applied in relation to a will, any requirement of that law whereby special formalities are to be observed by testators answering a particular description, or witnesses to the execution of a will are to possess certain qualifications, shall be treated, notwithstanding any rule of that law to the contrary, as a formal requirement only.

Construction of wills.

4. The construction of a will shall not be altered by reason of any change in the testator's domicile after the execution of the will.

* * * *

6. (1) In this Act—

"internal law" in relation to any territory or state means the law which would apply in a case where no question of the law in force in any other territory or state arose;

"state" means a territory or group of territories having its own law of nationality;

"will" includes any testamentary instrument or act, and "testator" shall be construed accordingly.

(2) Where under this Act the internal law in force in any territory or state is to be applied in the case of a will, but there are in force in that territory or state two or more systems of internal law relating to the formal validity of wills, the system to be applied shall be ascertained as follows—

(*a*) if there is in force throughout the territory or state a rule indicating which of those systems can properly be applied in the case in question, that rule shall be followed; or

(*b*) if there is no such rule, the system shall be that with which the testator was most closely connected at the relevant time, and for this purpose the relevant time is the time of the testator's death where the matter is to be determined by reference to circumstances prevailing at his death, and the time of execution of the will in any other case.

(3) In determining for the purposes of this Act whether or not the execution of a will conformed to a particular law, regard shall be had to the formal requirements of that law at the time of execution, but this shall not prevent account being taken of an alteration of law affecting wills executed at that time if the alteration enables the will to be treated as properly executed.

Short title, commencement, repeal and extent.

7. (1) This Act may be cited as the Wills Act 1963.

(2) This Act shall come into operation on 1st January 1964.

(3) The Wills Act 1861 is hereby repealed.

(4) This Act shall not apply to a will of a testator who died before the time of the commencement of this Act and shall apply to a will of a testator who dies after that time whether the will was executed before or after that time, but so that the repeal of the Wills Act 1861, shall not invalidate a will executed before that time.

THE FAMILY PROVISION ACT 1966
(1966, c. 35)

[As amended by The Family Provision (Intestate Succession) Order 1972.]

Increase of net sum payable to surviving husband or wife on intestacy.

1. (1) In the case of a person dying after the coming into force of this section, section 46(1) of the Administration of Estates Act

1925, as amended by section 1 of the Intestates' Estates Act 1952 and set out in Schedule 1 to that Act, shall apply as if the net sums charged by paragraph (i) on the residuary estate in favour of a surviving husband or wife were as follows, that is to say,—

(a) under paragraph (2) of the Table (which charges a net sum of £5,000 where the intestate leaves issue) a sum of £15,000 or of such larger amount as may from time to time be fixed by order of the Lord Chancellor; and

(b) under paragraph (3) of the Table (which charges a net sum of £20,000 where the intestate leaves certain close relatives but no issue) a sum of £40,000 or of such larger amount as may from time to time be so fixed.

(2) Accordingly in relation to the estate of a person dying after coming into force of this section sections 46, 48 and 49 (as so amended and set out) of the Administration of Estates Act 1925 shall be further amended as follows:—

(a) in the Table in section 46(1)(i) for the words "net sum of £5,000" in paragraph (2), and for the words "net sum of £20,000" in paragraph (3), there shall in each case be substituted the words "fixed net sum", and at the end of the Table there shall be added—

"The fixed net sums referred to in paragraphs (2) and (3) of this Table shall be of the amounts provided by or under section 1 of the Family Provision Act 1966";

(b) in sections 46(4) and 48(2)(a) for the words "the net sum of £5,000 or, as the case may be, £20,000", and in section 49(1)(aa) for the words "the net sum of £5,000 or £20,000", there shall in each case be substituted the words "the fixed net sum";

and any reference in any other enactment to the said net sum of £5,000 or the said net sum of £20,000, shall have effect as a reference to the corresponding net sum of the amount fixed by or under this section.

(3) Any order of the Lord Chancellor under this section fixing the amount of either of the said net sums shall have effect (and, so far as relates to that sum, shall supersede any previous order) in relation to the estate of any person dying after the coming into force of the order.

(4) Any order of the Lord Chancellor under this section shall be made by statutory instrument, and a draft of the statutory instrument shall be laid before Parliament.

LEASEHOLD REFORM ACT 1967
(1967, c. 88)

7. (8) In Schedule 2 to the Intestates' Estates Act 1952 (which gives a surviving spouse a right to require the deceased's interest in the matrimonial home to be appropriated to the survivor's interest in the deceased's estate, but by paragraph 1 (2) excludes tenancies terminating, or terminable by the landlord, within two years of the death) paragraph 1 (2) shall not apply to a tenancy if—

(a) the surviving wife or husband would in consequence of an appropriation in accordance with that paragraph become entitled by virtue of this section to acquire the freehold or an extended lease under this Part of this Act, either immediately on the appropriation or before the tenancy can determine or be determined as mentioned in paragraph 1 (2); or

(b) the deceased husband or wife, being entitled to acquire the freehold or an extended lease under this Part of this Act, had given notice of his or her desire to have it and the benefit of that notice is appropriated with the tenancy.

WILLS ACT 1968
(1968, c. 28)

[See annotation to Wills Act 1837, s. 15; *ante*, p. 567.]

FAMILY LAW REFORM ACT 1969
(1969, c. 46)

PART I

REDUCTION OF AGE OF MAJORITY AND RELATED PROVISIONS

Reduction of age of majority from 21 to 18.

1. (1) As from the date on which this section comes into force a person shall attain full age on attaining the age of eighteen instead of on attaining the age of twenty-one; and a person shall attain full age on that date if he has then already attained the age of eighteen but not the age of twenty-one.

(2) The foregoing subsection applies for the purposes of any rule of law, and, in the absence of a definition or of any indication of a contrary intention, for the construction of "full age", "infant", "infancy", "minor", "minority" and similar expressions in—

    (a) any statutory provision, whether passed or made before, on or after the date on which this section comes into force; and

    (b) any deed, will or other instrument of whatever nature (not being a statutory provision) made on or after that date.

(3) In the statutory provisions specified in Schedule 1 to this Act for any reference to the age of twenty-one years there shall be substituted a reference to the age of eighteen years; but the amendment by this subsection of the provisions specified in Part II of that Schedule shall be without prejudice to any power of amending or revoking those provisions.

(4) This section does not affect the construction of any such expression as is referred to in subsection (2) of this section in any of the statutory provisions described in Schedule 2 to this Act, and the transitional provisions and savings contained in Schedule 3 to this Act shall have effect in relation to this section.

(5) The Lord Chancellor may by order made by statutory instrument amend any provision in any local enactment passed on or before the date on which this section comes into force (not being a provision described in paragraph 2 of Schedule 2 to this Act) by substituting a reference to the age of eighteen years for any reference therein to the age of twenty-one years; and any statutory instrument containing an order under this subsection shall be subject to annulment in pursuance of a resolution of either House of Parliament.

(6) In this section "statutory provision" means any enactment (including, except where the context otherwise requires, this Act) and any order, rule, regulation, byelaw or other instrument made in the exercise of a power conferred by any enactment.

(7) Notwithstanding any rule of law, a will or codicil executed before the date on which this section comes into force shall not

be treated for the purposes of this section as made on or after that date by reason only that the will or codicil is confirmed by a codicil executed on or after that date.

2. [Relates to *marriage*.]

Provisions relating to wills and intestacy.

3. (1) In the following enactments, that is to say—

(a) section 7 of the Wills Act 1837 (invalidity of wills made by persons under 21);

(b) sections 8 and 3 (1) of the Wills (Soldiers and Sailors) Act 1918 (soldier etc. eligible to make will and dispose of real property although under 21),

in their application to wills made after the coming into force of this section, for the words "twenty-one years" there shall be substituted the words "eighteen years".

(2) In section 47 (1) (i) of the Administration of Estates Act 1925 (statutory trusts on intestacy), in its application to the estate of an intestate dying after the coming into force of this section, for the words "twenty-one years" in both places where they occur there shall be substituted the words "eighteen years".

(3) Any will which—

(a) has been made, whether before or after the coming into force of this section, by a person under the age of eighteen; and

(b) is valid by virtue of the provisions of section 11 of the said Act of 1837 and the said Act of 1918,

may be revoked by that person nothwithstanding that he is still under that age whether or not the circumstances are then such that he would be entitled to make a valid will under those provisions.

(4) In this section "will" has the same meaning as in the said Act of 1837 and "intestate" has the same meaning as in the said Act of 1925.

4.–8. [Deal with *maintenance of infants; committal of wards of court to care of local authority;* and *medical treatment of infants.*]

Time at which a person attains a particular age.

9. (1) The time at which a person attains a particular age expressed in years shall be the commencement of the relevant anniversary of the date of his birth.

(2) This section applies only where the relevant anniversary falls on a date after that on which this section comes into force, and, in relation to any enactment, deed, will or other instrument, has effect subject to any provision therein.

10. [Modifies enactments relating to *children of Her Majesty*.]

11. [Repeals certain enactments relating to *minors*.]

Persons under full age may be described as minors instead of infants.

12. A person who is not of full age may be described as a minor instead of as an infant, and accordingly in this Act "minor" means such a person as aforesaid.

Powers of Parliament of Northern Ireland.

13. Notwithstanding anything in the Government of Ireland Act 1920 the Parliament of Northern Ireland shall have power to make laws for purposes similar to any of the purposes of this Part of this Act.

PART II

PROPERTY RIGHTS OF ILLEGITIMATE CHILDREN

Right of illegitimate child to succeed on intestacy of parents, and of parents to succeed on intestacy of illegitimate child.

14. (1) Where either parent of an illegitimate child dies intestate as respects all or any of his or her real or personal property, the illegitimate child or, if he is dead, his issue, shall be entitled to take any interest therein to which he or such issue would have been entitled if he had been born legitimate.

(2) Where an illegitimate child dies intestate in respect of all or any of his real or personal property, each of his parents, if

surviving, shall be entitled to take any interest therein to which that parent would have been entitled if the child had been born legitimate.

(3) In accordance with the foregoing provisions of this section, Part IV of the Administration of Estates Act 1925 (which deals with the distribution of the estate of an intestate) shall have effect as if—

(a) any reference to the issue of the intestate included a reference to any illegitimate child of his and to the issue of any such child;

(b) any reference to the child or children of the intestate included a reference to any illegitimate child or children of his; and

(c) in relation to an intestate who is an illegitimate child, any reference to the parent, parents, father or mother of the intestate were a reference to his natural parent, parents, father or mother.

(4) For the purposes of subsection (2) of this section and of the provisions amended by subsection (3) (c) thereof, an illegitimate child shall be presumed not to have been survived by his father unless the contrary is shown.

(5) This section does not apply to or affect the right of any person to take any entailed interest in real or personal property.

(6) The reference in section 50 (1) of the said Act of 1925 (which relates to the construction of documents) to Part IV of that Act, or to the foregoing provisions of that Part, shall in relation to an instrument *inter vivos* made, or a will or codicil coming into operation, after the coming into force of this section (but not in relation to instruments *inter vivos* made or wills or codicils coming into operation earlier) be construed as including references to this section.

(7) Section 9 of the Legitimacy Act 1926 (under which an illegitimate child and his issue are entitled to succeed on the intestacy of his mother if she leaves no legitimate issue, and the mother of an illegitimate child is entitled to succeed on his intestacy as if she were the only surviving parent) is hereby repealed.

(8) In this section "illegitimate child" does not include an illegitimate child who is—

(a) a legitimated person within the meaning of the said Act
of 1926 or a person recognised by virtue of that Act or
at common law as having been legitimated; or

(b) an adopted person under an adoption order made in any
part of the United Kingdom, the Isle of Man or the
Channel Islands or under an overseas adoption as defined
in section 4 (3) of the Adoption Act 1968.

(9) This section does not affect any rights under the intestacy
of a person dying before the coming into force of this section.

*Presumption that in dispositions of property references to children
and other relatives include references to, and to persons related
through illegitimate children.*

15. (1) In any disposition made after the coming into force
of this section—

(a) any reference (whether express or implied) to the child
or children of any person shall, unless the contrary
intention appears, be construed as, or as including, a
reference to any illegitimate child of that person; and

(b) any reference (whether express or implied) to a person
or persons related in some other manner to any person
shall, unless the contrary intention appears, be construed
as, or as including, a reference to anyone who would be
so related if he, or some other person through whom the
relationship is deduced, had been born legitimate.

(2) The foregoing subsection applies only where the reference
in question is to a person who is to benefit or to be capable of
benefiting under the disposition or, for the purpose of designating
such a person, to someone else to or through whom that person is
related; but that subsection does not affect the construction of
the word "heir" or "heirs" or of any expression which is used to
create an entailed interest in real or personal property.

(3) In relation to any disposition made after the coming into
force of this section, section 33 of the Trustee Act 1925 (which
specifies the trusts implied by a direction that income is to be
held on protective trusts for the benefit of any person) shall have
effect as if—

(a) the reference to the children or more remote issue of the
principal beneficiary included a reference to any illegiti-

mate child of the principal beneficiary and to anyone who would rank as such issue if he, or some other person through whom he is descended from the principal beneficiary, had been born legitimate; and

(b) the reference to the issue of the principal beneficiary included a reference to anyone who would rank as such issue if he, or some other person through whom he is descended from the principal beneficiary, had been born legitimate.

(4) In this section references to an illegitimate child include references to an illegitimate child who is or becomes a legitimated person within the meaning of the Legitimacy Act 1926 or a person recognised by virtue of that Act or at common law as having been legitimated; and in section 3 of that Act—

(a) subsection (1) (b) which relates to the effect of dispositions where a person has been legitimated) shall not apply to a disposition made after the coming into force of this section except as respects any interest in relation to which the disposition refers only to persons who are, or whose relationship is deduced through, legitimate persons; and

(b) subsection (2) (which provides that, where the right to any property depends on the relative seniority of the children of any person, legitimated persons shall rank as if born on the date of legitimation) shall not apply in relation to any right conferred by a disposition made after the coming into force of this section unless the terms of the disposition are such that the children whose relative seniority is in question cannot include any illegitimate children who are not either legitimated persons within the meaning of that Act or persons recognised by virtue of that Act as having been legitimated.

(5) Where under any disposition any real or personal property or any interest in such property is limited (whether subject to any preceding limitation or charge or not) in such a way that it would, apart from this section, devolve (as nearly as the law permits) along with a dignity or title of honour, then, whether or not the disposition contains an express reference to the dignity or title of

honour, and whether or not the property or some interest in the property may in some event become severed therefrom, nothing in this section shall operate to sever the property or any interest therein from the dignity or title, but the property or interest shall devolve in all respects as if this section had not been enacted.

(6) This section is without prejudice to sections 16 and 17 of the Adoption Act 1958 (which relate to the construction of dispositions in cases of adoption).

(7) There is hereby abolished, as respects dispositions made after the coming into force of this section, any rule of law that a disposition in favour of illegitimate children not in being when the disposition takes effect is void as contrary to public policy.

(8) In this section "disposition" means a disposition, including an oral disposition, of real or personal property whether *inter vivos* or by will or codicil; and, notwithstanding any rule of law, a disposition made by will or codicil executed before the date on which this section comes into force shall not be treated for the purposes of this section as made on or after that date by reason only that the will or codicil is confirmed by a codicil executed on or after that date.

Meaning of "child" and "issue" in s. 33 of Wills Act 1837.

16. (1) In relation to a testator who dies after the coming into force of this section, section 33 of the Wills Act 1837 (gift to children or other issue of testator not to lapse if they predecease him but themselves leave issue) shall have effect as if—

(a) the reference to a child or other issue of the testator (that is, the intended beneficiary) included a reference to any illegitimate child of the testator and to anyone who would rank as such issue if he, or some other person through whom he is descended from the testator, had been born legitimate; and

(b) the reference to the issue of the intended beneficiary included a reference to anyone who would rank as such issue if he, or some other person through whom he is descended from the intended beneficiary, had been born legitimate.

(2) In this section "illegitimate child" includes an illegitimate child who is a legitimated person within the meaning of the

Legitimacy Act 1926 or a person recognised by virtue of that Act or at common law as having been legitimated.

Protection of trustees and personal representatives.

17. Notwithstanding the foregoing provisions of this Part of this Act, trustees or personal representatives may convey or distribute any real or personal property to or among the persons entitled thereto without having ascertained that there is no person who is or may be entitled to any interest therein by virtue of—

(a) section 14 of this Act so far as it confers any interest on illegitimate children or their issue or on the father of an illegitimate child; or

(b) section 15 or 16 of this Act,

and shall not be liable to any such person of whose claim they have not had notice at the time of the conveyance or distribution; but nothing in this section shall prejudice the right of any such person to follow the property, or any property representing it, into the hands of any person, other than a purchaser, who may have received it.

Illegitimate children to count as dependants under Inheritance (Family Provision) Act 1938.

18. (1) For the purposes of the Inheritance (Family Provision) Act 1938, a person's illegitimate son or daughter shall be treated as his dependant in any case in which a legitimate son or daughter of that person would be so treated, and accordingly in the definition of the expressions "son" and "daughter" in section 5 (1) of that Act, as amended by the Family Provision Act 1966, after the words "respectively include" there shall be inserted the words "an illegitimate son or daughter of the deceased".

(2) In section 26 (6) of the Matrimonial Causes Act 1965 (which provides, among other things, for the word "dependant" to have the same meaning as in the said Act of 1938 as amended by the said Act of 1966), after the words "as amended by the Family Provision Act 1966" there shall be inserted the words "and the Family Law Reform Act 1969".

(3) This section does not affect the operation of the said Acts of 1938 and 1965 in relation to a person dying before the coming into force of this section.

19. [Deals with *the entitlement of illegitimate children to policies of assurance*.]

20–25. [Make provisions for *use of blood tests in determining paternity*.]

Part IV

Miscellaneous and General

Rebuttal of presumption as to legitimacy and illegitimacy.

26. Any presumption of law as to the legitimacy or illegitimacy of any person may in any civil proceedings be rebutted by evidence which shows that it is more probable than not that that person is illegitimate or legitimate, as the case may be, and it shall not be necessary to prove that fact beyond reasonable doubt in order to rebut the presumption.

27. [Relates to *the registration of the births of illegitimate children*.]

Short title, interpretation, commencement and extent.

28. (1) This Act may be cited as the Family Law Reform Act 1969.

(2) Except where the context otherwise requires, any reference in this Act to any enactment shall be construed as a reference to that enactment as amended, extended or applied by or under any other enactment, including this Act.

(3) This Act shall come into force on such date as the Lord Chancellor may appoint by order made by statutory instrument, and different dates may be appointed for the coming into force of different provisions.

(4) In this Act—
  (a) section 1 and Schedule 1, so far as they amend the British Nationality Act 1948, have the same extent as that Act and are hereby declared for the purposes of section 3 (3) of the West Indies Act 1967 to extend to all the associated states;

(b)–(e) [Relate to sections of the Act not reproduced here.]
(f) section 13 extends to Northern Ireland;

but, save as aforesaid, this Act shall extend to England and Wales only.

SCHEDULES

SCHEDULE 1

STATUTORY PROVISIONS AMENDED BY SUBSTITUTING
18 FOR 21 YEARS

PART I
ENACTMENTS

	Short title	Section	Subject matter
c. 18.	The Settled Land Act 1925.	Section 102 (5).	Management of land during minority.
c. 19.	The Trustee Act 1925.	Section 31 (1) (ii), (2) (i) (a) and (b).	Power to apply income for maintenance and to accumulate surplus income during a minority.
c. 20.	The Law of Property Act 1925.	Section 134 (1).	Restriction on executory limitations.
c. 49.	The Supreme Court of Judicature (Consolidation) Act 1925.	Section 165 (1).	Probate not to be granted to infant if appointed sole executor until he attains the age of 21 years.

PART II
RULES, REGULATIONS ETC.

	Title	Provision	Subject matter
1954 S.I. 796.	The Non-Contentious Probate Rules 1954.	Rules 31 and 32.	Grants of probate on behalf of infant and where infant is co-executor.

NOTE: Only the Acts and Rules relevant to the law of succession have been included from Schedule 1.

SCHEDULE 2

STATUTORY PROVISIONS UNAFFECTED
BY SECTION 1

1. The Regency Acts 1937 to 1953.

2. The Representation of the People Acts (and any regulations, rules or other instruments thereunder), section 7 of the Parliamentary Elections Act 1695, section 57 of the Local Government Act 1933 and any statutory provision relating to municipal elections in the City of London within the meaning of section 167 (1) (a) of the Representation of the People Act 1949.

3. Any statutory provision relating to income tax (including surtax), capital gains tax, corporation tax or estate duty.

SCHEDULE 3

TRANSITIONAL PROVISIONS AND SAVINGS

[not reproduced here]

ADMINISTRATION OF JUSTICE ACT 1969
(1969, c. 58)

PART III

POWER TO MAKE WILLS AND CODICILS FOR MENTALLY
DISORDERED PERSONS

Provision for executing will for patient

17. (1) In the Mental Health Act 1959 (in this Part of this Act referred to as "the principal Act"), in section 103 (1) (powers of the judge as to patient's property and affairs) the following paragraph shall be inserted after paragraph (d)—

"(dd) the execution for the patient of a will making any provision (whether by way of disposing of property or exercising a power or otherwise) which could be made by a will executed by the patient if he were not mentally disordered, so however that in such cases as a nominated judge may direct the powers conferred by this paragraph shall not be exercisable except by the Lord Chancellor or a nominated judge;".

(2) At the end of section 103 (3) of the principal Act there shall be inserted the words "and the power of the judge to make or give an order, direction or authority for the execution of a will for a patient—

(a) shall not be exercisable at any time when the patient is an infant, and

(b) shall not be exercised unless the judge has reason to believe that the patient is incapable of making a valid will for himself".

Supplementary provisions as to wills executed under s. 103 (1) (dd)

18. The following section shall be inserted in the principal Act after section 103—

"103A. (1) Where under section 103 (1) of this Act the judge makes or gives an order, direction or authority requiring or authorising a person (in this section referred to as 'the authorised person') to execute a will for a patient, any will executed in pursuance of that order, direction or authority shall be expressed to be signed by the patient acting by the authorised person, and shall be—

(a) signed by the authorised person with the name of the patient, and with his own name, in the presence of two or more witnesses present at the same time, and

(b) attested and subscribed by those witnesses in the presence of the authorised person, and

(c) sealed with the official seal of the Court of Protection.

(2) The Wills Act 1837 shall have effect in relation to any such will as if it were signed by the patient by his own hand, except that in relation to any such will—

(a) section 9 of that Act (which makes provision as to the manner of execution and attestation of wills) shall not apply, and

(b) in the subsequent provisions of that Act any reference to execution in the manner thereinbefore required shall be construed as a reference to execution in the manner required by subsection (1) of this section.

(3) Subject to the following provisions of this section, any such will executed in accordance with subsection (1) of this section shall have the like effect for all purposes as if the patient were capable of making a valid will and the will had been executed by him in the manner required by the Wills Act 1837.

(4) So much of subsection (3) of this section as provides for such a will to have effect as if the patient were capable of making a valid will—

(a) shall not have effect in relation to such a will in so far as it disposes of any immovable property, other than immovable property in England or Wales, and

(b) where at the time when such a will is executed the patient is domiciled in Scotland or Northern Ireland or in a country or territory outside the United Kingdom, shall not have effect in relation to that will in so far as it relates to any other property or matter, except any property or matter in respect of which, under the law of his domicile, any question of his testamentary capacity would fall to be determined in accordance with the law of England and Wales.

(5) For the purposes of the application of the Inheritance (Family Provision) Act 1938 in relation to a will executed in accordance with subsection (1) of this section, in section 1 (7) of that Act (which relates to the deceased's reasons for disposing of his estate in a particular way)—

(a) any reference to the deceased's reasons for which anything is done or not done by his will shall be construed as a reference to the reasons for which it is done or (as the case may be) not done by that will, and

(b) any reference to a statement in writing signed by the deceased shall be construed as a reference to a statement in writing signed by the authorised person in accordance with a direction given in that behalf by the judge."

Other amendments of Mental Health Act 1959

19. (1) In section 107 of the principal Act (preservation of interests in patient's property), in subsection (3), after the words "or other dealing" there shall be inserted the words "(otherwise than by will)".

(2) In section 117 of the principal Act (reciprocal arrangements in relation to Scotland and Northern Ireland as to exercise of powers), after subsection (2) there shall be inserted the following subsection:—

"(2A) Nothing in this section shall affect any power to execute a will under section 103 (1) (dd) of this Act or the effect of any will executed in the exercise of such a power".

(3) in section 119 of the principal Act (interpretation of Part VIII), at the end of subsection (1) there shall be inserted the words " 'will' includes a codicil".

LAW REFORM (MISCELLANEOUS PROVISIONS) ACT 1970
(1970, c. 33)

Orders for maintenance of surviving party to void marriage from estate of other party

6. (1) Where a person domiciled in England and Wales dies after the commencement of this Act and is survived by someone (hereinafter referred to as "the survivor") who, whether before or after the commencement of this Act, had in good faith entered into a void marriage with the deceased, then subject to subsections (2) and (3) below the survivor shall be treated for purposes of the Inheritance (Family Provision) Act 1938 as a dependant of the deceased within the meaning of that Act.

(2) An order shall not be made under the Inheritance (Family Provision) Act 1938 in favour of the survivor unless the court is satisfied that it would have been reasonable for the deceased to make provision for the survivor's maintenance; and if an order is so made requiring provision for the survivor's maintenance by way of periodical payments, the order shall provide for their termination not later than the survivor's death and, if the survivor remarries, not later than the remarriage.

(3) This section shall not apply if the marriage of the deceased and the survivor was dissolved or annulled during the deceased's

lifetime and the dissolution or annulment is recognised by the law of England and Wales, or if the survivor has before the making of the order entered into a later marriage.

(4) It is hereby declared that the reference in subsection (2) above to remarriage and the reference in subsection (3) above to a later marriage include references to a marriage which is by law void or voidable.

(5) In section 26 of the Matrimonial Causes Act 1965 (orders for maintenance from deceased's estate following dissolution or annulment of a marriage), in the definition of "net estate" and "dependant" in subsection (6) (as amended by subsequent enactments) for the words "and the Family Law Reform Act 1969" there shall be substituted the words "the Family Law Reform Act 1969 and the Law Reform (Miscellaneous Provisions) Act 1970".

Citation, repeal, commencement and extent

7. (1) This Act may be cited as the Law Reform (Miscellaneous Provisions) Act 1970.

(2) [As to repeals.]

GUARDIANSHIP OF MINORS ACT 1971

Appointment, Removal and Powers of Guardians

3. *Rights of surviving parent as to guardianship*

(1) On the death of the father of a minor, the mother, if surviving, shall, subject to the provisions of this Act, be guardian of the minor either alone or jointly with any guardian appointed by the father; and—

(a) where no guardian has been appointed by the father; or

(b) in the event of the death or refusal to act of the guardian or guardians appointed by the father,

the court may, if it thinks fit, appoint a guardian to act jointly with the mother.

(2) On the death of the mother of a minor, the father, if surviving, shall, subject to the provisions of this Act, be guardian of the minor either alone or jointly with any guardian appointed by the mother; and—

(a) where no guardian has been appointed by the mother; or

(b) in the event of the death or refusal to act of the guardian or guardians appointed by the mother,

the court may, if it thinks fit, appoint a guardian to act jointly with the father.

4. *Power of father and mother to appoint testamentary guardians*

(1) The father of a minor may by deed or will appoint any person to be guardian of the minor after his death.

(2) The mother of a minor may by deed or will appoint any person to be guardian of the minor after her death.

(3) Any guardian so appointed shall act jointly with the mother or father, as the case may be, of the minor so long as the mother or father remains alive unless the mother or father objects to his so acting.

(4) If the mother or father so objects, or if the guardian so appointed considers that the mother or father is unfit to have the custody of the minor, the guardian may apply to the court, and the court may either—

(a) refuse to make any order (in which case the mother or father shall remain sole guardian); or

(b) make an order that the guardian so appointed—

(i) shall act jointly with the mother or father; or

(ii) shall be the sole guardian of the minor.

(5) Where guardians are appointed by both parents, the guardians so appointed shall, after the death of the surviving parent, act jointly.

(6) If under section 3 of this Act a guardian has been appointed by the court to act jointly with a surviving parent, he shall continue to act as guardian after the death of the surviving parent; but, if the surviving parent has appointed a guardian, the guardian appointed by the court shall act jointly with the guardian appointed by the surviving parent.

5. *Power of court to appoint guardian for minor having no parent etc.*

(1) Where a minor has no parent, no guardian of the person, and no other person having parental rights with respect to him, the court, on the application of any person, may, if it thinks fit, appoint the applicant to be the guardian of the minor.

(2) A court may entertain an application under this section to appoint a guardian of a minor notwithstanding that, by virtue of a resolution under section 2 of the Children Act 1948, a local authority have parental rights with respect to him; but where on such an application the court appoints a guardian the resolution shall cease to have effect.

14. (3) For the purposes of sections 3, 4, 5 and 10 of this Act, a person being the natural father of an illegitimate child and being entitled to his custody by virtue of an order in force under section 9 of this Act, as applied by this section, shall be treated as if he were the lawful father of the minor; but any appointment of a guardian made by virtue of this subsection under section 4 (1) of this Act shall be of no effect unless the appointer is entitled to the custody of the minor as aforesaid immediately before his death.

ADMINISTRATION OF ESTATES ACT 1971
(1971, c. 25)

1. (1) Where a person dies domiciled in Scotland—

(a) a confirmation granted in respect of all or part of his estate and noting his Scottish domicile, and

(b) a certificate of confirmation noting his Scottish domicile and relating to one or more items of his estate,

shall, without being resealed, be treated for the purposes of the law of England and Wales as a grant of representation (in accordance with subsection (2) below) to the executors named in the confirmation or certificate in respect of the property of the deceased of which according to the terms of the confirmation they are executors or, as the case may be, in respect of the item or items of property specified in the certificate of confirmation.

(2) Where by virtue of subsection (1) above a confirmation or certificate of confirmation is treated for the purposes of the law of England and Wales as a grant of representation to the executors named therein then, subject to subsections (3) and (5) below, the grant shall be treated—

(a) as a grant of probate where it appears from the confirmation or certificate that the executors so named are executors nominate; and

(b) in any other case, as a grant of letters of administration.

(3) Section 7 of the Administration of Estates Act 1925 (execu-

tor of executor represents original testator) shall not, by virtue of subsection (2) (a) above, apply on the death of an executor named in a confirmation or certificate of confirmation.

(4) Subject to subsection (5) below, where a person dies domiciled in Northern Ireland a grant of probate of his will or letters of administration in respect of his estate (or any part of it) made by the High Court in Northern Ireland and noting his domicile there shall, without being resealed, be treated for the purposes of the law of England and Wales as if it had been originally made by the High Court in England and Wales.

(5) Notwithstanding anything in the preceding provisions of this section, a person who is a personal representative according to the law of England and Wales by virtue only of those provisions may not be required, under section 25 of the Administration of Estates Act 1925, to deliver up his grant to the High Court.

(6) This section applies in relation to confirmations, probates and letters of administration granted before as well as after the commencement of this Act, and in relation to a confirmation, probate or letters of administration granted before the commencement of this Act, this section shall have effect as if it had come into force immediately before the grant was made.

(7) In this section "confirmation" includes an additional confirmation, and the term "executors", where used in relation to a confirmation or certificate of confirmation, shall be construed according to the law of Scotland.

2. [Deals with recognition in Northern Ireland of English and Scottish grants.]

3. [Deals with recognition in Scotland of English and Northern Irish Grants.]

Evidence of grants

4. (1) In England and Wales and in Northern Ireland—

(a) a document purporting to be a confirmation, additional confirmation or certificate of confirmation given under the seal of office of any commissariot in Scotland shall, except where the contrary is proved, be taken to be such a confirmation, additional confirmation or certificate of confirmation without further proof; and

(b) a document purporting to be a duplicate of such a confirmation or additional confirmation and to be given under such a seal shall be receivable in evidence in like manner and for the like purposes as the confirmation or additional confirmation of which it purports to be a duplicate.

(2) In England and Wales and in Scotland—

(a) a document purporting to be a grant of probate or of letters of administration issued under the sale of the High Court in Northern Ireland or of the principal or district probate registry there shall, except where the contrary is proved, be taken to be such a grant without further proof; and

(b) a document purporting to be a copy of such a grant and to be sealed with such a seal shall be receivable in evidence in like manner and for the like purposes as the grant of which it purports to be a copy.

(3) [Deals with Scotland and Northern Ireland.]

5 and 6. [Apply only to Scotland.]

Consequential amendments

7. Schedule 1 to this Act [not reproduced here], which contains amendments consequential on the preceding provisions of this Act, shall have effect.

8. [Provides new s. 167, Judicature Act, 1925; see *ante*, p. 622.]

9. [Provides new s. 25, Administration of Estates Act 1925; see *ante*, p. 583.]

Retainer preference and the payment of debts by personal representatives

10. (1) The right of retainer of a personal representative and his right to prefer creditors are hereby abolished.

(2) Nevertheless a personal representative—

(a) other than one mentioned in paragraph (b) below, who, in good faith and at a time when he has no reason to believe that the deceased's estate is insolvent, pays the debt of any person (including himself) who is a creditor of the estate; or

(b) to whom letters of administration had been granted solely by reason of his being a creditor and who, in good faith and at such a time pays the debt of another person who is a creditor of the estate;

shall not, if it subsequently appears that the estate is insolvent, be liable to account to a creditor of the same degree as the paid creditor for the sum so paid.

Sealing of Commonwealth and Colonial grants

11. (1) The following provisions of section 2 of the Colonial Probates Act 1892, that is to say—

(a) subsection (2) (b) which makes it a condition precedent to sealing in the United Kingdom letters of administration granted in certain overseas countries and territories that a sufficient security has been given to cover property in the United Kingdom); and

(b) subsection (3) (power of the court in the United Kingdom to require that adequate security is given for the payment of debts due to creditors residing in the United Kingdom);

shall not apply to the sealing of letters of administration by the High Court in England and Wales under that section, and the following provisions of this section shall apply instead.

(2) A person to whom letters of administration have been granted in a country or territory to which the said Act of 1892 applies shall on their being sealed by the High Court in England and Wales under the said section 2 have the like duties with respect to the estate of the deceased which is situated in England and Wales and the debts of the deceased which fall to be paid there as are imposed by section 25 (a) and (b) of the Administration of Estates Act 1925 on a person to whom a grant of administration has been made by that court.

(3) As a condition of sealing letters of administration granted in any such country or territory, the High Court in England and Wales may, in cases to which section 167 of the Supreme Court of Judicature (Consolidation) Act 1925 (power to require administrators to produce sureties) applies and subject to the following provisions of this section and subject to and in accordance with probate rules and orders, require one or more sureties, in such amount as the court thinks fit, to guarantee that they will make good, within any limit imposed by the court on the total liability of the surety or sureties, any loss which any person interested in the administration of the estate of the deceased in England and Wales may suffer in consequence of a breach by the administrator of his duties in administering it there.

(4) A guarantee given in pursuance of any such requirement shall enure for the benefit of every person interested in the administration of the estate in England and Wales as if contained in a contract under seal made by the surety or sureties with every such

person and, where there are two or more sureties, as if they had bound themselves jointly or severally.

(5) No action shall be brought on any such guarantee without the leave of the High Court.

(6) Stamp duty shall not be chargeable on any such guarantee.

(7) Subsections (2) to (6) above apply to the sealing by the High Court in England and Wales of letters of administration granted by a British court in a foreign country as they apply to the sealing of letters of administration granted in a country or territory to which the Colonial Probates Act 1892 applies.

(8) In this section—

"letters of administration" and "British court in a foreign country" have the same meaning as in the Colonial Probates Act 1892; and

"probate rules and orders" has the same meaning as in the Supreme Court of Judicature (Consolidation) Act 1925.

Repeals and savings

12. (1) The enactments specified in Part I of Schedule 2 to this Act (which include an enactment of the Parliament of Northern Ireland) are hereby repealed to the extent specified in the third column of that Schedule and the Government of Ireland (Resealing of Probates etc.) Order 1923 [not reproduced here] is hereby revoked.

(2) So far as they relate to England and Wales only, the enactment specified in Part II of Schedule 2 to this Act are hereby repealed to the extent specified in the third column of that Schedule.

(3) Nothing in this Act shall affect the liability of any person for, or alter the incidence of, estate duty, including estate duty payable under the law for the time being in force in Northern Ireland.

(4) The following provisions of this Act, that is to say—

(a) section 8;

(b) section 11 (other than subsection 2)); and

(c) the repeals specified in Part II of Schedule 2 to this Act, other than the repeal of section 34 (2) of the Administration of Estates Act 1925;

shall not apply in relation to grants of administration made by the High Court before the commencement of this Act or to sealing by that court before the commencement of this Act of administration granted in any country or territory outside the United Kingdom.

(5) Any administration bond given before the commencement of this Act under section 167 of the Supreme Court of Judicature (Consolidation) Act 1925 or under the Colonial Probates Act 1892 may be enforced and assigned as if this Act had not been passed.

(6) Section 10 of this Act and the repeal by this section of section 34 (2) of the Administration of Estates Act 1925 shall not apply in relation to the estates of persons dying before the commencement of this Act.

Extension of powers of Parliament of Northern Ireland

13. No limitation on the powers of the Parliament of Northern Ireland imposed by the Government of Ireland Act 1920 shall apply in relation to legislation for any purpose similar to the purpose of any provision in sections 8 to 12 of this Act so as to preclude that Parliament from enacting a provision corresponding to any such provision.

Short title, commencement and extent

14. (1) This Act may be cited as the Administration of Estates Act 1971.

(2) Section 13 of this Act and this section shall come into force on the passing of this Act and the remaining provisions of this Act shall come into force on 1st January 1972; and, notwithstanding anything in section 36 of the Interpretation Act 1889, any reference in this Act, or in any Act passed after the passing of this Act, to the commencement of this Act shall be construed as a reference to 1st January 1972.

(3) Sections 1 and 8 to 11 of this Act and subsections (2) and (4) to (6) of section 12 of this Act extend to England and Wales only.

THE NON-CONTENTIOUS PROBATE RULES
1954
(S.I. 1954 No. 796/L6)

[These rules are printed as amended by the Non-Contentious Probate (Amendment) Rules 1961 (S.I. 1961 No. 72), the Non-Contentious Probate (Amendment) Rules 1967 (S.I. 1967 No. 748), the Non-Contentious Probate (Amendment) Rules 1968

(S.I. 1968 No. 1675), the Non-Contentious Probate (Amendment) Rules 1969 (S.I. 1969 No. 1689), and the Non-Contentious Probate (Amendment) Rules 1971 (S.I. 1971 No. 1977), and (in relation to rr. 31 and 32) by the Family Law Reform Act 1969. The rules had also been amended by S.I. 1962 No. 2653, but that instrument was superseded by S.I. 1967 No. 748.]

Citation and commencement

1. These Rules may be cited as the Non-Contentious Probate Rules, 1954, and shall come into operation on the first day of October, 1954.

Interpretation

2. (1) The Interpretation Act, 1889 shall apply to the interpretation of these Rules as it applies to the interpretation of an Act of Parliament.

(2) In these Rules, unless the context otherwise requires—

"The Act" means the Supreme Court of Judicature (Consolidation) Act, 1925;

"Authorised officer" means any officer of a registry who is for the time being authorised by the President to administer any oath or to take any affidavit required for any purpose connected with his duties;

"The Crown" includes the Crown in right of the Duchy of Lancaster and the Duke of Cornwall for the time being;

"England" includes Wales;

"Gross value" in relation to any estate means the value of the estate without deduction for debts, incumbrances, funeral expenses or estate duty;

"Oath" means the oath required by rule 6 to be sworn by every applicant for a grant;

"Personal applicant" means a person other than a trust corporation who seeks to obtain a grant without employing a solicitor, and "personal application" has a corresponding meaning;

"The President" means the President of the Family Division;

"The principal registry" means the principal registry of the Family Division;

"Registrar" means a registrar of the principal registry and includes—

(i) (except in rules 45 and 46) in relation to an application for a grant made or proposed to be made at a district probate registry;
and

(ii) in rules 24 and 42, in relation to a grant issued from a district probate registry,

the registrar of a district probate registry;

"Registry" means the principal registry or a district probate registry;

"The Senior Registrar" means the principal registrar of the Family Division or, in his absence, the senior of the registrars in attendance;

"Statutory guardian" means a surviving parent of an infant who is the guardian of the infant by virtue of section 3 of the Guardianship of Minors Act 1971;

"Testamentary guardian" means a person appointed by deed or will to be guardian of an infant under the power conferred by section 4 of the Guardianship of Minors Act 1971;

"The Treasury Solicitor" means the solicitor for the affairs of Her Majesty's Treasury and includes the solicitor for the affairs of the Duchy of Lancaster and the solicitor of the Duchy of Cornwall;

"Will" includes a nuncupative will and any testamentary document or copy or reconstruction thereof.

(3) A form referred to by number means the form so numbered in the First Schedule; and such forms shall be used wherever applicable, with such variations as a registrar may in any particular case direct or approve.

Probate sub-registries

2A. Sub-registries may be established at such places and under the control of such registrars as the President may from time to time direct.

Applications for grants through solicitors

3. (1) . . . a person applying for a grant through a solicitor may apply by post at such registries at any registry or sub-registry and may apply by post at such registries or sub-registries as the President may direct.

(2) Every solicitor through whom an application for a grant is made shall give the address of his place of business within the jurisdiction.

Personal applications

4. (1) A personal applicant may apply for a grant otherwise than by post at any registry [or sub-registry] or to an officer attending at such place as the President may direct.

(2) A personal applicant may not apply through an agent, whether paid or unpaid, and may not be attended by any person acting or appearing to act as his adviser.

(3) No personal application shall be received or proceeded with if—

(a) it becomes necessary to bring the matter before the court on motion or by action;

(b) an application has already been made by a solicitor on behalf of the applicant and has not been withdrawn;

(c) the registrar otherwise directs.

(4) After a will has been deposited in a registry by a personal applicant, it may not be delivered to the applicant or to any other person unless in special circumstances the registrar so directs.

(5) A personal applicant shall produce a certificate of the death of the deceased or such other evidence of the death as the registrar may approve.

(6) A personal applicant shall supply all information necessary to enable the papers leading to the grant to be prepared in the registry, or may himself prepare such papers and lodge them unsworn.

(7) Unless the registrar otherwise directs, every oath, affidavit or [guarantee] required on a personal application (other than a [guarantee] given by a corporation in accordance with rule 38) shall be sworn or executed by all the deponents or [sureties] before an authorised officer.

(8) No legal advice shall be given to a personal applicant by any officer of a registry and every such officer shall be responsible only for embodying in proper form the applicant's instructions for the grant.

(9) (Deleted.)

2 5

Duty of registrar on receiving application for grant

5. (1) A registrar shall not allow any grant to issue until all inquiries which he may see fit to make have been answered to his satisfaction.

(2) The registrar may require proof of the identity of the deceased or of the applicant for the grant beyond that contained in the oath.

(3) Except with the leave of two registrars, no grant of probate or of administration with the will annexed shall issue within seven days of the death of the deceased and no grant of administration shall issue within fourteen days thereof.

[(4) The registrar shall not require a guarantee under section 167 of the Act as a condition of granting administration to any person without giving that person or, where the application for the grant is made through a solicitor, the solicitor an opportunity of being heard with respect to the requirement.]

Oaths in support of grant

6. (1) Every application for a grant shall be supported by an oath in the form applicable to the circumstances of the case, which shall be contained in an affidavit sworn by the applicant, and by such other papers as the registrar may require.

(2) On an application for a grant of administration the oath shall state whether, and if so, in what manner, all persons having a prior right to a grant have been cleared off, and whether any minority or life interest arises under the will or intestacy.

(3) Where the deceased died on or after the 1st January 1926, the oath shall state whether, to the best of the applicant's knowledge, information and belief, there was land vested in the deceased which was settled previously to his death and not by his will and which remained settled land notwithstanding his death.

(4) Unless otherwise directed by a registrar, the oath shall state where the deceased died domiciled.

Grant in additional name

7. Where it is necessary to describe the deceased in a grant by some name in addition to his true name, the applicant shall state in the oath the true name of the deceased and shall depose that some part of the estate, specifying it, was held in the other name, or as to any other reason that there may be for the inclusion of the other name in the grant.

Marking of wills

8. Every will in respect of which an application for a grant is made shall be marked by the signatures of the applicant and the person before whom the oath is sworn, and shall be exhibited to any affidavit which may be required under these Rules as to the validity, terms, condition or date of execution of the will:

Provided that where the registrar is satisfied that compliance with this rule might result in the loss of the will, he may allow a photographic copy thereof to be marked or exhibited in lieu of the original document.

Engrossments for purposes of record

9. (1) Where the registrar considers that in any particular case a photographic copy of the original will would not be satisfactory for purposes of record he may require an engrossment suitable for photographic reproduction to be lodged.

(2) Where a will contains alterations which are not admissible to proof, there shall be lodged an engrossment of the will in the form in which it is to be proved.

(3) Any engrossment lodged under this rule shall reproduce the punctuation, spacing and division into paragraphs of the will and, if it is one to which paragraph (2) of this rule applies, it shall be made bookwise on durable paper following continuously from page to page on both sides of the paper.

(4) Where any pencil writing appears on a will, there shall be lodged a . . . copy of the will or of the pages or sheets containing the pencil writing, in which there shall be underlined in red ink those portions which appear in pencil in the original.

Evidence as to due execution of will

10. (1) Where a will contains no attestation clause or the attestation clause is insufficient or where it appears to the registrar that there is some doubt about the due execution of the will, he shall, before admitting it to proof, require an affidavit as to due execution from one or more of the attesting witnesses or, if no attesting witness is conveniently available, from any other person who was present at the time the will was executed.

(2) If no affidavit can be obtained in accordance with the last foregoing paragraph, the registrar may, if he thinks fit having regard to the desirability of protecting the interests of any person who may be prejudiced by the will, accept evidence on affidavit from any person he may think fit to show that the signature on the will is in the handwriting of the deceased, or of any other matter which may raise a presumption in favour of the due execution of the will.

(3) If the registrar, after considering the evidence—

(a) is satisfied that the will was not duly executed, he shall refuse probate and shall mark the will accordingly;

(b) is doubtful whether the will was duly executed, he may refer the matter to the court on motion.

Execution of the will of blind or illiterate testator

11. Before admitting to proof a will which appears to have been signed by a blind or illiterate testator or by another person by direction of the testator, or which for any other reason gives rise to doubt as to the testator having had knowledge of the contents of the will at the time of its execution, the registrar shall satisfy himself that the testator had such knowledge.

Evidence as to terms, condition and date of execution of will

12. (1) Where there appears in a will any obliteration, inter-lineation, or other alteration which is not authenticated in the manner prescribed by section 21 of the Wills Act, 1837, or by the re-execution of the will or by the execution of a codicil, the registrar shall require evidence to show whether the alteration was present at the time the will was executed and shall give directions as to the form in which the will is to be proved:

Provided that this paragraph shall not apply to any alteration which appears to the registrar to be of no practical importance.

(2) If from any mark on a will it appears to the registrar that some other document has been attached to the will, or if a will contains any reference to another document in such terms as to suggest that it ought to be incorporated in the will, the registrar may require the document to be produced and may call for such evidence

in regard to the attaching or incorporation of the document as he may think fit.

(3) Where there is doubt as to the date on which a will was executed, the registrar may require such evidence as he thinks necessary to establish the date.

Attempted revocation of will

13. Any appearance of attempted revocation of a will by burning, tearing or otherwise, and every other circumstance leading to a presumption of revocation by the testator, shall be accounted for to the registrar's satisfaction.

Affidavit as to due execution, terms etc., of will

14. A registrar may require an affidavit from any person he may think fit for the purpose of satisfying himself as to any of the matters referred to in rules 11, 12 and 13, and in any such affidavit sworn by an attesting witness or other person present at the time of the execution of a will the deponent shall depose to the manner in which the will was executed.

Wills not proved under section 9 of Wills Act, 1837

15. Nothing in rule 10, 11, 12 or 13 shall apply to any will which it is sought to establish otherwise than by reference to section 9 of the Wills Act, 1837, as explained by the Wills Act Amendment Act, 1852, but the terms and validity of any such will shall be established to the registrar's satisfaction.

Wills of persons on military service and seamen

16. If it appears to the registrar that there is *prima facie* evidence that a will is one to which section 11 of the Wills Act 1837, as amended by any subsequent enactment, applies, the will may be admitted to proof if the registrar is satisfied that it was signed by the testator or, if unsigned, that it is in the testator's handwriting.

Wills of naval personnel

17. Every application for a grant in respect of the estate of a person who has at any time served in a capacity to which the Navy and Marines (Wills) Act, 1865, applies shall be supported by a certificate of the Inspector of Seamen's Wills as to the existence of any will in his custody:

Provided that no such certificate shall be required where—

(a) the application relates to a will made after the deceased had ceased to serve in such capacity as aforesaid which revokes all previous wills made by him, or

(b) the deceased was at the date of his death in receipt of a pension in respect of his service.

Evidence of foreign law

18. Where evidence of the law of a country outside England is required on any application for a grant, the affidavit of any person who practises, or has practised, as a barrister or advocate in that country and who is conversant with its law may be accepted by the registrar unless the deponent is a person claiming to be entitled to the grant or his attorney, or is the spouse of any such person or attorney:

Provided that the registrar may accept the affidavit of a solicitor practising in Scotland, Northern Ireland, the Channel Islands, the Isle of Man or the Republic of Ireland as to the law of the country in which he practises, and may in special circumstances accept the affidavit of any other person who does not possess the qualifications required by this rule if the registrar is satisfied that by reason of such person's official position or otherwise he has knowledge of the law of the country in question.

Order of priority for grant where deceased left a will

19. Where the deceased died on or after the 1st January, 1926, the person or persons entitled to a grant of probate or administration with the will annexed shall be determined in accordance with the following order of priority, namely:

(i) The executor;

(ii) Any residuary legatee or devisee holding in trust for any other person;

(iii) Any residuary legatee or devisee for life;

(iv) The ultimate residuary legatee or devisee or, where the residue is not wholly disposed of by the will, any person entitled to share in the residue not so disposed of (including the Treasury Solicitor when claiming *bona vacantia* on behalf of the Crown) or, subject to paragraph (3) or rule 25, the personal representative of any such person:

Provided that where the residue is not in terms wholly disposed of, the registrar may, if he is satisfied that the testator has nevertheless disposed of the whole or substantially the whole of the estate as ascertained at the time of the application for the grant, allow a grant to be made (subject however to rule 37) to any legatee or devisee entitled to, or to a share in, the estate so disposed of, without regard to the persons entitled to share in any residue not disposed of by the will;

(v) Any specific legatee or devisee or any creditor or, subject to paragraph (3) of rule 25, the personal representative of any such person or, where the estate is not wholly disposed of by the will, any person who, notwithstanding that the amount of the estate is such that he has no immediate beneficial interest therein, may have a beneficial interest in the event of an accretion thereto;

(vi) Any legatee or devisee, whether residuary or specific, entitled on the happening of any contingency, or any person having no interest under the will of the deceased who would have been entitled to a grant if the deceased had died wholly intestate.

Grants to attesting witnesses etc.

20. Where a gift to any person fails by reason of section 15 of the Wills Act, 1837 (which provides that gifts to attesting witnesses or their spouses shall be void), such person shall not have any right to a grant as a beneficiary named in the will, without prejudice to his right to a grant in any other capacity.

Order of priority for grant in case of intestacy

21. (1) Where the deceased died on or after the 1st January, 1926, wholly intestate, the persons having a beneficial interest in the estate shall be entitled to a grant of administration in the following order of priority, namely:

(i) The surviving spouse;
(ii) The children of the deceased ... or the issue of any such child who has died during the lifetime of the deceased;
(iii) The father or mother of the deceased ...

(iv) Brothers and sisters of the whole blood, or the issue of any deceased brother or sister of the whole blood who has died.

(2) If no person in any of the classes mentioned in sub-paragraphs (ii) to (iv) of the last foregoing paragraph has survived the deceased, then, in the case of:

(a) a person who died before the 1st January, 1953, wholly intestate, or

(b) a person dying on or after the 1st January, 1953, wholly intestate without leaving a surviving spouse,

the persons hereinafter described shall, if they have a beneficial interest in the estate, be entitled to a grant in the following order of priority, namely:

(i) Brothers and sisters of the half blood, or the issue of any deceased brother or sister of the half blood who has died . . .

(ii) Grandparents;

(iii) Uncles and aunts of the whole blood, or the issue of any deceased uncle or aunt of the whole blood who has died . . .

(iv) Uncles and aunts of the half blood, or the issue of any deceased uncle or aunt of the half blood who has died . . .

(3) In default of any person having a beneficial interest in the estate, the Treasury Solicitor shall be entitled to a grant if he claims *bona vacantia* on behalf of the Crown.

(4) If all persons entitled to a grant under the foregoing provisions of this rule have been cleared off, a grant may be made to a creditor of the deceased or to any person who, notwithstanding that he has no immediate beneficial interest in the estate, may have a beneficial interest in the event of an accretion thereto.

(5) Subject to paragraph (3) of rule 25, the personal representative of a person in any of the classes mentioned in paragraphs (1) and (2) of this rule or the personal representative of a creditor shall have the same right to a grant as the person whom he represents:

Provided that the persons mentioned in sub-paragraphs (ii) to (iv) of paragraph (1) and in paragraph (2) of this rule shall be preferred to the personal representative of a spouse who has died without taking a beneficial interest in the whole estate of the deceased as ascertained at the time of the application for the grant.

(5A) The provisions of the Adoption Act 1958 shall apply in determining the entitlement to a grant as they apply to the devolution of property on intestacy.

(6) In this rule references to children of the deceased include references to his illegitimate and legitimated children and "father or mother of the deceased" shall be construed accordingly.

Right of assignee to a grant

22. (1) Where all the persons entitled to the estate of the deceased (whether under a will or on intestacy) have assigned their whole interest in the estate to one or more persons, the assignee or assignees shall replace, in the order of priority for a grant of administration, the assignor or, if there are two or more assignors, the assignor with the highest priority.

(2) Where there are two or more assignees, administration may be granted with the consent of the others to any one or more (not exceeding four) of them.

(3) In any case where administration is applied for by an assignee, a copy of the instrument of assignment shall be lodged in the registry.

Joinder of administration

23. (1) An application to join with a person entitled to a grant of administration a person entitled in a lower degree shall, in default of renunciation by all persons entitled in priority to such last-mentioned person, be made to a registrar and shall be supported by an affidavit by the person entitled, the consent of the person proposed to be joined as personal representative and such other evidence as the registrar may require.

(2) An application to join with a person entitled to a grant of administration a person having no right thereto shall be made [to a registrar and shall be supported by an affidavit by the person entitled, the consent of the person proposed to be joined as personal representative and such other evidence as the registrar may require.]

Provided that there may without any such application be joined with a person entitled to administration—

(a) on the renunciation of all other persons entitled to join in the grant, any kin of the deceased having no beneficial interest in the estate, in the order of priority described in rule 21;

(b) unless a registrar otherwise directs, any person whom the guardian of an infant may nominate for the purpose under paragraph (4) or rule 31;

(c) a trust corporation.

(3) [Deleted.]

Additional personal representatives

24. (1) An application under subsection (2) of section 160 of the Act to add a personal representative shall be made to a registrar and shall be supported by an affidavit by the applicant, the consent of the person proposed to be added as personal representative and such other evidence as the registrar may require.

(2) [Deleted.]

(3) On any such application the registrar may direct that a note shall be made on the original grant of the addition of a further personal representative, or he may impound or revoke the grant or make such other order as the circumstances of the case may require.

Grants where two or more persons entitled in same degree

25. (1) A grant may be made to any person entitled thereto without notice to other persons entitled in the same degree.

(2) A dispute between persons entitled to a grant in the same degree shall be brought by summons before a registrar of the principal registry.

(3) Unless a registrar otherwise directs, administration shall be granted to a living person in preference to the personal representative of a deceased person who would, if living, be entitled in the same degree and to a person not under disability in preference to an infant entitled in the same degree.

(4) If the issue of a summons under this rule is known to a registrar, he shall not allow any grant to be sealed until such summons is finally disposed of.

Exceptions to rules as to priority

26. (1) Nothing in rule 19, 21, 23 or 25 shall operate to prevent a grant being made to any person to whom a grant may or may require to be made under any enactment.

(2) The rules mentioned in the last foregoing paragraph shall not apply where the deceased died domiciled outside England, except in a case to which the proviso to rule 29 applies.

Grants to persons having spes successionis

27. When the beneficial interest in the whole estate of the deceased is vested absolutely in a person who has renounced his right to a grant and has consented to administration being granted to the person or persons who would be entitled to his estate if he himself had died intestate, administration may be granted to such person or one or more (not exceeding four) of such persons;

Provided that a surviving spouse shall not be regarded as a person in whom the estate has vested absolutely unless he would be entitled to the whole of the estate, whatever its value may be.

Grants in respect of settled land

28. (1) In this rule "settled land" means land vested in the deceased which was settled previously to his death and not by his will and which remained settled land notwithstanding his death.

(2) The special executors in regard to settled land constituted by section 22 of the Administration of Estates Act, 1925, shall have a prior right to a grant of probate limited to the settled land.

(3) The person or persons entitled to a grant of administration limited to settled land shall be determined in accordance with the following order of priority, namely:

(i) The trustees of the settlement at the time of the application for the grant;

(ii) [Deleted.]

(iii) The personal representative of the deceased.

(4) Where the persons entitled to a grant in respect of the free estate are also entitled to a grant of the same nature in respect of settled land, a grant expressly including the settled land may issue to them.

(5) Where there is settled land and a grant is made in respect

of the free estate only, the grant shall expressly exclude the settled land.

Grants where deceased died domiciled outside England

29. Where the deceased died domiciled outside England, a registrar may order that a grant do issue—

(a) to the person entrusted with the administration of the estate by the court having jurisdiction at the place where the deceased died domiciled,

(b) to the person entitled to administer the estate by the law of the place where the deceased died domiciled,

(c) if there is no such person as is mentioned in paragraph (a) or (b) of this rule or if in the opinion of the registrar the circumstances so require, to such person as the registrar may direct,

(d) if, by virtue of section 160 of the Act, a grant is required to be made to, or if the registrar in his discretion considers that a grant should be made to, not less than two administrators, to such person as the registrar may direct jointly with any such person as is mentioned in paragraph (a) or (b) of this rule or with any other person:

Provided that without any such order as aforesaid—

(a) probate of any will which is admissible to proof may be granted—

(i) if the will is in the English or Welsh language, to the executor named therein;

(ii) if the will describes the duties of a named person in terms sufficient to constitute him executor according to the tenor of the will, to that person;

(b) where the whole of the estate in England consists of immovable property, a grant limited thereto may be made in accordance with the law which would have been applicable if the deceased had died domiciled in England.

Grants to attorneys

30. (1) Where a person entitled to a grant resides outside England, administration may be granted to his lawfully constituted attorney for his use and benefit, limited until such person shall obtain a grant or in such other way as the registrar may direct:

Provided that where the person so entitled is an executor, administration shall not be granted to his attorney without notice to the other executors, if any, unless such notice is dispensed with by the registrar.

(2) Where a registrar is satisfied by affidavit that it is desirable for a grant to be made to the lawfully constituted attorney of a person entitled to a grant of administration and resident in England, he may direct that administration be granted to such attorney for the use and benefit of such person, limited until such person shall obtain a grant or in such other way as the registrar may direct.

Grants on behalf of infants

31. (1) Where the person to whom a grant would otherwise be made is an infant, administration for his use and benefit until he attains the age of eighteen years shall, subject to paragraphs (3) and (5) of this rule, be granted—

(a) to both parents of the infant jointly or to the statutory or testamentary guardian of the infant or to any guardian appointed by a court of competent jurisdiction, or

(b) if there is no such guardian able and willing to act and the infant has attained the age of sixteen years, to any next of kin nominated by the infant or, where the infant is a married woman, to any such next of kin or to her husband if nominated by her.

(2) Any person nominated under sub-paragraph (b) of the last foregoing paragraph may represent any other infant whose next of kin he is, being an infant below the age of sixteen years entitled in the same degree as the infant who made the nomination.

(3) Notwithstanding anything in this rule, administration for the use and benefit of the infant until he attains the age of eighteen years may be granted to any person assigned as guardian by order of a registrar . . . in default of, or jointly with, or to the exclusion of, any such person as is mentioned in paragraph (1) of this rule; and such an order may be made on application by the intended guardian, who shall file an affidavit in support of the application and, if required by the registrar, an affidavit of fitness sworn by a responsible person.

(4) Where, by virtue of section 160 of the Act, a grant is required to be made to not less than two administrators and there is only

one person competent and willing to take a grant under the foregoing provisions of this rule, administration may, unless a registrar otherwise directs, be granted to such person jointly with any other person nominated by him as a fit and proper person to take the grant.

(5) Where an infant who is sole executor has no interest in the residuary estate of the deceased, administration for the use and benefit of the infant until he attains the age of eighteen years shall, unless a registrar . . . otherwise directs, be granted to the person entitled to the residuary estate.

(6) An infant's right to administration may be renounced only by a person assigned as guardian under paragraph (3) of this rule and authorised to renounce by a registrar . . .

Grants where infant co-executor

32. (1) Where one of two or more executors is an infant, probate may be granted to the other executor or executors not under disability, with power reserved of making the like grant to the infant on his attaining the age of eighteen years, and administration for the use and benefit of the infant until he attains the age of eighteen years may be granted under rule 31 if and only if the executors who are not under disability renounce or, on being cited to accept or refuse a grant, fail to make an effective application therefor.

(2) An infant executor's right to probate on attaining the age of eighteen years may not be renounced by any person on his behalf.

Grants in case of mental or physical incapacity

33. (1) Where a registrar is satisfied that a person entitled to a grant is by reason of mental or physical incapacity incapable of managing his affairs, administration for his use and benefit, limited during his incapacity or in such other way as the registrar may direct, may be granted—

(a) in the case of mental incapacity, to the person authorised by the Court of Protection to apply for the grant, or

(b) where there is no person so authorised, or in the case of physical incapacity—

(i) if the person incapable is entitled as executor and has

no interest in the residuary estate of the deceased, to the
person entitled to such estate;

(ii) if the person incapable is entitled otherwise than as
executor or is an executor having an interest in the residuary
estate of the deceased, to the person who would be entitled
to a grant in respect of his estate if he had died intestate;
or to such other person as a registrar may by order direct.

(2) Unless a registrar otherwise directs no grant of administration shall be made under this rule unless all persons entitled
in the same degree as the person incapable have been cleared off.

(3) In the case of mental incapacity, notice of intended application for a grant under this rule shall be given to the Court of
Protection, except where the person incapable is an executor
with no beneficial interest in the estate.

(4) In the case of physical incapacity, notice of intended application for a grant under this rule shall [unless a registrar otherwise directs] be given to the person alleged to be so incapable.

Grants to trust corporations and other corporate bodies

34. (1) Where a trust corporation applies for a grant through
one of its officers, such officer shall lodge a certified copy of the
resolution authorising him to make the application and shall
depose in the oath that the corporation is a trust corporation within
the meaning of section 175 of the Act as extended by section 3
of the Law of Property (Amendment) Act, 1926, and that it has
power to accept a grant:

Provided that it shall not be necessary to lodge a certified copy
of the resolution where the trust corporation is a person holding
an official position if the person through whom the application
is made is included in a list filed with the Senior Registrar of
persons authorised to make such applications.

(2) Where a trust corporation applies for a grant of administration otherwise than as attorney for some person, there shall be
lodged with the application the consents of all persons entitled to
a grant and of all persons interested in the residuary estate of the
deceased, unless the registrar directs that such consents be dispensed with on such terms, if any, as he may think fit.

(3) Where a corporation (not being a trust corporation) would,

if an individual, be entitled to a grant, administration for its use and benefit, limited until further representation is granted, may be granted to its nominee or, if the corporation has its principal place of business outside England, its nominee or lawfully constituted attorney, and a copy of the resolution appointing the nominee or, as the case may be, the power of attorney, sealed by the corporation or otherwise authenticated to the registrar's satisfaction, shall be lodged with the application for the grant, and the oath shall state that the corporation is not a trust corporation.

Renunciation of probate and administration

35. (1) Renunciation of probate by an executor shall not operate as renunciation of any right which he may have to a grant of administration in some other capacity unless he expressly renounces such right.

(2) Unless a registrar . . . otherwise directs, no person who has renounced administration in one capacity may obtain a grant thereof in some other capacity.

(3) A renunciation of probate or administration may be retracted at any time on the order of a registrar . . . :

Provided that only in exceptional circumstances may leave be given to an executor to retract a renunciation of probate after a grant has been made to some other person entitled in a lower degree.

(4) A direction or order under this rule may be made by either the registrar of a district probate registry where the renunciation is filed or a registrar of the principal registry.

Consent of administrator of enemy property

36. On an application for a grant—

(a) in respect of the estate of a deceased person who was at the date of his death resident in Bulgaria, Germany, Hungary, Japan or Roumania, or

(b) to any person resident in one of those countries or to the attorney of any such person,

there shall, if the deceased died before the 6th October, 1952, be lodged the consent in writing of the appropriate authority, which shall be obtained through the Administration of Enemy Property Department of the Board of Trade.

Notice to Crown of intended application for grant

37. In any case in which it appears that the Crown is or may be beneficially interested in the estate of a deceased person, notice of intended application for a grant shall be given by the applicant to the Treasury Solicitor, and the registrar may direct that no grant shall issue within a specified time after the notice has been given.

Guarantee

38. (1) The registrar shall not require a guarantee under section 167 of the Act as a condition of granting administration except where it is proposed to grant it—

(a) by virtue of rule 19 (v) or rule 21 (4) to a creditor or the personal representative of a creditor or to a person who has no immediate beneficial interest in the estate of the deceased but may have such an interest in the event of an accretion to the estate;

(b) under rule 27 to a person or some of the persons who would, if the person beneficially entitled to the whole of the estate died intestate, be entitled to his estate;

(c) under rule 30 to the attorney of a person entitled to a grant;

(d) under rule 31 for the use and benefit of a minor;

(e) under rule 33 for the use and benefit of a person who is by reason of mental or physical incapacity incapable of managing his affairs;

(f) to an applicant who appears to the registrar to be resident elsewhere than in the United Kingdom;

or except where the registrar considers that there are special circumstances making it desirable to require a guarantee.

(2) Notwithstanding that it is proposed to grant administration as aforesaid, a guarantee shall not be required, except in special circumstances, on an application for administration where the applicant or one of the applicants is—

(a) a trust corporation;

(b) a solicitor holding a current practising certificate under the Solicitors Acts 1957 to 1965;

(c) a servant of the Crown acting in his official capacity;

(d) a nominee of a public department or of a local authority within the meaning of the Local Government Act 1933.

(3) Every guarantee entered into by a surety for the purposes of section 167 of the Act shall be in Form 1.

(4) Except where the surety is a corporation, the signature of the surety on every such guarantee shall be attested by an authorised officer, commissioner for oaths or other person authorised by law to administer an oath.

(5) Unless the registrar otherwise directs—

(a) if it is decided to require a guarantee, it shall be given by two sureties, except where the gross value of the estate does not exceed £500 or a corporation is a proposed surety, and in those cases one will suffice;

(b) no person shall be accepted as a surety unless he is resident in the United Kingdom;

(c) no officer of a registry or sub-registry shall become a surety;

(d) the limit of the liability of the surety or sureties under a guarantee given for the purposes of section 167 of the Act shall be the gross amount of the estate as sworn on the application for the grant;

(e) every surety, other than a corporation, shall justify.

(6) Where the proposed surety is a corporation there shall be filed an affidavit by the proper officer of the corporation to the effect that it has power to act as surety and has executed the guarantee in the manner prescribed by its constitution, and containing sufficient information as to the financial position of the corporation to satisfy the registrar that its assets are sufficient to satisfy all claims which may be made against it under any guarantee which it has given or is likely to give for the purposes of section 167 of the Act:

Provided that the Senior Registrar may, instead of requiring an affidavit in every case, accept an affidavit made not less often than once in every year together with an undertaking by the corporation to notify the Senior Registrar forthwith in the event of any alteration in its constitution affecting its power to become surety under that section.

39. [Revoked by S.I. 1971 No. 1977.]

40. [Revoked by S.I. 1971 No. 1977.]

Resealing under Colonial Probates Acts, 1892 and 1927

41. (1) An application under the Colonial Probates Acts, 1892 and 1927, for the resealing of probate or administration granted by the court of a country to which those Acts apply shall be made in the principal registry by the person to whom the grant was made or by any person authorised in writing to apply on his behalf.

(2) On any such application—

(a) an Inland Revenue affidavit shall be lodged as if the application were one for a grant in England;

(b) if a registrar of the principal registry so requires, the application shall be advertised in such manner as he may direct and shall be supported by an oath sworn by the person making the application;

(c) [Revoked.]

(2A) On an application for the resealing of a grant of administration—

(a) the registrar shall not require sureties under section 11 of the Administration of Estates Act 1971 as a condition of resealing the grant except where it appears to him that the grant is made to a person or for a purpose mentioned in paragraphs (a) to (f) of rule 38 (1) or except where he considers that there are special circumstances making it desirable to require sureties;

(b) rules 5 (4) and 38 (2), (4), (5) and (6) shall apply with any necessary modifications; and

(c) a guarantee entered into by a surety for the purposes of the said section 11 shall be in Form 2.

(3) Except by leave of a registrar of the principal registry, no grant shall be resealed unless it was made to such a person as is mentioned in paragraph (a) or (b) or rule 29 or to a person to whom a grant could be made under the proviso of that rule.

(4) No limited or temporary grant shall be resealed except by leave of a registrar of the principal registry.

(5) Every grant lodged for resealing shall include a copy of any will to which the grant relates or shall be accompanied by a copy thereof certified as correct by or under the authority of the court by which the grant was made, and where the copy of the grant required to be deposited under subsection (1) of section 2 of the

Colonial Probates Act, 1892, does not include a copy of the will, a copy thereof shall be deposited in the principal registry at the same time as the copy of the grant.

(6) The registrar shall send notice of the resealing to the court which made the grant.

(7) Where notice is received in the principal registry of the resealing of an English grant, notice of any amendment or revocation of the grant shall be sent to the court by which it was resealed.

Application for leave to sue on guarantee

41A. An application for leave under section 167 (3) of the Act or under section 11 (5) of the Administration of Estates Act 1971 to sue a surety on a guarantee given for the purposes of either of those sections shall, unless the registrar otherwise directs under rule 60, be made by summons to a registrar of the principal registry, and notice of the application shall in any event be served on the administrator, the surety and any co-surety.

Amendment and revocation of grant

42. If a registrar . . . is satisfied that a grant should be amended or revoked he may make an order accordingly:

Provided that except in special circumstances no grant shall be amended or revoked under this rule except on the application or with the consent of the person to whom the grant was made.

Certificate of delivery of Inland Revenue affidavit

43. The certificate of delivery of an Inland Revenue affidavit required by section 30 of the Customs and Inland Revenue Act, 1881, to be borne by every grant shall be in form 3.

Caveats

44. (1) Any person who wishes to ensure that no grant is sealed without notice to himself may enter a caveat in any registry.

(2) Any person who wishes to enter a caveat (in this rule called "the caveator") may do so by completing form 4 in the appropriate book at the registry and obtaining an acknowledgement of entry from the proper officer, or by sending through the post at his own risk a notice in form 4 to the . . . registry in which he wishes the caveat to be entered.

(3) Where the caveat is entered by a solicitor on the caveator's behalf, the name of the caveator shall be stated in form 4.

(4) Except as otherwise provided by this rule, a caveat shall remain in force for six months from the date on which it is entered and shall then cease to have effect, without prejudice to the entry of a further caveat or caveats.

(5) The Senior Registrar shall maintain an index of caveats entered in any registry and on receiving an application for a grant in the principal registry, or a notice of an application for a grant made in a district probate registry, he shall cause the index to be searched and shall notify the appropriate registrar in the event of a caveat having been entered against the sealing of a grant for which application has been made in a district probate registry.

(6) The registrar shall not allow any grant to be sealed if he has knowledge of an effective caveat in respect thereof:

Provided that no caveat shall operate to prevent the sealing of a grant on the day on which the caveat is entered.

(7) A caveat may be warned by the issue from the principal registry of a warning in form 5 at the instance of any person interested (in this rule called "the person warning") which shall state his interest and, if he claims under a will, the date of the will, and shall require the caveator to give particulars of any contrary interest which he may have in the estate of the deceased; and every warning [or a copy thereof] shall be served on the caveator.

(8) A caveator who has not entered an appearance to a warning may at any time withdraw his caveat by giving notice at the registry at which it was entered and the caveat shall thereupon cease to have effect and, if it has been warned, the caveator shall forthwith give notice of withdrawal of the caveat to the person warning.

(9) A caveator having an interest contrary to that of the person warning may, within eight days of serving of the warning upon him inclusive of the day of such service, or at any time thereafter if no affidavit has been filed under paragraph (11) of this rule, enter an appearance in the principal registry by filing form 6 and making an entry in the appropriate book, and shall forthwith thereafter serve on the person warning a copy of form 6 sealed with the seal of the registry.

(10) A caveator having no interest contrary to that of the person warning but wishing to show cause against the sealing of a grant to that person may, within eight days of service of the warning upon him inclusive of the day of such service or, at any time thereafter if no affidavit has been filed under paragraph (11) of this rule, issue and serve a summons for directions, which shall be returnable before a registrar of the principal registry.

(11) If the time limited for appearance has expired and the caveator has not entered an appearance, the person warning may file in the principal registry an affidavit showing that the warning was duly served and that he has not received a summons for directions under the last foregoing paragraph, and thereupon the caveat shall cease to have effect.

(11A) Upon the commencement of a probate action the principal probate registrar shall, in respect of each caveat then in force (other than a caveat entered by the plaintiff), give to the caveator notice of the commencement of the action and, upon the subsequent entry of a caveat at any time when the action is pending, shall likewise notify the caveator of the existence of the action.

(12) Unless a registrar of the principal registry by order made on summons otherwise directs—

(a) any caveat in force at the commencement of proceedings by way of citation or motion shall, unless withdrawn pursuant to paragraph (8) of this rule, remain in force until an application for a grant is made by the person shown to be entitled thereto by the decision of the court in such proceedings, and upon such application any caveat entered by a party who had notice of the proceedings shall cease to have effect;

(b) any caveat in respect of which an appearance to a warning has been entered shall remain in force until the commencement of a probate action;

(c) the commencement of a probate action shall, whether or not any caveat has been entered, operate to prevent the sealing of a grant (other than a grant under section 163 of the Act) until application for a grant is made by the person shown to be entitled thereto by the decision of the court in such action, and upon such application any caveat by a party who had notice of the action, or by a caveator who was given notice under paragraph 11A of this rule, shall cease to have effect.

(13) Except with the leave of a registrar of the principal registry, no further caveat may be entered by or on behalf of any caveator whose caveat has ceased to have effect under paragraph (11) or (12) of this rule.

(14) In this rule "grant" includes ... a grant made by any court outside England which is produced for resealing by the High Court.

Citations

45. (1) Every citation shall issue from the principal registry and shall be settled by a registrar before being issued.

(2) Every averment in a citation, and such other information as the registrar may require, shall be verified by an affidavit sworn by the person issuing the citation (in these Rules called "the citor") or, if there are two or more citors, by one of them:

Provided that the registrar may in special circumstances accept an affidavit sworn by the citor's solicitor.

(3) The citor shall enter a caveat before issuing a citation.

(4) Every citation shall be served personally on the person cited unless the registrar, on cause shown by affidavit, directs some other mode of service, which may include notice by advertisement.

(5) Every will referred to in a citation shall be lodged in a registry before the citation is issued, except where the will is not in the citor's possession and the registrar is satisfied that it is impracticable to require it to be lodged.

(6) A person who has been cited to appear may, within eight days of service of the citation upon him inclusive of the day of such service, or at any time thereafter if no application has been made by the citor under paragraph (5) of rule 46 or paragraph (2) of rule 47, enter an appearance in the principal registry by filing form 6 and making an entry in the appropriate book, and shall forthwith thereafter serve on the citor a copy of form 6 sealed with the seal of the registry.

Citation to accept or refuse or to take a grant

46. (1) A citation to accept or refuse a grant may be issued at the instance of any person who would himself be entitled to a grant in the event of the person cited renouncing his right thereto.

(2) Where power to make a grant to an executor has been reserved, a citation calling on him to accept or refuse a grant may be issued at the instance of the executors who have proved the will or of the executors of the last survivor of deceased executors who have proved.

(3) A citation calling on an executor who has intermeddled in the estate of the deceased to show cause why he should not be ordered to take a grant may be issued at the instance of any person interested in the estate at any time after the expiration of six months from the death of the deceased:

Provided that no citation to take a grant shall issue while proceedings as to the validity of the will are pending.

(4) A person cited who is willing to accept or take a grant may apply *ex parte* to a registrar for an order for a grant on filing an affidavit showing that he has entered an appearance and that he has not been served by the citor with notice of any application for a grant to himself.

(5) If the time limited for appearance has expired and the person cited has not entered an appearance, the citor may—

    (a) in the case of a citation under paragraph (1) of this rule, apply to a registrar for an order for a grant to himself;

    (b) in the case of a citation under paragraph (2) of this rule, apply to a registrar for an order that a note be made on the grant that the executor in respect of whom power was reserved has been duly cited and has not appeared and that all his rights in respect of the executorship have wholly ceased;

    (c) in the case of a citation under paragraph (3) of this rule, apply to a registrar by summons (which shall be served on the person cited) for an order requiring such person to take a grant within a specified time [or for a grant to himself or to some other person specified in the summons].

(6) An application under the last foregoing paragraph shall be

supported by an affidavit showing that the citation was duly served and that the person cited has not entered an appearance.

(7) If the person cited has entered an appearance but has not applied for a grant under paragraph (4) of this rule, or has failed to prosecute his application with reasonable diligence, the citor may—

(a) in the case of a citation under paragraph (1) of this rule, apply by summons to a registrar for an order for a grant to himself;

(b) in the case of a citation under paragraph (2) of this rule, apply by summons to a registrar for an order striking out the appearance and for the endorsement on the grant of such a note as is mentioned in sub-paragraph (b) of paragraph (5) of this rule;

(c) in the case of a citation under paragraph (3) of this rule, apply by summons to a registrar for an order requiring the person cited to take a grant within a specified time [or for a grant to himself or to some other person specified in the summons];

and the summons shall be served on the person cited.

Citation to propound a will

47. (1) A citation to propound a will shall be directed to the executors named in the will and to all persons interested thereunder, and may be issued at the instance of any citor having an interest contrary to that of the executors or such other persons.

(2) If the time limited for appearance has expired and no person cited has entered an appearance, or if no person who has appeared proceeds with reasonable diligence to propound the will, the citor may apply [by summons to a registrar of the principal registry] for an order for a grant as if the will were invalid.

Address for service

48. All caveats, citations, warnings and appearances shall contain an address for service within the jurisdiction.

Application for order to bring in a will or to attend for examination

49. (1) An application under section 26 of the Court of Probate

Act, 1857, for an order requiring a person to bring in a will or to attend for examination may, unless a probate action has been commenced, be made to a registrar of the principal registry by summons, which shall be served on every such person as aforesaid.

(2) An application under section 23 of the Court of Probate Act, 1858, for the issue by a registrar of the principal registry of a subpoena to bring in a will shall be supported by an affidavit setting out the grounds of the application, and if any person served with the subpoena denies that the will is in his possession or control he may file an affidavit to that effect.

Limited grants under section 155 of Act

50. An application for an order for a grant under section 155 of the Act limited to part of an estate may be made to a registrar, and shall be supported by an affidavit stating—

(a) whether the application is made in respect of the real estate only or any part thereof, or real estate together with personal estate, or in respect of a trust estate only;

(b) whether the estate of the deceased is known to be insolvent;

(c) that the persons entitled to a grant in respect of the whole estate in priority to the applicant have been cleared off.

Grants of administration under discretionary powers of court, and grants ad colligenda bona

51. An application for an order for—

(a) a grant of administration under section 73 of the Court of Probate Act, 1857, or section 162 of the Act, or

(b) a grant of administration *ad colligenda bona*,

may be made to a registrar, and shall be supported by an affidavit setting out the grounds of the application.

Applications for leave to swear to death

52. An application for leave to swear to the death of a person in whose estate a grant is sought may be made to a registrar and shall be supported by an affidavit setting out the grounds of the application and containing particulars of any policies of insurance effected on the life of the presumed deceased.

Grants in respect of nuncupative wills and of copies of wills

53. (1) An application for an order admitting to proof a nuncupative will, or a will contained in a copy, a completed draft, a reconstruction or other evidence of its contents where the original will is not available, may be made [to a registrar];

Provided that where a will is not available owing to its being retained in the custody of a foreign court or official, a duly authenticated copy of the will may be admitted to proof without any such order as aforesaid.

(2) The application shall be supported by an affidavit setting out the grounds of the application and by such evidence on affidavit as the applicant can adduce as to—

(a) the due execution of the will,

(b) its existence after the death of the testator, and

(c) the accuracy of the copy or other evidence of the contents of the will,

together with any consents in writing to the application given by any persons not under disability who would be prejudiced by the grant.

Grants durante absentia

54. An application for an order for a grant of special administration under section 164 of the Act where a personal representative is residing outside England shall be made to the court on motion.

55. [Revoked by S.I. 1967 No. 748.]

Notice of election by surviving spouse to redeem life interest

56. (1) Where a surviving spouse who is the sole personal representative of the deceased is entitled to a life interest in part of the residuary estate and elects under section 47A of the Administration of Estates Act, 1925, to have the life interest redeemed, he may give written notice of the election to the Senior Registrar in pursuance of subsection (7) of that section by filing a notice in form 7 in the principal registry or in the district probate registry from which the grant is issued.

(2) Where the grant issued from a district probate registry, the notice shall be filed in duplicate.

(3) A notice filed under this rule shall be noted on the grant and the record and shall be open to inspection.

Information as to grants in district probate registries to be sent to principal registry

57. (1) The notice of an application for a grant made in a district probate registry required by subsection (1) of section 152 of the Act to be sent to the principal registry shall be in the form of an index card, stating the full name and address of the deceased, his age, if known, and the date of his death.

(2) The list of grants made by a district probate registrar required by subsection (5) of the said section 152 to be sent to the principal registry shall be sent once in every week, and shall include the full name of every person in respect of whose estate a grant has been made and the name of the county or town in which he resided, and a copy of every grant mentioned in such list shall be sent by the district probate registrar to the principal registry for filing.

Issue of copies of original wills and other documents

58. (1) Where copies are required of original wills or other documents deposited under section 170 of the Act, such copies may be photographic copies sealed with the seal of the registry and issued as office copies and, where such office copies are available, copies certified under the hand of a registrar to be true copies shall be issued only if it is required that the seal of the court be affixed thereto.

(2) Copies, not being photographic copies, of original wills or other documents deposited under the said section 170 shall be examined against the documents of which they purport to be copies only if so required by the person demanding the copy, and in such case the copy shall be certified under the hand of a registrar to be a true copy and may in addition be sealed with the seal of the court.

Taxation of costs

59. (1) Every bill of costs (other than a bill delivered by a solicitor to his client which falls to be taxed under [the Solicitors Act 1957]) shall be referred to a registrar of the principal registry for taxation and may be taxed by him or such other taxing officer as the President may appoint.

(2) The party applying for taxation shall file the bill and give to any other parties entitled to be heard on the taxation not less than three clear days' notice of the time appointed for taxation, and shall at the same time, if he has not already done so, supply them with a copy of the bill.

(3) If any party entitled to be heard on the taxation does not attend within a reasonable time after the time appointed, the taxing officer may proceed to tax the bill upon being satisfied that such party had due notice of the time appointed.

(4) The fees payable on taxation shall be paid by the party on whose application the bill is taxed and shall be allowed as part of the bill.

Power to require application to be made by summons or motion

60. (1) A registrar may require any application to be made by summons to a registrar or a judge or to the court on motion.

(2) A summons for hearing by a registrar shall be issued out of the principal registry and heard by a registrar of that registry.

(3) A summons to be heard by a judge shall be issued out of the principal registry.

Exercise of powers of judge during Long Vacation

61. All powers exercisable under these Rules by a judge in chambers may be exercised during the Long Vacation by a registrar of the principal registry.

Appeals from registrars

62. (1) [Deleted.]

(2) Any person aggrieved by a decision or requirement of a registrar . . . may appeal by summons to a judge.

(3) If, in the case of an appeal under [the last foregoing paragraph], any person besides the appellant appeared or was represented before the registrar from whose decision or requirement the appeal is brought, the summons shall be issued within seven days thereof for hearing on the first available day and shall be served on every such person as aforesaid.

Service of notice of motion and summons

63. (1) A judge or registrar of the principal registry may direct that a notice of motion or summons for the service of which no other provision is made by these Rules shall be served on such person or persons as the judge or registrar may direct.

(2) Where by these Rules or by any direction given under the last foregoing paragraph a notice of motion or summons is required to be served on any person, it shall be served—

(a) in the case of a notice of motion, not less than five clear days before the day named in the notice for hearing the motion;

(b) in the case of a summons, not less than two clear days before the day appointed for the hearing, unless a judge or registrar of the principal registry, at or before the hearing, dispenses with service on such terms, if any, as he may think fit.

Notices etc.

64. Unless a registrar otherwise directs or these Rules otherwise provide, any notice or other document required to be given to or served on any person may be given or served by leaving it at, or by sending it by prepaid registered post to, that person's address for service or, if he has no address for service, his last known address.

Affidavits

65. Every affidavit used in non-contentious probate business shall be in the form required by the Rules of the Supreme Court in the case of affidavits to which those Rules apply.

Time

66. The provisions of Order 3 and Order 65, rule 7 of the Rules of the Supreme Court shall apply to the computation, enlargement and abridgement of time under these Rules, except that nothing in the former Order shall prevent time from running in the Long Vacation.

Application to pending proceedings

67. Subject in any particular case to any direction given by a judge or registrar, these Rules shall apply to any proceeding which is pending on the date on which they come into operation as well as to any proceeding commenced on or after that date:

Provided that where the deceased died before the 1st January, 1926, the right to a grant shall, subject to the provisions of any enactment, be determined by the principles and rules in accordance with which the court would have acted at the date of the death.

Revocation of previous Rules

8. (1) The Rules, Orders and Instructions set out in the Second Schedule are hereby revoked.

(2) [Revoked rr. 7-12 and amended r. 73 of the Contentious Business Rules dated the 30th July 1862 (since wholly revoked)]. (The forms in the Schedule are not reproduced here but for an example of a Surety's Guarantee, see *post*, p. 700).

FAMILY PROVISION (INTESTATE SUCCESSION) ORDER 1972
(S.I. 1972 No. 916)

Made - - -		21*st June* 1972
Coming into Operation		1*st July* 1972

The Lord Chancellor, in exercise of the powers conferred on him by section 1(1)(*a*) and (*b*) of the Family Provision Act 1966, hereby makes the following Order:—

1. (1) This Order may be cited as the Family Provision (Intestate Succession) Order 1972 and shall come into operation on 1st July 1972.

(2) The Interpretation Act 1889 shall apply to the interpretation of this Order as it applies to the interpretation of an Act of Parliament.

2. In the case of a person dying after the coming into operation of this Order, section 46(1) of the Administration of Estates Act 1925, as amended by section 1 of the Intestates' Estates Act 1952 and section 1 of the Family Provision Act 1966, shall apply as if the net sums charged by paragraph (i) on the residuary estate were:—

(*a*) under paragraph (2) of the Table, the sum of £15,000, and

(*b*) under paragraph (3) of the Table, the sum of £40,000.

OATH FOR EXECUTORS

Extracting Solicitor: *Fairey, Tayle & Co.,*
20 King's Bench Walk,
Temple, E.C.4.

IN THE HIGH COURT OF JUSTICE.
Family Division.
The Principal Registry.

IN the Estate of *Mollie Twanky*, deceased.

I, *Teddy Bear* of *14 The Mall, London, S.W.1, Zoologist*, make Oath and say, that I believe the paper writing now produced to, and marked by me, to contain the true and original last Will and Testament of *Mollie Twanky*, of *114 The Mall, London, S.W.1, Widow*, deceased, who died on the *ninth* day of *March, 1973*, domiciled in England and Wales; that to the best of my knowledge, information and belief, there was *no* land vested in the said deceased which was settled previously to her death, and not by her Will, and which remained settled land notwithstanding her death; And I further make Oath and say that I am the lawful son of the whole blood of the said deceased and the sole executor named in the said Will, and that I will (i) collect, get in and administer according to the law the real and personal estate of the said deceased; (ii) when required to do so by the Court, exhibit on oath in the Court a full inventory of the said estate and when so required render an account of the administration of the said estate to the Court; and (iii) when required to do so by the High Court, deliver up the grant of probate to that Court: and that the whole of the said Estate amounts in value to the sum of £21,220.16 and no more, to the best of my knowledge, information and belief.

Sworn by the above-named deponent

in the City of Westminster

this *17th* day of *April, 1973*   *T. Bear*

Before me,

V. Profane

A Commissioner for Oaths.

698

OATH FOR ADMINISTRATORS

Extracting Solicitor: *Fairey, Tayle & Co.,*
20 King's Bench Walk,
Temple, E.C.4.

IN THE HIGH COURT OF JUSTICE.
Family Division.
The Principal Registry.

In the Estate of *Snow White*, deceased.

I, *Winnie Pooh* of *The Nest, 16 Acacia Drive, Surbiton, Surrey, Married Woman*, make Oath and say that *Snow White* of *"Seven Dwarfs", Frimley near Camberley, Surrey,* deceased, died on the *twenty-ninth* day of *March, 1973,* domiciled in England and Wales Intestate a widow; that no minority or life interest arises under the intestacy; and that to the best of my knowledge, information, and belief there was no land vested in the said deceased which was settled previously to her death and which remained settled land notwithstanding her death: And I further make Oath and say that I am the lawful *daughter and the only person entitled to the estate* of the said Intestate; that I will (i) collect, get in and administer according to the law the real and personal Estate of the said deceased; (ii) when required to do so by the Court, exhibit on oath in the Court a full inventory of the said Estate and when so required render an account of the administration of the said Estate to the Court; and (iii) when required to do so by the High Court, deliver up the grant of letters of administration to that Court; and that the whole of the said Estate amounts in value to the sum of £43,499.70 and no more, to the best of my knowledge, information, and belief.

Sworn by the above-named deponent

in the City of Westminster

this *23rd* day of *June, 1973*   *W. Pooh*

Before me,

I. Administer

A Commissioner for Oaths.

GUARANTEE

IN THE HIGH COURT OF JUSTICE
The Principal Registry.

In the Estates of *Snow White* deceased.

WHEREAS *Snow White* of *"Seven Dwarfs"*, *Frimley near Camberley, Surrey* died on the twenty-ninth day of March 1973 and *Winnie Pooh* of *The Nest, 16, Acacia Drive, Surbiton, Surrey*, Married Woman (hereinafter called "the administratrix") is the intended administratrix of her estate.

NOW THEREFORE:

1. We Tweedle Dum and Tweedle Dee both of Muckyacre Farm Cheltenham Gloucestershire hereby jointly and severally guarantee that we will when lawfully required to do so make good any loss which any person interested in the administration of the Estate of the deceased may suffer in consequence of the breach by the administratrix of her duty:

   (a) to collect and get in the Estate of the deceased and administer it according to law;

   (b) when required to do so by the Court, to exhibit on Oath in the Court a full inventory of the Estate and, when so required, to render an account of the Estate; or

   (c) when so required by the Court to deliver up the grant to the Court.

2. The giving of time to the administratrix or any other forbearance or indulgence shall not in any way affect our liability under this guarantee.

3. The liability under this guarantee shall be continuing and shall be for the whole amount of the loss mentioned in paragraph 1 above, but our aggregate total liability shall not in any event exceed the sum of £43,499.

Dated this *23rd* day of *June* 1973.

SIGNED SEALED and DELIVERED
by the above named TWEEDLE DUM
and TWEEDLE DEE in the presence
of

Tweedle Dum [LS]
Tweedle Dee [LS]

I. Administer
A Commissioner for Oaths

GRANTS

GRANT OF PROBATE

IN THE HIGH COURT OF JUSTICE.
The Principal Registry of the Family Division.

BE IT KNOWN that *Mollie Twankie* of *14 The Mall London S.W.1* died on the *9th* day of *March 1973* domiciled in *England and Wales*

AND BE IT FURTHER KNOWN that at the date hereunder written the last Will and Testament (a copy whereof is hereunto annexed) of the said deceased was proved and registered in the Principal Registry of the Family Division of the High Court of Justice and Administration of all the estate which by law devolves to and vests in the personal representative of the said deceased was granted by the aforesaid Court to *Teddy Bear* of *14 The Mall aforesaid Zoologist son of the deceased and the sole executor named in the said will.*

And it is hereby certified that an Inland Revenue affidavit has been delivered wherein it is shown that the gross value of the said estate in the United Kingdom (exclusive of what the said deceased may have been possessed of or entitled to as a trustee and not beneficially) amounts to *£21,220.16* and that the net value of the estate amounts to *£19,762.84.*

And it is further certified that it appears by a receipt signed by an Inland Revenue Officer on the said affidavit that *£1,190.71* on account of estate duty and interest on such duty has been paid.

Dated the *19th* day of *May 1973.*

I. B. Quick

Registrar

Extracted by *Fairey, Tayle & Co, Solicitors,*
20 King's Bench Walk, Temple, London, E.C.4.

GRANT OF LETTERS OF ADMINISTRATION
SIMPLICITER

IN THE HIGH COURT OF JUSTICE.
The Principal Registry of the Family Division.

BE IT KNOWN that *Snow White* of *"Seven Dwarfs" Frimley near Camberley Surrey* died on the *29th* day of *March 1973* at *Frimley Cottage Hospital Camberley* domiciled in *England and Wales* Intestate *a widow*

AND BE IT FURTHER KNOWN that at the date hereunder written Letters of Administration of all the Estate which by law devolves to and vests in the personal representative of the said intestate were granted by the Family Division of the High Court of Justice at the Principal Registry thereof to *Winnie Pooh* of *The Nest 16 Acacia Drive Surbiton Surrey married woman the lawful daughter and the only person entitled to the estate of the said intestate.*

And it is hereby certified that an Inland Revenue affidavit has been delivered wherein it is shown that the gross value of the said estate in the United Kingdom (exclusive of what the said deceased may have been possessed of or entitled to as a trustee and not beneficially) amounts to £43,499.70 and that the net value of the estate amounts to £36,341.95.

And it is further certified that it appears by a receipt signed by an Inland Revenue officer on the said affidavit that £6,469.35 on account of estate duty and interest on such duty has been paid.

Dated the *4th* day of *August 1973*

I. Scrutinize

Registrar.

Extracted by *Fairey, Tayle & Co, Solicitors,*
20 King's Bench Walk, Temple, London, E.C.4.

INDEX

WILL—*continued*

living person, of, depositories of, 623
lodging with registry, 273
lost, 92
 evidence as to, 301, 303
 grant of administration, 287
 probate, 274
  draft, of, grant of, 278
 proof in solemn form, 297
lucid interval, made in, 33, 36
marriage—
 conditional on, 103
 made in contemplation of, 102, 568
 revoked by, 26, 101, 102, 568
material on which written, 53
mental element. *See* animus testandi, *above*
mental incapacity—
 after solicitor instructed, 39
  will made, 39
 burden of proof, 34
 delusions, effect of, 37
 knowledge of contents, essential, 41
 lucid interval, will made in, 33, 36
 presumptions as to, 34, 35
 seeming irrationality, 31, 32
 standards, 30
 test of, 30, 31, 32
 will made by court in case of, 39
  execution, 65
  limitations, 65
  statement of reasons, 212
minor, by, invalid, 565
mistake—
 contents, as to, 50
 meaning of words, as to, 50
 motive, as to, 50
 wrong document executed, 49
more than one page, on, 56 *et seq.*
mutual. *See* MUTUAL WILL
nature of, 6 *et seq.*
not available, grant of administration, 287
nuncupative, 72
objects of, 7
obliterations. *See* ALTERATION OF WILL
option granted by. *See* OPTION
other transactions, distinguished from, 9
personal representatives, clause relieving from liability, 431
planning of, 3
privileged. *See* PRIVILEGED WILL
probate in solemn form. *See* PROBATE

WILL—*continued*

republication, 112 *et seq.*
 ademption, following, 466
 codicil, by, 112
 contrary to testator's intention, 116
 effect of, 113 *et seq.*
  gifts to persons, on, 150
 illegitimate children, reference to, 114
 intermediate codicils, 116
 persons, description of, effect on, 114
 property—
  adeemed, effect on, 115
  descriptions of, effect on, 114
 purpose of, 113
 re-execution, by, 112
restrictions on freedom, 2
review of, importance, 85
revival, 116 *et seq.*, 569
 codicil, by, 117, 569
 document must be in existence, 118
 effect of, 119
 intention must be shown, 117, 569
 re-execution, by, 117, 569
 requirements, 116, 569
 revocation of revoking document, 118
revocability, 9
revocation. *See* REVOCATION OF WILL
satisfaction. *See* SATISFACTION
scope of, 7
seamen's. *See* PRIVILEGED WILL
secret trust, witness benefiting under, 63
seemingly irrational, 31
ship, executed on board formal requirements, 67, 638
signature, 54 *et seq.*
 end, must be at, 55, 56, 565
 envelope containing will, on, 58, 59
 meaning, 54
 pages after, 57, 58
 position of, 55, 565
  more than one page, 56
  single sheet, 55
 witnesses to. *See* witnesses, *below*
simultaneous death. *See* COMMORIENTES
slaying testator, rule as to, 470
soldier's. *See* PRIVILEGED WILL
solemn form, proof in. *See* PROBATE
speaks from death, 9, 570
taxation implications, 3